TEXTBOOK REDS

Schoolbooks, Ideology, and Eastern German Identity
TEXTBOOK **REDS**

John Rodden

The Pennsylvania State University Press
University Park, Pennsylvania

Library of Congress Cataloging-in-Publication Data

Rodden, John.
Textbook reds : schoolbooks, ideology,
and Eastern German identity / John Rodden.
p. cm. — (Post-Communist cultural studies)
Includes bibliographical references and index.
ISBN 978-0-271-05856-6 (pbk : alk. paper)
1. Textbooks—Germany (East) 2. Education—Germany (East)—Curricula.
3. Communism and education.
I. Title. II. Series.
LB3048.G3R63 2005
371.3′209431
2005026151

Copyright © 2006 The Pennsylvania State University
All rights reserved
Printed in the United States of America
Published by The Pennsylvania State University Press,
University Park, PA 16802-1003

The Pennsylvania State University Press is a member of
the Association of American University Presses.

It is the policy of The Pennsylvania State University Press
to use acid-free paper. This book is printed on stock
that meets the minimum requirements of American National
Standardfor Information Sciences—
Permanence of Paper for Printed Library Materials,
ANSI Z39.48–1992.

Cristen Carson Reat
Meine alte Kameradin

Contents

Foreword by Wolfgang Strauss xi
Acknowledgments xiii
List of Abbreviations xvii
Glossary xxi
Prologue: Creating Young Comrades xxv

Introduction: Ideology as Core Curriculum 1
   1945: Textbooks and German Re-Education 1
   From Brown to Red? 3
   The (East) German Ideology 7

PART I: OF POLITICS AND LETTERS—AND NUMBERS

1 German for the East Germans: Language and Literature 13

   Reared in the DDR 15
   Mother-Tongue Education 21
   Socialist Fatherland Education 27
   EXCURSUS: Thälmann *über alles?* Vicissitudes of a Socialist
     State Icon 33
   Living Heroes, or the DDR Cult of Personality 41
   Canon Fodder for Young Revolutionaries 47
   EXCURSUS: A *Bruderland* Comparison: Soviet and Post-Soviet
     Textbooks 56
   The Advanced High School Curriculum 65
   Books Are Weapons 68

2 Terra Verde, Terra Rosso: Geography 69

   The Expanding Red Earth 69
   EXCURSUS: "Our Socialist Fatherland": How Fifth-Graders Learned to
     Love the *Heimat* 72
   EXCURSUS: "Elementary" Political Geography 74
   EXCURSUS: Amerika Through Eastern Eyes 81
   The Upper Grades 84
   Of Class and Soil 87

3 My Country, Left or Wrong? Civics   89

   Marxed *Menschen*   89
   EXCURSUS: Socialist Morality for Tenth Graders   94
   In Lenin's Corner: The Model Socialist Citizen   95
   Education for Hatred   97
   "Trust Is Good, but Control Is Better"   109

4 Progressive Lessons of the Past: History   111

   The Past is KA   111
   History Class / Class History   112
   Modern Times   121
   EXCURSUS: Marx and Engels as Role Models   124
   "Socialism Is Winning!"   126
   "Made in East Germany," or the Historical (Re)Invention of the DDR   129
   Overtaken by History? 1989 and the Perestroika of DDR Historiography   136
   EXCURSUS: The *Black Book* as Anti-Textbook: History Turns a Corner?   138
   Bearing the Double Burden of History   145

5 Socialist Science: Biology, Chemistry, Mathematics   147

   Science, Western versus Eastern   147
   Biology   148
     Biopolitics?   149
   EXCURSUS: Social, a.k.a. Socialist, Hygiene   152
   Chemistry   155
     Chemical Reactions, Progressive Results   155
   EXCURSUS: "Organic" Chemistry, or the Law of M-L   156
     Of Applied Science and Agitprop   158
   Mathematics   161
     The Simple Arithmetic of Progressivism   161
   EXCURSUS: Army Algebra for Ninth-Graders   165
     Party Figures, or the Higher Calculus of M-L   167

PART II: THE VOICES BEHIND THE PAGE: CONVERSATIONS ABOUT POST-COMMUNIST EDUCATION AND EASTERN GERMAN LIFE WITH FACULTY AND STUDENTS

6 Arts and Humanities   195

     1. "History Lessons" for Would-Be Revolutionaries   195

2. Pedagogy of the Distressed: A German Teacher's Self-Criticism   198
3. "My Post-Communist Brecht": A Weimar Student's *Weltanschauung*   207
4. West Side (Hi)Story I: A *Wossi*'s Postcommunist Critique of Humboldt Historians and *Jammerossis*   220
5. The Strains of Silence: A Music Teacher's Brave (New) Career   232
6. "My Teachers Ignored the Ideological Crap"   243
7. "French Leave": A Gifted Language Student Goes AWOL   247
8. West Side (Hi)Story II: A *Wossi* in Wittenberg   265
9. Running On, or Training for the (Russian) Olympics   271
10. Varieties of Academic Experience: A German View   279
11. "Proud to Be German"   288

7 Physical and Social Sciences   299

1. Of Biophysics and Metaphysics: Post-Communism Meets McUniversity   299
2. Post-Communist Social Studies? A Teacher-Student Conflict of Generations   313
3. "I Was a True Believer": A Convinced Communist Student Looks Back   321
4. "My Father Was in the Party": A Daughterly Diptych   329

8 Education for Tolerance: Of Ideology, Identity, and Intolerance, or Among (German and Jewish) Schoolchildren   345

1. Border-Crossing after Checkpoint Charlie   348
2. Forward and Never Forget—Tolerance? A Berlin Teacher's Post-Communist "Class" Struggles   362
3. Return of the Pink Rabbit?   367
4. Breaching Walls, Breaching Faith   375
5. The Strains of Silence II: Hospitality or Hitlerism in Weimar?   379
6. "Re-Education for Tolerance": A Civic Leader Speaks Out   383

Epilogue: Curriculum Without a Core   391
Notes   393
Bibliography   421
Index   433

Foreword

This book is a comprehensive overview of the East German school curriculum that is unequalled for scholarly thoroughness, stylistic verve, and sheer human interest. It is far more than merely a chronological report about the subject matter that was taught in the classrooms of the German Democratic Republic (Deutsche Demokratische Republik, DDR). The book furnishes keen insight into the true nature of communism and the historical processes that ultimately resulted in the overthrow of this system. I have not read such a brilliantly executed book about the aims and substance of DDR education in years. *Textbook Reds* exhibits a detailed knowledge of how communist ideology penetrated all school subjects and a firm grasp of the entire cultural and philosophical context of DDR education.

Textbook Reds falls into two parts. In Part 1, Rodden explores how a broad cross-section of school subjects, such as German language and literature, geography, civics, history, biology, chemistry, and mathematics, contributed to the pedagogical goals of East German education. "Ideology as Core Curriculum," as the author has titled his introduction, was indeed both the governing principle of textbook production and the prime pedagogical directive from the Ministry of Education to all classroom teachers. Among the specific topics addressed in Part 1 are: socialist patriotism, international proletarianism, socialist morality, the capitalist-imperialist enemy, the duties of socialist citizenship, and the DDR identity. It becomes evident that culture and education were thoroughly based on the dogma of Marxism-Leninism not only in the Stalinist period but also later in the seemingly "liberal" Honecker era.

Rodden covers in Part 1 how the manifold twists and turns in DDR ideological indoctrination, dependent on the "weather conditions" in global policy, manifested themselves in the nation's schoolbooks, especially in ideologically sensitive subjects such as German language and literature, history, geography, and civics. Though the Soviets had defeated the Germanic ideology of the Nazis, they immediately imposed an equally authoritarian ideology on eastern Germany, and this ideology rapidly evolved from a *Schein*-democratization at the beginning to a strict Sovietization and Stalinization by the 1950s. As a result, the DDR became more staunchly authoritarian than, for example, the neighboring states of Poland and Czechoslovakia. Rodden shows meticulously, based on a sophisticated analysis of both elementary and secondary school textbooks, how effectively DDR schoolbooks fulfilled the tasks of shaping the minds and capturing the souls of the younger generation.

Part 2 concentrates on teachers and students who experienced the DDR educational system in the 1970s and 1980s. Rodden has interviewed eastern Germans who were influenced in varying degrees by the textbooks used in the communist classroom. His intention is to suggest how the DDR textbooks have continued to exert influence on the minds of eastern Germans long after the DDR's demise—and to provide insight thereby into how the "textbook mentality" exemplified by the rigid indoctrination policies of the DDR endures.

Rodden is more concerned with people's lives than with pedagogical materials. In his interviews throughout Part 2, which span a range from former supporters and true believers in the system to resistant or even outspokenly critical individuals, he shows in a most subtle manner the diverse emotions prompted by the collapse of the DDR educational system and its transformation and abrupt "integration" into the West German system: disappointment, frustration, ignorance, self-criticism, expediency, and pragmatic acceptance of the new reality. In these portraits, as well as in his analytical sections, Rodden maintains an unusual stance that is both sympathetic and critical at the same time, which facilitates his explanations of the essential purposes and aspirations of DDR curricular policies.

I say all this as a man who himself lived through most of the history of DDR educational and cultural politics, first as an idealistic supporter of the system and then, later, increasingly in opposition to the dictatorship, a man who experienced the events of 1989–90 as a personal and intellectual liberation from an ideological straitjacket. I can, therefore, on the basis of my own intimate knowledge of that history, confirm that this book is an outstanding achievement as a work of scholarship and human empathy. *Textbook Reds*—and most especially its portraits and interviews—makes absorbing and compelling reading, and it addresses a public far beyond academic specialists. It is accessible to the general reader and deserves the widest possible audience. May it be a source of stimulating reflection for everyone who is interested in this period of the Cold War and in the future of German education.

Wolfgang Strauss
Professor Emeritus
University of Jena
June 2005

Acknowledgments

I began writing this book a decade ago, and in my ten years of work on it I have gained many comrades and acquired many debts. Friends and family suffered my obsessive preoccupation with amiable tolerance, patiently listening to my hard-to-translate jokes and puns as well as my stories and satires of East German life, many of them taken directly from my personal archive of DDR schoolbooks.

To Lynn Hayden, I am grateful for the opportunity to acknowledge a considerable personal debt publicly. A true friend, she has opened her home to me and provided me unwavering support, limitless forbearance, and constant encouragement. I am also indebted to Beth Macom, who offered me superb criticism, all of it welcome even when I lacked the wherewithal to implement it. A great many of the nonscholarly lessons that I have learned in the years during which this book has occupied my life have been learned with Beth, and the process of learning them together has proved as fulfilling for me as the knowledge itself attained. My brother Paul has also been indispensable to my work on this project, as he listened carefully to my unfolding argument, astutely edited my infelicitous phrasing, and offered sage advice. I am again grateful to other family members—to my parents, John and Rose Rodden, and my brothers, Edward and Thomas Rodden—who have welcomed another book into their lives and recognized the labor and value of such a birth.

Like its predecessor, *Repainting the Little Red Schoolhouse* (2002), this study is a tribute to German largesse. It was written without the aid of any fellowships, foundations, or university affiliations. It owes its existence to more direct and personal forms of human interaction—long-established friendships, chance encounters with strangers on trains, and midnight conversations with students who offered me floor space on which to rest before departing the next morning. In the course of several research trips totaling twenty-seven months, I rarely spent more than a single night in an eastern German hotel or rented room. In other words, this book was assisted by countless random acts of generosity committed by individual Germans.

In western Germany, Ilse Kathinka Robaschik introduced me to eastern

ACKNOWLEDGMENTS

friends, opened her home to me, and catered to my vegetarian peccadilloes. Gisela and Hubert Stuchly fed me and chauffeured me, repeatedly extending me more hospitality than I could ever hope to repay. Tine Traute and Karolin Wyneken adopted me as their "Black Forest Philosopher"; they are young western Germans of such intelligence and character that I feel glad for Germany's future. Rudi and Karin Walter, my editors at Verlag Herder in Freiburg, challenged my mind with their stimulating conversation and warmed my stomach with their delicious vegan meals.

In Berlin, Karin Hasselblatt and Ulrike Henderson remain valued friends whose support fortifies and uplifts. As in the past, I am once again grateful to the staff members at the following archives in Berlin: the Stiftung Archiv der Parteien und Massenorganisationen der DDR (SAPMO), the Deutsches Institut für Internationale Pädagogische Forschung, the Kinder- und Jugendbuchabteilung at the Staatsbibliothek zu Berlin-Preussischer Kulturbesitz, and the Deutsches Historisches Museum.

My sincere thanks also go to the many eastern Germans who corresponded with me, granted me interviews, and donated their old schoolbooks to their odd American visitor so absorbed in their rapidly receding and oft-forgotten past. They did more than any interviewer or foreign guest could ever expect, and many of them have since become cherished friends as a direct consequence of this work.

Above all, five eastern German friends have been of invaluable help by listening to my ideas about East Germany as they were forming. Stefan Schwarzkopf, critic and comrade, inspired me in our many conversations about DDR history and culture and helped me immensely in the late stages of the manuscript, reading it closely and spotting numerous errors of fact and interpretation. Christine Lösch in Apolda and Annaliese Saupe in Plauen hosted me on several trips, and their cogent observations led me to compose my ideas more sharply and boldly than I otherwise might have done. Matthias Pietzonka and his family in Meissen displayed extraordinary hospitality during numerous visits, showing me how the spirit of true socialism lives in the east, even if the corrupt DDR system does no more.

I am particularly grateful to Professor Wolfgang Strauss of the University of Jena, who contributed this book's foreword, was unfailingly ready with reminiscences from his extraordinary memory, devoted many hours to conversation with me about this project, and made shrewd suggestions about translation. (*Junge Sozialisten vom Reissbrett*, he suggested as the German translation of my title; I countered with *Kommunisten wie im Buche*.) As both a linguist and a scholar of DDR educational history, Professor Strauss was keenly interested in my research findings, read the first draft of this manuscript meticulously, and was both searching and specific in the extended criticism that he provided these pages.

Several other American friends and colleagues also graced me with immediate and open-handed generosity. Jay Alejandre worked with steady diligence and laser-beam concentration to prepare the manuscript for submission to the press. Tanya O'Neil, Jean Harrison, Michael Haydel, Sara Enright, Megan Giller, and Pablo Ormachea saw the book through its seemingly endless revisions. I am also grateful to Randy Bytwerk, the late Sterling Fishman, Vince Kling, Jim McAdams, Kathleen O'Connor, George Panichas, Craig Pepin, David Pike, Gerhild Rogers, James B. M. Schick, Christian Söe, and Denise Weeks, all of whom read portions of the manuscript and furnished me perceptive criticism. Peter Potter remained an exemplary editor throughout—available, insightful, and forever patient.

Still other friends and colleagues in the United States also assisted me, either via correspondence or in conversation, with their kind words of encouragement and knowledgeable observations about European history, German culture, and/or comparative education: Mitch Baranowski, Rafe and Jack Bemporad, Benita Blessing, Erica Carson, Thomas Cushman, Peter Dougherty, Catherine Plum, Jonathan Rose, Mary Triece, Claire Van Ens, and Greg Wegner.

I dedicate this book to my long-time *Kameradin*, Cristen Carson Reat, who contributed to the excursus in Chapter 1 on Soviet and post-Soviet textbooks. She was my first research assistant on this book and has had much to do with sustaining my commitment to this project and shaping its outcome, with helping me keep faith with it and with myself. Throughout my decade of work on *Textbook Reds*, Cristen not only drew on her years in Germany and the former Soviet Union to provide me with perceptive criticism but uplifted me with her sparkling wit and joyful wisdom.

I am blessed to know her.

J. G. R.
November 2005
Austin, Texas

List of Abbreviations

Although I have sought to minimize the use of acronyms in the main text, the following list includes abbreviations used in selected chapters of the book and throughout the notes, either for purposes of illustration or economy.

German-language acronyms, included here for ease of reference, are translated on first citation in the text.

APW — *Akademie der Pädagogischen Wissenschaften.* Academy of Pedagogical Sciences.
BRD — *Bundesrepublik Deutschland.* Federal Republic of Germany. Used by communist officials to refer to West Germany, in order to place West Germany on an equal level with the DDR; avoided by West German officials for this same reason.
CDU — *Christlich-Demokratische Union.* Christian Democratic Union party or Christian Democrats.
CPSU — Communist Party of the Soviet Union
DDR — *Deutsche Demokratische Republik.* German Democratic Republic, 1945–89.
DEFA — *Deutsche Film Aktiengesellschaft.* DDR state film production agency.
DFD — *Demokratischer Frauenbund Deutschlands.* Democratic Women's League of Germany, the major government-sponsored mass organization for women in the DDR.
DIAMAT — Dialectical Materialism. Shorthand term, along with M-L, for required university courses in Marxism, as well as for Marxist philosophy itself.
DKP — *Deutsche Kommunistische Partei.* German Communist Party of West Germany and, since 1990, of reunited Germany. Its current membership has shrunken to fewer than 5,000.
DSF — *Gesellschaft für Deutsch-Sowjetische Freundschaft.* German-Soviet Friendship Society.
EOS — *Erweiterte Oberschule.* The advanced high school of the DDR (eleventh and twelfth grades).

FDGB	*Freier Deutscher Gewerkschaftsbund.* Federation of Free German Trade Unions. The unique government-sponsored, national trade union of the DDR that negotiated labor contracts for the state, administered the pension system, and represented workers' interests in labor-management disputes. The FDGB was the largest mass organization in the DDR.
FDJ	*Freie Deutsche Jugend.* Free German Youth. The DDR's mass youth organization for fourteen- to twenty-five-year-olds.
GST	*Gesellschaft für Sport und Technik.* Society for Sports and Technology. The main DDR athletic association, paramilitary in orientation.
HJ	*Hitler Jugend.* Hitler Youth. The mass youth organization of the *Nationalsozialistische Deutsche Arbeiterpartei,* the National Socialist German Workers' Party.
JP	*Junge Pioniere.* Young Pioneers. The DDR youth organization for first through third grades. The acronym was not in use orally in the DDR, but is frequently found in official DDR publications.
KA	*Kapitalistisches Ausland.* Capitalist foreign country.
KJVD	*Kommunistischer Jugendverband Deutschlands.* Communist Youth League of Germany or Young Sparticists. The pre-war youth organization of the KPD.
KPD	*Kommunistische Partei Deutschlands.* Communist Party of Germany. The pre–World War II party founded in 1919.
LDPD	*Liberaldemokratische Partei Deutschlands.* The Liberal Democratic Party of Germany. A DDR "bloc" party.
LPG	*Landwirtschaftliche Produktionsgenossenschaft.* Agricultural cooperative.
M-L	*Marxismus-Leninismus.* Marxism-Leninism. See also DIAMAT.
MFS	*Ministerium für Staatssicherheit.* Ministry of State Security of the DDR. Also known by the shorthand term "Stasi."
NVA	*Nationale Volksarmee.* National People's Army.
PDS	*Partei des Demokratischen Sozialismus.* Party of Democratic Socialism. The reconstituted, successor party of the SED. Originally known as the SED-PDS, the PDS has since moved toward the center and become a left-wing social democratic party with a current membership of approximately 65,000.
POS	*Polytechnische Oberschule.* The ten-year uniform, general education DDR school.

RGW *Rat für gegenseitige Wirtschaftshilfe.* Council for Mutual Economic Assistance, generally known as COMECON in English. The East bloc equivalent of the Common Market.

SBZ *Sowjetische Besatzungszone.* Soviet Occupation Zone.

SED *Sozialistische Einheitspartei Deutschlands.* Socialist Unity Party of Germany. The Communist Party of the DDR.

SMAD *Sowjetische Militäradministration Deutschlands.* Soviet Military Administration of Germany. The occupation-era government of the SBZ.

SPD *Sozialdemokratische Partei Deutschlands.* Social Democratic Party of Germany or Social Democrats.

TP *Thälmann Pioniere.* Thälmann Pioneers. The DDR youth organization for fourth through seventh grades, the equivalent of Boy and Girl Scouts. The abbreviation was used only in West German publications, never in the DDR.

VEB *Volkseigener Betrieb.* People's Own Enterprise, official DDR term for state-owned and -run enterprises.

Glossary

The following list includes German-language terms appearing in the main text, except those items already noted in the List of Abbreviations, along with a number of terms not appearing in the book. I have included the latter for interest's sake and because they are germane to the topic at hand.

Abitur. German school-leaving examination, which qualifies a student for university admission.

Abwicklung. Wrapping up or winding down. Euphemism used for the dismantling of DDR institutions and the laying off of thousands of eastern German employees.

antifaschistischer Schutzwall. Anti-fascist Wall of Protection. Official DDR government term for the Berlin Wall.

Asylanten. Asylum seekers.

Ausländerfeindlichkeit. Xenophobia.

Besserwessi. A smart-aleck or know-it-all *Wessi*.

Blueshirts. Nickname for Free German Youth.

Bruderländer. Brotherlands. A communist term for the international fraternity of socialist nations.

Bundestag. The lower house of the (West) German legislature.

COMECON. Council for Mutual Economic Assistance. The mutual economic aid organization of the communist world.

das bessere Deutschland. "The better Germany." Term often applied both to the German socialist tradition and to the DDR.

Demo. Short for demonstration or protest march.

Demosprüche. Protest slogans.

DIAMAT. Dialectical Materialism. Shorthand term, along with M-L, for required university courses in Marxism, as well as for Marxist philosophy itself.

drüben. Over there. Used both in West Germany and the DDR to refer to "the other Germany."

Erbe. Heritage. DDR term for that part of the German past admissible to progressive DDR historiography.

Erdkunde. Geography.

Erziehung zum Hass. Education for Hatred. DDR school program in military training. Generally used to describe the proper attitude of socialist patriots toward imperialists and warmongers.
Erziehung zur Toleranz. Education for Tolerance. Administered by UNESCO and endorsed by most EU nations, this worldwide program seeks to foster interracial respect and international cooperation through teacher and student exchange programs, professional courses in "diversity appreciation," and numerous intercultural projects. Germany is a strong supporter of such initiatives.
Feindbild. Enemy image.
Freiraum. Free space, freedom.
Freundschaft! Friendship! A communist greeting.
Geschichte. History.
Grenzgänger. Border crossers.
Grepos. Short for *Grenzpolizei*, the DDR border police. Chiefly used by West German media.
Gymnasium. German high school.
Heimat. Homeland. A German term with patriotic overtones.
Heimatkunde. Local and regional studies. A DDR school subject (known in the early post-war era as *Deutschkunde*).
Historikerstreit. Historians' debate. The 1986–87 controversy among West German historians about the status and uniqueness of the Holocaust.
Hort. After-school child care center.
Jammerossi. A complaining *Ossi*, or eastern German.
Jugendweihe. Youth consecration ceremony. A communist confirmation rite administered to youth at the age of fourteen. Inaugurated in pre-war Germany under the auspices of the SDP, it had been voluntary until the 1950s.
Komsomol. The Soviet mass youth organization.
Land, Länder. State(s).
Mensch. Human being.
die neue schule. The new school. The uniform, democratic school of the DDR, a term chiefly employed by early post-war DDR educators.
Neues Deutschland. New Germany. Formerly the official SED newspaper; associated since 1990 with the PDS.
Neulehrer, Neulehrerin. New teacher. Mainly used to refer to teachers of anti-fascist convictions hired in the early post-war era of the DDR.
Oberschule. Generic name for DDR and pre-war German high school.
Ossis. Eastern Germans. Term used since 1989/90.

Planmensch. Planned human being, the "new socialist man." Chiefly used by West German media.

Realschule. Technically oriented German school.

Republikflucht. Flight from the Republic. Escape from the DDR; an official term of reprobation.

Staatssicherheitsdienst. State Security Service. Also known as Stasi, MFS, or SSD.

Stabü, Staatsbürgerkunde. Citizenship studies, or civics. DDR school subject.

Überprüfung. Audit, investigation. Term for formal screening conducted of all DDR teachers.

Umerziehung. Re-education. German-language term (used more frequently in the SBZ than western Germany) for Allied program of anti-fascist, democratic renewal.

Unterrichtshilfen. Lesson aids. Term used by Volk und Wissen for its teaching guides.

Vergangenheitsbewältigung. Coping with the past. German short-hand term for the national challenge of coming to terms with the legacy of the Holocaust.

Volk. People, nation.

Volk und Wissen Volkseigner Verlag. The official name of the DDR state publishing house for educational and pedagogical materials, including textbooks and teachers' handbooks. It was typically referred to by its shorter name, *Volk und Wissen Verlag.*

Volkskammer. People's Chamber. The DDR parliament.

Wehrerziehung, Wehrkunde. Defense education, military studies. DDR school subject.

weltanschauliche Erziehung. Education for a world outlook. The Marxist-Leninist philosophy of education.

Weltanschauung. Worldview.

Wende. The "turn." Used in the DDR and eastern Germany to refer to the change from SED rule to parliamentary democracy during 1989/90.

Wessis. Western Germans. Term used since 1989/90.

Wossis. Western Germans living or working in eastern Germany.

Prologue

CREATING YOUNG COMRADES

I

Books have long been weapons in cultural wars—it's no secret that education is one way of transmitting culture. American parents and school district administrators have wrestled for decades over what kinds of lessons those novels and plays assigned for classroom use should teach. In recent years, the fiercest struggles among educators, parents, and religious authorities have centered on what textbooks to adopt. The textbook campaigns have introduced new rules and expectations into the age-old book wars.

In these battles American educators have banned many a classic—from *Brave New World* and *Nineteen Eighty-Four* to *The Grapes of Wrath, Huckleberry Finn,* and *Catcher in the Rye*—that failed to satisfy cultural vigilantes on the lookout for four-letter words, sex scenes, evolutionary theory, or Commies between the covers. Traditionally, in the case of a novel or play, schools either use it or ban it, but they don't change it. That's not the case with textbooks, in which the content is insidiously malleable.

As the twenty-first century unfolds, the textbook wars rage on, with small watchdog groups disproportionately influencing textbook adoption policy. In the state of Texas, where I live, the state board of education, which purchases K–12 textbooks for the entire state, holds public hearings that witness no-holds-barred matches among family planning, pro-life, gay advocacy, fundamentalist Christian, and other lobbying groups on the merits of proposed textbooks—and those hearings often result in one or more textbooks being withdrawn from consideration for adoption or even in the reconsideration of previously approved texts.[1]

Though textbooks undeniably fulfill important tasks in the school systems of all states and nations—capitalist as well as communist, democratic as wells as authoritarian—nowhere were textbooks more consciously and completely turned to propagandist purposes than in the DDR (*Deutsche*

Demokratische Republik, German Democratic Republic). Throughout the forty-year existence of the DDR (1949–89), the Ministry of Education controlled textbook content tightly, and, in turn, the textbooks and teachers' guidebooks kept a tight rein on DDR teachers. The task of writing textbooks was entrusted by the Ministry of Education to scholarly "collectives" (groups of academics, each headed by an elite Party member) who could be trusted to adhere to the communist line on all questions.

The most important of these were the editorial collectives at Verlag Volk und Wissen, the central state publishing house in East Berlin.[2] To guarantee that there would be no ideological deviations among members of the collective, recalls Helmut Roske, formerly an editor at Volk und Wissen, his superior always took special precautions. Roske's department chief, Heinz Frankewicz, would regularly summon collective members to his office and remind them of the educators' ideological mission.[3] In his memoir titled "The Textbook Factory," published in the December 1963 *Atlantic Monthly,* Roske recounts one such meeting, during which the political lessons that DDR textbooks sought to indoctrinate became painfully clear:

> The editors would listen in silence while he [Frankewicz] read out a perfectly correct sentence from the text[book] and then proceeded to smother it beneath a mountain of objections.
>
> For instance, he would read: "Because the German Democratic Republic is poor in hard coal resources, soft coal is used here in great quantities." "This is what you have written," he would say, "and let me quote further": "Soft coal contains a high water content, very little hydrogen, and its heat potential is limited." "This kind of thing could be found in any book, even in a capitalistic one."

According to Roske, Frankewicz proceeded to ask:

> "And what is the student supposed to infer? That the German Democratic Republic is weak? That we are unable to build up any industry, or what? Teaching material must serve to instill patriotic feelings and political conviction. A textbook like this might just as well be published in West Germany. It is false and useless. We are political beings and are educating young communists. Where is there anything here about the Ruhr barons? Where is there anything about the warmongering monopolies in West Germany?

Why are the tables for water content in soft and hard coal placed right next to each other? So that the student can instantly compare them? Use the tables in which water doesn't appear and which build up a more favorable picture. It all sounds different when you say, "The German Democratic Republic has the greatest soft coal output in the world." Then list the collectivized industries we have treating soft coal. Show pictures of the [coal] plants. Quote from the plan, describe the activities in these various [firms]!"

Roske goes on to recount the futile attempts of the editorial collective to preserve the textbook's scientific integrity:

> "But this is a book on chemistry," the editors protested.
> "No," said Frankewicz. "This is a textbook whose job it is to work up student enthusiasm over the Party's output. It must show the teacher how and with what methods to instill this enthusiasm. Take a look at *Neues Deutschland,* our Party's paper."
> "But a newspaper," objected the editors, "is no source for a scientific textbook!"
> "Not *a* newspaper—*this* newspaper! It's the organ of the Party," said Frankewicz. "In it, Party Chief Walter Ulbricht outlines the prospects for our chemical industries, which today live off coal but which tomorrow will be fed by petroleum supplied from our Soviet friends. That's what we mean by science.
> "At least two socialist examples must be introduced on every page, deliberately, you understand. I'll see you in three weeks' time."
> With that he dismisses the team.

This exchange serves as ironic evidence of the single-minded intention of the Ministry of Education's policymakers. As the DDR *Pedagogical Encyclopedia* confidently pronounced: "The textbook is one of the most important lesson materials . . . and it effectively fulfills the cultural and educational tasks of the socialist school."[4]

II

Textbooks did indeed form a cornerstone of the DDR school curriculum—though, as East Germany's defunct status doubtless suggests, their effectiveness was disputable. But the lessons that they sought to impart are indisputable. DDR primers and school readers told schoolchildren who and what to admire and abhor. Civics textbooks exalted a model of German socialist youth and instructed DDR pupils what to think about the West, especially the United States, and what to think about the Soviet Union. History textbooks shaped pupils' views about the major events of DDR and world history. Even textbooks in the sciences and mathematics reflected the doctrine of so-called DIAMAT (dialectical materialism).

Textbook Reds examines how—and how effectively—DDR textbooks fulfilled these tasks, as it explores how a broad cross-section of school subjects contributed to the pedagogical goals of East German education. My title is intended to be thought-provoking rather than politically provocative: I do not mean to suggest that all DDR citizens were lock-step, ideologically benighted, card-carrying communist functionaries—or even to imply that lifelong Party supporters rigidly conformed to official DDR views. Rather, my title is meant to convey that what we can term a "textbook mentality"—which equated citizens' critiques of the Party and DDR government with disloyalty and such bourgeois sins as individualism, negativism, and cosmopolitanism—imprinted itself deeply on generations of DDR pupils. Those DDR citizens who broke free of such indoctrination still bore marks of its influence, even, as we shall see, long after their leaving school—and long after the DDR's collapse.

No book-length English-language study has discussed how the East German textbook sought to shape the *Weltanschauung* of DDR youth and form the young citizen's mind.[5] But if one wants to know what DDR students were told to think about their nation, their governing Party and its leaders, their so-called Soviet friends, and their class enemy, no better source than textbooks exists. For here we have the dogmas of the SED (*Sozialistische Einheitspartei Deutschlands*, Socialist Unity Party) communicated in their most simplified form and manufactured in the millions for mass consumption.

It is perhaps impossible to reconstruct at this date what DDR citizens actually thought about their state and its place in the world. Few reliable records and no public opinion polls existed in the former DDR (at least none that were ever published in the West). Some demographic information and research data were available from the Zentralinstitut für Jugendforschung (Central Institute for Youth Research), but for the most part Western scholars could only estimate or speculate about what DDR citizens actually thought. Specifically because of this scarcity of survey data the

DDR textbook is invaluable, for it reveals in detail what citizens were *supposed* to think.

In light of these facts, Textbook Reds draws extensively on teachers' manuals and handbooks in order to illuminate how the Ministry of Education directed teachers to present classroom material. Yet my main concern is not with classroom teaching methods or with an empirical analysis linking student attitudes and curricular content. Nor does this work seek to establish the dense post-war historical context in which the textbooks were produced and received, let alone to present a full-scale history of the DDR educational system, a story that I have recently told in Repainting the Little Red Schoolhouse: A History of Eastern German Education, 1945–1995 (Oxford University Press, 2002). Rather, this book scrutinizes the imprint of communist ideology in curricular materials and suggests how the thinking of eastern Germans has evolved beyond the worldview inscribed in the DDR textbook.

Part 1 is a detailed textual and thematic study of the role of ideology in making "textbook Reds" and how the promotion of that ideology served the purpose of state legitimation for the DDR. It concentrates on DDR educational materials and on how the state philosophy of M-L (Marxism-Leninism) permeated every school subject. Chapter 1 addresses the schoolbooks used in German language and literature classes, ranging from the primary school readers found in the POS (*Polytechnische Oberschule*) elementary school to the EOS (*Erweiterte Oberschule*) secondary school anthologies. Given the centrality of German class in the DDR curriculum—the DDR devoted up to 30 percent more class hours to German than did some West German *Länder*—its presentation in DDR textbooks receives the most extensive attention. Chapters 2 through 5, respectively, treat curricular materials in geography, *Staatsbürgerkunde* (civics), history, and the physical sciences and mathematics. Among the specific topics addressed are: socialist patriotism, international proletarianism, socialist morality, the capitalist-imperialist enemy, the duties of socialist citizenship, and the DDR identity.[6]

Drawing on a rich and varied collection of materials—a total of more than two hundred textbooks, teaching guides, school songbooks, educators' professional journals, and school examinations—*Textbook Reds* engages in close sociological and cultural readings of these materials and spotlights the role of M-L in East German pedagogy. For reasons of both space and the availability of primary materials, I have chosen to concentrate chiefly on the elementary (POS) curriculum and the post-Wall era

(1961–89). Periodic attention is also given to secondary school (EOS) schoolbooks and other educational resources from the early post-war years. My focus in Part 1 is, therefore, on the DDR era, especially the 1970s and 1980s, and on DDR textbooks, with occasional attention directed to textbooks published since 1990.

Each chapter in Part 1 features numerous examples and other data from the textbooks, whereby I mean to show the ubiquity of the ideological contents. Certainly the textbooks of every nation reflect its political culture and values. But the sheer volume and variety of ideologically conditioned material is the most striking feature of East German textbooks, and thus I deem it essential to offer an ample demonstration of both its pervasiveness and its significance.

Moreover, in order to show what role textbooks played in ideological indoctrination and national self-legitimation, the book not only investigates their contents, but analyzes how those contents evolved across the history of the DDR. In select instances, I have compared the textbooks of the DDR with those of West Germany or the Third Reich—and also with American, Soviet, and recent Russian textbooks. These cross-cultural comparisons serve to highlight the distinctive character of DDR schoolbooks. My hope is that these diverse approaches to understanding the DDR educational system will prove valuable not only to educators, but also to cultural historians, political scientists, sociologists, and communication theorists. Although I discuss periodically why certain school subjects were more vulnerable to ideologically motivated material, I am not concerned to specify what proportions of the texts are ideological in nature or to pinpoint the relative level of propaganda to which East German students were subjected. Instead my emphasis is on comparative historical analysis and interpretive methodology, whereby I also aim to render *Textbook Reds* accessible to a wide audience via the aid of the excursus sections, which are designed to shed light on the reception and impact of the textbooks.

These excursus sections in Part 1 warrant additional comment. Each chapter therein includes one or more such sections that highlight and further explore the topics pursued in the main narrative of the chapter. Each excursus broadly illustrates how eastern Germans were influenced by ideology in the schools or inspects some dimension of post-communist educational life. More specifically, each excursus examines a particular issue or theme in the curricular subject under discussion in its respective chapter, or devotes extended attention to how a single grade or class year was handled by the textbooks, or engages a topic in comparative education.

III

Part 2 of this book takes the story of the making of East German "textbook Reds" up to the year 2005. It discloses how cultural and educational policies enter the lives of real people even after the regime that promoted this ideology and issued its textbooks has passed from the scene. For the fact is that textbooks are often too narrowly analyzed according to their texts alone—rather than in the context of real readers—and therefore these analyses fail to capture any sense of the impact and imprint of the textbooks on people's lives.

This study attempts to redress that imbalance by devoting Part 2 to a series of portraits and interviews of eastern Germans influenced by the textbooks already discussed. Some of my interlocutors were, by their own admission, "convinced communists" (a.k.a. "textbook Reds"), while others were resistant to or even outspokenly critical of the DDR regime. Nonetheless, all of my interviewees grew up with the worldview of the textbooks as the official horizon of their thinking.

The three chapters of Part 2 thus feature both "school portraits" and interviews with teachers or students, each of whom reflects on his or her educational experience in the DDR. My aspiration is to illustrate suggestively how the *Weltanschauung* of DDR textbooks has been renegotiated in easterners' lives—rather than, once again, to argue whether or how DDR schoolbooks continue to exert influence on the minds of eastern Germans long after the DDR's demise and German reunification.

That is also the reason I have limited my formal analysis of textbooks to the DDR era. For I am more interested to trace into the post-communist era the developments that occurred in people's minds than in pedagogical materials; i.e., I am more concerned to disclose the ongoing imprint of the "textbook mentality" on the citizens who grew up in the DDR than to identify alterations in schoolbooks since reunification. In short: I am more concerned with people's lives than with propagandists' lessons. Part 2 concentrates on teachers and students who experienced the DDR educational system in the 1970s and 1980s; this focus suggests the mode of thinking of a generation, and it suggests the persisting—if quite indefinite—influence of the DDR textbooks in the process.

Among the questions that the portraits and the interviews raise are the following: How do the communist past and the post-communist present fit together in eastern Germany? How have education and teaching in the region evolved since 1989? What influence does "Ostalgie" exert on memory of the communist past and the direction of eastern German education? How did eastern Germans adapt in the classroom? How did they respond to the orthodoxies embodied in the textbooks? How much continuity existed between the idealistic era of the 1940s and early 1950s and the backlash that occurred toward the Soviets in the late 1950s and 1960s? And what remains in eastern Germans' attitudes of the DDR's determined campaign "to win the minds of men," its ceaseless struggle to form the East German identity?[7]

Most of the portraits and interviews in Part 2 concern an eastern German who passed through the DDR school system. I have not attempted to analyze closely how a particular textbook left its imprint on any of the minds of my conversation partners. (Who, indeed, remembers school that well?!) Rather, I have sought to present snapshots of eastern Germans coming to terms with their textbook learning during the decade following German reunification.[8] Because the majority of my interviews were conducted during 1990–97, the first seven years after German reunification, they also have a particular documentary value as oral history of a vanished past.

Indeed, this special documentary aspect of the conversations in Part 2—which function as "eyewitness testimony" of a gut-wrenching transitional moment in eastern Germany's history—was stressed to me by several early readers of this book in manuscript, who found the transcripts of my interviews invaluable as a historical record and urged me to edit them for this study. (All of the interviews were conducted in German.) The enthusiastic responses of these readers reminded me of my original motivations for scheduling these interviews: to serve as a witness to witnesses. For I was a visitor during a fleeting, evanescent moment in German history, when East German socialism had not yet disappeared and Western-style capitalism had not yet established itself.

In hindsight, many of my conversations and experiences in the early 1990s could only have happened at that precise historical moment. Before 1990, it was impossible for a Westerner, or indeed practically any non–East German, to travel freely in the DDR—and near-impossible to have conversations with East Germans who possessed the temerity and transparency to express themselves freely and openly. After the early 1990s, the old DDR way of life receded so quickly that older adults wanted to move beyond that past and young eastern Germans had no memory of it. Moreover, as numerous eastern Germans told me, I was distinctive because I am an American; they felt antagonism toward western Germans (the so-called *Besserwessis,* or western German know-it-alls), and they felt either hatred or incuriosity toward Russians and Eastern Europeans from the old Soviet bloc; but most of them had never spoken to an American, and now that it was safe to do so, they were passionately curious to share their stories with me—and almost equally so to hear about my impressions of their country and themselves.

So I was uniquely positioned both temporally and culturally to witness an extraordinary and defining instant in world history that has left very few traces in eastern German society today. Part 2 of this book represents an attempt to capture that unique experience.

Furthermore, the portraits and interviews in Part 2 represent an attempt not just to include the responses of readers but to bring alive how the textbooks reflected their worldview—even more than a decade after the fall of the Berlin Wall. For I am not simply analyzing the sober contents of now-moribund communist schoolbooks but suggesting how these books functioned in DDR education—and, in many cases, how they continue to influence their readers' lives. Thus the larger aspiration behind my examining "the textbook in the classroom" is to capture the human implications of East German curricular policy and spot the amplitude and register of political tones in the symphony of unsung citizens' lives. In this way, I have sought to establish a context in *personal* histories for better understanding the curricular materials. The study thereby becomes not only an investigation of DIAMAT pedagogy as communicated via DDR textbooks, but also a motley chorus of voices that discloses how the DDR *Weltanschauung* manifested itself in the outlooks of its ordinary citizens.

By inviting DDR teachers and students to tell their stories—to share the high and low notes of their experiences in the educational system—I have striven to make available the drama of DDR history from below, of *erlebte Geschichte* (lived/experienced history). Rather than interview top school administration officials, I sought out rank-and-file teachers and students whom I met through friends and acquaintances. The fact is that most well-known people tend to be somewhat removed from ordinary life; this book aspires precisely to draw American readers to re-experience a near-universal experience in the industrial world—school life—and thereby draw them into lives apparently dissimilar yet ultimately not so unlike their own.

Indeed, a special comparative feature of the portraits and interviews—

which should be of compelling interest to American readers—is the periodic commentary on American education and American values. In many cases my interviewees were drawn to make extended comparisons between Germany and the United States, especially between the values of capitalist America and the socialist heritage and their counterparts. This reflects both the new orientation of eastern Germans toward the West and, quite often, these easterners' recent experiences of studying in and or visiting the United States. In many cases, eastern German students preferred to compare their socialist values not with western German values but with American values, because they considered the latter most representative of capitalism—and because American capitalism seems to them an extreme version of the capitalist ethos that they have encountered in western Germany.

Because these interviews and portraits function as an informal social history of DDR education and tell its story from below, they may be considered a "school supplement" to Lutz Niethammer's revealing 1991 anthropology of everyday life in the DDR, *Die volkseigene Erfahrung* (The People's Own Experience) that showed the gap between claims of the Party (which professed to speak always for the *Volk*) and the lived reality of East Germans' lives. The conversations in the present volume expose a similar gulf, thus giving belated voice to onetime teachers and students from the former DDR. These "school portraits" might be titled: *Die volkseigene Schule*—"The People's Own School."

IV

Textbook Reds thus presents not just an interpretive analysis of communist textbooks, but also offers a glimpse of post-communism with a German face, indeed what might be called "the textbook with a human face," thereby to see how the ideology of the textbooks was variously concretized in the consciousness of the teachers and students who read them. "Post-communism" is a charged, indeed loaded and over-determined phrase in contemporary Europe. *Is* communism "post-"? Or can it be revived? Will it become just another school or movement of thought? Or can it serve as the basis for a reconstituted political and economic system? These are questions with which both thinkers and policymakers are still grappling, and they have particular relevance to citizens of former communist nations such as the DDR. At minimum, as the portraits and interviews in Part 2 evince, the past lives on in the present: the DDR communist regime exists no longer, but elements of the communist ideology remain alive in the minds and hearts of millions of eastern Germans.

Post-communist education is also, in a very real sense, post-*German* education. That fact is vividly illustrated in the final chapter of Part 2, about which an extended comment is appropriate here. Chapter 8 devotes consideration to a topic not found in the DDR textbooks and never explicitly advanced by DDR educators. Indeed, it is a topic that may be seen as a post-reunification counterpart to the old DDR program of "Education for Hate." The new program is broadly known as "Education for Tolerance" and it has received attention throughout Germany, yet most especially in the east. An entirely new dimension of education is raised with the introduction of tolerance as a leitmotif in the curriculum. For tolerance is not simply a matter of pedagogical approach or course content.

Among those most concerned with education for tolerance are Germany's Jewish citizens and residents. And arguably, the setting in which the success or failure of the program will prove most crucially apparent is the German-Jewish school. Thus a special feature of this book is its attention in Chapter 8 to Jewish themes and to the rebirth of Jewish education in Germany in the shadow of the Holocaust.

Finally, in a brief epilogue, I shift back from the school portraits to the DDR system, offering a final meditation on the high toll that its ideological core curriculum exacted.

IDEOLOGY AS CORE CURRICULUM

1945: Textbooks and German Re-Education

Nazi rule placed the entire course of German education, from nursery through university, in the service of fascist ideology, racial hatred, spiritual and physical preparation for war, chauvinistic baiting, and military drilling. . . .
—KPD-SPD Joint Declaration on Education, 11 June 1945

Even before the Russians occupied eastern Germany in May 1945, the topic of German schoolbooks was already one that occupied Soviet leader Joseph Stalin and the Kremlin. Like the western Allies, the Soviets wanted to avoid giving Germans the impression that their children would be stuffed with Allied propaganda. Above all, the Soviets sought not to repeat the fiasco that the British and Americans had unwittingly created during the early months of the Italian occupation. In 1944, after the successful Anglo-American invasion of Italy in late 1943, schools had been reopened in 1944 under Allied administration. London and Washington had decided, on a temporary basis, to continue using the fascist schoolbooks and simply excise those pages that glorified fascism. But some families had retained old—and intact—copies of the books at home, and predictably, the excised pages had become the object of intense interest among Italian schoolchildren. Allied policy thus had achieved exactly the opposite of its main goal, the political "re-education" of the vanquished fascist enemy.[1]

Plans to implement German re-education with non-Nazi textbooks hit an immediate roadblock: The Nazis had burned all German schoolbooks printed before 1935. And so the Allies were forced to search outside Germany for old German textbooks. The biggest source was Teachers College, Columbia University, which sent microfilms of twenty textbooks to London shortly before the war's close. These books were republished in Germany, with some alterations made for political content, and remained in use until 1947.[2]

But these textbooks were circulated only in Germany's western zones. By the war's end, political tensions between the western Allies and the Soviet Union had become so exacerbated that the two sides could not agree on how German re-education should be conducted. Both the western Allies and the Soviets concurred that re-education was a program of moral reconstruction that would entail a complete revamping of Germans' traditional (i.e., not just pro-Nazi) values. The aspiration was to foster a new Fatherland: Whereas the West sought a Germany committed to popular democracy and to the freedoms of speech, press, and religion, the Soviets wanted a Germany committed to Marxism-Leninism under the guidance of the Communist Party and the Kremlin. Thus the Allies' fight about re-education policy eventually became a battle over which "un-lessons"—the democratic or the Bolshevist—would be taught in German schools.

Of course, disagreement over textbook content was just one aspect of a larger battle—extending far beyond education policy—between the western Allies and the Soviets. The conflicts would ultimately lead to the complete end of cooperation between occupation authorities of the West and the Soviets—and, after the 1946–47 Berlin airlift and a series of other small crises, to the formation of separate Germanies: the Federal Republic of Germany (Bundesrepublik Deutschland [West Germany]) in May 1949 and the DDR (Deutsche Demokratische Republik, German Democratic Republic [East Germany]) in October 1949.

Although textbooks that had been in use during the Weimar Republic were now easily available, Soviet educators considered them insufficiently progressive, just as the western Allies regarded them as insufficiently democratic. (Both the USSR and the western Allies also judged them to be proto-fascist.) Unwilling to use the textbooks from the Weimar era—especially after they were revised by the western Allies to show strong sympathy to capitalism and hostility to socialism—the SMAD (Sowjetische Militäradministration Deutschlands, Soviet Military Administration of Germany) decided to issue its own textbooks.[3] Having located a few Weimar-era textbooks that could serve as models, Soviet educators worked with returning German socialist émigrés to write several textbooks for grades one through four. Volk und Wissen Volkseigener Verlag, the newly founded educational publishing house, rushed out these temporarily usable books in late 1945 for the 1945/46 school year. (Given paper shortages, fiscal crises, and the quickly changing political lines in the

Kremlin, the Ministry of Education issued no non-science textbooks until 1951. Even in the sciences and mathematics, teachers in the upper elementary school and secondary school grades had no textbooks until the founding of the DDR in 1949.)

From Brown to Red?

The old Party slogan trumpeted *"Stürmt die Festung Wissenschaft!"* ("Storm the citadel of learning!"). Marshal Stalin himself had issued the call to arms, declaring educational institutions "the citadel of learning" that "we must capture at any price. This citadel must be taken by our youth, if they wish to take the place of the old guard."[4] The youth could be persuaded of the superiority of communism, even if their elders were a lost cause. The Soviets called their agitprop educational campaign *vospitanie* (moral-social development); the East Germans termed it *weltanschauliche Erziehung* (education for a world outlook). Whatever the name, the intent was the same: creating the new socialist human being.

From the earliest days of the SMAD, textbooks were the foundation in eastern Germany that undergirded the "citadel of learning." As we shall see, no subject—not even spelling, penmanship, inorganic chemistry, or linear algebra—escaped the Red paintbrush. Marxist-Leninist (*Marxismus-Leninismus*, M-L) indoctrination thus "replaced" fascist propaganda in eastern German textbooks: "the Red replaced the Brown."

Of course, that formulation is a vulgar and misleading oversimplification. The word "replace" suggests a simple historic transfer from the Nazi regime to East German communism. There was no such easy transfer. The totalitarianism theory behind this oversimplification, first propounded by Hannah Arendt in *The Origins of Totalitarianism* (1951), is too reductionist to grasp the historical intricacies of the transition in German society between 1945 and the official founding of the two German states in 1949. Those four intervening years were crucial in the formation of two entirely new societies, whose complex development defies the simplistic "from Brown to Red" theories of East German society.

That new starting point in German history after 1945 in *both* German societies does not accommodate for a simple "replacement theory" of "Red = Brown." The theory of a mere replacement of the Nazis by the communists overlooks the liberties that the communist regime offered. It underplays the gravity of the racial hatred that the Nazis stamped in the minds of many Germans—including committed communists and political liberals. Moreover, generational change that was taking place within East German society in the late 1950s and 1960s, which reoriented DDR youth toward atheistic, progressive beliefs, also goes unnoticed. Thus, the "Red = Brown" concept only serves to obscure the complexities of East German society. DDR society was founded upon the belief in the equality of all human beings (black, white, Jewish, Muslims, men and women)—and it upheld that creed in the main (despite a degree of anti-Semitism and sexism).

Here again, I do not say that social and political reality ever matched these beliefs; in numerous cases I think they turned out to be vain beliefs. Nevertheless, as mental and social constructs, these beliefs were *part* of DDR reality. A "Red = Brown" approach thus ignores the many layers of East German social and political reality. Quoting from school textbooks and pressing the citations into an artificial framework of "Nazi-era → DDR transition" promotes a myth rather than illuminating history.

So the "Red" did not simply "replace" the "Brown"—the historical transition to the DDR was complex and partly discontinuous with the immediate past. Moreover, at least in 1945 and 1946, it was not evident that M-L would come to dominate eastern German education. Largely to satisfy the western Allies—and to preserve the possibility that a reunited Germany would one day stand in the socialist camp—the policy of the SMAD was anti-fascist rather than explicitly pro-communist: anti-Brown rather than overtly pro-Red. A directive on syllabus revision published by the Ministry of Education in October 1945 makes it clear that SMAD re-education policy sought merely to assure that eastern Germans would learn to scorn Nazis and fascist Brownshirts and to appreciate socialist and Soviet culture:

> In *Biology,* Nazi racial ideology and the teaching on which it is based—the supposed superiority of the German people over other peoples—is to be removed. Likewise to be removed is the application to human society of the teaching about the struggle for existence in the animal world. Students are only to learn about the lawfulness of nature and the development of plants and creatures, and to see how human beings learn to master nature through the recognition of these laws.
>
> In *German,* selection and interpretation of materials must consist not only of aesthetic and literary viewpoints, but also correspond to the introduction of the comprehensive educational goal [i.e.,

anti-fascism]. This requires that the youth be introduced to our classics, our current democratic [i.e., socialist] literature, and the great works of world [including Russian] literature.⁵

German communists began to speak of "the new school" (*die neue schule*)—the anti-fascist, democratic school—that they were building in the SBZ (*Sowjetische Besatzungszone,* Soviet Occupation Zone). The phrase was deliberately lower-cased to trumpet the DDR's democratic intentions. To staff their schools, the Ministry of Education fired almost all teachers who had been members of the Nazi Party (almost two-thirds of the teaching profession), leaving the median age of SBZ teachers at fifty-two and one-half (fifty-nine in Berlin). (Roughly 70 percent of teachers had been Nazi Party members during the Third Reich.)⁶ These teachers were replaced by "new teachers" (*Neulehrer*), some of whom were as young as sixteen years old, and some of whom had not even completed elementary school.⁷ But the SMAD ordained that educational attainment was not a decisive criterion for selection as a new teacher. Political reliability—an anti-fascist and, preferably, pro-socialist or pro-communist orientation—was the key. For the new teachers were to be the cornerstone of the SMAD's re-education efforts to transform the German character and eradicate German militarism. As part of this re-education, the SMAD banned all kinds of military games and ordered that the production of war toys be halted. These measures, along with the progressive ideological perspective provided by the new teachers, revolutionized the eastern German classroom. And by "spread[ing] the truth about the Soviet Union," the new teachers revolutionized the classroom in a pro-Soviet, M-L direction, as the words of one DDR historian make clear:

> Many young people began to understand [in 1945–46] that participation in democratic reconstruction which stamped out the roots of war—and not death on a battlefield in an imperialistic war—was meaningful and honorable. Concepts such as "love of the Fatherland," "heroism," and "courage" received new, humanistic content, completely opposed to imperialistic conceptions. Insofar as the new school told schoolchildren of the genuine heroism and real patriotism of the anti-fascist resistance fighters, insofar as it spread the truth about the Soviet Union, it helped to make the poison of anti-communism ineffective for the first time in German educational history.⁸

But Nazi, or at least anti-Soviet, attitudes could not be changed overnight: Most students had belonged to the HJ (*Hitler Jugend*, Hitler Youth) organizations, and most families harbored anti-communist sentiments. It was not easy for the Soviets to overcome years of propaganda against the "Bolsheviks" and the "Slavs"—and German hostilities were exacerbated by the widespread raping of German women by Soviet troops, by the shame of the Nuremberg Trials of 1945–46, and by the dismantling of eastern German industry by the SMAD. Some local school districts were hard to bring under control: A 1946 report in the state of Saxony on fascist tendencies in the schools noted that "military propaganda is still to be found" and even that teachers were teaching from "schoolbooks . . . that were published after 1933 and are considered fascist books." Indeed, defiance toward the SMAD even went further: "In various schools, there are still pictures of Hitler and other so-called Nazi 'leaders'; even Nazi placards and mottoes haven't been entirely removed."[9]

But resistance to the SMAD and the German communist educational authorities did not last long. By 1948, the citadel—at least at the elementary and secondary levels—had been successfully stormed (the university would take almost another decade of struggle). And by the early 1950s, it had been taken over and transformed completely. At least some of the credit for the victorious campaign after 1951 must go to the schoolbooks and teaching guides (which gave explicit instructions on how to conduct every single class hour), because it was through these materials that the Party controlled the teachers themselves. Since individual teachers, especially non-Party members, could not be trusted to support (or even grasp) subtle changes in the Party line,[10] every teacher was told to "teach the textbook to the letter"; the textbook and syllabus thus functioned like military orders issued from a rigidly centralized, hierarchical command structure—and SED (*Sozialistische Einheitspartei Deutschlands,* Socialist Unity Party of Germany) educational authorities permitted no deviations—at least not officially.[11]

Indeed, until the mid-1980s and the *glasnost* initiatives under Mikhail Gorbachev, it is fair to say that—long after the SMAD was gone—the USSR continued to control the East German educational apparatus, though of course not directly, since hard-line SED *apparatchniks* were available to write the texts and select the illustrations. Or rather, one should say, to *translate* the texts. For there was seldom much difference between the contents of the DDR and the USSR schoolbook: What Hänschen learned to read was usually very similar to what little Ivan was learning to read. What East Berlin mandated had already been handed down from Moscow.

But the combination of the Nazi past, the lost war, and the Soviet occupation also produced significant differences, often in the direction of a much more orthodox, rigid communism than in the post-Stalinist USSR. Hänschen's and little Gretel's textbook world was black and white—or better, Red and black—populated by good comrades and evil strangers, by friends of the Fatherland and enemies of the People.

This context makes the study of the DDR's schoolbooks especially significant. Virtually every classroom in the nation used the assigned textbook for each subject and grade level. The textbook was the ultimate source of information for many pupils—and even for many *Neulehrer*. Most DDR citizens had little or no formal education after their ten-year polytechnical school (or, in the early post-war era, their eight-year school). Above all, it was the information that was taught in school, not at the university or in adult education courses, that shaped the average citizen's beliefs. And beliefs implanted in school, especially given DDR travel restrictions and limited access to outside sources of information, took root and grew. So the textbooks taught the young how to perceive their nation and world. For many DDR citizens, the lessons lasted most of a lifetime—and the re-educational "unlessons" were hard-won indeed.

The (East) German Ideology

And what constituted, we may ask, the content of these textbook lessons—or unlessons?

The textbooks transmitted a factory myth of the First German Workers' and Peasants' State, a set of doctrines that might *in toto* be termed "the East German ideology." In *The German Ideology* (1845), Karl Marx and Friedrich Engels castigated the "illusions" of German Hegelianism, which promoted a system of false ideas, or "ideology," based on dishonest reasoning and the distortion of facts designed to justify the position of the ruling class. In the 1930s, the National Socialists glorified nationalism and perpetuated myths that gave special emphasis to *Deutschtum* (Germanness), representing the culmination of decades of increasingly aggressive emphasis on German soil and blood, and thereby creating what scholars such as Fritz Stern have termed "the Germanic ideology." Out of the defeat of the Reich in 1945 arose new ideologies, western and eastern, reflecting the opposing *Weltanschauungen* of the respective Allied occupation powers.

In the SBZ, the new German ideology soon emerged to be a wintry version of Soviet ideology transplanted—direct from the Kremlin and with little adjustment for environment or climate—westward. Thus the new Germany on the Elbe became, as it were, Soviet Germany. As we shall soon see in detail, however, though the Soviets had defeated the Germanic ideology of the Nazis, they immediately imposed an equally authoritarian ideology on eastern Germany. And it rapidly evolved, more and more showing its real colors: from *Schein*-democratization to Sovietization to Stalinization. Ultimately, the DDR of the 1950s and 1960s became more staunchly authoritarian than even the USSR.

And so, almost exactly a century after Marx and Engels had deplored the German ideology of their day, East German communists were inculcating their own official ideology, an ideology that turned out to bear striking resemblance to the Teutonic false consciousness that the German forefathers of the socialist Fatherland had excoriated: Stalinism, or M-L. But, as I have suggested, the emphasis in DDR Stalinism was definitely a matter of "L" before "M": Lenin, not Marx; Russian, not German. And Marx's definition of ideology—i.e., a false consciousness that masks from the protagonists themselves the causes, grounds, and motives for their actions—characterized M-L even more than it had the German nationalism and philosophical idealism of his own day. Indeed, for all its denunciations of fascism and Hitlerism, the only close counterpart in German history to the new East German ideology was, ironically, the recently defeated Germanic ideology of the Nazis. Just as Soviet ideals displaced Teutonic ones, Soviet nationalism replaced *Deutschtum*. Where the Nazi educators had prized German blood as the mark of the *Herrenmensch* (master race), DDR schools presented workers' children as superior to bourgeois children, and asserted that workers' problems had nothing to do with individuals and everything to do with economic structures. Soviet pedagogues and M-L "science" were treated as omniscient, eerily recalling the Nazi elevation of Aryan pedagogy and vilification of "Jewish" science. And so the new democratic socialist *Mensch* of East Germany would be reared on a *Weltanschauung* recognizably similar to that which the USSR had sacrificed 20 million citizens to conquer. The school stories in DDR readers highlighted the East German ideology, taking special pains to lionize the Soviet Union.

A common tactic was to portray Stalin's alleged love for German children, partly to counteract the enduring anti-Soviet sentiment among East Germans.[12] One story, which features Stalin's towering presence at the Potsdam conference in 1945, is titled "When Stalin Came [to Germany]": "Whether Stalin is sunk deep in thought at his work table or at the conference table seeking peace, always his mind is on the People. He thinks about every child, especially about German children. No one will ever know war or fascism again; there will only be peace and friendship among the children of the whole wide world." Under the picture of Marshal Stalin runs the caption: "Never, so long as the world turns, will the People forget their great and loving father and teacher."[13]

But the lessons of socialism's great march to victory were traceable to and projected upon events occurring long before the twentieth century. Consider, for instance, the introduction to the DDR fifth-grade history text of the 1980s, which covered the period from prehistory to classical Greece and Rome:

> In fifth through tenth grade you will become acquainted with the important events in the history of humankind. You will learn why working people often did not possess what they created and how the exploiters came by their riches. You will understand how wars came to be and why courageous persons battled for peace. But one thing above all should be investigated and answered:
>
> How does it come that human society, from its beginnings to the present, has steadily developed itself, and that this development already in many countries has led to socialism—and in all countries will lead to it?[14]

Whether referring to the Stone Age or ancient Mesopotamia or Periclean Greece, DDR textbook historians made it clear that animals and human beings were distinguishable by their different relations to work, that human history was the history of a class struggle between workers and non-workers, and that the glorious past battles of workers and peasants were the heroic antecedents of the First German Workers' and Peasants' State. The SED operated with its Marxist-Whig interpretation of history: History was the story of the rise of socialism, and "real existing socialism" could be found in the DDR and its *Bruderländer*. Following the guidelines issued by the Ministry of Education and Volk und Wissen, DDR textbook writers faithfully followed the Party summons that "authors of textbooks should take as their model the works of Marx and Lenin, which are permeated with boundless faith in the victory of communism and unrelenting hatred for its enemies. A textbook should be written so that not a single fact leaves the student indifferent."[15]

As we shall soon see, DDR textbooks did not leave the citizenry indifferent—as the outrage reflected in the popular demonstrations and mass protests that led to the toppling of the Berlin Wall in November 1989 evinced. That the textbook "facts" selected to persuade DDR pupils ultimately failed to do so, despite more than four decades of ceaseless effort, was not, however, for lack of trying. Nor should we Americans remain indifferent about the relentless textbook wars in the United States, when the state assumes ever greater control of education, whether in the name of the "No Child Left Behind" initiatives, or raising performance goals, or establishing uniform and comparative quality standards. For such justifications resemble what DDR educators also claimed, albeit in different language. So let us Americans remain vigilant and self-critical. A politicized curriculum led the DDR school to become an instance of "illiberal education" at its most extreme. We should heed the lesson of that mistake.[16]

But what were the particular "facts" chosen to inspire DDR youth? How exactly did DDR schoolbooks help breed the German democratic socialist *Mensch*?

Let us turn to the central subject in the DDR curriculum for our first glimpse at the answers.

PART I

OF POLITICS AND LETTERS—
AND NUMBERS

ONE

GERMAN FOR THE EAST GERMANS
Language and Literature

> Books are not only friends, they are weapons—revolutionary weapons! Create weapons! Create weapons!
> —Otto Grotewohl, DDR Prime Minister, greeting inscribed in the Dietz Verlag guest book, 1950

DDR schools devoted more hours per week (in some grades, twelve or more) to German language and literature than to any other subject. Whereas instruction in all other subjects (except mathematics) started in the middle or upper grades, German was taught in every grade, beginning in the first. East German schools also dedicated 40–80 percent more instructional time to German than did any West German state. For instance, whereas Hamburg schools (grades one to ten) devoted a total of 1,576 hours to German per year, DDR students in the POS (*Polytechnische Oberschule*, general education school) received an average of 2,853 hours annually.[1]

Much of my analysis of DDR textbooks in this and subsequent chapters is descriptive and explanatory, not based on *Ideologiekritik*. But before proceeding to a scrutiny of the textbooks, a brief word both about my own standpoint as an American cultural historian and about the daunting rhetorical and political challenges faced by DDR textbook writers is appropriate.

My research into the ideological and militaristic aspects of East German schoolbooks has confronted me not only with the stark reality of communist propaganda efforts, but also with a forceful adversarial perspective on the geopolitical intentions of the United States and the capitalist world. While I dispute that perspective, I do not mean to imply that the Soviet

Union (and Eastern Europe) constituted a black-and-white "evil empire." Nor do I deny either the complexities of the Cold War (in which the United States also took self-compromising positions) or the validity of some aspects of the Marxist analysis (or of other scholars critical of American foreign policy).[2] Rather, I respect the seriousness of the DDR *Weltanschauung* and textbook authors' critiques by engaging their work seriously, indeed sometimes combatively, as I offer here a self-consciously Western (American) response to the claims of these textbooks.

Certainly, I do not want to imply that DDR textbooks were nothing but agitprop. Yet even a casual glance through them makes clear that a significantly greater part of East German than Western schoolbooks was devoted to ideological claims, which were usually advanced in far sharper, blunter terms than in their western counterparts. These facts need to be acknowledged and evaluated, while avoiding both red-baiting and whitewashing.

Maintaining that critical stance is especially important when one assesses the DDR German curriculum. The curricular importance that SED educators accorded German reflected its central role in (East) German ideology. Indeed, its significance in molding textbook Reds—particularly through its emphasis on socialist virtue—cannot be exaggerated. German class, noted a second-grade teaching guide, contributed to "the all-around development of the socialist personality, the growth of young socialist citizens." And for all these reasons, this study devotes more attention to German textbooks than to any other DDR school subject.

And what was the specific content of German for the East Germans?

Whatever the grade level, German classes were integral to DDR *weltanschauliche Erziehung*, which, like Soviet *vospitanie*, was essentially character training or moral education devoted to forming "socialist personalities." While all elementary textbooks throughout the industrial world focus on such virtues as, for example, honesty, courtesy, and respect for property, East German textbooks put special emphasis on qualities such as team spirit, sobriety, industriousness, a high sense of public duty, intolerance of actions harmful to the public interest, good physical hygiene, and respect for manual labor, the military, and marriage and family life. East German textbooks held to a hard-line, M-L *Weltanschauung* whose great commandment was socialist patriotism. The precepts included revolutionary communist morality, militant atheism, devotion to the Party, the collectivist attitude toward labor, the class-oriented approach to social life, the international brotherhood of communist nations, undying solidarity with the Soviet Union, faith in the historic superiority of socialism over capitalism, an irreconcilable opposition to bourgeois ideology, and hatred toward the imperialists and other enemies of the socialist Fatherland.

Reared in the DDR

Reading—*that* is class struggle!
—Bertolt Brecht, "In Praise of Communism" (1932)

Of the three parts of German instruction—reading, letters, and culture—reading was the most important and received the most attention. SED educators outlined the POS German curriculum in three stages: (1) first through fourth grades, which focused on heroes and enemies, increasingly emphasizing historical context and current affairs in the higher grades; (2) fifth through seventh grades, which introduced literary genres, including longer selections (e.g., the novella); and (3) eighth through tenth grades, which added literary history, focusing upon the socialist and DDR heritage.[3] This section will proceed chronologically through the school grades. Following this section, the chapter devotes extended, separate attention to selected topics such as the language arts, culture, and role models in the primary and middle school years, before it treats the German curriculum of the upper grades.

First Through Fourth Grades

German textbooks for the lower and middle grades introduced pupils to life in socialist society. The primers in first through fourth grades are organized by theme, as shown by the section headings in the tables of contents of two representative primers:

> *Lesebuch 3*
> 1. Blowing in the Wind, Our Blue Flag!
> 2. Our Energy and Our Love for Our Socialist Fatherland!
> 3. Fighters for Peace, Progress, and Socialism!
> 4. Through the Seasons
> 5. I Want to Tell You
> 6. Excerpts from Children's Books
>
> *Lesebuch 4*
> 1. For Peace, Friendship among Peoples, and Socialism
> 2. For a Happy Life for All Peace-Loving Human Beings

3. In the Steps of Revolutionary Fighters
4. Reading, Learning, Being Cheerful
5. On the Seasons and Animals and Plants in General
6. Stories of the Olden Days and from Around the World
7. Excerpts from Children's Books[4]

These section titles furnish a good idea of the books' contents—and of the relative distribution of overtly ideological and non-ideological selections; at least half were devoted to the former. (The frequent use of exclamation marks is a notable feature of the ideologically tinged selections, both in the primers and throughout DDR textbooks.)

Primers for first grade contained lists of the chief DDR holidays and the Commandments of the Young Pioneers (JP, Junge Pioniere). The latter were composed in the fashion of the Ten Commandments of Socialist Morality formulated by SED Party Chief Walter Ulbricht in 1958. (Unlike this model, however, each Young Pioneer commandment did not begin with a thunderous "Thou shalt . . . .")

1. We Young Pioneers love our German Democratic Republic.
2. We Young Pioneers love our parents.
3. We Young Pioneers love peace.
4. We Young Pioneers maintain friendship with the children of the Soviet Union and all countries.
5. We Young Pioneers study diligently and are well-behaved and disciplined.
6. We Young Pioneers play sports and keep our bodies clean and healthy.
7. We Young Pioneers honor all working people and help them everywhere.
8. We Young Pioneers like to sing, dance, and play.
9. We Young Pioneers are good friends and help each other.
10. We Young Pioneers wear our blue neckerchief proudly.[5]

The second- and third-grade primers concentrate more on what a teacher's guide calls "moral norms" (e.g., "Take other people into consideration!"). Toward this end, teachers were instructed to give "special attention to the classes on Ernst Thälmann."[6] (Thälmann, who headed the KPD [Kommunistische Partei Deutschlands, Communist Party of Germany] in the 1920s, was the DDR's leading martyr-hero, as the subsequent Excursus in this chapter makes clear.) The 1973 teaching guide specifies that second-graders should be informed about "the leading role" of the

SED in East German society and about how "everywhere [in the DDR] working people labor for the welfare of all citizens."[7]

In first through third grades, such themes as collectivist virtue and socialist fellow-feeling occupy more than half of every primer section. These selections are usually simple message-poems or tendentious agitprop stories, sometimes even two-page "memoirs" (credited to leaders such as Ulbricht).[8] A scattered survey of early post-war readers suggests that this was less the case before the 1970s, but the 1965 Education Act specified that the study of literary genres begin only in the upper grades. As a result, few lower-grade primers of the 1970s and 1980s include any examples of "literature" at all; even authors exalted by the DDR, such as Johannes Becher or Bertolt Brecht, rarely appear.[9]

Instead, the elementary school readers revisit JP themes and contain numerous non-literary selections on the duties of the Young Pioneer, such as "Be Prepared!" "The Pioneer March," "Greetings and Thanks from the Young Pioneers at the Ninth Congress of the Socialist Unity Party of Germany," and "We, the Youngest Helpers of the Party."[10] Included are also official JP documents, such as "The Oath of the Young Pioneers" ("I promise to be a good Young Pioneer. I will act according to the Commandments of the Young Pioneers"). The oath and JP commandments are followed by a poem on the Tenth Commandment, "My Blue Neckerchief," the emblem of the JP, which was mandatory to wear on certain school days and to certain JP functions. The poem begins:

> My treasure is my neckerchief
> It's blue, look at it
> I keep it clean
> It covers my neck wonderfully.[11]

Solidarity with the USSR was another recurrent theme in these early years. For instance, a letter from "Misha in Moscow" explains the origin of the name of the "October Pioneers" in the Great October Revolution ("That's why we proudly call ourselves 'October Children'"), and "A Sunday of Friendship" celebrates the help given by a child to Soviet soldiers devoting their Sunday to building a bridge in a DDR village. Some selections make clear that power worship survived the Nazi era. One story, titled "The German Democratic Republic Has Strong Friends," begins: "The Soviet Union is the biggest and most powerful nation of the earth."[12]

Often the Soviet theme was linked to the JP Fourth Commandment, sometimes quite explicitly, as in poems such as "We Young Pioneers

Maintain Friendship with the Children of the Soviet Union and All Countries," whose title mirrors the Fourth Commandment:

> I love Misha Kugelrund
> who plays funny pranks.
> He brought to me the gift
> of a guest—Ivan from Leningrad.
> When I look at Ivan
> I think of Natasha and Masha and Ivan too.
>
> I greet the children in the Soviet Union.
> Our friendship is firm.
> I extend my hand to all the children of the world
> in the east, north, south, and west.

The primers in the early grades do not contain any fiction, at least not identifiably so; all stories are presented as dramatic nonfiction and therefore "true." Some stories are situated historically, so that the USSR is not depicted merely as a current ally but a longtime friend. (Some of these selections are translations from Russian.) For instance, in a story in *Lesebuch 2* titled "Dimitri Saves Two German Children," a tank gunner rescues a German boy and girl from a burning house at the close of the war. The story concludes: "And both children, who are long since grown up, will certainly not have forgotten Dimitri. And you can be sure that they are good friends of the Soviet Union."[13] Such a historical context—often established through stories that presented the official SED view of major events in DDR history or current affairs—becomes predominant in primers for grades three and four. For example, *Lesebuch 3* exalts a *Grepo* (*Grenzpolizist*, DDR border policeman) killed on patrol of the Berlin Wall in 1964 and personalizes the Vietnam War by featuring "Doan," a North Vietnamese boy whose family was killed by American bombers. *Lesebuch 4* includes two powerful agitprop documents, both delivered in the first person. The first is a report from an NVA (Nationale Volksarmee, National People's Army) soldier on a joint maneuver conducted in 1966 with his Czech and Hungarian brothers-in-arms. (Neither the story nor the editors allude to the DDR's unbrotherly—or Big Brotherly—suppression of the Prague Spring two years later.) The second selection is eyewitness testimony from two soldiers on the building of the Berlin Wall and its aftermath. One soldier tells of provocations at the Wall by American military units in October 1961:

> Right here American soldiers sought to push their way through [the border control]. They wanted to force open a passageway for one of their vehicles. When they couldn't achieve that, they took off. Then they set up a chain of tanks. Terror ran through every part of my body.
>
> Before the line of [enemy] vehicles . . . an officer in our People's Army stood with his hands behind his back.
>
> The first American tank rolled with lowered cannons right toward him. My thoughts at that moment were: Will the Americans dare? Will the officer stand fast? Will it come to war if they shoot?
>
> But our officer didn't move a single step. He forced the American tanks to stop on that spot.[14]

Fifth Through Seventh Grades

Ideologically oriented material in German language and literature was also present in the middle grades, but beginning in fifth grade, the balance begins to move toward letters and away from crude politics; German readers now include "literary" selections, not merely tendentious verse and prose. The fifth- through seventh-grade German texts draw from the "literary heritage" and "socialist youth literature," organized by genre. The aim is to give the pupil a social sensibility and a "literary-aesthetic picture of humanity."[15]

Lehrbuch 5 is divided by genre into five sections: fairy tales, fables, poems, stories, and excerpts from children's books. Poems and stories from Goethe, Theodor Fontane, Theodor Storm, Brecht, Becher, Erwin Strittmatter, Stephan Hermlin, Gorky, and Mark Twain (a snippet from *The Adventures of Tom Sawyer*) appear next to agitprop prose ("A Good Deed," "Red Berries") and verse ("Our *Heimat* [homeland]," "To A Soldier of the People's Army," "You Must be Useful to the Workers' State"). The fifth-grade teaching guide prescribes M-L genre criticism for the textbook selections. Fables are meant to contribute to the "moral training" of the young socialist, while pupils should learn that narrators of fairy tales "come from the working people, and that literary characters furnish insight about our ancestors and their status in society." The fairy tale also provides readers with "experiences of the methods of exploiters and oppressors of the People. These methods are condemned [in the tales] as inhuman, low, and small-minded."[16]

As these guidelines suggest, ideological concerns remained overwhelmingly dominant in fifth-grade German. For example, a teaching guide published in 1979 opens with a quotation from "Comrade" Erich Honecker on the value of literary works as "characterized by fidelity to reality, solidarity with the People, and partisanship," though no mention is made in the guide that "Comrade" Honecker is the SED chief and the head of state. The teaching guide then distinguishes DDR literature from that of West Germany, "where imperialistic mass literature, with its glorification of crime, brutality, and sex, influences the masses and especially the youth, day after day." By contrast, the teaching guide notes, DDR authors can and should adopt a stance of partisanship or "party-mindedness" toward all texts. Teachers should stress, whenever possible, "the struggle against fascism," and should "place the qualities of the socialist view of humanity in the foreground," focusing on themes that will "fulfill the motto 'Books are weapons.'"[17]

Lehrbuch 6 expands the range of genres taught in German class. For instance, the study of legends (e.g., about Prometheus, from passages from *The Odyssey* and the *Niebelungenlied*) invites "a stronger historical approach to literature." Even more significantly, sixth-graders encounter "texts belonging to the national [DDR] heritage and socialist literature from other lands."[18] Here the word "literature" is fully justified: the ideologically oriented prose and verse has almost disappeared. Instead, M-L doctrine is now expressed near-exclusively through distinguished Marxist writers and SED supporters such as Brecht, Becher, Strittmatter, Anna Seghers, Kurt Bartel, and Louis Fürnberg, whose works appear alongside ballads, nature poems, and stories by classical writers such as Goethe, Fontane, Eduard Morike, and Johann Peter Hebel.

Lehrbuch 7 features the first systematic presentation of "socialist" literature from "the present [i.e., DDR literature] and the heritage." Gone are most of the genre distinctions; the sections are divided simply into "stories" and "poetry" that introduce a wide selection of post-war literature.[19] *Lehrbuch 7* also contains Oliver's famous plea for more porridge from Dickens's *Oliver Twist*, a full novella (Gottfried Keller's *Clothes Make the Man*), and lengthy excerpts from three juvenile books (a Russian and a DDR author, along with Victor Hugo's *Gavroche*).[20] Outright M-L selections amount to less than 20 percent; the literary artillery is limited to an occasional fusillade of small arms such as the poems "A Tractorist Regales," "Socialist Spring in the Village," "We Saw Sputnik First!" "Cuban Ballad," "How Far is Vietnam, Mother?" Becher's "The State," and Brecht's "The Great October."[21]

These more mature selections, notes the seventh-grade teaching guide, "confront the pupil with a variety of human and social problems of adults. . . . The socialist hero—of the kind that the pupil meets in everyday life—is placed in the center of literature class." The socialist hero "teaches [the pupil] human greatness and exemplary behavior in daily work, and [how] to recognize and live similarly in his own actions."[22] The juvenile book excerpts faithfully fulfill Soviet pedagogue Anton Makarenko's call that the child reader "distinguish and recognize heroes at first glance" who will stimulate "positive or negative feelings." Teachers are instructed to present authors such as Keller in a "bourgeois-humanist" light. Keller's *Clothes Make the Man* shows "the progressive actions and humanity of the literary hero in an antagonistic class society [as he engages in his] passionate struggle against the ruling class's moral norms."[23]

Mother-Tongue Education

While the German literature selections for DDR elementary through junior high school pupils were covered in the *Lesebuch*, the language units for first- through tenth-graders were contained in a separate textbook. *Muttersprache* (Mother Tongue) indicates the scope of these language units. It is organized, in its first- and second-grade editions, into sections devoted to grammar, penmanship, vocabulary, spelling, and literary style.

Grammar

Grammar exercises at all grade levels of *Muttersprache* mix "politics" with "letters." Lessons on verb usage, sentence structure, and adverbial modifications are treated as opportunities for *weltanschauliche Erziehung*. For instance, passages on "Productive Work" and "The Vietnamese People's Struggle for Freedom" are occasions for building simple and complex sentences;[24] "Murder of a Fighter for the Human Rights of the Colored People in the USA" (about Martin Luther King) teaches proper comma usage; a text on the "slave work" suffered by Cubans under an American puppet regime before Castro's revolution treats active and passive voice.[25]

Quite literally, DDR children were schooled in a DDR version of Orwellian Newspeak ("Ostspeak") from their earliest years. One learned the mother tongue by learning the ideological syntax and semantics of M-L—or rather, that was the *intention* of the Party. That the SED's intention often went unfulfilled, or at best only partly fulfilled, was not for lack of sustained effort.

For example, here are a few seventh-grade grammar exercises:

1. Substitute appositives for any word groups in these sentences!
   a. In 1917, revolutionary Russian workers stormed the Winter Palace.
   b. In 1959, the Soviet Union put the first ship powered by atomic energy into service.
   c. On October 7, 1975, a treaty for friendship, cooperation, and mutual support was signed by the German Democratic Republic and the Soviet Union.
   d. In the furnaces of Eisenhüttenstadt factory, ore from the Soviet Union and coal from the People's Republic of Poland are refined into valuable steel.[26]
2. This text contains names of persons, places, events, organizations, factories, etc.! Copy the proper nouns! State what they mean!
   As they returned from *Warsaw, Erich Honecker* and his entourage were warmly greeted at *Schönefeld* [Airport]. The signing of the state treaty between the *German Democratic Republic* and the *People's Republic of Poland* is another step toward the security of peace in *Europe*.
3. Use *das* [article; "the"] or *dass* [conj.; "that," "because"]! Support your choice!
   a. It was in the last days of April 1945. . . . Terrified and distrustful, we waited; _____ first Soviet soldiers were coming. . . . An interpreter told us _____ the war was over. The soldiers took care _____ we received food. The *Angst* dissolved, and _____ feeling of trust in the Soviet soldiers grew fast. . . . When I later heard of the endless suffering _____ fascist army had inflicted on the Russian people, I thought back to my first meeting with the Soviet soldiers.[27]
   b. We know _____ the Soviet Union struggles insistently for the preservation of the peace.
   c. The Soviet Union is _____ land with the most modern weapons.[28]

Grammar exercises in other grades are similar:

1. [Fifth grade; keywords.] *Socialism* and *socialist*.
   a. Use the substantive in sentences! Write: "In the DDR _____ is being built up."[29]

2. [Second grade; suffixes.] [Note the] adjectives with suffixes: *-ig, -lich, -isch, -bar, -haft,* and *-sam.*

    Many citizens of our Republic spend their vacation in other socialist countries. The people that they meet there are friendly and diligent. We experience feelings of friendship toward them. A vacation on the coast of the Bulgarian or Romanian Black Sea, or spent enjoying any of the wonderful landscapes of our neighbors, is not only refreshing, but it also leaves one with many enduring impressions of the beauty of nature.

3. [Second grade; punctuation.] Copy the sentences! Put in the correct punctuation!

    Peter and Ines are proud of their mother. She has become an Activist today.³⁰

Even the upper grades included ideological instruction veiled in grammar exercises:

4. [Ninth and tenth grade; substantives.] We Young Pioneers wear our blue neckerchief with honor.
    a. What characterizes the substantive *Pioneer*?
    b. What characterizes the substantive *Young Pioneer*?
    c. Tell why the blue cloth of the Pioneers is a neckerchief!

5. [Ninth and tenth grade; verb tense.] What tenses are used in this resume?

    In eighth grade, I joined the Society for German-Soviet Friendship. As president of the Russian club of our school I sought to make contact with the House of the DSF [*Deutsche-Sowjetische Freundschaft,* German-Soviet Friendship]. . . . Last year I was elected secretary of our FDJ [*Freie Deutsche Jugend,* Free German Youth] group. I am responsible in this function for our political-ideological education and for the improvement of learning performance. . . . I have the desire to become an officer in our National People's Army.³¹

A variety of grammar exercises for upper grades also guides pupils to ideological "conclusions" about the United States and American capitalism:

1. [Ninth and tenth grade.] Put adverbs in the blanks!

    [1945.] Anglo-American bombers _____ dropped their death cargoes on German cities and residential areas. . . . In the morning shift he _____ performed his work, and was ready to protect his city, his family, and also his factory from the attacks of the Anglo-American bombers. . . .

2. [Ninth and tenth grade; main and dependent clauses, infinitive formation.]
   a. The colored population of the United States is struggling to receive the same rights as their fellow white citizens.
   b. The battle of the colored population for equal rights.
3. [Ninth and tenth grade; main and auxiliary verbs.]
   . . . West Germany *had* a greater population, and the political, business, and military leaders of German capitalism *had concentrated* there. The reactionary forces of West Germany thus *believed* that the capitalist BRD (Bundesrepublik Deutschland, Federal Republic of Germany) *would*, with the help of the American imperialists, *gain* superiority, so that, in the short or long run, the German Democratic Republic *would have to buckle* under the massive pressure.[32]

Military motifs were especially favored in the upper grades in DDR mother-tongue education:

1. [Ninth and tenth grade.] [Practice] the forms *to have* and *to become* in the present and imperfect tenses:
   His brother was a good student. After finishing his apprenticeship, he became a soldier. Now he is a university student. And what is your desired occupation?
2. [Ninth and tenth grade.] Underline the words that occur in the future! Examine exactly how the words "attempt" and "seize" are used to express future action!
   Dear Fighter!
   In our maneuver today, we assume that enemy agents are hiding in the forest, beyond the canal. The enemy will attempt to cross the canal in the dark. By 17.00, Group 1 of our unit will seize the Lenin Bridge. Groups 2 and 3 will secure the canal bank. . . . Pay attention to every noise! At 24.00 the maneuver is over. Now: Synchronize your watches!
3. [Ninth and tenth grade.] Name the predicate in every sentence. . . . Decide which word is the subject. . . . Underline the predicates and their corresponding subjects. . . .
   Bernd's father is a member of the military unit of his factory. On many a Sunday he gets up early, puts on his uniform, and goes to

his maneuver. His Comrade Fighters register themselves, arrive at the site, and receive their assignment.
4. [Ninth and tenth grade.] Name the verbs that must be completed with an object if the statement is to be complete! . . . Decide the case of the object. . . .
   a. We compose in class.
   b. Pioneers arrive.
   c. Pioneers receive.
   d. We are writing in class.
   e. The freight train arrives.
   f. NVA soldiers defend.
   g. NVA soldiers march.
5. [Ninth and tenth grade.] After the war the soldiers of the Soviet Army helped the German population. They distributed food. . . . The people thanked their liberators for this great assistance.
   a. Determine the predicates and objects!
   b. Name the verbs in each sentence! Determine the objects!
6. [Ninth and tenth grade.] Practice words with *g* and *ch:*
   a. *dive* [tauchen] into the depths
   b. *smoke* [rauchen] the pipe
   c. *guard* [bewachen] the border
   d. *risk* [wagen] the jump
7. [Ninth and tenth grade.] The soldiers of the NVA defend [*verteidigen*] our *Heimat*. Day and night they are prepared for defense [*zur Verteidigung*].
   a. Write the words with the prefix "ver."[33]

Vocabulary, Spelling, Penmanship, and Rhetoric and Composition

As with lessons on grammar, "letters" was not without politics even in units on handwriting, as the examples of suggested penmanship exercises in three teaching guides establish. Teachers were often required to devote several minutes of class time to the discussion of these ideologically conditioned topics, followed by having their pupils imitate the class selection or write paragraphs addressing the content of the topics (as in example 2).

1. Poem: "Armed Peace" (W. Busch)
   Sing Together: "We Carry the Blue Flag"
   "We Young Pioneers love our German Democratic Republic."[34]
2. Lenin: Our Model[35]

3. Acquire knowledge about the hard struggle that the working class had against their exploiters and oppressors, and for the peace and happiness of humankind. [For example:]
   Despite its influence on jazz melody and harmony throughout the world, the original folk-blues remains to this day the exclusive possession of the Negro population of America. The cradle of blues arose in the last century in the American South—in the wide, dusty country roads, on farms and plantations and cotton fields, in prisons and jails, in cheap bars and poor huts.[36]

Vocabulary and spelling lessons have a similar flavor:

1. [Second grade; vocabulary.] Fill in the blanks with those words that complete the meaning of the sentences!
   a. The Vietnamese *Volk* are building their land up again. _____ are supported by all decent human beings in the whole world.
   b. The opposition between socialism and imperialism is incommensurable. Because of _____ there can't be any ideological co-existence.[37]
2. [Sixth grade.] Words with *k* and *z*. [e.g., *Aktivist*]
   October 7: Every year on the birthday of our Republic, the most active workers, comradely farmers, and scientists are honored. Many of them receive the honorary title "Activist."
3. [Sixth grade.] Write out the full names of the social organizations characterized by the following abbreviations!
   SED, FDJ, GST, DSF, FDGB, DFD[38]
4. [Fifth grade.] Exercises for comprehension of words borrowed from foreign languages with the suffix *-mus:*
   socialist, socialism, communist, _____, _____, Marxism-Leninism . . . .[39]

Examples of exercises in rhetoric and composition for the upper grades are in the same vein. They include:

1. [Ninth and tenth grade.] [The following is a list of prescribed themes for student compositions.]
   a. Ernst Thälmann—Our Model.
   b. The first president of the DDR [Wilhelm Pieck].
   c. We celebrate International Women's Day.
   d. All children need peace.

e. We are practicing solidarity.
   f. Our correspondence with the Soviet Pioneers.
   g. What we experienced in vacation camp.[40]
2. [Ninth and tenth grade.] Present in a short composition your main ideas on the topic "Young Revolutionaries Yesterday and Young Revolutionaries Today! . . ." Try to include the following quotation: "Whoever seeks the truth must fight lies; whoever wants the good must have contempt for the bad; whoever loves man must hate his enemies."[41]
3. [Eighth grade.] To what conclusions about the value of human rights . . . in the U.S. do the following facts lead you?
   The U.S. / one of the richest industrial nations of the world / many millions of unemployed people / poverty across the broad mass of the population / exclusion of a great part of the people from the possibility of an all-around education and the development of personality / racial discrimination. . . . [42]

Socialist Fatherland Education

POS German classes in first through fifth grades also featured a unit in culture, in which mother-tongue education had its counterpart: *Heimatkunde*, which might have been termed "socialist Fatherland" education. *Heimatkunde* formally consisted of the cultural study of the "home" region, including its history, native traditions, and topography. But it was often even more overt in its promotion of the (East) German ideology than the literature and language units.

Heimatkunde textbooks were organized thematically. For instance, *Heimatkunde 3* accented the DDR government and post-war history, and *Heimatkunde 4* stressed the socialist tradition before 1945 and social life in the pupil's local district. The following are the section headings for the two texts:

> *Heimatkunde 3*
> 1. On the Work of the People's Delegates
> 2. Our Socialist Firms
> 3. The DDR—Our Socialist Fatherland
> 4. From the Life and Struggle of Workers in Earlier Ages
> 5. The Soviet Union Defeats German Fascism
> 6. The Difficult Beginning [1945–49]

7. The Further Formation of the Developed Socialist Society in Our Republic
8. The Life of the "Ernst Thälmann" Pioneer Organization

Heimatkunde 4
1. On the Buildup of Socialism in Your Home District
2. Maps of the Home District and of the DDR
3. The DDR—Our Socialist Fatherland [1949–1960]
4. On Nature[43]

Specific topics in the two books include "How Comrade Farmers Work," "Berlin, the Capital of Our Republic," "Important Cultural Spots and Memorials," "How Karl Marx Lived and Worked in London," "Battles Against War," "Workers Greet the Ninth Congress of the SED," and "Karl Liebknecht." (Liebknecht was the socialist leader who became—like Thälmann—a martyred hero after he was murdered, along with Rosa Luxemburg, in 1919.)

Despite its formal emphasis on DDR culture, instruction in *Heimatkunde* was highly ideological in character, as the foregoing section headings and sample topics evince: cultural politics was its real focus. The teacher's guide for fourth-grade *Heimatkunde* stresses that its chief purpose is to inspire loyalty toward the socialist Fatherland: "Finally, the discipline of *Heimatkunde* should especially contribute to the political-ideological education of the pupil. It must—just like the subject of German—contribute to the further development of his education in citizenship and to his socialist patriotism and proletarian internationalism."[44]

The most notable aspect of both the German primers and the *Heimatkunde* readers is their focus on role models, a theme that warrants separate and extensive attention before we turn to the German literature curriculum in the upper grades. SED educators sought to form "socialist heroes" and believed that "German plays an especially great role in this process (especially in literature and *Heimatkunde*). . . . The close familiarity with outstanding personalities in the *Heimat* of the children must be used purposefully, in order to give the pupils their first insights into the significance of work and of the battle of exemplary persons to secure the present and future welfare of this generation. In their studies and behavior, the pupils should take such persons as models."[45] Or, as a leading SED educator phrased it in a lecture titled "Good Germans: Models for Our Youth," delivered at the German Central Pedagogical Institute in East Berlin in 1961: "Every young person needs and seeks ideals—models—with whom he compares himself and whom he imitates. . . . The superiority of socialist society over capitalist society manifests itself in our bestowing our youth with true, great models."[46]

German primers—above all in grades one through five—traditionally offer schoolchildren numerous exemplary models of "Good Germans," idealized men and women worthy of admiration and imitation, all of whose lives are presented as stories of daring and romantic adventure. In the DDR textbooks, the models range from the lower platforms on History's stage of loyal adults and intrepid youth (heroic *Grepos,* valiant student revolutionaries, brave older Pioneers or FDJ Blueshirts, "ordinary" heroes such as Adolf Hennecke)[47] to the higher scaffolds of public exploits populated by great personalities (historical personages, statesmen, Party leaders).

At the lower levels, the primers specialized in scouting "the bloody crossroads where literature and politics meet": soldier stories.[48] The textbooks exalt *Grepos,* NVA soldiers, Soviet soldiers, and East bloc "brothers-in-arms," showing them all as grown-up versions of perfect Pioneers. A poem in *Lesebuch 5,* "To a Soldier of the People's Army," opens:

> When we're older
> We want to be just like you some day.[49]

Other selections personalize military heroes so that children can readily identify with them.[50] A pair of fourth-grade stories exalts two young communist martyrs: Artur Becker, a Spanish Civil War hero, and *Grepo* Egon Schultz. Pupils learn that Becker is "a model for all members of the Free German Youth." (The Artur Becker Medal was the highest FDJ honor.) Becker was president of the KJVD (Kommunistischer Jugendverband Deutschlands, Communist Youth League of Germany or Young Sparticists) in the 1930s and Party secretary in the Thälmann Brigade in the Spanish Civil War. He was wounded and captured by the fascists, and then murdered.[51] "A Son of Our Republic" is a two-page biography of Egon Schultz, who was "murdered by cowardly West Berlin agents" on October 5, 1964. "He is a model for many young people in our Republic, an inspiration to perform good deeds." We are told that Egon was an excellent first-grade teacher who resigned his post and soon became group leader of the Friedrich Engels Barracks. His comrades remember his words: "You must not only work well. You must protect what you have created with your weapons." Egon was "very much loved" by his acquaintances, one of whom said: "I can't imagine a better comrade. He knew a lot, but he never bragged. He was very modest and understood us all." And another said: "Egon Schultz was a model for all of us. He was smart, modest, helpful, and friendly." The biographical portrait goes on to report that a few months before his death, Egon became a candidate member of the SED. On a visit home in Rostock, his father said to him: "Well, my boy, with this decision you're on the right track." A number of streets and schools are named after Egon Schultz, including an *Oberschule* in Rostock. The story concludes with the words of a Young Pioneer from this school: "We will emulate Comrade Egon Schultz and live as he did: diligently, sincerely, and faithful to our State."[52]

Some *Lesebuch* and *Heimatkunde* selections present Young Pioneers themselves as miniature soldiers, whose own activities contribute to the peace. In the poem "Peace Fighters, Border Soldiers" in *Lesebuch 4*, for instance, the soldiers "protect our studying and other tasks / day and night," while "our work consists in good deeds, / because we're Pioneers."[53]

Above all, the primers aim to inculcate love of the Fatherland—and the national fathers. Even long after Stalin's definitive fall from power in the early 1960s, personality cults around other leaders—especially Lenin, Thälmann, and Ulbricht—endured into the 1970s and 1980s. Communist heroes became atheistic substitutes for saints, and their celebration in the state calendar was systematically institutionalized. The DDR curricula featured countless stories glorifying communist leaders as heroes to be emulated. Among foreign leaders, the revolutionary deities were Lenin, Mao, Tito (after the USSR's reconciliation with Yugoslavia in the late 1950s), and later Ho Chi Minh.[54]

The four greatest German figures exalted by DDR educators were Marx, Thälmann, Pieck, and Ulbricht.[55] The former pair—the dead fathers—were the Immortals and dwelt on a Marxist Olympus perched on lofty pedestals just below Lenin; the latter pair stood on a lower plane as minor deities, the living models of Good Germans, the objects of veneration in the DDR's native cult of personality. But, like Marx and Thälmann, Pieck and Ulbricht too were "stalinized"—sanitized and lionized—via tales highlighting their relationships with young people, especially their own children: the first three were presented in the DDR stories of the 1950s as kind, omniscient father figures, and Ulbricht was beatified shortly after Pieck's death in 1960.

Consider, for instance, a story in *Lesebuch 4* titled "The Forest Ants." We are told that Marx wrote books that workers throughout the world read today, but that he was often exhausted and got headaches from writing. "Then he put down his quill, took his big black hat from the cloak stand, called to his youngest daughter, and they went walking together." And so, one day, as Marx and his five-year-old daughter Eleanor stroll through the woods, she asks her father (pictured with a top hat and walking cane) whether ants work for their food, as human beings do. Marx tells her that they do indeed work. The story continues:

> "Do you see what the ants are doing?" he asked his daughter.
> "Those are soldiers, they're standing guard," Eleanor explained eagerly. . . .
> "Yes," answered Marx, "they are standing watch, so that the others can work in peace. And many ant children are in that treehouse. . . ."
> "Do the ants go to war, Papa," she asked, "and take away the houses of the other ants?"
> "No," explained Marx. "They protect only their own house and their children. Only when someone wants to do something evil to them do they defend themselves."
> "Those are good soldiers, right, Papa?" asked the girl.
> "Yes," said her father, "those are good soldiers."

The message was clear: Like good ant soldiers, Marxists fight only in self-defense.[56]

Although *Heimatkunde 4* includes extensive treatment of Marx and Engels as socialist models and as exemplary workers,[57] the readers of the post-Wall period are dominated by Lenin and Thälmann—and, to a lesser extent, Pieck and Ulbricht.[58] It is almost as if the SED *dared not* elevate Marx and Engels—the founders of "scientific socialism"—too high. To do so might have threatened the privileged place of Lenin (and, in earlier years, also Stalin)—and suggested too explicitly what even many loyalist SED intellectuals secretly held: that the German radical tradition was equal (or superior) to that of the Bolshevist.

Indeed, DDR German textbook writers made sure to keep Lenin and his example in the center of the curriculum: Virtually every primer in the early grades contains a story or poem honoring him. *Lesebuch 2*, for example, features the poem "When the Grown-Ups Honor Lenin," showing how and why everyone pays posthumous homage to Lenin in 1970 on the 100th anniversary of his birthday. It begins:

> When the grown-ups honor Lenin
> we children do our part too.

>Because he fought that the future
>should be happy for all of us.
>
>And just like the grown-ups
>we follow his advice
>to study, study, and still more study
>that's really our first task.
>
>Second, we never forget
>How things are for the children in Vietnam
>And collect paper and bottles
>to show our solidarity.
>
>Third, we greet the children
>of the *Heimat* of Lenin.
>Many thousands of greeting cards
>are being sent by us to them . . . .[59]

Stories dramatizing Lenin's pure and noble life are staples of the primers. "The Special Pen," for instance, is a third-grade story about Lenin's generous gift of a pen to a Russian boy.[60] *Lesebuch 3* also includes a letter from Lenin's wife, Nadezhda Krupskaya (who was a teacher and "loved children just as Lenin did,"[61] the editors tell us), urging youth to "continue the work of Lenin": "If you see paper lying around, pick it up. If you see that a light is on, turn it off. . . . If you see that someone can't read or write, teach him." *Lesebuch 4* includes "On the Bridge," a story of Lenin's exploits in the Russian Civil War.[62] And *Heimatkunde 4* has three Lenin stories: on young Lenin's effort to organize hungry factory workers in 1893 and his narrow escape from injury by avenging capitalists; on his life in exile in Siberia (1897–1900), when he first "took Marx and Engels as his models" and established friendships with the neighboring workers; and on his ingenious plans to overthrow the capitalists and landowners.[63]

Perhaps the best example of the myth-making effort to elevate Lenin as the "father of socialism" occurs in "Lenin Lives Over There," a story in *Lesebuch 2*. It portrays a humble Lenin, leader of the USSR yet so much a man of the people that he stops to chat with a small Russian country boy for a half-hour—without identifying himself—about the boy's fascination with the great Vladimir Ilyich. The boy knows that Lenin lives somewhere "*drüben.*" Amused, Lenin incognito replies that people sometimes say that he himself resembles the great leader. "But surely Lenin has a nice suit and jacket," protests the boy, noting that the stranger is quite modestly dressed. The conversation proceeds without Lenin ever revealing his identity. When the boy returns home, a relative who saw the two talking asks him what he has had occasion to speak about at such length with Lenin. Astonished, the boy runs back to the spot where the conversation occurred—"but Lenin was no longer there."

EXCURSUS: Thälmann *über alles?* Vicissitudes of a Socialist State Icon

I

And what about the man lionized for decades in the DDR as "the German Lenin"? Ernst "Teddy" Thälmann (1886–1944) was the leading German communist hero commemorated by SED educators. He was memorialized in countless speeches and Party placards as the "Son and Leader of the Working Class." FDJ and SED meetings, especially during the 1950s and 1960s, rang with the words from a Party hymn: "Thälmann, Thälmann, Germany's immortal son has never died!" The song's refrain declared:

> Thälmann, to you
> we swear our steadfastness!

Thälmann was indeed regarded as the DDR's Lenin—the Ernst Thälmann Pioneers (*Thälmann Pioniere*) were founded in 1948 and modeled on the Lenin Pioneers—and the DDR primers feature Thälmann almost as prominently and frequently as Lenin. Ulbricht found the creation of a Thälmann cult just as useful as Stalin had found the posthumous Lenin cult: dead men pose no threats. And Ulbricht realized that, because Thälmann had been an obedient follower of Lenin and Stalin, he also posed no threat to the Soviet "friends."

Thälmann's life was rich fodder for DDR glorification. In 1903, at the age of 17, Thälmann joined the SPD (*Sozialdemokratische Partei Deutschlands*, Social Democratic Party of Germany). Later he assumed several minor SPD posts as he earned his livelihood through odd jobs. In 1915, he was drafted into service in World War I and served on the French front near Verdun and Nietz; the experience turned him into a pacifist and uncompromising radical. He withdrew from the SPD on account of its support for the war. By 1921, he was head of the Hamburg KPD and had met Lenin and Trotsky. He became KPD chief in 1924 and was also elected that year to Reichstag. In 1925, he ran for the presidency as the KPD nominee. A spellbinding orator, Thälmann was the leading German communist for two decades. His arrest by the Nazis on 3 March 1933, shortly after KPD informants tipped off the Gestapo about his whereabouts and about his attendance at an underground KPD meeting, ended his political career. (The illegal and secret KPD gathering on 27 February 1933 was memorialized in DDR history schoolbooks as "the final meeting of the KPD Central Committee.") His imprisonment in Bautzen by the Nazis laid the groundwork for the communist image of him as a suffering hero; in honor of his tribulations, many KPD members fought in the "Thälmann Brigade" in Spain. After eleven years in prisons and concentration camps, orders were issued for his execution in the wake of the abortive plot in July 1944 against Hitler. News of Thälmann's murder in Buchenwald on Hitler's direct orders—although the Nazis claimed that he died during an allied bombing raid on Buchenwald—transformed him into a permanent martyr for the cause.

One indication of Thälmann's status in the DDR was that celebrations occurred on the days of both his birth (April 16) and death (August 18)—a practice that continued right up through the 1980s. Unlike the case with other DDR icons, Thälmann remained an object of veneration even after the Stalin-inspired cults of personality had long ceased. For instance, the deaths of Pieck, who died January 3, 1960, and Otto Grotewohl, who died March 11, 1962, were each recognized for several years with schooldays in their honor. However, these commemorations ceased in the 1970s, and they were dropped from the official calendar by the 1980s. By contrast, Thälmann received two official holidays in the DDR calendar. That fact alone makes clear his exalted stature in DDR hagiography. He was the only German ever to be so honored. (Lenin was accorded the same honor on the dates of his birth and death, April 22 and January 21, respectively; Engels was remembered on November 28 and Marx on May 5.)[64]

And how was Thälmann depicted in DDR textbooks? The SED's plaster saint version of Thälmann is presented frequently in the *Heimatkunde* texts in connection with the Thälmann Pioneers. For instance, *Heimatkunde 3* contains the Oath of the Thälmann Pioneers: "Ernst Thälmann is my model. I swear to study, to work, and to fight as Ernst Thälmann taught. I will act according to the laws of the Thälmann Pioneers. Faithful to our greeting, I am always prepared for peace and socialism." The text then enumerates the laws of the TP, which closely echo those of the JP:

1. We Thälmann Pioneers love our socialist Fatherland, the German Democratic Republic.

2. We Thälmann Pioneers love and respect our parents.
3. We Thälmann Pioneers love and protect peace and hate warmongers.
4. We Thälmann Pioneers are friends of the Soviet Union and all socialist brotherlands and maintain friendship with all children of the world.
5. We Thälmann Pioneers study diligently, are well-behaved, and disciplined.
6. We Thälmann Pioneers love work and respect all working people.
7. We Thälmann Pioneers love the truth, are reliable, and are friendly to one another.
8. We Thälmann Pioneers familiarize ourselves with technology, research the laws of nature, and acquaint ourselves with the treasures of culture.
9. We Thälmann Pioneers keep our bodies clean and healthy, play sports regularly, and are cheerful.
10. We Thälmann Pioneers wear our red neckerchief with honor and prepare ourselves to become good members of the Free German Youth.[65]

In a manner similar to their treatment of Lenin, many textbook stories teach of Thälmann's heroic path: how he gained awareness of social injustice as he met working-class children; how he learned at the Hamburg harbor during the 1896 dock strike that resistance, active protest, and organization could achieve results. The textbooks are filled with chronicles of his life. "All peace-loving people will never forget Ernst Thälmann," announce the editors of *Lesebuch 2*, which contains a story of Thälmann's childhood titled "Hang Together!" Young Ernst sees two working-class boys fighting and shouts to them: "Why are you hitting each other? Make up! Be friends! . . . Working-class boys are friends!" The story concludes: "The boy . . . was called Ernst Thälmann. Later, as head of the Communist Party of Germany, he said to all workers: 'Hang together, so that you can beat your enemies!'"[66]

"Encounter with Teddy" in *Heimatkunde 3* personalizes Thälmann by showing him through the eyes of a fellow "anti-fascist" Bautzen inmate. We are told that Thälmann's presence alone caused all anti-fascist prisoners to find courage. The story includes two large photos of Thälmann and concludes with the following exercises:

1. List the names of any anti-fascists from your hometown!
2. List any streets, institutions, and places in your hometown that are named after anti-fascists!
3. Inquire how these anti-fascists battled against the fascists!

Lesebuch 3 contains a story set in 1943 in Ravensbruck, a women's concentration camp. The story features two Russian girls and a German girl who have been imprisoned for giving bread to a Soviet prisoner of war. One of the Russian girls draws Thälmann's picture on the dusty window. The German girl does not recognize the image or even know much about Thälmann. This gives the Soviet girls the opportunity to tell the story of his life. An SS guard comes by and wants to know what the window drawing means, but the girls say nothing. From then on, all comrades who pass by the window learn about Thälmann on asking about the window drawing. "Every day, though threatened by beatings and death, they hear about his struggle and about his powerful Party."

In fourth grade, when JP members become Thälmann Pioneers, the primers feature Thälmann even more prominently. *Lesebuch 4* includes "The Song of the Thälmann Pioneers," composed by the poet Ernst Weinert, which closes with these lines:

> We've proudly given our young organization
> the name Ernst Thälmann.
> We've sworn to live
> every hour according to his model example.
> And if we're worthy of his name
> we will learn what he taught us
> And dedicate all our energies to a more beautiful future—
> Pioneers are always prepared.[67]

Lesebuch 4 also contains a typical story representing Thälmann as "father" of German socialism. The tale, "Christmas Eve," was adapted from a biography of Thälmann written by his daughter Irma. The editors declare that the purpose of the story is to show how Thälmann was "a happy, courageous, sincere person and an uncompromising fighter against war and fascists."

In an elementary school German reader of the 1960s, an even more saintly image of Thälmann is presented. Here he appears not just as a suffering shepherd but as a slain martyr of German socialism, murdered by the fascist devils. And yet he has arisen. Like Christ, he "died and yet is not dead," and his teaching lives on in the hearts and minds of all Good Germans. This excerpt, which is titled "Thälmann Lives," alludes to a phrase in a Party hymn that echoed through countless FDJ and SED meetings during the entire history of the DDR.

Thälmann died and yet is not dead;
for that which he taught, when he lived,
that which he strove,
lives as a memorial in millions of hearts,
lives as knowledge in millions of minds.

Look at the millions of workers' hands,
which, without shrinking, reach for the stars.

Next comes the rote, incantatory invocation, whose rhetorical flourish sounds absurdly excessive to ears not accustomed to personality cults:

Thälmann lives in all railways,
which travel over the fields,
Thälmann lives in all ovens,
which just yesterday were without fire,
Thälmann lives in all waves of feeling,
that stimulate the love of peace in the people,
that announce the truth,
that spread optimism,
until they can stretch and straighten their bowed backs.

Thälmann lives in every ton of coal,
which is pulled out of the shaft in a special shift,
Thälmann lives in every red flag,
which proles wave on the hill,
Thälmann lives in the sound of the tractors,
lives where buddies struggle to scoop ore from mountains,
and Ernst Thälmann lives in every book
from which Marx and Lenin's words speak.

Thälmann lives where there is struggle
and the striving for unity,
where creation unites city and country,
where the Germans who love Germany
see themselves, despite the zones, as brothers.

Thälmann lives wherever one takes away
everything from the war profiteers
who make money from weapons,
Thälmann lives wherever brides, women, and mothers
call for the defense of the peace.[68]

The hagiography of Thälmann was not confined to the classroom textbook or the Thälmann Pioneer meeting. Even a saint needs a hallowed site—like Lenin's tomb—where his relics are preserved and venerated. DDR schoolchildren were regularly bused like pilgrims to the Ziegelhaus sports stadium, just outside Berlin, which by 1953 became an official communist shrine because it was the site of Thälmann's last public speech.[69]

Another mainstay of the Thälmann curricular cult was the official documentary film made about him. Millions of DDR children were shown *Ernst Thälmann, Leader of His Class* in school. Produced in 1955 by the DEFA (*Deutsche Film Aktiengesellschaft*), the state production agency, and widely regarded as one of the best films that East Germany ever made, the movie portrayed Thälmann as a secular saint whose entire life, from boyhood to his death, was impeccable and devoted exclusively to liberating the masses from oppression. Thälmann Pioneers received a similar message in youth meetings. They were taught to identify with the Christ-like Thälmann and to sing still another Thälmann Pioneer hymn, the "Thälmann Song":

> Homeland, open your eyes
> dazzling and decked with flags is the day
> Full-shouldered he stands there before us
> Thälmann, just as he was.
>
> Thälmann and Thälmann above everyone
> Germany's immortal son
> Thälmann hasn't died
> Voice and fist of the nation
> Thälmann hasn't died
> Voice and fist of the nation.
>
> Endlessly brutalized and tortured
> he remained faithful to us and held firm
> In his name we are united
> and struggle for Our State!
> Thälmann and Thälmann above everyone. . . .[70]

After a rousing performance of the "Thälmann Song," a typical youth group meeting would end with the children rising from their places and bursting forth with a round of the "Pioneer March" as they filed out:

> May our young hearts blaze
> Like Ernst Thälmann's,
> So faithful and bold!

II

"Good-Bye Forever," the title of Irma Thälmann's memoir of her father abridged and adapted for use in *Heimatkunde 4*, might be an appropriate title for Thälmann's eclipse with the passing of the DDR as well. This excerpt discusses her last visit with her father in 1943, in Bautzen prison, before he was shipped to Buchenwald. Given that her visits were attracting attention both in the prison and in the surrounding neighborhoods, the Gestapo insisted that Irma Thälmann visit her father under an assumed name; her father refused to submit to this demand with the words: "If my daughter is supposed to come to me under a false name, then she won't come at all." (Thälmann's wife did, however, subsequently visit him under her maiden name.)[71] Since 1990, he has utterly disappeared from eastern German textbooks in *Heimatkunde* and *Deutsch;* only briefly and in passing is he mentioned in chapters of *Geschichte* textbooks devoted to the KPD and twentieth-century Germany.

What has instead begun to appear in scholarly books and articles—and which will doubtless one day enter the textbooks—are revelations about Thälmann's feet of clay. For instance, a recently published collection of Thälmann's letters to Stalin, written during Thälmann's Buchenwald years, shows him to have been not just a loyal Stalinist vassal, but also a passionate supporter of the show trials and purges—indeed an advocate of every aspect of Stalin's brutal regime of terror toward all potential opponents.[72] Between 1928 and 1933 he "bolshevized" the KPD in Stalin's image. Thälmann likewise rhapsodized later about Stalin's foreign policy genius in negotiating the Nazi-Soviet Non-Aggression Pact in August 1939. His policy was to follow Stalin's "social fascism" to the letter, whereby he branded the German Social Democrats, rather than the Nazis, as the workers' enemy (despite the fact that Thälmann had formerly been a member of the SDP for fourteen years). Despite this unconditional servility, Stalin never attempted to negotiate Thälmann's freedom from Buchenwald, which (presumably) could easily have been arranged after the Nazi-Soviet Pact. Evidently, Stalin preferred to leave Thälmann behind barbed wire, a martyr for Stalinism.

But Thälmann's subservience to Stalin never discredited him in the DDR, even long after de-Stalinization had rendered Stalin himself an "unperson." More recently, however, less important facts about Thälmann's personal life seem destined to tarnish his image even among the SED old guard. For instance, he was apparently a lifelong alcoholic and would repair to a secluded, luxurious private residence in Fichtenau to indulge.

Moreover, in 1928, Party member John Wittorf, an old buddy of Thälmann, stole a substantial sum of KPD funds; Thälmann covered it up. When this was discovered, the KPD Central Committee removed him from power—but Stalin intervened and Thälmann was returned to his post as KPD chief.[73]

Thälmann's ignominy in present-day Germany is reflected in the fate that has befallen the monuments to him—those towering statues that were once the object of DDR pupils' school excursions and whose images appeared in countless DDR textbooks. For instance, in 1949 the Wilhelm Square in the Prenzlauer Berg district of Berlin was renamed Thälmann Square, and a Thälmann statue was erected there on the hundredth anniversary of his birth in 1986, whereupon the meadow surrounding it became known as Ernst Thälmann Park. Gorbachev and Boris Yeltsin attended the October 1986 dedication. "We recognize Thälmann as a passionate tribune championing the brotherhood of the German and Soviet worker," said Gorbachev. Honecker pronounced the Thälmann monument "beautiful and dignified." Designed by the famous Soviet sculptor Lew Kerbel, it stood fourteen meters high, fifteen meters wide, weighed fifty-five tons, and was made of granite from the Ukraine. Sporting his docker's cap, Thälmann stands defiantly with his upraised fist before a fluttering flag, on which appears the hammer and sickle. (In reality, the monument resembles Lenin far more so than Thälmann—perhaps unsurprisingly, given that Kerbel had chiseled several award-winning Lenin sculptures.) But in 1998, the Commission on Post-war Political Monuments in the Former East Berlin decided to remove the monument. The Commission pronounced a verdict soon to be reflected in German textbooks: "The idealized, uncritical representation of [Thälmann's] person in the form of a monumental sculpture is in no way appropriate for his real historical significance." The mayor of Prenzlauer Berg added: "That monstrosity flatters neither our district nor Thälmann."

And so, Marx and Engels may stay, ruled the Commission, but Ernst Thälmann must go. The statue of Marx and Engels that dominates Alexanderplatz was allowed to remain. But the monument depicting Thälmann—whom only a decade earlier East German schoolchildren were being taught to idolize as a near-deity, a selfless fighter, and a martyr to Nazi terror—had to go. The Berlin commission concluded: "He organized the Party along Stalinist lines and led it on an uncritical pro-Soviet course. Although he was a firm opponent of Nazism, his policies helped contribute to the collapse of the Weimar Republic. Portraying this person heroically and uncritically is in no way justified by his true historical meaning."

Numerous German socialists continue to disagree with that judgment, and they have successfully lobbied the SPD/PDS-controlled Berlin Senate to reject the ruling of the Oversight Commission that it had sponsored—despite renewed calls from centrists and conservatives to raze the statue. And so, to this day, children and teens in their blue FDJ shirts, most of them affiliated with socialist youth groups, meet in Ernst Thälmann Park and hold huge Thälmann portraits up to the monument.

In September 2001, the Thälmann monument was secretly cleaned up by a Berlin group of communist and socialist activists. Thälmann's bronze head had been smeared completely with graffiti since the demise of the DDR; this was the first of many such cleanups for the statue, which is a prime target of Berlin street artists and spray painters. Meanwhile, a few hundred kilometers away in western Germany, a placard that had been preserved seven decades suffered the fate that the Thälmann statue in Prenzlauer Berg had so far averted. "Vote Thälmann," ran a large placard in Essen, which was a campaign sign in the March 1932 presidential election, when Thälmann earned 22 percent of the Essen vote. Despite arguments from the Essen city planner's office to preserve the placard, it was removed in the spring of 2002: "It's too bad," the city planner said. "Here was an opportunity to document a piece of history, so that it wouldn't just be in schoolbooks but which you could experience by seeing it 'on site.'"

Living Heroes, or the DDR Cult of Personality

If Thälmann was the object of DDR veneration in textbooks and in the context of everyday life, how were other prominent figures treated? The only DDR figure elevated to a status rivaling Thälmann in the school curriculum was President Wilhelm Pieck (1876–1960). Already in his eighties by the mid-1950s, Pieck was officially treated as the grand old man—an orotund, ceremonial statesman, rather like an aged Hindenburg of the DDR, or, in American terms, a cross between George Washington and Ben Franklin. "Father Pieck," as he was called by the press, was portrayed as the guiding spirit of the infant republic. (His detractors considered him a fat, pompous clown, an uncrowned Kaiser, and labeled him—privately—Wilhelm III.)

From the founding of the DDR until his death in 1960, and even into the 1970s and 1980s in DDR primers, Pieck was a national symbol, representing the last link to socialism's legendary years in the late nineteenth century, an age of underground resistance and revolutionary glory. An outspoken SPD Reichstag opponent of German participation in World War I, a cofounder of the KPD in 1919, a guard of honor at Lenin's funeral in 1924, and a comrade of early left-wing SPD leaders Karl Liebknecht, Rosa Luxemburg, Franz Mehring, and Clara Zetkin, Pieck had been present at the creation. Escaping Germany in 1933, he had gone to Moscow, serving after 1935 as the chairman of the KPD Central Committee in exile. He became co-chairman of the SED in 1946 and DDR president in 1949.

A characteristic effort to inculcate love of the newborn DDR by personalizing it through Pieck was the third-grade story, "From Wilhelm Pieck's Youth."[74] Derived from the opening chapter of the Pieck biography for children (written by Walter Bartel, Pieck's official biographer), the story presents Pieck as a model young socialist from an exemplary working-class family. His parents raised him "with love, but sternly." Young Wilhelm "especially liked math and penmanship." He was "diligent and finished his schoolwork and homework punctually and properly." He was equally conscientious during his four-year apprenticeship as a carpenter, during which time he received no wages. But the master carpenter cared not at all about him, only that he worked hard. After a conversation with another young man who had also received no wages during his apprenticeship, Wilhelm decided, at the age of 18, to join the SPD, which stood opposed to the factory owners. But his real moment of truth came two years later. For the first time, Wilhelm resolved to participate in the May Day parade and to carry the red flag. His boss warned him that he would fire him—and he did. He was unemployed for a long time, "but he always remained true to the workers and their children, because he knew suffering and need from his own experience."[75]

Pieck's adulthood was also meticulously recounted to DDR schoolchildren. *Heimatkunde 3* portrays Pieck's return to the SBZ from abroad: the dramatic day of Pieck's inauguration in October 1949 is told in "Wilhelm Pieck: the First German Working-Class President," which includes a photograph of twenty-two-year-old Margot Feist (then the youngest representative in the DDR *Volkskammer* [parliament]) presenting "Father Pieck" with a congratulatory bouquet.[76] The captain forgoes mentioning that Fräulein Feist was by then [1979] DDR Minister of Education and the wife of SED chief Erich Honecker.

Several *Heimatkunde* selections underline Pieck's bona-fide working-class credentials, seeking to show him as a real man of the People. In one story, meeting with a group of building tradesmen, Pieck mentions that he had once also done skilled carpentry work. A skeptical carpenter says that such work requires a very steady hand. "Well, let's see if I still have one," Pieck replies. Surrounded by critical eyes, Pieck then rolls up his sleeves and burnishes a piece of fine wood. "Hats off to you!" says an old worker. "*Ja*, we can really trust a president like you."

Songs learned by the JP and Thälmann Pioneers also bore tribute to "Father Pieck." In his later years, he was a figurehead, a homegrown Stalin, beloved and unblemished. The following tune even refers to him as a "symbol":

"Greetings and Thanks to Our President"

Choir: Today let's greet the one whom we all love,
The President of our Republic.
He is written in each young heart
As true friend and father, Wilhelm Pieck.

A girl: He builds new nice schools.
Proclaiming our happiness with joyful songs
At vacation periods in the field and in the woods
We express our thanks to our beloved president!

A boy: His shining presence shall always inspire us
To serious studying and joyful playing
Then we will be able to manage life.
He shows us the safest way to the goal.

Choir: His example makes us strong, and we eagerly strive to emulate him,
He has devoted himself to the young Republic.
Good health and a long life, that's what we wish for
The friend of the children, our Wilhelm Pieck!

Upon Pieck's death, the growing cult of Walter Ulbricht (1893–1973), who inherited Pieck's offices, entered the schools. Already by the early 1950s there were Walter Ulbricht streets, Walter Ulbricht factories and youth brigades, a Walter Ulbricht SED Academy, and a Walter Ulbricht Stadium; especially after construction of the Wall, educational leaders openly began to exalt Ulbricht as a socialist paragon. At a pedagogical conference in October 1961 on educating young patriots, one professor contrasted the exemplary Ulbricht with Western antiheroes, especially "sad figures such as E. Presley, and killers like the top American and West German fascist soldiers, who live completely without direction." By contrast, the SED instead spotlighted "positive heroes" with whom children could identify. The Party elevated citizens who lived according to what it termed "socialist ideals." Above all, socialist workers were exalted: "This orientation enables us to show the youth how to grow like the leaders of the working class, especially that man, whose life and efforts are inseparably linked to the decades-long struggle and sacrifice of German workers, to the workers of the First German Nation of Peace, and to the bright outlook for the future of our entire people: Walter Ulbricht."[77] Party education officials made clear that the Party slogan *"Walter Ulbricht—das sind wir [alle]!"* (Walter Ulbricht—that's us!) was to be carried into the schools, as the following speech from the 1960s of one Ministry of Education functionary evinced:

> Our *Volk* is represented via a truly great human being, one who is honored by the entire progressive world. He is for us the quintessential Good German. His road from worker's son to their leader and excellent statesman is perfectly suited to help the youth to understand the most complicated questions of our time and their own desire to find a clear, concrete, and attractive model. . . .
>
> Workers have coined this slogan: *"Walter Ulbricht—das sind wir!"* This deep insight directs us how to work. We must lead all children to the consciousness that, under Walter Ulbricht, our *Volk* is in the best possible hands. In all young people we must stimulate pride in our strong, smart party of the working class, in the Central Committee, and in the man who is at its head. His life and his struggle, his thinking and his actions should serve youth as bridges to the thinking and action of the workers and peasants . . . .[78]

And so, throughout most of the 1960s, DDR readers praised Ulbricht as a living example of the "new socialist *Mensch.*"[79] The details of his working-class origins and exemplary activist life were often—if selectively—told. Son of a tailor, Ulbricht had become a leader of the local KPD and a Reichstag member in the 1920s. Known as *"Genosse Zelle"* ("Comrade Cell") for his skills in political organization—the KPD's chief activity was to establish communist cells in every factory—Ulbricht succeeded Pieck in 1929 to become the top official in the Berlin Party organization. When Hitler was appointed chancellor in 1933, the forty-year-old Ulbricht went underground; in 1934 he fled to Prague, then Paris, then to Loyalist Spain, where he aided the KPD in its support for German communists who were fighting against the Spanish fascists. In 1938, as Franco was emerging victorious, Ulbricht escaped to Russia. Amid a decade of mass purges of both Russian and foreign comrades, Ulbricht assiduously worked his way up through the Moscow-based Party hierarchy, partly by following every twist and turn in Stalin's line (including a vigorous defense of the 1936–38 Moscow show trials and the 1939 Molotov-Ribbentrop Pact), and partly by out maneuvering less adroit rivals. Supported by Stalin, he rose during the war to become KPD deputy chairman; he and Pieck, then sixty-nine and titular leader of the Party, returned to Berlin in April 1945 with the victorious Red Army. Although Pieck was the official Party head until his death, his age and poor health limited his activities, and the real power in the SED was Ulbricht.

Resembling to a degree their treatment of Thälmann, DDR primers of the immediate post-Wall era lionize Ulbricht unreservedly, omitting any mention of his slavish loyalty to Stalin or his accommodations with fascism during 1939–41. For example, one fourth-grade story burnished Ulbricht's anti-fascist record, portraying his courageous outspokenness at a local Nazi Party meeting in 1931. Another typically flattering Ulbricht story is "Mission: Shavings," in *Lesebuch 4,* which portrays Ulbricht as a twenty-five-year-old soldier in World War I, trying to persuade his comrades to lay down their arms and shorten the war. "We must act just like the Russian soldiers, workers, and peasants under Lenin's leadership," Ulbricht declares. "Then there will be peace." He calls his plan of noncompliance with the Prussian military leaders the "Shavings Mission," and several comrades leave the battlefront to fight on "the peace front."

A fifth-grade primer features a worshipful poem about Ulbricht, "And you can confidently trust him!" Written in the hallowed cult-of-personality style, the poem links Ulbricht to the rest of the SED rosary of Marx, Lenin, Thälmann, and Pieck. It concludes:

> Whoever is such a human being and fighter
> Is a true Communist
> On whose word you can build
> And whom you can confidently trust.[80]

Ulbricht's youth was also highlighted. For example, one fifth-grade reader included two selections about young Walter: "How They Celebrated May 1" and the autobiographical "Memories of My Youth."

Ulbricht modeled himself above all on Lenin, becoming an avid sportsman and even adopting the Master's trademark goatee. DDR citizens accordingly bestowed Ulbricht with the mock sobriquet "Old *Spitzbart.*"

DDR pedagogical materials designed for teachers discussed Ulbricht in similar terms to those employed in the textbooks themselves. One Leipzig kindergarten teacher spoke for her colleagues when she discussed in *Neue Erziehung im Kindergarten* her innovative lesson plan to "awaken the feeling of love and affection for him in the children entrusted to me." After unveiling a portrait of Comrade Ulbricht, the teacher proceeded to "carry out a project":

> *Method:* Look at the picture; pronounce the name. I tell the children: Walter Ulbricht is a good man. He was a worker. Good people—Berni's father, Angela's mother, Frau M., and I—all like him. He takes care of us.
> We practice pronouncing his name. (Some children say, instead of Ulbricht, the forename Ulrich!)
> We hang his picture above the class cupboard. We put flowers in the vase hung beside it.
> I remind the children that we want always to put fresh flowers before the picture of this good man.
> *Evaluation:* The children listened to me very attentively. All except one boy pronounced the name correctly. I also had the impression that, through my project, I have awakened in them their first positive feelings toward Walter Ulbricht.[81]

But a fate very different from Lenin's befell Ulbricht less than a decade after this act of homage. The public encomia to Ulbricht halted abruptly upon his stepping down from his post as Party Chairman in 1971. Although he continued to be exalted as a model socialist in a few DDR primers into the 1980s, that status prevailed merely because any textbooks still in use in the 1980s had been designed in the early 1970s, before "de-Ulbrichtization" had reached the schools; many primers were simply reprinted, rather than revised, in later editions.

And what about the last two decades of the DDR's life? Did a personality cult continue to prevail—and to pervade DDR curricula? Erich Honecker succeeded Ulbricht as SED head at the Eighth Party Congress in 1971. He had been Ulbricht's favorite and heir apparent since 1958, when he had sided with Ulbricht against Ulbricht's moderate Politburo rivals.

As in Ulbricht's case, a cult of personality grew up around Honecker briefly during his leadership, chiefly from the mid-1970s to early 1980s, and it included the ubiquitous photos in *Neues Deutschland* and ritualistic ten-foot portraits in DDR parades.

But otherwise the Honecker cult remained comparatively subdued. With exceptions such as Honecker's portrait on the opening page of the 1978 edition of *Heimatkunde 3*, the beatification was confined to homage paid in official Party organs and did not result in Honecker's enshrinement in DDR curricula. Respecting Leonid Breshnev's wishes—and no doubt fearing that he too might be ousted like his predecessor if he aggressively promoted his own cult of personality—Honecker adhered far more than had Ulbricht to Lenin's principle of collective leadership and thus disavowed the grosser manifestations of leader worship. Even the FDJ, which Honecker headed from 1946–55, did no more than print numerous photographs of him and cite his speeches frequently in its official publications.

Canon Fodder for Young Revolutionaries

The cult of personality—at least in its most egregious forms—was restricted to textbooks in the lower POS grades. And yet, though the choice of weapons grew in sophistication in eighth through tenth grades, and even more so in the EOS (*Erweiterte Oberschule*, advanced high school), SED educators never ceased to regard the German literature textbook as indispensable war materiél.

Upper-grade POS syllabi specified that the curriculum should "strengthen socialist ways of behavior, especially striving for knowledge and readiness both to assume full responsibility and to make class-conscious decisions."[82] And a teaching guide further advised:

> The pupil should recognize that socialist art and literature help him to master his life, and that they possess great significance for the development of the human being in socialist society.... What in late bourgeois society, which is characterized by the alienation of human beings, is often pushed into the sealed sphere of private interest, receives in our socialist social order a publicity that it was never before granted. An essential educational task of the literature curriculum, therefore, is to lead the pupil to the insight that the humanism of art and literature is inhibited from its full developmental flowering when it is only cultivated in isolation. One of the greatest achievements of our socialist social order is

to have created the pre-conditions whereby the most various expressions of humanity needn't any longer hide in the shadows; because of the triumph of the revolutionary worker class, they have entered the public stage. This constant interaction is required if real humanism is to develop to its fullest.[83]

But the cultivation of "real humanism" evidently does not prescribe any relaxation of ideological fervor or tolerance toward opposing *Weltanschauungen:* "The pupils will therefore be able to approach the role of literature in the class struggle from a partisan position, and in this context to grasp the different conditions of the social function of the writer."[84] In eighth-grade German, SED educators formally commenced what Western literary scholars term "canon-formation." Here began the study of German literary history: textbooks now divided literature into historical periods and specified major authors and their lines of influence.[85] In ninth and tenth grades, a systematic presentation of the "progressive canon" was provided. Literary periodization occurred along M-L lines, according to the doctrines of materialist history; the twentieth-century offerings for the upper grades included an odd assortment of distinguished literary masters and Party hacks, as the table of contents for editions of *Unser Lesebuch. Klasse 8* during the 1970s evinces:

1. *German Literature from its Beginnings to 1700*
   (Walter von der Vogelweide, folk songs, Sebastian Brant, Friedrich von Logau, Paul Fleming, excerpts from Johann Jakob Christoffel von Grimmelshausen's *Simplicissimus,* Johann Christian Günther)
2. *Poems and Sayings of Classical German Literature*
   (Goethe [short lyrics], Schiller's "The Cranes of Ibykus")
3. *Revolutionary-Democratic and Early Socialist German Literature of the Nineteenth Century*
   (Georg Büchner, Heine's "The Silesian Weavers" and other selections, excerpt from Gerhart Hauptmann's "The Weavers," Georg Weerth's "Hunger Song," Johann Christian Luechow, Ferdinand Freiligrath, Hoffmann von Fallersleben, Adolf Glassbrenner, Georg Herwegh)
4. *Bourgeois-humanist and socialist German literature after 1917*
   (Ricarda Huch, Kurt Tucholsky, Friedrich Wolf, Johannes Becher, Erich Weinert, Brecht, Anna Seghers, Jo Schulz, Louis Fürnberg, Heinz Kahlau, Franz Fühmann, Eberhard Panitz, Günther Deicke, Helmut Preissler, Fritz Raebiger, Erwin Strittmatter, Günther Kuhnert, Heinz

Senkbeil, Stephan Hermlin, Erich Kästner, Jens Gerlach, Hermann Kant, Hartmut König, Joachim Nowotny)

5. *Literature of other lands*
(Pushkin, Chekhov, Alphonse Daudet, Guy de Maupassant, Jaroslav Haek, Bogdan Czesko, Mykolas Sluckis, Konstantin Pastowski)[86]

Not only were world classics taught alongside Party literature, however; the eighth-grade teaching guide stressed that the classics themselves were to be approached for their "progressive" ideas. Aleksandr Pushkin, for example, was highly recommended because Lenin and Gorky admired him. On introducing Goethe and Schiller, the teaching guide for eighth grade advises: "Special value should be laid on their historically progressive ideas, their discoveries about the human being and his life. . . . [This approach] can furnish the first insights into how classical German literature developed its *Weltanschauung* and morality in opposition to feudalist-absolutist society."[87] Thus, for example, the pedagogical approach toward the "Easter Stroll" scene in *Faust II*, in which Faust soliloquizes that "the streams and rivers are being freed from ice by the sacred, life-giving eye of spring," should emphasize the investigation of this process, its dialectical character, and above all the optimism that one can draw from it. For in this process, the classical humanistic conception is recognizable:

> There is genuine progress in the world, and it will ultimately win out. This optimistic world outlook . . . can be presented as a general law.
>
> The development of nature proceeds contradictorily; it is a battle of opposites: the new against the old, the outdated, and the inhibited. Faust's feeling of happiness and his optimism correspond to his perception that the spring—the new, the developing—will triumph over the winter, the old.[88]

Progressivist themes received even sharper accent in the study of nineteenth-century literature belonging to the DDR heritage. For instance, Heine's "Silesian Weavers," written out of sympathy for a worker's uprising in 1844, was presented as "an impressive artistic picture of the decisiveness of the proletariat, who regarded the extant feudalist-capitalist order as 'the false Fatherland' and resolved to send it through force to its grave." As a supplement to teaching the poem, teachers were instructed to play a recording dramatizing the relationship between Heine and the young Marx in Paris.[89] The poem achieved canonical status partly because it was originally translated into English and given a Marxist interpretation by Engels, who admired Heine for his fierce criticism of church authorities and German nobility.

DDR literature was unabashedly chosen and presented in the textbooks for its potential influence on young revolutionaries. According to the eighth-grade teaching guide for *Lehrbuch für den Literaterunterricht*, Brecht's one-act play "Señora Carrar's Rifles" (1937), an anti-Falangist tract set in civil-war Spain and arguing that force must be met with force, represents

> literature as a weapon of the international proletariat, in that it affords [the teacher] various means of showing the way of the revolutionary worker from an oppressed and exploited person to a fighter and victor.... [The play shows that] every person must decide to engage in the class struggle. Pupils should experience and deeply understand the significance of active intervention for human progress and the avoidance of tragic events. They comprehend that it is fatal, after temporary setbacks, to give up the struggle, and that it is impossible to remain neutral toward an uncompromising class enemy.[90]

The pedagogy of hate animates the play; as the teaching guide notes, Teresa Carrar's "transformation" into a woman of "decisive readiness for militant action" is "triggered by her insight" about the Falangists: "Those aren't people. They are a leprosy, and they must be burned out like a leprosy." The pedagogy guide does not mention, however, that Brecht himself considered the play a large step backward in his dramatic development.[91]

Literaturunterricht 9/10 laid even greater stress on a systematic historical-materialist approach to literature; East German teachers did not speak of "medieval poetry" or "the Romantic era," but rather "the poetry of high feudalism" and "the revolutionary-democratic age," respectively. The later editions of *Literaturunterricht* 9/10 followed DDR literary scholarship and refined the periodicization of German and world literature into the following six epochs.

1. High feudalism
2. The early bourgeois revolution and the Thirty Years' War [including Shakespeare]

3. Progressive bourgeois literature [Enlightenment, Sturm und Drang movement, Classical period]
4. Revolutionary-democratic and early socialist literature of the nineteenth century
5. The Great October Revolution until the defeat of fascism
6. DDR literature

Literaturunterricht 9/10 reintroduces some authors encountered in eighth grade and even earlier; but fewer authors and selections are included, and the major emphasis therein, as a teaching guide notes and as also occurs in the EOS curriculum, is on twentieth-century literature and on "cultural politics, artistic production, and the reception of literature."[92]

For instance, *Literaturunterricht 9/10* treats high feudalism by concentrating on the anti-clerical political poetry and populist love poetry of minnesinger Walther von der Vogelweide (c. 1170–c.1230). Considered a progressive Chaucer of medieval Germany, Walther attacked the corruptions of Pope Innocent III and was the first in a chivalrous epic to sing of love for a peasant girl.[93]

Early bourgeois literature centers on Shakespeare's *Macbeth*, which is not discussed in terms of Renaissance faculty psychology or ideas about regicide, but rather for its "dialectical interplay of individual and social attributes" and its "optimistic ending," which "Shakespeare chooses . . . in order to express his commitment to a humanistic picture of mankind, against which the title character stands in crass contrast." The teaching guide recommends Shakespeare as a "model": "He was against every kind of dictatorship, possessed bourgeois-humanistic convictions, and had a bourgeois-progressive conception of freedom, happiness, and the relationship of human beings to one another."

Progressive bourgeois literature—referred to as "our classical national literature"—is treated at greater length in *Literaturunterricht 9/10*. Goethe's "Prometheus" (1774), for example, was regarded as important not least because Marx, in the epigraph of his doctoral dissertation, explicitly declared Prometheus as his inspiration and model. But DDR teachers did not stress how the poem expresses Prometheus's harsh portrait of modern humanity, his feeling of isolation and tone of bitterness, and his championing of individuality. Rather, Goethe's Prometheus is "the triumphant rebel, who is superior and triumphs not only in the long run, but in the present" and thus "expresses the revolutionary potential of the young bourgeois class of 1770."

Early socialist literature is divided into two categories. The first type is titled "Writers from Capitalist Countries Who Chose Peace and Humanism" (elsewhere called "Bourgeois-Realistic Literature in the Battle against Imperialism and War")—e.g., the story "The Old Man at the Bridge," written in 1938 in Spain when the "bourgeois-humanist writer" Ernest Hemingway was a war correspondent. The second and more important type is "Socialist Humanism in Soviet Literature"—e.g., Nikolai Ostrowski's *How Steel Is Made Hard,* Mikhail Sholokhov's story "Fate of a Man," and Vladimir Mayakovsky's poetry. Ostrowski's 1934 novel was one of the biggest sellers throughout the communist world. Its protagonist, Pavel Korchagin, a patriotic supporter of the Russian Revolution and model of the young hero in new Soviet literature, was based on Ostrowski himself, a former soldier and *Komsomol* leader. DDR teachers were advised that Korchagin represents "the essence of the uncompromising, fearless fighter for communism and the embodiment of the moral superiority of the communist *Weltanschauung.*"

Sholokhov's "Fate of a Man" (1957) delivered the same message in a context even more serviceable for SED educators: a socialist realist portrait of a meeting between a Soviet soldier and an SS soldier in a German concentration camp. The German plans to execute the Soviet prisoner, but first offers him a last shot of vodka. The Soviet soldier refuses any food, however, even after the second and third shots; finally he does accept some food. Astounded at the strength of his enemy's body and spirit, the German spares his life. DDR educators admired the story for its stark contrast between the fascist and socialist visions, and for its affirmation of the superiority of the latter. The story is typical of Sholokhov, a long-time member of the CPSU (Communist Party of the Soviet Union) Central Committee and a pitiless hard-liner (who once called Solzhenitsyn a "Colorado beetle" deserving extermination and suggested that dissident writers Yuli Daniel and Andrei Sinyavsky should be shot).[94]

Mayakovsky was the canonized poet of the Russian Revolution, a favorite writer of Stalin, and a staple of DDR upper-grade German. Written in late 1928–29, shortly before his suicide in April 1930, both his "Verses from My Soviet Passport" ("Go ahead, read it, envy me, see who I am: / Citizen of the Soviet Union") and "The Secret of Youth" give voice to the SED claim that the USSR is a socialist paradise and that its *Komsomol* members represent the glorious future of the species. In the latter poem, Mayakovsky (who was also an editor of the Soviet youth magazine *Komsomolskaya Pravda*) expresses what the teaching guide calls his "love of youth."[95] The "secret" of youth lies in both its idealism and its utopianism, says Mayakovsky. His poem lionizes its "militant cheerfulness" and heroic strivings, but it also condemns the irresponsibility of youth "who bum around evenings, under the spring heaven, behaving like fashionable fools." The teaching guide suggests: "It is completely imaginable that he read his poem aloud to young people and perhaps directly from that experience concluded that 'to be eighteen' is no excuse [for political ignorance or irresponsibility]."[96] DDR teachers were also encouraged to play Hanns Eisler's song "The Secret of Youth," an adaptation of Mayakovksy's poem, and to take the poem as an occasion for examining both the relation of young people to "the revolutionary traditions of their class" and the changing historical meanings of the words "revolutionary" and "young."[97]

Pre-1945 progressive German literature received close attention, especially in the EOS, with such selections as Friedrich Wolf's *Professor Mamlock*, Heinrich Mann's *The Vassal*, Thomas Mann's "Mario and the Magician," and Kurt Tucholsky's satirical prose taking their place as mainstays in the canon.

Not all of the writers in the POS-EOS twentieth-century canon were faithful Party supporters, let alone Party members; but all of them were socialists or social democrats. For instance, while Wolf did join the SED, "bourgeois-realistic writers" such as the Mann brothers and Tucholsky were viewed sympathetically as fellow travelers in fundamental agreement with the communist *Weltanschauung* and the aspirations of the DDR.

The teaching guides stress such affinities. For instance, ninth-grade teachers are advised that Wolf's committed play, written in 1933 and subtitled "A Tragedy of Western Democracy," bemoans the "lame resistance" to the rise of Hitler of the Weimar Republic and of neutral, liberal-humanist professors such as Professor Mamlock. Heinrich Mann's *The Vassal* (1914), a satirical novel of a servile yet authoritarian and nationalistic paper factory owner in Wilhemine Prussia, portrays "in masterly fashion the arrogant, cowardly, brutal, and sentimental physiognomy of the bourgeois type of his epoch, the German vassal." "Mario and the Magician" (1929), which depicts a demonic, deformed hypnotist whose mesmerizing stage illusions allegorize Mussolini's psychic captivation of millions, expresses Thomas Mann's "timely warning against the danger of fascism and his uncompromising rejection of the fascist power-grabbers in Germany." The teacher's guide also notes that Mann's remark that "anti-communism is the fundamental idiocy of our epoch" demonstrates his "active humanism," which was also proved by his decision to accept an invitation to preside at the DDR's celebration of the 150th anniversary of Schiller's death in 1955. Although the teaching guide mildly disapproves of Tucholsky's "resignation" in his later years (after emigration from Germany), the satirist is praised for his "passionate hatred of the poisoners of Germany and strong sympathy for working people."[98]

DDR literature received the most attention in the upper-grade POS and EOS textbooks, featuring works such as Brecht's *The Mother*,[99] Dieter Noll's *The Adventures of Werner Holt*,[100] Anna Segher's *The Duel*, and Bruno Apitz's *Naked among the Wolves*. A teaching guide explained:

> With the unit "The Development of the Socialist National Literature of the German Democratic Republic" the literature curriculum of the ten-year general POS reaches its climax and also its conclusion. This material places a special measure of responsibility on the teacher to exploit the great political, ethical, and aesthetic power of this unit for the development of the socialist personality of the pupils. His goal must be to make fully effective the picture of the socialist person presented in these works for the all-around education of the pupil.
>
> Only in this way can he make the pupils aware that the great process of becoming the socialist person is manifested . . . in the heroic battle of the working class against imperialism and fascism, in their historical triumph in the anti-fascist-democratic and socialist revolution, and in the making of great writers of world stature, as well as in the creation of a younger generation of DDR authors.[101]

Two excellent examples of how a writer successfully portrayed "the heroic battle of the working class against imperialism and fascism and their historic triumph" are the selections from Seghers and Apitz. Seghers' *The Duel* has direct relevance to the educational history of the DDR. The novella deals with the SED's battle in the late 1940s and early 1950s to capture the DDR universities, and it exemplifies the author's skill in combining socialist realism with psychological and moral analysis. The work is a frank attempt to persuade DDR youth of the superiority of the socialist educational system. The title alludes to two professors' duel for the allegiance of a young working-class student, a contest that pits Professor Winkelfried against Professor Bötcher. Professor Winkelfried is an outstanding scholar and professor, but has no sympathy for Marxism or the historic role of the working class. Professor Bötcher is a communist who was removed from his position during the Third Reich and sent to a concentration camp by the Nazis. The teaching guide stresses Winkelfried's "reactionary class standpoint. He sees no connection between the reactionary educational system that he defends and the catastrophic results of the politics of German imperialism." Ultimately, the student sides with the communist professor. The teaching guide advises: "Pupils should grasp why it is necessary for the working class, after taking power, to break up the educational monopoly and create educational opportunities for the entire *Volk*. The pupils become aware that the pre-conditions of our educational system were created in the early post-war years."[102]

Apitz suffered eight years in Buchenwald, and his novel *Naked among the Wolves* (1958), normally assigned in ninth grade, centers on a true story: the rescue of a four-year-old Polish Jewish child from murder by the SS. The novel became the leading best-seller in DDR history, with editions in the millions of copies. The syllabus specifies that "the deep emotional effect and actual content of the novel should seize every pupil."[103] Pupils were supposed to "identify with the heroism of the anti-fascist resistance fighters." The ninth-grade teaching guide specifies that five "important insights" should be gained from a reading of the novel, "insights" of broad scope that themselves yield insight into a main priority of the DDR German canon: state legitimation. The novel should teach that:

1. The achievement and the sacrifice of the revolutionary representatives of the German and international working class in their battle against the barbarism of the fascists earn for all time the highest recognition, respect, and honor.
2. The communists have proved themselves in the development of history, especially in their battle against fascism. Because of their Marxist-Leninist *Weltanschauung*, they are the most faithful, consistent, and successful representatives of the working class, as well as of the interests of the People and of all Humanity. They are therefore also legitimized for the future as the leading force in the battle for the social progress of Humanity.
3. In building the theoretical foundation of the teachings of Marxism-Leninism, and in the praxis of their battles, the revolutionary representatives of the working class have developed the essential characteristics of the socialist picture of humanity: militant humanism, solidarity and proletarian internationalism, solidarity with the People, unshakable loyalty to the working class and its revolutionary Party, strength of principle, collective action, courage, responsiveness, willingness to sacrifice, optimism toward life, decisiveness, and confidence of victory.

4. Militant humanism is the defining attribute of the socialist picture of humanity. The genuine revolutionary holds this to be his most important task: not only to proclaim humanistic ideas and goals, but also to fight for their actualization in social praxis.
5. A dialectical relationship exists between the individual and society, between personal and collective responsibility. . . . One side is unthinkable without the other. The power of the collective is the power of the individual, and the preservation of the individual is the cornerstone for the preservation of the collective as a whole.[104]

The teaching guide lays special emphasis on the conclusion of *Naked among the Wolves,* urging that teachers particularly devote time to the lines: "We often had to submerge the human being in ourselves. . . . We are leaving this place as inmates no longer! From this hour forward, we are human beings!" These lines illuminate the "contrast between the inhumanity of the fascists and the fundamental humanistic outlook of the anti-fascists."

True–but not at all the whole truth. Although *Naked among the Wolves* is indeed based on a true story of heroism, the novel freely alters the facts to fit DDR ideological priorities, a fact that the teaching guides suppress. For example, the liberation of the camp by U.S. General George S. Patton's Third Army goes unmentioned in the teaching guide, which misleadingly claims that "the open battle of the inmates against the SS at the end of the novel enabled the saving of tens of thousands of people." And later: "The armed uprising assured the saving of the 21,000 inmates still in the camp." Making no mention of the collaboration by some leading communists in the camp (the "Red *Kapos*") with the Nazi guards, the teaching guide concludes: "Fascists and anti-fascists opposed each other in an irreconcilable battle to the death."[105] Teachers were urged to show the film adaptation and to play the "Song of Buchenwald," which was written and sung by the inmates themselves. The novel was also meant to serve as a preparation for the class visit to the Buchenwald Memorial, which was a regular part of ninth-grade preparation for the *Jugendweihe* (youth consecration ceremony).

EXCURSUS: A *Bruderland* Comparison: Soviet and Post-Soviet Textbooks

I

In our discussion of the DDR textbooks' treatment of "bourgeois humanism," we noted that the interpretive approaches highlighted "progressive themes" in eighteenth- and nineteenth-century German literature, showing how it contained the seeds of the "real humanism" that would ultimately come to flower under the "really existing socialism" of the DDR. Of course, this argument of DDR educators, as in so much else, followed the lead of their Soviet counterparts, who were also seeking to claim the great art of the pre-socialist era as part of their "revolutionary heritage."

For both Soviet and East German educators, such claims were often difficult to stake persuasively: in numerous cases, it was not at all easy to reconfigure an aristocratic author who defended the royalty and nobility into a supporter of democratic (let alone revolutionary and proletarian) ideals.

This excursus looks at one difficult case handled by Soviet policymakers, with various degrees of success. As we will see, just as the DDR had a complicated relationship with Goethe and *Faust*—and attempted to integrate them into its "bourgeois realist" tradition of German classicism—so too did Soviet educators have an ambivalent relationship with their native literary genius and his *chef d'oeuvre:* Leo Tolstoy and *War and Peace.* In both cases, the authors and their masterworks were too ideologically incompatible and too artistically powerful simply to co-opt as exalted socialist precursors—and too culturally significant simply to ignore. They had to be embraced—but partially, in both senses of the word: a partial image of the whole, to which orthodox educators were extremely partial.

And so, with the example in mind of Goethe's treatment in the DDR and because key features of DDR textbooks were based significantly on their Soviet counterparts, let us now examine how schoolbooks differed between the Soviet and post-Soviet eras via a single significant example: how two textbooks treat the masterwork of the leading Russian novelist, Leo Tolstoy.

This excursus compares and contrasts Soviet and post-Soviet pedagogical treatments of Tolstoy by examining *War and Peace* as it is presented in secondary school literature textbooks. It is an attempt to place the textbook within the world of Soviet and post-Soviet pedagogy and education.[106] The schoolbooks selected for analysis are from two representative moments in the Soviet and post-Soviet eras: a 1973 ninth-grade literature textbook (edited by Boris Bursov) and a 1996 tenth-grade literature textbook (edited by Yuri Lebedev). Our attention to the treatment of Russia's greatest author and greatest work—Tolstoy, then and now—does not merely illuminate the changing historical approach to Tolstoy and his work, but also suggests further how ideology reflects both literary cultural policy and conceptions of national identity.

For it warrants emphasis that the Soviet textbook was integral to the goals of the Ministry of Education. As one literary scholar put it: "At all times the teacher is supposed to bear in mind that the subject outline and the textbook are his main tools in the teaching of literature."[107] Although Soviet instructors did have access to supplementary teaching materials, the textbook was the primary source for class lessons: "The textbook is the only source of literary history encountered by a pupil at school, and therefore the manner in which it is presented is of utmost importance for understanding the material covered."[108] Such convictions have re-emerged in the Russian pedagogy of the post-Soviet era with a Tolstoyan accent on the existential power of art. Lebedev writes in his 1996 edition that Tolstoy regarded literature as "the textbook of life."[109]

II

An examination of the historical and institutional context of our two secondary school literature textbooks from the 1970s and 1990s raises first this question: How did Soviet literary critics of the Brezhnev era and post-Soviet textbook authors approach Tolstoy?

In the 1910s and 1920s, Georgi Plekhanov and Anatoly Lunacharsky sharply criticized Tolstoy largely because of his doctrine of non-resistance to evil and his calls for moral self-perfection.[110] This critique came at a time when the social aspects of literature and the class position of a writer were emphasized, while discussions of form and aesthetics were treated as bourgeois criticism. In the 1920s and 1930s, Lenin's respectful essays on Tolstoy were not yet widely known and cited by Soviet literary critics.[111] In the early Soviet era (primarily pre–socialist realist), Tolstoy was often condemned as a reactionary who had aristocratic biases and was therefore unsuitable for a central place in the Soviet pedagogical heritage. A marked tendency among Soviet critics of the 1950s and 1960s was to interpret *War and Peace* largely in terms of class and country, showing the cleavage between the people and the aristocracy—and the moral superiority of the former over the latter.[112]

Tolstoy's artistic writings—even after his religious conversion in the 1880s—were condemned in the 1920s and 1930s as depicting only the nobility and the wealthy. Before Lenin's literary essays on Tolstoy became canonical, *War and Peace* and *Anna Karenina* were denounced as counter-revolutionary.[113] Only after World War II did changes occur in teaching Tolstoy. Lenin's critical articles on Tolstoy became the guiding authority for the view that a more unified approach to Tolstoy as an artist-thinker should be undertaken. These essays did not address the literary heritage of Tolstoy, but instead focused on the political and social struggle taking place around Tolstoy's personality. Lenin emphasizes the contradictions in Tolstoy, but insists that they are a reflection of contradictory conditions in Russia of the last decades of nineteenth century. Lenin's article "Tolstoy as the Mirror of the Russian Revolution," written in 1908 to celebrate Tolstoy's eightieth birthday, figures prominently in the 1973 textbook.

Lenin's articles are concerned with social issues rather than art, but they do devote time to the study of genre, composition, and other aesthetic problems that had been ignored previously. Lenin describes traits that are considered positive or negative depending upon how useful they can be to the cause of the working class. Tolstoy's idea of moral self-perfection seems to contradict Marxist teaching as an excessively individualistic pursuit, but Soviet ideologists argue that revolutionary change in society occurs at various rates, so moral self-perfection can actually be useful.[114]

In the 1950s, there was a great effort to bring interpretations of Tolstoy closer to the problems of contemporary reality, just as was done with other nineteenth-century classics. During this period, ideological aspects were re-emphasized in the study of literature. There was an increased stress on patriotism, as well as criticism of the Orthodox Church, the judicial system, and the corrupt social order.[115]

Because the textbook collectives demanded that teachers highlight the historical process in teaching literature, the textbooks focused on the role of the *narod* (the people) in the historical process. The key to handling *War and Peace* became the image of the people, i.e., the three main characters' close association with the *narod*. Educational functionaries thus sidestepped the fact that the protagonists in the novel are aristocrats—like Tolstoy himself. By taking advantage of Tolstoy's genius of creating unforgettable characters and presenting the heroes as embodying the sensibility of the People in the context of the sweeping events of history, the textbook writers repositioned *War and Peace* as a pre-socialist novel.[116]

III

The organizing principles for the two schoolbooks differ dramatically: The 1973 textbook thematizes the *narod* and history, whereas the 1996 edition highlights language, aesthetics, and spirituality. Attending to History in the earlier edition means focusing on the appearance of revolutionary proto-Decembrists within the framework of the character discussions, whereas the 1996 emphasis turns to religion, featuring the eternal soul, an ahistorical matter. Let us now examine these divergent orientations of the two textbooks in closer detail.

The 1973 edition. During the Soviet era, given the cultural authority of Lenin's *obiter dicta* and Tolstoy's great popularity among readers, cultural commissars and textbook authors realized that it was impossible to exclude Tolstoy from the socialist literary heritage. Tolstoy was unquestionably part of the Russian literary tradition, but how could he be part of the communist heritage? Excluding his works would be too great a loss, so the textbook collectives had to find some way of claiming this heritage in part and rejecting or remolding those facets of it that did not conform to M-L ideological criteria. Tolstoy was not the only bourgeois writer embraced in the M-L cultural policymakers' reclamation project: because they perceived that Soviet culture needed a pre-1917 literary pedigree, they sought to claim the great bourgeois authors as part of the socialist heritage.

The dialectical dilemma was fundamentally a didactic one: how could Soviet cultural functionaries teach both Tolstoy and M-L truth? How could they claim the greatest prose writer in the Russian language and the spiritual and religious sage of millions and yet also promote communist ideology? How was it possible both to expose readers to the literary power of Tolstoy and simultaneously to advance M-L ideology? How would textbook authors resolve this dilemma of focusing on politics and not aesthetics when presenting Tolstoy?[117]

The first half of this dialectical dilemma, which is largely pedagogical, occurs at the level of *War and Peace* itself. The textbook policymaker's most immediate problem regarding Tolstoy was how to handle the aristocratic protagonists as a means to promote class consciousness. The character approach in the table of contents of the 1973 textbook is faithful not to M-L pedagogy, but to Tolstoy. Typically, M-L pedagogy would feature plot via history, or emphasize setting via social structure, whereas characters were used to symbolize class and critique class types. Such an approach highlights political issues, not aesthetic ones. However, the textbook authors could not avoid acknowledging the importance and centrality of the main characters in *War and Peace* by merely presenting the novel's greatness as consisting in its brilliant plot lines and skillfully drawn settings. They had to concede that Tolstoy had created immortal characters, but their task involved portraying these unforgettable characters as types who are closely identified with the *narod* and who reflect nineteenth-century social historical developments.

It must be re-emphasized that Tolstoy's power of characterization was the essence of his literary achievement. Its unique features stand in opposition to the M-L ideologists' claim that Tolstoy's characters must be understood in relation to the people. Such a claim justifies the 1996 return to aesthetics because if Tolstoy is introducing a new kind of characterization in Russian literature in the nineteenth century, then it merits explanation as to what he does differently than other authors and why readers find his characters immortal and unforgettable. Tolstoy's protagonists develop during the course of the action without having any tendency to betray their true selves. Such character development runs counter to the approach of M-L ideology, which implies that they are static characters for the most part, especially Pierre and Andrey.

Lenin's essays on Tolstoy figure prominently in the 1973 Bursov edition. His view of Tolstoy, which focused on the contradictions in the man and in his work, dominated and determined the limitations of Tolstoyan criticism in the Soviet Union. Lenin's criticism made it easier for Soviet critics to appropriate Tolstoy as part of the Soviet cultural heritage. To accommodate the restrictions of Soviet didactics, *War and Peace* had to be viewed as a mirror of nineteenth-century Russia.[118]

That was how the novel was presented as historically faithful and socially accurate. Lenin himself highlights Tolstoy's contradictions, which can be invoked as one of the tactics of claiming him—via the argument that his great novel serves as a magnificent mirror because it contains and reflects all of these contradictions. The Marxist and socialist realist approach emphasize man's social nature, whereas Tolstoy emphasized the eternal nature of man's soul, but such religious beliefs were characteristic of nineteenth-century society.

The second half of the dilemma focuses on Tolstoy the man. He was not simply a writer or an artist; he was the moral and spiritual exemplar of the nation. However, his status as an aristocrat posed a great problem: M-L pedagogy had to both lionize an aristocrat as *the* great writer of his age and explain that he still speaks to the socialist realist era. The educational functionaries had to demonstrate that they recognized the literary value of *War and Peace* and that Count Tolstoy anticipated the events of 1917.

The task of the textbook writer thus became a virtuoso challenge of claiming the past, constructing a canon, and rehabilitating the bourgeois-humanist heritage. In the U.S., such dilemmas are typically discussed in terms of canon formation, but this problem extended far beyond the realm of an academic issue in the communist world: it was a national problem, a problem of communist culture, and a problem of reconceiving the past. What would this past include?

In order to claim Tolstoy, educators had to recast history to make it seem as if the author were actually a peasant champion at the time he wrote it. Lenin's attraction to Tolstoy centers on the fact that Tolstoy became a peasant champion and peasant himself *after* writing *War and Peace*. So the early Tolstoy is downplayed and the later Tolstoy is highlighted. The attention that the 1973 textbook gives to literary history is not exactly historically accurate, but it manages to stretch Tolstoy to fit the ideological mold. It is historically anachronistic, but the textbook authors downplay the Tolstoy who was actually the author of *War and Peace* and claim the later Tolstoy as their own. When discussing Tolstoy's life, they had to portray him as a progressive bourgeois humanist trying simultaneously to liberate the people and himself, but ultimately failing.

Although Tolstoy was obviously foremost a spiritual revolutionary, in order to be acceptable to M-L ideology he had to be recast as a political revolutionary. Ironically, it looks as if the Russian Revolution led by Lenin did indeed owe a debt to Tolstoy. Lenin's essay on Tolstoy clearly states: "Tolstoy decisively broke with the views and interests of the landowning class and came out as a great spokesman of those ideas and moods which developed among the millions of peasants until the time of the attack on the bourgeois revolution in Russia."[119] This approach to Tolstoy focused on the contradictions of the writer-thinker from a sociopolitical point of view, whereby Tolstoy was caught in the social and historical contradictions of his bourgeois age.

The strategy that was implemented thus approached Tolstoy via Tolstoy, so to speak, but twisted him in such a way to make him suitable for M-L pedagogy. Just as Tolstoy in his art and aesthetics highlights character because of the deep sincerity and emotional power they hold for the reader, Soviet critics to some extent approached Tolstoy according to character, but manipulated the concept for their own ideological purposes.

The same can be said for Nikolai Chernyshevsky's idea of the "dialectic of the soul" when it is applied to Tolstoy's art. Soviet critics socialized Chernyshevsky's conception of "soul" into "the spirit of the Russian people" and eliminated his emphasis on religion and the *Christian* conception of soul. The overall tactics consisted in reworking the idea of "soul" to make it suitable for M-L pedagogy. By adopting this strategy—to "leninize" and "marxify" Tolstoy—it is possible to omit discussing topics such as religion. And where it was impossible to avoid discussing a problem area such as Tolstoy's membership in the aristocracy, Soviet critics could acknowledge that Tolstoy does not fulfill all M-L criteria perfectly.

The 1973 textbook's work focuses on the problems and the role and importance of the People in the war with France. To leninize Tolstoy, and to claim him for a canon in which socialist realism was the canonical approach, entailed shifting some values. The strategic process for claiming Tolstoy was twofold: first, by narrowing down the focus on Tolstoy to his relationship and the relationship of all the characters to the *narod;* secondly, by treating Tolstoy's personal history, which was mired in contradictions, as simply that of a man of his time caught in those historical contradictions.

The claiming of Tolstoy thus involved taking parts of him that were salvageable and advancing those acceptable parts in the textbooks by focusing on history and populism—not on religion and pacifism, which were reactionary and deplorable. These latter elements were either criticized or omitted entirely.

The 1996 edition. The re-education process, in which the rewriting of textbooks plays an important role and reflects the ongoing struggle for competing ideologies, is still evolving. A textual analysis of the 1996 Russian textbook shows that critics and educational bureaucrats of the 1990s were grappling with these ideological issues.

Whereas Tolstoy was leninized and marxified in the era of Soviet literary criticism, a much more complex phenomenon occurred in the 1990s. Nonetheless, despite the intricacies and the difficulty of making any overall assessment, what is evident is the step away from a materialistic toward a spiritual interpretation. Such a move involves a shift away from the human being as a social and political creature, toward attending to man's "inner needs."[120]

The introduction to the 1996 literature textbook addresses issues that textbook authors deem crucial to students' understanding of nineteenth-century literature. Within the larger context of the contrasts between Slavophiles and Westerners, attention is devoted to exploring the differences between the development of Western thought in terms of Catholicism and Protestantism versus the Eastern Orthodox tradition. The West, on the one hand, traditionally considers evil as manifesting itself in the external material world, so that human reason and intellect join forces to create a so-called heaven on earth and focus on material conditions. The Slavophiles, on the other hand, believe that worldly evil resides within man himself. As a result, Russian philosophical thought and especially literature are concerned with improving man's spiritual inner life—by practicing moral self-perfection.

The textbook thus discusses the psychological analysis of Tolstoy as revealing the endlessly rich possibilities in man for self-renewal. Social circumstances very often limit these possibilities, but in general they are not in a position to be destroyed. The "fluidity of man," i.e., his ability to change, most concerns Tolstoy. The textbook editor, Yuri Lebedev, asserts that the most important theme of Tolstoy's biography and work is the evolution of man through practicing moral self-perfection. Tolstoy considered this idea to be the prerequisite for transforming the world. The 1996 textbook explains that the youthful Tolstoy belonged to the revolutionaries and materialists, though he soon abandoned them. It seemed to him that the revolutionary transformation of the external, social conditions of human existence was unlikely to have long-term prospects. By contrast, Lebedev explains, Tolstoy considered moral self-perfection a simple activity, which can be chosen freely by each person. The textbook summarizes Tolstoy's philosophy for the student: "to have goodness around you, you must become good yourself: with moral self-perfection you can begin to transform your life."[121]

Lebedev provides a complex set of issues to orient the student's reading of Tolstoy in the 1996 textbook. A new emphasis on spirituality and moral self-perfection pervades the text. Tolstoy is intensely interested in the experiences and changes of his heroes—their ability to renew themselves and increase their attunement to the spiritual world. He believes that his art brings light to human souls and wishes to teach people "how to love life," for literature is (in the editor's words) "the textbook of life."[122]

The shift from the Soviet to the post-Soviet treatment of Tolstoy in literature textbooks involves replacing a purely political and ideological interpretation with one that is more concerned with ethical and spiritual issues. This shift is not merely a simplistic movement from ideology to interpretation, but reflects a complex series of interrelationships ranging from interpreting Tolstoy in M-L terms to discussing him in more aesthetic terms. The divergent emphases are clear. The 1973 edition devotes little aesthetic attention to Tolstoy, let alone to addressing literary issues and poetics; i.e., to approaching Tolstoy via Tolstoy. The 1996 edition devotes much greater attention to aesthetic issues and places less emphasis on M-L pedagogy.

Yet both editions contain common strands of political and textual interpretation that allow for seeing the richness of themes in the work. Both of these interpretations also include historical contradictions. It seems implausible that the 1973 edition would emphasize character. However, given the dialectical dilemmas, the textbook collectives did address character, but in relation to the *narod* and history. It is also implausible that the 1996 edition would place *War and Peace* in any kind of M-L framework. Yet because of understandable continuities between the Soviet and post-Soviet eras, the 1996 edition's emphasis, while not explicitly on M-L pedagogy, is nonetheless on social questions and on class issues, and thus still displays vestiges of quasi-Marxist elements.

Thus, whereas the 1973 edition is overtly ideological in nature, the 1996 edition attempts a new approach to interpreting Tolstoy that is tinged but not dominated by M-L ideology. The post-Soviet textbook allows today's Russian students reading *War and Peace* to discuss several topics that were omitted during the Soviet era—linguistic problems, cultural issues, and Tolstoy's own religious-ethical views. Such a shift does not indicate that M-L ideology has been cast aside for something completely new, but it does reflect a sharp turn from a progressive interpretation to a more literary or formalistic one. The 1996 literature textbook's commentary on *War and Peace* is, therefore, not by any means a complete refutation of the 1973 edition: there are as many continuities as discontinuities.

The Advanced High School Curriculum

Art for me is a sort of intellectual appendix, and when its propagandist role, essential to us, has been exhausted, we shall—flick! flick!—cut it out.
—Lenin, in conversation, 1921

Let us return to the East German schools and address now the upper grades: The EOS German curriculum continued the main themes of the POS curriculum. Cultural politics, especially the issue of the DDR's radical *Erbe* (heritage), remained a focal point, as did the concentration on nineteenth- and twentieth-century literature. The priorities of *Literatur. Klasse 11 und 12* are reflected in the order of its sections; only after introducing both the radical humanist tradition and DDR and Soviet bloc literature does the textbook address earlier works—and then only in order to establish "their significance for socialist national culture." The section headings run as follows:

1. Realistic Literature in Capitalist Society
2. Socialist Realist Literature as a Representation of Socialist Society
3. The Literature of Socialist Realism in the Battle for Socialist Progress and against Imperialism and War

4. Humanism and Realism in Classical Literature, and their Significance for Socialist National Culture[123]

But the canon fodder fed to young revolutionaries in *Literatur. Klasse 11 und 12* was also much more refined than that of previous grades: the EOS German curriculum featured a much wider and less orthodox selection of works for study than had the POS. For instance, in addition to standard authors such as Brecht and Gorky (and even, in an obvious concession to *weltanschauliche Erziehung*, Wilhelm Pieck), excerpts from important Marxist theoreticians (Franz Mehring on naturalism and on proletarian culture), Enlightenment philosophers and men of letters (Kant, Lichtenberg, Herder), and critically-minded leftists (Ernst Toller, Henri Barbusse) find a place in *Literatur. Klasse 11 und 12*.

Numerous forgettable (and now forgotten) Soviet writers, as well as several foreign writers sympathetic to the Marxist revolution (Pablo Neruda, Federico Garcia Lorca, and James Baldwin) are predictably included in *Literatur. Klasse 11 und 12*. Moreover, unsurprisingly, the ideological aim behind most choices is not hard to decipher—Aeschylus on "Prometheus in Chains," a friendly exchange of letters between Heine and the young Marx, a scene from Dickens' *Oliver Twist*, Brecht's poetic hymn to Lenin, a Pieck speech to the 1946 KPD Cultural Congress, James Baldwin's "Open Letter to Angela Davis," a Hermann Kant speech to the 1978 Writer's Congress. And yet, the innovative selections are worth remarking: several writers formerly condemned as formalist or as anti-socialist and even anti-humanist (Hölderlin, Rimbaud, Verlaine, Georg Trakl, Kafka, Rilke, and Hugo von Hofmannsthal) are present. Even more unexpectedly, *Literatur. Klasse 11 und 12* also includes contemporary selections that arguably gave ammunition to "the enemy." And these come straight from the enemy camp itself, i.e., works by significant West German and Swiss writers who expressed both sympathy toward and criticism of the DDR (Martin Walser, Ingeborg Bachmann, and Max Frisch).

But this limited official openness in the German curriculum of the DDR's advanced high schools should not be exaggerated. To weigh properly the pedagogical accents, I believe, it is invaluable to supplement analysis of EOS textbooks with examination materials—and also conversations with DDR-era teachers and pupils. Freya Klier found during her survey of the cultural literacy of DDR secondary school pupils that practically none had ever even heard of dissident or exiled DDR authors whose works were published in small DDR editions or were unavailable.[124] My own informal survey of several dozen EOS teachers and students between 1990 and 1995 likewise indicated that the (admittedly narrow) latitude suggested by the EOS textbooks proved largely illusory: the official *Freiraum* was greater in theory than in practice. My interviewees reported, for instance, that as a result of the focus in DDR syllabi on the socialist "heritage," pressure to "cover" all the required material led to a time shortage, so that DDR émigrés and Western authors "skeptical" toward socialism were seldom discussed in class—even if to be rebutted.

And yet that is not the whole story. According to my informants, the unofficial latitude in DDR curricula also heavily depended on the particular teacher—and could often be surprisingly wide. Once the classroom door was shut, many teachers did not parrot the textbook's line—even if they did not go so far as to say anything incautious that would come to haunt them if it were circulated by any young true believers among their pupils. Such teachers did not defy SED orthodoxy; they simply declined to regurgitate it. The bottom line was that, in a minority of DDR classrooms, a noticeable gap opened up between the textbook tenets and the classroom discussions. As we will learn in several of the portraits and interviews in Part 2, many DDR teachers did not all "teach by the book": either the syllabi or the *Abitur* (school-leaving) examinations.

Nonetheless, this did not mean that they taught "outside" or against them. The overwhelming majority of both teachers and pupils knew that public obeisance, or at least acquiescence, to SED orthodoxy was essential in order to get ahead in DDR society—or even to simply avoid running afoul of SED authorities.

Indeed, perhaps the most conclusive evidence as to what "counted" in the EOS German curriculum was the *Abitur* exam, which was taken by twelfth-grade EOS pupils and which was a significant criterion for university admission. The following are the two main questions for the 1986 German *Abitur* exam.[125]

1. "Our life demands a socialist realist literature and art characterized by Party loyalty, the spirit of the People, and high socialist ideals. It must also convey new enthusiasm for thinking, feeling, and action in practical activities."
   From: Report on the Central Committee of the SED,
   by Comrade Erich Honecker.

   In order to reflect more deeply on the function of socialist literature, address these aspects of the content of any literary work that has especially engaged you.

2. *Interpret the following 1985 poem of Uwe Berger:*
   In our work live on
   those who once stood at the barricades,
   who in the face of persecution, hatred, and murder
   discovered in the struggle for our rights,
   that their dying words
   were of the Red flag.

   We oppose the night on the strength of
   the bond that unites us;
   thus do the People enjoy happiness and power
   thus do flowers bloom from stones
   thus is freedom prized
   which we value as humans, not as [fascists] wolves.

   We must cast our lot fully,
   on good days and on hard days,
   with those who liberate themselves,
   who as comrades prove themselves
   and what we have will prosper
   because we will preserve and increase it.

Books Are Weapons

"Books are weapons": Such *Abitur* exam questions recall again our opening main epigraph to Chapter 1: the summons that Otto Grotewohl entered in the guest book of the Dietz Verlag in 1950: "Books are not only friends, they are weapons—revolutionary weapons! Create weapons! Create weapons!" And such *Abitur* questions should indeed leave no doubt about the ideological orthodoxy ultimately expected in EOS German classes. Or as Friedrich Wolf expressed it in his play *Cyankali* (1929):

> Shatter the wall of your silence!
> Demand your life, your joys,
> Create them yourself, Proletarian!
> Art is a weapon!

But art and literature were not the only ammunition ready to hand from the DDR Ministry of Education: the cultural front had other materiél available too.

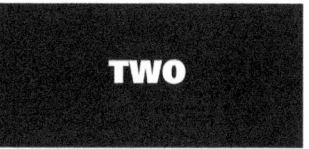

TERRA VERDE, TERRA ROSSO
Geography

> Forward and never forget
> wherein our strength resides!
> Whether famished
> or whether fed
> Forward and never forget!
> Solidarity!
> —Bertolt Brecht, "The Solidarity Song" (1931)

The Expanding Red Earth

However central German language and literature was in the DDR schools, however important SED educators regarded the task of constructing a progressive literary canon, German was ultimately only one part of a comprehensive core curriculum of ideology, from whose influence even the sciences and mathematics were not wholly free.

Moreover, if German literature in the upper POS grades and the EOS seemed to take the high, less ideological road, that was partly because *Heimatkunde* stopped in fifth grade; its topics of concern were thereafter mainly taken up by geography and *Staatsbürgerkunde* (citizenship studies, colloquially known as *Stabü*), both of which aggressively promoted the DDR and the socialist *Bruderländer*. That was these subjects' main aim: to convince pupils that, when all was said and done, they were socialists and DDR citizens first and last. Right or wrong—no, Left or wrong—the DDR was still their country, still their socialist Fatherland.

Succeeding *Heimatkunde* in fifth grade, *Erdkunde* ("earth studies" or geography) took up its topographical aspects, leaving overt agitprop for *Staatsbürgerkunde*, which we will discuss in the next chapter. But like DDR civics, geography was highly political. It served as one half of what might be termed "advanced socialist Fatherland education."[1]

DDR *Erdkunde* thus focused not merely—and often not chiefly—on the "green earth," i.e., the physical features of a region (i.e., climate, elevation, soil, vegetation, population, and land use), but rather on the rapidly expanding "Red earth." What educators sometimes termed "socialist geography" frankly argued the superiority of socialist nations' use of the earth's resources—which post-war History was rapidly demonstrating by the spread of communism across the globe. Indeed, the inside front cover of the POS atlas of the 1950s through the 1970s gives graphic testimony to these aspirations: three maps covering Europe and Asia appear; they are dated 1914, 1917–45, and 1945–61, respectively. The first map contains no red; the next map is half-covered in red, and the third is dominated by red. The title: "*Der Vormarsch des Sozialismus*" ("The Advance of Socialism").[2] The military connotation of the subject noun seems deliberately chosen.

Yes, the message was graphic: *Der Sozialismus siegt!*

Erdkunde in East German classrooms was, therefore, frequently less concerned with the study of the earth than with the revolutionary advance of socialism upon it. And geography teachers were supposed not merely to describe that advance but to contribute to it. "Forward and never forget! / wherein our strength resides," as Brecht's "Solidarity Song" expressed it. Or as the familiar FDJ slogan, derived from a speech of SPD leader Wilhelm Liebknecht in 1872, put it: "*Wer die Jugend hat, hat die Zukunft*" ("Who has the youth, has the future").

DDR geography possessed the same ideological orientation as *Heimatkunde*. But its range and depth were greater, especially in the upper grades of the POS, where it addressed polytechnical educational issues as well as cultural and moral ones. In the introduction to the 1980 edition of *Geographie 5*, pupils received a glimpse of what lay in store in upcoming years:

> We already know from *Heimatkunde* a great deal about our home locale, our home *Kreis* [small region], our home *Bezirk* [district], and Berlin, the capital of the German Democratic Republic. We've also heard about the life of people in the Soviet Union and in other socialist nations. So we have already gained our first acquaintance with geography. But that isn't enough at all. . . .
>
> Many working people need geographical knowledge in their daily work. Construction workers and engineers and architects

have to understand the layout of the ground when they build new houses. Farmer comrades must observe the contents of the soil exactly, in order to raise their agricultural production.³

Or as the geography teaching guide phrased it, in a unit titled "The Significance of Geography Class in Fifth Grade and in the Following School Years":

> The material of fifth-grade geography is especially well suited to further the acquisition of *knowledge about the socialist Fatherland* and *a feeling of pride in [our] achievements and a feeling of solidarity with working people.* In geography the pre-conditions for the educational effectiveness of [other subjects in] later grades is created, above all in the units treating other socialist states, especially the Soviet Union; here and in the treatment of West Germany and other capitalist states, the pupil gains a *partisan perspective.* Beyond all this, the pupil should already in fifth grade acquire the *foundations of a materialistic Weltanschauung and a socialistic way of behaving within his learning collective.* In these ways, geography class makes an essential *contribution to the formation of socialist personalities* who are accustomed to adopt—ambitiously, critically, and independently—the task-oriented, socially necessary perspective.⁴

The geography syllabus for the POS and EOS proceeded in two phases. In the first stage (fifth through ninth grades), the emphasis—at least formally—was on physical geography. The regions of the world were studied according to topographical and ideological categories, i.e., by continent and hemisphere (and, secondarily, by political system—whether socialist or capitalist). In the second stage (ninth through twelfth grades), pupils also studied economic geography, especially "the socialist world system," concentrating chiefly on economic development. Upper-grade POS and EOS geography concerned itself more with M-L theory. But all grades celebrated the economic successes in the socialist camp (especially the Soviet Union and eastern Europe, with West Germany's failures serving as counterexamples illustrating the weaknesses of KA [*kapitalistisches Ausland,* capitalist foreign territory]). The next two excursus sections take an indepth look at those topics emphasized in the first two years of the curriculum.

Excursus: "Our Socialist Fatherland": How Fifth-Graders Learned to Love the *Heimat*

The fifth-grade curriculum covered the physical geography of the DDR itself. Much attention is given in *Geographie 5* to East Germany's topographical distinctions: the plains and valleys of the north, the hills and mountains of the south. But the political dimension of such facts is never forgotten. For instance, *Geographie 5* repeatedly stresses that the DDR land mass is "tended with care" by socialist agriculture and industry. Unsurprisingly, no mention is made of the DDR's dying forests, poisoned rivers, and polluted air. The paragraph on socialist agriculture concludes: "The land is the most important natural foundation of agricultural production. In order that its bounty may be maintained and even increased, it is carefully tended in socialist society."[5]

If DDR German mixed politics with letters, DDR geography mingled ideology with geology and topography. Passing reference was made to the relation between the "laws" of physical science and scientific socialism; the teaching guide advises teachers to mention the "dialectical aspect" of physical geography, i.e., how M-L and Nature share the same "general lawfulness."[6] But the teaching guide notes that this theme will be handled systematically in the upper grades and should remain in the background in fifth grade. Thus *Geographie 5* is less "ideology and geography" than a counterpart to Western political geography, though this de-emphasis on agitprop is more true of the texts from the 1970s and 1980s than of those from earlier decades.

Geographie 5 is divided into two parts based on the topography of East Germany: the plains of the north and the mountains of the south. The textbook's sub-chapters, however, are organized according to the DDR's administrative system of fifteen *Bezirke*;[7] this allows for a political emphasis to the text, with local political achievements and economic geography featured. For instance, sub-chapter and unit titles include "The Development of Rostock," "Big Chemical Firms," and "The New Residential City of Eisenhüttenstadt."[8]

The first chapter of *Geographie 5*, "The DDR—A Socialist State," sets the tone for the text. It presents a map of the *Bezirke* and an overview of the physical facts of the DDR: size, population, population density, major rivers, and so on. The opening paragraphs make clear, however, that a strong political emphasis in geography class is to be expected:

> Under the leadership of the Socialist Unity Party of Germany, the working class rules in the DDR. In alliance with the comrade

farmers, the intelligentsia, and all other working people, the working class promotes the interests of the whole *Volk*. All the important means of production are the property of the *Volk* or Party. . . . The DDR is cordially allied with the Soviet Union and all other countries in the socialist community of nations. Many socialist countries cooperate closely in the RGW [*Rat für gegenseitige Wirtschaftshilfe*, Council for Mutual Economic Aid]. In this way, people from the allied countries get to know and understand one another better and better.

The DDR maintains diplomatic relations with almost all nations of the earth. It conducts peaceful trade with many nations and helps young national states with economic reconstruction.[9]

Featuring units titled "The DDR—a Socialist State" and "Berlin—Capital of the German Democratic Republic," the chapter on East Berlin is the longest and most detailed in *Geographie 5*. East Berlin—always referred to simply as "Berlin" in official language (West Berlin was termed "Westberlin")—is described as "the political center of our Republic," "a modern socialist capital." In the style of the *Heimatkunde* textbooks—and anticipating the more extensive attention to the political history of modern Berlin in history class (tenth- through twelfth-grade history)—the opening unit on Berlin in the 1967 edition gives a quick, five-paragraph overview of wartime and post-war Berlin.[10] For example:

> In the Second World War, large parts of Berlin were destroyed. After the liberation of Berlin by the Soviet Army, the city was occupied by troops from the Soviet Union, the U.S., Great Britain, and France. A separate administration was introduced in the three western zones with the support of the western occupation powers. These measures destroyed the unity of the city. Berlin was split into two parts. . . .
>
> The three former western sectors form the politically autonomous area of *Westberlin*. From this center the economy of the DDR was damaged year after year. Therefore, on August 13, 1961, our government decided on protective measures on the border of our Republic and Westberlin.[11]

The unit concludes: "Berlin, the capital of the DDR, is a major, modern socialist city. Working people from all *Bezirken* of our Republic cooperate to make the city ever more beautiful."[12]

The East Berlin chapter also spotlights the DDR's political structure, featuring photographs of the State Council headquarters and of "Red City Hall," the site of the municipal administration of Berlin that was built with reddish brick. In the 1967 edition, the unit begins: "Our capital Berlin is the site of the highest body of the People in the DDR, the *Volkskammer.* ... Between the meetings of the *Volkskammer,* the direction of the state and society lies in the hands of the State Council. It is under the direction of *Walter Ulbricht.* ... The leading party of our state is the party of the working class."[13]

This paragraph exemplifies how socialist educators determined that geography could make a contribution to *weltanschauliche Erziehung.* The various regions of the DDR are primarily treated as occasions to present the state philosophy and structure of government of the DDR, as the end of the closing chapter of *Geographie 5* evinces: "The DDR is a socialist state. All measures of the Party and state are directed toward the constant improvement of citizens' lives. The economy is developed systematically, under the direction of the Party, in the interest of all citizens. ... On account of their productive labor, all working people have a share in the development and execution of the plans [Five-Year Plans]."[14]

Excursus: "Elementary" Political Geography

Geography in sixth through eighth grades devoted roughly equal attention to both capitalist and socialist nations: sixth grade covered Western Europe (often referred to as KA) and "the socialist countries of Europe"; seventh grade treated the USSR and Asia; eighth grade addressed North and South America, Africa, and Australia.

Geographie 6 is divided into two parts. The division is not geographic (west versus east), however, but political: "Capitalist Countries of Europe" and "Socialist Countries of Europe." And the introduction ("Overview of Europe") signals that the textbook will be blending geography and ideology in order to develop a "partisan perspective." The textbook begins with a table that orders by rank the length of rivers in Europe: the Volga and Donau are first and second; the table then skips to the Rhine, which comes in a poor ninth. (The Elbe is tenth.) The editors then state:

> One can order the states of Europe according to their geographical position. ... All of Eastern Europe belongs to the European

> part of the Soviet Union. The entire Soviet Union is the biggest country of the world.
>
> If one divides the states of Europe according to their political organization, they belong partly to the socialist and partly to the capitalist countries. Until the end of the Second World War, the Soviet Union was the sole socialist country in Europe. Since then, the number of socialist countries in Europe has significantly grown.

The introduction concludes with this sentence: "The biggest part of the land mass of Europe is occupied by socialist countries."[15]

Given its division into east and west on the basis of political systems, Europe was the perfect setting for comparing the relative successes of socialism and capitalism—and, of course, of the two Germanies—and it is fascinating to see here how *Geographie 6* employs geographical facts, often in the form of charts or lists, to imply—without ever actually stating—that socialist nations are superior to capitalist ones. Nothing is falsified. But the impression of the overall superiority of socialism is effectively communicated. That socialist nations occupy a greater land mass than the capitalist ones implies other sorts of superiority. That the USSR contains the biggest rivers (the Rhine is the only western European river even mentioned in the chart) and is the "biggest" country in the world geographically leaves the implication of its greatness in other areas of importance.

But a word about the difficult task that faced the editors of *Geographie 6* is necessary. When writing a geography textbook about capitalist nations—above all those of Europe, and particularly West Germany—SED educators of the post-Wall era had an especially thorny problem that entered every young reader's mind yet that the textbooks could not directly address: the irony (indeed frustration) of studying countries that you were forbidden to visit. Even some socialist countries—especially countries outside eastern Europe, such as Cuba—were near-impossible to visit. And yet nowhere do the textbooks, nor even the teaching guides, ever breathe a word about travel restrictions. It was a topic just too hot to handle.

Still, the issue lurked in the shadows, above all in units that dealt with the German border and the Berlin Wall. Like the Wall, it was *there*. With pupils in the uncomfortable position of learning about numerous nations to which they could never travel until retirement age, the question that dared not speak its name crouched in catatonic anguish on the tip of even children's lips: Since we can't go anywhere, what do we need this subject *for?*

The agitprop in the geography teaching guides tried, of course, to head off that question; but in the units on the capitalist world, SED educators had to perform a virtuoso balancing act. They had to justify the value of studying the capitalist world and yet condemn KA. They had to douse the desire to travel to the West by making the capitalist world seem not even worth visiting. And yet, the very treatment of the capitalist world fueled the DDR citizenry's obsession with it.[16] In the end, however unsuccessfully, the textbooks attempted simply to annihilate the question by force of sheer invective.

Consider, for instance, the presentation of West Germany and Great Britain in the chapter "Capitalist Countries of Europe" in part 1 of *Geographie 6*. More than a third of this part is devoted to the BRD. In the opening paragraphs, under the heading "The BRD, a Capitalist Nation," which is accompanied by photographs of young workers on strike, we learn that:

> As in all capitalist countries, the raw materials, industrial firms, and banks belong principally to private property owners, the capitalists. Even the land and terrain is, in largest part, private property. The capitalists represent only a small part of the population, but they govern the economic wealth of the state. The actual earnings of the working people are really received by them as profit. . . .
>
> There is only one political party in the BRD that openly and fearlessly battles for a just order. That is the German Communist Party (DKP).[17]

This text is followed by one lone unit question: "Contrast property and power relations in the BRD with those of the DDR! Prove why there cannot be any exploitation of people here!"[18] The section on Britain is cast in similar terms: "Great Britain is the *country where capitalism originated*. . . . Back then, the ruling classes of Great Britain governed the greatest merchant and war navy. They had conquered huge territories in Asia, Africa, and North America and had oppressed the peoples there. Such a subordinated and exploited country is called a colony."[19] The summary for part 1 then opens:

> All capitalist countries possess these distinctive features:
> 1. The same property and power relations prevail in capitalist countries. Almost all the means of production, above all the industrial firms, belong to a small minority of the population. The

great mass of the working people is exploited by the capitalists for their own profit. All essential measures of the government serve to maintain these capitalist relations.

2. The capitalist class is opposed to the working class. The workers battle for improved working and living conditions. They struggle for secure jobs, good educations for their children, and suitable medical insurance as well as a beautiful and natural environment. The capitalists ultimately have only one interest: the protection and increase of their profits.[20]

By contrast, the chapters on the "Socialist Countries of Europe" in part 2 are an inspiring story of progress, persistence, courage, and human dignity. After contrasting the distinctive features of *"socialist relations of production"* point for point with those of capitalism, the introduction explains the "developmental path" of eastern Europe with a short historical overview. Interestingly—perhaps to heighten pride in the success and independence of the *Bruderländer*—any expression of gratitude to the USSR for its role in this history is omitted:

> In the era of capitalism (until 1944–45), Poland, Hungary, Romania, and Bulgaria—already-industrialized Czechoslovakia was an exception—were among the most economically backward countries. . . . The need became even greater during the Second World War (1939–45), when troops from fascist Germany invaded. . . .
>
> With the liberation in 1944 and 1945, the peoples drew the correct conclusions from their experiences suffered during the capitalist era. They first altered the political relations. The *Volk* assumed rule. . . . Then property relations were altered. Against the bitter resistance of the capitalist exploiters, the exploiters were dispossessed of their firms, which were acquired by the *Volk*. Under great hardships, the *Volk* proceeded to overcome their war losses and develop the young socialist countries from backward rural countries into modern industrial countries with sophisticated agricultural production. In all this, they have proved that workers and peasants are able to govern a state successfully and to develop its economy for the welfare of all.[21]

Geographie 6 stresses that, despite their awful past, socialist countries are committed to peaceful cooperation with their capitalist neighbors and can rest confident in their superiority. Class conflicts will continue under capitalism; under socialism, all conflicts are resolved in comradely fashion. The future belongs to the socialist nations, because the laws of History are on their side. As the summary for part 2 notes:

> With the Great Socialist October Revolution, the lawful transition from capitalism to socialism began. The Soviet Union forged ahead on this path as the first country. . . . [Under socialism] emergent difficulties and problems are overcome and dissolved in the common socialist interest and in comradely character. . . .
>
> The socialist countries of Europe decisively campaign, in the interests of their peaceful reconstruction, for cooperation between socialist and capitalist nations.[22]

Similar arguments and modes of presentation are to be found in seventh-grade geography, which covers the USSR and Asia. Unlike other texts, however, *Geographie 7* lionizes the USSR explicitly and in unrestrained language:

> Everywhere in the Soviet Union, modern science and technology are used. . . . For the first time in the history of Humanity, affairs are decided by working people. . . . The successes since the Great Socialist October Revolution show that no other social order can produce such achievements. . . . The socialist world order has become the decisive force of the present. . . .
>
> A close friendship exists between the Soviet Union and our Republic. . . . The working people in the Soviet Union and in our Republic pursue common goals: Under the direction of the Party of the working class, they both are building a future that offers peace, security, prosperity, and happiness for all people. That's why the citizens of our Republic have such heartfelt feelings of friendship toward the Soviet Union.[23]

As the seventh-grade teaching guide notes, the emphasis should be on "*socialist ideological education*":

> In the foreground is the goal of making the pupils aware of the political significance and economic strength of the first and most important socialist country of the world. . . .
>
> In the sense of proletarian internationalism, the conviction

should be deepened that the Soviet Union conducts a consistent peace politics, is a model for the further development of socialist states, and that close friendship exists between them and the USSR. These educational goals constitute the leitmotifs in the entire handling of the Soviet Union.[24]

The seventh-grade units focus on the leading nations in socialist Asia: China, Korea, and Vietnam. The "educational emphasis" when discussing the "historical-geographical" dimension of China, according to the teaching guide, should be "Education for Hatred against the oppression and plundering of peoples by the imperialists."[25] The opening paragraph of the unit on the Democratic Republic of Korea—North Korea—runs: "Korea was divided by the imperialists. The attempt of the U.S. to annihilate the Democratic Republic of Korea failed."[26] The Vietnam unit is accordingly titled "The War of Independence of the Vietnamese *Volk*." "Education for Hatred" against U.S. imperialism and "solidarity" with the Vietnamese *Volk* is the "educational emphasis" in all editions of the teaching guide.[27]

> Pupils recognize especially in the portrait of the criminal war of aggression by the U.S. that imperialistic nations are not above even making war in order to halt Asian progress. But their wars are opposed by aid for economic reconstruction from the Soviet Union and other socialist countries. . . . The victory of the Vietnamese *Volk* should be especially honored. [1978][28]

> The heroic struggle that the Vietnamese *Volk* have carried on for years against the aggression of U.S. imperialism is the focus in the treatment of the Democratic Republic of Vietnam. The portrait of the development of this battle for liberation serves, on the one hand, as an example for the national liberation movements in Southeast Asia, and on the other hand, characterizes the brutality of imperialism, which violates human rights and sovereignty in the service of its interests. . . .
> The pupils must gain the conviction that U.S. imperialism, which has taken over the positions of the earlier colonial powers, tries with all its means to halt the independent and progressive development of peoples, but that in Asia too, developments are increasingly defined by the growing strength of the socialist world system. . . . The pupils can establish with emotionally effective

and current press clippings that the U.S. is conducting a barbaric war of aggression in Southeast Asia. [1968][29]

Geographie 8 focuses on Africa and the Americas, particularly the United States.[30] In keeping with the DDR's ideological slant on geography, the opening paragraph on Africa heralds the liberation movement that has led to "fifty independent nations" in the post-war era, concluding with the question: "How has it happened that the African independence movement has achieved success and imperialistic colonialism has almost collapsed?" The answer is not hard to fathom:

> The cornerstone for this development was laid with the Great Socialist October Revolution. For the first time, in a sixth of the globe, capitalism was overcome and workers and peasants began to erect the first socialist state, the Soviet Union . . . . With the victory of the workers and peasants in the Soviet Union began *the epoch of the worldwide transition from capitalism to socialism*. A characteristic of this epoch is the independence movement among the colonially enslaved peoples of Asia, Africa, and Latin America.[31]

Geographie 8 extensively discusses neocolonialism in Africa, which is described as a continuation by the capitalists of the old imperialistic aims of the colonial powers. "The imperialist powers exploit toward these ends their *monopolies* and the *dependence on exports and imports* of the African states."[32] Teaching guides advise referring to "so-called 'economic aid'" from "the imperialistic states."[33] Special attention is given in *Geographie 8* to the "Suez aggression" of 1956 and the "Israeli aggression" of 1967. The text spotlights model socialist states such as Zaire, which gained independence in 1960 and, under the socialist government of Sese Seko Mobuto, nationalized the mining industry in 1967. Pupils encounter the following unit questions:

1. Review: a) In what form and under what conditions do the monopolies draw their profits from Africa? b) What possibilities do the imperialistic states exploit in order to gain influence over the developing countries?
2. Explain via the example of the historical development of the Republic of Zaire the features of colonialism and neocolonialism!

3. Report on the penetration of BRD monopolies in Africa! Take a position![34]

Recognizing that identification with the continent of Africa is hard for DDR pupils, the teaching guide on the Africa units issues classroom instructors a challenge: "Educational success will essentially turn on the partisan position of the teacher."[35]

Excursus: Amerika Through Eastern Eyes

Of greatest interest to an American reader, of course, is the treatment of the United States in *Geographie 8*. Not surprisingly, the picture is wholly negative, buttressed by quotations from observers such as "V. I. Lenin, who studied the U.S. intensively."[36] Following Lenin's remarks, the text organizes its discussion of the United States into the "industrialized North," the "formerly slave-holding South," and the "colonized West." Lenin's approach testifies to the truth of the "dialectical-materialist *Weltanschauung*," for it proves that "social relations, not Nature, are the decisive factors" in economic development.[37]

Indeed, each unit in *Geographie 8*, as the teaching guide makes clear, is meant to convey an ideological point. "Pupils should grasp societal oppositions" when studying New York; Appalachia teaches that "monopolies only lead to the striving for maximum profit"; the iron-ore and steel industries in Detroit, Chicago, and Pittsburgh reveal how "automation, under capitalist conditions, has negative consequences for the workers (greater danger of unemployment)"; the wealthy petrochemical industry in Texas, New Orleans, and Tennessee instructs how "oil monopoly" gets "high profits" from nations such as Venezuela; American agriculture shows the "contradiction between the possibilities of productive means and the inhibiting role of [capitalist] productive relations."[38]

According to *Geographie 8*, racial discrimination and nationwide poverty dominate the American scene. No positive aspects of "the American way of life" are depicted, nor are advances in the United States toward racial tolerance, equality, and economic well-being noted. Photographs of protest demonstrations against racial discrimination and Mississippi tenant huts accompany passages such as the following, which are representative:

> The contempt for human beings of the ruling classes shows itself especially in the treatment of the *Negro population*, who are only

assigned subordinate work and receive only a percentage of the wages that white workers—who had to fight hard labor battles—receive.

> The obsessive struggle for profit produces horrible misery, crime, and immorality. . . . The country has 256 hunger areas, above all in the South. . . .
> That is the U.S. today. While the leading classes, year after year, could pay out $30 billion for the criminal Vietnam War, there reigned in their own country mass misery, crime, and immorality. A horrible indictment against the capitalist system![39]

The unit questions highlight this unrelievedly dark portrait, often inviting the pupil to draw on knowledge gained either from history class or from geography units on other continents:

1. Explain, given your knowledge from history class, how the U.S. developed into a monopoly state and into the most powerful capitalistic and imperialistic country!
2. With which countries have you already become acquainted in which U.S. monopolies occupy a ruling position?
3. Name the reasons why the U.S. monopolies are compelled, in spite of their high profits in their own land, to exploit the raw materials of other countries![40]

The summary for this unit both approaches U.S. imperialism from a "socialist world system" perspective and examines its domestic consequences:

> The Soviet Union, the leading state of the socialist world system, has melted the earlier great [economic] lead of the U.S. as a result of the former's lightning development. . . .
> U.S. monopolies control more than four-fifths of the industries in Western Europe, making calculating machines, a considerable part of the auto, oil and chemical industries, airplane construction, and other decisive industrial branches. . . .
> Just as they function against progressive forces throughout the world, so too do the reactionary powers-that-be of the U.S., in order to bolster their exploitative position, move against the progressive movement in their own country with the cruelest meth-

ods. They even kill politicians on their own side, as the example of the murdered Kennedy brothers shows in terrifying fashion. The leaders of the Negroes have suffered and still suffer the same fate on racial grounds, as happened to Dr. Martin Luther King.[41]

The teaching guide reflects these same priorities, and indeed functions as a kind of keyword index to DDR agitprop against the United States:

> The treatment of the political divisions in America is meant to emphasize that the U.S. is the most aggressive imperialistic state. It constantly tries to expand its spheres of influence and to influence the countries of Latin America politically and economically. This fact should be a leitmotif throughout the entire treatment of the following sections of the syllabus.
>
> [Highlights to] elaborate: The U.S., the most powerful, but also most aggressive imperialistic country; leading power of NATO; rejection by the population (also the colored peoples) of its imperialistic politics; its racial discrimination; its rule of power (murder of Dr. Martin Luther King, Ku Klux Klan); demonstrations against the Vietnam War; colored medal winners in [1972] Olympics admit membership in Black Power movement and are expelled from U.S. team.[42]

All of this should be contrasted with the new *Geographie 8*, which was issued in late 1990–early 1991. The editorial closing date (*Redaktionsschluss*) is listed as 2 July 1990. So the book was written right in the middle of the accelerating breakdown of the DDR system. Among the most notable changes are that the back cover of the new *Geographie 8* depicts an African American couple . . . and they smile! In DDR textbooks from the 1970s and 1980s, all Africans and South Americans look stern or unhappy, even (or especially) if they are portrayed as class-conscious freedom fighters for socialism. (Indeed, before 1990, all "natives" in DDR textbooks—whether Native Americans in the United States, Africans in Africa, Asians in Asia, or South Americans in South America—were shown either as suffering or as working together "in solidarity" with aid workers from the eastern Bloc.) But now, as *Geographie 8* depicts, they have apparently rejoined (as eastern Germans in early 1990 would do) the larger family of their former enemies, evidently becoming part of one big family that's all happiness and smiles.

Another significant change in the new *Geographie 8* is that questions marked with an asterisk are ones for "stronger and more intelligent pupils"; one never saw such "elitist" or "bourgeois" questions in the DDR's "uniform polytechnical" schoolbooks before 1990. Likewise, in the reference section, the citations are revised: Odo Marquardt and other Western sources are used, along with traditional M-L sources. The eastern German Gymnasium graduate who sent me a photocopy of his *Geographie 8* textbook for 1990/1991 wrote to me about still another change that continued to impress him in 2004:

> One thing you can't see from the Xerox is the remarkable change in the printing quality compared to our old textbooks. Whereas the old ones were made of cheap paper, the new one came in a very good printing quality (soft and heavy paper). Also the design surprised all of us. I remember that during the first lesson, we just flicked through the book and (the boys especially) were amazed at the pictorial content of the book: there were pictures of skyscrapers, American cars, a picture of a truck in the chapter on Canada (like the ones we saw on TV in American series like Knight Rider). I even cut out some of the pictures and pasted them in my notebook just because I liked the colorful pictures of the "New World."[43]

The Upper Grades

Although the last two POS years focused increasingly on economic geography, ninth-grade pupils also received a global overview of physical geography, which stressed "above all the great possibilities under socialistic relations for the transformation of agriculture."[44] It is noteworthy that environmental pollution is never addressed, except in relation to the abuses of imperialism. Indeed, the ninth-grade syllabus finds it easy to reconcile the DDR's scientific-technical revolution and ecological concerns. "Socialist society is convinced that the structure and lawfulness of the geosphere will be ever more comprehensively understood and that socialist productive processes should constantly use the environment better and intervene into the processes of the geosphere systematically and more strongly."[45]

Economic geography in ninth through twelfth grades treats the relation of physical and economic relations to the production of raw materials and their manufacture into finished products. Textbooks are divided into units on industry, agriculture, and economic relations (within "the socialist community," with "imperialist" nations, and with "young nation-states"). The ninth-grade curriculum focuses on the USSR and the socialist countries of eastern Europe (especially Czechoslovakia and Poland);[46] the tenth-grade curriculum covers the same ground and includes the DDR (and, until the 1970s, the BRD).[47] Units on subjects such as the economic development and socialist transformation of Cottbus are common, followed by unit questions such as "Compare the present state of economic development in the Cottbus Bezirk with that of 1945!"[48]

The following passage from *Geographie 10* serves as a touchstone of POS economic geography:

> In 1976, the People's Republic of Bulgaria constructed in Varna a bridge 2 km long and 48 meters high over the passageway from the Black Sea to the Varna Sea. Since then, ships weighing up to 100,000 tons can travel within 20 km away from the coast, where the chemical firm Devnya lies. In the direct vicinity of the firm, they can dock in a new harbor or be loaded up. Therefore they need not repeatedly load and unload coal imported from the Soviet Union or dung, cement, and other products slated for export. Now many workers can be transferred to other areas of the People's economy. The total economic advantage justifies the extraordinarily high costs of the bridge construction. Moreover, the construction work has made shorter travel times possible for ships that want to leave Varna toward the south. The bridge is part of a future *Autobahn* from Varna to Burgas.

The passage concludes by stressing the dialectical "unity" between the economy and the *Volk* under socialist planning: "The use of land in socialist countries must proceed in unity with the further improvement of the working and living conditions of the population."[49]

Much of ninth- and tenth-grade economic geography is devoted to the analysis of the "economic laws" of M-L that define the modes and relations of production. Attention is given to such concepts as socialist economic integration (the law of economic cooperation of socialist nations in the RGW) versus imperialist market competition (inconsistent and rivalrous Common Market interaction). One unit question, for example, asks: "Prove that the countries of the RGW constitute the most stable and dynamic economic region of the world!"[50] Similarly, the texts address theories such as systematic socialist economic development (the law of equal or proportional development of all socialist regions) versus haphazard and unequal capitalist economic development (e.g., nations versus colonies, wealthy neighborhoods versus slums, the boom-bust cycle of prosperity and recession). Pupils also study neocolonialism more rigorously and are informed of the differences between mutual aid among socialist nations and exploitative "developmental aid" from imperialists.

But upper-grade POS geography is not meant to dwell on theory; the teaching guides also stress the "dialectical unity" of theory and praxis. Indeed, the Varna bridge project serves as an example both of socialist economic integration, which is a "lawful, long-range process" and a precondition for the optimal use of a region's resources, and of equal socialist economic development, which shows how the USSR aids the *Bruderländer* to achieve a living standard equal to (or even better than) its own. Teachers are also urged to pose practical questions derived from socialist theories of economic geography, e.g., "What must we do in order to raise our living standard even more?" "Why does the systematic use of land contribute to the increase of worker productivity and to the improvement of our life?" "How do socialist countries achieve better use of the social and natural resources of their land, so that a rise in worker productivity is made possible?" "Why are the centers of great American cities deteriorating?" (The guide proposes that pupils' class reports take Detroit or St. Louis as examples, though "for variation" Tokyo and Yokohama are also suggested.) Pupils "must gain the conviction," concludes the teaching guide, that problems such as "traffic chaos, bad living conditions in slums, minimal opportunities for recreation in city centers, and unemployment are of the essence of capitalism, and that it is not possible in capitalism for all working people to be guaranteed a high material and cultural living standard."[51]

EOS pupils also studied both physical and economic geography. But the curriculum differed in two ways from that of the POS: EOS geography emphasizes specific industries (e.g., chemical, steel, iron ore) and their relation to the "socialist world system," and it focuses near-exclusively on socialist nations, even giving substantial attention to smaller socialist countries such as Hungary (e.g., its prairie region of Hortobagy is featured in and pictured on the back cover of *Geographie 11* [2nd ed., 1983]).[52] In physical geography, this socialist focus means excluding or limiting discussion of certain topographies and climates (e.g., tundras, tropics), since few or no socialist nations could illustrate them. Economic geography for eleventh and twelfth grade reviews many regions that earlier grades addressed, developing the extant "partisan perspective" via newly gained M-L theories on topics such as socialist economic development and neocolonialism.[53] Especially in earlier textbook editions, this partisanship is often quite aggressive. And, in hindsight, it is sometimes ironic, such as when modest productivity increases are claimed to signal the impending "triumph of socialism in the economic competition between the socialist and capitalist systems."[54]

Of Class and Soil

But SED geography did not require "positivist" evidence to support such claims. Hard evidence or no, "dialectical unity" or not, M-L theory was to guide the young revolutionary's spirit. It was to be imbued with the progressive faith encapsulated in the refrain of Brecht's "Solidarity Song," which we cited at the outset of this chapter: "Forward and never forget! / Solidarity!" Yes, however long the march, however slow and halting the fulfillment of History's "laws," M-L theory insisted: *terra rosso* is the future.

And the present?

"Who has the youth, has the future."

To sustain the socialist believer in the present, "conviction" was all: "My country—Left or wrong."

And a crucial subject for reinforcing that revolutionary conviction was the other half of "advanced socialist Fatherland education": *Staatsbürgerkunde*. For in the battle between German socialism and German capitalism, the DDR needed well-bred textbook Reds to brandish the hammer-and-sickle flag.

MY COUNTRY, LEFT OR WRONG?
Civics

> Don't let anyone talk you into it,
> Examine it for yourself!
> Whatever you yourself don't know
> You don't know at all.
> —Bertolt Brecht, "In Praise of Learning" (1932)

Marxed *Menschen*

The study of civics in the DDR did not merely involve rights and responsibilities to the community; because the socialist citizen was fundamentally a collective being, the subject defined the identity of East Germans. More than any other subject, it aimed to breed "the new socialist *Mensch*."

Unlike other subjects, *Staatsbürgerkunde* did not have to contend with literary or geographical or historical "facts": it was almost pure ideology. Its textbooks cited virtually no authorities except sacred Party documents and leaders. And unlike the case in most other subjects, most *Staatsbürgerkunde* teachers joined the Party. (A strong majority of history and Russian teachers did too.) *Staatsbürgerkunde* textbooks were written by scholarly collectives headed by distinguished senior professors at the East German Academy of Sciences or in departments of philosophy, M-L, or history at the leading DDR universities.

With DDR civics, a POS subject introduced in seventh grade, DDR pupils received their "first level of systematic political-ideological training and education."[1] Although the emphasis of that sentence, of course, should be on "systematic"—*Staatsbürgerkunde* was, after all, a continuation of the political units of *Heimatkunde*—SED educators did in practice regard *Staatsbürgerkunde* as the cornerstone of ideological indoctrination. It aimed to develop a "clear political standpoint" on socialism and imperialism, and to bolster socialist patriotism and proletarian internationalism.

Created in 1957 to replace *Gegenwartskunde* (current events), which had been an unsystematic, discussion-oriented class,² *Staatsbürgerkunde* was conceived as the explicit political education of DDR pupils. Its task was to convince them of the superiority of socialism over capitalism, of the Party's adherence to true M-L principles, and of the legitimacy of the DDR state. Unlike *Heimatkunde,* it was less oriented toward studying socialist leaders than toward the state and citizenship responsibilities. Its importance increased after the erection of the Berlin Wall: in 1965, its first textbooks and teacher training programs began; in 1968, it was introduced into seventh and eighth grades as a key discipline. Before the erection of the Wall, *Staatsbürgerkunde* chiefly attacked West German capitalism and the crime of *Republikflucht* (flight from the Republic). After 1961, its main topics were the sovereignty and achievements of the DDR and the "eternal" bond with the Soviet Union, respectively.³ The civics curriculum of the 1970s and 1980s moved in stages, from emphasis on the DDR to a more international focus (chiefly on the "socialist state community"), and from a focus on history and DDR state institutions to the theory and laws of M-L.

In seventh grade, *Staatsbürgerkunde* covered four related issues: twentieth-century Soviet and German history,⁴ the formation of the SED, the DDR's basic political institutions, and the DDR's unshakeable friendship with the USSR. "You and Your Time" is the title of the 1979 edition's opening chapter, which discusses the consequences of the October Revolution for progressive humanity and features a photograph of Lenin in 1917 and a prominently displayed quotation from Honecker. The general approach could be summed up in a line from the Danish Marxist Martin Anderson Nexø, à la Cervantes on friendship, which various *Staatsbürgerkunde* textbooks quoted with approval: "Tell me where you stand toward the Soviet Union, and I'll tell you who you are." Nexø's line gave voice to Article 6 of the DDR constitution: "The DDR is always and forever irrevocably allied with the USSR."

Although the approach of eighth-grade *Staatsbürgerkunde* was more theoretical and systematic, it too left no doubt about where young revolutionaries should stand. Rather than learn about historical events and political institutions, however, pupils were reintroduced to the historical mission of the working class and its Party, the interdependent relations among the working class and other classes, socialism's historic superiority over capitalism, and the rights and duties of the citizen under socialist democracy.[5] Via concepts such as socialist property and economic planning, pupils learned about the rudiments of M-L economics and the political foundations of the socialist state. Unit questions included the following:

1. Explain why the DDR and the USSR, and the SED and the CPSU, cooperate especially closely!
2. What causes can you name that explain why even the most aggressive imperialistic countries are increasingly compelled to recognize the politics of peaceful co-existence of the community of Peoples?
3. Show as a result of your investigation that the statements of Lenin are as relevant today as they were fifty years ago![6]

Questions for class use from the teacher's guide yield further insight into the pedagogical orientation of the eighth-grade curriculum:

1. What fundamental transformation of social relations did the working class and its Marxist-Leninist party seek since the time of the difficult beginning [1945]?
2. What causes explain the DDR's historical achievements and its superiority over capitalism?
3. Name and prove the most important conditions that have led to our greatest successes!
4. What is the basis of the claim to leadership of the working class in socialist society?
5. Why does the working class need the Marxist-Leninist party as an advance guard?
6. Why is there such a close alliance between the SED and the other Marxist-Leninist parties [of the world], especially the CPSU?
7. What is the necessity and significance of the alliances of the working class with the class of the comrade farmer, the intelligentsia, and all other working people?
8. Why is the leading role of the working class and its party, as well as the alliance with other working people, an indispensable political foundation of our society?
9. What is the essence of socialist property and its significance for society and its further development?
10. What does one understand by "central state direction and planning of the economy," and why are they possible and necessary?

11. Why is the central direction and planning of all areas of social life under socialism necessary?
12. How is the leading role of the working class and its Marxist-Leninist party manifested in the direction and planning of our economy?
13. What are People's Economic Plans? What significance have they in the directing and planning of the economy?
14. What gives our socialist society the right to place such comprehensive and high demands on our youth?
15. What do you understand by the phrase "a clear class standpoint"?
16. As FDJ members and functionaries . . . , how do you properly evaluate [your] assigned tasks [under socialism]?[7]

The teaching guide for eighth-grade *Staatsbürgerkunde* also notes that lessons should develop socialist patriotism:

> Pupils should comprehend more deeply the objective advantages of socialist society and grasp its superiority to that of the exploitative states. . . . From insight into these objective conditions, conclusions for everyone, including all pupils, apply: Our society possesses dignity, one must campaign for it actively, one assists it through work, and one defends it. Insofar as the lesson in this unit deepens the conviction that the working class and its Marxist-Leninist party are the leading force in socialist society, it contributes to deepening the love of pupils for the working class and its Marxist-Leninist party, to strengthening their patriotic and international attitude, and to raising their readiness for class-conscious action consistent with the requirements of socialist society.[8]

Pupils in ninth grade moved on to learn about the "laws" of History and of M-L economics. Special emphasis was placed upon more theoretical issues in historical materialism. Pupils studied the modes and relations of production in tribal, slave, feudal, capitalist, and socialist societies, along with related topics such as the dynamics of class struggle and the dialectic of productive forces and relations. Several units focused on the predictability of capitalism's collapse and socialism's triumph. Above all, teachers were to highlight the central role of the working class in these processes and events.[9] For example, the first sentence of the ninth-grade teaching guide specifies: "*Staatsbürgerkunde* class in ninth grade should lead pupils to the insight of the lawfulness of social development and prove that the working class is objectively summoned, under the direction of the Marxist-Leninist party, to overthrow capitalism, the last exploitative political order, and to build socialism and communism."[10]

Units for ninth grade in the 1968 textbook such as "Marx and Engels: the Great Teachers of the International Working Class" describe the fathers of scientific socialism as "explorers" and "discoverers" who plumbed the "laws" of social science. Engels's eulogy for Marx, which compared Marx with Darwin as a scientist of human history, is quoted at length to this end.[11] The following passage in the opening chapter of the 1979 edition of *Staatsbürgerkunde 9* is representative of the theme of socialism's laws as well:

> The transition of Humanity to socialism and communism is a lawful process. It will not occur automatically, however, but rather will be carried out through fierce class struggle by the international working class in alliance with other working people.
>
> A necessary, general, essential relationship between things and processes exists in the laws of Nature and Society, which proves itself constantly through repetition.[12]

Here again, the teaching guide questions designed for classroom use provide insight into the orientation of the entire civics curriculum:

1. Why is capitalism being replaced by socialism throughout the whole world?
2. Why is the working class alone able to overthrow capitalism and to erect socialism and communism?
3. What relations did Marx discover between the means of production and the systems of social relations?
4. What shows that the transition from capitalism to socialism will occur in our time?
5. What indicates that the working class is the main force that will carry through this transition?
6. Why is class opposition between bourgeoisie and proletariat irreconcilable?
7. Why is the overthrow of capitalism historically necessary and lawful?
8. What supports the law of the correspondence of productive relations and productive forces?[13]

The theoretical and international focus of *Staatsbürgerkunde* continued in the tenth grade, with particular attention given to the theory of socialist economic integration and its relation to socialist "alliance politics," and to the strategies and tactics of world imperialism against socialism and vice versa. Emphasis also shifted from citizenship duties per se to socialist morality.[14]

Excursus: Socialist Morality for Tenth-Graders

Of special interest is this last topic: socialist character formation. In tenth-grade *Staatsbürgerkunde,* pupils were clearly told that nobody was permitted to have "purely personal cares and difficulties in a socialist collective." One unit in the 1971 edition is titled "Socialist Consciousness of Freedom," which introduces the Orwellian concept of "socialist freedom." Pupils learn about "the class content of socialist freedom": "The individual realizes his freedom when he activates all individual powers and abilities in all areas of social life—work, politics, and culture. . . . In socialist society, there is no freedom for the restoration of the old society, for the reintroduction of exploitation. *Socialism proclaims no abstract freedom, but rather economic and political freedom for the vast majority of society.*"[15]

Specific "socialist" virtues are also enumerated in the 1983 edition:[16] respect for humanity, justice, integrity, love of truth, simplicity, modesty, friendship, and love. These virtues, understood from a specifically socialist perspective, are to be sharply distinguished from their bourgeois counterparts. For instance, the socialist love of truth *"strives toward the whole."* Enemies must be identified. *"A half truth is no truth, and a half friendship is no friendship."* In a similar vein, the text insists: *"Our love is not uncritical. . . . It doesn't cover mistakes and weaknesses of others with the 'coat of brotherly charity,' but rather is devoted to helping a person to recognize and overcome his mistakes and weaknesses."* (For such purposes, Party "criticism" may be necessary.)

The text even ventures to prescribe the requisite "M-L *Weltanschauung*" for what might be termed "socialist romance" (a topic not covered in subsequent editions), which certainly has a pre-feminist ring:

> Marxists are no apostles of abstinence, and in answer to the question of young people—when they may have sexual relations—one can give no simple date.
>
> A girl is no boy, and therefore a young man cannot behave toward his girlfriend exactly as he does toward his own sex. This difference occurs because of our special respect for the dignity of

the woman (in this sense a girl is also a woman) and because of her own bodily and spiritual-moral singularity....

Young people often ask: How does one recognize genuine love? ... The frequently insistent urge, "love at first sight," is mostly no more than "infatuation at first sight." That is why the first commandment for young people in love is: Examine your feelings thoroughly![17]

If such positions hardly seemed revolutionary, SED educators had recourse to the holy Marxist trinity to bolster their authority on such problems of unscientific socialism. "Two people participate in love," the text quotes a newspaper article of Lenin, "and a third, new life emerges from that. So there is also a hidden social interest in love; there grows a duty toward the collective." Society's "interest" doesn't automatically mean that a couple must marry; on the question of whether sexual relations must lead to marriage, pupils learn that Engels had already pronounced in *The Origin of the Family, Private Property, and the State*: "Love is not tied to marriage. That means it does not first arise within marriage, but rather generally ahead of it. Love is that deep, intimate affection of two people for each other, which awakens the passionate desire to be together forever and to lead a common life and build a family." To illustrate the proper socialist attitude, this passage is followed by a love letter from Karl to Jenny Marx.[18] A similar sentiment concludes a more recent edition of *Staatsbürgerkunde 10*, whose last unit is titled "The Meaning of Life" and closes with a tribute to Marx's "beautiful family life."[19]

In Lenin's Corner: The Model Socialist Citizen

But "socialist morality" occupied only one-quarter of the tenth-grade *Staatsbürgerkunde* curriculum. The range of topics may be guessed by the titles of various units: "Socialism Defines the Revolutionary World Process"; "The Task of Anti-Imperialist-Democratic Forces in Latin America in their Battle for National and Social Liberation"; "Ideological Diversion [by Imperialists]"; "The Law of Systematic and Proportional Development of the Economy"; "The Law of the Constant Rising of Worker Productivity"; "Democratic Centralism in the Economy"; "The Lawfulness of Socialist Economic Integration"; "The Relation Between Scientific-Technical Progress and the Advantages of Socialism." "The Indivisible Relation Between Proletarian Internationalism and Socialist Patriotism."

A sample of tenth-grade teaching guide questions for classroom use suggests, once again, the specific approaches that teachers took toward these topics:

1. Is the human being in our society an appendage of the economy, or does the economy serve the person?
2. What interactions occur between productive forces and productive relations in today's capitalist society?
3. What concrete demands does the law of constant increase of worker productivity place on working people?
4. Why does the party of the working class expect an ever better correspondence between its achievements in the scientific-technical revolution and the [inherent] advantages of socialism?
5. How were the productive forces in the Floeha cotton mill developed?
6. Why are the working people from Floeha ready to contribute their scientific-technical expertise to their partners in the USSR, Czechoslovakia, and Hungary?

The importance of these topics is underscored by recourse to Lenin's authority on matters ranging from class consciousness to morality to economics:

1. What significance did Lenin attach to worker productivity?
2. What were Lenin's criteria for characterizing classes?
3. How is the place of a class in a social order decided?
4. When you think of Lenin's definition of a class, how do you distinguish the working class and the class of comrade farmers?
5. What did Lenin characterize as the morality of the exploiter class?
6. What did Lenin consider good mores?
7. How do the basic interests of the working class find expression in Lenin's explanations of mores?
8. Prove through Lenin's explanation of morality what relation exists between socialist morality and the historical mission of the working class!
9. What does the following statement of Lenin's mean for our concrete historical situation: "If one is a communist, morality consists in a constant battle for the masses . . ."?

Many teaching guide questions were concerned with the role of the Party in developing socialist morality and the proper "class standpoint":

1. How do you explain that all workers do not yet possess the qualities of their class in fully realized form?
2. What influence does the development of the socialist qualities of the working class have on the development of all members of socialist society?
3. What is the principal task of the Party?
4. What do we understand by the term "patriotic duty"?
5. How is the responsibility of the individual for the class collective developed?
6. How are helpfulness and comradely readiness developed?
7. Is there a proper stance toward [Party] criticism and self-criticism?

Finally, numerous questions addressed the proper role of the DDR citizen toward the imperialist threat across the border:

1. What significance does the alliance politics of the working class and the Party possess for realizing the historic mission of the working class?
2. Prove through examples from current politics what Engels meant in his statement that the working class is "in its essential nature international."
3. How do the imperialists oppose the main tendencies in international developments toward relaxation [of tensions]?
4. What is the essential cause for the constant push toward war and aggression by the imperialistic countries?[20]

The answers to these drumbeat questions were self-evident; most answers were, implicitly or explicitly, contained in the questions themselves.

Education for Hatred

To a Western reader, this last theme likely stands out above all as conspicuous in *Staatsbürgerkunde* texts: the aggressive, relentless criticism voiced against "imperialists" and "capitalists," not excepting references to "hatred." As the teaching guide for seventh-grade *Staatsbürgerkunde* notes, teachers should aim to "stimulate anti-imperialistic solidarity among the peoples of the world and hatred against imperialists and militarists."[21] Or as the 1968 edition of ninth-grade *Staatsbürgerkunde* phrases it, under the heading "Who is a Good German?":

> The love of the working people of our Republic for their socialist Fatherland is love for the German *Volk,* for their language, culture, and history—and simultaneously hatred toward the imperialistic enemies of our people in West Germany.
>
> Nothing could be falser and more hypocritical in Bonn's propaganda on the German question than the slogan about "Brothers this side and beyond the Wall."[22]

This "hate pedagogy" toward inculcating socialist patriotism warrants special attention, including some reference to the history of this unique DDR program (which endured because of the perceived threat of the BRD) and to its manifestations outside textbook policy. For if POS German and *Heimatkunde* textbooks stressed love of the Fatherland, the *Staatsbürgerkunde* texts highlighted equally hatred of the enemy, an addition they justified on the grounds of "dialectical unity." Both emphases were integral to the DDR's conception of socialist patriotism.

Indeed, if the personality cults were intended to stimulate love for the Fatherland through identification with their leaders, SED propagandists did not neglect the power of negative emotions to arouse patriotism. East German ideology strictly defined the regime's enemies as well as friends. The offensive to generate *Vaterlandsliebe* was merely the affirmative half of an aggressive agitation campaign in the schools, known in the 1950s and 1960s as Education for Socialist Patriotism. As we have seen, the notorious negative half of the campaign, launched in 1952 and much criticized in the West, was known as *Erziehung zum Hass* (Education for Hatred), a phrase the GST specifically used for its school exercises in paramilitary training that took its spirit from Stalin's own words: "Soviet patriotism is indissolubly connected with hatred toward the enemies of the socialist Fatherland. It is impossible to conquer an enemy without having learned to hate him with all the might of one's soul."

Education for Socialist Patriotism thus emphasized not only love for the *Heimat,* the USSR, and socialism, but also hatred toward all antagonists. It continued in the DDR with various modifications, as we shall see, into the 1980s. Love and hate: love for the Fatherland, the Party, and the nation's leaders; hatred toward all class enemies, both within (class traitors, "enemies of the People") and without (the KA, the decadent West). These messages were summed up in two slogans that millions of DDR schoolchildren heard ad nauseam. The first could be heard at almost any

SED meeting for decades: Louis Fürnberg's hymn to the SED, *Die Partei hat immer recht:* "The Party, the Party / It's always right!" The second motto was a favorite during the early post-war era and up through the 1960s, especially in the *Erziehung zum Hass* curriculum: "Carry hatred in your heart!"[23]

Likewise, the textbooks for *Staatsbürgerkunde* pulled no punches against the DDR's main enemies, the capitalists and imperialists of the West.[24] Contrasting tables in the seventh-grade text portray the "brotherhood-in-arms" of the Soviet Army and NVA, working together on a rocket launcher, and the rise in NATO expenditures since 1949. A large chart, titled "Military Aggressions of Imperialism After 1945," presents a "partial" list of twelve capitalist wars, including the French Indochina War, the Portuguese-Angola conflict, and the U.S. invasion of Cambodia. The language is pointed: "Exploitation and oppression are the eternal goal of capitalism. . . . Violence, war, robbery, oppression, and lying characterize imperialism."[25]

DDR-BRD relations are a focal point of seventh-grade *Staatsbürgerkunde*, featuring such questions as "Express your opinion about the statement: Everything is better without capitalists!"[26] Historical conflicts between the DDR and BRD illustrate the point; *Staatsbürgerkunde* went to far greater lengths to defend the erection of the Berlin Wall than other subjects did. The text recounts various provocations from the BRD and NATO in the years before 1961 and then explains Ulbricht's decision of August 13 as follows:

> The enemies of socialism didn't even stop at dastardly crimes. On August 7, 1961, a fire was started in the VEB Great Berlin Butchery. A few days later, a fire was set in Humboldt University. On the state border of the DDR, attacks and disruptions increased. Near the DDR coast, the NATO maneuver "Wallenstein II" took place.
>
> The imperialists dreamed how the West German army's invasion would succeed. Peace was endangered in the extreme by the imperialistic BRD and her allies. In order to bridle imperialism, grab the war torch from its hand, and secure peace, important decisions faced the socialist countries.[27]

The Wall is described as an unqualified DDR success, both for its contribution to securing the peace and for establishing a new balance of power in Europe: "The measures of August 13, 1961, brought a new balance of power between the forces of peace and socialism and the forces of war and imperialism, both in Germany and in the world."²⁸ But pupils learn that imperialism unfortunately remains a disruptive and dangerous presence throughout the world:

> Imperialism has changed neither its peace-hating and anti-progressive nor its aggressive goals. That is the case because the heads of monopolies keep striving for ever greater profits and ever greater economic and political power. . . .
>
> The BRD strives at the side of the U.S. for the destruction of socialism in the DDR and in other socialist states. The BRD supports the warmongering of other imperialistic states and helps them with the oppression of other peoples.²⁹

Such language exemplifies the relentlessly hard-driving, head-on approach of most *Staatsbürgerkunde* passages.

But *Staatsbürgerkunde* texts also made use of other styles and genres. In our discussion of German literature, we noted that upper-grade POS textbook selections were more literary and less overtly ideological. To a degree, this arose because *Staatsbürgerkunde* took over these agitprop functions, especially in literature and music, wedding the literary to the ideological in this subject as well.³⁰

For instance, seventh-grade *Staatsbürgerkunde* pupils studied poetry by Becher ("Great October") and Mayakovsky ("Good and Beautiful"), both of which celebrate the Russian Revolution. Teachers were also encouraged to play socialist hymns such as "The Song of the Fatherland" or "Toward the Sun, Toward Freedom, Brothers." Or Louis Fürnberg's "Our Song," which posits that socialist patriotism functions dialectically, entailing love of the Fatherland and hatred of all enemies:

> Our song did not fall out of the raging clouds [as mere]
> Colorful kling-klang that would delight romantics!
> Our song did not rise out of a fairy-tale sea
> A colorful lie that would deceive us!
>
> It was a dream that gave it birth
> Not a dream that will dissolve in mist by day
> But one that was also Lenin's:
> "Thunder! Strike! But also dream!"
>
> Our song is quaked from anger
> Into beautiful words, resonant tones.

Life and time reflect their contents
Our sons have written the words and notes.
We have lived every syllable
Every note is written with blood. . . .

Our song is love and is hatred
Just like the battle to which we've sworn ourselves![31]

To strengthen pupils' "partisan perspective" toward controversial events such as the erection of the Wall, the Ministry of Education created special pedagogical materials, e.g., the handbook *Songs About August 13, 1961* (which "can wield a strong emotional effect"). Education officials also promoted official DEFA (*Deutsche Film Aktiengesellschaft*, DDR state film company) documentary films about August 1961 (e.g., "Stories About That Night").[32] As happened in *Heimatkunde,* inflammatory songs by outstanding writers such as Brecht and unofficial poet laureate Johannes Becher were often drafted into service. For instance, ninth-grade pupils were taught the "irreconcilability of class oppositions" by singing Brecht's "Song of the Class Enemy":

When I was small, I went to school
and I learned what was mine and yours
and as all of that was learned
It appeared to me not to be everything
For I had no breakfast to eat

But others—they had one!
And so I did indeed learn everything
About the essence of the class enemy.

And I learned why and wherefore
A cleft runs through the world
And it remains between us
Because the rain flows from high to low . . .

Because we're class enemies
as is always said
Whoever among us won't risk fighting
Will risk starving.

We are class enemies, drummer!
Your drumming can't cover that up!
The factory owner, the general, and the landed aristocrat
are our enemy, that means you!

> Nothing of this will be deflected
> Nothing of it twisted around
> Rain doesn't fall upwards
> And it is also given to the upper classes!
>
> The decorator may paint
> But he can't cover over the cleft
> One of us stays and one must leave
> Either it's me or you.
>
> And what I even now am learning
> Which is nothing more than basic math
> I don't have anything in common
> With the interests of the class enemy.
>
> The word will not be found
> That can unite us
> Rain flows from above to below
> And you are my class enemy.[33]

The evils of imperialism were a focal point in the *Erziehung zum Hass* units. We have already looked at a few tenth-grade teaching guide questions on imperialism; the following ninth-grade textbook questions show further how central education toward "hatred of the imperialist enemy" was to the curriculum:

1. How does the aggressiveness of imperialism influence the development of productive forces?
2. What examples of the aggressive foreign policy of imperialism do you know?
3. What is the goal of imperialistic foreign policy?
4. Where do the limits of the aggressive politics of imperialism presently lie?
5. Why does imperialism concentrate in increasing measure on the intellectual manipulation of working people?
6. Which goals does imperialism pursue against socialist countries through its ideological diversions?
7. What methods and means does it apply?
8. What messages do imperialist radio and TV stations distribute?
9. What declared goals do they pursue? What results are achieved?
10. What is the evidence that the monopolistic ruling system expends

incredible material resources for the purpose of intellectual manipulation and ideological diversion?
11. What facts confirm the statements of Lenin about imperialism when one looks at imperialism today?[34]

Teachers are also encouraged to play cassettes such as "The Quality of Life under Imperialism" and "What is Hidden Behind BRD Propaganda about Humanity?"[35]

But the enemies were not only outside; they were also within, as a tenth-grade poem in *Staatsbürgerkunde* reminded pupils. "The Report of the Garbage Collector Manfred K. on the Failure of his Best Friend" was the main discussion assignment for the unit titled "The Relation of Personality and the Collective Under Socialism." The speaker is the title's Manfred K., who mourns that, in the face of his own ideological lapses, his best friend never "accused me. So it emerged / that his friendship / wasn't strong enough." Manfred had begun to goof off and skip his shift to cavort with girls or just to indulge a whim. The best friend "warned" him confidentially, but didn't "accuse" him publicly. So Manfred was finally caught by the supervisor and accused by the collective, which "washed my cloudy eyes . . . / and showed me my filthy inside / . . . and beat my rumpled soul." The best friend kept silent throughout the humiliating public "criticism." And Manfred concludes:

> I blamed him then / that he didn't defend me
> Today I blame him / that he didn't accuse me.
> But I blame him today just as yesterday
> That he remained neutral.

"Genuine comradeliness is not possible without sincerity and helpful criticism," advises the text.[36] Manfred's friend should have put his duty to the state and Party above personal feelings of friendship. The "higher" friendship demands reporting a friend's negligence, whereupon the wayward offender receives the proper "criticism" from the Party. According to the teaching guide, the poem shows "the objective correspondence between the interests of socialist society and the interests of the collective and the individual, [which] is an important basis for the development of the socialist personality and indeed the socialist lifestyle. . . . We develop ourselves as socialist personalities above all when we understand how to carry out the policies of the Party in our active socialist work."[37]

Staatsbürgerkunde class was also linked to activities of the Pioneers, where the cult of personality was sometimes used to demonize as well as lionize. A favorite song of the Thälmann Pioneers—"Thälmann's Young Guard"—spared enemies no mercy. Its refrain re-echoed:

> Yes, Thälmann, you rock of the [working] class.
> Clear as the source [river-bed] is your word
> strong in love and terrifying in hate
> Thälmann, you continue to live in us.
> Thälmann, you continue to live in us.[38]

The Christian allusions in such lyrics are transparent: much as the Nazis had done, the SED hoped to replace the Christian saints with their own paragons and the compassionate ethics of Christianity with a pedagogy of hate toward enemies. For all their differences, the Nationalist Socialists and the SED (especially in the early post-war era) conducted relentless "hate" campaigns against their ethnic and class "enemies," respectively. Under Hitler, the enemies were Jews, communists, Gypsies, Russians, and homosexuals; under Ulbricht and Honecker, they were capitalists, imperialists, and Americans. Socialist "saints" such as Lenin and Thälmann were "good haters," whose here-and-now commitment to harsh class justice would displace the soft, otherworldly Christian morality of mercy and love for one's enemies. Thus was the East German ideology effectively also an East German theology, complete with pseudo-religious "sacraments" (the *Jugendweihe* and other rites), orthodox creed (DIAMAT, dialectical materialism), "holy days" (the birthdays and death days of sanctified communists), "hymns" (e.g., the "Workers' Silent Night"), and even "commandments of socialist morality."

The FDJ devised similar agitprop. Take, for instance, the popular FDJ song of the 1950s and 1960s, composed by Johannes Becher, "We Are Soldiers of the People," which predicted that DDR youth would become the gravediggers of capitalism—and capitalists.

> You don't have a chance
> With your warmongering in German lands
> Take your robber band back to your own land
> Our step keeps time to a song
> Full of power and courage.
> German blood will never flow
> For Wall Street profits.

You, rich lord, had better share
Otherwise we'll cut you to shreds
You'll be taught respect
For People's Property.
No German can calculate
Germany's suffering and misery
No one will cry
For the Wall Street generals!

We are the glory of the *Heimat*
the dawn of Freedom
Hearts are burning
with the call to arms of the youth
and the honor bestowed by Peace,
and they sing full of power and courage.
German blood is too good
For Wall Street's billionaires![39]

Because the preceding curricular examples span the 1950s to the 1980s, a word about the evolution and the larger historical context of the remarkable SED policy of Education for Hatred is of value here.

Although "hatred of the enemy" reached its maniacal peak during Stalin's lifetime, *Erziehung zum Hass* remained part of DDR education policy to the regime's very end. Even among university students and professors, and especially during crisis moments in DDR history, the subject of *Erziehung zum Hass* received attention in meetings of Party academics. For instance, the campaign intensified, sharply if temporarily, after the Wall's erection in August 1961. Just as the FDJ was first declaring its notorious slogan "Carry hatred in your heart!" educators at an October 1961 conference on patriotic youth were justifying hate pedagogy in high-toned language that metamorphosed dialectical materialism into dialectical terrorism. One professor made clear that passionate hatred was the historically necessary way to peace, despite the reservations of critics about its central role in DDR schooling:

> Insofar as we teach the students to learn from Walter Ulbricht, we help them to find their place in life more easily, to distinguish between friend and enemy, to love all people who are for peace and socialism, but also to hate out of the depths of their hearts all those who would turn the wheel of history backwards.

> There are in this matter, as you know, misunderstandings, intentional and unintentional. Hatred, so people tell us occasionally, cannot be the content and goal of pedagogy; true human education must strive rather to ban hate from human relations.
>
> That's what we want to do! Our entire striving is for a communism and a world without weapons and without war, a world in which human beings are friends and brothers of one another. Therefore, to achieve this goal, we must, today in 1961, not only have the better, stronger weapons, but also be able to hate out of passionate hearts. . . .
>
> But we want a love and a hate that are conscious, strong, and genuine, and not blind, fanatical, and moody. Therefore the students require solid, certain knowledge that will clarify and regulate their feelings and passions.[40]

The new hate campaign was geared to legitimate the Wall and was coordinated with new syllabi for *Staatsbürgerkunde* (and history), which were introduced in October 1961.[41]

Margot Honecker enforced this view stringently upon her appointment in 1963 as Minister of Education. As ideological tensions heightened with the arrival and crushing of the Prague Spring in 1968, SED hate rhetoric reached a second crescendo in the post-Stalin period. Frau Honecker ever more enthusiastically championed *Erziehung zum Hass,* unceasingly proclaiming the need for a "burning hatred against the imperialistic enemies of our *Volk* and Humanity," for "passionate hatred against the West German imperialists," and to "see through the motives of the enemy."[42] Or, as she declared in her keynote address to the Seventh Pedagogical Congress in May 1970, just as the DDR was establishing university departments of military studies and founding a series of new military academies for the NVA, as she explicitly invoked the authority of *The Communist Manifesto:*

> The bourgeoisie knows no Fatherland. It knows only profit. German imperialism in particular has proved again and again that it will, without any consideration, endanger the interests and even the existence of the People, and that it is always ready to betray and sell out the People.
>
> Educating youth to a deep love of their *Heimat,* the German Democratic Republic, and educating them toward socialism means: to teach them to hate imperialism.
>
> To all those who sanctimoniously question us, How do you

reconcile *Erziehung zum Hass* with your conception that one must love human beings, we answer with the question: Shouldn't our youth hate a system that is the enemy of humanity, the hearth of wars, unfreedom, and insecurity, the cause of the exploitation and the enslavement of human beings? Shouldn't our youth hate a system that brutally suppresses every free impulse, that becomes an ever greater danger for all of humanity, that calculates war and the annihilation of peoples in unknown quantities?

Because we educate our youth to a deep love of human beings, we also teach them to hate the inhumanity that imperialism embodies; we educate them to a love for socialism, which is the humanistic perspective of all of humanity.[43]

During the long campaign in the 1960s and 1970s to ban or restrict Western music and promote socialist popular art, Frau Honecker also supported "hate music," songs that, as one music group explained, "have the power to arouse hatred against the enemies of our republic and against the enemies of peace from Bonn to Saigon." An example of the new hate music was Bernd Walter's "October Ballad," written in 1967 to honor the fiftieth anniversary of the Great October Revolution:

On an empty stomach
But with a heart full of hate
They drive the enemies away.
And a thousand years of servitude
Now break in two.
And our world, yes, our new world
Thereby exists.

Some observers had hoped that the *Ostpolitik* of the 1970s would dampen the DDR's hate campaigns, as was happening in Hungary and Romania. But with the introduction of mandatory *Wehrerziehung* (military studies) into DDR schools in September 1978, *Erziehung zum Hass*—which some Western commentators now called "ideological *Wehrerziehung*"—heightened yet again. Fearful that Western influences, now pervasive as a result of détente, would undermine the DDR from within, the SED instituted its policy of *Abgrenzung* (demarcation). This policy carefully circumscribed relations with the BRD after the movement toward détente during 1970–72. And it was a policy that sought to defend the DDR from imperialist subversion: capitalist encirclement was now primarily an ideological concept, not a geographical one. So détente didn't temper the fires of hate, but rather stoked them. *"Je stärker der Sozialismus, um so sicherer ist der Friede!"* rang a new SED slogan. "The stronger our socialism, the safer the peace!"

More than ever before, hate education now sought to personify hatred and justify its "dialectics" to doubters. This included the regular showing of NVA films in school classes; anti-imperialist themes from ninth-grade *Wehrerziehung* and ninth-grade *Staatsbürgerkunde* would invariably be coordinated.[44] Helga Labs, head of the Thälmann Pioneers, urged educators in 1978 "to openly call the enemies of socialism, the enemies of our peaceful life, by their right names."[45] "There is nothing hateful about hatred toward the imperialist enemy," maintained the editor of *Armeerundschau*. "Such hatred is born out of love for our socialist Fatherland, and gives us the power to do everything possible for its defense and protection." TV commentator Eduard Schnitzler, whose weekly show, *Der schwarze Kanal* (The Black Channel), included a regular segment called "Portrait of the Enemy" that was often discussed in *Staatsbürgerkunde* class, insisted that hatred of the enemy "is of a high moral order, an indispensable part of love." (For a teacher's recollections of Schnitzler's program, see Chapter 6, "Pedagogy of the Distressed.") In an essay titled "Education for Peace," one educator even sought to justify the hate pedagogy via the Bible, arguing that the New Testament contained no universal condemnation of hate, but rather demanded the hatred of oppressors: "This kind of hatred of the enemy excludes blind hatred, but not insightful, creative hatred, because it grows out of solidarity with the exploited."[46]

Evidently, one must hate not just the sin, but the sinner—even if he appears to be your brother:

> He stands over there with a weapon
> could be my brother
> but what is a brother?
> Cain murdered Abel.
> Fairy tales tell of enemy brothers,
> but this is no fairy tale!
>
> He could be my brother over there
> might be nice and peaceful
> but he has a weapon
> he serves the authorities
> and they are my enemies.

> He stands over there with a weapon
> could be my brother.
> But he also seeks to incorporate us into his Reich
> a cheap tool of the conquerors
> an unfeeling weapon of the murderers and robbers
> a man, perhaps a brother
> but is exploited to murder
> and is therefore my enemy!

The hate pedagogy thus sought to make clear to DDR youth that the battle was not German against German, but imperialist against socialist: the children of darkness against the children of light.

"Trust Is Good, but Control Is Better"

And yet Cain did indeed look—and even speak—like Abel.

Yes, but what *is* a brother? Might he be a Good German too? If one didn't know his past, and looked merely at his current record, a West German might seem unthreatening, even benign.

Even a Good German, too.

And so SED educators put their trust in Lenin's famous statement: "Trust is good, but control is better." Preferring trusty control over chancy trust, they made sure that History was also on their side—even if systematically "rectified," à la the DDR language of Ostspeak.

Which is to say that they aimed to take yet another page from Orwell's *Nineteen Eighty-Four*:

> Who controls the future controls the present;
> who controls the present controls the past.

FOUR

PROGRESSIVE LESSONS OF THE PAST
History

> The past is a foreign country; they do things
> differently there.
> —L. P. Hartley, *The Go-Between*

The Past Is KA

Modern Germany, especially post-war Germany, is a land awash in history, and DDR historians were assigned the vital task of establishing a definitive break with the German past, addressing the immediate legacy of Nazism, and explaining the new nation to itself. In DDR history textbooks, the past was a foreign country—indeed a capitalist (or pre-capitalist) country: the past was KA.

This orientation ultimately resulted in a history curriculum more ideological than even that of the Nazis. And for a simple reason very much connected with history: time. Nazi educators had less than a decade to develop their curriculum (which included hurriedly devising an intellectual pedigree that featured Nietzsche as its only luminary) and Nazi history effectively "stopped" in 1939–40, before the Stalingrad catastrophe. By contrast, DDR educators had four decades to refine the DDR "heritage," not to mention the advantages of drawing on Soviet history since 1917 and a distinguished radical German and European legacy stretching back long before Marx and Engels.

History occupied a central place in DDR *weltanschauliche Erziehung*. But whereas *Staatsbürgerkunde* classes were to approach that task conceptually, focusing primarily on class consciousness and socialist institutions, history teachers were to approach it developmentally, emphasizing how lives and events either sail gloriously atop the tidal wave of Progress or drown in the contradictions of feudalism or advanced capitalism. As a Ministry of Education directive of the early 1950s ordained: "The historian is in the first line of the class conflict, at the head of the cultural front."[1]

DDR educators' control of how the past was presented should not be underestimated. Since most DDR citizens, even non-history majors in DDR universities, did not study history after secondary school, SED schoolbook history had an overwhelming impact in shaping the populace's view of the past. Even East Germans sympathetic to the West often considered it "imperialist," usually on the basis of historical events filtered through a Marxist-Leninist historical lens. In general, history could be analyzed by asking, as Lenin put it, *cui bono?*

And when DDR historians asked "What is history *for?*" they had a quick answer: to teach lessons—Marxist lessons. DDR historians fully exploited history's didactic possibilities, using it to promote the lessons of "progressive" history, lessons that taught socialist patriotism and the related values that we have already discussed. DDR school history concentrated on political and military history, touching only briefly on cultural and intellectual history, given the focus on cultural politics in the literature texts. The history textbooks argued that the historical process is progressive; those who understand the materialist, scientific laws of development are no longer victims of historical forces, but rather historical agents who direct History.

History Class / Class History

History education began in the fifth grade. The Introduction to *Geschichte 5*, which addresses the prehistoric and ancient world, opens:

> In the lessons of your first school years you have already learned a great deal about the development of our German Democratic Republic. The DDR could only be created through the long sacrifice and struggle of the working class. Both this battle of the revolutionary workers and the indispensable years after the end of the Second World War, when the DDR was founded and the construction of socialism was begun, today already belong to history.
>
> History class will bring you numerous insights. But above all an important question will be examined and answered in grades five through ten:

How is it that human society has constantly developed itself, from its beginnings to today, so that in many countries it has already led to socialism, and in all countries will lead to it? To answer that we need good insight into the origin and development of Humanity. That is why we begin our lessons for fifth grade with the lives of the earliest human beings.[2]

Long before the West discovered social history, DDR historians were writing their own version, a relentless story of exploitation, oppression, and victimization. Quite often, however, discussions of modern history were not exactly "history from below" in the Western sense—i.e., history that gave voice to the lower and working classes—but Party history or the history of socialism. Most of the sources cited in the textbooks are Party documents or writings by the great historical figures of socialism and communism, especially Marx and Lenin. But because the Party represented *das Volk,* SED historians viewed their socialist historiography as the story of "the common people." This posed something of a problem for the teaching of history of the pre-socialist era. Original documents imbued with a "socialist" consciousness were scarce, and thus fifth-graders had to be instructed about the revolutionary difference between bourgeois and progressive history. Once again, this is not to say that DDR history teachers *did* conduct their history classes according to the edicts of the teaching manuals, or that DDR pupils embraced such teachings when their teachers did follow such official instructions. It is merely to note that teachers were *supposed* to adhere to these guidelines. Strong evidence suggests that in the ideologically sensitive subjects—*Staatsbürgerkunde* above all, but also German and history—a majority of teachers did so. But by no means did all of them do so (as the interviews in Chapter 6 evince).

Let us turn again to *Geschichte 5*. The introduction to *Geschichte 5* continues: "Scholars have researched and established through exhaustive work almost everything that you will learn in history class. Much can be learned about the past from documents. But these are mostly the legacy of writers serving onetime rulers. And they interested themselves little in the life of the common people."[3]

DDR history textbooks make no attempt to glorify the distant past, especially the German past. Rather, they condemn the conditions of pre-socialist history as the work of tyrants and exploiters, beginning with the decline of the *klassenlose Urgesellschaft* (classless primitive society), which knew no private property. From the very dawn of recorded history in ancient Mesopotamia, exploitation—the handiwork of robber priests who headed the "temple economy"—prevailed. This reading of pre-modern history is similar to that of other communist nations, but DDR historians placed special emphasis on the antecedents of the First German Workers' and Peasants' State. The past was a foreign country, but it was one of the few borders that DDR citizens could cross, and SED textbook writers—their xenophobia toward KA notwithstanding—proved themselves intrepid travelers.

Geschichte 5 is not subtle about drawing the first lessons of progressive history:

> The peasants and craftsmen were dependent on the temple. The fruits of their work in the temple economy belonged to the priests. What the peasants and the craftsmen in the temple economy produced, however, amounted to a great deal more and had much greater worth than what they were conceded in food and clothing. Insofar as the priests gave the peasants and craftsmen less for their work than the latter produced, *they exploited them.* The peasants and craftsmen had to supervise the workers assigned to them without resistance. The supervisors belonged to the temple staff and also *were oppressed by the priests.* . . .
>
> The overseers, foremen, administrators, and head shepherds received bigger allowances of grain and wool than the peasants and craftsmen. They also received hectares of fields, whose returns increased their incomes. These people stood in the service of the priests and helped them to exploit the dependent peasants and craftsmen. The merchants also received more from the temple warehouses, because they had to undertake dangerous and wearying journeys in the mountains to do business for the priests.
>
> The priests were the most important part of the *ruling class* in society. Insofar as they were enriched by the profits of the peasants and craftsmen, they belonged to the *exploiter class.* On the other side were peasants, craftsmen, and slaves. They were exploited and oppressed. They were the *oppressed and exploited class.* The ruling class and the oppressed class stood opposed to each other. *A class war* occurred between them. A society that is divided into classes we call a *class society.* Thus the first class society in human history was born about 3000 *v.u.Z.*[4]

Thus, the lesson is that in ancient Mesopotamia, which constituted the first "class society," ruling priests benefited from private property. Although the term "alienation" is not yet used with fifth-graders, the texts describe in detail how the priests did no productive work yet owned the means of production and thereby exploited the peasants/workers, who suffered because they did not receive the fruits of their labor.

> The opposition between the ruling priests and the oppressed peasants and craftsmen was fierce, which was proved by the fact that the temple property and the means of production belonged to the priests. Their power was not limited to the immediate temple economy. The priests also ruled the remaining population, since the temple within the city was the power center of a whole residential area. Every peasant had to obey the will of the priests of the nearby village, even if the peasant didn't directly belong to the temple economy. And they could be forced to work in the fields of the temple. They delivered to the temple offerings and sacrifices that the priests received.[5]

Discussion of the Mesopotamian "temple economy" provided DDR historians with an opportunity to attack religion as primitive and reactionary, and to promote atheism, science, and scientific materialism as advanced and enlightened, thus facilitating SED attempts to undermine the DDR churches and institute Party youth rituals such as the *Jugendweihe*. How did religion come about? Its origins were in pre-class society, in the absence of any scientific, i.e., Marxist-Leninist world view. Why does it remain despite the advance of civilization? Because the ruling class exploits superstition to secure its private property and promote its class interests.

The schoolbooks encourage DDR youth to view such analyses in light of contemporary struggles between Christianity and Marxism, as a battle between the forces of reaction and progress. Accordingly, from its earliest beginnings, religion is depicted as the priest-manufactured and -administered opiate of the people:

> The [Mesopotamian] people couldn't explain events according to Nature, because they knew too little about nature. They also believed that the gods ruled the lives of the people. They thought the priests were the representatives of gods. They believed that the priests stood in close relationship to the gods. They regarded the experiences and the knowledge of the priests, as well as their success in the organization and leadership of the irrigation work, as proof that the priests acted with the authority of the gods.

> When the peasants therefore wanted to receive the favor of the gods, they had to bring sacrifices into the temple and honor the priests. The priests demanded that the people believe in the gods, they spread religion among the population. The priests could rule the oppressed better when they explained: We have access to the powerful gods and act according to their will. Thus they used religion for the oppression of the peasants and craftsmen.[6]

The Greek city-states, including Athens and Sparta, are also discussed in Marxist developmental terms; despite their class injustices, they represent more advanced forms of social organization, the first "slave societies":

> The *citizens* owned their own land. They grew grains, wine, olives, or vegetables, and thereby fed themselves. Other citizens worked as craftsmen and merchants in their own small workshops and stores.
>
> They all provided for their own needs as *private property owners*. The citizens were free and had the right to hold state offices. They were obligated to obey the laws and the civil servants and to protect their city state against enemies. . . . The *slaves* were people stolen or sold from other lands and possessed no rights.[7]

Ancient Greek culture is reduced to a secondary theme in *Geschichte 5;* the rise and dominion of Rome is also strictly portrayed as a narrative of exploitation and enslavement, with three-fourths of the units on classical antiquity devoted to slave life. The contrast with textbooks from the Third Reich is extreme. Whereas Nazi history schoolbooks had portrayed Greece and Rome as the rise of the "Nordic race" and the origins of the heroic German *Volk,* DDR books emphasize the "life and work of the slaves," a theme that occupies more than half the pages of *Geschichte 5*. The "lesson" of the Nazi history of Rome was that the Romans were a master race, a superior Nordic race, which declined because it sacrificed its racial purity; SED history shows the Romans to be class exploiters ultimately overwhelmed by the march of progressive History.

But this contrast is not meant to put Nazi and DDR historiography on the same level. Indeed, the difference is obvious: it is absurd to call the Greeks a Nordic race or to analyze history along the lines of race, but it makes sense to analyze Greek history along the lines of economic differences within the society. Most Western historians today also do that—though they strongly differ as to how much "class struggle" they see within a given society or age. Generally speaking, Marxist historians see more and other historical schools see less "class" in history. This should not imply that a Marxist orientation was limited to DDR historians: several fine British historians of the last generation (e.g., E. P. Thompson, Eric Hobsbawm) were Marxists who analyzed British history along the lines of working-class consciousness and class formation. None of this is to say, therefore, that DDR historians simply replaced race with class, whereby they restructured history in ways comparable to the Nazis. No indeed: but it *is* to note that official SED historiography was also schematic and one-dimensional, a hopelessly oversimplified story of economic conflict and oppression, of haves versus have-nots.

For instance, the "forms of class struggle" undertaken by the Roman slaves against their masters are described as "lower" and "higher": "lower" forms include "mutual aid, indolence at work, and escape"; the "higher" form is revolt. The major event of the ancient world, according to *Geschichte 5,* was the slave revolt led by Spartacus (73–71 BC), the first underclass revolt in recorded history—an event rarely given more than passing reference in Western school texts on classical history. Indeed, Spartacus is the sole admirable figure in ancient history, a model for all exploited people, especially in his final battle. The past is a foreign country—but not completely foreign, not completely different.

Spartacus and his fellow slaves illustrate both the "lower" and "higher" forms of class struggle, and even in defeat provide an enduring, uplifting lesson to all those battling class injustice:

> Spartacus himself fought heroically. He wanted to push back the Roman general Crassus, and he killed two high Roman officers as he made his way. But he remained in the thick of the Romans and was wounded in the thigh by a heavy spear. He gave up his horse and still battled, kneeling, his shield held before him. He and the remaining slaves round him fell in battle. No one could locate his corpse. . . .
>
> The revolt by Spartacus was the high point in the struggle of the slaves against the slavemasters. In the heart of the Roman Empire a strong slave army had arisen, defeated Roman legions several times, and threatened the Roman state.[8]

Lest the fifth-graders fail to absorb the inspirational power of Spartacus's example even in defeat, the chapter on the classical world closes: "Neither in Greece nor in Rome, however, was the slave merely a piece of property without his own will. He defended himself against the slave masters. Lazy work, flight, or armed rebellion were forms of *class struggle* that the slaves introduced against the slave owners."⁹

And lest the teacher fail to understand the drift of *Geschichte 5*, the teaching guide includes explicit "pedagogical emphases" for each of its units—including, when necessary, hate education. For example:

> [Egypt]: You know that exploitation is only possible where there is private property. Capitalists are private property owners, and regardless of what language they speak, and regardless of where they rule, the capitalists today also claim to the workers that they're not exploiting them!

> [Mesopotamia]: The confrontation with the picture of this divided class society should stimulate in pupils a well-grounded partisanship for the oppressed and, at the same time, place before them the question of whether this development constitutes progress.

> [Rome]: By means of an emotion-laden, partisan portrait, via words and with pictures, pupils gain a concrete appreciation of the dignified humanity of the exploited slaves and of the luxurious life of the slaveowners. Through identification [with the slaves], pupils should evaluate these relations. Their solidarity with the slaves and their hatred toward the slaveowners should be deepened. In this way, pupils' love for all working people and their hatred toward all exploiters will be strengthened.

> [Spartacus]: By means of an emotion-laden portrait, via words and with pictures, pupils should relive the Spartacus uprising and evaluate it in partisan terms. Respect and sympathy for the courageous and decisive slaves, who were against exploitation, and hatred against the inhuman cruelty of the slaveowners should be deepened. In this way, we strengthen the love of pupils for working people, their solidarity with all those who struggle for a better life, and their hatred against all exploiters and oppressors.¹⁰

Other exercises invite the teacher to draw comparisons between antiquity and the twentieth century. One wonders if the following suggestion about the Spartacus rebellion might not, in the decades after June 1953, inadvertently have caused DDR teachers to muse privately about analogies between the Roman masters and the SED's Russian "friends": "[The lesson] should lead pupils to condemn wars of conquest as unjust. In this way, the hatred of pupils will be deepened toward those people who conquer foreign regions and plunder them. . . . Name [contemporary] examples of how we support the battle of human beings against exploitation and oppression!"[11]

In DDR history textbooks for the sixth and seventh grades, the Middle Ages, Renaissance, Reformation, and French Revolution are presented in similar Marxist terms, according to the periodicization that we have already encountered in our discussion of the POS-EOS literary canon. These events occurred during the periods known to DDR historians as "feudalism" and "emergent capitalism," the latter of which witnesses "the existence of two new classes." "The *bourgeoisie* and the *proletariat* now enter upon the stage of history, and they become in England and later in other countries, in varying degrees, the leading actors."[12] The introduction to *Geschichte 6* tells pupils:

> You will learn about the origins of feudalism from previous social orders, its full development, and its collapse. . . . History class for sixth grade will answer the following important questions:
>
> 1. How did this new social order, feudalism, arise?
> 2. What distinguishes it from previous social orders?
> 3. How has production developed under feudalism?
> 4. How did the oppressed classes conduct the class struggle against the ruling class?
> 5. What new form of exploitation arose from feudal ownership of the means of production?
> 6. How did the ruling class organize the state?
>
> Especially via this last question, you will hear for the first time about the history of our people and about the first German state.[13]

The question of the place of religion carried over into the sixth-grade curriculum as well. Even in their later editions, after Honecker had heralded "the church in socialism," DDR textbooks took a dim view of Christianity. Early editions of *Geschichte 6* were especially severe. "Christianity was originally a religion for the poor and exploited," but the rich Christians eventually took control and, along with the [Roman] emperors, turned it into an exploitative religion. The text notes that Christian bishops never pushed for the abolition of slavery, only its "softening." One unit about the medieval church is titled, "Wealth of the Church and Preaching about a Life of Poverty."[14] The bloodshed of the Crusades is said to have arisen from "the envy and greed of the Pope and the European feudal lords. . . . In order to find a motive for the war of conquest, the Pope spread the lie of the alleged murdering of Christian pilgrims by the Mohammedans." Despite Luther's support of the princes against the revolutionary peasants, the textbooks manage to keep Luther in the DDR pantheon by this description of the Peasants' War of 1525: "The early bourgeois German Revolution began with the Reformation that Luther triggered. Thomas Müntzer led it further toward a People's Reformation by giving the revolutionary People's Movement a goal and proving their right to liberate themselves from their godless lords."[15]

SED historiography approached all history through this rigid Marxist-Leninist lens. For example, in *Geschichte 7*, Thomas More's *Utopia* is claimed as a precursor to Marxism; the Thirty Years' War is an example of late feudal exploitation of the peasants; and the French Revolution too is described, following Marx, as a historical "locomotive" delivering the Industrial Revolution and modern European "bourgeois" revolutions.

And the teaching guide for *Geschichte 7* stresses the contemporary lessons that the latter two events offer. Teachers are advised to write on the chalkboard about the former:

> *What feeling do you have after hearing all these cruelties that the population had to suffer?*
>
> *[Answer:] Sympathy with the tortured people; hatred toward the guilty and the beneficiaries of this war of plunder and conquest.*[16]

Similarly, advises the teaching guide for *Geschichte 7*, the French Revolution should teach "readiness to fight for the goals of revolution and the liberty of the Fatherland. Our age also knows examples of such behavior. (The Soviet *Volk*'s battle against the fascists, Vietnam's battle against the U.S. invaders)."[17]

The interpretations of all the foregoing historical events are supported by citations and quotations from the classical M-L canon. In fact, the textbooks rarely cite any sources except Marx, Lenin, and especially Engels[18]—not even DDR or Soviet historians, doubtless given the founding fathers' unquestioned authority and the ever-present possibility that the "line" might change and a non-canonical source would be rendered suspect.

Right up to the DDR's end, an M-L straitjacket on history held SED historians tight. Even in history texts published for EOS eleventh- and twelfth-graders in November 1989, the transition from the Middle Ages to the Renaissance is approached via extensive quotation from such sources as Engels's *obiter dicta* on the decline of feudalism and the rise of the bourgeoisie in *The Dialectics of Nature* and Marx's remarks from book 1 of *Das Kapital* on forms of capital punishment meted out to unruly slaves or lazy workers; similarly, Thomas More's *Utopia* is treated as a brief for a communist utopia. Meanwhile, the reign of Frederick the Great, who is partially rehabilitated, is explained as a historical "contradiction" between "enlightened theory" and "feudal praxis"; formerly regarded as the tyrant of Absolutism, Frederick is now credited with a historically progressive role, i.e., for having "doubtless helped promote capitalist tendencies."[19]

Modern Times

Upper-grade POS history education concerned chiefly modern history, i.e., the history of the rise of socialism and communism. As in the case of the Nazi education, which also stressed the twentieth century because it was the era of the new Reich, DDR history treated virtually all events before the socialist era as a preparatory run at the DDR.[20]

The DDR emphasis on modern history, however, was even greater than that of the Nazi *Gymnasium*, which continued to devote substantial time to classical and medieval history; after seventh grade, virtually no attention was given in DDR schools to pre- nineteenth-century history.[21] The differences had to do merely with different historical "locations" that, once mined, yielded the rich ore of state legitimacy; in both cases, the goal was to ferret out the glorious "lessons" that history provided: pre-modern history was essentially a selective search for a useable past.

And so, given their emphasis on race and national glory, the Nazis found the distant German past quite serviceable. They invented a "Germanic" past, e.g., the Nordic race, "national" philosophers such as Fichte, and national heroes such as Frederick and Bismarck; indeed Nazi textbooks focused on "Germanic" heroes, developing what might be termed "Great *Mensch* History." Declaring Marxian socialism "un-German," the Nazis celebrated "true" socialism, i.e., *German* or "national" socialism, whose philosophical origins they located in Fichte. Thus they promoted race consciousness and divided the world into the Nordic master class and the *Untermenschen* .

By contrast, SED educators preferred modern history since the French Revolution, or so-called revolutionary-democratic history, which highlighted the rise (and the risings) of the working class. Turning to Hegel and Marx for their own philosophical origins, the SED focused on the history of German and Russian communism, including "world-historical" personalities such as Marx and Lenin. Thus *Geschichte 8* begins with the 1848 revolutions and ends with the German Left's failed "November Revolution" of 1919; *Geschichte 9* ranges from the Russian Revolution to the end of World War II; *Geschichte 10* covers the post-war era. EOS history classes in eleventh and twelfth grades dealt mainly with Party history and background issues, i.e., the pre-history and history of the SED and CPSU.

The cover of *Geschichte 8* exemplifies the style and subject matter of DDR hagiography: a painting of Lenin declaiming to an ocean of enraptured Russian factory workers in May 1917 from the perspective of one of the crowd. The introduction makes clear that the significant moments in modern history consist of rebellions and uprisings, and it makes clear why the revolutionary events in 1871 Paris and twentieth-century Russia warrant priority:

> In between [1848 and 1919] lie the first examples—even if its conquest was triumphant for only a short time—of the proletariat wresting political power: [the Paris Commune] in 1871, the convulsions that shook czarist rule in 1905 and 1907, the overthrow of czarism in February 1917, and the first great world-historical triumph of the Russian proletariat in Red October. For the first time in world history the bourgeoisie was defeated by the proletariat. A new epoch of world history now dawned, the epoch of the transition from capitalism to socialism, the period in which we now find ourselves. In this book the development and contradictions of capitalism will be addressed. You will learn about the struggle of the proletariat and its first steps toward the realization of its historical mission.[22]

Geschichte 8 offers a clear answer as to why the 1848 revolutions throughout Europe did not meet with success. "Why did the revolution suffer defeat? The *main blame* for the failure of the revolution rests with the bourgeoisie." Similar to the emphasis in *Geschichte 5* on the revolt led by Spartacus, *Geschichte 8* concentrates not on the founding of the Second German Reich in 1871, but on the Paris Commune, the uprising of the Paris workers during the Franco-Prussian War of 1870–71—"the *first prole-*

tarian revolution in world history."²³ Again one notices that an event treated cursorily, if at all, in Western textbooks here receives exhaustive scrutiny: thirty pages of pictures, graphs, charts, and photographs of its guiding revolutionaries. The eighth-grade teaching guide also specifies, in a checklist fashion, the contemporary "pedagogical emphasis" that teachers should give the Commune: "Insight that this new proletarian power is the highest form of democracy. Declaration of the DDR as a socialist state in which the inheritance and legacy of the Paris Communards is maintained as a tradition of the international workers' movement. Education toward international solidarity and sympathy and admiration for the heroic battle of the Paris Communards, with consequences for their own behavior."²⁴ The teaching guide adds: "Despite its defeat, the Communards' battle was not for naught. The Commune furnished the international working class with the insight that the working class can only fulfill its historical mission if it is allied—under the leadership of the Marxist party—with other classes, especially working farmers, and if it destroys the old bourgeois state apparatus and actualizes the political rule of the working class."²⁵

Geschichte 8 spotlights the leaders, milestones, and culture of German socialist history. The text includes workers' hymns, such as the *Internationale* and the SPD *Socialist March,* and it offers thumbnail biographical sketches of the leading socialists of the nineteenth and early twentieth centuries: Ferdinand Lassalle, August Bebel, Wilhelm Liebknecht, Karl Liebknecht, Franz Mehring, Rosa Luxemburg, and Clara Zetkin. Lenin and the first year of the Russian Revolution are also prominently portrayed, though limited to one chapter; chief attention is reserved for German history and the background of the KPD. The dangers of "Opportunism" and "Revisionism" receive extensive treatment—particularly the nefarious influence of the gradualist, parliamentary-oriented socialist Eduard Bernstein, the "spokesman of the Opportunists" who "fell under the influence of bourgeois British social reformers" such as the Fabians. (That Lenin translated Sidney and Beatrice Webb's *Industrial Democracy* goes unmentioned.) Indeed, Bernstein's relevance to the DDR's long history of difficulties with critically minded intellectuals such as Wolfgang Harich, Robert Havemann, and Wolf Biermann, followed by numerous Gorbachev-inspired dissidents in the 1980s, is strongly implied: "Bernstein claimed that Marxism in the form in which it had developed until now was no longer valid; it had to be reworked, transformed, revised. So Bernstein was one of the first revisionists. Revisionism played a sinister role, because it was so difficult to see through."²⁶

Excursus: Marx and Engels as Role Models

Pride of place in *Geschichte 8*, however, is reserved for Karl Marx and Friedrich Engels, whose heroic presences and brilliant writings are ubiquitous. Turn to the 1848 revolution, and the founding fathers are there; turn to the 1871 Paris Commune, and they are there; turn to the First International debates and the political infighting with the followers of Lassalle and the German Workers' Association, and they are there. For good measure, *Geschichte 8* also implies that Marx was an exemplary family man; the text includes pictures of Jenny Marx and the Marx daughters, and depicts Marx as though he were a diligent scholarship boy that DDR students should imitate: "Karl Marx and his family underwent self-denial and great sacrifices to serve the cause of the working class. In the library of the British Museum and then at home, until late into the night, Karl Marx studied tirelessly.... Engels did everything possible to support Marx and his family financially."[27]

This last point warrants additional comment. The idealized presentation of the Marx family in *Geschichte 8* burnishes, with greater detail and authoritativeness, the rosy image of domestic harmony that the primers and *Heimatkunde* schoolbooks painted, as we have already seen in Chapter 1. The pedagogical fit between these textbooks and *Geschichte 8*, exemplified by the use of highly selective bibliographical emphases and omissions, was obviously part of SED educators' deliberate curricular design. For instance, a *Lesebuch 4* selection in full alignment with and anticipating the themes of *Geschichte 8* is "A Sunday Morning at Karl Marx's House," which portrays Marx's happy family; the story refers to family members by their family nicknames: Marx is "Mohr" ("darky," referring to Marx's black beard, the swarthy Moor of Venice), the housekeeper Helene Demuth is "Lenchen," and Engels is Uncle Frederic, Uncle Angel, or General.[28]

Needless to say, the story does not mention that Marx fathered a son by Lenchen (named Frederick Demuth, whom Marx never recognized)—or that he persuaded Engels to claim paternity, so that Jenny would not find out about the transgression, and then soon thereafter conducted a *menage à trois* that he forced Jenny to accept.

Once again, as in the case of the DDR's school readers, Marx and Engels are presented not just as political heroes but also as moral exemplars.[29] DDR historiography proudly exalted Marx and Engels as the Romulus and Remus of modern history. They became the founding fathers not just of the DDR but of the entire socialist tradition. Given that status, they could do no wrong. *Geschichte 8* makes no mention that the Marx family's "self-denial and great sacrifices" had much to do with the father's bohemianism: Marx's decades of carousing and gambling, his scandalous neglect of his wife's and children's health, and his failure to provide them with even a minimum of economic support. During their early years in London, the Marx household of eight lived in a two-room attic without a lavatory, bath, or running water. Four of the Marx children died in infancy of malnutrition and disease; two of his three grown daughters (Eleanor and Laura) committed suicide. The only male who survived was the maid's child by Marx, Freddy. Marx never held a job, and instead borrowed money constantly from Engels—for rent, housekeeping expenses, and alcohol—resulting in Engels's frequent outrage about Marx's casual expectations (especially after 1870) that his younger colleague would finance Marx's middle-class household in grand style, including such proletarian necessities as maids and butlers.

Of course, American elementary school readers also have traditionally placed our founding fathers in a positive light—with little or no attention paid, say, to Thomas Jefferson's alleged affair with Sally Hemings, the slave girl on his Monticello estate with whom he purportedly had children. Likewise, American schoolchildren typically learn that young George Washington admitted that he chopped down a cherry tree because he "could not tell a lie." They do not learn that he had dozens of slaves on his Mount Vernon plantation estate.

Nonetheless, the difference between these examples and the DDR readers is one of scale: the degree of cover-up and whitewashing of Marx's history is extreme. By any reasonable standard, Marx's personal failings are much greater than those of any comparable Anglo-American figure—and their effacement is, after all, not just for reasons of national pride or because of children's innocence, but for ideological reasons related to the communist cult of personality. Frank Manuel, the great historian of the European radical and utopian traditions, remarks on Marx's "scorn for most human beings," noting that he maintained "consistently amicable relations" with "almost no one" (besides Engels). Manuel adds: "Outside of Engels and the family circle there is not much sympathy for human beings in Karl Marx. But while officially condemning a surrender to pathos or sentimentality as a character flaw, he himself could not always rise up from the swamp of self-pity."[30]

Echoing the German literature selections designed to honor "the fathers" of socialism, the eighth-grade teaching guide specifies the "pedagogical emphasis" of the unit as follows: "to awaken love and reverence toward Marx and Engels." Not surprisingly, these stories do not allude to Marx's utter egocentricity, his irresponsible bohemianism, his cruel exploitation and mistreatment of his family, or his financial irresponsibility. Instead, unit questions ask: "Which qualities of Marx can you take as a model?" "What was the basis of the friendship of Marx and Engels?" (Lenin is quoted as saying that their friendship was "more touching" than any of the relationships depicted in myth and literature.) The text provides excerpts of pathetic letters from Jenny Marx about the cruelties of capitalist landlords and shopkeepers as well.[31]

Another notable feature of *Geschichte 8* and other history textbooks is their quotation from "primary sources" in their narratives. In practice, this meant ceaseless, irrelevant citation of the M-L Holy Trinity of "historical scholars": Marx, Engels, and Lenin.

Indeed, the history textbooks are a *locus classicus* of what, at various times in SED history, constituted the Party sacrilege known as "citationism." This practice, wondrous to read and purportedly a proof of authoritative historical scholarship, is seen in lengthy quotations about the slaves of the ancient Orient or the Roman economy taken from Engels's *Origins of Private Property, Family, and the State*. Or sober reference is made to Lenin's *On the State* in a unit on ancient Sumeria. Or definitive-sounding pronouncements about the Greek writer Diodor are cited from Marx's *Capital*. Or edicts about Aristotle and Copernicus from Engels' *Dialectic of Nature*. Or conclusions about feudalism from Lenin's *The Development of Capitalism in Russia*. And on and on. And never a single Western scholar quoted—at most, an occasional reference to legitimate (if Party-approved) Marxist historians such as Mehring or Kuczynski.[32] Dozens of other similar references to Marx's *Critique of Political Economy* or *German Ideology*, to Engels' *History of the Ur-Germans* or *Anti-Duhring*, or to Lenin's letters abound in other textbooks, testifying fully to the Party's claims for all three men (and, in earlier eras, Stalin too) as universal geniuses.

"Socialism Is Winning!"

As the grades progressed, so too did the march of communist and socialist history progress through time. The key chapters in *Geschichte 9* and *Geschichte 10* spotlight the world-historical triumph of communism from 1917 to the present, concentrating on the USSR and DDR, as if to trumpet the

Party cry: "*Der Socialismus siegt!*" ("Socialism Is Winning!"). Pictures and paintings of Lenin are everywhere throughout the texts: Lenin addressing factory workers in Rasliv, Lenin entering Petrograd in April 1917, Lenin arguing heatedly at a 1920 Central Committee meeting.[33] Ulbricht is likewise a notable presence in editions during his tenure in office; ironically, while not even mentioning Stalin's name, chapters on World War II include pictures of his lieutenant Ulbricht talking to German war prisoners and in exile in Moscow.[34]

Geschichte 9 and *Geschichte 10*—as well as the EOS history texts and the majority of university courses in history—focused on twentieth-century socialism because, as the introduction to *Geschichte 9* explains, the most direct and applicable progressive lessons are to be found in "the socialist struggles of our own century":

> In ninth-grade history you will learn about the fundamental *Wende* [turn] in human history, which began with the triumph of the Great Socialist October Revolution in 1917. . . . You will learn at length of the international significance of this social transformation—the greatest one in history, which confirmed the correctness of the teachings of Marx, Engels, and Lenin—and which directed the way for all of humanity into the socialist epoch.
>
> Great attention will be devoted in the textbook to the intensification of the international contradictions of imperialism under the conditions of the worldwide battle between socialism and imperialism. . . . The heroic battle of the armies and peoples of the socialistic Soviet states, which endured the main burden of the war against Hitler's Germany, will be introduced. . . . [The textbook] will also enable you to draw the correct lessons of the battle against imperialism, militarism, and war, as well as of the fortification of the socialist German Democratic Republic.[35]

Some chapters in *Geschichte 9* and *Geschichte 10* even close by spelling out the "lessons" under headings such as "The Lessons of the November Revolution." For example, *Geschichte 9* draws five lessons for would-be revolutionaries from the November Revolution of 1918–19. The passage reads as though it were written to instruct slow learners, such as wayward DDR intellectuals Wolfgang Harich and Robert Havemann, on what both men called the "Central Administration's Eternal Truths":

1. The basic question of revolution is *the question of power,* in which it is demonstrated that no "third way" exists between the rule of the monopolistic bourgeoisie and the working class. Only when the power of monopoly capital and militarism is broken and the power of the working class, the *dictatorship of the proletariat,* is established, can peace, liberty, and democracy be achieved and secured.
2. The working class cannot use the *state apparatus* for its purposes, but must rather break it and replace it through organs of the working class.
3. To maintain its rule in the new world-historical epoch, the monopolistic bourgeoisie needs *Opportunism,* so that it can split the working class and prevent its unified action.
4. The working class can fulfill its historical mission only when it is led by a *Marxist-Leninist party of class struggle,* which has been freed of all bourgeois, petty bourgeois, and opportunistic influences. . . .
5. The working class can only triumph in *closest alliance with the Soviet Union.* . . .

Or as the teaching guide instructed, under the heading "The Lessons of the Revolution": "It taught great portions of the *Volk* who their real enemies were and who fought for the interests of the entire German *Volk*."[36]

Similar to the case of the civics textbooks in Chapter 3, DDR Education for Hatred is a running leitmotif through the units on twentieth-century history, as the teaching guides evince. Classes on colonialism should "stimulate contempt and hatred toward the inhuman system of imperialist colonialism." World War I units should instill the "conviction that the German imperialists are deadly enemies of the German *Volk*" and "hatred against imperialism as a system." Discussions of Karl Liebknecht and Rosa Luxemburg, both of whom were murdered in 1919, should emphasize not only "love and reverence for the leaders of the revolutionary working class, but also hatred and contempt toward imperialists, militarists, and even the actions of right-wing SPD leaders."[37]

The character of DDR history textbooks can best be appreciated by examining in greater detail the issues most relevant to the DDR that *Geschichte 9* and *Geschichte 10* addressed. The bowdlerizations of certain sensitive moments in German history for SED members—such as the Nazi-Soviet Pact of August 1939—is indeed a textbook illustration of Nietzsche's aphorism from *The Gay Science*: "I have done that, says my memory. I cannot have done that, insists my conscience. At last, memory yields."

"Made in East Germany," or the Historical (Re)Invention of the DDR

Understandably, SED historians devoted most attention to the background and history of the DDR itself. The treatment of the following wartime and post-war events suggests how SED textbook historians served the Cold War cultural front and heeded the Party injunction to write "committed" history.[38]

The German Resistance and World War II

For decades after the war, BRD history texts fudged the history of the Third Reich, downplaying or sketchily addressing the Nazi era. Not until the mid-1960s did the subject begin to be treated openly and accurately.[39] By contrast, SBZ/DDR textbooks gave it full attention twenty years earlier—though always, then as later, from a Soviet-slanted perspective. Readers of *Geschichte 9* received the impression, for instance, that the main effect of Hitler's rise to power was the destruction of the KPD, and that the German resistance to Nazism was limited to the KPD leadership and their resistance groups. Several are discussed, including the *Rote Kapelle*, named after Heinz Kapelle, a young KJVD member who distributed anti-Nazi pamphlets, was arrested, and purportedly cried out in the courtroom before being sentenced to death in July 1941: "*Es lebe die Kommunistische Partei!*" ("Long live the Communist Party!"). By contrast, a half-sentence suffices to describe the White Rose resistance group, organized by Hans and Sophie Scholl in 1943 at Munich University. And the July 20 Movement to overthrow Hitler, led by Count Klaus Schenk von Stauffenberg, was a circle drawn from the "monopolistic bourgeoisie and reactionary military" that simply sought to "rescue the remaining power positions of German imperialism."[40] Hitler's own rise to power is attributed to rotting capitalism.

The testimony to communist heroism, on the other hand, is exhaustive, particularly the heroism of the KPD leadership. A photograph secretly taken of KPD chairman Ernst Thälmann in Buchenwald, along with two of Georgi Dimitroff, head of the KPD faction in the Reichstag, accompanies a discussion of Thälmann and Dimitroff. The text highlights excerpts from Thälmann's speech to the KPD Central Committee in early February 1933—just one month before his capture and arrest—and honors Dimitroff for his open defiance of Hermann Goering in the December 1933 trial following the Reichstag fire on February 27. Dimitroff's assertion that the Nazis started the fire in order to have a pretense for mass terror is quoted, sympathetically and at length.[41] The text also features pictures of the 1935 KPD Central Committee in exile, including Wilhelm Pieck and Walter Ulbricht. Thirteen photographs of KPD and Red Orchestra members who died at the hands of the Nazis are shown, along with extensive commentary. The section on concentration camps concludes that eleven million people "from different nations and classes—mainly workers, communists, Soviet citizens, Poles, progressive intellectuals, and Jews—were brutally murdered."[42] The rank-ordering in this list is notable.

Meanwhile, the presentation of World War II in *Geschichte 9* lionizes the USSR and castigates or patronizes the western Allies at every turn. (One chapter is titled "The Triumph of the USSR and Her Allies in the Second World War.") The text spares only a single sentence for the Nazi-Soviet Pact of August 1939, justifying it as a "normalization" of relations designed "to destroy the Western powers' plans to solve the inner contradictions of capitalism at the cost of the socialistic Soviet Union."[43] Stalin's name appears only once,[44] in connection with Germany's invasion of the USSR in June 1941,[45] as the head of the CPSU and leader of the "Great War of the Fatherland" against the Nazis. Coverage of the Battle of Britain and the Allies' North Africa campaign is limited to a single sentence each.

Geschichte 9 presents the D-Day invasion as follows: "When the Western powers recognized in 1944 that Soviet troops and their People's Allies could liberate the oppressed countries throughout Europe from the fascist yoke on their own, they landed their troops in Normandy on June 6, 1944."[46] Implying that the Americans and British sought to destroy the SBZ even before its creation (and failing to note that the territory that would become the SBZ was U.S.-occupied at war's end), the chapter concludes: "In the last months of the war, the [Anglo-American bombing] attacks centered principally on the cities of the future Soviet occupation zone. This was intended to cause the USSR and the German anti-fascists insurmountable difficulties in post-war reconstruction."[47] Here too, then, the DDR texts echoed their immediate Nazi forerunners: both painted Britain and the United States as reactionary, aggressive, and imperialistic.[48]

But the DDR texts explicitly deflected any such perceptions of their similarity with the Nazi era. For instance, whenever possible, the DDR officials referred to the Third Reich as "fascist" rather than "Nazi" or "National Socialist": the aim was precisely to avoid any association of Nazism with "socialism"—and any comparisons between the totalitarian tendencies of the DDR dictatorship and the Nazi Reich.

Geschichte 9 closes with study questions to reinforce these distinctions. For instance:

1. Explain why the signing of a Non-Aggression Pact with Hitler's Germany was, for the Soviet Union at that time, necessary and correct!
2. Show with concrete historical facts that the Second World War was, in its first phase, an unjust imperialistic war!
3. Explain why the goals of the fascists for the invasion of the USSR corresponded to the interests of the most reactionary elements of German monopoly capital!
4. Compare the goals of the conspirators of the July 20 Movement with those of the NKFD [National Committee for a Free Germany, composed of German émigrés based in Moscow], and explain which group's goals corresponded to the interests of the German *Volk!*
5. Prove that the main burden of the war against fascism lay on the shoulders of the Soviet Army, even in the last period of the war!

Topped off by the now-familiar exclamation marks—which a former POS history teacher whom I interviewed in Part 2 derided as "DDR punctuation"—such "study questions" left no doubt about how East German ninth-graders were supposed to reflect on the origins and course of the Second World War.

The Marshall Plan

The Cold War is the prime focus of *Geschichte 10*. The text devotes separate sections to themes such as "The Imperialistic Politics of Aggression under the Leadership of the USA" and "The Plans for World Conquest of U.S. Imperialism and the Struggle of the USSR for a Peaceful Post-War Order." The American bid for world domination and the "immeasurable arrogance" of American politicians, reports *Geschichte 10*, began with the atomic bombing of Hiroshima, which should not been seen "as the last military act of the Second World War, but rather as the first act in the Cold War against Russia. It was designed to intimidate the Soviet Union."[49] The text grants no other military or strategic aims to Hiroshima or the Marshall Plan.

Geschichte 10 portrays the Marshall Plan, proposed in June 1947 and instituted in April 1948 by the Truman administration, as the centerpiece of U.S. post-war imperialistic strategy. Via the Truman Doctrine, the United States "promised protection and help for all reactionary regimes of exploitation," whereby "the rights of the peoples to self-determination were treated with open contempt." Although the United States "formally" offered Marshall Plan aid to the USSR and its allies, "the offer was mainly a diplomatic maneuver to veil the anti-Soviet character of the Plan," since the West canceled the offer when the USSR signaled a willingness to accept aid on condition of "strict respect for its sovereignty and economic independence."[50]

The economic credits that the Marshall Plan granted to the reactionary regimes for reconstruction, explains *Geschichte 10*, constituted "a new level" of "preparation for a war of aggression against the emergent socialist world system."[51] The Marshall Plan advanced three specific U.S. postwar aims:

1. Strengthening of the economic power positions of the reactionary forces in the Western European nations, in order to repress the democratic forces.
2. Surmounting the inner [economic] crisis in the U.S. through improvement of its trade and profit possibilities in Europe.
3. Creation of the economic and political conditions for a military bloc against socialism in Europe.[52]

The textbook goes on to argue that Marshall Plan aid to the western zones of Germany was in violation of the Potsdam Agreement, according to which the victorious Allies would jointly determine post-war German reconstruction. In a characteristic act of projection, *Geschichte 10* accuses the United States of abrogating Potsdam, which in fact was official Soviet policy in the SBZ: "In view of the fact that a part of Germany was removed from its imperialistic sphere of power, the U.S. decided, against [the provisions of] the Potsdam Agreement, to restore German imperialism and set up West Germany as part of its anti-communist spearhead."[53]

The DDR Workers' Revolt and the Soviet Invasion of Hungary

Although the history texts are mum about Stalin's show trials and purges, the Gulag, or Khrushchev's Secret Speech denouncing Stalin's cult of personality—nor hardly a word about the Berlin blockade and the Berlin airlift of 1948–49[54]—SED historians obviously felt that they could not remain silent about embarrassing crises that occurred during the DDR era and were directly experienced by or deeply affected thousands of DDR citizens, such as the June 1953 revolt and the USSR's invasion of Hungary in 1956.

But what to tell DDR students, many of whom had parents, neighbors, or older siblings who had participated in *der 17. Juni* and in anti-Soviet protests over Hungary? Without wanting to go into the circumstances of either event in detail—the two together are granted a combined total of nine paragraphs—the authors of *Geschichte 10* neatly handle them under a section heading titled "The Increasing Failure of Imperialistic 'Cold War Politics.'" The discussion is revealing for the overwhelming body of evidence it suppresses that both the DDR and Hungarian revolts were indigenous, mass rebellions by a broad cross-section of citizens.

Geschichte 10 advances the familiar DDR position that the West organized and funded the revolt of June 17. The "growing horror" of "unscrupulous" "BRD imperialists" sparked the uprising, the text explains. With the DDR economy experiencing "disturbances" due to BRD subterfuges, the "imperialistic forces" launched a "counter-revolutionary putsch" through "agents of various secret polices." These agents, operating out of West Berlin, induced small groups of "provocateurs and criminals" to commit arson and to murder "functionaries of the workers' movement." But the workers of the young state, under the "leadership of the Party," stood fast:

> The workers drove the provocateurs back. In defense of the campaign to build socialism, factories had worker defense units, which were organized into armed *battalions of the working class*. Many workers distanced themselves from the counter-revolutionary putsch as soon as they saw its hidden motives. They went back to their factories and helped capture the provocateurs. Through this decisive action of the progressive section of the working class and their allies, in cooperation with the Soviet forces and the armed organs of the DDR, the counter-revolutionary putsch collapsed within twenty-four hours. The attempt to destroy socialism in Germany had failed.[55]

The Soviet attack on Hungary in the fall of 1956 is similarly presented as a response to "criminal actions" by the West, which triggered "distribution problems and discontent" within the Hungarian populace. According to *Geschichte 10*, the West "actively supported fascist bands with weapons" in preparation for "a counter-revolutionary uprising." Pseudo-socialistic slogans such as "Democracy and Decentralization" and "Hungarian Communism" quickly became turned into "anti-communist calls." The "blood terror against communists and state functionaries" that began in late October 1956 was met on November 3 by "the class-conscious workers of Hungary . . . with support from the Soviet units stationed in the country," who "brought *the counterrevolution to an end.*"⁵⁶

The failure of both June 17 and the Hungarian uprising showed the futility of Cold War putsches against socialism, concluded *Geschichte 10*, and "underscored that the balance of power in the world in the 1950s had shifted more and more strongly in favor of the forces of peace, democracy, and socialism."⁵⁷

The Erection of the Berlin Wall and the Soviet Invasion of Czechoslovakia

The two major events in DDR domestic and foreign policy of the 1960s are likewise heavily rewritten in *Geschichte 10* according to the SED line.

Doubtless because the Berlin Wall was a continuous presence in the DDR, one that did not simply dim in the citizenry's mind with time—and perhaps also because Erich Honecker and the Party leadership were striving to make DDR citizens proud of the Wall—SED historians devoted a full chapter, complete with photos and a litany of the earliest heroic *Grepos* killed on Wall duty, specified by name and place and date of death, to "The DDR's Measures on August 13, 1961."⁵⁸

The erection of the "Anti-Fascist Wall of Protection" (*antifaschistischer Schutzwall*) was a response to "*the intensification of tensions by the aggressive circles of imperialism.*" "Although the DDR government, along with the Soviet Union and the other socialist *Bruderländer*, had done everything possible to induce the BRD toward a politics of reason and good will," explains *Geschichte 10*, military stockpiling by "*BRD* imperialism" continued relentlessly. In the spring of 1961—as in 1956 in Hungary—Western forces generated "distribution problems and discontent" within the DDR populace. Western "agents and secret police," engaged in "sabotage," "brutally exploited the open border with West Berlin, in order to damage the DDR." In the summer of 1961, NATO started testing maneuvers for "a limited war against the DDR and other socialist states."⁵⁹

In August 1961, continues *Geschichte 10*, the West's "military preparations were accompanied by a *wave of harassment against the DDR.*" No mention is made of the fact that, disgusted with restrictions on freedom of speech and movement—and fearing that the borders might close soon—two to three thousand DDR citizens were fleeing through West Berlin daily. *Geschichte 10* instead presents as groundless rumor what had become the plain truth: DDR citizens "were supposed to believe that a majority of the people were against socialism and that it would be a gesture of Humanity to overthrow the Workers' and Peasants' State."

With the approval of the USSR and the *Bruderländer*, concludes *Geschichte 10*, the government took the necessary "security measures" on August 13. "The war inciters in West Berlin were thus brought under reliable control." The measures "surprised" the BRD, whose politicians "raced agitatedly from one meeting to another," but everything in "the DDR capital went on as normal."⁶⁰ The chapter ends on an upbeat note:

> The majority of the labor force *greeted and supported the security measures*. Numerous Berliners visited the armed troops in the following days. Delegations from factories and many individual citizens brought gifts and flowers as expressions of their gratitude. . . .
> As a result of the security of the state borders, it was no longer possible to take the fruits of their labors from the labor force and plunder the DDR without punishment.⁶¹

No reference is made, either in this chapter or elsewhere in *Geschichte 10*, to the hundreds of DDR citizens murdered by *Grepos* as they scaled the Wall or otherwise tried to circumvent "the measures of August 13."

Moving on to discuss Czechoslovakia, *Geschichte 10* presents the USSR's abrupt cancellation of the Prague Spring in August 1968 as the high point of a chapter on "The Defeat of the Politics of 'Bridge-Building.'" The term was used by the DDR—after a remark by President Lyndon Johnson on "building bridges" to non-capitalist nations—to denote the allegedly devious means by which the West sought to export counter-revolution by laying economic and ideological bridges to socialist countries and the Third World. Having realized that direct attacks on socialism were futile and that socialism was winning the Cold War, American imperialists tried a clever new strategy: promote "socialist-looking" policies aimed at sowing division within the socialist bloc and, quite specifically, breaking the Warsaw Pact alliance. "Counting on admiration of the West by ideologically confused people," explains *Geschichte 10*, the United States aimed "to get a foot in the door of socialist countries. Caught in this illusion, American imperialism hoped to be able, step by step, to propel an anti-socialist wave toward the re-establishment of capitalism."⁶²

"The planned model case" for the U.S. "bridge-building politics," continues *Geschichte 10*, was the fomenting of a "*counter-revolutionary uprising*" in Czechoslovakia. Much as had happened in Hungary, "right-wing forces" pretended to campaign for the "improvement" of socialism, while actually seeking to restore capitalism. Perhaps because the pain and indeed anger of the USSR's crushing of the Prague Spring—with military support provided by the NVA—was still a sore spot in DDR citizens' minds in the 1970s and 1980s, the text does not remind the reader either of the Soviet or DDR military action. *Geschichte 10* merely notes that the counter-revolution "failed" because of "*the class solidarity of the socialist states*": "The international help from the Warsaw Pact states protected Czechoslovakia from a civil war and frustrated the threat to socialism. The politics of 'bridge-building' had failed."[63]

Overtaken by History? 1989 and the Perestroika of DDR Historiography

The interpretations of the foregoing watershed events in DDR history changed little through edition after edition of DDR textbooks. By late 1989, however, with the DDR finally—if belatedly—participating in the ferment sweeping the USSR and eastern Europe, SED history textbook writers began taking steps toward writing less tendentious history.[64]

On December 7, 1989, prominent Party and non-Party history educators, textbook writers, historians, political leaders, and church representatives attended a conference sponsored by the APW (*Akademie der Pädagogischen Wissenschaften,* Academy of Pedagogical Sciences) on the future of history teaching in the DDR. A diverse APW working group that emerged from this conference repudiated the traditional, exclusive claim staked by Party historians to the M-L economic interpretation of history. Instead, by February 1990, the APW circulated a tentative POS curriculum that rejected collectivism, socialist patriotism, and the glorification of the East German state and sought to "strengthen the individuality of each pupil." The new guidelines stressed the "the need for differentiation, for pluralistic thinking, and for consideration of different social forces" besides the economic.

The specifics of the APW curriculum for the POS grades were never fully worked out. By March 1990, History had overtaken DDR historians' belated attempts to restructure the German history curriculum. Still, the ferment in the field was felt at the secondary school level. Even before the December 7 meeting of the APW, older students in the EOS began unlearning the lessons of progressive history: The past, they now discovered, was not entirely KA.

Within three weeks of the opening of the Wall on November 9, 1989, the Ministry of Education published new history texts for EOS students in the eleventh and twelfth grades: *Geschichte: Lehrbuch für die Abiturstufe,* which replaced the study of SED and CPSU history and constituted a dramatic—if still limited—departure from the orthodoxies of decades past. Originally scheduled for publication in September 1990, the new two-part text was rushed out in November–December 1989—a vain attempt at a liberal official response to the tide of events—without photos, pictures, charts, or graphs.

The new text was a complete revision of history from Mesopotamia through World War II. The authors' collective acknowledged implicitly in their introduction that previous DDR history texts had been inadequate, even as it seemed to sense that the SED-sponsored unlearning was arriving too late and that the new Party-lined texts would not meet the growing demand for full disclosure, for a genuine DDR *glasnost:* "The editors are aware that many problems with which historiography is now coping cannot be considered at this time. Nevertheless we hope that the decision to print this book early is useful both for classes and in light of the sharp deficiency of historical materials."[65]

The 1989 EOS *Geschichte*—which covered only the years up to 1945 and did not touch upon SBZ or DDR history—broke numerous DDR taboos, most of them dealing with the Soviet past. For example, the text condemned, at length, Stalin's "dictatorial regime," his "crimes" against the CPSU and USSR, and the personality cult that he fostered. It also acknowledged, if vaguely, that Stalinism had claimed "many millions" of victims and had inflicted "extreme damage" on Soviet science and culture.[66]

The 1989 EOS textbook also termed the Stalin personality cult "the ideological centerpiece of Stalinism": like those who try to minimize Nazism by treating it as "Hitlerism," SED historians still insisted that the horror of Stalinism had primarily to do with one man's corruption, rather than with the broader phenomenon of Marxism-Leninism itself. Trying to keep pace with changing events, the text even excerpted a Gorbachev speech from November 1989 on Stalin's "deformation of socialism."[67]

Criticism of Stalin from his erstwhile opponents, especially from Leon Trotsky on the left and Nicolai Bukharin on the right, receives prominent display in the last EOS *Geschichte.* Trotsky's theory of permanent revolution is, however, dismissed as "unrealistic . . . just decorative, revolutionary-sounding slogans"; he cared less for "the ideals of the Revolution" than about his own "personal vanity." The text notes that Stalin ordered Trotsky's murder, and that Bukharin was rehabilitated in 1988 by USSR courts.[68]

Once again, History had changed overnight. "What did you unlearn today?" DDR parents could again ask their children—just as in the late 1940s, during the transition from Nazi "Brown" to Soviet "Red." Still, the SED was obviously not ready to unlearn all its progressive lessons. "Ostspeak" and doublethink were still the order of the day, as DDR historians essayed a middle, or fallback, position.

Above all, Lenin remained sacrosanct. The 1989 EOS *Geschichte* quotes most of Lenin's famous "Letter to the Party Congress" of December 1922, in which the sick leader cautioned the CPSU that Stalin might not be "careful" in the use of his "immeasurable power." The text seeks thereby to establish that Stalin's reign represented a "break from [Lenin's] political legacy." Stalin's USSR was "a long way off from socialism, as Lenin had understood it." That Lenin founded the murderous Cheka, which by 1920 had 250,000 agents and was conducting a thousand political executions per month, still goes unmentioned. The February 1921 massacre of the Kronstadt sailors likewise goes unmentioned. The 1989 *Geschichte* mourns Lenin's death as "a terrible loss not only for the peoples of the Soviet Union but for all of progressive humanity."[69]

World War II became open to partial truth-telling as well in the 1989 EOS *Geschichte*. For instance, the textbook calls the Nazi-Soviet Pact, which included secret clauses that gave the USSR title to Poland, a "violation" of Poland's international rights. (The subject of the "violation" of the rights of Finland and the Baltic republics, however, is not broached; and while Nazi Germany's motives in the pact are condemned as "based on *short-term*, tactical interests," the USSR is defended as having "wished only *permanent* peace on its borders.")

Moreover, although discussion of the non-communist German Resistance is still restricted to the July 20 Movement, the group is given more attention and called "progressive." Count Stauffenberg and his co-conspirators are now described as "patriotic and peace-loving" men who, in cooperation with Social Democrats and labor leaders, sought to establish "a bridge with the leaders of the communist underground resistance."[70]

EXCURSUS: The *Black Book* as Anti-Textbook: History Turns a Corner?

And how has the historiography of the DDR developed since the upheaval of 1989–90? One index may be seen in the ferment aroused in Germany by a thousand-page scholarly tome that reads like a textbook—or perhaps "anti-textbook": *The Black Book of Communism,* a comprehensive catalogue and analysis of the crimes of communism.

It is worthwhile to examine the debate triggered by the *Black Book* among German intellectuals and professors, for it seems likely soon to leave its imprint on German—especially eastern German—history classes. So let us take a very different approach in this excursus and look not to a schoolbook or classroom or interview with a schoolteacher or student. We are focusing here not on history teachers but on historians—i.e., on those educators who shape history and educate history teachers. Thus we are concentrating not on secondary but rather on higher education debates as we attend to the impact within the German academy and intelligentsia of a work envisioned to exert a shaping influence on Germany's history textbooks.[71]

The *Black Book* appeared in Germany in May 1998—significantly, on the 150th anniversary of the publication of the *Communist Manifesto*. Since that date, it has been impossible to view the communist past so benignly as before—especially the past of the SED's "Russian friends"—yet also the DDR past. Even staunch German leftists and PDS (*Partei des Demokratischen Sozialismus,* Party of Democratic Socialism) supporters have been defensive about the crimes dated and listed—in sober textbook fashion—in the *Black Book*. The arguments and statistics will probably soon find their way into new German schoolbooks devoted to twentieth-century history (and ultimately those of other nations as well).[72] It is often compared with *The God That Failed* (1950)[73]—as well as with numerous other works that shook generations of European leftists (from Viktor Kravchenko's *I Chose Freedom* [1947] to Alexander Solzhenitsyn's *Gulag Archipelago* [1973]). One reason for its likely influence is that the *Black Book* is not a memoir—it is based on archival research. Scholars quote eyewitness testimony of communist crimes from archival documents, rather than presenting it in the form of political autobiography. Perhaps that is also why it has been harder for the European Left to dismiss it: "anti-anti-communism" could always brand the work of ex-communists—and even of figures such as Solzhenitsyn—as conservative, nationalist, even fascist axe-grinding. But the *Black Book* merely cites contemporary statements of Communist Party functionaries in good standing, beginning with Lenin himself. Moreover, it is beside the point to dismiss the *Black Book* as "unoriginal" scholarship—indeed as "a mere textbook compiled by a committee"—which many historians have done. For its chief aim is not to break new scholarly ground, but instead to channel discussion of communist crimes into the intellectual mainstream and transform the "damnable heresy of anti-communism" (as Francois Furet termed it in *The Passing of an Illusion*) into a fully legitimate topic of inquiry.

Originally published in 1997 in France as *Le livre noir du communisme* under the general editorship of Stéphane Courtois, the *Black Book* stayed for months near the top of the German nonfiction bestseller list in 1998 (just as *Le livre noir du communisme* had done in France a year earlier), and one of the Berlin discussions even provoked a minor riot.[74] Tensions ran so high in eastern Germany about the *Black Book*'s denunciations of communism that angry leftists tried to disrupt these discussions. Waving banners ("Who is counting the victims of capitalism?") and shouting insults ("Enlightenment, shit! Jump out of your ivory tower!"), three dozen protesters sought to drown out Courtois in a Berlin meeting. Their flyers proclaimed: "In the land of the culprits of Auschwitz, the relativizing of this crime against humanity must not be taken as an acceptable topic for discussion."

This public outcry reflected how and why the *Black Book* is particularly relevant to German history and German readers. Given its provocative comparative treatment of Nazi and communist crimes, and the fact of the recent experience of communism by millions of former East Germans, many German historians expected that Courtois's book would command special attention from the German public. But they underestimated how the German Left would attempt to whitewash the crimes detailed in the *Black Book*, as well as how a professional *Politikverdrossenheit* (exhaustion/ frustration with politics) affected the German intelligentsia generally, which had already fought three internecine battles related to German history in the mid-1990s and saw little new either in the volume's scholarship or in the historical questions that it raised.

My exploration of all these issues places the *Black Book* in the larger context of recent German cultural politics. Although my focus is on the distinctive conditions that shaped Germans' response to the *Black Book*, I also allude to its French reception in the spirit of Courtois's urging that the "crimes of communism" need to be judged "via an "approach call[ing] for cross-country analysis."[75]

I

Written by Courtois and ten other scholars and journalists associated with the Centre National de la Recherché Scientifique in Paris, which works with younger Russian historians to analyze material from Soviet archives, the *Black Book* summarizes the murderous legacy of communism in seventeen nations; in the German edition, two separate chapters were added on the history of the DDR, bringing its length to a hefty 992 pages (150 more than in the American edition). One of those added chapters was authored by Joachim Gauck, the post-reunification director of the *Stasi* files compiled by the SED. The other was written by one of his assistants, Erhard Neubert, administrator of the education/research branch of the Stasi files and a historian of DDR communism.[76]

Along with Courtois himself, Gauck participated in several of the discussions designed to promote discussion of the *Black Book*. Invariably, these discussions—which also included distinguished German historians such as Hans Mommsen and Wolfgang Wipperman—centered on the book's claims about the comparative evils of communism and Nazism, claims that German historians are especially well qualified to assess given Germany's singular, Orwellian distinction of having been home both to communist and Nazi tyrannies. The combative Courtois—whose full-length beard and extravagant gestures remind one of a young Solzenitsyn—even declared in a May 1998 discussion in Berlin that the *Black Book* "should have been written here in Germany." Why? Because, according to Courtois, Germans have a "fuller perspective for understanding totalitarianism," given that they were both the victimizers and victims of Nazi and of communist states.[77]

Courtois argues in his introduction that a double standard has prevailed in measuring degrees of totalitarian evil. The Western intellectual establishment prefers its dictators Red: it has demonized the Nazis but has refused to judge—or has even remained silent about—the crimes of communists around the world. Courtois accuses the European Left of complicity in those crimes. The "black books" of fascism and Nazism have been published and publicized, he notes, but the crimes of communism have never been judged with the same severity or scrutiny. His words possess special credibility because they come from a former Maoist. (Indeed, it is chiefly because the contributors are all former communists or former fellow travelers[78] that the *Black Book* has been read as a successor to *The God That Failed*, that powerful collective memoir written by six ex-communist intellectuals, including chapters by Arthur Koestler, Richard Wright, Stephen Spender, and Ignazio Silone, among others.)

In his public statements in Germany, Courtois declared that European leftists have been responsible for "manipulating" the German public into having a permanent "guilty conscience" for Nazi crimes—which conveniently has taken the focus off of communism's still greater crimes. That view elaborates on his more general contention that the Left-dominated academic intelligentsia has orchestrated a "cover-up" of communism's evils. As he writes in the introduction to the *Black Book:*

> One cannot help noticing the strong contrast between the study of Nazi and Communist crimes. . . .
> [S]cholars have neglected the crimes committed by the Communists. . . . Why such a deafening silence from the academic world regarding the Communist catastrophe, which touched the lives of about one-third of humanity on four continents during a period spanning eighty years?[79]

Courtois variously attributes this "cover-up of the criminal aspects of communism" to the romantic glamour of the idea of revolution, the exaggerated esteem accorded "anti-fascism" borne of gratitude toward the Soviet Union for its crucial participation in the Allied victory over Nazism, and the privileged status of the Holocaust as a "unique" historical event.

II

It was this last factor that received most attention in the German reception of the *Black Book.* Peter O. Chotzejitz ridiculed Courtois for attempting to create a "Bolshicaust" that would lead to the "extinction" of the idea of communism and the "apotheosis" of capitalism. Wolfgang Wipperman pronounced that the *Black Book* contributed merely to the "relativization of the Holocaust." Rather than treat the *Black Book* as an occasion for the Left to reevaluate its positions in reunified Germany now that a Social Democratic government was in power for the first time in sixteen years, "the infallible Somehow-Still-Socialists," said Reinhard Mohr, responded "with their traditional schemata of allergic reactions" to a challenging critique. Christian Semler, a former Maoist in the 1970s who had traveled a path similar to Courtois, pronounced a final diagnosis of the German intelligentsia's response to the *Black Book:* "A miserable leftist attempt at self-inoculation."[80]

By and large, the German Left's response thus confirmed Courtois's charges in the book's introduction as to how the "unique" status granted to the Holocaust operates to preclude any comparison of fascism and communism:

> After 1945 the Jewish genocide became a byword for modern barbarism, the epitome of twentieth-century mass terror. After ini-

tially disputing the unique nature of the persecution of the Jews by the Nazis, the communists soon grasped the benefits involved in immortalizing the Holocaust as a way of rekindling anti-fascism on a more systematic basis. . . . More recently, a single-minded focus on the Jewish genocide in an attempt to characterize the Holocaust as a unique atrocity has also prevented an assessment of other episodes of comparable magnitude in the communist world.[81] (23)

In his public comments during his German book tour, Courtois also castigated the prohibition on voicing public criticism of communism, noting that the taboo was especially severe in Germany. My own experience confirms Courtois's claim: silence about communism's crimes is a form of German political correctness, traceable to Holocaust guilt.[82] To criticize the Gulag in Germany can seem to compare it with the Holocaust—and thus to relativize and thereby minimize the latter, whereby a chain of allegedly anti-Semitic implications can be deduced: If the Holocaust is not uniquely horrible and the Gulag is comparably awful (or even worse!)—then the Germans (or even Hitler) are less guilty as a result—and indeed their collective guilt and shame are properly shouldered by other nations too, starting with Stalin's Russia.

The German edition of the *Black Book* does not address how German political correctness figures in a discussion of the comparative historiography of communism and Nazism. But Courtois hit directly on it when he remarked about the Germans to *Die Woche:* "How long do you want to behave as if you're the condemned defendants at Nuremberg?" Referring to Auschwitz, he added: "At some time you have to draw the line and say it's over."[83]

That, of course, is precisely what the code of German political correctness forbids—a code that even the German edition of the *Black Book* does not explicitly violate. That is why I also draw attention to the politically incorrect, German-specific comments by Courtois during his public appearances. For when I suggest that the *Black Book* will eventually influence the next generation of German schoolbooks devoted to modern European history, it is primarily because of its potential to raise the "Auschwitz factor," which is not at all past but still viscerally present in Germany, an oozing, festering, always-open wound in German public life.[84]

Auschwitz obviously occupies a different, much more oppressive and central place in the German national consciousness than it does in France (or elsewhere). Whereas Courtois's criticism of French communism amounted to a declaration of ideological civil war in France (where the French Communist Party had been in the ruling socialist government coalition and remains powerful),[85] the Holocaust is the key sensitive issue in Germany. To "draw the line" on the Holocaust in Germany is the most explosive, politically incorrect topic—usually taken as equivalent to "forgetting the past" and thereby endorsing a resurgence of German national pride or even neo-Nazi activity. Long after reunification, even as it struggles to integrate and rebuild the eastern states, the BDR of the twenty-first century is still battling to overcome the long, seemingly inescapable shadow of Nazi crimes.[86]

III

Are eastern Germans—and western Germans too—ready to deal with the nation's post-war past? The communist state that befell East Germany had much to do with the outcome of World War II, the Holocaust, the Allied occupation, the rise and course of the Cold War, and developments in capitalist West Germany. Perhaps Germans will not be able to confront fully their relationship to communism until some kind of national consensus has been reached about this matrix of events—which inevitably also means reaching consensus about the Nazi past. And so it may be that Germany will have to proceed "layer by layer" in its grief work.[87] As many commentators have noted, the ongoing ferocity of controversy about the Nazi years—and the virtual silence about the DDR—suggests a compensatory relationship, as if the two regions, east and west, were deliberately and strenuously avoiding criticism of the DDR past in order to avoid further exacerbating the ongoing labor pains of German reunification. And all this suggests that resistances on the German scene to a completely honest accounting of communism's crimes and those of the DDR will remain.

The "burden of the past" from Auschwitz still weighs heavily on an elder western German generation—unlike the case with communism. But eastern Germans bear a "double burden" of the past: the weight of both Nazism and Stalinism. Nonetheless, elder western German intellectuals shape the national dialogue, and their preoccupation remains with the Holocaust. So it may be that the Holocaust will only recede from the center of German national life once this generation leaves the high stage of German culture.

And perhaps only then will the legacy of communism win a place in the moral-political landscape of Germany (and elsewhere) sufficient for a full and open discussion of its own history of crimes. For that to happen, as Courtois acknowledges, a "sense of duty to history" must receive priority. "A good historian leaves no stone unturned. No other factors or considerations, be they political, ideological, or personal, should hinder the historian from engaging in the quest for knowledge."[88] Or as Jürgen Habermas has warned: "Historical scholarship degenerates into historical politics as soon as the view of the observing analyst blurs with that of participants hostage to beliefs they hold self-evidently true."[89]

Bearing the Double Burden of History

The last two sections both show the transition that eastern history classrooms have been experiencing and suggest some issues that soon may arise. As we have seen, even in the closing days of the DDR regime in 1989–90, Party historians were still writing tendentious textbook history that enshrined Lenin and defended the history of the USSR and the CPSU. East German historians had not yet renounced the old Party aim to produce impassioned *überzeugte Kommunisten* (committed communists)—instead SED historians aimed to promote a new, more subtle version of "textbook Reds." The tone had changed, but not the target: the formation of "socialist personalities." Today, however, as eastern educators and pupils struggle with and face their checkered history—especially with regard to their double burden of the Nazi and communist pasts—some confrontation with the decades of ideological indoctrination represented by the DDR's history textbooks is ultimately part of that onerous challenge.

And that specifically eastern struggle must also be undertaken in a comparative framework and related to the ongoing western German encounter with the Nazi and post-war legacies—and examined in light of western German textbooks as well. The fact is that the DDR's history textbooks had, already in the 1940s—at least two decades before West German texts unequivocally denounced the Nazi regime—quite properly condemned Hitler and the role of monopoly capitalism in his rise to power. But, to their credit, West German educators eventually did take a self-critical approach to both German and world history, even including most aspects of the Cold War. By contrast, SED historians proceeded to become Party mouthpieces. Today, though DDR history has now itself passed into history, its textbooks remain—and they show how Party historians helped the DDR breed an M-L ideology all its own.

Thus did the educators' relentless campaign proceed: a carefully screened leftist history curriculum joined a thoroughly vetted social studies regimen and a reliably revolutionary literary canon to form the main triad of the DDR curricular offensive. But even that stockpile was not quite enough ideological ammunition for SED educators. As our next chapter evinces, politics had to be integrated into even the most ostensibly non-ideological subjects—not just into letters, but into numbers.

SOCIALIST SCIENCE
Biology, Chemistry, Mathematics

> Our youth must learn to see through the enemy, under whatever masks they seek to distinguish themselves in a decent appearance. . . . Our youth must remain impervious to the influence of our opponents. In this respect all the school subjects have their specific contribution to make.
> —Margot Honecker, Address to the Seventh Pedagogical Congress, 5 May 1970

Science: Western versus Eastern

The humanities and social sciences were indeed the main fields whereby the SED directly promoted M-L. But—not surprisingly, given the educational campaigns we've already described—the hard sciences and even mathematics were also integrated into the ideological core curriculum.

Unlike the case with humanistic subjects such as history and German literature, however, the physical sciences were not subjected to fine alterations in ideological calibration according to a changing Party line. Nonetheless, DDR educators did hold that the sciences, physical as well as social, were indeed determined by the dialectical laws of M-L. And there was a competition with the West as to which version of science—Western or communist—reflected more accurately the laws of nature. Whereas "natural science" was proudly held by Western scientists to operate according to a marketplace of ideas, whereby meritocratic ideals prevailed, à la capitalism, dialectical materialism held that basic and applied science adhered to the laws of "scientific socialism." A further major difference between the two conceptions, however, prevailed: Western science more closely followed the traditional scientific method, whereas the theory—if not the practice—of "socialist science" readily sacrificed scientific principles to

Marxist ideology. (Scientists from the former DDR did, however, tell me that Marxist theory meant very little to them once they entered the laboratory or sat down to write up their experimental results. If theory conflicted with practice, they claimed, a gesture toward dialectical materialism might appear as a rhetorical flourish in a scientific paper, but M-L played no role whatsoever in the actual analysis and interpretation of their data.)

Still, DDR educators were careful to adhere to a Party line when it came to writing textbooks and communicating the Marxist understanding of "scientific socialism" to East German schoolchildren. "Socialist science" was clearly formulated to reflect and support the communist worldview—even though the "natural" sciences by no means always conformed in their experimental results to the ideological tenets of M-L. In effect, natural science was conceived to uphold social science, above all the dogmas of Marxism-Leninism, even though such a "dialectical" relationship necessarily entailed numerous omissions as well as distortions of the facts.

All this was especially evident when it came to applied science. Such topics as environmental science and its relation to DDR economic performance goals, or the hygienic sciences and socialist morality, or the presentation of the atom bomb—let alone the use of SED leaders' names for naming the state chemistry factories—is evidence that "socialist science" was the servant of the state.

To Western ears, all this sounds rather odd, if not outrageously misconceived. To Westerners, "nature" is less socialist than Darwinist: it tends toward "survival of the fittest," that is, toward capitalist values. To SED theorists, however, "nature" was socialist because it reflects the laws of scientific socialism, and whatever did not reflect the laws of M-L was branded "unscientific," as we shall see.

This chapter opens with a presentation of the two most important school subjects of DDR "socialist science": biology and chemistry.

Biology

The most important subject in the DDR science curriculum was biology, which began in fifth grade. DDR biology was not just the study of living matter in its diverse forms, or a survey of the origin, growth, and reproduction of plant and animal life. For "the human being is not only a biological, but also a social essence," as one EOS textbook put it.[1] Or, as the fifth-grade teaching guide for biology specifies:

Along with other subjects, biology class has its own specific *contribution to the socialist education* of pupils to make. In our socialist school, education is essentially directed to the formation of the will and feeling—in the service of a scientific *Weltanschauung*—of conscious political-moral behavior from the standpoint of the working class, and of an optimistic attitude toward life. If it is relevant to life, oriented toward the subject matter and the realities beyond, based on exact observation and investigation, and founded on independent interpretation and pursuit of problems—as well as on applying what is learned in praxis—a scientific biology class offers numerous *sources for developing a worldview*. The *weltanschauliche Erziehung* of the pupil is above all directed toward an understanding of the world.[2]

It should be emphasized that most pages in biology (and other science) textbooks themselves are not overtly marked by ideology, at least not after the late 1960s, by which time Lysenkoism had long been discredited in the USSR; less than a quarter of the units in biology textbooks of the 1970s and 1980s have any M-L dimension.[3] Still, the teaching guides evince that the "M-L *Weltanschauung*" was meant to serve as the pedagogical framework.

Bio-Politics?

Teachers were told that "biological events" based on such "scientific principles" as materialism, causality, determinism, and prediction mirrored the "events" of the social world, as demonstrated by scientific socialism. And the biology curriculum makes clear that biological science is to serve scientific socialism, not the other way around. "The social relations of human beings among one another reveal new laws, which are objectively available and apply specially to human society: the socioeconomic laws discovered by Karl Marx. The position of the human being in nature is therefore only properly defined when results from the natural and social sciences are based on historical and dialectical materialism."[4]

The DDR approach to biology is thus founded upon M-L philosophy. Natural science is not only about life forms and processes observable in Nature, but also about empirical evidence testifying to the truth of Marxism-Leninism. The first pedagogical priority, which is the development of the M-L worldview, is to see how the laws of Nature and the laws of History and Society mirror each other, as the fifth-grade teaching guide notes:

> A biology curriculum based on the principles of dialectical materialism furnishes the pupil the way to the fundamentals of the Marxist-Leninist *Weltanschauung*. It is not the task of biology class at this level [fifth grade], however, to employ or prove philosophical categories. Rather, the biology teacher must, through generalizing about a number of concrete biological facts about plants and mammals, develop understanding for the complicated and contradictory—but lawful—processes of living nature, so that, at the appropriate age, observations about a [socialist] worldview can be derived.[5]

Passages such as this one make clear that, although DDR science teachers were less often Party members and clearly had more teaching *Freiraum* than did those in more overtly ideological subjects (e.g., *Staatsbürgerkunde*), official SED guidelines for the science curriculum were also strongly influenced by political considerations. Class time devoted to the "philosophical" aspects of biology increased in sixth and seventh grades, when teachers were directed to draw connections with the "laws" introduced in history and geography class.[6] However, because the fundamentals of such considerations did not substantially change over the decades, most science texts—in contrast to the other DDR subjects we have examined—also did not alter much over the years. Ironically, whereas changes in the Party line necessitated periodic adjustments of texts in a subject such as history or even German, this was not the case in biology; conversely, whereas scientific advances in the West typically render science textbooks outdated after just a few years, some DDR texts, which were more driven by ideology than science, remained in use for two decades or more.

The second and third pedagogical priorities in biology were socialist morality and "aesthetic" education. The latter had nothing to do with Schiller's ideas or other Romantic notions;[7] DDR biology class was to contribute to "an optimistic attitude toward life." Pupils should feel the "joy" of living beings. (Even if they "thought that turtles, snakes, and mice were disgusting," according to the teaching guide, pupils' attitudes should change in biology class "in a positive direction.") Similarly, "political-moral education" entailed developing in pupils the following attitudes and habits:

1. Joy in the care for and observation of plants and animals.
2. Respect for living animals and plants.

3. Love for life forms in the immediate *Heimat.*
4. Support and striving for the protection of Nature and the preservation of the environment.
5. Heeding simple rules of hygiene.
6. Respect for order in the workplace.
7. Respect for treatment of tools and materials in the biological laboratory.[8]

The "political" aspect of biology, given the "scientific" character of the subject, should also undermine religious belief, according to the teaching guide. With its respect for "objective data" and development of "exact biological perceptions and convictions," biology class will "destroy any residual element of superstition" in pupils. The teacher is instructed to emphasize the materialist basis of natural science, so that biology directly contributes to atheistic education, which otherwise was inculcated in history, literature, and *Staatsbürgerkunde* class: "The pupil must learn to understand that Nature functions through its own inner forces, and that the development, regulation, order, and structure of material facts are immanent in the living materials themselves; there are no other [nonmaterial] forces at work."[9]

Upper-grade POS biology class pursued these topics further: eighth-grade biology stressed ecology, especially the relationship between nature and socialist morality; the ninth-grade and EOS curriculum laid emphasis on personal hygiene and "social hygiene" (community health, population control, etc.). Once again, these topics do not dominate the textbooks. They are granted only a few pages; but they are conspicuous and their importance is underscored in the teaching guides.

The presence of such topics also makes clear that the themes of *Heimatkunde* were continued not only in geography, *Staatsbürgerkunde,* and history, but also in biology class. As in *Heimatkunde,* biology classes devoted to ecology units dealt with more than relations between organisms and their environment; unlike in *Heimatkunde,* where the focus was on the "socialist homeland," the stress in biology class was on labor and technology: i.e., the value of environmental awareness for industrial gains.

Biologie 8 devotes entire units to topics such as "Nature Protection in the DDR" or "The Influence of Humans on the Habitat of Our *Heimat*" (what Western scientists would term our "ecological niche," our position within the environment). Although SED educators were unwilling to admit that the DDR's industrial policies were destroying its forests and polluting its air and water, these units in *Biologie 8* suggest some recognition of the environmental havoc that the DDR's "economic miracle" was wreaking. They are written in a slightly more reflective tone than the self-congratulatory geography units on the scientific-technical revolution that we examined in Chapter 2—even if they, too, assert that the ultimate goal of environmental awareness is greater economic productivity.

> We see everywhere today attacks by humans on the cultural landscape, which is the living room [within the natural landscape] that humans have created [for themselves]. But the economy of every location is dependent on its natural condition. Within such limits, the capacities for the development and preservation of the location largely define the human economy. Humans can, through careful measures, not only maintain the location in its natural productive power, but also essentially improve it. On the other hand, humans can, through one-sided, excessive claims and misuse, exhaust [the environment] and worsen it into a worthless swampland. This is why knowledge of the relationships and interactions in nature are of economic and cultural necessity.[10]

Such an approach remained far removed from trends toward *biophilia,* Gaia theory, and other radical, organicist topics being broached in Western environmental education. SED biology classes stressed the human—indeed the industrial and economic—advantages of environmental education. *Biologie 8* notes that the maintenance of a favorable biological balance in nature is the "precondition for a healthy, productive environment, in which the fruitfulness of the land and its acreage return can be raised. That is why nature protection is so important." Pupils studied the basic provisions of the 1954 Environmental Protection Law, which, according to the textbook summary, was designed not to "protect Nature *from* human beings, but *for* human beings."[11]

EXCURSUS: Social, a.k.a. Socialist, Hygiene

In ninth-grade and EOS biology class, separate units focus on human beings themselves, rather than on the natural environment. Here the stress is—as in the case of the DDR's environmental laws—on socialist policies that preserve and enhance human dignity, such as special DDR legislation for pregnant women and working mothers. Socialist success in population policy and longevity is also noted (though the text does not mention that longevity was up to six years *less* for DDR citizens than for West Germans).

Nor does the text mention that the longevity of the average Russian citizen was even shorter than for East Germans. Fears about overpopulation are ascribed to capitalist "theories":

> Population increases and a raising of living standards can go together if the proper social conditions prevail, as the socialist countries have proven. . . . The Soviet Union is a highly developed industrial state without economic crises or unemployment, which refutes the unscientific neo-Malthusian theories that talk about the danger of overpopulating the earth. [These theories] lead capitalists to proclaim the necessity of decimating the world's population through wars and hindering the reproduction of the lower classes and "inferior" races.[12]

Nor were the units on child health and development immune to biopolitics:

> A sudden change in inherited factors leads almost always to a disturbance in development and therefore—when the fetus is able to live at all—to deformations. . . . So it is in Japan that—as a consequence of the atomic bombings—many children of women from the cities of Hiroshima and Nagasaki are deformed.
>
> The demands of the Soviet Union and all socialist countries for an immediate stop to all atom bomb experiments and the banning of the production, storage, and application of atomic energy of all kinds is therefore one of the most humane demands in human history. It is not only strongly supported by the population of the socialist countries, but also by responsible persons throughout the whole world. Its realization will not only protect people from death or long illness, but also combat the increasing appearance of deformations in children and protect the health of succeeding generations.[13]

The preservation of human health is also studied in units on hygiene, where practices conducive to health are placed in a socialist context. Cleanliness is approached from a labor perspective and praised as important for "bodily and mental work." Because of socialist conditions, "labor hygiene" is easily maintained in the DDR. "Working conditions weren't always so favorable as they now are here," the text notes. "Only under socialist conditions is care taken that all work-saving machines and devices are introduced insofar as possible. . . . In modern socialist firms there are also sanitation rooms and special relaxation lounges for women [*Frauenruheräume*]."¹⁴ Similarly, waste and drinking water issues are handled well under "comradely agricultural production," in the "socialist village," and in the "socialist factory." "New institutions ease work for the comrade woman farmer, such as [state] nurseries, common washing facilities, and bathing areas that are gathered together in a village house."¹⁵

All this is in sharp contrast to the non-progressive conditions prevailing in earlier ages and in the non-socialist world. The ninth-grade text gives an overview of hygienic practices across various cultures and eras, noting that hygienic practices have "almost exclusively served the ruling classes and the ruling class order." The text explains that "superstitions" explained illnesses for centuries, but "the more that Nature was explored, the stronger science pushed back false, superstitious conceptions [as the explanations for] illnesses." Nevertheless, superstitious ideas persist, because "the inhabitants of capitalist countries are offered many 'wonder remedies' from unscrupulous business people who seek to deceive sick people." Fortunately, the socialist world is free of such hucksterism: "People's Own Firms deliver to us today a number of valuable health products. [But] as great as the importance of scientific knowledge may be, it is also the case, as in other areas, that the most important thing about hygiene is that humans apply their knowledge for their own welfare. In the socialist countries—for instance, in our Workers' and Peasants' State—maintaining the health of the population receives great attention."¹⁶

In units on "social hygiene," biology teachers went beyond issues of personal health to the general health of the DDR population and the influence of the environment on public health. Here too, a doctrinal M-L purity—an orthodoxy that might be termed "ideological hygenics"—governed SED educators' thinking. Pupils learned that the "hygienic sciences" are especially outstanding in socialist society because, under socialism, science is conducted according to the material and cultural needs of the entire society, not those of a privileged elite.¹⁷

EOS biology, which included attention to human anatomy and the theory of evolution,¹⁸ also dealt with hygiene. It discussed the history and sub-fields of the subject in detail ("hygienic air," "the hygienic water supply," "food hygiene," "labor hygiene") and included thumbnail sketches of important hygienists such as Max von Pettenkofer. Not a word appears about DDR deficiencies in these areas. Instead, as an example of "unclean air," an excerpt from an article in the *Berliner Zeitung* on London smog is presented. Additionally, the unit on food hygiene notes that the DDR has a special law designed to speed the process of passing new laws based on path-breaking scientific discoveries.[19]

One interesting claim in the EOS biology text is that the DDR preserves the importance of hygiene as a scientific field because the subject is centrally concerned with "social conditions." (The same claim, however, could perhaps be advanced for the Nazis' notorious "racial hygiene.") Hygiene in pre-war Germany became "an appendage of microbiology," the eleventh-grade text maintains, because "German imperialism was more interested in the liquidation of diseases than in the problems of the environment, [adequate] clothing, housing, work, etc."[20]

Chemistry

An even more reliable Leninist "transmission belt" than biology for the M-L *Weltanschauung* was chemistry. Thus ideology also pervaded DDR study of the applications of natural laws and processes involving organic and inorganic chemistry. Long before the advent of the scientific-technical revolution of the 1960s, SED educators had "revolutionized" the scientific and technical subjects—even the physical sciences.

Our discussion in this section will be limited to POS-EOS chemistry. Before we turn to the study of chemistry, it bears noting here that DDR physics also contributed to the M-L metaphysics. DDR physics was far more than a science of matter and energy expressed in terms of motions and forces. When DDR physics pupils grappled with hypotheses and theories and their applications, they learned the concept of the dialectic; when they studied the atom, they learned about materialism and atheism; when they worked on electricity and mechanics, they learned the relation between abstract theory and practical results (in the form of DDR production increases and the success of the Soviet space industry).[21]

Chemical Reactions, Progressive Results

So chemistry, which was introduced in eighth grade, became not just a science dealing with the properties, reactions, and elementary forms of matter, but a history and sociology of DDR industries related to chemistry. Next to units on the structure of the alkaline molecule, polycondensation, and the attributes of chemical catalysts, one finds units on pig iron and steel, coal processing, glass, oil and natural gas, plastic, and artificial fiber-making.

Indeed, both DDR organic and inorganic chemistry texts devoted dozens of pages to the successes of these industries, including tables showing the important factories in each industry, such as the Karl Marx Sodium Plant, the Walter Ulbricht Coal Processing Plant, the Unity Glassworks, the Wilhelm Pieck Chemical Fibers Plant, the Clara Zetkin Silk Factory, the Otto Buchwitz Textile Factory, and the May 8, 1945, Gem Processing Plant. Discussion of pure chemistry slides regularly into such topics as DDR state planning, the fruitful relationship between the DDR and the Soviet oil and gas industry, and the profitability of DDR chloride products. (Another little-known DDR "first" was trumpeted in the textbooks: The DDR ranked first in the export of chloride products, including potassium chloride and magnesium chloride.)[22]

Excursus: "Organic" Chemistry, or the Law of M-L

As might be expected, these emphases reflected SED educators' view that chemistry, too, had its contribution to make to the M-L *Weltanschauung*. For instance, the reaction in molecular chemistry stood as a model of dialectical determinism; the atom was a miniature model of the world. To take the atom as a starting point for reflection supported a materialist *Weltanschauung* governed by the precepts of M-L. Change is materially conditioned and Life is lawful, i.e., the same laws that govern physical life apply to social life—and vice versa. And these were the laws of Marxism-Leninism, which was the only philosophical system having both a materialist basis and a unity of theory and praxis. As one chemistry teaching guide noted:

> The teacher should constantly proceed from the principle of the unity of science, partisanship, and Life, so that he contributes effectively to the education of the pupils to become socialist personalities. Political-ideological, philosophical, and economic problems are to be addressed whenever they arise in the textbook units. [These units] also contain a collection of the most significant aspects of polytechnical education and acculturation, along with suggestions for the perfection of the polytechnical orientation of the pupils.[23]

As an example of the relation between physical science and social life—of the unity of theory and praxis under socialism—the teaching guide added:

> Treatment of the physiological effects of ethanol should contribute toward developing the capacity to respect and heed the norms of cooperative social life in socialist society. . . . The example of the chemical reaction between carbon monoxide and hydrogen into methanol should explain the unity of parts and their interactions. The perception should be deepened of the general validity of the theory of the chemical reaction in both organic and inorganic chemistry. . . . Pupils should appreciate that the application of theory brings practical results. . . . In connection with explanations about the further development of the chemical industry in the DDR, socialist economic integration should be explored.[24]

Chemistry class also furnished an opportunity to bolster anti-imperialist convictions and develop socialist morality:

> Observations about the misuse of phenol and diethyl oxide under imperialism [for poison gases and explosives during World Wars I and II] give the chemistry pupil examples whereby to examine the inhuman character of that social order. Through these examples, the connection will be underlined between the use of scientific knowledge and the [character of the] social order. . . .
> Chemistry also contributes [to a socialist *Weltanschauung* and socialist morality] insofar as it promotes pupils' recognition of the essence of socialist patriotism and internationalism (e.g., cooperation among RGW members on petrochemical trade), of international solidarity (on uses of phenol and diethyl oxide), and social norms of behavior (conclusions about the consequences of alcohol misuse).[25]

In eighth-grade inorganic chemistry, chapters are devoted to carbon, silicon, iron and steel, phosphates, and electrolysis. But the first sentence of the eighth-grade inorganic textbook yields insight into the approach taken to these topics: "Our Republic is a big socialist construction site." Above the sentence is portrayed a series of cement silos. The next page features, amid a technical discussion of graphite, a discussion of the VEB electrochemical factories in Berlin-Lichtenberg and Bitterfeld.

A detailed chapter in eighth-grade inorganic chemistry, dealing with the steel industry, gives the impression that even the physical sciences were meant to perform in the upper grades some of the functions of *Heimatkunde*. A map of the DDR appears, complete with locations of major iron deposits, steel factories, iron ore foundries, and rolling mills. The chapter opens with the modest production figures of 1946, discusses the success of the DDR's first Five-Year Plan in boosting productivity, and even mentions a heroic Soviet steel worker à la Alexei Stahkanov.

> Since 1948 steel production has been significantly raised. A productive exchange of experiences between the steel-melting workers of the Soviet Union and the DDR took place.
> Following the model of the steel-melting worker AMOSSOV, the speedy steel-melting movement began in our Republic's steel mills.[26]

Meanwhile, a chapter on the DDR nitrogen industry, which features the Walter Ulbricht Nitrogen Plant at Merseburg, is the occasion for a short history of German monopoly capitalism and worker heroism. A brief summary of this chapter gives the flavor of DDR "socialist science" at its most overtly political. In this unit, ostensibly on nitrogen production, the political events connected with the Walter Ulbricht plant receive prime attention. The plant served the munitions industry during World War I, but in 1917 the workers organized a mass strike in order to halt the "criminal war." They also organized strikes to protest the failure of the November 1918 revolution, and they fought against government police who sought to occupy the plant in 1921. "After days of battling, the heroic fighters were overcome. Their war of defense belongs to the most glorious deeds of the German workers' movement." During the Third Reich, the plant was again "misused for war production" by IG Farben. More than 80 percent of the plant was destroyed during the war; occupied by Soviet troops in 1945, it was up and running "in the shortest time." The plant was returned to East German hands in 1954, and hundreds of fighting groups at the plant "today protect it against attacks from enemies of our Workers' and Peasants' State."[27] A photo of a marching militia of workers illustrates the text. Significantly, the text does not mention that the "enemies" may be within: the plant's workers were among those who participated most enthusiastically in the June 1953 uprising against the DDR regime.

Of Applied Science and Agitprop

Apart from such agitprop interwoven into practically every chapter in the chemistry textbooks—to a far higher degree than in the biology textbooks—one notices here that DDR "socialist science" meant applied science. However much the DDR promoted the "scientific-technical" revolution, its textbooks are noteworthy for their emphasis on the second word in that pair—on *technical* applications. Hard science is indeed discussed at length, but always with an eye toward technological applications and the DDR's industrial achievements. With the exception of repeated assertions about Lenin's theory of reality—whereby "true" scientific abstractions "reflect" Nature and have a corresponding relation to social life—the chemistry texts seldom discuss M-L theory or the M-L *Weltanschauung*. A representative exception is the treatment in ninth-grade inorganic chemistry of the work of Dmitri Mendeleev (1834–1907), who developed the periodic law of elements. This law states that the properties of elements are periodic functions of their atomic numbers; their properties recur periodically when the elements are arranged in order of their atomic weights.

The DDR textbook mentions aspects of the law, but its emphasis is on Mendeleev's "recognition of the necessity to connect theory and praxis." We are informed that Mendeleev was no mere theoretician; he was also concerned with air travel and air balloons. Thus Mendeleev is a great dialectician, a forerunner of the great Soviet scientists of the twentieth century. He was "insufficiently respected during the era of the Czars" and "provoked mistrust from the regime" because he campaigned for progressive school reform. The unit on Mendeleev concludes: "Only after the triumph of the Great October Revolution were Mendeleev's great achievements properly honored in his *Heimat*."[28]

Such discussions of dialectical "laws" are normally reserved for the teaching guides. The EOS texts, however, are often adorned with various pronouncements from the fathers of "scientific socialism." Indeed, as in the case of the history textbooks, it is startling to see respectful quotations of Lenin and Engels in twelfth-grade chemistry units on the atom. The reader encounters Lenin's "dialectical law" ("Development is the struggle of opposites"), and finds his view about the independent existence of atoms from the human brain (from his *Materialism and Empirico-Criticism*) enshrined as the last word on the primacy of material reality. Then a letter from Engels on social "need" as the motor for scientific advances, followed by a biographical summary of Lavoisier, which features Engels's praise for the Frenchman's refutation of the theory of phlogiston.[29]

But such explicit intrusions of socialist "science" occur no more than four or five times apiece in most DDR science textbooks. Rather, attention is chiefly given to DDR industry. This emphasis prevailed both in the upper POS and EOS grades. In organic chemistry, pupils learned not just about carbon compounds but also about the history of the coal-processing industry: e.g., that by 1964, DDR output doubled that of Nazi Germany in 1936. (Another world first: The DDR was first in the export of brown coal, fulfilling 35 percent of global demand.) These proclamations in the ninth-grade text are accompanied by a list of the nine leading coal factories in the DDR, complete with large drawings of their insignias. A similar chart appears in the chapters on the plastic and artificial fibers industries, followed by chapter questions such as "Name the most important plants in our People's Own Plastic Industry!"[30]

The special USSR-DDR relationship in industry—a model of socialist economic integration—is exemplified by cooperative efforts in the oil and natural gas industries. As the text explains: "The development of the oil processing chemistry industry would only have been possible, however, with the help of the Soviet Union. Oil and gas production could be raised through improved Soviet means of exploitation of the appearance and tapping of new sites. . . . That is why the *Friendship Oil Pipeline,* which is several thousand kilometers long, was laid from Soviet oil regions into our Republic."[31] The achievements of socialist economic integration can be used not only to deepen solidarity among socialist *Bruderländer,* but also to sharpen antipathy toward imperialists. A teaching guide notes that the unit on oil and natural gas

> should strengthen pupils' convictions about the essential advantage of cooperation among the socialist states belonging to the Council of Mutual Economic Assistance [RGW]. Historical and current examples about the misuse of chemistry by imperialistic states should be shown to pupils. In this connection, one should discuss the moral responsibility of the scientist for the results of his research. And that should lead the pupil to recognize the humanistic character of the socialist social order, where scientific research is exclusively employed for the benefit of Humanity.

Needless to say, such research "exclusively employed for the benefit of Humanity" as the steroid experiments on DDR Olympic candidates (conducted at leading DDR research institutes) goes unmentioned in the text.

Succeeding chapters in a textbook for ninth and tenth grades note that the chemical industry is the "most comprehensive" branch of DDR basic industry; a ninth-grade teaching guide praises its "world fame."[32] The textbook for ninth and tenth grades quotes Ulbricht at a 1958 conference of chemists, and it features official SED pronouncements about the importance of promoting "the natural sciences and technology." The DDR's success in the chemical industry is attributed to its "socialist work community," which exemplifies "how science and production can grow ever stronger together and thereby raise worker productivity."[33]

Mathematics

Except for German, mathematics was the only subject taught in all POS and EOS grades. The curriculum ran as follows:

Grades 1–3: arithmetic
Grades 4–7: arithmetic, geometry, and algebra
Grades 8–9: geometry and algebra
Grades 10–12: geometry, calculus, advanced mathematics

Although a relatively small number of units in DDR mathematics textbooks bear direct ideological traces—as in the case of biology—SED educators did exploit "M-L math" to strengthen solidarity with the working class, promote socialist patriotism and internationalism, and deepen hatred of Western imperialism and militarism. And it is these ideological uses that concern us here.

The Simple Arithmetic of Progressivism

The typical method of fostering "socialist personalities" through M-L math was via workbook problems, which sometimes functioned as subliminal indoctrination. Alongside exercises on magnitude, on the relations between figures and forms, and on quantities expressed symbolically, there would suddenly appear a multiplication problem on DDR brown coal exports, a decimal problem on Soviet space records, a geometry problem on the potato yield from a Czech collective farm, or an algebra problem on American arms expenditures. As in the case of the German grammar and spelling examples discussed in Chapter 1, a sampler of such math problems furnishes insight into the ideological convictions that SED educators felt most important to inculcate at different ages.

Consider, for instance, the following second-grade problems. Pupils are asked to compute something more than just whole numbers; the problems introduce Pioneer or work-related topics relevant to school field trips and to the child's immediate experience. The pair of exercises below concerns a trip to a model factory site shortly before the DDR's national holiday, Worker's Day:

1. Multiplication with the number 9:
   a. In the days before May 1, the best pupils of the school visited workers in their factories. At the factory entrance, they were divided into groups of 9. How many pupils formed 5 groups?
   b. Every group was introduced by members of the brigade sponsor. 2 groups visited the factory carpentry room. 3 groups went to workers in the foundry. How many guests did the workers in the factory carpentry room and foundry have?[34]

The math problems in fourth through seventh grade cover a wider ideological territory, including DDR industry and world socialism vs. imperialism. Here are several questions from the fourth-grade text:

1. Workers in the DDR water industry presented 10 water pumps, valued at MDN 40,000, to the Democratic Republic of Vietnam [North Vietnam], so that the irrigation lines destroyed by U.S. bombers could be repaired.*
   What was the total value of this gift?
2. At a solidarity meeting, three apprentices gave 1.35 M in October. In November, each of them gave 65 Pf more than in October. In December, each of them gave 10 Pf less than in November.
   How much did the three apprentices give in November all together?
3. The number of residents in a city in the Soviet Union was 2,150,000. It rose by 200,000.
   How big is the population total of this city?
4. An NVA jet fighter flew 18 km in 1 minute.
   How far would it travel in a half-hour flight?
5. A supersonic plane of the NVA flew 25 km in 1 minute.
   How far would it travel in 15 minutes?
6. A tractor driver harvests potatoes. In a shift he harvested 6.09 hectares and needed 5.9 liters of fuel. The projected production norm is 5.85 hectares and 6.3 liters per shift.
   a. What percent of the acreage of his norm did the Traktorist fulfill?
   b. How many liters of fuel did the tractor driver save with an acreage completion of 6.09?[35]

*MDN = *Mark der Deutschen Notenbank*, the official name for DDR currency from August 1964 through December 1967.

The fourth-grade teaching guide for math expressly notes that "especially good possibilities are available" to select textbook problems that demonstrate "the great success of our socialist reconstruction.... It is, therefore, an essential task of the teacher, both in the [selection of] material and in his presentation, *to actualize with full effectiveness its potential for socialist education.*"[36]

The middle-grade math texts offer numerous examples of this "potential," what might be thought of as "progressivist arithmetic" or "the higher math, DDR-style." A pattern is not hard to detect here:

1. In 1950, the DDR had a total of 75,000 cars. After 10 years, the number had quadrupled. In 1970, the total was already above one million cars. In comparison with 1960, the number of cars had increased by 1,500,000!
   Calculate the number of cars [in 1970]!
2. In 1960, the DDR had 500,000 mopeds. After 10 years, this number had tripled. In 1974, there were 2 million mopeds. In comparison with 1970, the number by 1975 was up 600,000.
   Calculate the number [for 1975]!
3. The production of whole milk rose 500,000 tons between 1960 and 1975. In 1960, it was 1,000,000 tons.
   Calculate the production of whole milk for 1975!
4. The time required to produce electrical ovens has been reduced $1/6$ since 1955. How long does it take to make ovens that had required 552 hours in 1955?
5. By means of a new experiment, a brigade of People's Own Firms raised its performance of cable production threefold. It had been 780 meters.
   a. How many meters more of cable were produced?
   b. How many meters of cable did the brigade produce altogether?[37]
6. The oil processing factory at Schwedt delivered 300,000 filled-up wagons. Each wagon is 10 meters long.
   How long would the line be, if one placed these wagons next to one another?[38]
7. An LPG [*Landwirtschaftliche Produktionsgenossenschaft*, agricultural cooperative] raised its acreage results in rye from 2,200 tons to 2,500 tons through better cultivation of the ground, good fertilizer, and timely pruning. In the previous year, 74 hectares were harvested; this year it is 81 hectares.
   How many tons more were harvested?[39]

8. A factory raises its production annually by 8 percent. How high is the production increase at the end of 1970 compared with the beginning of 1965?[40]

Some arithmetic problems seem designed to accompany a well-known FDJ song of the 1950s and 1960s: "My Friend: The Plan," which rhapsodized about how the Five-Year Plan was a child's comrade who was changing DDR life for the better. Consider, for instance, these problems:

1. The fulfillment of the three-month plan plus an over-fulfillment of the plan resulted in a production total of 15,000 bicycle covers in these three months.
   How many covers were produced in one month?
2. The fulfillment of the six-month plan plus an over-fulfillment of the plan by 30,000 bicycle pumps resulted in a production of 270,000 pumps in these six months.
   How many pumps were produced in one month?
3. A factory delivered 18,000 tons of cement per month over five months. The half-year plan expects 100,000 tons.
   How many tons of cement are still to be delivered to fulfill the plan?
4. A factory delivered 15,000 tons of industrial limestone monthly. The half-year plan demands 80,000 tons of limestone.
   How many tons of limestone are still to be delivered to fulfill the plan?[41]

Whatever else may be said about such exercises, there is a noticeable dearth of problems illustrating production losses or the under-fulfillment of DDR norms.

The fourth-grade teaching guide offers special exercises to supplement the textbook problems. These themes also exemplify the guide's concern with realizing M-L math's "potential for socialist education." As in the case of the grammar exercises in POS German class, military themes are especially popular.

1. Three classes of a grade are competing in the donation drive "Help for Vietnam." Class 4A collected 33.75 M. By collecting old clothes, Class 4B reached four times the total amount of Class 4A. Class 4C only collected 1/3 the amount of Class 4A.
   a. How many more marks did Class 4A donate than Class 4C?
   b. How many marks did the three classes together donate?

2. An NVA unit conducts a practice march. It leaves its barracks at 06.00 and heads back at 13.30. The average tempo of the soldiers was 5 km per hour.
   How long is the length of the march on a map designed with a ratio of 1:100,000, if one considers that a half-hour break was taken during the march?
3. The LPGs "Peace," "Unity," and "Solidarity" agree to become a larger cooperative. The LPG "Peace" possesses 684 acres of land, the LPG "Unity" has half as much, and the LPG "Solidarity" has three times as much as the LPG "Peace."
   Calculate how many total acres of land the newly founded cooperative possesses![42]

EXCURSUS: Army Algebra for Ninth-Graders

Upper-grade POS and EOS math was linked to *Wehrerziehung*, the defense education class that included rifle practice and grenade-throwing, which began in the ninth grade and was closely coordinated with math classes in linear and non-linear algebra. Upper-grade math textbooks contain a higher percentage of ideologically oriented problems—and more prominently displayed, often with illustrations—on topics central to the scientific-technical revolution such as computers, electronics, or electrical energy.[43] Most conspicuous is the increased appearance of NVA soldiers, missiles, warships, and tanks in math problems. All of these changes aimed "to prove once again that the socialist social order is superior to the capitalist."[44] This problem on the 1988 *Abitur* exam for mathematics—which doubtless would have given Euclid pause—is exemplary:

> At a practice session of the missile unit of the National People's Army, a flying object at Point P (-6, 9, 7) is pinpointed. It is cruising at a constant speed of S_1. Twenty seconds later it is identified at Point Q (2, 1, 11).
> At Point A, a defensive missile rocket is launched in the direction of the vector $a = i + 2j + 5k$. The cruising speed S_2 of this rocket is straight. The defensive missile meets the flying object at Point S.
> *Calculate the average speed of the rocket if its launch at A followed 2 seconds after its pinpointing at Point Q.*

Mathematik 9 offers a variety of other examples of such M-L math. Indeed, this textbook is a stunning reading experience for the Western reader. Bannered on the front cover of the 1979 edition is Lenin's celebrated quotation—often cited in DDR textbooks—that abstract science leads one "not further from the truth, but nearer to it. . . . [A]ll scientific abstractions reflect Nature more deeply, more truly, more completely."

The placement and content of this quotation suggest how important SED educators regarded math's potential contribution to the Marxist-Leninist *Weltanschauung*. Perhaps the decision was made—in the wake of the introduction of *Wehrerziehung* into DDR schools in the fall of 1978—to feature the Lenin quote even more prominently than in previous editions. (The 1967 edition of *Mathematik 9* used the same quotation as its epigraph, placed on the inside cover of the front page. The text added the obvious: "These thoughts of Lenin also apply to the highest levels of abstraction—to the formal speech of mathematics.")

Mathematik 9 is often startling in its abrupt shift from standard algebra formulae to M-L exercises in "Politics and Numbers." Repeatedly, after a series of polynomials with complex coefficients, or between routine problems on sets and vectors, comes an exercise such as "Calculate the flight path of six NVA rockets."

Consider, for instance, the following passages that introduce chapters in *Mathematik 9*. The first passage leads off a unit titled "Quadratic Functions and Quadratic Equations," which is illustrated by three NVA jet bombers:

> The socialist camp is equipped with the best defensive weapons. These modern fighter bombers of the NVA can fly with the speed of supersonic planes. A higher altitude and more energy are therefore required. . . . One can calculate the movement of a body with the help of the equation
>
> $$W = (m/2)(v/2)$$
>
> The kinetic energy of a body grows with constant mass at an exponential speed. This physical law is an example of a quadratic function.[45]

A second unit, titled "Powers and Functions," begins with a photograph of a platoon of NVA soldiers firing tank shells. Above it appear the words: "After they are fired, shells move in a ballistic curve whose width and height depend on the trajectory of the firing, among other things. If air resistance doesn't influence the flight, the path will be a parabola. The pictures of special exponential functions are, therefore, parabolas. Paths of firings can, with the help of mathematical functions, be measured and the site of firing also calculated."[46] A third unit, titled "Exponential Functions and Logarithms," portrays a Soviet nuclear ship. The text reads:

> The first nuclear-powered ice breaker, the *Lenin*, entered into service in 1960 and belongs to the Soviet ice fleet. The nuclear material, Uranium 235, decays in the reactor of the icebreaker and releases warm energy. The decay of a radioactive element occurs according to the following law of decay:
>
> $$n = f(t) = n(e/2)$$

As happened in earlier grades with arithmetic and geometry, *Mathematik 9* also contains military-oriented problems for solution:

1. A tank of the National People's Army traveled a distance of 230 km. In its original fuel tank it still had 40 liters of fuel. If the fuel consumption per 100 km was reduced by 15 liters, this tank would have a mobile radius of 270 km.
   How large is the capacity of the fuel storage tank? How much fuel is consumed in a distance of 100 km?
2. A transport column of National People's Army vehicles received the command to reach, at top speed, a point 120 km away. By raising their speed 10 km per hour, they reached the stated point 1 hour earlier than they would have by the original speed.
   How much time did the column take to reach the stated goal, if one presumes that their advance remained constant?[47]

Party Figures, or the Higher Calculus of M-L

"How much time . . . ?" That last question was indeed the computation that should have been on SED educators' minds by the late 1980s, and it also represents a sardonic reminder that SED ideologists miscalculated the most crucial "applied math" equation of all: the problem of reckoning their own immediate future.

And that reminder stands as a fitting note on which to close Part 1. As historical hindsight now makes clear, the policies of SED leaders would soon run out of time to reach their stated goals—and would instead delegitimize the DDR itself.

Nonetheless, the "socialist schools" of the DDR left their ideological imprint upon millions of citizens. Its demise notwithstanding, they survive today.

Let us turn now to these "voices behind the pages" of the DDR textbooks—and hear them in their own distinctive registers and inflections. To do so enables us to discern the continuities and discontinuities of citizens' outlooks from the DDR past to the post-communist present—and thereby to comprehend better the ways in which vestiges of a "textbook mentality" persist in the minds of many eastern Germans.

JOHANNES R. BECHER

Der Staat

Ein Staat, geboren aus des Volkes Not,
und von dem Volk zu seinem Schutz gegründet –
Ein Staat, der mit dem Geiste sich verbündet
und ist des Volkes bestes Aufgebot –

Ein Staat, gestaltend sich zu einer Macht,
die Frieden will und Frieden kann erzwingen –
Ein Staat, auf aller Wohlergehn bedacht
und Raum für jeden, Großes zu vollbringen –

Ein solcher Staat ist höchster Ehre wert,
und mit dem Herzen stimmt das Volk dafür,
denn solch ein Staat dient ihm mit Rat und Tat –

Ein Staat, der so geliebt ist und geehrt,
ist unser Staat, und dieser Staat sind Wir:
Ein Reich des Menschen und ein Menschen-Staat.

Poems such as "Der Staat" ("The State") formed a significant part of the elementary school German literature textbook, as in the case of *Unser Lesebuch* for seventh grade. The last two stanzas read as follows:

"Such a state warrants the highest honor,
and the People vote for it with their hearts,
for such a state serves them in word and deed –

This state so beloved and honored
is our state, and we are this state:
an empire of human beings and a human state."

The poem was composed by the erstwhile German expressionist Johannes R. Becher, who was the DDR's most prominent state poet and served as its Minister of Culture during the 1950s.

Ernst Thälmann, the head of the Communist Party in Germany during the late 1920s and 1930s, was the crown figure in the SED cult of personality throughout the existence of the DDR. Here Thälmann speaks to Berlin supporters during the early 1930s. The leading German communist for two decades, Thälmann's arrest by the Gestapo in March 1943, imprisonment by the Nazis, and execution in Buchenwald in August 1944 transformed him into a permanent martyr of German communism in the DDR. (Photo courtesy of Deutsches Historisches Museum Berlin)

President Wilhelm Pieck (seated in center) is surrounded by Young Pioneers in their blue neckerchiefs during a visit to a Pioneer summer camp, circa 1953. The SED cultivated the image of Pieck as a grandfatherly statesman beloved of children, referring to him as the "Father of the Nation." (Photo courtesy of Deutsches Historisches Museum Berlin)

Literature textbooks stressed that, in Brecht's phrase, "Reading is class struggle!" Such a summons was often illustrated by an inspirational photo from a socialist youth rally or an image of studious pupils that testified to the DDR's claim to be "the Land of Reading." Here FDJ Blueshirts "carry forward" the great heritage of Marxism-Leninism. Pictured in their wagon are outsized tomes by the socialist trinity that prevailed in the communist world after de-Stalinization occurred in the late 1950s: Marx, Engels, and Lenin.

Above the books is a globe in which a portion of the land mass is depicted in red and attached to a red wreath. The globe is balanced on an axis pole that reads: "Marxism is all-powerful because it is true," which is a statement often attributed to Lenin. In the background is a banner that reads: "Our achievements will lead to the happiness of German youth." This parade occurred during the German Rally in Berlin on May 16–18, 1964. (Photo courtesy of Deutsches Historisches Museum Berlin)

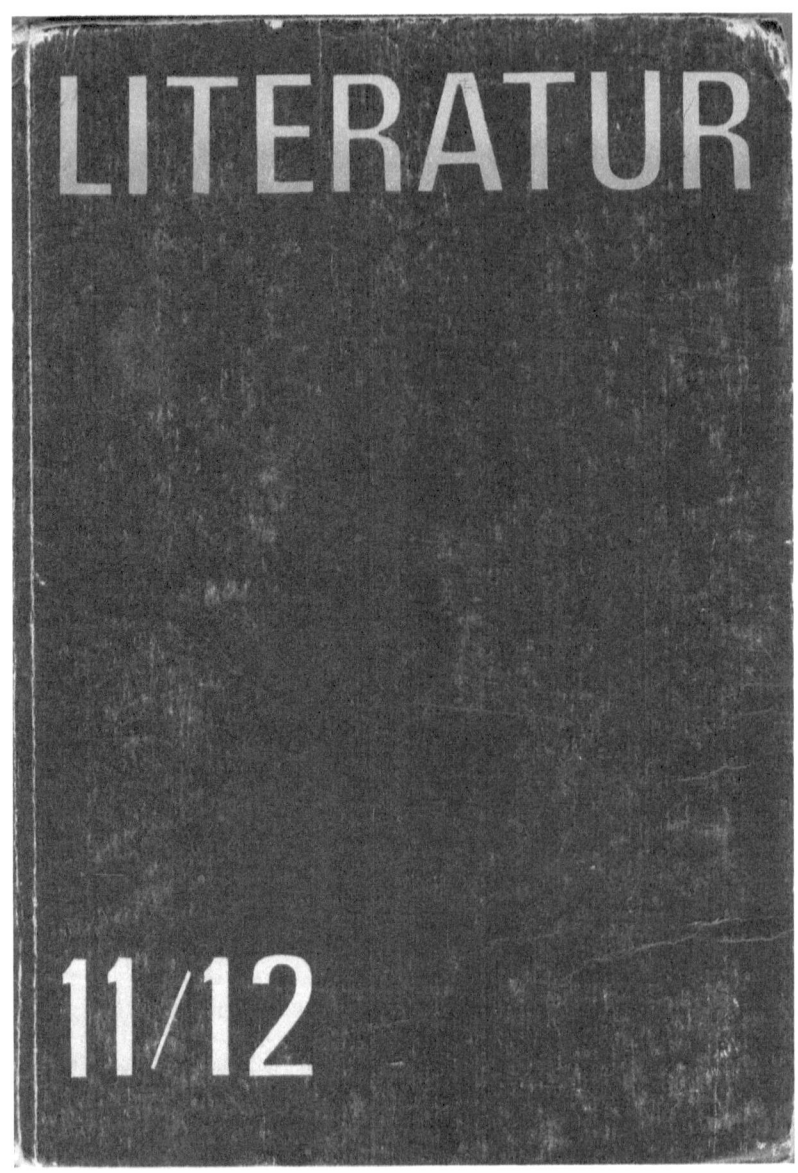

The German literature course for the advanced high school of the DDR, known as the EOS, covered nineteeth- and twentieth-century literature "from the beginnings of the workers' movement to the Great Socialist October Revolution." Special attention was given to "literature of socialist realism as a contributor to socialist society." This allowed the inclusion of such works as Wilhelm Pieck's 1946 Party speech on culture, a Mayakovsky interview conducted with "Comrade Lenin," and agitprop verse from Party poets such as Kuba, Boris Sluzki, Gunther Deicke, and many others.

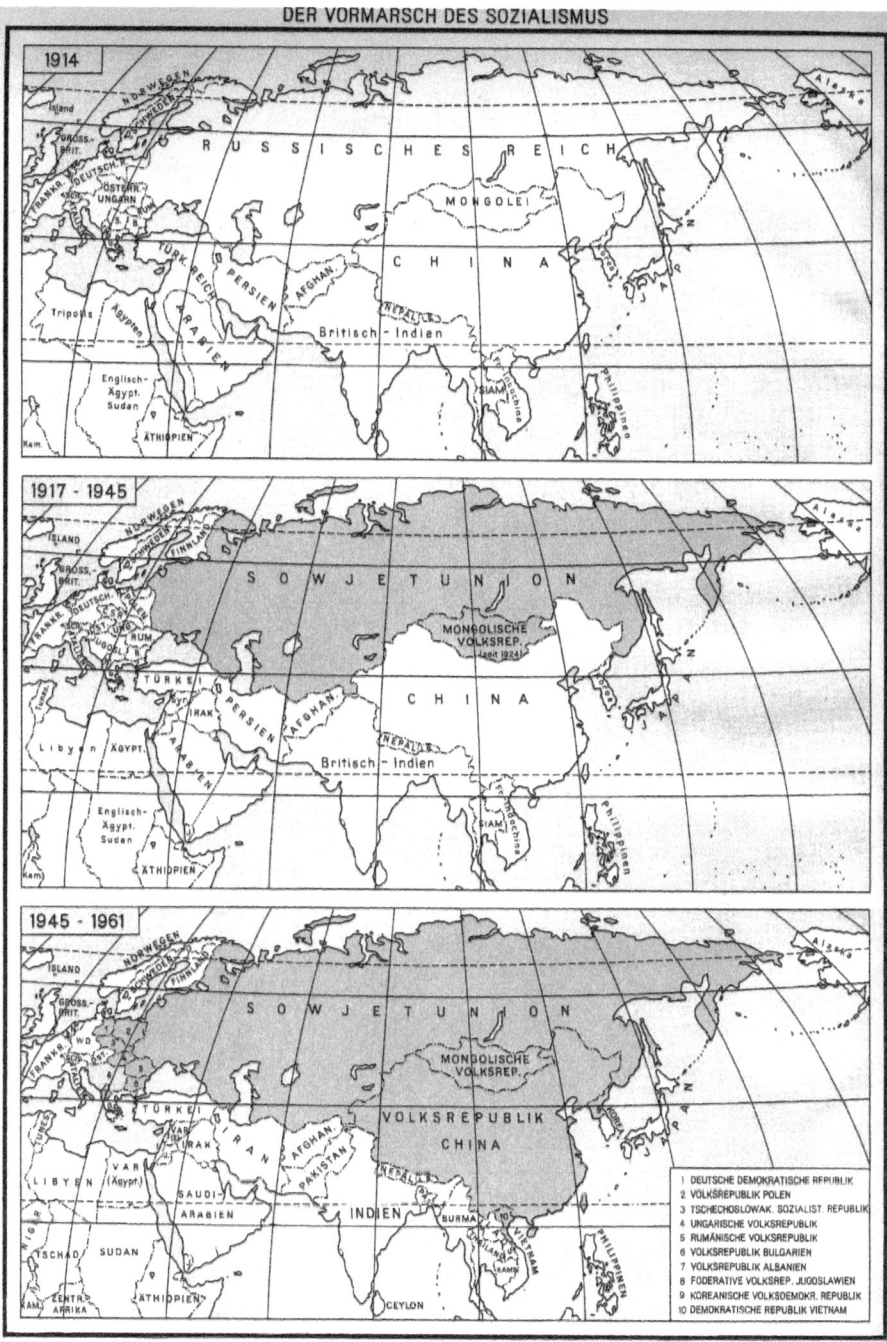

Geography pupils of the 1960s through the 1980s studied from this atlas, which was used in all elementary grades in the DDR. First published in 1962, it shows the widening influence of communism in the early postwar era. The caption above the 1914 map (at top) reads: "The Advance of Socialism." The connotations of the military term *Vormarsch* make the idea of a "Cold War" between East and West explicit.

The teaching of history in DDR schools began in the fifth grade. *Geschichte 5* covered antiquity and devoted special attention to "the formation of slave society." The introduction to *Geschichte 5* makes clear that an important purpose of historical study is to show the rise of socialism. The opening paragraphs read: "Only through the long and arduous struggle of the working class could the DDR be formed. . . . In fifth through tenth grades . . . you will learn why working people often have not possessed what they themselves created, and how their exploiters achieved riches.

"Above all, we will investigate and answer this question: How has it happened that human society from its beginnings until today has constantly progressed, and why has this development already led to socialism in many lands and will ultimately lead to it in all countries?"

In *Geschichte 8*, which deals with the period between the revolutions of 1848 and World War I, a full chapter (among only eight chapters in the entire book) is devoted to the Paris Commune. It is hailed as "the first proletarian revolution in world history, a first attempt of the working class to wrest political power from the hands of the bourgeoisie."

The opening page of chapter seven in *Geschichte 8*, which deals with "The Great Socialist October Revolution," includes a well-known cartoon from the 1920s. It depicts Lenin bestriding the globe as he sweeps away feudal royalty and wealthy capitalists alike. The caption reads: "Comrade Lenin cleanses the earth of exploiters."

This cartoon from a chapter in *Geschichte 10* is titled: "U.S. imperialism's plans for world conquest and the USSR's battle to establish a peaceful postwar order." The frames' triadic sequence portrays the shrinking power of Western capitalism. The cartoon's caption reads: "World capitalism before the First World War . . . after the Great Socialist October Revolution . . . and after the World War II." Uncle Sam is depicted in a top hat and shown losing more than half his global weight by 1949, after the establishment of communist rule that February in the most populous nation on earth, the People's Republic of China.

A unit of *Geschichte 10* titled "The Founding of the SED and Its Historical Significance" shows an illustration of the famous handshake between the leaders of the Communist Party and the Social Democratic Party in the Soviet zone of occupation in February 1946. Underneath the handshake are a frustrated yet impotent Konrad Adenauer (in top hat) and western German socialist leader Ernst Schumacher, both of whom protest lamely as the eastern German newspaper *Tagesspiegel* proclaims the news: "You'll not divide these hands again, for we are creating THE SOCIALIST UNITY PARTY."

Karikatur von Alfred Beier-Red aus der Zeit der Gründung der SED

Geschichte 10 also reproduces a placard devoted to launching the GDR's Two-Year Plan in 1949–50. A happy worker is contrasted with a bored, lazy, bourgeois drone slouching behind him. The caption reads: "1949: Forward with Equality! Produce More—Live Better!"

Das Wunder der Wiederherstellung (Herluf Bidstrup)

A unit in *Geschichte 10* on "the construction of the monopolistic ruling relations in the leading imperialist countries" shows a cartoon whose caption reads: "The miracle of recovery." The cartoon shows how the Russian army disposed of the Nazis, only to have capitalist America and Britain sneakily refurbish West Germany with American dollars in the form of Marshall Plan aid, whereupon re-nazified West Germany becomes a powerful country capable of issuing orders to the rest of the West.

The history of the SED was a focal point of the EOS (advanced high school) curriculum in history, with eleventh-grade history devoted exclusively to Party history. This scene portrays the Third Party Conference of the SED, which took place on July 20–24, 1950, in Berlin. After proclaiming the "early fulfillment" of the Two-Year Plan, SED leaders announced the definitive introduction of economic planning modeled on the planned economy of the Soviet Union in the form of a DDR Five-Year Plan. This SED conference underscored the primacy of communist leadership within the SED, which was reflected in the insistence of Party leaders on abolishing free elections and shifting to a single candidate list. The four leading heroes of the Stalin-era SED are pictured in radiant splendor presiding loftily over events from the rear of the auditorium: Marx, Engels, Lenin, and Stalin. By the early 1960s, Stalin was no longer included in the Party pantheon and his image (and even the very mention of his name) vanished from DDR school textbooks. (Photo courtesy of Deutsches Historisches Museum Berlin)

This photo from a regional conference of SED delegates convening in Eberswalde (11 June 1950) reflects well the DDR cult of personality during the early postwar era, before Stalin's death. It portrays a typical scene. Enshrined behind the speaker's podium is a portrait of Joseph Stalin. On the far right side is an equally large portrait of Lenin, both of which make clear that the SED at mid-century is under strict tutelage in its adherence to Soviet-style Marxism-Leninism. The German leaders of the SED are relegated to positions of lesser prominence: DDR President Wilhelm Pieck to Stalin's right and Prime Minister Otto Grotewohl to Lenin's left.

In the center of the stage is an outsized medallion bearing the full name of the SED (Socialist Unity Party of Germany), which appears in white lettering around the famous SED trademark, the brotherly handshake that occurred on that fabled day of March 21, 1946, when the Communist Pieck and the Social Democrat Grotewohl shook hands in the Admiralspalast in East Berlin, dramatizing their mutual willingness to unify their parties and form the SED. The unity handshake also appears on the podium. By 1950, however, the "unity" handshake had become a death grip that crushed the Social Democratic Party in the DDR, as the "Sovietization" of the Party (reflected in the dominance of the portraits of Lenin and Stalin) evinces. Below the stage level is a portrait of Karl Marx. Noticeably absent is Marx's colleague Friedrich Engels, who along with Marx had been enshrined in a prominent position in SED meetings just a few years earlier.

Above the portraits is a statement reflecting the Leninist turn in the SED: "Through the party of the new type, we create the best conditions for the triumph of the National Front of Democratic Germany and for a lasting peace in Europe." This phrase of Lenin — "party of the new type" — also signaled the new Bolshevik emphasis at mid-century: the SED would become a Marxist-Leninist vanguard party, rather than a "socialist unity" party committed to democratic socialism and a politically diverse membership. (Photo courtesy of Deutsches Historisches Museum Berlin)

DDR schoolchildren aspiring to be "model comrades" joined affiliate organizations of the Young Pioneers such as the Timur Helpers, who ran errands for retirees in their neighborhoods and assisted them with household chores. They upheld the twelve Pioneer Laws ("#1. Young Pioneers respect people. #2. Young Pioneers show respect for other nations...."). The name "Timur Helpers" was inspired by the Soviet bestseller, A. Garzin's *Timur and his Troop*. Young Pioneers listened with rapt attention for hours to the adventures of Bolshevik boy scouts such as Timur, a heroic young Russian communist who exerted himself in the service of others. (Photo courtesy of Deutsches Historisches Museum Berlin)

A unit in *Staatsbürgerkunde 8* addresses "the duty to protect and defend the Socialist Fatherland." This accompanying photo depicts a Russian and an East German soldier working together as comrades. The caption reads: "Brotherhood in arms. Friendly visits in the 'Regiment Next Door' program are part of everyday life for our soldiers, because you understand the other better when you have mastered the language of your friend."

The latter comment was, of course, designed to justify the required school subjects of *Wehrerziehung* (defense education), introduced in 1978 into the upper grades, and Russian, which was extremely unpopular among DDR pupils and continued to be compulsory even throughout the university years.

Staatsbürgerkunde 8 exalted the DDR worker. This unit in chapter 1 was entitled: "The Leading Role of the Working Class in Socialist Society." The illustration depicts a miner who has received the Hero of Labor award for the outstanding performance of exceeding his work norm.

This drawing from *Staatsbürgerkunde 8* depicts an unemployment office in West Germany, outside of which are thousands of job seekers who are frustrated, angry, and impoverished. The caption reads: "Work? —That's not a human right."

The images of Marx and Engels introduce Part One of *Staatsbürgerkunde 9*, which is entitled "The Laws Governing the Social Development Toward Socialism: The Communist Manifesto." Below the images of the fathers of communism is their famous cry from that book: "Workers of the world, unite!"

This cartoon from *Staatsbürgerkunde 9* shows the capitalist West dominating both the communist and Third World (frame 1) until the communist rises up against the capitalist (frame 2), and the Third World also then rebels, at which point the imperialist powers fall (frame 3) — and the world belongs to the communists and the developing nations. The caption reads: "The Modern Era."

This cartoon in *Staatsbürgerkunde 9* portrays racial discrimination against minorities and their poverty in the U.S. in the 1960s. The caption reads: "Would you like to fly to the moon, Joe?" The starving companion answers: "Why? Is there work there?"

The evolution of class relations under capitalism only increases the gap between the rich and poor, contends this cartoon in *Staatsbürgerkunde 9*. The four frames show the movement from colonialism to mercantilism to imperialism to the advanced capitalism of the 1970s, in each stage of which the rich only get richer. The captions reads: "Capitalist Development."

This caricature from *Staatsbürgerkunde 9* shows a miserly Uncle Sam launching the Alliance for Progress. The program claims to provide aid to developing nations, but in actuality makes the Third World more dependent on Uncle Sam and only increases his wealth. The caption reads "The 'generous' Uncle Sam."

The following illustration from *Staatsbürgerkunde 9* for Bertolt Brecht's "Song of the Class Enemy" is a lithograph by Fritz Cremer, made in 1965. The image exemplifies the thrust of the DDR program *Erziehung zum Hass* (education for hatred), as it depicts a worker who is enflamed with righteous class hatred. The caption includes a stanza from Brecht's "Song of the Class Enemy": "What I also keep on learning / which is always an open-and-shut equation: / I have never had anything in common /with the interests of my class enemy."

Superior athletic achievement was held by DDR educators to reflect the superiority of the socialist state. SED leaders promoted competitive sports vigorously. This photo shows (from left to right) FDJ chief Erich Honecker, Wilhelm Pieck, and Rosa Thälmann applauding the performances of Young Pioneer athletes atop a victory stand in Dresden, 1954.

By the mid-1970s, after its Olympic successes, the DDR was known internationally as a *Sportwunder* (athletic miracle). The DDR's successes were no accident. Nursery school teachers scouted for talent over a three-year period; by school age, the coaches were ready to step in, with some schools sponsoring Spartakiads, or socialist mini-Olympiads, for children as young as five. "In the spirit of Socialism, Peace, and Friendship and for the honor of the German Democratic Republic and the Glory of Sport" ran the Spartakiad oath that the children recited before competitions. Top-performing second- and third-graders eligible for the DDR's special sports schools received extensive ten-day batteries of tests from doctors, psychiatrists, and coaches, including computer measurements of their physical abilities ranging from endurance to lung capacity, after which experts assigned children to sports programs based on their physical aptitudes, regardless of the child's preferences. Parents had to sign releases that granted the state complete charge of their children, whom they were allowed to visit twice a month. In exchange for this waiver, parents received special state favors, such as bigger apartments and increased salaries. (Photo courtesy of Deutsches Historisches Museum Berlin)

Most DDR higher education students belonged to the Free German Youth (FDJ). Many FDJ meetings were devoted to the study of the works of Marx, Engels, Lenin, and other Party-sanctioned authors and documents. The pennant on the wall depicts the FDJ emblem: "sunrise in the east," topped by the FDJ logo, all of which symbolized that DDR youth represented the great future of socialism and the East German state.

A 1969 demonstration outside Humboldt University drew 300,000 East Berlin students and residents. The banner reads: "Enough Crimes by the American Barbarians in Vietnam! Long Live the War of Liberation of the Vietnamese People!"

Staatsbürgerkunde 10 devoted special attention to socialist morality, including a chapter titled: "The foundations of the socialist worldview and morality." Separate units were devoted to "socialist patriotism," "the development of personality and the socialist collective," and "the class basis of socialist morality."

DDR chemistry textbooks highlighted activities of the chemical industry, especially in relation to DDR polytechnical education. This flag was presented by the District Commission of Greater Berlin to the state chemical factory of the city for the best work in political education in the Children's Vacation Campaign of 1969. The pennant reads: "For best political education work in the Children's Vacation Campaign." (Photo courtesy of Deutsches Historisches Museum Berlin)

THE VOICES BEHIND THE PAGE

Conversations about Post-Communist Education and
Eastern German Life with Faculty and Students

SIX

ARTS AND HUMANITIES

How much do the contents of textbooks actually influence peoples' identities? That question is impossible to answer precisely. What is clear is that the social beliefs of the DDR are still alive today amongst eastern Germans. And included in those beliefs—usually in complex form and function—are the lessons learned from DDR textbooks. But it is one thing to claim generally that aspects of the ideological content of the textbooks live on, and it is quite another to analyze how and why.

The portraits and interviews in Part 2 attempt something much more modest: to invite reflection on such matters by depicting eastern Germans' troubles with finding their way into the new westernized society and building a new social/cultural identity. Part 2 also features several interviews with western Germans (sometimes referred to as Wessis, especially during the early 1990s). These conversations provide yet another point of view on eastern German education, namely, the perspective of both transplanted Wessis residing in the east (known as Wossis) and of western Germans commuting to work there.

1. "History Lessons" for Would-Be Revolutionaries

In 1999, I am interviewing teachers and students in eastern Germany to ascertain whether and how the "textbook mentality" of DDR schooling endures in the minds and hearts of its erstwhile pupils. Renate, thirty-five, has brought her old DDR history textbooks and teaching guides to our interview. She taught history and civics for five years (1986–90) in a Leipzig POS. When the Wall fell, she decided to leave teaching. She has made a new life for herself as a travel agent specializing in *Studienreise* (educational tours) to eastern Europe. But the decision to launch her new career has nothing to do, she says, with anxiety about her activities as a DDR teacher. She believes that she would have passed the *Überprüfung* (audit, screening). "I was in the Party," she says, "but I had no official position in the school and never had anything to do with the Stasi."

Renate says that she hasn't thought much about her teaching years since reunification. But she finds herself in a "didactic mood" with me, the curious American. She proposes to "begin at the beginning," with *Geschichte 5*.

"Even to fifth-graders studying prehistoric and ancient civilizations, the priority of contemporary socialist history was made explicit," Renate says. She turns to the introduction in *Geschichte 5*, which closes with the observation:

> There are many important events in history, and we must know when—on what date—they occurred.
> Every student knows:
> 1949 was the founding of the German Democratic Republic.
> 1945 was the end of the Second World War and liberation of the German *Volk* from fascism.
> 1917 was the Great Socialist October Revolution.

Renate points out how "cleverly" the textbook study questions "smuggle" ideology into even the basics of historiography. For instance, she notes, to elucidate the reckoning of historical chronology and concepts such as *v.u.Z.* and "century," the editors of the 1982 edition of *Geschichte 5* repeatedly ask questions such as: "In which century did the revolt of Spartacus take place?" "How many years ago did the revolt of Spartacus begin?" "How many years before the revolt of Spartacus did Hammurabi reign?"

Renate notes that the Spartacus revolt was considered the exemplary model by DDR historians for all ideological claims involving the major historical revolutions that followed, including the French Revolution and the Bolshevik Revolution, because it symbolized uncompromising resistance to powerful exploiters—regardless of whether or not victory was possible. The concept of "revolution from below" was a key one for DDR historians. "Revolution" meant resistance and defiance of unjust oppressors, and all underclass revolutions shared that feature. Renate illustrates her point by flipping to her teaching guide for *Geschichte 7*, which advises that the French Revolution should teach readiness to fight for the goals of revolution and the liberty of the Fatherland. More recent events from history also provide examples of such behavior, such as the Soviet *Volk's* battle against the fascists and Vietnam's battle against the U.S. invaders (p. 226).

The teaching guide for the 1983 edition of *Geschichte 7* also stresses the contemporary lessons that the latter two events offer. Teachers are advised to write on the chalkboard about the former:

> What feeling do you have after hearing all these cruelties that the population had to suffer?
> [Answer:] Sympathy with the tortured people; hatred toward the guilty and the beneficiaries of this war of plunder and conquest. (p. 124)

All "revolutions" were part of the East German "inheritance," Renate says. Just as in the case of Spartacus, they possessed ongoing value and relevance to the present—and taught pertinent lessons.

But most of the "lessons" were drawn from the twentieth century: DDR history classes focused on the recent past, Renate says.

She pulls out the 1986 edition of *Geschichte 9*. "Even German events that occurred decades before World War II and the DDR's founding were interpreted in a way that could 'lead up' to the DDR's birth," Renate says. "Every historical event contained a lesson."

She points out that some chapters in *Geschichte 9* even close by spelling out the "lessons" under headings such as "The Lessons of the November Revolution." For example, she directs my attention to the passage in *Geschichte 9* that we discussed in Chapter 4: the five "lessons" for pupils to draw from the November Revolution of 1918–19.

Geschichte 9 also includes a section titled "The Lessons of World War II." Among the chief lessons—which make no mention of the Nazi-Soviet pact, the total unpreparedness of the USSR to wage war in 1941, or the positive contributions of the Western Allies—are the following:

1. Only the *closed front of workers of all nations can turn jingoist forces from their course of war*.... On the eve of the Second World War, only the USSR, the most advanced section of the working class, and their allied forces in the capitalist countries prepared for the danger of war.[1]
2. German fascist imperialism embodied the historical survival of a dying capitalism, which had been condemned to death, in its most reactionary, barbaric form.... The *defeat* of German imperialism was *unavoidable*.

3. The most important factor in the defeat of Hitlerite Germany was the heroic battle of the *Volk* of the USSR.
4. After the triumph over fascism and its allies, the *balance of power* in the world altered *in favor of peace and socialism.* (p. 78)

The ninth grade teaching guide is especially passionate about the Nazi invasion of the USSR. Teachers are to "establish the connection between the heroic battle of the peoples of the USSR and the related superiority of the socialist social order.... *Pedagogical emphases:* Honoring of the heroic defensive war of the Soviet people. Solidarity with them. Condemnation of the criminal attack on the Soviet Union."

As we discussed in Chapter 4, *Geschichte 9* closes with study questions that leave little room for questioning. Recall, for instance, this assignment: "Explain why the signing of a Non-Aggression Pact with Hitler's Germany was, for the Soviet Union at that time, necessary and correct!"

Renate and I laugh at the ubiquitous exclamation marks that trumpet the study questions' messages. She refers to the practice as "DDR punctuation." "Writers in the DDR textbook collectives were not subtle," she remarks. But Renate is quick to assure me that secondary school texts used in West German history courses during the Cold War had their own shortcomings. Until the 1970s, pupils in history classes were rarely taken beyond World War I. (Although this is certainly no longer the case today, it apparently continued—in at least a few select instances—until the late 1980s in CDU-governed [*Christlich-Demokratische Union,* Christian Democratic Union] *Länder.*)

Here again, Renate is quoting from the actual text that she used in class—the third edition (1986) of *Geschichte 9*. She notes archly that the text was virtually unchanged from its first edition (1970), which had been issued when she was a schoolgirl—and that this was generally the case with DDR textbooks of the 1970s and 1980s. Once aligned with the "laws" of dialectical materialism, says Renate, the "lessons of progressive history" were apparently unchanging and irreversible. "Until," she adds, "October 1989," when the East German *Volk* embraced the example of Spartacus as their own.

2. Pedagogy of the Distressed: A German Teacher's Self-Criticism

"It's easier for you in the West," she says. "You've been educated to think critically. I haven't. And it's still a great difficulty for me."

I am speaking in October 1994 with Frau Bärbel Hintze, a German teacher at the Schiller Gymnasium in Weimar, formerly the Schiller EOS, one of the elite communist secondary schools in the DDR. We have just left her twelfth-grade double period class on Brecht's *Life of Galileo*. I have been asking her whether she taught *Galileo* any differently during the DDR era. No, she says. *Galileo* expresses Brecht's views as a socialist, anti-fascist, and critic of religious dogma. I suggest that the play also offers an opportunity to criticize the communist dogmas of the DDR regime, which never tolerated any freethinking Galileos.

Frau Hintze, fifty-three, a thin, slight woman with red-tinted hair, and a former Party member herself, nods her head.

"When I teach the *Galileo* again, I'd like to explore that. But that approach feels very unfamiliar—threatening even, though exciting."

I ask why; her answers are various. She was never educated in "critical thinking." Her studies and her continuing education seminars never suggested such an approach. She feared losing her job if she said anything too controversial.

We discuss Brecht's famous line: "Whoever doesn't know the truth is an idiot. But whoever knows it and calls it a lie is a criminal."

Frau Hintze resists my attempt to apply Brecht's line to the DDR.

"We weren't criminals or idiots. Just human beings—with vulnerabilities and weaknesses. Just ordinary people who never lost hope that they could one day improve things." She reminds me that such a faith in ordinariness was precisely one of Brecht's key points. "He was challenging the notion that little people are helpless, and that only the extraordinary people—the heroes—can change things." Frau Hintze pauses. Then she draws the connection. Holding to a faith in ordinariness is precisely "why October 1989 finally arrived."

"But there were many good things long before that," Frau Hintze continues. "In my own life too—for example, the teachers in this school. Many outsiders seem to think that it was just a Red school. That's not so. The former director, it's true, was not a critical thinker. He was loyal to the system and a careerist. He was really an old Stalinist."

But the protest marches of 1989, which led to the fall of the Berlin Wall that November, proved that people like him were the exception, Frau Hintze says.

She repeats the phrase "critical thinking" several times. It seems to be a term of high approbation for her, somehow related to the strongest virtues of "Western" speech: a bold questioning of hierarchy and of received answers, a searching inventory of one's responsibilities in the face of unjust authority, a healthy scrutiny of oneself.

"I had no open debate in my studies, only M-L. We were fed teachers' opinions and the verdicts of authorities. I learned to cite authorities—a Party document, a state official, a Marxist touchstone—as proof and defense of all positions. And so I never really took seriously any *oppositional* viewpoint. An opposing view wasn't an occasion for thinking about my own viewpoint. It was 'incorrect.' It was just 'oppositional,' and an energetic standard response would neutralize its power.

"Only one opinion on a topic reigned in the DDR," Frau Hintze says. "And I didn't take into account other opinions. Not really. There were never any other opinions to take seriously into account.

"Everything was walled in—quite literally. You've heard the phrase? It's true: The Wall was in our heads.

"And one doesn't unlearn all this quickly. At least not at my age! Until you spoke in class, I never thought about non-Marxist ways of teaching Brecht—even though, I grant you, it's been five years since the *Wende*. I could give lip service to the statement, 'There are a variety of interpretations possible,' but I never really conceived of any serious opinion outside the Marxist *Weltanschauung*.

"You have to understand all this historically," Frau Hintze continues. She is a "product of the DDR." During and after her studies at the Dresden College of Pedagogy (1960–64), she says, she never encountered anyone who thought "critically."

"Even after Prague [the Soviet and DDR invasion of Czechoslovakia in 1968], I never met a critical thinker. I never learned how to do that, I never encountered anybody who was doing it. We were directed in our course of studies in college to think a certain way. And I learned that particular way of thinking. This is probably very hard for you to understand, because it is just as natural for you to think critically as it was for me to think dialectically."

What about the younger, post-reunification generation?

"The pupils here still aren't being educated to think critically," Frau Hintze says. "Because their teachers don't know how to do it. And because 'thinking' is very hard to do at all in the midst of the confusion and turmoil and upheaval of this transition from the DDR to the BRD. Too many teachers still teach ideologically: they begin with the ready-made answer. And they emphasize rote textbook learning, rather than foster independence of mind and the awareness of diverse viewpoints. The kids go by others' cues and escape into distractions and sloganeering, rather than do the hard work of 'thinking'—whether 'critically' or 'dialectically.'

"And they still feel self-constrained and are biased against critical thinking, which really starts with what the Party called 'self-criticism.' But 'self-criticism' for us was really an apologia to the Party for individualistic excesses."

Self-criticism, says Frau Hintze, was what one hoped to avoid: it was a public act of repentance for one's hubris or disloyalty—an acknowledgment of having been a bad Marxist. She continues: "The idea of your western self-criticism—that one includes oneself in all criticism, or even begins with oneself and one's own side—is very unfamiliar and threatening to us.

"I didn't see any role models. Christa Wolf and [Anna] Seghers [the DDR's leading literary women in the Party] remained silent about most injustices [in the DDR]," she explains. Such silence was considered a sign of "loyalty to the Party."

In the early 1980s, Frau Hintze continues, just two or three years after she arrived at the Schiller EOS, a stricter syllabus was introduced. That syllabus was a reaction by SED conservatives to the liberalization policies developing in the USSR under Gorbachev. Margot Honecker and SED leaders were sending the Party rank-and-file a clear message that *glasnost* and *perestroika* were not on the agenda for DDR schools.

"I was a new, young teacher at the time," Frau Hintze says. She adds that the Schiller EOS was the only EOS in the area. It had the best-trained faculty; positions at the school were coveted.

"In 1978, I began teaching at this school. In 1985, I joined the Party. It was a pragmatic decision. The Schiller EOS was one of the best schools in the state. It was an important school for producing university candidates, and the director wanted more Party members, above all in my subjects, German and history. The director told us that if there were any transfers, Party members would have the best chance of remaining at the school. So I joined.

"Everybody had been saying for years that an EOS German and history teacher like me should be in the Party. I had a tough time fending off the pressure to join. And teaching history was so hard—especially eleventh grade, which dealt with the worker's movement since 1848, and twelfth grade, which covered the history of the Communist Party since 1945. At times I hated it. That had to do with my family: my parents were skeptical about the Party and the DDR. My father had a position in church administration; before the war, he was a civil servant. When he joined the church and began working for it, he naturally gravitated toward the opposition voices and was constantly among people who were suspected by the regime of activities hostile to the state.

"I was never really a supporter of the regime, but I conformed. I was a careerist like most of my friends and colleagues—we constituted 85 percent of the Party.

"We had absolutely no *Freiraum* in history or German. We could never have taught Brecht in the critical way you've suggested!"

What about events that were contested between East German and West German historians? Did you ever have any doubts about the Party line?

"Strangely enough, no. For instance, the Nazi-Soviet Pact in 1939 was skipped in my studies. And in later years, I don't remember ever discussing it, even once, with a colleague. I never knew about it. And not just that event. When *Sputnik* [Russian newspaper for youth] was banned in 1988, I was shocked. Before *Sputnik*'s revelations about Stalin's crimes, I never knew much about Stalin. When all the news about his regime of terror came out, I couldn't believe it. I never knew about all that. Then *Sputnik* was banned, and I was flabbergasted that a new cover-up was set to occur in the DDR.

"You see, I 'knew' the historical truth about Stalinism—and I didn't know. I had heard various things over the years, but I had never discussed Stalin—he was effectively screened out of my course of studies and the history curriculum of the school. There was a wall around him. I never knew that he murdered millions of people."

Even though you could watch West German television?

"We didn't watch it much until the 1980s. But you're right: I may have heard things about Stalin from West German television. But I had a *Feindbild* [enemy image]—I attributed any negative reports to the Cold War and screened them out. We had Eduard von Schnitzler and *The Black Channel* [a TV program that propagandized for the DDR via critiques of West German events], but Matthias Walden did the same thing for RIAS [*Rundfunk im amerikanischen Sektor*, Radio in the American Sector]. He was a propagandist too.

"I used to smile at Schnitzler—I never really believed him. I had a certain built-in defense mechanism toward him—I was never a Schnitzler true believer.

"Who was telling the truth—Schnitzler or Matthias Walden? I didn't know."

As Frau Hintze speaks, my mind drifts back to Brecht and his famous

1934 essay "Five Difficulties with Writing the Truth": "Whoever wishes to fight against lies and ignorance and write the truth today, has at least five difficulties to overcome. He must have the *courage* to write the truth, even though it is everywhere suppressed; the *intelligence* to recognize it, even though it is everywhere concealed; the *art* to wield it as a weapon; the *judgment* to choose in whose hands it will be effective; and the *cunning* to spread it among them."

"And, as I say, I didn't inquire too deeply into who was telling the truth," she continues. "In the end, I simply assumed that much of what both sides were saying was false, but that our side was less so.

"Yes, that was a blind spot of mine. Pupils would occasionally ask in history class: But did the *Volk* know about the Holocaust? I would say: the Nazi grandparents could have known if they chose to see.

"*Should* they have known? I took a hard line on that: Who wanted to know, did know. But who really *wanted* to know? The very knowledge made you complicit—or put you in great danger. And who would take the risks? For most people, it all depended on the people with whom you were in close contact and whether they were being directly victimized or not.

"Who wanted to know, did know: I always said that about the Nazi years. That's what I believed—and, for the most part, still believe."

Frau Hintze pauses. Her eyes are pools of tears. The unspoken question—or self-accusation?—hovers in the air.

"And what about us?" Frau Hintze finally asks. "Us"—she means citizens of the DDR. She does not imply that the crimes of the Nazis and the communist dictatorship are equivalent. Her question simply exemplifies, she says, Western-style "critical thinking."

"I gathered that there were some 'excesses' of Party zeal [in Stalin's USSR], attributable to the difficult post-revolutionary [post-1917] conditions and, later, the war. I knew that Khrushchev spoke about a 'cult of personality' around Stalin, but I had never participated in that cult, and I didn't think it was anything more than hero-worship. I was a fourteen-year old girl in 1956, very unpolitical. Khrushchev's speech, Poland, Hungary—they all swept by me. In the 1970s and 1980s, I heard the name Solzhenitsyn. But I knew nothing about his work. It simply never filtered down to me."

And if you—as a German and history teacher in an elite school—didn't know any of this, then certainly the general population of the DDR would have had little likelihood of knowing, of developing the informed skepticism of "critical thinkers."

"Right. *Die Mauer im Kopf* [the Wall in the head] prevailed. The Wall was in their heads too."

What about the erection of the Berlin Wall in August 1961? Certainly that event was—and remained—inescapable.

"Yes, but I was studying in Dresden at the time. We were far from Berlin. I never really reacted strongly to the erection of the Wall. The West was already inaccessible to us—you couldn't go there unless you had special reasons. And I never thought of emigrating. I couldn't have taught school in West Germany—DDR teaching credentials weren't recognized there. And though I had been to Cologne and West Berlin a few times in the 1950s, all my relatives were in the DDR. And they were aging and needed me to help care for them. I had a strong *Heimatgefühl* [feeling of home]. The Wall didn't change anything for us—just made us turn further inward.

"In 1988, I read *One Day in the Life of Ivan Denisovich*. Then I read Sholokhov's *New Country Under Way*, which showed how necessary it had been to collectivize agriculture in the 1930s. But no other critically minded socialist authors were accessible to us during the DDR era."

We discuss the exciting Russian literature newly approved for the official Soviet curriculum in the late 1980s, which one of her students experienced during her years at Leipzig University in the early 1990s: Solzhenitsyn, Pasternak, Alexandr Blok. Then she recalls the works by DDR and Soviet authors that were once curricular staples at the Schiller School and are no longer assigned today: Hermann Kant's *The Auditorium*, Anna Seghers' *The Seventh Cross* and *The Duel*, Becher's poetry, Louis Fürnberg's songs and poems, Erwin Strittmatter's fiction, Mayakovsky's verse, Sholokhov's *Fate of a Man*. Some DDR authors are still discussed, if seldom taught, adds Frau Hintze: Christa Wolf, Stefan Heym, Christoph Hein. Almost all of them have now been replaced by Western authors, many of whom were largely untaught (and not even officially published) during most of the DDR era.

"Kafka was only introduced in the late 1970s," Frau Hintze recalls. "We teachers had to wait for the literary scholars to blaze the trail. Only long afterwards would such 'problematic' authors gain admission to the school curricula. That was also because the centralized curriculum required suitable secondary materials, and that took time to develop."

Here again, I am reminded of how integral textbooks were to the rigid, top-down DDR curriculum. If an author did not enter DDR textbooks (which was well-nigh impossible if he or she violated ideological orthodoxies), that author was simply never taught—and thus remained on the edge of ignominy, unknown to DDR pupils and obscure to the DDR populace as a whole.

How about your pedagogical approach? Did you teach the DDR or socialist authors much differently then, as opposed to now?

"Not really," Frau Hintze answers. She looks at me quizzically and repeats what she said at the outset of our conversation: she says that she handles Brecht as she did before the *Wende*.

"I still emphasize his anti-fascism. We don't usually read his more aggressively pro-socialist works anymore, such as the "Solidarity Song" or "Señora Carrar's Rifles."

Frau Hintze falls silent. The digression into literary topics peters out. Then she says in a low monotone devoid of feeling:

"Nobody in the DDR ever mentioned that Stalin murdered twenty or thirty million people."

She pauses.

"But I did know it—vaguely.

"The truth was kept at a distance from us," she continues. "The government kept it from us and didn't cultivate, or even allow, critical thinking."

And so that is the question: In a society like the DDR, how *do* you get to the truth?

The truth is difficult, Frau Hintze acknowledges, and poses difficulties once it is ascertained. Difficult to discern, difficult to express if discerned, difficult to share publicly if capable of expression.

"Take Stalin's mass murder," Frau Hintze says. "We in the DDR simply never thought to ask about it. If you did ask, you would receive only a confused, ambiguous answer anyway. And if you kept on asking: that would be dangerous. You had to be ready to go to jail. You had to be prepared to part forever from your family. You had to be ready to lose your career and your friends."

Frau Hintze looks out the window. Then she turns and faces me.

"You had to be a hero. But I don't mean a 'positive' hero. I just mean a person of extraordinary moral courage."

She is referring to the socialist concept of the model socialist personality, the socially conscious "positive" hero of labor, the champion of working-class solidarity—as opposed to the so-called decadent Western, individualistic negative heroes—or antiheroes—who rebelled against society.

"Well, I was never a hero. I couldn't be a hero. I just didn't have it in me.

"But I had a limit," she continues. "I wouldn't inform. I never did—and never would have—worked for the Stasi. That was a line I wouldn't cross, and I have little sympathy today for those who did."

Her voice is steady. She looks me direct in the face.

"Should I be ashamed that I'm not a hero? Well, I'm not ashamed."

Her voice remains low and even. The statement betrays neither defiance nor defensiveness.

Again and again the exchange between Andrea and Galileo in Brecht's *Galileo* runs through my head: "Pity the land that has no heroes," says Andrea, a pupil of Galileo. "Pity the land that *needs* heroes," Brecht's marxified Galileo corrects him.

Which is it, really?

Frau Hintze continues: "Although I now judge all the lying and deception to have been wrong, I just wasn't strong enough to pursue the truth. In hindsight, I couldn't have done things much differently. I wish that I had developed a mode of critical thinking, but I hadn't."

Only now is she beginning to think "critically" about the communist dogmas of the DDR era, she says. She is confronting the overwhelming task of *Vergangenheitsbewältigung* [coping with the past].

"Havemann and Reiner Kunze—how I can teach them? I haven't yet really confronted them myself.

"But I am ashamed in another sense—not of myself, but rather of the nation that I lived in, a nation that effectively dictated that the only truly decent human beings were those with the courage to be heroes. It was a nation that, by cutting us off from the truth, made cowards of us all."

Do they—do *we*—need heroes?

Perhaps it is my own weaknesses—or only the relative immaturity of the Andrea in me—but I conclude that we all still do. It would be soothing and self-satisfying to think that we do not. But the assumption of Galileo—and Brecht too—that a special few heroes exclude the possibility of heroism for the rest of us, that public heroism elevates those special few at the expense of the vast majority—may be misconceived.

Maybe indeed just the reverse is the case. Might not heroes show us what we're *all* capable of? Such persons might blaze a trail for the rest of us to follow, in whatever way, and help us become heroes in our own right—men and women with the courage to speak truth to power.

As Frau Hintze escorts me to the bus stop, we talk of her career in the Schiller School. She mentions the names of some of the pupils that I met during my last visit—a few of whom are now teachers in the school themselves. As we shake hands, she hands me several textbooks and official teacher guides published in the 1970s and 1980s by the DDR Ministry of Education in East Berlin that she has retrieved from a closet in the teacher's lounge.

"Valuable historical documents," she jokes. "I've saved them from oblivion."

She smiles and pauses. She says that her first name is Bärbel.

Waiting for the bus, I look at the faces of the playing children as they scamper by me.

The old Party slogan of the DDR youth organizations comes to mind: "Who has the youth, has the future."

3. "My Post-Communist Brecht": A Weimar Student's *Weltanschauung*

Interview in October 1996 with Stefan, twenty, a twelfth-grade pupil in the Goethe Gymnasium for the Humanities in Weimar. He expresses his view of Brecht after a German class devoted to Brecht's poetry written in exile. I've told him I'm especially interested in the DDR textbooks and the DDR era. Unlike in the DDR days, Stefan notes, his literature class uses no textbooks; the "textbook" is a selection of Brecht's poetry, prose criticism, and dramas. He remarks that using the primary text allows the class to read Brecht "unfiltered." Stefan's teacher, a western German from Bremen, has just returned Stefan's essay (on Brecht's poem "To Posterity") with a grade of fifteen points, virtually the highest mark one can receive and only rarely granted in German schools.

Q: What was the topic of your class today?

A: Brecht is concerned with exploitation, especially with how powerful people manipulate ideology. In "To Posterity," Brecht doesn't think that life is just meant to be fulfilling or enjoyed; rather, it must be *used*—for constructive social ends. One should organize one's life so that it is as useful as possible for others, too. It shouldn't be wasted on dreams of the future, but lived in the here and now, according to whatever possibilities can be concretely realized. He wants to promote a society as rational as possible, a society that wants to improve on the present.

Q: Do you agree?

A: I find myself drawn not so much to agree or disagree with him as to understand his historical situation. I also see how I am quite literally a descendent and am doing what Brecht talks about as inevitable in the poem, that is, judging my predecessors. I'm faced with exercising judgment on Brecht and the generation of Germans that fought the war or resisted or fled it.

Q: That doesn't sound like "socialist commitment." Would Brecht have approved of such a disengaged stance?

A: No, it isn't—and he wouldn't have. I admire his work. But mine is a post-communist Brecht.

Q: What does that mean?

A: I don't feel forced to judge—as he and his generation did. I feel instead called to understand.

Q: You're a historian rather than a partisan of Brecht.

A: I do admire him but perhaps that's true.

Q: What do you admire about him?

A: Well, less his person than his work—I admire his uncompromising anti-fascism, and indeed his skepticism toward both capitalist and DDR ideology.

Q: Yet you could seem to be an apologist for him. There is a saying: To understand all is to pardon all.

A: I'm not apologizing for anything.

Q: "Do not judge us too harshly," writes Brecht at the close of the poem. But you're not judging him at all. Might not this poem actually be Brecht's attempt to justify, or at least pardon, himself and his generation for their cooperation or acquiescence with the Hitlers and the Stalins?

A: True. Yes, I agree. He wrote this poem between 1933 and 1938 when both the Nazis and Russian Stalinists were committing unimaginable atrocities. Brecht seems to be referring to the shortcomings that his generation possessed. These are the weaknesses of his generation and time period. As a German, he obviously feels himself in some way implicated in the crimes of Hitler—and as a Marxist in the crimes of Stalin. He asks that his descendents view all of this with *Nachsicht* [kindness, patience, care]. Having inherited these burdens, the people of the future will feel themselves somewhat guilty, and Brecht asks them to have empathy and to forgive his generation. The sins of the fathers will be visited as guilt upon the sons, but the sons are asked to pardon the fathers.

Brecht also hopes that somehow this time period will nevertheless lead to a better future, that somehow it will be transformed into an improvement for mankind. Moreover, many people of his time didn't know about these criminal sins or couldn't do anything to oppose them. Or they were suffering under such burdens elsewhere in their lives, they had to repress much of what was happening before them. Brecht had to flee Germany in order to save his life. Others who did remain died in concentration camps for their resistance.

Q: Did your teachers typically discuss it that way in class?

A: No, that would have been too defeatist or too traitorous—and also too personal—an approach. But I do think that approach reflects Brecht's situation. The poem is an expression of helplessness toward such towering events in history: "I couldn't do anything more than this, flee. Please think on me and my generation with a generosity of spirit. I feel guilt towards you, people of the future. I can't erase that debt of guilt."

The poem is an expression of Brecht's and his generation's weakness and vulnerability and incapacity to meet the challenges of their time. I imagine him saying: "We simply didn't measure up. The times demanded superhuman capacities and we responded in merely human terms. Nothing in history had ever matched the Nazi dictatorship. We had no idea what we were up against until it was too late, so please have consideration for us."

Q: Perhaps it's appropriate, especially in Weimar, in light of the revelations about the mass graves from the Stalin era found at Buchenwald—which had been reopened as a labor camp by the Soviet occupation authorities from 1945 to 1950—that one now look back differently on the poem. After all, 120,000 Germans were herded back into Buchenwald—and tens of thousands died of malnutrition or outright starvation. So today we can say that the poem applies not only to the Hitler years, but also to the Stalinist period in the DDR. Both periods witnessed grave crimes against humanity. Both dictatorships imprinted themselves on Brecht's generation.

A: I don't quite follow you.

Q: Might we now say that Brecht's request at the close of "To Posterity" appeals to his descendants to understand not just the German situation, but also the Soviet? The poem was written not only during Hitler's excesses, but during the show trials, the purges, and the beginning of the Gulag in the USSR. In this respect, Brecht is also apologizing for his silence about these Stalinist atrocities—about which Brecht knew something. He's apologizing because he only criticized Hitler and the Nazis—and not Stalin and fellow Marxists.

A: I see what you mean. That's not something I ever thought of, but it's possible. Yes, it could well be that some part of him was trying to apologize for his own relationship to Stalinism, and if one does concede that possibility, then it's easier to come to an even more comprehensive, detailed, and multifaceted picture of him. One can see all the pressures and contingencies facing his generation and facing him as a German leftist.

Q: He predicts that later generations will have it easier because his generation made the hard choices and endured the agony of being forced to choose.

A: Yes. He says: "You who emerge from the flood and speak of our weaknesses, you escapees have evaded this dark time." Of course, he could well mean not just in Germany, but also in the Soviet Union and elsewhere—and not just the dark time under the Nazis.

This remark reminds me of Helmut Kohl's statement of "the blessing of late birth." Brecht is telling us descendents: "You are blessed to have been born in a later time, in which these hard choices and these agonizing possibilities don't confront you."

Many younger Germans have little empathy for the earlier generations. They say: "Why didn't you protest, rise up, or flee the country?"

Maybe Brecht would answer: "It wasn't so easy. We didn't have the knowledge or information from the media that you have today. You are lucky to have been born later. If you had been in our shoes, you probably wouldn't have acted any differently. Don't be so priggish and self-righteous, don't act so superior. Understand instead what we suffered from the limited possibilities that we faced."

Q: This is all so ironic. It puts Brecht on the same plane as Kohl, and even makes him sound like those patriotic Germans who are pleading with their grandchildren and great-grandchildren today for more understanding and less criticism.

A: Ironic—but true in that limited aspect.

Q: Right. Brecht believed in *Realpolitik*. He writes in his poem: "Think on our weaknesses. We didn't have enough resources to remain friendly in the face of the terror."

A: Brecht held his tongue about Stalin because he stood on Stalin's side and believed that Marxism would lead toward a good end. It had to commit some atrocities. It had to have some bad means in order to reach that end. As Lenin said, "You can't make an omelet without breaking a few eggs." Brecht believed that, whatever Stalin's excesses, Marxism was the lesser of two evils. "You must choose, and you must choose between these two ideologies of the future, between the Right and the Left. And so, my descendents, I hope you understand that we only have two choices and I chose not the better one, but the less evil one."

Q: Would such an interpretation ever have emerged in a class during the DDR era?

A: No. During the DDR era, one never would have criticized Marxism, or even Stalinism, in connection with this poem. Today, however, it's possible to see that the shadow of the poem extends beyond Hitler to Stalin, beyond Nazism to Marxism, and that, at least psychologically, Brecht would have felt even more responsible for what was happening under Stalinism, after all, since he came to view himself much more as a leftist than as a German in the 1930s. It's not necessary to equate the two or to say that Brecht was putting equal emphasis on the two, but the criticism of Marxism is also within the sphere of the poem.

Q: Your teacher is an "imported" westerner, a *Wossi*. Yet he is a great admirer of Brecht. Why?

A: I think he had the opportunity as a West German student to see all sides of Brecht, not just the orthodox DDR side or Party careerist side. As a result, he has developed a rounded picture of Brecht. Our teacher uses examples from Brecht again and again to illustrate different literary motifs, themes, and so on. His love of Brecht is clear from the way in which he admiringly discusses these themes and motifs. Whether we discuss committed literature, modernism, or certain dramatic principles, Brecht is often the case in point.

Q: By offering your classmates examples from the literature of their past and citing their most famous author as an example, might not your teacher be adapting himself to eastern Germans?

A: Possibly, but no, I don't think so. I don't think that pupils of my age have been ideologically conditioned so strongly that it would be necessary to do this. We have received the ideology, but in a subtler, less direct way than our predecessors. But citing examples using a Marxist author politically approved in the DDR days helps dissolve tensions between easterners and westerners. It builds respect for a western teacher teaching in the east and shows a grasp, from a westerner, of Marxist and eastern thinking rather than a sense of superiority or ignorance.

His enthusiasm is much too genuine and deep for that strategy, but it's plausible. Yes, I recall when he first began to do this. I asked myself: Why is this *Wessi* constantly citing Brecht? In the course of time, I've granted that his grasp of Brecht is sovereign. His mastery of Brecht has also deepened my appreciation of this teacher as someone who understands the east. I had never encountered a westerner who had such an intense connection to the DDR or to a Marxist author. That was unimaginable to me before I met this teacher. So yes, this has contributed to greater understanding of Brecht and sympathy for this teacher. And his enthusiasm has broken down the cliché: "Brecht is for easterners and Günter Grass is for westerners." It is very much in the spirit of a new Germany, in which both easterners and westerners share the German tradition together. The idea that Grass equals western is also dissolved when such passion for Brecht is demonstrated by a westerner. I'm glad to see these clichés swept away.

Now I realize: "Well, why not cite Brecht?" After all, he certainly was no DDR author who was in the pay of the state or wrote slavish lyrics supporting the state. He was no Party hack or some creature of the Politbüro who danced to their orders. Brecht served German culture and, above all, himself—not the DDR leaders.

Q: I notice that you have no textbook in this class. I've been told you always did during the DDR era. Which is preferable to you?

A: Almost everyone would rather read the primary texts, because you encounter the author himself—unabridged and without the filter of ideologically slanted editorial commentary.

I want to know what I'm reading and to have it available in its entirety—and not have it excerpted or bowdlerdized by censors. For instance, my old German teacher told me that the standard DDR schoolbook edition of *Galileo* did not end with the last sentence of the play, but rather with an earlier sentence: "Pity the land that has no heroes." Whereas the play as written by Brecht actually ends: "Pity the country that needs heroes." The authentic passage did appear in the DDR edition of the play that Brecht approved; the distorted ending was an "abridged version" that appeared as a school textbook selection from the DDR Ministry of Education.

Q: That's intriguing. How do you interpret that altered ending?

A: The DDR authorities changed the ending because they held that the "positive" or anti-fascist hero is necessary and desirable. Brecht's original closing line seems to sweep aside the positive hero along with other kinds of heroes. That would have been undesirable to DDR pedagogues. So much in the DDR referred to heroes—heroes of socialist labor, workers' heroes, and so forth—that Brecht's last line would have been an implicit criticism of M-L orthodoxy.

Everything in the DDR promoted a will to perform heroic acts for socialism. We heard constantly about Soviet heroes like Stahkanov, or Adolf Henneke in the DDR, or others who performed heroic acts against fascism during the Second World War. We also heard ad nauseam about heroic acts by underground resistance figures like Ernst Thälmann and other communist leaders. It was a goal of DDR pedagogy to educate young people to perform similar heroic acts for socialism and the socialist state. We took trips to Buchenwald for the *Jugendweihe* to reinforce our commitment to live lives of heroic excellence in the socialist tradition. A giant sculpture by Fritz Kremer at Buchenwald depicts resistance fighters in the camp heroically defying their Nazi oppressors. We were supposed to imitate them.

So "Pity the land that needs heroes" would have implied that it's a sad, sorry event when a country has to hold up such models. It implies that the people themselves can't be expected to be heroic in their own way, that they can't develop their personalities to the full without these pressures. So that's why this sentence would have been excised.

Q: To return to Brecht's "To Posterity," consider this line, "Don't let yourselves be tempted." Does that refer to the temptations of Western capitalism?

A: Yes, in the DDR we interpreted the poem's lines that way.

Q: Who are the tempters?

A: Brecht's and the DDR answer would have first been religion, Marx's "opiate of the masses." The idea that the afterlife will be more beautiful than this one is reversed in Marxism. The message is: We will create a socialist paradise here on earth. Heaven is brought to Earth and any non-material heaven of the afterlife disappears. The reality is that life consists of the here and now and there's nothing beyond it. Make everything possible out of the here and now. Seize the day.

Second, don't let yourselves be tempted by the promises of the class enemy. Every one of our literature textbooks promoted this hard, antagonistic, class-based analysis. History textbooks did the same. Class was the decisive mode of interpretation.

Brecht was easy to turn toward these ends. One could always refer to other agitprop writings of his that were overtly M-L.

Q: Did your class discuss his agitprop?

A: We read his poem "Questions of a Well-Read Worker." This poem lent itself quite directly to such treatment. Such poems were anthologized in DDR schoolbooks to portray Brecht as a writer of and for the proletariat, for a classless society, and for socialism and communism.

Q: What's your view today of that portrayal of Brecht?

A: It's very partial and limited. That textbook image of Brecht excluded all of the conflicts that he had in the 1950s with Party leaders like Ulbricht. It also excluded all his critical writings against the regime and how his private life defied many of the regime's edicts and orthodoxies. All of this was airbrushed out of any discussion of Brecht's personal or literary history. Our old Brecht image was based on concepts such as revolution, class, the proletariat, international workers' solidarity, and socialist peace among nations.

Q: How did your textbooks present such a partial view to you?

A: Teachers rarely commanded us, "You must understand it this way." It was a matter of perspective, of a Marxist worldview utterly enveloping us in such a way that no one could really think outside those terms. That was the textbook mentality: the world was cut to fit the textbook definition of reality. The fit was near exact. Since the aspects of Brecht that wouldn't fit were unknown to us, those aspects that we did learn were designed like a key to fit into the keyhole of an M-L *Weltanschauung*. At the same time, we pupils had been schooled to give the teacher the interpretation that he wanted. We knew what direction all interpretations should go in. We knew what concepts, what terminology, and what basic elements he wanted to hear. And the prescribed literature in the textbooks invited the use of those concepts. Everything was structured in such a way as to minimize any other critical standpoint being voiced.

Q: For example?

A: For instance, in a textbook section devoted to proletarian writing, we read a great deal of carefully selected worker literature. Of course that literature championed the proletariat, portrayed life in class terms, saw socialism as the system that honored and represented the workers, and featured [socialist] writers such as Brecht and Erich Weinert. It also included sayings of Marx and Lenin, heralding the cause of the worker.

Q: What was your experience of other aspects of DDR ideology?

A: Of course, I can really only speak of the DDR in its final years, beginning with my school years in 1980. By this time the DDR was extremely liberal in its policies in comparison with the 1960s and 1970s. But even in my time the teachers had lesson plans and grading books in which there were columns for commenting on academic performance and on ideological orthodoxy or conformity.

Q: So even a grading book was a kind of textbook for the teachers, explicitly instructing them how to judge the pupil.

A: Right. They would also make note of your social class. They would mark down the abbreviations for working class or intelligentsia. They wrote your name and next to it, they'd write your class position or affiliation. That fact alone suggests the role that class played in the estimate a teacher formed of a student and also the way in which workers' families received preferential treatment.

It wasn't as crudely done as it had been done in earlier decades, but it still played a role in my time. It was almost a throwback to old status distinctions prior to the French Revolution. There were different estates—nobility, clergy, and so on. This view certainly reigned in the time of Emperor Wilhelm. It was the same kind of categorization and narrowness in the classification of human beings. We were classified according to our [economic] class origin and then we were handled accordingly. I was the child of professionals. I came from an intellectual family. This made it difficult for me to get into EOS. It was difficult for me to obtain a university position—especially one in medicine or biology. If I didn't come from a working family and my parents weren't in the SED, I had grave problems.

There were quotas. A certain percentage of EOS students had to come from working-class families. I believe the minimum was two-thirds. The educational system gave working-class children strongly preferential treatment.

Q: Why weren't your parents in the Party [SED]?

A: I have never discussed that at length with them, but I know it had to do with their distaste for the entire system of the communist state. My parents themselves were working-class children. My father was the son of a weaver who worked in a factory in Frankfurt. His mother was a housewife and also a nanny for the children of a rich Jewish businessman. My mother was the daughter of a man who worked in quarry as a laborer. He had only attended four years of elementary school and was always a blue-collar worker. Her mother was a cleaning woman—a washerwoman in a laundry.

Q: Were you active in the Young Pioneers?

A: Yes. I held several offices. Pupils were elected to a group board [*Gruppenrat*] that consisted of seven functionaries, among them scribe [newspaper editor], agitator, vice president, and a president. The full group board met once a month for a conference. The leading functionaries of the group boards also belonged to the Friendship Council [*Freundschaftsrat*], which negotiated and organized with the school administration, and also with the local heads of Pioneers in order to coordinate various activities. Many of these activities included, for instance, interscholastic flag observances, visits from Soviet officials, and so forth.

In the seventh grade, I was president of the Friendship Council. I was twelve years old. My term began in 1988 and lasted until the spring of 1989. I was also delegated to attend the Pioneer Republic—a huge camp—the Wilhelm Pieck Camp just outside Berlin. It was a Pioneer camp that was also a cadre training camp for future leaders of the FDJ and possibly even the SED. It was really a Boy/Girl Scout camp. Pupils from all over the DDR were chosen to attend this elite camp to receive ideological training in M-L. In hindsight, it reminds me very much of what I've heard about HJ schools during the Third Reich—particularly the special SS schools, the Napola, where elite HJ members were sent in order to become the Nazi leaders of the future.

My summer Pioneer camp was similar. Perhaps not so bad, certainly not racially tinged, but there was ideological indoctrination. This cadre training began in the fifth grade. That was the earliest class. My only visit was in the seventh grade, although I probably would have continued attending in future years too, if the Wall had not fallen. The state knew what it was doing. What was uppermost in the minds of the students was that this was a great honor. This event was publicized widely beyond school in the local Pioneer newspaper, even in regional newspapers. It was a mark of distinction that was said to be the token of a great future in the DDR.

Every Young Pioneer and Thälmann Pioneer had a membership certificate that he carried with him and it had three signatures on it. One of these signatures belonged to the principal, another to the local head of Pioneers, and the other to the head of the Friendship Council. My name was on the membership certificate of every Thälmann Pioneer in our school for 1988–89. Everyone knew your name and knew you were the leading representative in school for everything having to do with extracurricular activities and Pioneer activities, and that you were the bridge to the teaching staff and administration.

Q: Tell me more about your involvement in Party youth organizations. What was it like to chair the Friendship Council?

A: As I said, I was head of the Council for a year. It was prestigious. Already as a member of the *Gruppenrat*, I could wear my Pioneer shirt, which displayed one red stripe. Members of the Friendship Council wore a shirt with two stripes, while the president wore three. So I wore a shirt with three stripes in seventh grade and that was really a prestigious honor. Only the best pupils did so. These pupils were also classified as "best" in the sense of academic performance. It was a great distinction to attain such a position. The school made certain that no one holding that position would bring embarrassment to the school or represent anything negative.

Q: But students elected you, right, so they wouldn't have known your grades, would they?

A: Well, there were a small number of students who were proposed by the teachers' board. Teachers proposed candidates and the students elected representatives from that pool of candidates. I shouldn't actually use the plural, because teachers proposed one candidate and pupils had to rubber stamp that candidate. That is, of course, typical of how the DDR operated. The SED operated in the same way. I was the only one to be proposed for the Friendship Council by teachers, so students simply ratified what teachers had already decided. In that sense, I wasn't really elected by students at all. Our student elections were not democratic. They were *Bestätitigungswahlen*, mere rites of confirmation posing as elections. They were democratic elections in appearance only.

Q: Was it unusual that you could attain that prestigious office even though you weren't a working-class child? How did that happen?

A: Well, that was not such a stringent criterion by the time that I was in school. That's the only explanation I have. Class differences were playing increasingly subordinate roles by the mid- and late 1980s. Grades, distinguished performance in the Pioneers, and the perception of one's capability to represent and reflect well upon the school were more important criteria. In other areas, such as admittance into EOS and into the university—those kinds of formal privileges—class played a greater role. In the Pioneers and FDJ, class played a secondary role.

The importance of class was also evident in professional life. A supervisor would be chosen only partly on the basis of class background. The head nurse on a hospital floor was preferably from the working class. Certainly that also applied to SED membership. The worker families did, in general, have a better shot at getting into EOS and into the university.

Q: Did you have angst, or at least reservations, about freely expressing your qualms about the Pioneers?

A: In the Friendship Council meetings, and as president of the Friendship Council, I would be in close discussion with the leader of the Pioneers about particular members. As *perestroika* and *glasnost* were in full swing, I remember that many discussions occurred about *Sputnik*, which was a newspaper our students read in and outside of classes. Then *Sputnik* was suddenly banned.

I was a very close and careful reader of *Sputnik* at the age of thirteen and fourteen and I could see how much it was changing into a different kind of newspaper in light of Gorbachev's *glasnost*, discussing all kinds of things that had been missing before in relation to weaknesses in Soviet policy or embarrassments in Soviet history. The biggest thing was the newest image of Stalin. One *Sputnik* issue covered a Stalin bibliography exhibit in Moscow that told much about Stalin's reign of terror.

I remember questioning the Pioneer leader and the principal at one meeting about some *Sputnik* reports and the reply from the Pioneer leader to me was: Good, you should question what this means and how *Sputnik* has changed, that's fine; but now you've questioned up to this point, so don't go any further. That reply indicated how much had been repressed. Everyone knew that there was some great black hole toward which all of this was heading. There was some massive set of crimes that we were all part of. The Pioneer leader was acting as if there was a tremendous undertow that would sweep us all away—so we could go just so far but no further. It was a difficult position to be in. It's hard to sympathize with this today.

Q: Yet there remained to the end a *Zusammengehörigkeitsgefühl* [feeling of togetherness].

A: Yes. And that also contributed to the de-emphasis on class in general and the privileged status of the working class in particular. Instead, solidarity was the theme; thus differences in class or other things were downplayed in order to promote a society-wide feeling of togetherness.

Q: What was your attitude toward the new eastern Germany as the Wall fell and afterward?

A: I had no great desire to make up for lost time and to get everything that the consumer society now offered—even though what was available to us expanded dramatically overnight. I was thirteen. I had never felt deprived, so I had no great lust to get what I had never had. Many of my classmates simply gave themselves over to a great indulgence, a spree. They reveled in the new luxuries. You could now have whatever kind of pop record or newspaper you wanted. Before, it was nearly impossible to come across things like that. It took most of my classmates at least two or three years to realize that you could renounce these things. They could be renounced. And with that insight you suddenly distanced yourself a great deal more from this consumer society.

I enjoyed a few aspects of this new capitalism. In particular, I enjoyed the freedom to travel. You could also enjoy some of the technological conveniences like computers. I looked on all this in a detached way from the start. I was really an observer just watching how the east was collapsing into the west in this *Rausch* [intoxicated revelry]. Easterners were jumping into the luxuries of the new world.

I had the perception by the age of fourteen or fifteen that you have to renounce a great deal in order to become a person who isn't merely externalized. You must conduct a search for self. You must ask: Where do I conduct that search? Do I conduct it in great department stores? Do I seek it in the newspaper and magazine stands, or in music stores? Do I search in the display windows of a new mall? Or do I conduct it within myself? I gave the latter answer almost from the start.

This new consumer society offers very little of value for that inner search, or for what really matters in life. But what it does offer is greater freedom of expression, and it also offers greater space in which to experience the new. In those respects, this society offers a great deal that contributes to the search. One is free to search in ways that were taboo before.

4. West Side (Hi)Story I: A *Wossi*'s Post-Communist Critique of Humboldt Historians and *Jammerossis*

Interview with Ludger, thirty-two, a so-called Wossi who has relocated to Treptow, a district in eastern Berlin. Ludger was a student at the Humboldt University writing a dissertation in history from 1991 to 1994, but he dropped out and began working for the newly formed Treuhand Agency, which was charged with selling and dismantling old DDR state-owned businesses and property. Already in his mid-thirties and ready to start a family, Ludger was tired of being an impoverished graduate student with little prospect of ever becoming a history professor. He saw his move from academe to the BRD bureaucracy as a practical, indeed necessary step.

As a transplanted westerner—a Wossi in eastern Berlin—Ludger was confronted daily by the deep differences between eastern and western Germans. Ludger comments extensively on what I have called "the textbook mentality" of eastern Germans, whom he considers to be far more "ideologically orthodox" than western Germans. From the ritualistic citation of Soviet scholars by history graduate students at Humboldt University to the tentative, circuitous patterns of speech among his Treuhand colleagues when they addressed superiors, easterners demonstrated repeatedly, said Ludger, a "subservience to authority."

This interview was conducted not long after Ludger had left his position at the Treuhand Agency in October 1996, a time of transition in Berlin when the last vestiges of the old DDR were fast fading away and the new BRD was fully emerging.

Q: How did the Humboldt students from eastern Germany differ from the western German students in the early post-reunification years?

A: They [easterners] always had to have an appropriate Marx or Lenin quote handy to back up any assertion they were making. They were still liable in that sense to fall back on their DDR conditioning. Ironically, the Russians took ideology in a looser way because there wasn't any competition with a western counterpart to Russia. Eastern Germans had to be more ideologically orthodox because they were constantly facing comparisons with western Germans and facing the realistic prospect of losing hundreds of thousands of citizens every year to the capitalist competitor across the border.

Q: So how did the easterners conduct themselves differently in the classroom?

A: A standard difference was—and still is—their subservience to authority. Consider their need to cite authorities in class—they can't just make their own argument; they feel they must cite an authority, which they regard as presenting evidence—but which is really just subservience out of a posture of fear. Even the daring M-L students avoided risks this way.

Q: So how would they speak in class?

A: For instance, a history student knew he could usually cite Russian authorities and be safe from reprimand. Here's an example from Soviet historiography: The so-called Moscow school of historians were the Soviet hardliners; the Leningrad school consisted of liberal Marxists. When you wanted to do something clever and devilish in DDR historiography, you checked out whatever the Leningrad school was doing, quoted them, and then presented that as the orthodox Russian position that could be followed in East Germany. Then you began by saying, "Our great Soviet brother has already established a new road for us. Professor Ivan so and so, as he states in . . ."

That strategy often worked in the DDR. And even if it didn't win you the argument, it allowed issues to be brought up and a viewpoint entered into the discussion that otherwise would be regarded as taboo. Something of the sort later happened on a much bigger scale society-wide, when Gorbachev came to power. Even though the SED opposed his ideas and didn't want them to be part of East German policy, it was legitimate to broach the topic of liberalization as soon as one referred to Gorbachev's *glasnost* or *perestroika*. That tactic was one of the crafty maneuvers often resorted to in order to bring something dicey up for discussion without paying a penalty. You chose this detour, which became known as "the unimpeachable stratagem of the Russian route." You could never say directly what you meant, but you could always cite authorities. The best authorities were always Russian.

A typical formulation would be, "I would like to say, following our great Soviet brother, blah blah blah." If you didn't get as far as being able to bring up specific citations from the great Soviet brother, and there was objection, you could always say, "That's not actually my opinion, it's just a suggestion that I've heard floating about."

Q: And you observed this pattern of behavior even after reunification?

A: I heard these formulations advanced by *Ossis* in Humboldt seminars long after the *Wende*. That pattern of thinking and speaking was deeply ingrained in easterners. The strategy was to be able to withdraw a suggestion immediately and without anxiety if it should be jumped on. So everything was formulated with as many conditions and reservations as possible.

Easterners were conditioned to fear that they were proceeding through a verbal minefield. That meant going very slowly and, if even the slightest tremor occurred, heading back to the trenches.

Q: So that put eastern students at a disadvantage.

A: Not at all. One advantage that eastern students had in Humboldt seminars was that they had such a clear *Weltanschauung*. So they could seem at times to assert their position much more firmly. Western students coming to the east were bombarded by new impressions and had to integrate these new experiences into a developing *Weltanschauung*, and even though the western picture was much more differentiated and complex, it was also more fragile, more in process.

This problem is gradually disappearing. That discrepancy was primarily attributable to [post-*Wende*] reconstruction. That situation prevailed when there were still many convinced communists at the university who were trying to save the old Humboldt M-L professors and saw all westerners as just *Wessis* who had invaded their university. I felt like an alien, a foreign element at Humboldt. Today there's a new generation of students, so that defensive attitude of eastern students of the early 1990s has disappeared.

Q: What about the attitudes of the eastern professors?

A: If the professor were an easterner, the categories in which things were discussed would very often be Marxist. We *Wossis* were unfamiliar with these categories in their intimate details. Here again, the eastern students had the advantage of speaking this language with native proficiency. They were able to move quickly and effortlessly from the concept to the example and back. They had learned to think better in abstract systematic conceptual terms but had fewer facts at their disposal. We had far more historical information, but our pattern of thinking was more empirical. Rather than know facts rooted in some theory, we proceeded inductively, from the information toward some larger conclusion. Eastern students proceeded deductively. They had the M-L theory and then a few examples, which they treated as illustrations in support of it.

Q: For example?

A: *Ossis* seemed to have all learned a particular fact along with a particular theory, so that they always had some ready illustration at hand, fully memorized. It was as if examiners had tested them for years as to which illustrations were best suited to the theory. As long as a discussion remained at a theoretical level, they were impressive. They could readily say, for instance, that a nobleman under King Otto III had 1,100 oxen which, were passed down to so and so . . ., and this arcane factoid somehow would illustrate the nature of feudal property. They had a structural advantage in those kinds of arguments because their examples so perfectly fit with the conceptual point that they were making, because they knew this conceptual terrain well, and because they had argued this point using that very illustration numerous times.

Once they offered their example, we had to respond to it and work with it even though they knew it in its nuances and had selected it for its applicability.

Q: Did you find eastern professors to be "authoritarian personalities"?

A: Seldom. Interpersonally, the eastern professors were not at all authoritarian, but very approachable. It was only in their intellectual orientation that authoritarianism emerged, not in their relationships with western students. In some ways, however, one could say that they were authoritarian by virtue of their almost exaggerated friendliness, that is, they demonstrated something approaching submissiveness toward the perceived intellectual authority of western Ph.D. students. Rather than simply treat them with an attitude of calm equality, they sometimes placed themselves beneath them.

Still, they came across as far more human to me than the westerner professors, far warmer—not cold, impersonal, or haughty like the stereotypical *Besserwessi* (know-it-all westerner). Because the eastern professors themselves were having difficulties with this transition, our common struggle amid the chaos fostered a certain mutual understanding. Western professors had no such difficulty.

By the way, even today, there remains a certain mutuality of interest between eastern professors and western students. Just as westerners want to find out what the east is like, eastern professors want to break out of their isolation and make contact with westerners. In the west, professors are more firmly established, and the views of students make no difference to them.

Of course, eastern faculty were being screened for their past by western review boards. No doubt they wanted to make sure they behaved well in front of western Ph.D. students and faculty. But I always had the impression that they treated us well on human grounds, not for tactical reasons. Their cordiality and generosity were even more discernible in a field such as geography because that department remained almost purely eastern. By the end of my time [1994] there were already many western professors in the Humboldt history department, but no longer any real orthodox M-L students. Instead you could really talk to all of them and think through ideas with them. They were not M-L parrots. Partly what made studying at Humboldt so stimulating was the meeting of two different worldviews, neither of which fortunately was so rigid that it didn't permit lively discussion.

Q: Did you form friendships with eastern students?

A: It was very difficult to establish any kind of personal relationship. They argued eagerly, but defended themselves against any closer contact with a western student unless he too shared their Marxist views. I had the feeling they just withdrew whenever I made a suggestion that we continue the conversation in a café. If I said, "Let's have a beer tomorrow evening," they always had some other appointment. Or "Let's go for coffee in the cafeteria," they said they had no time available. That experience wasn't unique to me, it was the same for many westerners that I knew.

But my experience was shaped by my moment of arrival: it was a new, uncertain beginning, both exciting and chaotic. I arrived in the middle of the great phase of upheaval and no one knew who was going to supervise me or even what courses were required in order to get approval for writing my dissertation. I was constantly running from one office to the next having to present my documents again and again in order to be eligible for admission. I was one of the first students from the west who had come to Humboldt in order to write a dissertation in history and they just didn't know what to do about my case. All the other students received either fellowships or teaching assistantships, so they didn't have to worry about registering and they were all easterners.

Western faculty members arrived first. Their way was paved because they already had positions. Then followed the Ph.D. students like me—and if they didn't have teaching assistantships they were in trouble. Then came regular undergraduate students, who enrolled out of curiosity or deeper commitment, to experience studying in the so-called wild East.

In the beginning, it was an exciting climate, the classes were small, the eastern professors wanted to impress western students and were eager just to meet them and hear their ideas. That was the advantage of this early period of upheaval. There was a fantastic professor–student ratio, in some cases only four or five to one.

Q: It was difficult to transfer to Humboldt, but transferring within the system was already difficult even within West Germany itself by the 1980s, right?

A: Yes, the German system became increasingly bureaucratized after 1968 and the student movement, when many students challenged existing regulations. Reacting to those challenges, the courts intervened and laid everything down far more precisely in strict legal language. This has led to difficulty in switching universities. In the decades before the war, it was common to study at two or three universities. Today, although that ideal is still exalted, in practice each state has its own strict regulations and they conflict with other states, so you can lose credits and time if you try it. That university tradition of students' easy mobility is dying out.

To some extent, the eastern states are more flexible, because they are still in the early period of adjusting to the new system and they have so many students with disjointed histories that they're more generous in their interpretation of such rules. Most western students still don't want to study in the east, even though the student-teacher ratio is almost as favorable as the one that prevailed during the DDR, about eight or ten to one, whereas the western ratio is about fifty to one. The introductory lecture course in history might have three hundred students in Freiburg. The introductory law course might have a thousand or fifteen hundred. Most students sit on the floor; there are never enough seats for them. In the east, it's common for a lecture to have less than twenty students—

sometimes less than half a dozen. With so few students, a professor will sometimes have the seminar in his office. That creates a much more personal atmosphere. In the west, if such a small number of students enrolled, the class would simply be cancelled.

By the mid-1990s, eastern universities were starting to get better reputations because their administrative advantages—their faculty ratios and better supervision—were appealing. That compensated for the poor living conditions in eastern dorms. Most eastern university students live in student housing because the apartments built by the SED are tiny and few. In the west, most students live in apartments, and there is very little student housing. In smaller, out-of-the-way places like Frankfurt an der Oder, Greifswald, Cottbus, and Rostock, it will probably take decades before living conditions are fully equal.

Q: How would you sum up the difference between eastern and western modes of thinking? Were the stereotypes of eastern students lacking "critical thinking" skills true in your experience?

A: We westerners think that they have been schooled in a form of communist dependence, while they think that we've been schooled in imperialism. Both of those views are caricatures; the fact is that they've been schooled in a mode of thinking that leads to passionate conviction, whereas we've been schooled in a criticism that leads to skepticism. Neither approach is perfect. We've been schooled toward intellectual independence. We're never totally successful; but I do think there's a qualitative difference between our independence and theirs.

Eastern schoolteachers were not trained to foster intellectual independence, and I saw the consequences at Humboldt. I was always told by fellow students: "Of course we couldn't talk about sensitive political issues in public, but within Party meetings we discussed all that very openly." But I don't believe they discussed anything openly—they learned to police themselves.

Q: Speaking of voicing public criticism, you worked after your Humboldt years as a staffer at the Treuhand Agency, an institution much criticized as a ruthless western German tool for exploiting the east. Its task has been privatizing and/or selling DDR-era businesses and property, and it has received withering criticism from the Left and from a majority of easterners—who regard it as corrupt and imperialistic. What was your experience of it?

A: The Treuhand Agency had five thousand staffers and seemed to be monolithic. This giant conglomerate was a caricature of capitalism and was stepping in to transfer all the state assets of the east to western hands. Western investors were coming in and buying everything up. So Treuhand was the big corporation that was officially authorized to dismantle the east [Abwicklung].

There were many mistakes made, but something like the Treuhand Agency was necessary to evaluate and distribute properties once the state and the SED no longer owned them. People forget that it wasn't set up by western Germany; it was set up by [DDR president Lothar] de Maiziere and the East Germans shortly before reunification. The DDR parliament set it up; it wasn't a western institution. Many of the staff and some of the managers were easterners. But westerners did dominate the very top positions.

When I worked for the Treuhand Agency, I always had to justify myself, even though I was only a staffer. I was always put on the defensive by leftists and by many critics. "How could you possibly work for this bureaucracy that is exploiting and raping eastern Germany of all its assets? It's so right-wing," people declared. My reply was that it's a necessary agency, it does some things wrong, it makes a lot of mistakes, but it is a defensible way of returning property owned by the East German state and the SED to private hands.

Q: How dramatically have living conditions improved since reunification?

A: Six years ago, East Berliners earned an average of six to eight hundred marks per month. Rent hasn't really gone up when one considers the rise in salary as well. So they'd pay maybe forty marks per month for rent while earning six to eight hundred marks per month. That's less than 10 percent. In West Germany, we pay at least a third of our incomes for rent. *Ossis* don't appreciate that. Rent in the east has gone up, but so have salaries. Autos and televisions cost more, but availability is far better. You get them immediately and don't have to wait five or ten years.

Very often, improvements are assumed by *Ossis* and hardships are emphasized. It's not so easy to find an apartment in western Berlin. That's why I'm living in eastern Berlin. We have a two-room apartment for less than five hundred marks. In western Berlin, a comparable apartment would be almost three times as expensive. We spend only twenty marks for heat and electricity per month! Western Berliners would spend eighty.

Q: Can you recognize an easterner by his speech or clothing?

A: Yes, sometimes immediately. As you go from eastern to western Berlin, some of the differences are quite distinct. The haircuts are different. Many easterners seem to be dressing themselves from a fashion catalogue. They see some western look and adopt it whole cloth. They simply put away their old look and put on the western look, but it is some caricature of the western look, so it doesn't quite fit them or it's too perfect, so it's quite conspicuous.

Whenever we get to the heart of eastern Berlin I always have the feeling that the passengers in the streetcars have been paging through fashion catalogues and have picked the look they prefer the most. Whatever is in fashion and is most current is what they've just bought. They want to be up to date and want the most stylish look available in advertisements. By contrast, western Berliners prefer to look quite individualistic, to have their own particular, individual look. They orient themselves not according to whatever trend is fashionable, but rather make a new look for themselves out of new and old trends and out of their own idiosyncrasies.

Western Berliners seek their own style, whereas eastern Berliners seem to have fallen victim to mass society. They embrace the "organization man" look. Eastern Berlin women always seem to have the same haircut. Old eastern Berliners don't pay much attention to this. They all look the same, as if they stepped out of the year 1970. Of course, differences blur in Berlin. All these visual differences are much more discernible if you go farther into eastern Germany, where western influences are still much smaller. I can't identify everyone as an easterner or westerner merely by appearance, but the great majority, yes, when I guess, I'm right.

Q: Can you generalize about other east-west differences?

A: Easterners are much more reserved or shy in their body language and speech. They are very cautious in their formulations and they withhold themselves. They don't say, "I think this," or "I believe that." They say, "It could be the case that," or "One might think that," or "Perhaps it is so that. . . ." They are far more indirect and circuitous in their formulations. They show much greater circumspection and pay keen attention to the reactions of a listener, especially if he's a westerner. They look for approval from the listener. It's a less decisive, weaker, tentative mode of self-presentation.

Q: But it served a useful function in the DDR days.

A: Yes. In the DDR years, it was a strategy for survival because the system required that you be circumspect even in the expression of personal opinions and certainly in political ones. You were safer if you checked out who your listener was and, when in doubt, said nothing. Or said the approved thing. Or proceeded cautiously, as if there were always a yellow traffic light in front of you. There was always the fear: "Whatever I say could be twisted or misinterpreted to my disadvantage." Along with that went the awareness of a very defined hierarchy in which there were inevitably people above you, so when you were speaking to people over you, you were especially cautious. You would phrase suggestions this way: "It could be the case that," "One could also perhaps say to that point that. . . ." That would be a typical circumlocution to a superior.

Q: So how would the boss [*Chef*] respond?

A: You'd start: "One could imagine that one could do such and such if this eventually arose." Then if the boss would say, "Yes, that's a very good suggestion," you might trust yourself to formulate things more clearly. Always it was better to begin carefully, in case it would be dismissed. Then you hadn't stepped out so far as to expose yourself or to be seen as committed to something that might have quite serious negative consequences. When I worked for the Treuhand Agency, whenever the boss said something, many of the employees from the east didn't attempt to voice their own opinions. Instead they took his position and repeated it in other words or found supporting arguments to bolster it. I felt that I was surrounded by "yes" men.

What was laughable was that their supporting arguments would be things that the boss never thought of or even disagreed with at times. So sometimes the "yes" men weren't sufficiently careful in formulating how they would say yes. All this is, of course, characteristic of bureaucracies, but I noted it was especially the eastern Germans, who tended to do this, not the westerners.

The differences in style of expression led to many management-staff conflicts between easterners and westerners. Of course, one problem was that the bosses were almost universally westerners, whereas the majority of the staff were easterners. The western staffers would reply to the boss when they were criticized: "Well, you can look at it this way." They would defend themselves. The easterners would not. They would admit their weakness, their wrong-headedness to the boss immediately, but when the boss left, they would immediately complain to all the staffers about their unjust treatment. But they wouldn't offer arguments when the boss had confronted them, even though many of the criticisms voiced by the boss were indeed unjust. They just didn't have the personal strength to stand up to a boss. They often did fit the western caricature of the *Jammerossi* [complaining easterner]. And they griped and carped about the bosses as if they were all *Besserwessis*.

Q: And that interpersonal dynamic became part of the social superstructure of the DDR, so to speak?

A: Yes. All that reflected the training of the "socialist personality." It's attributable to the socialist system of education and culture [*Bildung*]. Of course, in the west there are also countless examples of passive-aggressive behavior, or of evading confrontation, but not to the near-universal extent that existed in the east and not as a deliberate, systematic part of the training of youth.

In brief: What I noticed in the Treuhand Agency was that westerners trust themselves much more to speak out and the easterners don't trust themselves. The two mentalities were constantly colliding.

Q: Was this also the case when westerners were reporting to eastern bosses?

A: No. This craven behavior was not—and is not—exhibited by western staffers to the same degree.

Q: Can you elaborate?

A: The key is hierarchy. It isn't a matter of an unwillingness to express themselves in public, because easterners express themselves, complain, in fact readily in public among peers. But as soon as superiors are around, they orient themselves to those superiors and wait until they know their opinions. It's a form of obedience to authority. They only feel themselves safe when they feel they're among equals. One sign of the safety is the complaining.

Q: You've lived five years in eastern Berlin. Have you developed friendships with easterners since your student days?

A: Most *Wossis* have no personal contact with eastern Berliners except in the formal work setting or in impersonal situations like shopping. It's difficult to meet and develop new friendships when one is busy with family and already has an established circle of friends. But the discrepancy in mentalities of easterners and westerners is the biggest barrier. I have one genuine eastern friend, but she has turned herself into a westerner. She moved to western Berlin, dresses like a western Berliner, has a friendship circle made up almost entirely of westerners and specializes in telling ironic embarrassing jokes about easterners, which of course delights most westerners. She of course is not typical. Most easterners have remained among themselves and more or less continued the habits of their DDR years.

Q: Do you find that your eastern colleagues and neighbors are generally satisfied with developments under reunification?

A: They live in *Ostalgie* [eastern nostalgia]. Sooner or later when you talk with them they always say that things are worse now than ever before, even when you push them and they admit that things are better for them personally than before. But they insist that for eastern Germans generally things are worse. The DDR past is always viewed nostalgically. Everything that was really awful has been simply whitewashed.

When they say that something was far better, I always attempt to tell them that it had a particular function in the oppressive system. For instance, the kindergartens served the state's attempt to claim the children and ideologically indoctrinate them. Yes, there were more and cheaper child care programs, but they too were used for specifically ideological purposes that undermined them. It wasn't child care; rather, it was state care. Yes, it was the case that more women worked—but they provided the necessary manpower for the state. Because everyone was escaping, there were simply too few workers in the DDR. Millions—20 percent of the country—escaped, and as a result, the women were needed. It wasn't much different during the period before and after the First World War. Because of the population decline and the men who went away, more women entered the labor force.

You have to see all these so-called DDR advantages in the context of the oppressive system, not to mention the 10 to 20 percent of DDR citizens who were jailed, persecuted, or politically disadvantaged for protesting dictatorship. There were also various minorities that were exposed to oppression: the Gypsies, the Catholics. Eastern Germans forget all that today.

Easterners don't see the history and broader structure sometimes, they only see their own personal fate. So if they didn't suffer, those who did are invisible to them.

Q: If so, that's ironic—it's so individualistic. Didn't DDR ideology sensitize them to oppressive social structures and historical conditions?

A: Yes, but quite selectively. Today they're fixated on their own condition. That reflects the orientation of the DDR government, which sought to veil all those elements that didn't fit the Party line. Until 1989, people who protested had the feeling that they could only speak openly inside their own four walls. So their consciousness contracted to those four walls. Because there was freedom there, they have deluded themselves into believing there was freedom outside those four walls. There was not.

This led to isolation and a focus on themselves. They were very much turned inward; it was an inner emigration not unlike that of the Nazi period.

Ach, die Wende. [Ludger sighs.]

Q: That seems to say it all.

A: Well, after forty years of division between us Germans, we can't expect ourselves to become one happy family overnight—or likely ever. We're engaged in a complicated dance, the *Besserwessis* and the *Jammerossis*.

With the Wall down, there are great new opportunities for everyone—and that's what we must tell one another: "Look here, take advantage of all this! Seize the day!"

5. The Strains of Silence: A Music Teacher's Brave (New) Career

Interview in October 1994 with Frau Christine Ehspanner, thirty-six, formerly a music teacher and currently principal of the Goethe Gymnasium for the Humanities in Weimar. Contrary to the strict ideological guidelines ordained by the Ministry of Education for teaching music, Frau Ehspanner taught music without what she referred to as "DDR dogmas." She noted, however, that when she was formally evaluated, she said nothing that challenged SED educational doctrines, though she refused to teach according to "the hard Party line." Her observations are invaluable, for they shed light on how a teacher maneuvered betwixt and between the pedagogical prescriptions set down by Party educators.

Frau Ehspanner's comments also support further my surmise in Part 1 that the contents of DDR textbooks were not always taught "to the letter." Nor did those contents automatically flow into the minds of DDR pupils. Rather, both teachers and pupils selectively embraced certain tenets in the textbooks, rejected others, and in general constructed their own meanings, while screening out aspects of the textbooks that did not fit into their mental frameworks. Frau Ehspanner's approach to teaching Beethoven, which defied Party dictates to present Beethoven as a progressive and committed composer, is an excellent example of how teachers created their own Freiraum and practiced small yet significant forms of heterodoxy.

Frau Ehspanner's mention that her father was in the Party—and that his membership deterred her from joining it—stayed with me. As we shall see in Chapter 7, it prompted me to ask other interviewees about the roles of their parents in the Party. Whereas Frau Ehspanner's father did not go along with Party authorities and suffered for it, however, the fathers of my other interviewees basically did go along with the Party. Nonetheless, neither those men nor their children were spared perhaps even greater suffering.

Q: How did you become principal of this distinguished EOS?

A: In 1990, I was asked to take over this school as principal because I was never in the Party. I had a "white vest" ["pure" past, i.e., a politically uncompromised record].

During the DDR years, I had organized school concerts for every grade in this school. Each grade had an annual concert. I was also an adviser to the music teachers in this district and directed three different choirs, so I had contact with teachers and administrators throughout the region. These tasks required administrative experience and organizing skills, all of which apply to running a school and rendered my lack of formal experience as a staff administrator less important.

I was also not eligible to get a Ph.D. in the DDR because I refused to join the SED, but that came as no surprise to me. I knew that my refusal meant the end of educational opportunity for me. When you don't do what the others do, you will be punished. That was the lesson of my refusal to join the Party.

Q: You were courageous.

A: I found it difficult subsequently to live with that decision, but by that time I simply had to. I wasn't so courageous that I did anything like that again or that I sought to leave the DDR. I was born and raised in this region. I had a love for my family and friends and I wanted to make a life here. I made my peace through silence and through a kind of acquiescence with the system.

Q: Why did you never join the Party?

A: My father was in the Party. As a young man in 1949, he believed that he could help in building this new socialist state—far more so than by participating in the capitalist system of the West. He felt hopeful about the social programs that the DDR was establishing, which promoted child care, kindergartens, and employment opportunities for women. There was a great idealism at that time and there is no doubt that many people were well-intentioned, but what developed led to a communist takeover of these programs, which entailed a silencing or muzzling of many people.

This was impossible for my father to tolerate. He was an idealist and wanted to do something to help his country, but whenever he advanced criticisms, he was punished. As a teenager, I witnessed this and was hurt at how he was treated and how he was suffering from what he regarded as a betrayal of his ideals and youthful hopes. When he said, "No, I will not do that," he was then given a command by Party authorities to do it. As a man who respected Party discipline, he felt he had to carry out those orders.

That injured his human dignity. When I attended college in Weimar and was invited to join the SED, I refused. I told them that I didn't want to be a member of a Party that treated people the way they had treated my father. I had excellent grades, but as a result of that declaration, I didn't receive an offer to teach. This was unusual in the days of the DDR. I would have been preferred for almost any job in the region, given that my grades were high.

I was offered a job in outlying areas instead. I had to commute from my parents' home two hours each way to get there. I had to wake up at 4:00 A.M. in order to be at school on time. Because I had openly criticized the state, I began to suffer just as my father had.

I learned that the state would use its power to grind you down if you went against it. I could only get a job teaching music to blind children. Later, for ten years, I taught music at a POS.

Q: Many westerners would imagine music to be a school subject largely free of ideological content—aside, say, from learning to sing the national anthem or some other patriotic or religious hymn in class.

A: The DDR music class, unfortunately, was strongly ideologically conditioned. Sometimes it was hopelessly vulgar. Beethoven was presented as a communist composer, and Mozart was discussed as a revolutionary forerunner of socialism. It was clear to me that I wasn't going to teach these idiotic ideas; otherwise, it would tear my mind apart. The teaching guide prescribed these kinds of socialist pieties. It called for ideological blankets to be draped over these musicians.

Q: Did you ever teach music in the prescribed manner?

A: I simply refused to do it because it was a lie. Beethoven lived in his time and I wanted to illuminate his period. They wanted to rewrite it to fit the ideological straitjacket of a post-war socialist state.

I believe that it is important to understand art and literature in its own time. To that extent, historical interpretation is crucial, but not to the degree that it is distorted in order to be replaced by DDR dogmas. I couldn't empty Beethoven of his true historical content and fill him back up with the revolutionary bromides of our day. He had nothing to do with communism. The authorities wanted to see him as a progressive and a socially committed composer, but that was anachronistic. So I never taught him that way.

We were also mandated by the syllabus to teach the work of DDR composers who had composed mediocre music. Sometimes I went so far as to shorten the length of time devoted to them or even to say to students, "What do you think of this?"—rather than deliver the prescribed Party line. We had to cover certain people, but *how* we covered them was not closely supervised or sometimes not discernible by the authorities. I would ask rather innocently, "Do you like this music or not?" The pupils had some artistic sensibility. It was often the case that they would rave about Beethoven and Mozart and deplore the DDR composers. I never contradicted them on that; instead, I indirectly encouraged that preference.

Q: And your defiance of the orthodox pedagogy was never noticed?

A: When I underwent formal observations by other teachers or by the administrative staff, I would not teach in such an open way. Nonetheless, during these evaluations, I still would not deliver the hard Party line. I got by with leaving a lot of things unsaid. If I had acted as I often did when the evaluators were there, however, I would certainly have been in trouble with the authorities. So I never openly defied the prescribed Party line on these composers. My defiance consisted of acts of omission rather than commission. They certainly would have dismissed me if I had been more open. I simply couldn't reconcile what was in these textbooks with my conscience.

Q: How did you teach a theme such as "Beethoven and freedom"? What about the "Ode to Joy"? How did you handle with the pupils a topic such as the freedom to travel?

A: Yes, that was always a delicate topic. We would discuss French revolutionary ideals such as liberty, fraternity, and equality. The teaching guides always twisted what these ideals really meant. I sometimes believed that this "workers' paradise" had achieved these ideals. After all, this was the "workers' state," and workers did receive preferential treatment in many ways. It was difficult to see through these things in the DDR days. I never visited the West. I could only experience it through television, but how accurate was that? I wasn't sure.

We knew there were a lot of bad things about the DDR, but we didn't think everything was bad. We thought it was reformable, so we reconceived freedom to mean, "Well, we can't travel, but we have the freedom of knowing that we'll never fall into social deprivation because the state provides us with the minimum." Here you always have food, shelter, and warmth. Then a teaching guide would ask, "What's more important: my life on a day-to-day basis or the ability to travel past the borders for a week?" Most of the students would then answer, "Well, our state does have its priorities in the right order." We simply conflated freedom and security and often conceived of security in rather paternalistic, invasive terms.

This, too, got by DDR functionaries. "You can't have everything. You have to be mature about the available choices and know your limits." That was the approach that was drummed into us.

Mostly it was propaganda. Yet, when I look at things today, there's some truth in it. You *can* travel to a place like Australia if you have a lot of money, but you'll still spend fifty weeks a year right here at home; so this great freedom to travel is rather theoretical. Yes, you *can*—in the abstract—but you really can't, because most people don't have the financial means to take advantage of such capitalist freedoms.

This insight makes everything about the DDR past more difficult to judge, that is, everything is a matter of comparisons. Everything needs to be looked at from different perspectives. So, despite all the abuses, some ultimate condemnation isn't so easy to pronounce.

Q: Was the old DDR preferable to the current eastern Germany—was it "the better Germany"?

A: I would still say that we're now living in something much closer to a democracy. Everything that involved the Stasi was ultimately a betrayal of the ideals of freedom. That was criminal. But most of us never experienced that and certainly not on a daily basis. We were happy, more or less, because we had food, clothing, shelter, a sense of security, a job, and Gemütlichkeit.

Walking through our supermarkets today, I often ask myself, "Why does everyone need three dozen choices for one product?" Consumerism can't possibly be the meaning of life or the center of one's existence! It can't possibly furnish any deep satisfaction. I feel that the deception of consumerism—that it can somehow prop up your identity—is worse than most of what happened in the DDR. There is much more *Frieraum* for teaching today than there was in the days of the DDR. This doesn't mean that there is an unlimited freedom—that teachers and students can do as they please. Although this There are still regulations and rules that apply. There are limits that need to be respected. Education is partly a matter of receiving and understanding discipline.

Q: In what ways was the DDR superior?

A: I feel that the DDR had advantages—many of which pertained to education and that were also beneficial for working women. I still think that the child care system was excellent and its absence today is a real disadvantage for working families. Child care is extremely expensive.

The DDR in some ways was quite child-friendly even if it had ulterior motives, whereas Germany today is hostile to children. This is why parents choose to not bear any. There are crazy feminist ideas running around. Some feminists believe that children are like a ball-and-chain for a woman, because they shatter her life, destroy her potential, and ruin her chances of having fun. We were often accused by West Germans of having been brainwashed and therefore believing that we must send our kids into a child care program or to an after-school nursery, but that wasn't the case. We simply thought they were well provided for there.

Yes, it's true that I didn't stay at home with my kids, but my kids have turned out well because when I was there, I was *really* there. I was a good mommy to them. When I wasn't working, I immediately picked them up from child care. When I had free time, I spent every moment of it that I could with them. Most parents love their children and it isn't the case that the state creates these economic incentives as a tactic to take over their lives.

The youth here [in eastern Germany today] are adjusting well, unlike the older people. The older people don't understand the world anymore, because their old world has all gone by too far, too fast. The young ones are able to adapt easily and gain all the advantages of the new world, including the freedom to travel. We're finding that most young couples don't want to have children. It isn't because they want to have more pleasure, its because the future seems so "iffy."

The DDR was often accused of wanting children to prop up the economy, but that was rarely a deciding factor for young parents. What was a deciding factor was the belief that the future was fairly secure—that the husbands could keep their jobs, and their wives could work while child care services would still be provided free of charge. It's ridiculous that western German women have their first child at the age of thirty-eight. It's biologically bad. I feel that twenty-five is about the right age. If we don't have young people to support the state for the people who are going to receive pensions in the next twenty years, then who are we to rely on?

Q: Any other advantages in the old DDR system?

A: Another advantage was that basic foodstuffs were extremely cheap. A bread roll cost five cents until the late 1980s and you could eat meat for a couple of marks. For years, the price for a bottle of milk was fifty cents. The government underwrote these prices. The social safety net was there for you in the case that something went wrong in your life, such as in your career or health. The minimum was secured for you. There were very few rich people and the entire country was lower middle class.

I still think that it was not so bad. The more I hear about how people under capitalism live, the more I am convinced of its faults. It may sometimes seem glamorous, glitzy, and shiny on the outside; but it's sick or corrupt inside. It is sometimes the case that, because you can't work anymore or your occupational field is no longer in demand, your family is thrown into the abyss. That, in my opinion, is inhumane. Occurrences since reunification have led me to believe that every system has its pluses and minuses. Our state certainly had its grave injustices, which were contemptible: its hostage trades for money; its exploitation of the arms race; its warmongering and militarism; and, of course, the role of the secret police.

But there were also some positive things—especially at the beginning with the founding of the DDR. The hopes for a truly socialist state, however, dimmed with the passing of the decades and those advantages grew smaller as disillusionment set in and hopes dimmed. Nonetheless, in the end, there were good things about the DDR. I must admit that, even when things were worsening, I never had—and never would have had—the courage to climb the Wall like others did in an effort to escape. Nor would I have had the courage to legally apply for an exit visa.

All the while that my friends were being punished for their attempts [to emigrate legally], I never gave it a second thought because I had my children and my husband; furthermore, I felt that capitalism had its own problems. I think I still harbored a small hope that somehow the DDR would reform despite forty years of heading in the wrong direction, but that hope was naive. The entire economy was in shambles. It should have been obvious that the country was on the verge of collapse and that almost nothing could be done to save it. Yet I still never imagined that the Wall would fall when it did.

Q: When did you imagine that it would fall?

A: We always believed that a great climactic battle, which would arise due to the tensions between the East and West, would be the only way to bring down the Wall. It would be a prelude to, or at least a seeming foretaste of, World War III. I always had great angst about the possibility of weapons being deployed on both sides of the border. The 1989 *Wende* occurred without violence, which is good. I am grateful that everything transpired peacefully. Of course, we have problems today in the eastern states, but we should have patience. Prosperity wasn't achieved in a day for West Germany after the war, and we must cope with these problems if we want to renew eastern Germany. We had a lot of patience in the old system, so it is a virtue we are familiar with. When we forget it, we need to look back on the old system and remember how much patience it required of us.

Q: How did you become principal of this school?

A: Sixty applications from teachers in western Germany and many others from teachers in eastern Germany were submitted, but the regional education administration wanted a native Weimar principal. This was advantageous for me because I had worked at a POS in Weimar and the special school for the disabled was also in Weimar. My first job was three hours away in Arnstadt, yet I didn't relocate to that area because I had already begun my family and my husband was working in Weimar. All my relatives are here as well. Unfortunately my decision led to a long and exhausting daily commute.

Q: What staffing changes occurred here in your school in the wake of reunification?

A: *Abwicklung* played no significant role in our *Gymnasium* as a result of the *Überprüfung* process. Everyone had to reapply for employment and everyone was screened but no one was fired. The only changes that occurred were that some teachers of Russian and civics were let go because their subjects were no longer taught here. They were taught only in the EOS. Correction, one teacher who was a Party secretary in the EOS was fired, but she was later rehired as the result of a judgment from a lawsuit she'd filed against the state. She was rehired on the grounds that many senior Party educational officials managed to keep their jobs and it was unjust that she, a mere teacher who had assumed the Party's main responsibilities in this school, should be fired.

It was determined that it would have to be proved that she was in collaboration with the Stasi. Without that evidence, the grounds for firing were deemed insufficient. In the DDR days, there was a Party board within the school; once a month, all the Party members attended this meeting. She ran that board. It doesn't necessarily mean that she harmed people in the school. I was not a Party member, and therefore I was not privy to these Party meetings. Everybody knows that people had diverse reasons and motives for joining the Party. Some entered in order to reform the DDR, while others exploited their Party status in order to excel in their careers.

These screenings required extremely precise differentiations as to the motive and quality of the work in DDR days, and we haven't always been successful in drawing these fine distinctions, partly because of the passage of time and the loss of memory. That is, pupils who experienced these teachers in class are gone and very few got in touch with screening boards when questions came up about their teachers' pasts. Other people felt it was better to let bygones be bygones, let sleeping dogs lie, or leave skeletons in the closet rather than raise the dust all over again. Still others with shady pasts managed to make use of their Party connections to protect themselves or even to rouse students and fellow colleagues to defend them.

Parents that had children in school knew their children would be disadvantaged, in a sense, if the teachers were let go. This would result in a loss of continuity with that particular classroom subject, and those students preparing for the *Abitur* would be deprived of a teacher familiar with the process. As a result, often on very pragmatic grounds or due to a teacher skillfully becoming a turncoat [*Wendehals*], the teacher was able to rally support from colleagues—who, perhaps, also feared dismissal. Such clever teachers were thus also able to gain support from parents and pupils who knew nothing of those teachers' pasts and had never experienced harmful ideologically based judgments from them.

Q: Do you think that the screening process was fair?

A: There was an attempt to do a better job than was done during the Nazi period, but the same complexities that arose during Nazi days arose in a different form after reunification. Many teachers were unjustly fired in 1945 because they had been Party members. This time, it was decided that Party membership would play no role. Grounds for termination would stem from prior collaboration with the Stasi or from prior responsibilities with significant Party functions, which would have necessitated high-level decisions that were harmful to DDR pupils and teachers. This meant that relatively few teachers would be fired, unlike in the early post-war days when 80 to 90 percent of the teachers were fired in some regions because of past Nazi affiliations.

Q: How did the school system evolve after the initial stage of upheaval and the *Überprüfung* process?

A: In August 1991, Thuringia introduced a new educational system that was modeled after that of the west. Our partner states were Bavaria and Rhineland Palinate. These two states cooperated with us to draft new models for the educational system for our state. The model was structured as follows: elementary school consisted of the first through fourth grades attended by pupils of ages six through ten. After the fourth grade, children could attend either a *Realschule* [technical school]—also known as *Regelschule*—or *Gymnasium* and receive the *Abitur*.

Pupils could also finish school at the age of sixteen with the *Mittlere Reife* [GED certificate]. At the age of sixteen they are placed into a job-training program. They also have the option of transferring to *Gymnasium* if they attain grades that are sufficiently high. In 1994, there were no longer any differences between the old and new states except in equipment and financial wherewithal. Our schools are not so well equipped as those in the west. We still do not have a thirteenth grade, so our students graduate after the twelfth. Sometimes high-school graduates choose to not attend the university and begin the job-training program instead.

Q: What percentage of pupils choose religion class, now that it is available?

A: A majority of students register for ethics rather than religion. For instance, in our fifth grade there are ninety-four students. Eighteen want a Catholic religion class, twenty want a Lutheran, and the others want ethics, so about 60 percent prefer ethics. We don't have ethics and religion in all grades yet. These classes begin in the fifth grade, continuing throughout [the subsequent grades] as the pupils get older. We began teaching religion and ethics last year in the eleventh grade. Until 1993 there were no ethics or religion classes in higher grades, but we began them in the fifth grade in 1991.

We simply don't have enough well-trained teachers in these subjects to be able to staff all grades. I am not permitted to offer an ethics class, which we can staff adequately, unless I staff corresponding classes in Catholic and Lutheran religion. These three options must be equally open to pupils at all times. So this year we are offering both religion and ethics in the eleventh and twelfth grade.

The first grade in elementary school has also recently begun with these three subjects. As elsewhere in eastern Germany, there are very few Catholics here, a few more Lutherans; most pupils are not affiliated with any religion, so they choose ethics. We are still hiring religion teachers from western Germany because we don't yet have higher education programs in the east to train teachers for this type of education.

Q: Are most Russian teachers being retrained?

A: Yes, we are also retraining former Russian teachers to teach ethics and Latin—both of which were absent in the DDR curriculum. Civics teachers are also being retrained to teach ethics. The pupils who were learning Russian when the Wall fell still have the option of continuing with the study of Russian as their main language through upper grades. The younger pupils have started with English as the main language. Russian is being phased out and being replaced by English or French—sometimes by Latin.

Q: But I've heard that Russian is popular among a small group of pupils.

A: During the DDR era Russian was a requirement; now it's an elective. Beginning in 1992, pupils were given the option of selecting it—it was no longer required. Ironically, although it was seldom a favorite subject in the DDR days, Russian is making a comeback. We offer it beginning in the seventh grade. It is far more popular than Latin or even French. We also offer Spanish. English begins in the fifth grade and a second language is taught beginning in the seventh. Our Russian teachers are superior to those in the west. Many of them have years of experience and have studied quite intensively in Russia. They are quite distinguished. Russian was taught in only a few West German schools. That is still the case today in the west.

Twenty per cent of the pupils who studied Russian in 1990 here have continued with it. The others switched to English. The main reason was political: Russian was disliked because of the Russians. A secondary factor was that English is the international lingua franca and the language of European business; but the political component was the dominant reason. Also, reverse psychology played a role. Because Russian was required, it was disliked. It's making a comeback now in part because it's an elective.

6. "My Teachers Ignored the Ideological Crap"

Another exchange with Stefan, now twenty-nine, the Gymnasium pupil whom we met earlier in this chapter when he discussed his classroom experience of Brecht. We had become friends and maintained contact during the course of my writing this book. Hearing about my research, Stefan voiced interest and we spoke at length in October 2003 about his memories of DDR schoolbooks. He told me that he wanted to "challenge" any simplistic notion that the DDR was a giant schoolroom consisting "textbook Reds." Instead he insisted that teachers in most subjects (except Staatsbürgerkunde) ignored the ideological imperatives laid down in the textbooks and teaching manuals.

Q: Did you ever encounter a subject being taught "to the letter" according to the ideological content of the textbook?

A: My experience as a pupil in the DDR from grades one to seven [from 1983 to 1989] was simply that teachers would leave out everything that openly smelled like stupid ideology. This might sound weird—since nearly every page was infested with that openly ideological crap. But all teachers—except the teacher for *Staatsbürgerkunde*, who was the only one who went through the book page by page—ignored that stuff.

For example, consider music. You spoke to Frau Ehspanner, she was actually my teacher in grades five, six, and seven. We talked in class about

Mozart and Beethoven and their music, but not about their music as examples of socialist revolutionary theory. Teachers (in my school at least, but I strongly doubt it was different elsewhere) simply blocked out the ideological part of the books and constructed their own curriculum. Yes, my teachers just ignored the ideological crap! It is hard to believe—but that was my experience and that of many others.

Q: Travel restrictions and the state-controlled media limited access to outside sources of information. Did that render the official media—including the DDR textbook—more important as sources of knowledge and information?

A: Well, historical research since reunification into the DDR as a media society has shown that, by the late 1970s, West German television and radio stations effectively replaced the East German media as primary sources of information. In 1983, when the DDR was granted a billion-dollar credit by West Germany, it was the beginning of the end, since that move made clear that the DDR was effectively bankrupt.

Also, everyone who traveled to the USSR could see with his own eyes the reality of the alleged "superiority" of the USSR. My father traveled to Moscow twice in the 1960s. He came back with horrible stories about the poor living standards of Russians. People there were living on the streets, had no shoes, and were begging for money from the tourists. These stories were then brought back into the DDR and told in families and in offices amongst colleagues. Thus, *that* knowledge (Western media, traveling to the USSR, and so on) was influencing decisively the worldview of many DDR citizens—not the textbooks. Everyone—including the teachers—knew that the textbooks were written by Party officials and did not adequately mirror the reality of the outside world.

Q: It was the *intention* of the Party that every child should learn to read and write according to the ideological syntax and semantics of M-L. But to what extent did that aim of the Party actually match the reality in the classroom?

A: Not at all. My German and history teacher from grades four to eight [in the Goethe Gymnasium in Weimar] was Frau Mühlpfordt, a woman with a strong humanistic-bourgeois background (as was indeed the case for many of the humanities teachers in towns and cities like Weimar, Dresden, and Leipzig). Her husband worked in the Museums and Research Center in Weimar on German literature of the Weimar classical period [eighteenth to early nineteenth centuries]. When we talked in class about Goethe's poetry, we would analyze it as the work of a young man fighting against the older generation and against oppressive power exerted "from above" (as in the case of the "Prometheus" poem), or in terms of angst, superstition, and reactionary attitudes to imaginations (as in the case of the "Erlkönig" poem).

Q: How did that differ from the way these poems are discussed in classes today?

A: In the 1970s and 1980s, everyone knew that the Party wanted us to interpret these poems in defense of the working classes. The teaching material told teachers like Frau Mühlpfordt to do so.

But did she? No, she did not. No one really abided by Red ideological teaching guidelines—at least not in my school (except my *Staatsbürgerkunde* teacher).

My recollections are that both teachers and pupils silently and implicitly agreed on ignoring and masking the ideological parts of the textbooks. It was a quiet agreement that emerged over decades in the DDR.

Q: Here's a quote from the fifth-grade geography teaching guide of the 1980s: "Teachers should mention the dialectical aspect of physical geography." Did they?

A: Seldom. I was in that class [which used *Geography 5*] in 1987. My teacher was Frau Ludwig. I can't remember that we ever talked about ideology.

True, we were introduced to the existence of the RGW (COMECON) as the counterpart of the EU, but in a straightforward, factual language. A teacher who actively taught what was written in the teaching guide would have made a fool out of himself! And everyone knew that. It was this silent agreement to be guided by selective perception that defined DDR reality, not the blunt ideological content of Party pamphlets, textbooks, official television speeches, and so on.

Q: What about *Staatsbürgerkunde*? You said earlier that your *Stabü* teacher did follow the Ministry of Education approach in his classroom. Was he typical of DDR civics teachers?

A: Yes. Unlike the cases of music or geography, *Staatsbürgerkunde* textbooks were taught "to the letter." Most *Stabü* teachers were ideological hard-liners. But that's why both *Staatsbürgerkunde* and its teachers were perceived among pupils in our school as naive, stupid, rigid, outdated, ideological, and so on. *Staatsbürgerkunde* textbooks left no space for un-ideological interpretations or discussion of exceptions.

Indeed, after the events of Autumn 1989, the only teacher who had to leave my school for political reasons was the *Staatsbürgerkunde* teacher, Herr Lebede. All the other teachers were kept. That actually applied to most of the schools in my home state of Thuringia. Principals of some DDR schools were dismissed (or were demoted to teachers), and so were some teachers whose main subject was *Staatsbürgerkunde* as well as teachers who were Party hardliners, but nobody else on political grounds.

Q: Here's a quote from a fifth-grade history teaching guide: "Fifth-graders should be instructed about the revolutionary difference between bourgeois and progressive history." Was this actually taught?

A: No. I was in that class with Frau Mühlpfordt. These things just did not receive prominent attention.

Q: What about the sciences?

A: The same holds for the sciences. Sure, teachers were *supposed* to do that. But very few of them did. I'd estimate that 70 percent of math and science teachers seldom mentioned the so-called laws of M-L.

Whenever there was a mathematical question in the textbook that featured Russian tanks or the overwhelming achievements of the Bulgarian computer industry, math teachers would just ignore the problem in the textbook, go to the blackboard, and replace the tanks with everyday real-life examples.

The same applied to chemistry: we never talked about atoms as examples of the truth of DIAMAT; we talked about atoms and molecules, period. The fact that the teaching manual advised chemistry teachers to teach DIAMAT does not mean it was actually taught!

Q: How much did all this change after reunification?

A: In some subjects, only a little, but in others, a great deal, especially in subjects such as history. Of course, *Staatsbürgerkunde* ceased even to exist by 1990. In fact, after November 1989, nobody paid attention to schoolbooks in civics and history. When I was at the Goethe Gymnasium between 1992 and 1995, we used West German history textbooks. The old DDR ones were superseded by events—and we hadn't yet received new textbooks. Everything was in upheaval, and educators hadn't yet decided what to enshrine as the new curriculum. We learned from mimeographed materials and from discussions—which I much preferred to dry textbooks.

7. "French Leave": A Gifted Language Student Goes AWOL

Interview with Kersten, thirty-one, a former DDR interpreter, in October 1996. She defected from the DDR in 1986, at the age of twenty-one, during her first week on assignment in Paris. Subsequently, she lived and studied in western Germany until she returned home permanently in 1992. At the time of the interview, Kersten was a Ph.D. student in French at Humboldt University in Berlin.

On a few occasions in our conversation, Kersten seemed uncertain of past events and seemed to contradict herself. But I deemed it more important to adopt an empathetic than a critical stance, i.e., to let her tell her own story and use this interview to wrestle with her memory and explore her past—rather than to interrupt and challenge her (sometimes painfully) constructed version of events.

Kersten's wrestling with her history struck me as yet another instance of how one worked through the "textbook mentality" that many young eastern Germans acquired—and with which they are still struggling today. Because of her intensive ideological indoctrination during her years in DDR special language schools and later, Kersten had indeed embraced elements of the DDR worldview—despite her daring act of committing Republikflucht. *It also became clear to me during the interview that what is often judged as evasion from the outside is experienced from the inside as ambivalence and confusion. Part of Kersten's difficulty was from bewilderment about how to reconstruct a past that quickly became far removed from the reality in which she came to live. She considered the interview a valuable opportunity because it was the first and only time that she had even spoken with anyone outside her family about her DDR years.*

Q: Why did you become an interpreter?

A: I simply wanted to do something practical with the foreign language skills I had acquired—with my French, English, and Russian. I wanted to speak and write the language with native speakers in a live situation, not the artificial classroom situation that I had been limited to for the past fifteen years.

The courses of study for interpreters and doctors were the two most desirable career paths in the DDR. Even subjects like law were unattractive because they were so ideologically tainted. But there was nothing necessarily ideological about developing linguistic gifts or gaining knowledge on how to handle diseases and cure people. By and large these two fields were exempt from the negative connotations of many other DDR courses that, although prestigious in official DDR propaganda, were polluted in Western eyes—and in our own—by ideological indoctrination.

You earned a lot [as an interpreter], but the most attractive aspect of the interpreter degree was that you were automatically one of the *Reisekader* [traveling cadre]. You could leave the country. Not even doctors could do that. Doctors were attracted by the relative purity of science and the fact that doctors did earn a great deal more than other professionals, whereas interpreters were attracted by the freedom to travel. If you didn't make it as an interpreter, you became a teacher. Those who didn't make the standard or were excluded for political reasons and didn't make it into the traveling cadre became teachers of various languages, and they began to train others who had the chance to become interpreters. So there was a great deal of status attached to an interpreter, less so to translating, because that didn't necessarily involve travel.

Interpreters were at the very top of the linguistic hierarchy; translators followed, and teachers (including university instructors) were much lower.

Q: What was the balance between ideological indoctrination and technical proficiency in the training programs for becoming an interpreter?

A: There was, of course, a large ideological component in all the courses. But that fact notwithstanding, the training was not just technically competent but excellent. Even the training to become a language teacher was excellent. We used to say: "Well, if you don't make it as an interpreter you'll at least become a teacher."

But becoming a language teacher in the DDR meant reaching a very high level of proficiency. I was enrolled in elite schools beginning in my earliest years as a result of specializing in languages and my proficiency, and also because of my outstanding grades. It was the same for other pupils who specialized in music, in math, and in sports. There were a select number of elite schools to promote a cadre of talented, strictly loyal DDR citizens who would excel in these spheres. What gained all of us initial entry to these schools was our membership in loyal Party families. But we had to excel in order to remain in such schools.

My parents supported and promoted my language fanaticism eagerly. They also saw it as a way for me to distinguish myself in the DDR. Getting me into that school reflected and conferred special advantages on our family. We were a very, very loyal Party family. As soon as I finished my course of studies in the tenth grade in a special school, I decided to go for the *Abitur* and I entered the EOS for the eleventh and twelfth grades.

After I completed my studies in French and English, I was sent abroad on one of the most prestigious assignments—a job in Paris. I had just turned twenty-one. It was the first time in six years that anyone new had been sent to Paris to work as an interpreter. None of my friends had a chance like this. Even the best of my fellow graduates were simply assigned to East German government agencies in Berlin to interpret for visiting Western dignitaries.

Q: How did you manage to defect?

A: During the second week that I was in Paris, I slipped away and went to the West German embassy and asked for asylum. That, of course, came as a total shock to my parents. I never said a word to them about it. I never indicated in any way that I harbored any ideas about not coming back. I wasn't sure if I would be able to do it. I didn't want to say anything, because in some way or another, when they would be interrogated, it would be squeezed out of them if they did know. They would never be able to pretend they didn't. I knew what I thought I would do, and if I had the chance to do it, I knew I would, but I kept it all to myself until that moment.

It was October 10, 1986. I simply walked through the streets—though I'm sure I was being periodically observed by spies from the DDR that were in Paris—to the door of the West German embassy and entered.

Q: What led you to make that momentous decision?

A: The key event for me was meeting my oldest brother's best friend, who was applying for an exit visa and was being put through hell for doing so. He was put in jail for a period of time. He lost his job and had to do manual labor for months. His exit visa was ultimately refused, so his career prospects were over at that time. But he was still stuck in the country. I realized the consequences of having the fanatical idea that I had. I wanted to see the world and there was no state-legitimized means to get out. Now I had the means. So I vowed to myself: "I'll keep it to myself, but when the moment arises, I'll seize the day."

That's when my eyes really began to open and I began to see through his eyes that there was so much corruption in the DDR system. I'm sure that my parents suspected that I could never spend my entire life in the DDR. They knew from the earliest days of my passion to find out about what was going on in the world. But when they heard the excitement in my voice about going to Paris, they didn't dare ask me if I was coming back. They were proud of that assignment. It was *la crème de la crème* for any interpreter in the DDR.

I wonder if they guessed what was on my mind, but like me, didn't want to say anything for fear that the question might plant an idea in my mind. If anything had gone wrong, they would have felt guilty. I wanted to protect my parents. I knew they would be questioned immediately by the Stasi as soon as I made the move. They would be interrogated endlessly.

Q: And what did happen to your family?

A: My father was given one opportunity to keep his position. He was ordered to put in writing that he disowned me as a daughter, and that I was a traitor to the DDR and its ideals of peace and socialism. My father was willing to say that he promised he would never have any contact with me. "You can demand a lot from me, but I'm no pig and I won't do that to my daughter," he said. "You can't force my wife not to have any contact with her." That proposal was completely insufficient for the state. He also refused to disown me or criticize me at all. He simply said that in order to preserve everything he'd done, he would have no contact with me, and that the authorities could interpret that in whatever way the state mandated.

So he accepted that his reservations meant he would be fired. I felt terribly guilty. I felt that I had ruined his life and the lives of everyone left in my family. But he told them, "Look, this girl is twenty-one years old and she can do what she wants in her life, and I support whatever decision she makes. She's made this decision, and I can't lead her by the hand through life. I'll stand by her."

He was deemed a traitor to the state and dismissed with both a dishonorable discharge and a severe reduction in his pension. My defection also damaged the careers of my brothers. Later, my father's discharge was changed to "retired due to poor health," but his pension was not raised. Although my father had heart palpitations and delicate health by the time he was removed from his position, the health claim was a trumped-up justification.

Q: Did he maintain his connection to the SED?

A: He remained in the Party up until the very end, but thereafter he had no positions of responsibility. They had been taken away. In general he lived a much less active life. He basically turned inward.

Of course, the forced retirement sent him into a deep depression, and he became disappointed by everything in the DDR. For the first time, he admitted to himself how bad the system was, but after the *Wende,* he began to think the same thing about the western system. All the negatives that had been preached about the West German system in the DDR were now being realized before his very eyes, so he concluded that it really wasn't any better either. Probably the main reason that my father stayed in the Party so long was that he had looked forward to an extremely comfortable retirement. He was a prison warden in a large institution that included a section for political criminals. His pension would have been much greater than the salaries of most DDR citizens. But after he left his job in disgrace, he had a very small pension. When the *Wende* came in 1989, his pension was less than what a cleaning lady was earning in West Germany.

He was angry because he felt he deserved a pension that was equivalent to that of a West German civil servant who had contributed as many years of service as he had. Of course, prices began to skyrocket due to inflation, but his pension remained constant at less than 1,000 marks per month, which is difficult to live on. He felt as if he had been a pawn in the large game of East-West relations. As a result, today he doesn't vote any more. He is constantly saying, "What's the point? As a little man you really don't have any voice about what happens." That's the attitude of many people of his generation. They've never been able to cope with all of the upheaval associated with the *Wende.*

After my father was forced to retire from his job, he broke off contact with almost all of his Party comrades. He retained contact with his friends, some of whom were certainly in the Party, but ceased to have contact with any acquaintances whom he knew merely from Party meetings. I think some part of that decision certainly had to do with me. He was aware of the attitude that many Party figures had. Many claimed that his daughter was an enemy of the state or a class enemy, and that she betrayed the DDR. My father didn't want to have anything to do with people who thought like that.

Q: Why did your father join the Party?

A: To work his way up through the system, he was forced to become a comrade or an active Party member. This was distasteful to him, because he had come from an active Protestant Lutheran family that had participated in church activities that were hostile to the state or at least to the atheistic indoctrination that the DDR state was promoting.

When he joined the Party, he was forced to leave the church. This was a condition of membership in the 1950s. You couldn't be a member of both. If he wanted to go further, he would have to join the Party and be active in it.

My father simply wanted the best for his children. He wasn't a political person at all; he rarely talked about politics at home. His interest in politics was limited to figuring out which new state system would make his children and grandchildren's lives smoother, more successful, more pleasurable, most meaningful, and most challenging. The best working opportunities were available through the Party. Of course, he mouthed the proper ideological slogans. As children we always knew there were two worlds: the world at home, which was not political and which despised some of the play-acting and hypocrisy of the public world; and the larger public and political world, wherein everything was ideological and you had to know what to say, when to say it, and when to remain silent.

My father was an *Oberleutnant* [colonel] of the prison system—a chief warden. This was in a correctional facility, which wasn't a directly political job—although anyone at that level of responsibility had to have a history of service in the Party. Father came from a simple working-class family. Mom was a secretary at the punishment/rehabilitation center. He was a product of the climate of strict hierarchy in the criminal justice system. He was extremely submissive toward authority.

I have sympathy for him. Look at how much he suffered during the war years and post-war years and during the petty tyranny of the DDR. Now that the country is reunified and he is in his old age, he still isn't able to enjoy economic freedom because he has so little, even though he worked like a dog for decades. He waited so long and now it will never work out his way, that is, receiving a decent civil servant's pension by western German standards. He's completely disappointed. So are most of the people of his generation. He's sixty-seven years old and there's not much time remaining for him.

That was the most difficult decision of my life in Paris and I didn't breathe a word of it to anyone I knew—not to my parents, nor my two brothers—even though my younger brother also wanted to leave. He eventually did leave legally in 1988 through the official emigration process.

Q: Did you have any contact with your family before the Wall fell?

A: We all met in secret once before the Wall fell. My mother died in March 1989, shortly before that.

A rendezvous was worked out for me with the family. Through third parties, we were able to arrange a meeting in Hungary. I think that's one reason that Hungary has become my favorite country in the world, because it provided us asylum. I would have never otherwise been able to meet them. Hungary was one of the countries that East Germans could easily go to, and I was also able to get there without too much spying occurring.

In November 1988, we were granted official permission to have an intermittent correspondence, though I would never have been able to mention anything like a meeting in it. The correspondence, of course, was opened and noted by the Stasi. It was actually useful to them, because they could keep tabs on my family's correspondence.

The letters were, naturally, completely non-political. Sometimes I made quite specific attempts to help my parents. I presented things in the letters to imply that they had strongly discouraged me from attempting to do anything like this, but that I had defied them. I implied that they were completely against my *Republikflucht* and had begged me not to do it.

I also pretended that it was a love affair, that it was non-political, even though my whole reason was broadly political. I wanted freedom of travel. I wanted to see the world.

But I presented it all as if I had defected only because of Andreas, whereas the truth is that he was only a secondary reason. I wasn't in love with him. He was just a good West German friend that I had once met [before leaving for Paris]. That way, my parents could still say that they had raised me to be a loyal socialist and it was only for "personal reasons" that I had defected. They could present me as a kind of superficial, impulsive girl. But there wasn't any love relationship; he was just a friend that I met.

Q: So you imagined that your defection would have major costs for your family—and you were right—and these letters were largely a subterfuge designed to ease what you imagined would be the harsh state penalties.

A: Right. I was aware that my decision would expose my family to all kinds of disadvantages and financial hardships, potentially. But I viewed this trip that I was given to Paris as a gift from God. I had dreamed of Paris since I was a little girl and suddenly—of all the possible assignments

I could get—I got the ideal one. The hardest thing I faced in 1986 was to cope with the fear that if I didn't take advantage of that opportunity, I would not get another. I thought "No one else in my class is abroad. I'm the first one here in six years. When I get sent back who knows how long I'll have to stay or who knows what turns my life might take? This is my chance, right now. If I pass it up I will never forgive myself."

I made the decision on emotional grounds, not rational ones. I didn't hate the DDR. I wasn't in despair about having a future there. I simply wanted to breathe deeply the atmosphere of other cultures and other peoples and that was not permitted. I wanted that particular freedom.

On the other hand, as a result of knowing this friend of my brother, I was increasingly beginning to perceive injustices and I hated the injustices that the state was imposing. I hadn't yet generalized so widely beyond my brother's friend's case as to condemn the DDR as a state. I really saw it simply as a matter of isolated cases, for people like him, and possibly me, who wanted what the state wouldn't permit. I didn't have the political consciousness to see it in broader ideological terms.

Q: So you would have been glad to return if you had been allowed to do so without punishment?

A: Yes! I loved my parents, I had good friends, and I didn't want to leave permanently. I had this passionate desire to learn. I had this love of languages. I knew that this curiosity and love could never be satisfied if I were to stay in the DDR. I would have had a great future in the DDR: I was being hailed as one of the leading young interpreters as a result of getting this plum assignment. I would have been in the traveling cadre. The likelihood is that I would have gotten more assignments abroad. Once you'd proved yourself trustworthy in a place like Paris, you would have been selected again. But that wasn't certain and also there was a rotation process. Plus I was impatient. I had waited so long already. I was probably going to be hired next by Intertext, which was the language translation interpretation bureau in the DDR. Although it was based in Berlin, they assigned people to various delegations that were traveling abroad.

Q: You must have often wondered during those three years away, before the Wall fell, what your life would have been like if you had stayed.

A: All the time. I probably would have eventually been an interpreter for members of the Central Committee of the Party. I would have gotten a lot of western currency every time I went abroad. I would have had a comfortable, easy, high-status life in the DDR. On the other hand, that would have entailed my learning more and more state secrets, and that, in turn, would have led to more spying upon me and my family. The more responsibility and the more trust the state was investing in me, the tighter and tighter the net would have been drawn around my freedom to speak to a variety of people.

I felt this political cage that was closing in on me even in my first week in Paris. I vaguely feared already that what had happened to my father would happen to me. Once you're in, you never get out. He would have gotten out if he could have done so without facing negative consequences, but there were consequences.

Q: Why were the Party authorities willing to take such a big risk as to send you abroad? They had invested a great deal in you, and they turned out to have been disastrously wrong about your "political reliability."

A: I had excelled in English and French. Those were the key languages of Western Europe, so it was clear I would spend a great deal of time in KA [capitalist foreign nations]. Just to be permitted to study at university, I was subjected to a very extensive background investigation of my family, schooling, and political convictions. By the time I was taking advanced courses beyond university, I had already passed many state evaluations for what could be called political correctness. Moreover, I attended special language school courses for permission to travel to other countries as a member of the diplomatic corps. We had to take an oath that nothing said during the course would ever be mentioned outside the course. It was like preserving military secrets, yet it was absurd because our courses simply involved the learning of a language; nonetheless, it signified that there was a special need to train people to work abroad. The State wanted to be certain of our socialist convictions and loyalty to the DDR.

Beyond that, it was a great advantage that my mother and father were in the Party. Our family was a Party family. That automatically facilitated my acceptance.

It also helped that I was technically proficient yet not outspoken or especially politically minded. I wasn't a critical thinker at all, so I was one of the best FDJ advocates. I was a completely "convinced communist" when I was in my teens and early twenties. You needed two things: the highest grades, and your family had to be "clean." We had a word for a good loyal socialist lineage, for a good Party family: *astrein* [clean timber, spot-free, straight, without knotholes].[2] That's a funny Berlin expression, but we used it all the time. Both of my brothers had served in the NVA, on the border and with distinction. That was a huge plus for me. Border patrol was a delicate assignment to receive because escapes were so common on the border. It was a sign of your extreme loyalty to the DDR that you were chosen for such assignments.

Q: So *astrein* meant that you had to be not only politically reliable, but of a pure ideological lineage, i.e., politically untainted.

A: Yes, with no relatives in the capitalist West and preferably none in other communist countries. That would guarantee that you would not only be completely loyal to the State out of conviction, but also out of fear, because if all your family was in East Germany, and if you did anything disloyal, something terrible would happen to them—all of them. And you would have nobody abroad to help you—no blood relations. You would be fearful on that score too. How could you trust anyone? So it looked as if I was an ideal choice to be sent to Western Europe. I had the political qualifications.

I also had the highest technical qualifications. As a child, I was sent to a special language school. In this school I learned to speak Russian beginning in the third grade. In fifth grade, I learned English and I received extremely good grades. On that basis, I was admitted to a special course of study at a university concentrating on languages. I was a language fanatic my whole life, so everything came together. It was what I loved to do and I was going to get the chance to do it at the highest level that the DDR permitted. At university, I studied French and English intensively. Then one day I was informed, as soon as my selection for a new elite course of study occurred, that we "chosen ones" would no longer have contact with Englishmen, Americans, or Frenchmen. "You will master the instrument, but you will not interact with them. You will not be spoiled and corrupted by their values and ideology."

Q: So you really didn't have any contact with Westerners before you defected?

A: Yes, but not much. Yet I shared the passion of millions of East Germans. I wanted to get out and see what was going on in the world beyond the borders of the tiny DDR! I had the curiosity and fascination of any young person. I wanted to breathe in all of the wondrous variety that the world seemed to offer. Of course, this desire was increased by the fact that I studied in Berlin. Even in East Berlin there were so many opportunities.

It was a metropolis and so I constantly saw people from elsewhere. Because I couldn't approach these foreigners, I would become frustrated. If there was to be any interaction between us, they would have to approach me. Seeing these people broadened my horizons and stimulated my curiosity about them.

On language grounds, I wanted to practice speaking with them, but that kind of opportunity was very limited in East Berlin. I wanted to experience them in the climate of their own language and culture. Very often, we did accompany Americans or Canadians into cafés to have English conversations, but that was forbidden and we had anxiety when we were doing it. The conversations were quite innocent, and there was always some worry that somebody might be watching us or that our conversation might turn to something politically sensitive. I feared that a professor who knew me would come into the café and report that I was conversing with a foreigner. I would lose my special place in his course of study and foil my chances of going abroad. So I was jeopardizing my future each time I did it, yet I couldn't resist the urge to speak with foreigners. But I refrained from speaking with them in private places, because the implications of such an action would make it difficult to downplay the conversation as something innocent. I could present it as something innocent that was suggested by the foreigner—that he was offering to pay for my meal. A dinner invitation could always be rewritten as some vaguely romantic and therefore non-political affair of the heart.

I was motivated to do all this on linguistic and cultural grounds—and the same thing with correspondence. I did begin writing to people for language practice and also to find out what their lives were like. There wasn't an iota of politics in it, and I was not interested in getting West German currency or in making contacts so that I could begin some kind of illicit love relationship and thus have grounds to apply for an exit visa on that basis.

Q: You were at the top of the academic hierarchy in the DDR at Humboldt University—the best of the best. You were an elite achiever in your field and you had become an interpreter abroad, which was a sign of both intellectual and political distinction.

A: Yes, I really could have made something of myself in the DDR if I had stayed. I was eligible for the highest tracks in salary, prestige, and honor. Perhaps within a few years I would have been working for the SED Central Committee.

I was simply one of the lucky ones to have had the opportunities that I did. It was a once-in-a-lifetime opportunity to go to Paris when I was twenty-one. So I seized it. The three years that I was out of contact with my family, from 1986 to November 1989, were extremely difficult for me despite the fact that I was living a new life abroad. It was a new and exciting life.

Q: How were you received in West Germany? You must have been very well treated, given your value as a high-status defector.

A: The West Germans were extraordinarily nice to me. I don't know if they regarded my defection as a coup, but they were so forthcoming and supportive. They never really interrogated me for whatever state secrets I was supposed to have in the eyes of the DDR. They thought that I had voted with my feet and was making a public statement by coming to them. So I suppose they did look at things in an ideological way.

Perhaps some West Germans did look upon my *Republikflucht* as a victory for them, or as a victory for the West over the East. But what I most experienced was the personal warmth. I felt that they treated me as a human being and not as a statistic or as a feather in their caps. I was in the refugee camp for only a single day. I was immediately put into contact with West Germans who showed me how everything in West Germany was run. I was also able to study at a university in West Berlin. They put themselves at my disposal. I immediately received a guest family and a guest mother who took great pains to introduce me to nice people and look after my welfare.

Q: Could you discuss further the ideological dimension of your education?

A: What I call my *rote Erziehung* [Red education] really began with kindergarten or in the *Hort* [daycare center] after nursery school.

The socialist lessons never stopped. Even during play we were encouraged not to pursue any kind of individualistic leisure activities; rather, in order to promote collectivist thinking, to have work groups or play groups in which we would undertake activities with a common purpose. So school lasted a half-day and the *Hort* was a half-day. Those children who had mothers at home (which was increasingly less the case by the 1970s, or even after the Wall went up) went home for the afternoon, but most of us were in the *Hort*. My mother arranged to have part-time work when I was small, so that I could come home after kindergarten for the afternoon.

In school and in the *Hort,* there were activities that we participated in, like memorizing Pioneer songs or Pioneer poetry that was explicitly political. They were designed to develop political consciousness. There were songs that preached the solidarity of the working-class children in the world. Of course, most of the slogans we were taught to chant spontaneously were designed to develop our socialist convictions. A great deal of the group work had to do with inculcating collective thinking. But this collective thinking also had positive consequences. I remember being taught to love red flowers, such as roses and carnations, more than any other flower. A girl was even called a "Red flower." In the Pioneers, that was a phrase of great praise.

I never thought of the DDR system as superior to other systems, but maybe that was because I was always so interested in other cultures and languages. What I gained most was a sense of proletarian internationalism or international solidarity with other workers. I was eager to gain exposure to other nations and cultures. I was always keying on the international aspects of our education and seeing this kind of outreach in linguistic and cultural terms, even if the real theme in the classes was ideological, such as "Socialism is winning," or "We are better than the capitalists"—that wasn't the way I responded to the lessons.

I was an extremely eager Young Pioneer. I was in the choir. I helped to organize a lot of the activities. I was the chairwoman of our little central committee, which was composed of the most active Pioneers that were in the class. I was the secretary of the Pioneers, the *Schriftführer.* I also helped edit the Pioneer newspaper in school. I was simply a good, decent, well-behaved pupil. Yes, I was a good little Pioneer.

The positions were like being an officer of the student council in America. I suppose I was simply a *Streber,* a striver in the sense of a swot, as the British call it. I always wanted to be doing something. I always wanted an official position and a position of honor. To be a *Streber* certainly wasn't something negative. It was something highly valued in the official eyes of the Pioneers: the model socialist personality.

The students who had the best grades, along with many awards for high achievement, usually received these positions in the youth organizations.

Q: Apart from regretting its impact on your family, you had no guilt, and even no major regret about defecting. Is that so?

A: True. Yet I must confess that there was still some residue of the DDR ideological browbeating in me. I had some residue of an anti-Western enemy image in those early years. And to prove to everyone, especially to myself, that I was as good as a West German, I worked like a crazy woman around the clock.

I don't mean that I harbored an enemy image toward particular West Germans; rather I had it about the whole system. I feared that, by tomorrow, I could be a helpless drug addict or a homeless person, lying in the street with no one to care about me and no financial cushion—no security whatsoever. Then the cruel system would close in on me. I would have to become a prostitute as a way of escaping from this misery. I would have to sell myself so I could have something to eat. I had such great angst toward capitalism that I feared these horrible scenarios. I imagined these scenes were happening all around me and that it was like an infection that could hit me.

Even though I was receiving quite a bit of money from the state, I still had the notion that there was no social net in capitalism, unlike the case in the DDR. I received 750 marks per month in basic needs, while receiving support from three other endowments that gave me at least as much income. I was quite comfortable. I had plenty of money and felt I was living in paradise because of all the things I could buy. West German life wasn't horrendously expensive as I was led to believe. I was experiencing the best of capitalism in every way.

I never had the feeling that I was being exploited as a Western billboard to be hung out in front of East Germans: "Daughter of the DDR Who Has Escaped." I never noticed a political dimension in any of my interactions. I don't think I was exploited at all. To the contrary, I thought I was *not* being exploited for the first time, that I was being dealt with and evaluated on some honest basis. I could express my opinions, and not be penalized for them. I didn't have to live a lie. What I especially liked at the university was that academic merit was valued over political affiliation.

Q: What did the West Germans whom you met think of most East Germans? Surely you didn't fit their stereotypes.

A: A lot of the snap judgments that West Germans have about East Germans since the *Wende* are accurate—especially those pertaining to East Germans' inability to compete. East Germans are not competitive. They don't know how to work hard. Most *Ossis* really didn't know how to compete. Those of us who were in special schools and attended places like Humboldt, or were in some other line of work in which high motivation and high performance were rewarded, proved the exception. In general, there was little incentive and, therefore, much mediocrity.

Q: Do you recall your first impressions of the DDR when you returned after the Wall fell?

A: I first returned to the DDR in November 1989, when it was safe to return. I was utterly shocked at how run-down the country was. It was collapsing economically, but what I noticed most was the grayness and dilapidation, because my experience in the West gave me a framework of comparison that I didn't have before. I had known this in the abstract. Previously, other people would say this, and much of what we saw on West German television confirmed it. I had never lived outside of the DDR before 1986, and so it was a shock to return. The sad fact was that my mother was no longer alive. She died when I was away. That was the really sad part of coming back home. I couldn't go to the funeral, because I knew the Stasi would be there waiting for me if I tried to slip in.

I did make one half-hearted attempt to apply legally to return to visit. I discovered that I had never been officially denationalized [*ausgebürgert*]; i.e., my citizenship was never formally revoked. I was still officially a DDR citizen even though I had forsaken the country. If I had returned, I would have also been subject to DDR law and the punishments that would come under the DDR judicial system. My West German citizenship wasn't recognized, so I had no protection. I would, no doubt, have been tried and convicted of "flight from the Republic" and been jailed for fifteen to twenty years.

I still had my DDR passport at home. I was never officially deprived of my DDR citizenship, so I continued through this technical legality to be recognized as a DDR citizen. [Kersten shows me her DDR passport; the last time it's stamped is in 1986 when she went to Paris.] I never qualified for any form of amnesty from the DDR and so that explains it. I never seriously tried to get back into the country. I had grave anxiety when I was in Hungary that it would have been easy to nab me—that there might be Stasi agents poised to grab me. I could have easily been kidnapped. One of the reasons that we also chose Hungary was that, by contrast, Czechoslovakia had a very close working relationship with the DDR to extradite escaped citizens. Hungary took all of that much more in stride. This was possibly done as a concession to the tourism industry, since a lot of West Germans were secretly meeting East Germans in Hungary under the pretense of vacationing.

Upon entering the refugee camp, I was immediately recognized officially as a West German citizen, and that's what I wanted. If the DDR had recognized me as a West German citizen I could have easily visited East Germany without facing political consequences. That's precisely what the

DDR didn't want to do. They wanted to punish me according to East German law, and this is why I didn't attend my mother's funeral. Through third parties, my father was able to give me a telephone call and warn me, under any circumstances, to not do anything stupid like try to attend the funeral. It was a bittersweet reunion in Hungary in 1989, because, as happy as my family was to see me, nothing was as it had been before.

Q: You say that you partly adopted the DDR's ideological mandate to "love the Fatherland," sometimes known as "education for socialist patriotism." How did you respond to its counterpart, Education for Hatred toward the West?

A: I never had that much of a *Feindbild*. We often found such talk about a capitalistic enemy image very amusing. We used to laugh about it. How could anybody be so naive to think that our fellow Germans across the border were so different from us? They just had a different economy. For example, we thought of the U.S. as a place where you could get good jeans; Spain was a place where you could have great vacations. That part of the propaganda never really got through to us, because we were so eager to experience everything we had associated these places with: the products, the dream images that our grandparents had, and what we saw on western television.

Even our family, though we had no relatives in the West, saw how happy the people were and how well everything was going for them. We couldn't believe that they were directing their lives toward hurting us or that they saw themselves in some sort of a rival campaign to outdo us. They were enjoying their lives! We saw that they could live reasonably well abroad. I saw this even as a convinced socialist. My socialism was, in that respect, somewhat defensive; I also thought that we could live good lives in our society. One life isn't necessarily better than another; it's just different, and this is the one we have, so let's live as well as we can within our system.

The whole black-and-white propaganda treatment seemed absurd to us. You could see on television that this wasn't true. The East German government's preaching was vastly oversimplified and it attempted to blacken the West in a far-too-exaggerated fashion. The West didn't only consist of discontented workers and homeless people. Of course it's true that the price of a roll or a piece of bread in the DDR was five or ten cents, while prices were five times that or more in the West, but, on the other hand, we saw that they were consuming such products as bananas, kiwis, and apples—rarities that we could only experience as special treats at Party events.

Q: What was different in your family, so that you learned to toe the Party line?

A: Once again, in my family, everything was discussed. There was, at least, a tolerance of varied opinion, but in other families, there was intolerance and a strict enforcement of the Party line. I can imagine even the intelligent teenagers in those families didn't allow their minds to roam in such a way that would jeopardize their future.

There were always two sides to any experience. There was what you could say in school and then there were the things that you had to remain silent about. We, of course, knew even as small children that our parents weren't as narrow-minded as the orthodox ideologues that were promoted in our schools or among our neighbors. Sometimes the orthodox lessons that were drummed into us in school were mocked or dismissed in our home. But in many families that were extremely strict and that didn't permit any western television at home, or didn't permit any discussion of western topics or dissident figures who had emigrated, that was never the case.

These other families were 100 percent communist families in which no other opposing political viewpoint would even be discussed at home, but our parents were never like that. A great deal was discussed, never or rarely in direct opposition to the DDR, but more just raising questions about DDR policy. I was always so content with the DDR because I never perceived, given the strong influence of my parents' home, that I lived in a pressure cooker. I could see that other people had more limited views, but I never experienced anything like the suffocating, unlivable, day-to-day agony of having to suffer in silence while living a lie. Our home was always a place where I could breathe and could say what was on my mind. My mind never ventured into dangerous areas that would have threatened the state. I was a convinced communist, but I was not a political creature or a political enthusiast. My fanaticism began and ended with languages.

Q: You described your younger self as a "convinced communist." In hindsight, was that conviction formed because the system worked to your benefit?

A: Yes, I could reconcile myself to the way that the state worked because I was a beneficiary of so many advantages, and my deepest love of learning languages and living abroad was being supported and promoted. So I was convinced of the goodness of a lot of things in the DDR. I believed in many of the ideals that it was promoting. I also believed that they were being realized: the equality, the fellow-feeling, the respect for the worker, and the solidarity among working classes of all countries.

Even today, I still think that not everything in the DDR was bad. I had, for instance, an excellent history education in school and obviously an excellent language training program. Education was, at least for those who qualified for these elite schools, outstanding.

I had numerous advantages and opportunities that many others in the DDR and abroad did not. We were upset by a lot of hypocrites, especially by those in the Party who maintained contact with Westerners and received a lot of Western currency yet weren't punished for it. We were also upset with Western visitors who would bring all kinds of goodies. We had none of that because we had no West German relatives and never developed any connections with West Germans. We were always annoyed by some of the Party elite, because they were the biggest hypocrites, in that they gained all kinds of financial benefits from the West, while denouncing the West as horrifyingly capitalist.

Of course, in the strictest sense, we were all hypocrites. In the election, we all voted for a single standard Party list. If you voted for some other candidate or refused to vote at all, you were endangering your place in society, so we all made our peace with the corrupt system by commission or omission. The question was "How much are you willing to suffer?" Many dissidents and regime opponents were willing to give up their freedom, or compromise their career possibilities, or even endanger their family's future. In a few cases, they would even give their lives. Nobody in our family was willing to go near that. So whatever discontent or questioning occurred, it remained within the four walls of our home and was conducted in quite modulated tones.

Our language training in modern languages was as good as it could be for such an artificial environment. It was grammatically outstanding and teachers were extremely well trained, but what limited it and made it impossible was that we couldn't spend every summer in England like West German English majors did or regularly visit France to freshen up our French. So on the one hand we didn't get enough practice, and on the other it wasn't real. That was also the case with Russian. We could talk about Party documents and string together prefabricated phrases in our sleep but we had difficulty conducting a typical conversation that normal Russian people would have had on the street. This was due to the lack of training in that area and also to the lack of travel opportunities that may have allowed us to pick that up.

8. West Side (Hi)Story II: A *Wossi* in Wittenberg

Interview in September 1994 with Herr Franz Weber, twenty-eight, a recently hired Wittenberg history and Latin teacher from Baden-Württemberg. Herr Weber majored in classics at Freiburg University and minored in history chiefly in order to get a job. (Classics is a subject seldom taught in German high schools.) He teaches twenty-five hours per week in Wittenberg, seventeen of which are in history, eight in Latin. Herr Weber has recently finished his teacher training period in Freiburg. He is commuting weekly between there and Wittenberg, because he was unable to find a teaching position either in his home state or anywhere else in western Germany. He had never set foot in an eastern school before his sudden hiring in Wittenberg. Because his firsthand contact is so new, his curiosity about eastern schools is keen and his impressions of eastern education are fresh. Particularly noteworthy are his observations on the post-reunification vogue in the east for Latin, the declining popularity of Russian, and the curricular changes pertaining to history and religion. "Anything that was missing in the DDR days and has taught in the West," says Herr Weber, "is assumed to be better."

Q: As a western German, are there any remaining differences today in the subject matter or pedagogical approaches between eastern and western history classes?

A: There are no differences as to what history is taught in eastern and western Germany now. The same textbooks are used in many of the states in the east and west even though there is no uniform textbook selection throughout Germany. It isn't as if there is a special eastern textbook and a different western textbook. However, there are differences in the way themes are treated if there is a connection to regional history. For instance, when we do the Reformation in Wittenberg, which is also known as the city of Luther, we go into immense detail and devote time to Luther's biography and his role in Wittenberg. That occupies a central place in our study of the Reformation. That would not be the case in regions outside Saxony-Anhalt.

I'm sure there are still some differences in how eastern and western teachers present the Cold War, the erection of the Wall, or the 1953 Workers' Uprising. Although we are all teaching from the same book, it is likely that our experiences condition how we present this material; therefore, we would treat such politically sensitive East/West crises differently in light of our own personal histories. Equally interesting is the tendency of eastern German students to react differently to western German teachers who discuss such material, in comparison to eastern German teachers. The students here seem much more receptive to western teachers—and very skeptical about everything their eastern teachers have to say on East/West historical issues.

I also applied to teach history in Saxony, and one school principal told me that he would prefer western teachers like me to fill the new history teaching positions, since old eastern teachers had a Marxist-Leninist *Weltanschauung;* he added that recent graduates from eastern universities were no freer of ideological taint because they had been taught by M-L professors. I didn't get that job, but I was struck by how strongly this Saxony principal felt that western teachers have fresh perspectives because they were not tainted by M-L ideology.

Q: Volk und Wissen no longer has a textbook monopoly in the east. How are textbooks now selected in the east and west?

A: Each German state determines which textbooks will be used and which publishing houses will receive contracts. There is no central publishing house or uniform selection process for textbooks throughout Germany—unlike in the DDR, in which the Volk und Wissen publishing house produced and distributed all textbooks. But there are two or three major schoolbook publishing houses that regularly produce new textbooks for most subjects, and they have cornered the entire German market.

Q: How has teacher training changed in the east since reunification?

A: That's a question I'm very familiar with, because principals and fellow eastern teachers have constantly been telling me how superior my western training in the classics and in history has been.

Depending on the subject, there was no student training period for many teachers in the DDR. Take, for instance, Latin teachers. They were simply left to fend for themselves and decide how to present material to pupils, so they had no pedagogical or didactic methods taught to them. Typically, they taught subjects as they were taught at the university or in the POS.

Eastern Germany now has a formal teacher training period to train teachers, unlike in its DDR days, wherein that wasn't always the case in every subject. There are many teachers still on staff who never went through a formal training period. Many western Germans criticize the DDR system for this deficiency. They say that, because those easterners never had any training in pedagogy, the quality of their teaching depended solely on the quality of the teacher's ability to communicate the material. Even the training that the easterners did receive was poor. There was an overemphasis on content at the expense of method—that is, at the expense of understanding the student and the class's group psychology.

Q: One hears that the teacher screenings for Party and Stasi connections have been especially close in Saxony. Have many teachers been released?

A: There was a very strict screening for DDR teachers who taught German, history, and civics, because those subjects were strongly ideological. Those screenings are now completed. Almost one-fourth of the teachers were fired or furloughed. Most teachers were retained. The strictest screenings occurred in this state [Saxony], where 20 percent of the teaching staff was fired on ideological grounds that were based on Party functions performed in school or in cooperation with the Stasi. Most of these teachers were in those three subjects as well as geography.

Q: Many eastern teachers object to the ongoing differences between eastern and western teachers—in salary, official status, and terms of appointment.

A: Yes. I hear it all the time: the gap in official status is large. For instance, all of the eastern teachers are merely employees rather than civil servants. After a testing period, all western teachers are given civil service status, which prevents them from being fired or furloughed. Employees can be released for any reason, whereas civil servants can't. In order to save money through retrenchment, teachers who are employees can be fired or furloughed. In other words, teachers in eastern Germany have no security. There is no difference in status or security between teachers who were in the Party and who weren't in the Party. It's impossible to tell who was a Party member and who wasn't, unless those former Party members had official functions; in which case, it's often true that their old attitudes are still discernible. There are many teachers who are turncoats and who have often, with some hypocrisy, adapted so well to the new system that one would never imagine they had any redness in their background.

Q: Is the "partner program," whereby western states are matched with eastern states to assist them in the transition, proving effective?

A: By and large, yes. It depends on how extensively an eastern state avails itself of the opportunity to receive help. Each eastern German state has selected a partner state in western Germany. For instance, Saxony-Anhalt has Lower Saxony as its partner state, accepting its syllabi as models for Saxony-Anhalt. That is, new federal states in the east have "big brother" federal states in the west who ship textbooks, send administrative personnel, exchange teachers, and offer guidance on making their transition.

Western partner states, in various ways, support their eastern partner states. For instance, Bavaria is partnered with Saxony. This partnership is not limited to education, but extends to legal and court matters, politics, law enforcement, and the exchange or loaning of civil servants.

Q: Given the widely recognized superiority of western teacher training, is it fairly easy for western teachers to get eastern positions?

A: Training was indeed considerably better in the west than in the east—both with respect to pedagogy and content, and especially true in subjects that were ideological. Nevertheless, despite the superiority, western teachers are not preferred in the east. Just as in the west, each eastern state still generally gives priority to its own institutions of higher education. It is easiest to get a job in your own state. It is difficult to move, as I have done, from one state to another unless one has unusual qualifications that are difficult to fulfill in the home state. For instance, I teach Latin and there are no higher education centers in eastern Germany that train Latin teachers. That's coming, but it's not yet here.

Q: What factors currently determine which teachers get hired?

A: The combination of fields that one majored in at the university, along with grades, is decisive. For instance, history and Latin are unusual combinations, and it is for this reason that I was able to get a job at Wittenberg. History is glutted with applicants. Latin is seldom taught in eastern schools, but because of the absence of university programs for Latin in the east, I had an advantage.

By the way, it is an extreme rarity that easterners are hired in western Germany. I know of no example whatsoever. I've never met an eastern teacher in western Germany, even though easterners would certainly prefer to be in western Germany for two reasons: the salaries are much higher; and one can be eligible for civil servant status, rather than simply remain an [untenured] employee.

Q: So easterners are not yet [1994] permitted to teach with civil servant status in western Germany.

A: Right, they are restricted to the eastern states. Their diplomas are not yet recognized in the west. That is also why eastern teachers are paid less. They are classified as BRD 3, whereas newly hired teachers in the west are immediately classified as BRD 2a. [These are employee rankings similar to civil servant rankings in the United States.]

Every state is trying to take care of its own graduates. Education is in the administrative jurisdiction of the local states, not the federal government. So, in the east, regional graduates are preferred for each state's schools. Outsiders are hired as exceptions. Because of the dominance of Russian in the DDR, Latin was not a school subject. The third language after Russian and English was French, yet it was only a special offering that was often restricted to the EOS.

One of the perceived strengths of western teacher training has been its rigor. There was very careful oversight. At the close of your teacher training period, you receive a grade consisting of your university grades and of your evaluation as a teacher trainee by your supervising teacher at *Gymnasium*. In subjects where there is a very strong need in the east, such as in English, grades are a decisive criterion and there is a ranking of teacher trainees based on these grades in each state. Trainees will generally be hired according to their grades. English is now in great demand in the east because it has replaced Russian as the chief foreign language. Many Russian teachers are trying to learn English well enough via an *Umschulung* [retraining] to gain qualification to teach it.

A second exam takes place after the teacher training period, known as the Second State Examination. So there is a complicated composite of evaluative criteria. One-third of your state exam grade consists of your grades in your courses at the university, and another third consists of four supervisions of your classroom conducted by your supervisory teacher throughout the year. The supervisory teacher is accompanied by another person, so two people evaluate your session during each of these four visits. Your supervisory teacher is responsible for the pedagogy. He also accompanies you throughout the year and teaches you didactics or discusses teaching methods with you. The accompanying evaluator focuses on content and is a specialist in your subject area. There is also a chair or president of testing evaluation, who is either a central administrative authority of the state or a member of the school administration.

The final third consists of oral examinations. These exams test knowledge on civil servant law, certain general pedagogical methods, courses that apply to your subject, and psychology. Each of these oral exams lasts for half an hour. Five or six percent of teacher trainees these days are hired, and they must be excellent across the board. They typically have a point total, no higher than 1 or 1.5 on a six-point scale. As a result, there has been a surge in unemployment among teachers. For instance, in Baden-Württemberg, 2,850 teacher trainees have applied for teaching positions in the state. Only 175—about 6 to 7 percent—have found a position; thus, well over 90 percent are unemployed for the upcoming year.

However, even outstanding performances in subjects that aren't in demand, such as Russian, don't open the door to a job offer. In Baden-Württemberg, there were only two Latin teachers hired out of 180 applicants in the entire state this year. So these two top students were really extraordinary. Their point total approached zero, which is perfect. That is "A+ + + +."

It's also possible that these cases had an extremely favorable subject combination if there were ties in point totals. For instance, mathematics and chemistry are always in high demand, because so many graduates go into industry rather than teaching. Sports for girls is also in high demand, since relatively few women are majoring in sports now; thus the female athletics graduates who have majors such as geography or political science—which are not highly sought—will nevertheless be hired. Most often, and sometimes entirely, their classroom hours will be devoted to sports.

History is also a subject that too many people study. There are opportunities for temporary substitute teachers in history.

Q: How has the introduction of religion been received?

A: Religion is such a new subject in the east that, typically, there isn't much of a demand yet. Generally there is not more than one student out of twenty-five in a class who is Catholic. Three pupils will be Lutheran, and the others will fall under the "agnostic or atheist without any religious affiliation" category. Lutheranism is stronger here [in Wittenberg] than anywhere else in the DDR, so that latter affiliation is actually quite minimal elsewhere.

I notice the difference between student believers and non-believers when I treat a topic like the Reformation in history class. The believers are very interested in how the division in the Church arose, and how Protestantism developed in Europe thereafter. They are keenly aware that the state-sanctioned atheism of the DDR raises the same issues of religious freedom and toleration that occurred during the Reformation and Counter-Reformation. But to the non-believers, all those issues are just dead "textbook" history—just something to memorize, inert facts or bits of knowledge.

The same distinction prevails with students who select Latin. Latin pupils usually come from ambitious religious families. Of course, Latin is associated with the Church, but there's also an oddly practical, indeed capitalist motive behind the selection of Latin by many students. There is a misunderstanding among students that—because Latin was never offered before and it was a western German subject—it will increase job opportunities! Parents think that the chances of success in the new Germany will improve for their children if they study Latin. These kids had Russian before, which they hated, and which didn't necessarily bring good job prospects. Latin has replaced Russian and is much more popular.

Anything that's western or anything that was missing in the DDR days and was taught in the west is assumed to be better. Not just better in the general sense, but better in a way that eastern German parents value in economic terms even when every bit of evidence that one could marshal speaks to the contrary.

Q: You mentioned the declining popularity of Russian among pupils. That has, of course, meant that Russian teachers have no pupils in their subject to teach. Have Russian teachers been able to retrain?

A: Often an eastern state still prefers to help its own teachers by not hiring western teachers who teach Latin, but rather retraining Russian teachers in quick-fix courses to teach basic Latin. These teachers are then assigned to teach first-year Latin. So, in some cases, Russian teachers do remain, but they switch languages to either Latin or, more commonly, English in order to do so. Of course, these teachers can't be compared with a western German teacher trainee who has studied the subject for four years or longer—sometimes even since *Gymnasium*.

9. Running On, or Training for the (Russian) Olympics

Another conversation with Kersten, now thirty-three, the former DDR interpreter whom we met earlier in this chapter. In this interview in October 1998, she explains how she mastered Russian in her special language school, which largely dispensed with textbooks in order to promote spoken fluency. Kersten's discussion of DDR pedagogical methods for promoting the mastery of Russian is most interesting, as is her contention that the pedagogy of the special language schools was "very different from the normal pupil's experience." She also stresses that the teachers in her special school were "very Red" and that they did teach the textbooks "to the letter." She remarks: "What was in the textbooks is what was taught in school by teachers." Her testimony is thus directly contrary to the reports of Frau Ehspanner and Stefan, whom we encountered in sections 5 and 6 of this chapter, and it once again suggests the diversity of educational experience of DDR citizens. The ideological emphasis, based on the classroom materials in all of Kersten's school classes, corresponds to Stefan's memory of his civics teacher. But otherwise, it is as if Stefan and Kersten attended schools in different countries. All of this makes clear that the phrase "DDR educational experience" is complex, contingent, and multidimensional, and that it is a virtually meaningless abstraction when it lacks a specific context and concrete content.

Why was Kersten's experience so different? One explanation is that the "special" schools were ideologically "special" too, necessarily so. Why? Because these schools trained the DDR elite to become the leaders or models or showcase performers in DDR society. So the DDR elite, who would make public statements and exercise privileges such as international travel, had to be loyal (or at least not openly rebellious) toward the DDR. They had to be monitored more closely than the average citizen for ideological purity. If that was so, then Stefan's and Frau Ehespanner's claims that most teachers maintained lax attitudes toward SED classroom directives was doubtless more representative of the typical DDR pupil's experience.

Q: You attended a special language school. Did you ever have textbooks?

A: No, not actual books—just mimeographed exercises and exercise booklets. The special language school began in the third grade. I had the opportunity to go to the post-secondary Russian language school. It was for *Abitur* graduates from the EOS who had already achieved the language proficiency certification, that is, for the elite pupils of Russian. There were only two of these schools in the entire DDR.

We mastered Russian. We were the geniuses of Russian in the DDR. We automatically qualified to be professors of Russian or interpreters or translators of difficult literary texts or employed in prestigious departments of the government. We learned Russian so well that it was a second mother language. The school was thought of as "the Russian school," because the chief language that was emphasized was Russian. It was really an intensive language program in the early grades. Most of us wanted to become interpreters, and the school was geared toward that.

Q: Did a family's Party affiliation play a role in admission to the school?

A: There were two important characteristics of the special language school. First, there were very many convinced communist kids. Second, there were children who were unusually interested in learning and they came from homes with parents who were extremely committed to education. The parents wanted very much that their children receive the best possible education. You had to either get a 1 or 2 [an A or B] in your grade in every subject. If you got a 3 [a C], you would be expelled if that continued through the academic year. So there was a great deal of pressure to keep your grades up and study hard. The standard of achievement was quite high. In order to gain admission, you had to get straight 1s in the first and second year of the POS.

The special school lasted just as long as the POS [up to tenth grade]. I got my *Abitur* in 1981 and then entered the EOS. The EOS was extremely competitive. We really had to *pauken* and *schuften* [cram and slog away, work like dogs]. I had to do homework until late into the evening every single day of the week, including weekends.

Q: How was Russian taught to you, if no textbooks were used?

A: We learned stock phrases by rote. When you knew a lot of stock phrases, you could very quickly build a monologue that sounded a lot like a Party speech or something you might read in Party document or DDR schoolbook. You just ran on and on, speaking prefabricated phrases that often would extend to the length of paragraphs, since you'd have so many interchangeable phrases that would apply regardless of the assigned topic. The topic could be on the Council for Mutual Economic Assistance [COMECON], it could be on the Warsaw Pact, or it could be on the transition to really existing socialism in East Europe. This kind of forced repetition was an excellent language learning tool. You developed a very firm foundation in language, even though it was limiting and stifling for creative thinking; insofar as repetition is the mother of learning, these phrases were repeated so frequently that we Russian [language] Olympic competitors did gain some facility in speaking that jargon.

Q: Did you participate in the Russian Olympics?

A: Yes, in fact I was really the champion. Officially, I was the second-place winner in the district. I was so angry about it! The girl who won was born in and attended kindergarten in Russia. She was from a Russian-Italian family and they were transferred to a nearby battalion in our area when she was in kindergarten. You were automatically disqualified if you attended any Russian school after the age of eight. She was only five or six, but I still thought that was an unfair advantage. This girl spoke as if she was a native speaker, so as far as I was concerned she should have been disqualified. In principle, she was a native speaker; she was able to slip in under a technical definition as an immigrant too young to be a native speaker.

I wasn't at the next Olympics because I was sent to an international competition in Poland. It was actually an international competition between the DDR and Poland. There was a cultural part where you memorized and delivered a poem and talked about some work of art. There was a conversational part where you had to speak impromptu about a particular topic, but the themes were pretty straightforward and simple, such as my hometown or my Russian pen pal or my professional future. There was a monologue part where you had to talk a little bit about your biography. This competition was held three or four times per year and it began at the school level and you worked your way up through local, regional, and district levels.

At these international competitions, we would represent East Germany. There were also, of course, math and sports Olympic competitions.

Q: Was your Russian Olympics training as well as Russian class at all ideologically conditioned?

A: Absolutely—both in content and approach. I had to learn to speak about a topic the way that you knew the Party authorities wanted you to speak about it. You knew how it should sound and what phrases to use. For instance, a frequent topic was the Council for Mutual Economic Assistance, the counterpart for the Warsaw Pact countries to the EU. That was my monologue topic at one of the Russian Olympics competitions and it was also my final exam question for my *Abitur* in Russian. You were allowed to prepare the monologue ahead of time and you would deliver it strictly in ideologically orthodox language.

For the Russian Olympics, the Russian teacher would select a topic and you had to write a composition that would be graded on language, but you were also being implicitly graded on content. I received one of the highest marks in class for one performance: "Contemporary Problems in the Struggle of the Socialist Unity Party."

Another topic I had at the Russian Olympics was based on "Selected Works of World Literature." I didn't even have to learn anything. I just had to parrot strings of phrases that I knew would be acceptable. In hindsight, it was a scandal, I consider it pathetic and shameful. We simply talked all the time like somebody who was at a Party meeting—as if we were all fellow comrades. But we were far less critical than at a Party meeting, because the sphere of M-L orthodoxies allowed for arguments. But none of us would challenge this teacher.

Here's another Russian Olympics topic: "How to Achieve Increased Productivity and Meet the Work Norm." We went to a factory and the goal was to learn how the DDR workers were so productive and how their productivity level could be raised even further. This monologue was designed both to praise the DDR factories and to show how they were in the process of becoming even more productive.

Being able to speak Russian jargon was not really a practical form of speaking. There were all kinds of things that we didn't know. We didn't know how to conduct a simple conversation, but we could talk about Party ideas with any official representative from a Russian delegation as if from a textbook.

Q: So that was a reason why your school didn't use DDR textbooks—the emphasis was on speaking and on a narrow mastery of Party jargon.

A: Yes—plus the fact that there were so few of us—it made sense for the teachers to work very closely with us. I'm sure they used a lot of material from textbook chapters devoted to Party jargon, but it probably didn't make sense to have special textbooks for us.

Also, our pedagogy was very different from the normal DDR pupil's experience. Written materials were all-important in most DDR language classes. But speaking is all-important for interpreters—and for us as interpreters at official Party functions, a mastery of Party jargon was crucial, so we learned it by parroting strings of phrases. It's a good method—but not your typical language-training method!

Q: Are there any particular phrases you remember?

A: A favorite phrase was "glorious victory of the great Soviet Army," pertaining to when Russians occupied the country in 1945. Two other phrases were "liberation from Hitlerite fascism by the glorious Red Army" and "our eternal bond of fraternity with our socialist brotherlands." All this was DDR German and also the official socialist German. This was what was in the schoolbooks and what was taught in school by teachers. It was a form of civics lesson through language. Everything that had to do with language and culture was filtered through the ideological prism. And ultimately language was used for the promotion of ideology, but it wasn't an end in itself. I made linguistic mastery an end in itself for me, but that wasn't how it was taught or why it was taught. But that was more or less the case with every humanistic subject, such as history, German literature, and even music—although the sciences were less capable of being twisted in this direction.

Q: So the teachers were also strongly "convinced communists."

A: Yes. Teachers in special schools were very Red. There were some that were less so, but even they were at best neutral and unpolitical. There wasn't anyone who was critical toward the regime. Even the neutral ones were only in subjects that were of secondary importance to us as language students such as math.

I worshipped a man who was my Russian and geography teacher. For me he was the greatest teacher there ever was. He was a completely convinced communist and he also taught history and did it with such ideological fervor. He was an idealist, honestly convinced of the superiority of socialism. He had a backbone. He always defended the DDR and the socialist system even though he acknowledged it had some weaknesses. He always rationalized the weaknesses as a part of the process of socialism moving to a higher stage of development. He was the Party secretary in our school. Nothing could shake his fervor. Either the alleged DDR weakness was capitalist propaganda, or understandable weakness in the system, or a fault of particular individuals who were corrupt, or it had to be seen against the march of history. Socialism was a living reality, it was evolving toward a greater period of maturity, and it understandably would have growing pains.

He was as Red as they come, but unlike many other Red teachers, there was nothing careerist or slimy about him. He wasn't an opportunist, he was an idealist. Nor was he the kind of comrade that you couldn't trust. You could trust him, you could raise some question with him. What he loved was argument. He wasn't closed-minded, even though the categories within which he operated were orthodox M-L categories. The *Direktorin* [principal] was also extremely dark Red [*dunkelrot*]. And we had a flag call [pledge of allegiance] every morning. That was the occasion for a great deal of civic breast-beating by official school leaders like the principal and the Party secretary.

Every time there was an official holiday or festival day, the principal, vice principal, or Party secretary would give a speech. Those speeches could have been printed in *Neues Deutschland*. I don't know if my high school Russian teacher remained a convinced communist right until the end, but at least until the mid-1980s he did.

Q: How was that possible?

A: The ideals of socialism were so deeply internalized in him as a result of the war and early postwar years that he never outgrew them or never was willing to re-evaluate them and put them to the fire completely. He was of the generation that was going to build the new Germany—"Sunrise in the east." He belonged to the founding generation of the Republic. They had the idealism and perhaps naiveté of founding visionaries. This was before countless socialist failures and corruptions led to a great deal of cynicism and careerism in the Party. People who joined the early postwar SED at a young age—he did so as a teenager in the mid-1950s—were still making a statement. If they came from left-wing families as he did, then members of his family had either suffered in the Third Reich or had been exposed to some risk.

But he was never so blind that he didn't see the limitations or corruptions of the regime, especially in later years. I last saw him when I'd just been admitted during my course of studies at the university to become an interpreter. He said, "I hope you're not going to study Russian." I was surprised. He said, "Don't be like that, get a chance for some varied experience and do something like French or Spanish, where you can be different and even see a bit of the non-socialist world for yourself."

That was the first time I thought that his private life and discourse among friends might be very different from what it was in public, in school, and on official occasions. That had never occurred to me before. It's still an open question to me whether he said that to me as some kind of joke or because I was clearly one of his favorite students. Or because he had changed his opinion about the DDR. I don't know.

Q: But that conversation planted a seed of skepticism in you.

A: Yes. But I remained a convinced communist until I was eighteen or nineteen. The first time I really began to call anything into question was after I left my parents' home. So long as I was there—despite the freedom to talk about things—my basic *Weltanschauung* as a supporter of the DDR regime and socialist system was unshakeable. My parents had protected me from everything, including opinions that would shake the foundations of my worldview. They just took care of everything. As soon as I began to live independently as an adult in East Berlin, I began to meet other kinds of people and began to have my horizons open as a result of seeing so many foreigners [in Berlin]. I began to meet some victims of the regime and some alternative thinkers and saw what was happening to them—admittedly at a distance, but enough to begin to ask questions.

Q: What happened to your teacher after reunification?

A: After I returned in 1989 to the DDR, I heard from old friends that he had become extremely depressed and disillusioned with how the DDR had betrayed itself and had collapsed. Yet he certainly was not able to affirm capitalism or West German political ideals.

Kersten then reads me her report card from twelfth grade when she achieved her diploma. It lists all her subjects and includes a certificate from this Russian teacher. "Kersten has consistently and faithfully represented within the FDJ the proper class perspective of the socialist world system. She has a firm world education perspective and has represented our class position consistently within the FDJ collective. Therefore she has earned the distinction in gold."

Q: How do you regard that achievement today?

A: I have to laugh about it as I look back on it. That commendation was for a political economy course. When you achieved a certain grade after an examination, you would get such a certificate from the FDJ, and usually a coin in gold, silver, or bronze, which signified you were *dunkelrot*. This kind of ideological competition was also very common. Probably the balance of criteria was about 50 percent intellectual or academic and 50 percent ideological. I'm listed on the report card as having "good organizational talents."

Q: Where was that demonstrated? Was that a matter of your activities in the Pioneers and the FDJ?

A: That had to do with my different roles as a functionary that I had in the group council [*Gruppenrat*] of the Pioneers and FDJ. So yes, this was an evaluation that derived from my activities in the youth organizations. That phrase—"good organizational talents"—is another way of expressing my faithful execution of collectivist ideals, my ability to cooperate within collective and for collectivist thinking.

As group council leader, I often had to organize activities for small collectives of a class or the school at large. This good organizational ability was the characterization of my facility in organizing different people in class and ascertaining if they carried out their assignments effectively. It was another way of saying that I was eligible for a leadership position: "She has good leadership talents." I also had different leadership positions in the summer camps. I was a Thälmann Pioneer and also a very active member of the FDJ in high school and at the university in the DDR. Originally these youth organizations had actually been part of the socialist workers movement [SPD] in the early decades of the century. They were turned into SED youth machines when the DDR became entirely Russified during the postwar period.

10. Varieties of Academic Experience: A German View

Interview in October 1994 with Dorothee, twenty-four, a University of Jena student in Germanistik. *Born in the eastern city of Apolda, she spent a semester in a Texas high school in 1991 and another at the University of Texas at Austin in 1993. She was struck by the differences between American and German students. Because she visited the United States not long after the fall of the Berlin Wall—before many adult eastern Germans, let alone eastern German pupils, had encountered American high school students—her impressions are largely uninfluenced by contact with the West and emerge from a DDR socialist perspective. In contrast to some of my other interviewees, she also spoke very personally throughout the interview, drawing her observations from her own experience. Dorothee's reliance on her own immediate experience, rather than on ideological categories and concepts, suggests that her range of experience extended far beyond the DDR "textbook mentality"—or indicates that, quite possibly, and much like Stefan, she was never much affected by it in the first place. Instead, Dorothee concentrates on differences in German and American* Alltagsleben *(everyday life), such as cheating in school and conversational interactions. But she does not merely comment on them in a naïve empirical way; she brings her sociological and semiotics training to her observations. I seldom witnessed this pattern of thinking,* which departs sharply from a Marxist schema, in the conversation of eastern German university students.

Q: Did you notice any differences between American and German high school pupils?

A: Yes. Cheating! In the U.S., it's practically a mortal sin to copy someone else's answers. If you see someone else doing it, you're supposed to report him—or prevent it at all costs. In Germany, it's just the reverse. It's a mortal sin if you're asked if you can copy something and you refuse. It's a gesture of solidarity to help out a classmate who doesn't have the work done. It isn't hurting you if he copies, so why not let him copy something? Whoever refuses is called a *Streber* [self-seeker].

Q: Are you referring to differences exclusively at the high school level? Or do you mean to include university students in this comparison?

A: Not only in high school, but even at university people cheat regularly. Yes, it's less common among university students than high schoolers, but it's still prevalent. University students and high school pupils simply cheat much more in Germany and it doesn't really bother them. "What's the big deal!" they think. University students, of course, are much more motivated to study and make something of themselves, whereas *Gymnasium* pupils study because they must in order to pass the *Abitur*. It's inconceivable that a high schooler would tell the teacher, "He asked to copy my answers."

Q: What would happen if one pupil did tattle on another?

A: If somebody did something like that, the rest of the class would never speak to him again. He would be regarded as hopelessly self-righteous and a real brown-noser. Yes, if a teacher discovers you've cheated, you'll receive a 6 [F] for that work. But I'm only speaking of the student attitude. But even teachers are tolerant. You'd never be reported to the principal, let alone be expelled or have it put in your records. It would simply be a private matter between you and that teacher. "You flunked this test."

Q: Why do German schools handle the problem—which we treat as a serious issue of "academic dishonesty"—so casually?

A: There's no wider disciplinary consequence because it's regarded as something that everyone does, and you just happened to get caught. But if it becomes part of a frequent and larger pattern of behavior, if you get caught several times plagiarizing and you rarely come to class and you're a discipline problem in class, then it would be part of some general indictment and could lead to your dismissal. But cheating in itself is not serious.

Q: Would you cheat? Or rather: have you done so?

A: Sure. It's no big deal. I know that I could never refuse other students if they asked me to copy my paper or test, even though I think that it's good that Americans try to think for themselves and work independently. It almost seems to me a merely technical exercise in honesty—an empty, rather moralistic, formal matter of following official rules. Unless somebody is constantly asking me to copy, I view it as a chance to help him. I would hope that he would help me out if I didn't have time over the weekend to complete my work. I don't view it as some kind of moral crime. To me, helping him out is a corporal work of mercy; it's giving someone a loan or a gift.

Q: American educators consider it a form of theft from all those who have worked openly and fairly for what they receive.

A: But we don't have anything like bell curves for grading. Grades aren't as important here as in your country. One grade that does matter is the *Abitur* exam. It is scored, not by one's own teachers, but by outside evaluators. Later examinations that are also important are the state examinations for university students. But your grades in the U.S. are much more significant and are accumulated on a month-to-month basis. So when American students cheat, people regard it as unfair because the others who don't cheat are disadvantaged. That isn't the perception in Germany. It's more a matter of "Please, let me too be able to make this checkpoint. I can be checked off as having submitted this. That doesn't hurt everybody else. If I don't ultimately study the material, I won't pass the *Abitur*."

Q: We prize "fair competition" and believe in performance graded on merit—at least in principle.

A: Yes. It's a different and fiercer context of competition in your country. It isn't really important in Germany if twenty-five pupils have good grades and only five have bad ones. That won't affect what their *Abitur* grades are. The competitive climate in the U.S. means that everyone is evaluated relative to one another, whereas in the *Abitur* and state examinations, students are evaluated relative to an absolute standard.

Q: Does the competitive U.S. climate in higher education foster a stronger work ethic there than in Europe? Many Germans who come to the States remark on how hard American students work.

A: You have so much homework at university because everything is just like school. Quantity is what counts there. There's nothing like that in humanities and social sciences in Germany. We practically never have homework in Germany at university, certainly not by the time of *Hauptstudien* [chief course of studies]. At most we have a *Referat* [an oral report] and perhaps one written assignment. One receives credit, not a grade, for the course. The class meets only once a week for two hours. I took fourteen semesters, seven years. One can go faster and complete the degree in only eight semesters, but then you'll work like a dog.

Q: Many Americans would say that seven years is too long to study for an undergraduate degree.

A: What does it mean to study too long? We really should study our whole life long, but should the state support that? The only matriculation requirement that I have to meet is finishing my basic course of study in four semesters. And passing the exam that allows me to become an advanced student. After that I can study as long as I want. It could be forty semesters. I think everyone should have the right to as much education as he wants. It should be a basic right. The state should guarantee free education in all public institutions regardless of age. I just don't know if that's financially feasible. Our prescribed course of studies is also like yours, four years, but it can also be extended two semesters. That is the prescribed length of time, but that was rarely enforced in the past. So once you've begun university, you can keep getting support from the state, almost indefinitely. When my course of studies began, nothing even had to be paid back. Now, it's a loan on marginal interest, so it's still advantageous to take this loan from the state. I never knew anybody who got a degree in eight semesters. Even ten was extremely rare. I took fourteen because I wanted to enjoy my life.

Q: Could you enjoy yourself and perform well as an American undergraduate?

A: When I arrived in the States for a year to study linguistics at the university, I realized I didn't know how to study. The quantity overwhelmed me.
Americans are like machines! The way you work! You just don't have

any life outside school in the States! There's just too much demanded of you. On the other hand, you're forced to learn how to study. I thought I knew how before I visited the States, but I didn't.

By the way, here's another notable difference about student performance and grading. In the States, students never compare their grades. But in Germany, the first thing you ask your neighbor is, "What did you get?" It was amazing to me that my university colleagues [fellow teaching assistants] told me to distribute the papers face down and not announce grades in class at all. That all hangs together: Grades are private. You don't cheat. It's competition. It's unfair if somebody gets an advantage. "This is my property. This is my future."

Q: Did you find your American university courses challenging?

A: No. I was shocked—it's all so basic. Everything seems like an introduction. The requirements at university are very much like high school subjects. You have to take them. That obviously changes the motivation of the student. If you Americans don't have homework, you do nothing. The German university student simply does what is necessary for his education.

The *Abitur* is really equivalent to an American B.A., and that's why we don't have anything like a baccalaureate degree. It's the same in France. The first degree in a university is an M.A. In America, people don't want to know what you've studied but, rather, where you've studied. The name of university as a brand label—that's what has shocked me.

Most universities in Germany have no difference in prestige; some departments are better or worse. For instance, some people would say: "Go to Berlin if you want to study German literature. The capital is where everything happens." But that has more to do with the vitality of urban culture and the intellectual ferment in Berlin than with university prestige rankings.

Q: I've met eastern Germans who believe western German universities have succumbed to this form of "Americanization."

A: Yes. I think a lot of these differences also apply to eastern German perceptions of western Germans. Everything really revolves around image, self-presentation, and selling yourself. It's something very distasteful to us easterners. For example, Americans exaggerate their accomplishments very much, because competition there is so great that one feels one has to inflate oneself. So do western Germans, though not as much. The practical consequence at the American university is grade inflation and inflation in letters of recommendation.

Take, for instance, an interview: if Americans are asked, "Can you do that?" they would say, "'Sure,'" because if you say no, then you'll never get the job. You think: "Besides, it can't be that hard. I'll learn it on the job or beforehand." Whereas an eastern German would say, "No, I have no experience with that. I think I could probably learn it, but I can't do it now." He's much more innocent or guileless. Or if your recommenders write, "We were content with his work," that's no recommendation. You have to write, "We have the greatest enthusiasm. His achievement was outstanding." That means he was good.

Professors in Germany have said to me that if they are recommending a student to Americans, they exaggerate everything. I can remember one conversation like the following: "We know in America that good means bad. 'Great' means good, and 'one of the very best I've ever seen' means excellent. So if I want the student to have a chance, I usually say something like the latter."

In Germany, we simply say he was pretty good or he has potential, but he's got such-and-such shortcomings. No one would ever think to write a letter of recommendation without emphasizing the weaknesses and shortcomings.

It's the inflation of value. It's capitalist self-packaging: since everyone is saying the other candidates are excellent, you have to talk him up a few notches just in order to keep your student in competition.

Q: Was that your own experience with grades as a visiting student in the United States?

A: Yes. I laugh when I recall how naive I was. I jumped for joy when I got an A in graduate school. Until I eventually heard about other students' grades, and one said to me, "Look, you've got to understand: if you don't get an A, something is seriously wrong with you. It's an unwritten law here that if you don't get an A or A-minus, you're mediocre and you may flunk out in grad school. You have to do really embarrassing work to get a B."

Q: What are the main differences that you perceive between German and American students?

A: American undergraduates are unbelievably more polite and politically conservative or unpolitical than German students. American students emphasize much more image, competition, and careerist considerations.

Q: Why the political differences?

A: It may be that German students are more politically active because we have more time. American students have much less time. Given the quantity of material in their classes, the number of small assignments and tests during a semester, and the fact that they must pay for their classes, they often must work part-time. This was also the case in East Germany. Students didn't have much time to do anything much outside of classes. Requirements took up so much time and energy that there was little remaining for activism.

Q: Any other notable differences?

A: Yes, I can think of a few other small yet revealing social differences, but they aren't limited to the student culture. I noticed, as a result of my Ph.D. research in semiotics and sociolinguistics, that one difference between German and American pupils consists in their informal interactions in and out of class. For instance, here's a typical example of how much more friendly Americans are. When I first came into a shop, a lady came up to me and said: "Hi, how are you today?" And I immediately thought she had confused me with a friend of hers! I didn't realize that this was simply the standard business practice in a shop.

In Germany, you don't get greeted like that. You'll get a polite *Guten Tag*, or sometimes only a nod of the head. Or American cashiers will say, "That's a nice blouse you have!" Or, "Where did you get those glasses?" Or a waitress begins to have a conversation with you in a restaurant about the bracelet you have on.

Nothing like that happens in Germany. When Americans do that in Germany, it's sometimes regarded as rude or intrusive. To ask a waitress, "Well, are you busy today?" or "How has business been this summer?" or "Are there a lot of tourists?" is impolite. The response is often an embarrassed short answer.

I didn't realize that was a normal way of speaking in the United States. I thought it was just a peculiarity of acquaintances of mine. Only later did I realize: No, this IS the American culture! It's just friendlier and filled with smiles and curiosity.

Oddly enough, I like all that. Many Germans regard it as superficial, but that doesn't really matter to me. It makes a more hospitable atmosphere possible. You don't get acquainted with people on the street or in a shop personally anywhere in Germany, so why not have something that's a bit warmer and friendlier? It doesn't mean that relations on the street or in service occupations are personal, they're not. It's simply nicer when people are handled in a friendlier manner. It's a little way of making life more pleasant.

A second difference is with introductions of casual acquaintances. When a trio meets another trio on the street, they stop and each person gets introduced. If that were to occur in Germany and only one from each group knew each other, those two acquaintances would talk to each other for a few moments, and the others would just stand around talking to themselves. They would not be introduced to the wider group and it would not be an inclusive conversation. That certainly must seem impolite to Americans, whereas the American way simply seems pointless and superficial to Germans.

A third difference is telephone behavior. We are trained to say always who we are when we open a conversation. That seems very business-like and arrogant to Americans, to always identify themselves first, at least in any detail beyond their names. It's very common in America to say hello and you'll be recognized by your voice. But even good friends in Germany will identify themselves, sometimes even with surnames. As a German, it's still an act of courtesy for me to state my full name.

A fourth difference is that when you're introduced to people in the United States, you're typically introduced to them with full names, not with *Herr* and *Frau*. You then refer to them by these names rather than with a title; for instance, for a friend of the family, you don't usually say "Frau so-and-so."

You say: "A friend of mine." We say: "Someone whom I know." Most of those whom you call your friends, I would never call a friend. That also has something to do with quantity over quality in the U.S. We would say: "Somebody I studied with," "somebody I worked with." You would say: "My friend."

The German language reserves the word "friend" for a special, close relationship. A "du" friend [*Duzfreund*] is a sign of greater intimacy, and that's especially the case with the older generation.

Q: Let me ask you about your background. You are a former DDR citizen, right?

A: Yes. My family has an odd history. My mother is from Dresden, where

I grew up. My father emigrated to East Germany shortly before the erection of the Wall in 1961. He was by that time divorced and last year got to see his first wife, who remained in West Germany, for the first time in forty-five years, just before she died. And he also attended the funeral. Because of his background, I was very interested about life in the West. But we had no contact, except through some letters with my father's family, until the Wall fell. They didn't come over to East Germany to visit us. I didn't apply to go alone to see them.

Q: Did you have any contact with your family in West Germany?

A: I had never known any of these people personally and my father's relations weakened with them over time as well. My only contact was with my two nephews. I was always fascinated, but I never really had any means whereby I could make a connection with my father's family. You couldn't really imagine [from inside the DDR] what was going on over there. We really couldn't write in our letters what we wanted to write. We self-censored and so did they; neither side ever had any concrete picture of what life was like across the border.

So I was only able to get a vague idea through the letters of what was going on over there. For instance, we could write about what we ate, what the other limited offerings were in the goods that were available. We used to always say that the only thing you could get in the grocery store in the produce section was carrots. Next month we'll have lettuce and other greens. There was no variety; it all depended on what was imported or what happened to be available in eastern Europe at the time. We might mention that we had to wait ten years for a car, or eighteen years for a telephone, or we'd discuss all kinds of practical day-to-day information. That's the kind of thing we could say in a letter. We really had no idea of the mentality of West Germans, because there was no point of comparison.

Q: What are your politics currently?

A: Most of my friends vote SPD. My ex-boyfriend is in the SPD. He is quite active, but I have always regarded politics as so boring. I never really got involved. Nowadays, I don't have any real political tendency. "Conservative" doesn't always mean automatically "western" German, or "leftist" "eastern" German—or the reverse. My own circle at the university isn't politically committed at all. One could say we're idealists, but more in the social sense rather than in an explicitly political sense. We want a decent life for everyone and we support equality for everyone, but that doesn't translate into political activism.

11. "Proud to Be German"

At the time of this interview in July 2001, Dorothee—whom we met in the last section—had just completed her dissertation research for a thesis addressing the broad theme of contemporary German literature and problems of identity. Her dissertation topic explores the question of "Germanness" and the issue of national and generational identity in the wake of the Holocaust. From an American standpoint, a striking feature of the interview was Dorothee's gratitude when Dutch or Jewish people expressed a willingness to look beyond the Nazi-era past. She seemed to expect that the sins of the grandfathers would be visited upon the grandchildren, i.e., that foreigners would hold her accountable for the crimes of the Hitler era, a prospect unthinkable in an American context. Indeed, such an attitude was also quite rare in the DDR, and it is clear that Dorothee's approach to her dissertation topic is one that DDR students would not have undertaken—or would not have been officially permitted to undertake, given her ready embrace of responsibility for the Holocaust. As we saw in our analysis of history textbooks in Chapter 4, SED educators denied that the DDR bore any responsibility for the crimes of the Third Reich.

Dorothee's outlook represents another way in which eastern Germans are "working through" their complicated "double burden" of the past, which entails loosening and breaking the "textbook mentality" that absolved DDR citizens of any responsibility for modern Germany's past and the fascist era.

My title for this interview alludes to the public debate that occurred in Germany during mid-2001 on whether or not it is offensive or politically incorrect for Germans to say they are "proud to be German." So a further word about the context of that debate, which formed the background of part of my conversation with Dorothee, is warranted.

In March 2001, CDU General Secretary Laurenz Meyer had answered a journalist's question by saying, "I am proud to be German" (Ich bin stolz, ein Deutscher zu sein). This was not merely a somewhat banal statement of national pride, but a coded formulation, which has been used for many years by groups of neo-Nazis. Not only can this slogan be found in Gothic script on skinheads' bomber jackets, but it also adorns the banners of the neo-fascist German National Party (NPD). Meyer was soon accused of choosing this phrase in order to tie extreme right-wingers to the CDU and set his party on a nationalistic course. Environment Minister Jürgen Trittin of the Green Party attacked the balding CDU *general secretary: "Laurenz Meyer not only looks like a skinhead, he has the mentality of one." Former* CDU *Chairman Wolfgang Schäuble then made the absurd claim that Trittin's criticism of the slogan "I am proud to be German" would drive millions of Germans who felt a "healthy national pride" into the arms of right-wing extremist organizations.*

So a national debate ensued around the question: In view of the past, can Germans be proud of their German identity?

The debate proved inconclusive, and the question is still alive in Germany today.

Q: Has your research on your dissertation topic made you more politically active?

A: Well, perhaps more reflective about politics and history. Certainly, my research lends itself to political discussions. I just returned from a trip to Holland. When you are in Holland you sometimes encounter this attitude: "You're a German, you must be a Nazi." There are those who say, "Germans are Germans and Germans are evil. It doesn't matter what generation they are, they all think alike and all have some bad seed." Yet others in Holland and elsewhere in Europe go to special lengths to tell me: "We have nothing against you. Whatever happened in the distant past, your grandparents and great-grandparents were involved in that. I want to assure you that there's no national or cultural prejudice toward you as a German." I find that extremely reassuring and hopeful.

Q: How do Americans respond to the fact of your being German?

A: My advisor during my stay in Texas [1994] was actually a Jewish woman. I didn't know that. One day I showed her a postcard. It was a picture of Freiburg, where I was studying at the time. And I said it was a lovely town. I went on to describe it further, and she said, "Well, but that is a city I think I'll never visit. I don't think I'll ever visit that country."

I became very scared at that moment. She went on to say that some of her relatives had been killed in concentration camps. Once, when her family was traveling in Europe, a change of plans announced that the plane they were supposed to get on was to make a short fuel stop in Frankfurt. Her parents refused to take that plane. They had such great anxiety about being in the Frankfurt airport even for a few hours. I believe that she had known before this conversation that I was a German, but it had never come up.

She was very nice to me, and I'm just grateful it didn't become an issue between us. All I said to her was that I can very well understand that she wouldn't feel comfortable in Freiburg, and that her parents would refuse to board a plane going to Germany. On the one hand, I think it's a shame that people would react this way. On the other hand, I think that anyone who had experienced this kind of history would be liable to think this way. She's really the only Jew I've gotten to know well.

Q: Are you open to friendship with Jews?

A: Yes, I could even imagine marrying a Jew. It is imaginable, but as I said, I'm really not a political person. So it's really a matter of indifference to me whether or not a person is Jewish. I really care about the humanity of the person, not the political orientation or cultural or racial background. After all, I wouldn't be marrying the entire Jewish people. I would be marrying a particular man. Of course, some of that history and racial identity is in him, but I don't view that as subsuming his identity or constituting the whole of him. I would be developing an intimate relationship to this particular person, not the entire Jewish people.

But I'm not going to force myself on a man. He would have to be a Jew who is quite open to marrying a German.

Q: I have an American Jewish acquaintance who told me that he would never entertain the possibility of marrying a German. It was utterly out of the realm of the imaginable for him.

A: I find that regrettable. I see that attitude perpetuating antagonisms down through the generations.

I should emphasize I don't want to be regarded chiefly as a German. I don't want my national or ethnic identity standing in the foreground of every interaction I have. I recognize that's more likely to happen abroad. But it only constitutes part of my identity, really a small part. I want people to be approached first as human beings, only later as representing a particular nationality.

Does that sound shameful? Escapist? I don't think it's a reaction to my shame; it is a step toward world citizenship. I'm German. I've grown up in Germany. I speak German, but that's not everything about me.

Everyone criticizes Helmut Kohl for saying that his generation received "the blessing of a late birth." He meant that if he had been older, he would have probably participated in the activities of the Third Reich, fought as a soldier, or even been active in the Nazi Party.

Q: Do you feel a similar kind of blessing?

A: Yes, I think I've also received the blessing of a late birth *two* generations later. I don't, however, believe in this idea of collective guilt or collective shame. I don't think that young people in Germany today have anything to be guilty about. *We* haven't done anything against the Jews. Yet what follows is a big "but." *But* this doesn't remove from us the responsibility to remember what happened and honor the victims and children of the victims. We must never forget and must act correspondingly in light of that memory.

So, yes, I do feel it's a blessing I was "born late." I am happy that I was not confronted with the horrible choice: either to stay and probably participate or to emigrate or risk my life in the underground. So the "blessing" means that I'm someone who wasn't faced with this awful choice. Therefore I don't bear any guilt or shame.

But I do bear *responsibility* because of my heritage as a German. My responsibility is that I must somehow help guarantee that this never occurs again—by my own words, my actions, my changed consciousness as a result of the relation of my heritage to those terrible events.

I would speak of collective responsibility, not collective guilt. I can't feel myself guilty for something that occurred before I was born. It is a responsibility to remember. The responsibility is to remember not just a chronological or historical past, not just a textbook past, but rather a past that lives on into the present and the future—whereby memory is directed toward a better future.

Q: What should Germany's role be on the world stage right now?

A: Tricky topic. For instance, during the [1991] Gulf War, there were many intellectuals and students who were against U.S. policy. These Germans seemed in world opinion against the Israelis, against defending them from Saddam and their position in the Arab world. There were many peace marches in Germany. This was misinterpreted in the U.S. as anti-Semitism. Being against the war was misperceived as being against Israelis.

Some people think that because we're German, we've lost the right to criticize anything like a war. "Look what you've done to Jews!" That statement should shut us up, they believe. And very often a word such as "Auschwitz" does shut us up. "Who are *you* to talk about crimes against humanity?! Who are *you* to talk about dictators?! *You* didn't stand up to Hitler!"

So how can we play any role in promoting peace on the world stage?

Often we feel we must swallow the criticism. That doesn't seem right to me. That's history as blackmail. It's exploiting some shameful event in the past from another generation to silence the current generation and intimidate it. It's history used as a power tool for intimidation. They know that our jugular is this horrible twelve-year period in our history that blackens everything else before and after it, and it's used to reduce our identity to a nation of mass murderers. And what does a convicted murderer have to say against any other potential act of murder? He's not a trustworthy witness. He would be immediately discredited on the witness stand.

Q: Can Germans be "proud to be German"?

A: Other Europeans are proud of their country and really *are* nationalists, and nobody resents that. If a similar attitude were expressed by Germans, it would be regarded as preliminary to right-wing radical politics or to launching some kind of neo-Nazi activity. When other peoples show their flag, everyone says, "Isn't it beautiful?" When a German does it, it is cause for international alarm. That's a shame. We can't even participate in what is extremely harmless elsewhere, like singing old folk songs, because those folk songs were apparently irretrievably spoiled during the Third Reich. On August 1 the Swiss fly their flag proudly, yet if we make much hullabaloo about it on October 3, say, other European nations think that we are getting ready to dominate them.

Because of the past, everything having to do with Germany is interpreted purely in political terms—when maybe instead it's just affection for a cultural symbol. In Germany you have to be so careful and that is kind of a shame. You have to tiptoe around anything that can be misinterpreted as power politics. And that extends well beyond the perception of a responsibility to remember. Some of us have developed a preternatural awareness of other nations' and other cultures' feelings. We try to anticipate what might offend them or make them uncomfortable, even if it's quite out of the realm of our immediate experience. And it all really relates back to that earlier generation.

It's amazing that German history before 1945 has practically disappeared. Ironically, even among Germans and certainly among Europeans, the idea of a zero hour in 1945 is so widely discredited by historians who say there are strong continuities between the German past and the postwar era. But as far as the awareness of people about concrete details of that past, we hear so much about Hitler and the Third Reich that German history, in practical terms, seems to begin and end there.

Frederick the Great, Bismarck, and other German figures are forgotten or tainted *post facto* by authoritarian perceptions linked to fascism. In light of the Nazi years, they begin to assume an extremely authoritarian look. So, even if they're remembered, they're remembered as forerunners to Hitler because everybody asks afterward, what came after them? What did they lead to? So it's a short step from an authoritarian figure like Luther to a totalitarian one like Hitler. These kind of pitiful simplifications are everywhere. The shadows of Hitlerism are everywhere.

Q: One sees them in the changes in the German language.

A: Yes. Certain words are irretrievably lost. No one could ever say *"Führer"* anymore, which is only an innocent word [leader]. And a whole range of words associated with it: "Leadership" [*Führerschaft*] is often used by German speakers only in the English now—it's become a German word because our language now has no such word.

Or take *Volk* traditions. Sometimes I will meet foreign visitors now who will sing a folk song of their nation and say: "Now it's your turn." Most Germans won't sing any. Sometimes Germans of my generation don't even know any. There is a sense of shame because of what these songs evoke, images and memories of nationalistic pride from the Hitler years.

Yes, it's a pity. And it's tragically unfair that an entire nation should have its long history blackened by a dozen years, and that—sixty years after the war's end—our flag, our folk songs, our views about current events should all be hopelessly historicized and politicized. The German people are no worse—and no better—than other people. I'm proud of my country. I'm proud to be a German—not a nationalistic German, but just a citizen of this democracy, this culture.

Q: Your father fought in the Wehrmacht. Does he share your sentiments?

A: For twenty years, my father met every year with his soldier friends in his company, until the age of seventy. He's now seventy-two, and he has decided he won't attend anymore.

There were two key experiences that changed his attitude toward celebrating with his old friends. On a boat on the Mosel River, suddenly some men began to sing battle songs [*Panzerlieder*] that they used to sing back in the war days and before, songs they sang as they were marching on the battlefield even. This upset my father, because it seemed to be an affirmation of what happened during those days. But maybe instead it was fond memory of solidarity. It's hard to know. It just made him uncomfortable.

Another time, during a soldiers' reunion, he was in a jewelry store. Somebody gave a buddy of his a nice piece of jewelry as a gift. The man asked where it came from. He was told, "Israel." Then he said, "I don't want that piece of jewelry." And he gave the gift back. My dad was so upset that he wrote a letter to the company commander and said he didn't want to participate anymore if there were veterans like that who were going to attend.

So I think that Germans need to be doubly careful because there are some Germans who still have these attitudes. By remaining silent in the face of expressing their attitudes, we implicitly support the attitudes. It's always very difficult to know when to intervene, when to take a stand, when to draw the line. But I would say this: When in doubt, speak out rather than remain silent. This horrible past has to be stamped out. "Never again!" Any attitudes that seem to be building a climate that would let any part of it return must be opposed.

Q: Is it returning?

A: Not like the 1930s, but some part still smolders. The embers still flicker. For instance, given our history, expressions used in private circles—such as "you're just as stingy as a Jew"—are problematic. My grandmother says that often. It is deeply inside her. She wouldn't think twice about it. Younger people do avoid the expression. It's a generational division. Even the word "Jewish" or "Jew"—especially "Jew"—is fraught with difficulties. Many Germans avoid using "Jew," because every time the word is spoken, it's charged. There's a certain emotional and political valence. This is why many people remain silent whenever the topic of Jews arises. Anything you say may be cause for embarrassment or misunderstanding. You're going through a verbal minefield and you may hit the mine called "Auschwitz."

When German children and young teens are insulted on the streets in Holland and elsewhere because they're German, it sometimes builds very negative attitudes in them. When they return home, they are often much less tolerant and instead predisposed toward hatred of foreigners or antagonism toward Jews.

This raises the question of whether there's a corresponding responsibility for non-Germans to forgive Germans, or at least forgive the present generation for what the elders did. Without forgiveness, we'll never get further, and I don't see any advantage in holding grudges and antagonisms across generations. Feuding like Romeo's and Juliet's families inevitably will lead to more tragedy. Other nations and peoples will be able to maintain that they hold the moral high ground. Forgiveness levels both sides. It says: "You're on the same plane as me. I'm not above you, looking down on you and demanding something from you. I'm canceling the debt."

Q: So that's why the world hasn't forgiven Germany for the Holocaust—whereas the Gulag and other crimes are not still "held against" a nation or a people?

A: Partly. Forgiveness means giving up advantages. Without it, here's the mentality: "We can always exploit these advantages as long as we haven't forgiven you. We can always claim that this unique event, the Holocaust, can't ever be forgiven."

So memory and lack of forgiveness begin to slide into each other. Again, here's the mentality: "What should be remembered must also never be forgiven. The Holocaust was unique and therefore remains unforgivable. Everything else can be forgiven, but not that." It's a power struggle, a power play: whoever wins, writes history. The stronger power will hold high the moral ground and continuously impose on the weaker one. As a result of losing World War II, Germans are in the weaker moral position.

Nobody ever talks about what happened with Americans in Vietnam as a cause for national collective guilt. Most people don't even remember what happened. That was thirty to forty years ago. But America was never occupied by a foreign power, so it never had driven into it any cause for collective guilt or shame. It is always being drummed into us in Germany and wherever we go in Europe. During my recent stay in Norway, every month there came some new report about the Third Reich, some new claim or discovery. Because the Nazi regime stands as the culmination and quintessence of evil, and because evil fascinates us so much, and because it seems to be a human tendency to need a scapegoat, German history—and specifically that period of history—is endlessly intriguing to everyone.

Q: My Jewish *Doktorvater* emigrated from Vienna in 1938. He told me that most Viennese in his class year joined the Party, or were at least fellow travelers. They didn't really believe in the ideals of the Party. Membership in it was just a way to be safe in society, a way to get a better job or situation, a matter of careerism. He said to me: "If I had been German or Austrian, rather than a Jew, I probably would have joined the Party myself. I wasn't morally superior to people around me. I was just like they were."

A: That's the most shocking statement I've ever heard!

Q: Of course, he means that a great deal of Nazism had little to do with nationalism per se. It had to do with the weaknesses of individuals. And all individuals have weaknesses. So it *can* happen here. It can happen everywhere.

A: Yes. Let's admit: It *did* happen here, so concerns that it could happen here again are justifiably greater, but that doesn't mean that other races and peoples are inherently superior to Germans.

Q: My *Doktorvater*'s humility and courage amaze me. I admire his self-critical admission that he is just as human as any German of his generation who yielded to a grave weakness and participated in some Nazi activity.

A: I think often about my father. It must have been so hard to be surrounded by this mentality, being swept along a wave as a young person of seventeen or eighteen, especially when there were no other sources of information. How do you develop other opinions that might take you outside that world? It's very easy for us to say today: "I never would have participated." Too easy! So many young people today scream accusingly, "Why didn't you get out? Didn't you see through it?" They don't understand that it was a matter of tiny steps being taken one by one, of sliding into something that everyone else was sliding into. Almost nobody in 1933—or even 1937 and 1938—had any idea about what was to happen in the mid-1940s: a world war in which millions of people would be murdered in concentration camps. Nobody outside the very highest circles of Nazis had any inkling that all that lay in the future. Perhaps even they didn't. We need distance to be able to judge something. When you're in the middle of something, you have no distance on it. The only way out, once it became clear around wartime what was happening, was to pay with your life. Very few people have that level of heroism, that willingness to lay down their lives for principles.

My father says he had no idea what was happening with the Jews. They were being deported, but he didn't know they were being murdered. He says a lot of people residing away from major cities had no idea. Only after the war did he learn what was happening on a mass scale.

Q: Do you believe that Germany's generally strong support for the EU is a reaction to collective shame or guilt?

A: Yes. Of course, many Europeans claim that Germans are enthusiastic about the EU because it will permit them to escape from their German identity. They can have a European identity, which will replace the German identity permanently destroyed by the Holocaust. Now they can adopt a European identity.

Q: Is there anything most Germans are allowed to be proud of?

A: Yes. German industry and the quality of German products. German products are automatically considered good. Certain German values are good for business: punctuality, order, cleanliness. So anything that can be easily kept in a contemporary context and doesn't relate to history, or automatically invoke some military or political dimension, is seen as something worth preserving. Europe is attracted to these values. They believe these values will promote prosperity. The Deutschmark, of course, traditionally was the strongest currency in Europe. German organization is always regarded as something good.

Years ago, [Jürgen] Habermas called it "D-mark nationalism." We are really proud of our economy, and that's really German culture: German products, prosperity, and economic culture. We're conceded that kind of pride by other nations. We can be proud about the good automobiles we produce. So we're allowed a measure of D-mark nationalism. So long as it doesn't slip into anything political. But with the arrival of the Euro, our D-mark nationalism is already being swallowed up—and that will be another step toward our acquiring a European identity.

SEVEN

PHYSICAL AND SOCIAL SCIENCES

1. Of Biophysics and Metaphysics: Post-Communism Meets McUniversity

Interview in July 1999 with Achim, twenty-eight, a biophysics student from Dresden who is enrolled at the University of Würzburg. He had recently visited the United States and studied for a year at the University of Texas at Austin. Achim had no qualms about severely criticizing American education—much more sharply and extensively than did Dorothee in Chapter 6. I found his frankness both shocking and refreshing—he was quite willing to violate norms of political correctness dictating that one doesn't castigate a former host country—at least not directly to its citizens' faces.

Achim's criticism of American capitalism was an intelligent critique, not merely a throwback to communist agitprop or an anti-American rant. Nonetheless, his class-based categorizing was sometimes so schematic that it was evident to me that his DDR education did live on into the present—as he quite candidly admitted at the outset of our interview. Our conversation suggested another complex way in which eastern Germans are renegotiating the terms of their political and economic outlooks. Achim reacted strongly against American (and western German) capitalist values, and this antipathy has served to deepen and strengthen his socialist worldview.

Q: Have your fifteen years of experience in a socialist educational system exerted a continuing impact on your world outlook?

A: Yes; especially given my last two years as a student in western Germany and my recent visit to the United States, my socialist convictions are stronger than ever.

Q: Why?

A: More and more, I see that capitalism conditions American professors and students to want status and image above all. They want to be associated with the very best universities. It's like joining the best club or living in the most exclusive neighborhood. And yet, except for the top researchers, the general quality of work is weak. American students are willing to work hard, but not in order to gain deeper understanding so much as to get a good grade. They are overconfident about their opinions, which typically lack strong supporting evidence.

Q: What surprised you as an eastern German science student about the United States and American higher education?

A: I thought western Germany was materialistic, but the United States really is the heartland of capitalism!

In the U.S. all values are associated with money. In Europe, many values are still independent of money, but all that is changing since Europe is imitating the U.S. nowadays. Therefore it's a schizophrenic situation, especially for eastern Germans who are playing catch-up with the Americanization of Europe. The process really began in 1945, but in eastern Germany it only began in 1990.

What is so ironic to me about the United States is the inverse relationship between money and culture. In almost every other land, it seems as if money and culture are directly related. In the U.S. for the most part—at least in Texas—the wealthier you are, the more uncultured you are. Money is spent on superficial entertainment and mindless distraction and not on self-enrichment [*Bildung*]. When I went to Mexico, I saw that the rich there are also cultured—just as in Europe. That's not case in the U.S.

Q: Are there any differences you noticed specifically between German and American universities?

A: Yes. There is no system of ranking universities to compare with the systematic rank-ordering of every college and program and department in the U.S. The old German universities, such as Heidelberg and Tübingen, are regarded as distinguished and good, but it's nothing like coming from Harvard or Yale. There's no Ivy League in Germany. And German universities don't have endowments. Particular departments are recognized as having excellent people, but there's a long tradition honoring the idea of students transferring from one university to the next—in order to expose themselves to different professors and curricula, not for elitist reasons.

There's nothing in Germany like the market system of buying credentials, including brand name educations, as occurs in the United States. Education is a product that one pays for in the U.S. One can pay a lot of money and buy, if not a good product, then the best packaging, the best name, which, in turn, will often deliver the desired result of a good job—or at least good connections to get a good job. Or one can buy the economy model and get a good local job or regional job. Or one can go "super-economy" to community college and then move up to a higher quality school and get a formal degree from there. There are all these educational options in the U.S., according to one's budget, high school record, talent, particular career aspirations, specialized areas of study and research, and so forth. It's like looking at U.S. supermarkets or department stores, where there are hundreds of items from different companies to choose from. It is pure capitalism.

In Germany, when I mention that I study at Würzburg University, outsiders understand nothing about it. In the U.S., when you say, "I study at Texas or Harvard," everyone on the outside has some idea of what it means socially. Of course, if someone says, "I study at Heidelberg," everyone knows the name, but it doesn't impress them. It doesn't mean anything because everything depends on the department of your course of study and how well you do, and not on the mere name of that university. Bremen, Marburg, Freiburg: these universities have traditions, but their traditions don't translate into automatic prestige in the minds of uninformed persons outside the university setting. There are some universities that have political reputations: Frankfurt and Bremen are left-oriented, while Heidelberg is very conservative. But these are a minority of the instances, and the tendencies are no longer as strong as they were decades ago. In any case, it is a matter of political reputation, not a prestige ranking.

Q: And you find this problematic—or even deplorable?

A: Of course. Education in the U.S. is just another superficial product. Everything is for immediate gain. But it's historically and culturally understandable.

Everything developed so quickly in the United States. After the war [World War I], the U.S. developed into a world superpower so quickly and suddenly became so technologically advanced, partly because it received all of the best people from Europe, especially Germany. The result, then as now, is that there is a highly qualified elite in the U.S.—with research resources that Europeans can only dream of—but a system of mass education that is a catastrophe. You learn nothing in secondary or elementary school. It's ridiculous. It's not education, it's babysitting.

All this is actually quite dangerous, because a dumb, uneducated American plays a significant role on the world stage, far more so than an intelligent, educated person from a small European country. Americans think their country is the greatest. They internalize strong identifications between themselves and the international ranking of the U.S.—that is, individual Americans think: "We're #1."

Many Europeans possess a superior knowledge of the U.S., especially its capitalist features. We rarely encounter Americans who know anything about their own system! The contrast between the role that the U.S. plays in the world and the qualifications of the broad mass of its populace is extreme.

Q: What is the basis for these strong views of yours?

A: The idea that the U.S. is the best country in world is refuted with a simple conversation with most of your citizens! They just don't know about anything going on in the world beyond their local community! They don't know any foreign languages. Nor do they know anything about the past. Nor do they seem to have active, inquiring minds that can discern trends pointing to the future.

Every major European nation has imagined itself at some time to be the best nation in the world. So it isn't surprising that America's turn has finally arrived. Still, it's shocking to encounter it. Possibly in no other country has there been this level of mass arrogance or have the claims to individual greatness ever been so untrue.

One way of assessing the broad spectrum of the population is by the quality of schooling. And all international surveys show that the quality of American schools in terms of math, the hard sciences, and other basic skills is among the lowest of developed nations.

I can confirm that. Teaching and tutoring American undergraduates—even at a reputable major university—is like working with average high school students in Germany.

Within the elite, of course, it's completely different. But it's also interesting to see how many members of the elite are foreigners or foreign-born. In the sciences, more than half of the graduate students are foreigners in most major research universities.

So the discrepancy between the mass and the elite is great. America is a nation of mediocre schoolchildren [*Hauptschüler*]. The danger is that this enormous world power is in the hands of a voting public that is so ignorant. That public is really entrusting decisions to an elite, which—though highly qualified technically—is claiming to represent this public and has no basis for such a claim.

Q: You mentioned earlier that you were appalled at the low level of international awareness and foreign language education in the U.S.

A: People in Europe still talk about Dan Quayle! You can have a vice president like Dan Quayle who can visit Latin America and announce that he very much regrets that he never took Latin in high school! It is painfully laughable. Or about how when Carter went to Poland and his chief interpreter for Polish blundered Carter's statement that he "loved the spirit of the Polish people" by giving the misinterpretation that Carter "lusts after Poles."

That the interpreter to the president would make such blunders is inconceivable in a European context.

Q: And the implications of such a gaffe aren't limited to such state occasions.

A: Right. The larger point is that Americans also don't understand the role of foreign languages in the world. They think they can go through the world and have a quality experience with English, but they can't. Travel is of an entirely different quality when you speak a native language. There is a difference between being a traveler and being a tourist. Americans think they are traveling to foreign countries when they are actually just receiving superficial impressions as tourists.

Of course, this is also a species of American arrogance. Here again is the failure to draw distinctions, as if the instrument of communication and the degree of precision afforded by that instrument make no difference.

Q: Your example would seem to indicate that even the American elite are incompetent.

A: Yes, if you take the example in a narrow sense. But I'm talking about the length and rigor of training that Americans consider sufficient to become "highly qualified." The lax training in your country promotes incompetence that masquerades as expertise.

Of course, on the one hand, in Germany, people take too long to get trained. It seems excessive, for example, that a two-year training program is required in Germany to teach; in most other countries, one year is the norm.

On the other hand, it means that the people at the base of the system really know the fundamentals. They're basically qualified. In the United

States, you might go through a short course or, at most, a semester before receiving a job such as grocer or manager of a McDonald's. But it's often the case that you've never learned how to do your job, even the basics. So there are masses of people, especially at the lower levels, who are utterly unqualified to be in the positions they're in.

Q: But the United States also has an international reputation for having the finest or most advanced research institutions in the world.

A: Indeed. Especially in the sciences, there's often an unbelievable reservoir of knowledge in the American elite, but it's never really applied or distributed at a mass level. On the one hand, the American idea of getting on with the task at hand, jumping in with both feet is very good. It makes for real spontaneity. On the other hand, it often does so at the cost of any serious grounding and thoroughness in preparation for the task. Americans often begin to study at the age of twenty-five or thirty, but in Germany that doesn't happen. American students are diligent and eager, but they learn less.

Most Americans know a great deal about very little and nothing about so much beyond. For example, I recall teaching about the development of the German language and noting that the Bible translation of Martin Luther contributed greatly to the unification of various dialects. It led, during the Reformation, to a standard German language. And to the birth of the printing press in Germany with Gutenberg.

And what did the students grasp? During the following week, a couple of students wrote a composition in which they stated that Martin Luther King had translated the Bible into German in the sixteenth century.

That's not just an error in the name; rather, it means that the entire context of American and German history is missing—that a student doesn't even know what century the leader of the black civil rights movement lived in, let alone know details about the Reformation in Europe. It simply doesn't fit that an American assassinated thirty years ago could have translated the Bible four centuries ago. It's not just a factual error, it means a whole series of relationships is missing.

Q: So that buttresses your argument that even so-called educated Americans lack basic skills.

A: Many American students are so wrapped up in their ambitions that they don't notice their appallingly low level of skills. And I'm astonished how badly they often respond to criticism. Instead of treating it as an opportunity to grow or learn, they consider it insulting and often begin to think thereafter of the seminar by that critical professor as a waste of time. They prefer admiration and praise to honesty. It's a form of narcissism. They're in love with their own reflection, which accounts for the grandiose sense of self-importance. That's why they exaggerate their achievements and talents, and why they expect to be recognized as superior without considerable accomplishments.

Success is everything in the States, and people become a means to a successful end. To those in authority from whom there is something to gain, they are deferential and cooperative. People against whom they compete either serve as an index of their own importance or as threats that must be eliminated.

They turn everything into a contest. Their professional accomplishments, their looks, their careers, their spouses. It is as if they are always saying, "Mine is better than yours." Because they are competing with everyone, they can't make friends with their peers. Competition makes them see others as threats and obstacles to their own success.

But they attempt to succeed in competitions not by improving themselves but by improving their self-presentation. They aim to make a favorable impression, whether or not the image they project is who they really are. It's style over substance. They see themselves as commodities. How others perceive them and their image becomes everything. It's all in the packaging. They come across extremely well, but in a rehearsed, synthetic way. They are smooth and slick. What is missing is a personal sense of engagement and commitment to anything but themselves.

Yet they oversell themselves with these extraordinary claims about themselves. They start to believe their own hype! They puff up their achievements to ludicrous extremes. It's so pretentious and they are so easily offended if you point out how unrealistic their evaluations of themselves or their expectations of success have become. They are never content seeing what they really are.

Q: And you view this as a phenomenon of advanced capitalism?

A: Essentially, yes. The worlds of advertising, marketing, sales, and fashion have taken over the American university. Americans engage in a public relations game. How they are perceived is everything. Rather than devoting their energies to the development of their genuine talents, they allocate their resources to managing the impressions of others about them.

It's as if they are always in a job interview. They are always trying to sell themselves. Being merely successful is eventually not enough. They need to be famous or important in some way. They need to be big stars who are known and celebrated for something. It's all bells and whistles. They are never sufficiently content to make a case on the numbers alone. They can't show how their interpretation is the logical choice based on supporting facts. They are intellectually sloppy.

American universities are expert at responding to the market. You don't ever get a sense that they believe that people are part of a community—or indeed, that there *is* such a thing as the university community.

On one campus building at your university in Austin it is written, "The truth will set you free." But Americans systematically deceive themselves and others about almost everything! If only you Americans would notice your tendency to embellish the truth and refrain from doing that! Even the question, "How are you?" seems always like a conversational nicety, never a genuine inquiry.

Q: Given this market-driven character of the American university, do American students get better treatment from their professors than is the case with the German system? Are the student buyers getting their money's worth?

A: In a narrow sense, yes. The student evaluations here are a very good practice. German professors get far too smug and comfortable in their positions. Maybe that's one reason why American lectures seem much better prepared. But much of it has to do with capitalism. The students are paying and insist on regular evaluations of faculty. Students are consumers here. They're paying for a service. Professors are compensated by students and are providing a service. That is an advantage of a system that is partly private and not entirely state-financed. There is more accountability.

Consider the German student's plight. The amount of contact existing between professors and students in Germany now is much less than three or four decades ago. The faculty-student ratio has gone up, so students are less well guided and less supervised than they were before the *Wende*. Now you need a good reason to approach a professor and ask something. Before, you could just stop by. It's much like the case in the traditional pre-war German university, in which a professor was a higher being—part of an elite. Nowadays, you sometimes have to chase down a professor. You have to run after him for two or more weeks before you can catch him to ask a simple question.

It is a great achievement to be a German professor and everyone recognizes that achievement. Traditionally, German professors have occupied an extremely high social position and that status endures to some extent. German professors are regarded much higher socially than professors in the U.S.

In Germany, the entire reputation of a department depends on the chairman [*Lehrstuhl*]. Typically he is the most distinguished professor of the department, and the others are less well known. So if I go to Heidelberg for medicine or Würzburg for zoology, I might be able to say, "I worked for professor so and so," or "I am a *Schüler* [pupil] of his." One is regarded then as a disciple. It's a laying on of hands from that particular professor to that student—like Heidegger being a pupil of Husserl and then Gadamer being a pupil of Heidegger.

Everyone in that field will know the *Doktorvater* [dissertation father], despite the fact that the direct, personal contact nowadays is often minimal or sometimes just a formal administrative connection. Perhaps he isn't at the university during one half of the year. He spends the other half doing his own research. Thus, you may seldom see him, but you are his doctoral student. You benefit from the formal guidance that he has been authorized to give you, but you don't actually receive regular contact. You only get his administrative title. You might meet with him twice a year. But if you are really intelligent, two hours of conversation with him will be more helpful to you than dozens with mediocre scholars.

Q: You said that the American student benefits from his greater access to professors in a "narrow sense." You mean that the quantity of contact doesn't translate into a better-quality education?

A: Yes. The ratio between professors and students and the quality of supervision in the U.S. is very good, but the *Ehrfurcht vor Bildung* [reverence for learning] is missing. *Bildung* [learning, culture] has great traditional value in Germany and a professor is considered a steward of that value. In the U.S., learning is regarded somewhat with mistrust: the image of the pointy-headed intellectual, the egghead, the Harvard know-it-all, the quiz kid, the brain trust member. There's a tradition of the common man and the common touch in the United States. It's a strain of populism that seems to mistrust not only the abuse of learning but learning itself. Reason and the mind are liable to remove one from life, whereas in Germany, the supreme value is traditionally the life of the mind.

Americans exploit learning, especially for personal gain and technological advance, but they don't value it for itself. It's a means to an end, not an end in itself—and there is no reverence for it. Instead, it is something to be used or turned to one's advantage—applied. The difference between applied knowledge and basic (or pure) knowledge is lost in the United States. But it is something still discernible to us. German professors value knowledge for itself. It doesn't necessarily lead to them professing wisdom, no more so than is the case with professors in the U.S. But they do indeed value knowledge that has emerged from a long tradition of taste or aesthetic refinement.

In Germany, knowledge is treated in the sciences and the academy generally—especially in a relatively new field such as biophysics—as a frontier without borders. You can always do more, learn more, and develop your skills more. In America, one has the impression that there are crash courses and quick fixes that will give you ability; also, there is no great differentiation of people with ability. That's why Americans will casually say that they can speak a language, when they can only express themselves in a few phrases. In contrast, a German who is quite capable in English would immediately say that his English is poor, because he's aware of what a complex language English is and where the frontier is. An American has no conception at all of what it might be to master a foreign language.

Q: But many eastern Germans speak about how the western German system is also enmeshed in a market system.

A: I'd agree. Take our growing obsession with credentials. Thirty years ago, the *Abitur* was a much more decisive credential in a German's future than was a university degree. Only 6 to 7 percent of the population had the *Abitur*. It didn't really matter if you went to a university: you were already a member of the elite at that point. Today 35 to 40 percent get the *Abitur,* which is roughly similar to the percentage of Americans who graduate from university. You call it a democracy, but you achieve mediocrity. Democracy is a euphemism for "more is less," more students equals less quality. That has been the result of mass education. Germany is also heading down that road. Nowadays a *Gymnasium* graduate wants a university education because society has mandated that everyone should have it. That's already the case in the U.S., and the result has been a few universities for the highly gifted and a mass education for the rest, in order that they too possess the credential of a so-called college degree.

Q: What do you think of the debate about political correctness in the American academy?

A: The basic claims of what is called "political correctness" in the U.S. are undeniably true. Their truth—for instance, the discrimination against minorities—is self-evident. It is just a matter of seeing reality.

But the problem in the U.S. has been that when somebody does see reality, it's immediately exaggerated, so people who are voicing statements reflecting political correctness are simply exaggerating the truth that they've seen. Minorities have suffered discrimination and are still disadvantaged in some respects, but this situation is so overblown that the truth is completely distorted. A false accent is placed on an insight, whereby it becomes a caricature.

It's just another example of everything in the U.S. being exaggerated. There's a certain lack of common sense in American university life, whereby these exaggerations take hold. They play into people's ideas of self-pity and victimization and so are often embraced as an alternative to seeing the reality of injustice that is in front of their noses, rather than doing something about it. Political correctness is a movement proclaiming tolerance that is, in reality, entirely intolerant. There's nothing like it in Germany, really. So the exaggeration consists in the fact that, yes, we should eliminate injustices, but it doesn't mean that minorities are right about everything or that everything is unjust.

Yes, reverence for learning is missing, so Shakespeare's *Hamlet* and Alice Walker's *The Color Purple* can be discussed as equally worth reading. But there are advantages to lacking this reverence and that has to do with the famed American enterprise and American willingness to try anything, do it differently, and not be bound by tradition. Americans aren't burdened by tradition the way Europeans often are. Instead of building on tradition and growing out of tradition, we are sometimes limited by tradition, hemmed in by it. It's an end rather than a point of departure for us.

But again, the extreme tendency in the United States! Instead of acknowledging that other authors besides Shakespeare are good, the political correctness movement says you *must* read these black authors, and if you don't, you're a racist. Of course, what is just as regrettable is that nothing really changes if you read Alice Walker or Toni Morrison. The bourgeois Wasp remains that. Getting these black authors into the curriculum is a matter of institutional politics, not of changing popular consciousness.

Q: Many Americans would consider the German system too lax and too lacking in evaluations of student performance—and as veiling that negligence with bogus claims about "reverence for learning."

A: No. Take the subject of grades. We Germans really don't have many grades in the university. Usually it's just pass or no pass and then you receive the *Schein* [credit]. There are no grade point averages; very few courses are even graded. A professor often records a grade and work is often assigned, but that grade doesn't appear on your record, so it doesn't matter. He retains it as a reference should you need a letter of recommendation. There are a lot of professors who simply don't give out a 1, or an A. The best student might get a 2+ because there are no grades of 1 ever dispensed. A grade of 1 is reserved for their colleagues or for God—whereas here, especially in graduate school, everyone gets an A. American hyperinflation has not hit the German university system yet.

My *Doktorvater* gave me a 2+ on my masters, then he said, "Now you've got something to shoot for in your dissertation . . . a 1." I only found out by talking with a couple of his colleagues that he felt the work was truly excellent. American professors sometimes think they're encouraging a student when they give them an A. They think that it will make them feel good and deepen their motivation. In Germany, however, it's the reverse. If you get a little less than you deserve, you'll keep striving and hoping to get the best grade possible.

It seems to us that if 60 to 70 percent are getting As, there is no motivation. An A doesn't mean anything. In Germany a 3 is *Befriedigend* [satisfactory]. You have reached an "adequate" level of performance—whereas in the U.S., if you don't get an A in graduate school, you're a failure. Letters of recommendation in the U.S. are also exaggerated. They have to be. If you say merely that a student is "good," since everybody is "good," it really means that he's not. So you have to say he's excellent in the greatest and lengthiest possible detail.

Foreigners have to realize how Americans quantify and belabor these recommendations in order to understand the educational rate of inflation in the United States. I've seen American résumés and they're amazing. "I was in a flute course and I worked at McDonald's for three months this summer and I also waitressed for four months in X restaurant last summer." Everything is put down. It has to be exhaustive. Every experience is exploited and rendered expedient. One would assume that it's no great achievement to have been able to waitress for three months in a restaurant. It's not something you think you would record for employment at a higher level after graduation; but Americans, because of their quantitative mindset, think that everything should be recorded. Everything is somehow portrayed as important.

Q: So the typical large institution in American higher education is the "McUniversity"?

A: Yes, "McUniversity"—that's Texas and the others. I realize that the small colleges are somewhat different. But the differences are relatively minor—and the smaller ones are still determined by the big ones.

In my typical conversation with an American, he'll say, "I can speak German too," and it turns out that he can say a couple of words: *Danke, Guten Tag*. Again, he has a tendency to exaggerate.

Everything that the American job applicant has ever done is played up—a modest level of ability is played up. Certainly, you see this in Germany on occasion, but it's the norm here. Much of it has to do with the mentality of competition in American capitalism. You try to distinguish yourself by having more than your competitor in order to be better qualified. If everyone is exaggerating, and I'm the only one who hasn't taken this flute course, then I'm disadvantaged, so I've got to exaggerate too.

Q: Of course, the German system is fully state-supported, so it doesn't have the same dynamics of competition as our American system.

A: There are only two private universities in all of Germany. There are only a couple of thousand students at these private universities. They are completely insignificant in terms of numbers, but as an experiment and model for new kinds of private education, they are very important. If students have to pay for universities, education will be much more closely evaluated. The tradition of a university or the independent status of a professor won't be accepted as having an inherent value. But if these new private universities don't receive strong support from German industry, this experiment won't be carried through on a wide basis.

Q: How do these differences between German and American universities bear on day-to-day campus life and student culture?

A: Most German students don't work part-time during the semesters. Unlike in the U.S., they only work during the semester break.

In a certain sense there's no student culture at American universities. Partly because of competition, people seem to speak less to one another.

They're always working or always running off to some other place. They don't sit around in cafés and debate about what happened in their classes. They don't reside in academic or field-oriented housing arrangements [*Zweckwohngemeinschaften*] as in Germany, where students band together in order to study better. These German *Zweckwohngemeinschaften* are really for study purposes. Sometimes they do also develop into common cooking arrangements and other forms of common life.

So there's less of a sense of community among the general student population in the United States. Of course, there are dozens of extracurricular activities that provide a sense of community in the U.S. The difference is that they're all organized by the university. In Germany, students simply band together on a cooperative basis and form their own organizations, which last as long as there is mutual interest among these students. In the U.S., you spend a lot more time on campus. I'm a biophysics student and, except for the labs and a few lectures that I attend, I have no relationship to the campus at all. For everything else, I get what I want from the city of Würzburg.

When I play sports, it's never affiliated with the university, let alone on campus. In the U.S., there's really an organized togetherness. Everything is run through the university, which in some sense is part of its capitalist offerings. In another sense it's part of the *in loco parentis* mentality. Undergraduates are no older than most of the high school students in Germany. A German university limits itself to actual programs of study, whereas American universities conceive of themselves as general activity centers that sponsor academic and other programs. The most important activities concern education, but they also include social and athletic activities. The old boy system in Germany, reflected in the dueling societies, still survives. This is the only analogue to U.S. extracurriculars.

There's nothing in Germany that resembles ceremonies such as parents' day in the United States. There are no huge commencements, which are as much for the benefit of the parents and alumni—and serve as fundraising devices—as for the students. In the U.S., student culture is largely organized and determined from above. In Germany, it's organized from below. In Germany, there is no "dean of students" office that supervises extracurricular activities or "athletic director's office" with a giant gymnasium and extensive intramural sports programs. Practically every German who has traveled has a stereotype of Americans as uneducated. And it's remarkable, when one spends time there, how many of these stereotypes are precisely accurate.

2. Post-Communist Social Studies? A Teacher-Student Conflict of Generations

Interview with Paula, nineteen, an eleventh-grade student in the Goethe Gymnasium for the Humanities in Weimar, after her social studies class in October 1994. The social studies class featured a debate on Marxism and Karl Marx, along with discussion about the PDS and SED. Politically active and a PDS supporter, Paula is an outspoken advocate in class 11B for social justice and political reform. Like Achim, the physics student whom we met in the previous section, Paula is a strong critic of capitalism and engages in a class-based analysis in the Marxist spirit. Perhaps because she is much younger than Achim, and has not yet visited the United States, Paula's emphasis is less anti-capitalist than pro-socialist. Paula emphasizes the spiritual and moral aspects of the socialist ethos, not just the economic issues. But she is more inclined to compare present-day Germany with the DDR past, but she is quite obviously a young woman who thinks for herself: her class-based analysis has nothing in common with the rigid categories and knee-jerk agit-prop of DDR civics textbooks. It is also obvious that her teacher, Frau Smute, is teaching against the grain of the old DDR socialist worldview.

Q: You seemed frustrated by the non-socialist and anti-socialist views of your teacher and some classmates.

A: The discussion we just had in class 11B enrages me because I have such different opinions from all my classmates. There's hardly anyone in school who is as left-wing as I am. But I also found it quite interesting.

Q: Did you feel yourself challenged or attacked?

A: No—even though there were many times when I wanted to get my two cents in, when I wanted to contradict people. But I restrained myself. I get agitated when I hear people defending this capitalist state [the BRD] so uncritically and celebrating it, blind to all of the suffering that has come in its wake. They are completely forgetful of some of the strengths of the previous system.

The spoiling of eastern youth began with all these western German goods coming in—chocolates, hamburgers, expensive clothes, and jewelry. All children wanted to have these things, but they didn't appeal to me at all. I still find it absurd to live in such excess and surplus. When you eat a banana that came out of Africa or Latin America, the natives have received one penny for that and we might charge a mark. They can't live on a penny. They're being exploited and we're the beneficiaries. We're exploiting them.

Q: That reminds me of Marx's chapter in *Das Kapital* on exchange value. Have you read it or heard your teachers talking about it? The example that Marx uses is coffee, but the principle is the same—how workers are alienated from the fruits of their labor and how consumers indirectly cause their misery.

A: Yes—and it applies even to us Germans since [reunification in] 1990! The worst features of the West German life have entered our lives here. We always saw on East German TV that there were beggars on the street in West Germany and it was true! There was never such a thing in the DDR. I believe that this difference may be one sign of the DDR having been "the better Germany." We wouldn't let our people fall to that level. Regardless of what abuses people were exposed to, they never had to suffer like that. Which is worse: to beg for your food or to be spied on? To starve, or hold your tongue?

Frau Smute had just asked us [during social studies class]: "How could you kids have been happy in the DDR?" But I find that question applicable in the present situation! How can I be happy when I see Germans all around me unemployed? My own countrymen? I never saw that in the DDR.

Q: So what should people do?

A: When people believe they're living in an unjust system, it's better to stand up and rebel. If the authorities don't agree, it's an act of courage and virtue to be willing to go to jail for your principles. People did that in the DDR. But I think it's an even more unjust system when people are starving in the streets. There were people who were fighting to make the DDR better, protesting against its inhuman elements such as the Stasi, and I think that is part of what it means to be a decent human being: the will to make things better. But I don't see anyone making a big sacrifice today in an effort to improve capitalism. People now think we're living in a just system.

The people who suffer are utterly invisible. We're not fighting for them, only for ourselves now.

Q: If 60 to 70 percent of the population eventually rose up against the DDR, does that make it a more unjust system?

A: Yes, when half the population is against it, that speaks for itself. In the Pioneers, I was an opponent of the regime in a modest way. We used to have flag-waving in a parade on the mornings of holidays, along with singing folk and battle songs. You were required to stand at attention, salute, and sing. It was explicitly militaristic. Everything—including the Pioneer greeting—was directed at either preparing you for the army or to cultivate your respect for the DDR military. There were demerits and black marks if you didn't behave exactly right during the flag ceremony. It was all nonsense. Most of us made a lot of jokes and irreverent gestures during the whole proceeding. That was the art of resistance that I and some of my friends expressed as Pioneers. It was a kind of open mockery of the whole process.

Q: Today your resistance is much more direct and politically assertive, given your real support for the PDS. Why are you a supporter of the PDS?

A: Because I think that the West is so unjust, so lacking in social justice, with the rich given all the advantages and the poor victimized. The rich are invited through unjust laws to exploit the poor, to make use of advantages that the system offers them. The system works for them. They would be fools not to take advantage of opportunities that are placed before them. Of all the political parties, only the PDS wants to devise definite social measures to change all this and create a more just, more socially equitable system. Human beings should never starve. There are people who don't have a warm room in the winter, even while others are having banquets every night in their home and have a ritzy apartment with five or six bedrooms, or own ten hotels. That shouldn't be, that simply shouldn't be.

Of course, you can't keep banging your head against the system. There are some things you have to tolerate. You have to decide on what fronts you can fight. Now we live in a capitalist society with a free market. And the PDS accepts that; its goal is not to overturn capitalism and institute socialism. That would be a violation of the constitution. Rather the PDS wants to humanize capitalism, make the market serve human beings, not the reverse. Nonetheless, there is so much to change even if it is done on a smaller basis than large-scale revolutionary aspirations. It won't be a revolution, but a gradual reformist approach might in the end result in changes just as significant, though slower to achieve.

Q: What do you think the relationship is between the PDS and Marxism? And between the PDS and the SED? Is the PDS Marxist?

A: No, the PDS is not. It can't be. It has certainly retained some of the ideals of Marxism; maybe you could say its ideal is still indebted to Marx. But the difference is that the PDS is content to remain in opposition. It is not seeking to overturn the status quo by force and thereby replace capitalism with socialism. It has taken a role as the conscience of a nation and as the critic of a capitalist society. I think that is a better role for it. You can't constantly be practicing revolution. History has shown us that Trotsky's idea of a permanent revolution doesn't work—it just leads to the kinds of injustices that plagued the DDR.

Anyway, you realize when you are a minority that you have to play a smaller role and tolerate the system. The PDS only wants to improve capitalism, at least in the near future, not transform Germany into a socialist society.

Q: What do you mean by "the near future"?

A: We need to remember that there really is no PDS in western Germany. The PDS has less than 1 percent there, whereas it gets 20 percent, and up to 50 percent, of the vote in some regions in the east. It's not even really a national party until it establishes a foothold in the west, which after all has three-quarters of the population of the country. It has to recognize that its capacity to promote change is modest. Of course, if all eastern Germans were voting for the PDS, then the seeds of some major change probably would be sown. And who knows what would happen then? It's the "Party of Youth"—the motto fits the eastern reality, since its strongest support comes from voters under the age of twenty-five. That reminds me of an old DDR slogan: "Who has the youth, has the future."

But, at present, the PDS has no chance of coming into power even in eastern regions. It's a minority party. The one thing that the majority parties agree on is that they don't want to form a coalition with the PDS. They don't want it to be allowed to enter into any policy-making role. It has been systematically excluded from attempts to form coalition governments.

Q: It sounds to me as if you reluctantly accept the capitalist system. To seek merely "improvement" means that the system possesses weaknesses, but it is basically all right. That's why I asked you about the near future. Your formulation seems to indicate that, perhaps in the long run, you hope for a non-capitalist or anti-capitalist government.

A: Yes, I hope that communism will one day return—but next time purified of the corruptions that brought down the DDR.

Q: So you don't believe that capitalism could ever progress toward a just society?

A: No. The system would have to contradict itself. It is defined by a competition that leads to radical injustice—a competition that leads to radical inequality. In practical terms, it supports the strong and lets the weak fend for themselves. Its goal above all is to stimulate the economy and it does so in a top-down fashion. This is social Darwinism. The strong will survive. The weak will perish, but they don't really count. Another belief is that when Germany has a stronger economy, then eventually the poor will also do better.

Q: This is what during the Reagan administration was referred to [by presidential aide David Stockman] as the "trickle-down theory," or what market economists sometimes refer to as the "rising tide" that "raises all boats."

A: That's fine in theory, but I think it's much better if the rich help the poor directly and the state tries to make everyone equal in their financial means. I would prefer that the economy function on that basis. Besides, if the poor had more money, they would buy more. It would stimulate the economy, but even if that weren't the case, the economy isn't that important to me. I think that the key is to have enough to eat and to have the basic needs for shelter and warmth met. I don't see any need for the economy to prosper much beyond that, but no one thinks the way I do. Everybody wants to live in a more prosperous country. Everyone wants their electric toothbrushes and their fancy gadgets for the kitchen. They don't *need* any of these things, but they want them.

Q: Your classmates in the other section [Section 11A] held a vote in class today. Between 40 and 50 percent of your classmates voted for the PDS in a mock election. Paula, that would seem to indicate that you're not alone in the school. Do you regard that percentage as representative or not?

A: That vote surprises me. I never thought of the Goethe Gymnasium as very Red. I feel like I'm surrounded by conservative Catholics most of the time. Maybe class 11A is different from mine. Maybe it's an exception. I don't think it's representative of the entire school, let alone Weimar. I rarely meet anyone who agrees with me, so it certainly seems unrepresentative. I suppose it could be a protest vote without any substantial content. It's one thing to vote against reigning bourgeois pieties, it's another thing to understand and support a socialist or radically socially conscious program.

Q: Do you come from a left-wing family? Were your parents Party members?

A: My parents are left-of-center but never joined the Party. They don't belong to the PDS. I'm not from a worker's family. My allegiance to the PDS derives from purely human feelings, not family history or background or parents' convictions or the relationship between my family and the SED. I'm prepared to live for this ideal, and I'm supporting this Party because it's the only one that projects high ideals and is willing to be frank about the need to renounce some material comforts. It's exactly the reverse with other parties. They want to secure material comfort and security first, and only then produce justice and a better society.

Q: Ironically, Marx never preached renunciation. He promised people they would be far more prosperous materially—especially the workers—if they supported socialism. He was completely against any kind of spiritual orientation that included material renunciation.

A: Well, maybe this is just my personal opinion. It isn't as if the PDS has been preaching renunciation. I don't believe the PDS can transform or revolutionize human nature. I certainly don't expect the PDS to adjust its political program to my *Weltanschauung*.

Q: The true Marxist believes that economics and politics condition nature, not that there is any essential human nature. Economics conditions consciousness, not the reverse. The reverse is the idealistic Hegelian position.

A: My position may be something like *Zwang zum Guten* [to be forced to be good].

Q: Or maybe just a strong stimulus to be good.

A: Yes.

Q: Have you heard of the slogan: Build a society in which "it's easy for people to be good" [the slogan for the American newspaper founded in the 1930s, the *Catholic Worker*, devised by Peter Maurin]? Many utopians have felt the same. "How different the world would be if it were easy for people to be virtuous!" The task then is to create a new society in which incentives would make it easier for people to do what is right.

A: Yes! By promoting individualism, capitalism makes it hard for people to do what is good for others.

Q: Frau Smute said in class that Marxism is contrary to human nature.

A: Yes, maybe because human beings are not good enough for Marxism. It raises the bar too high. It's too idealistic to live by.

Q: Perhaps the single true example of widely practiced Marxism is the monastery or religious life, with everything owned in common and no private property, so that most people are equal.

A: But at the cost of hypocrisy. I see this all the time with Christians around here. They can't live by Christian ideals. They're not up to it. They call themselves Christians, but they don't live a Christian life.

Q: There's a saying: "Christianity is wonderful, unfortunately there are Christians." Or from G. K. Chesterson: "It isn't as if Christianity has been tried and found wanting, but that it has been found difficult and not really tried." [Paula laughs.] Might it be that, in theory, communism is wonderful, like Christianity, but in practice it has not been so good because the majority hasn't been able to abide by it?

A: Yes. You could say the same thing about communism and communists.

Q: So, is it contrary to nature to have ideals that are as high as those projected by Christianity and communism?

A: No. You have to project a high ideal so that people will have something to shoot for, something by which to guide their lives. You have to be looking at the stars, not the shoestrings.

Even when you don't reach this ideal, you still have a standard. That furnishes a direction and a destination.

Q: Isn't that view quite dangerous? It's so abstract. What about living concretely according to available possibilities, rather than unavailable ideals or not-yet-available ideals? What about living more pragmatically than idealistically and seeing what can be done with what we already have?

Couldn't we say: Do not look at the stars, but be more earthbound and look less heavenward?

A: If we were to proceed by first looking at the limitations of human beings, seeing their flawed nature and not seeking to reform them and the society, then yes, that would be advisable. That's why I'm so convinced about the preferability of democracy, because I think tyranny exploits such limitations and imposes its policies, using such views as its rationalization. I don't want people to be living in dictatorship. There must be differences of opinion. The very idea of agreeing that we're going to proceed from a single set of assumptions is implicitly dictatorial or authoritarian, because it assumes that we all do agree on a norm. It tacitly snuffs out alternative opinions.

Q: You're very idealistic.

A: Yes, I believe that you should pursue high ideals, even if you never reach them. And you should fight for them, even if it's only on the small stage of your family and work life. At least communists have high ideals, but I think it would bring us so much if communists and Christians, both of whom share similar ideals, were to put aside their differences and unite on a humanitarian basis. They share the ideal of making the world better. Their orientations are different—the Christians look beyond this world, communists believe this is the only world—but the Christian goal of social justice resembles the communist goal of fraternity and equality. I wish we would battle together. We would achieve a lot more if we did, but instead there is a history of enmity between us.

Q: You're not a Christian, obviously.

A: No, I'm not. But I admit that Christians were badly handled in the DDR. That was another one of the black marks of the DDR under communism, the mistreatment of Christians. When they weren't actively discriminated against, they were, at best, tolerated.

Q: The DDR practiced a certain degree of "education toward intolerance." They were intolerant toward all non-communists.

A: That was never explicitly stated, but yes, you're right. I admit that the BRD is very tolerant. It still astounds me how many political parties there are and how many different opinions one hears. There are right-wing radicals and left-wing radicals, and all of them are vocal. And anyone can belong to any one of these parties or factions. They're all permitted. That's good. I think there should be a great diversity of opinions and oppositional standpoints.

Frau Ulrike Smute is Paula's social studies teacher, a Weimar native who spent two years in the west in Hamburg immediately after the fall of the Berlin Wall during 1990–92. I bump into her after leaving Paula. She disputes the validity of the PDS campaign slogan: "The Party of Youth."

Q: Frau Smute, I've just interviewed Paula, an ardent PDS *supporter in your class. As you know, she finds you and your class unreasonably critical of the* PDS.

A: Her memories of the SED only stretch up to the age of twelve or thirteen. She and the other pupils can remember only a beautiful time, which is draped in childhood. They rhapsodize: "What a wonderful experience it was to go to the [Pioneer] summer camps!"

The pupils in my class—and throughout the east—who vote PDS are too young to remember what the SED did. The PDS is the "Party of Youth" because the youth have no memory. At my age, having seen the horrors of socialism, I'm more realistic—and therefore more tolerant of the imperfections of capitalism.

Q: One pupil told me that you don't seem to realize that he and his classmates were children during the DDR years, and that children don't care about the freedom to travel or freedom of speech and association. Those are adult values, he said.

A: I'm astounded that so few students have asked their parents what the SED years were really like. I'm astounded that so many students seem to be defending the SED. They don't seem to have asked their parents or grandparents what living under that so-called socialist regime was really like.

3. "I Was a True Believer": A Convinced Communist Student Looks Back

Interview in May 1997 with Grit Pieper, twenty-six, a sociolinguistics doctoral student at Leipzig University. Her projected dissertation topic deals with language differences between eastern and western Germany before and after 1989. Grit was quite interested in my research because she too was studying the "categories of thinking" that distinguished citizens of the two Germanies. Her dissertation research is another example of how eastern Germans have moved far beyond the "textbook mentality" of the official dogmas of the DDR. *As in the case of Dorothee, whom we met in Chapter 6, where she discussed with me her dissertation on German identity and the Holocaust, Grit is pursuing an approach to German identity that would not have been possible during the* DDR *era. She is taking a comparative approach that would have been regarded as placing the two Germanies, quite unjustifiably, on the same level. Nonetheless, Grit has also maintained a good deal of her socialist outlook from earlier years and is a strong critic of western German society.*

Q: What is the main focus of your research in sociolinguistics?

A: I'm examining how differences that might be expressed in other cultural forms such as dress, or more overtly through opinions, get expressed instead through language differences: e.g., different words being coined or pronounced differently, different concepts for similar words, and the various indirect ways in which hostilities between the two Germanies were manifested. For instance, the official phrase in the West German newspapers for the DDR "the so-called DDR." Or the official DDR name for the Berlin Wall: "The Anti-Fascist Wall of Protection."

Q: So your research also concerns the relationship between language and social perception.

A: Yes. I'm also interested in different categories of thinking, what the relationship is between language and thought (including the Sapir-Whorf hypothesis), and how misunderstandings arose between East and West Germans because of language differences. I'm really investigating the divergent ways of thinking between the two Germanies and how that was expressed in language; for instance, one key has to do with geographical concepts, such as how the two Germanies designated the DDR, which was cited for decades in the West German press in inverted quotation marks. "East Germany," "middle Germany," "capitalist foreign country," "KA," "so-called DDR," and now the "former DDR." West Germans only rarely called their own country the "BRD"; they referred to themselves as the Federal Republic because they never wanted to use abbreviations; in doing so, they felt they would have been equated with the DDR—a mere abbreviation. The same thing occurred with the Wall. The West German media referred to it as the "Wall of Shame" or the "Wall of Outrage." The East German press referred to it as the "Anti-Fascist Wall of Protection."

I've also been exploring what the range of "us" and "them" meant—who was included and excluded by those pronouns. And the word *drüben* ["over there"].

Q: You spoke of changes in the use of formal and informal address since reunification. What do former Party comrades call each other now? When do they still speak in informal pronouns? Or have they reverted to the formal usage?

A: When my father was at a Party meeting, he used informal pronouns for everyone even if they were only acquaintances. I believe it's an interesting sociolinguistic issue, but I haven't yet explored it. He's not in the Party [PDS] anymore. He may avoid the use of a pronoun, if possible, or he may revert to using formalities or he'll find some middle way of using informal plurals which aren't as informal as informal singular terms.

Q: How was the choice of formal versus informal address handled among academic colleagues in the Party before the fall of the Wall?

A: In the old DDR days, it was quite possible that a senior professor would have spoken with you in a Party meeting with an informal pronoun, but then in auditorium or in office hours with a formal pronoun. You were a comrade during the Party meeting. But outside that meeting, you were a student and he was a professor; there was a sense of equality in the Party meeting and a sense of hierarchy outside in the university setting, the latter of which followed a long German tradition. I was in the FDJ but never in the Party.

Q: And how was it handled in the FDJ?

A: The Party president of the FDJ, when I was a student at the university, was forty or older and he always used informal pronouns with us. Party functionaries in the FDJ always used informal pronouns, but that wasn't limited to FDJ meetings because they always spoke informally on the street or anywhere we met them. When I spoke with the junior faculty, I always used formal pronouns. To be in the FDJ at university was different than to be in the FDJ of the Party. The university FDJ wasn't close-knit.

Q: Did it ever cross your mind to commit *Republikflucht?*

A: I could never have been someone who left and went to the West. It never even occurred to me to leave the country. The very thought of it would have been horrible. I considered it an act of extraordinary disloyalty to become a "traitor" to the state. In hindsight, I can hardly believe I thought that. To have still had those convictions in my late teens and early twenties was a bit naive. To have believed all that so completely—so that the thought would have never even crossed my mind—was a kind of willed naiveté, a will to not see certain things, to not see the evils of the state and how it was victimizing many people and how that tendency was at the root of how that state functioned.

Q: Do you feel strongly identified now with western Germans?

A: No, I always feel that they're "the Other." They're different—we're different—because of our manner of speaking, our worldviews, and our values; there often seems to be no point of connection between us easterners. I think many western Germans don't notice this, but it's very obvious to us and them. They just assume we're like them, but we're not. They think we'll adapt and we do, to some extent, but it doesn't mean we feel we're like them or that we're strongly related to them as fellow Germans.

Q: How do western Germans now view easterners?

A: As soon as they ask you where you come from, you feel as if they're thinking you're from *"Ossiland"*—this strange, backward place that has primitive or even corrupt ideas of communism and socialism. We're not perceived as equals and the idea of equal rights hasn't fully lodged in western German consciousness. We're second-class citizens in their view and we're on trial, in that we have to prove ourselves worthy of being part of the new Germany. As soon as they hear we're East German, they say, "oh," with a strange inflection in their voice. That inflection speaks volumes. It isn't arrogance or a sense of personal superiority; rather, it's a sign of pity: "Oh you poor *Ossi*. We come from a strong and good system, but you poor people are from that horrible east."

We sense that they are trying to say, "We'll have to teach you what a good system is, and how to live in that system, but you have to pay close attention and do it just the way we do it." The idea that they might learn something from us, or that our system had anything worth preserving, is inconceivable to them. Western Germans don't have anything to learn, they think, and there's nothing in the old East German system worth keeping; it should all be swept away. They feel a great sense of regional superiority, but most of them haven't visited the east even a single time! They know nothing about the east at all! They've never in their whole lives visited it—even now that the Wall has fallen.

It's astounding, but they have no curiosity about what has happened on the other side of Germany over the last half century! They have no sense of curiosity at all. And when there is any, it doesn't extend beyond the curiosity of a tourist who believes, "Well, the old East Germany is going to be invisible or gone in five years. So let's have a look at it while it's still there, and while we can still see these exotic traces of the past. In five years there won't be any difference between it and us; we'll have revamped the entire system in our image."

We're really more or less a museum for western Germans now. There isn't any kind of fellow feeling as a German. When they do visit, they could be coming from anywhere. They don't feel any relation to us. They just come and look at us as creatures from the past that are near extinction or already extinct, but that are being preserved in this transition period for their observation and appraisal. It's not much different from tourists observing at a zoo. The *Ossis* are gaped at like strange animals. We hardly ever get into serious conversation with a westerner about differences between the two countries, or the nature of our past, or how our consciousness was shaped. I still feel much more strongly connected to other East Germans. In fact, I feel myself more strongly connected to Czechs, Poles, and Yugoslavs than I do to western Germans. Despite the cultural and linguistic differences, we share a common consciousness, a common attitude about the relationship of an individual to a society, about the values of a community and the role of consumer products in our lives.

Q: You feel you have more in common with post-communist eastern Europeans than with western Germans?

A: Yes. I have a feeling of solidarity with them, and not at all with western Germans. Their individualism, their self-centeredness, their natural assumption of superiority, their certainty that their way at looking at the world is *the* right way. Those attitudes are repellent to me. That doesn't mean that I don't have something to learn from the western Germans, or that I don't need to have my own picture of them and of the world corrected at times. I'm just telling you how I feel.

Q: So shared history is more decisive for you than the ties of nationality and a common language.

A: For me, yes, I share with other eastern Europeans a common past. That past is rooted in a certain kind of collective thinking and a set of socialist values, even though I'm aware that much of it was orchestrated by organizations like the FDJ. Those values did influence how I think and still think. For me, there remains something comprehensible as "socialist Europe." That doesn't mean western Germans are bad people. I have western German friends. Just that we're different.

Q: Did you participate in the Leipzig marches in October–November 1989?

A: The only reason I didn't participate was because of the angst I had. I had all these fears—e.g., that there might be violence, or that we would be arrested or disadvantaged at the university, or that some Party-initiated retaliation would take place against my father, or that I would lose my university place or scholarship. I had all these fears and these were fears that my father voiced at home because we knew that in the early days, when the marches were small—up until September 1989 at least—that everyone who participated was closely observed by the Stasi and there were some quiet measures taken against some of them.

Given what happened in previous workers' uprisings, you simply had to be ready to put a great deal on the line to sacrifice something in your life or in your family's life for a principle, and I just wasn't willing to stake that much on a principle.

Q: The demonstrations were occurring right under your classroom windows, weren't they? How did that feel?

A: Yes, I happened to have a lecture at night on Monday evenings at Leipzig University, so I would see what was happening on the streets of Leipzig, but I never skipped lecture in order to go to any demonstrations. I remember one October coming out of one of my lectures and seeing many *Vopo* [People's Police] units with jeeps and cars, bobby sticks, even guns and helicopters, following marchers all at a distance, all peacefully, but clearly with the message that if this demonstration went beyond a certain point, stern measures would be taken. So there was a quite visible *Vopo* presence, which was generally not the case—actually quite an exception in the DDR—which was intended as a warning or form of intimidation to the marchers. There were at least three to four hundred policemen, and part of the march of late September 1989 occurred on the doorstep of Leipzig University when it was still a great risk to appear in those *Demos*.

Within a month, it had turned into a festive atmosphere—by late October 1989, marches had swelled to two or three hundred thousand people—and at that point it was clear that the government wasn't going to do anything to stop them or penalize demonstrators in any way. The marches were far too big for the government to respond with intimidation.

Q: Did any of your university friends march?

A: No.

Q: In retrospect, how convincing was the DDR propaganda?

A: Well, most of us ignored the state-controlled media. Some of the propaganda was so blatant!

Eduard Schnitzler's television program, *Der Schwarze Kanal* (The Black Channel), distorted abuses that occurred in the West to prop up this enemy image that the government wanted to inculcate among DDR citizens. The Black Channel was supposed to show the blackness of capitalism—its dark side—which indeed it did. But it naively blackened capitalism by showing *only* its dark side, in direct contrast to almost everything else that DDR citizens saw on the screen. Since most DDR citizens didn't watch that much DDR television, but rather West German television, the contrast was extreme. The Black Channel, rather than moderating our views of the West, was often treated as a joke. It departed so far from the images that we saw of the U.S. and West Germany! It didn't balance out the glamor of what we saw on West German television; it reinforced it, because it seemed such a pathetic attempt to undercut it.

But I should qualify that statement. Many of us partly believed the DDR stereotypes of the West because of another reality that we suspected was true: the mass homelessness, the ruthless competition in which people lost their jobs at the drop of a hat, the lack of any economic security, no financial security blanket for retirement, and so on. Those parts of the enemy picture did sink in for us and remained intact for millions of DDR citizens even after the turn. That is largely because we ourselves are losing our jobs in a major transition to a capitalist future.

Q: What's worth keeping from the old system?

A: It isn't clear what was good from the old system that is reconcilable with the capitalist system, but it had to do with a sense of security, setting a floor underneath people. Like nurseries for children, so a mother can find it easy to work because they are state-supported and -funded. I think it's a crime such nurseries are gone. Women had a different position in the DDR than in West Germany. Almost 95 percent of women worked; they could do so because the state took care of children.

Q: Was the state really interested in taking care of children or simply in increasing the number of people in the workforce to boost the economy since so many people had fled? Were such nurseries a way of taking control of the kids away from their mothers so that the state could fill their minds with ideology?

A: [Pause.] It was unusual for West German mothers to work, whereas for East German mothers it was the norm. I was in daycare since the age of two and also attended kindergarten. I think it was good for me. I'd never say I was badly raised because I didn't spend as much time with my mother as a West German girl. Today kindergarten costs 500 marks per month—and child care in nursery school may cost double that. In general, the work versus family struggle of women under capitalism is regrettable. The reduced competition and lack of anxiety that East Germans had about the work world would have been something worth preserving in some form.

Q: Is that really compatible with achieving Western prosperity levels? It seems that the socialist view that economic incentives are not necessary for people to work harder was disproved in 1989–90. DDR citizens voted to join the BRD partly because they wanted a better economic life, including the freedom to own their own business and some private property, and the sense that this is theirs and can be protected, cultivated, and passed onto their children.

A: [Long pause.] I don't know. You immediately perceive in western Germany that there is unfreedom, just as in eastern Germany. It only seems to be much freer in the west. There is private property, so there is economic freedom in that sense, but no greater social freedom, no more room to maneuver as a social being. I still have the feeling that the human element counts more in the east than in the west. Despite all the abuses by the Stasi and all the violations of human rights by the East German regime, I feel very uncomfortable in Germany today because I did identify with the DDR and it doesn't exist anymore. Sometimes I think about participating in building up eastern Germany into a different kind of left-oriented region than it was, but other times I feel it's not my mission.

That's when I think, "What is there to build up?! Everything has been swept away! There is something new already put in place! Alien." So I wonder what my own future is. To be identified with the DDR is to have no future in the new Germany. So I think a lot about emigrating, but I'm not sure where to go.

4. "My Father Was in the Party": A Daughterly Diptych

In August 2003, I had the opportunity to interview Grit again. Later that month, I also spoke again with Kersten, whom we met in Chapter 6. At the time of these interviews, Grit was still pursuing her dissertation research on sociolinguistic differences between eastern and western Germans. Now a mother of three, Kersten worked privately as an interpreter/translator of Russian and English in Berlin.

My concern in these new conversations with Grit and Kersten was to explore how the burden of the communist past for eastern Germans possesses an inter-generational dimension. Both interviews highlighted the ambiguous legacy of communism within the eastern German family, and both show how the fathers of these women are morally compromised and partly alienated from their children by their years of affiliation with the Party.

Just how was the difficult issue of negotiating a life within the communist regime handled within the family? Kersten's father is from a Christian family and joined the Party for practical reasons: to help his family and promote his own career. By contrast, Grit's father comes from a staunchly communist background and joined the Party for ideological reasons. As Kersten's father went further up the ladder in the prison system, he got mired deeper in Party duties and also reported regularly to the Stasi—all of which seemed unavoidable to him. He and his family members lived in denial of his self-compromising choices, but nevertheless the effects are deep.

And what about Grit's father? Though she dismisses the idea that her father had close Stasi contacts, it is clear that he has also been traumatized by his Stasi cooperation as well as his Party activities—and most especially by his role in suppressing the 1953 Workers' Uprising and in erecting the Berlin Wall in 1961.

So this diptych emphasizes aspects of eastern German experience that have heretofore not emerged in this book: how "the sins of the fathers" are revisited upon the daughters in succeeding generations. It also shows the diverse ways in which eastern Germans bear the burden of the communist era—a past that is a distinctively eastern phenomenon. Each interview depicts how the burden is passed on from one generation to the next, from the parents to the children. The children are burdened with the choices and compromises that their parents made, indeed that their parents sometimes made on behalf of their children.

Interview #1: Kersten

Q: Why did your father join the Party?

A: He felt that joining the Party was necessary because he was fatherless by the end of the war and was the only male in his family. He took it upon himself to support his mother as well as six sisters until they were all married. He was poor, and he had to work as an unskilled laborer in different factories. He wanted to learn, and he wanted the opportunity to improve himself through higher education. He later accepted a job with the People's Police. That was the beginning of his entry into the system, although he wasn't yet a member of the Party. At that time, he met my mother, so he became more concerned with establishing enough security to start a family. He was proud that he was going to be a good provider for his family, and the best way to establish stability to do so was through the Party.

Soon he began achieving better positions in the People's Police. He worked very hard, and he was being rewarded financially for that—at least by DDR standards. Sometimes he worked twelve to fourteen hours per day. That was very unusual in the DDR, except in the highest echelons, but he was earning a good living and our family had all that we could ask for in the DDR. He always thought it was important to be guaranteed good retirement pay and benefits. At his level, it was guaranteed and it would be extended to my mother. So he was thinking economically, but actually more in a capitalist direction. He wasn't concerned with the good of the whole society or even our local community. He was concerned about our family. "How can I provide for my family and their future?" And "family," during his youth, also meant his six sisters.

Q: So he was not ideologically committed to the Party?

A: My father knew exactly what was going on in the DDR. He understood the system and he was rather shrewd, even though he was essentially unpolitical. He learned where the invisible lines were, and he knew the distinction between work and home. He also knew the public and private language, and how much free space one was allowed. But he wasn't supposed to speak about his work at home, and in order to protect us, he didn't. He also didn't because he'd developed a cautious, submissive posture in his work environment. He would say, "Why make waves or cause problems? Let's just go along."

His willingness to conform slid into something close to cowardice at times. When he saw something scheduled on West German television, he wouldn't forbid us to see it; he just wouldn't reply to it. My mother was usually the one who would agree with West German programs critical of the DDR. Or she would tell us about the context of these programs.

My father later said to me, "Child, of course I knew everything that was going on, but I didn't know how to explain it to you and I didn't see the point." The political side, he always said, was just part of the crap he had to wade through. But he did wade through it in order to get what he wanted. He eventually became the warden—not of a political jail, but of one containing hardened criminals who had committed violent crimes. But there was still a lot of politics and he was ill suited to it. He simply wasn't a political creature. He could go along, but he was never enthusiastic, let alone fanatical, about M-L ideology. He was simply familiar with it. He could talk it.

To rise to his position, he had to enter the Party. He said, "This is a lot of *mist*" [shit], but he entered. The Party was a means to an end. He never supported its aims or agreed with its ideology. His Christian rearing and the hardships undergone by his parents for resisting the Party, as well as his distaste for ideology that had already occurred in reaction to the Nazi years, were probably deeply embedded in him. Communism wasn't much of an improvement over Nazism, he said. It was just another system. It was a bit better, but it wasn't something he wanted to support actively.

Q: Tell me more about his political and religious background.

A: My grandparents were very Christian and tradition-minded. They were not interested in politics. My maternal and paternal grandfathers died before I was born. My grandmothers were basically unpolitical. They never understood why they couldn't visit their girlfriends in West Germany. "All these ideologies and political issues don't concern me," they both said. They were born in the 1890s and they could remember the Kaiser and Germany before the Nazis, the Russian occupation, and the DDR. What mattered to them were family and local matters—their little garden, the market's produce selection this week, or the neighbors' gossip. They lived in a small world and it contented them. They had always lived in such a world, and they turned even more inward when I was growing up.

My paternal grandparents came from Silesia in Poland and were expelled at the end of the war [1945] by the Poles. As a result, they lost everything. They fled into eastern Germany. In the course of escaping, my grandfather was murdered by the Russians. My father was in the *Pimpf* [the Cub Scout counterpart to the Hitler Youth]. He was too young to be in the *Volkssturm* [People's Army] at the end of the war, so he never became a soldier. Thus, my grandparents had neither a left-wing nor a Nazi heritage or background, but rather a conservative Christian orientation that my parents eventually put aside in order to get ahead in the DDR.

Our family history made it natural for us to feel that the limits of the DDR were our horizon—and to accept life within its tight box. My grandparents on my father's side settled in Magdeburg and Brandenburg, and my mother's parents were from Berlin. So all of my grandparents lived in East Germany. That explains why we had no relatives beyond the DDR borders when the Wall went up—and why no officials ever thought that I'd commit *Republikflucht* during my first visit to Paris.

Q: Was your father able to maintain that stance of being "in" but not "of" the Party?

A: In the later years, it changed a little. He was appointed to the Party as a *Wohnbezirkfunkzionär* [district official]. He accepted that responsibility in the Party reluctantly. Unfortunately, it got him in deeper. He had to make sure that everyone in the district voted in the elections. He had to attend a lot of certain meetings. He had to keep tabs on some Party activities that were occurring in the district, such as the May Day parades and special ceremonies (to honor a visiting Russian official or a junior DDR Politburo member). He wasn't in charge of those visits, but he would be told that his district must be in order.

As a young man, my father had a certain innocence—or a kind of idealism—toward the Party. With the passage of time, it turned to skepticism, if not cynicism. He became more and more enmeshed in Party activities and became more a *Realpolitiker* [hard-nosed realist]—more of a Party careerist. "You've got to get your hands a little dirty, and you've got to be willing to make compromises," he would say. And that's what he did.

So he slid into things, as I said. An undertow was pulling him out. He also felt that the only way he could change things was to be involved in the system. A piece of his idealism did remain. He rationalized his Party work by saying that if you wanted to improve things, you could only do so if you had access to power, or at least to those who could influence those who were in power to change things. You couldn't do so from the outside, as a dissident, and certainly not from jail.

Q: So your father was never a believer in socialism?

A: Not really. My father joined in the early to mid-1950s, when the battle for socialism was still being fought quite earnestly. At that time, there was a great deal of hope that the horrible Nazi past could be overcome. He was partly induced to join the Party because he harbored a sense of idealism—he dreamed of a better world.

But in the last years of the DDR, my father was a disgusted complainer—though he was in too deep to say anything against the Party, let alone get out. In late 1989, he threw away his Party book and resigned from the Party, but by then, everyone was doing it. He was genuinely disillusioned by that point. Before 1989, he reasoned that he couldn't jeopardize the future of the family and he wasn't going to throw away his entire career and the security that he'd fought for. When you're in, there's no turning back. That was the lesson in the Party. The advantages were yours, but the disadvantages for pulling out were far greater than for those who never joined.

He had a lot of responsibility. To be running this large prison was an extremely demanding and anxiety-producing job. There were always things going wrong, and there were always things to worry about.

Q: Your brother also joined the Party. Did he share your father's opinions of the Party?

A: My brother, Uli, became a candidate member of the Party at the age of eighteen. He entered the Party completely convinced of the virtues of communism yet knowing the system's falsities, but he emphasized the good sides and believed that the system was capable of reform. People like my brother were Party members in order to try to improve the state. Socialism was still a system in process, they held, it wasn't yet fully realized. The phrase "really existing socialism" was only a theoretical phrase, because true socialism did not yet exist. It merely existed as a seed—not a full-grown tree. My father and brother wanted to change the Party. There were a lot of idealists like them. And, of course, my brother's experience of the Party and the DDR school was different from mine. He is sixteen years older. He grew up at a time when there was still more hope that everything could be reformed.

Q: Your father was raised in a religious home. Did he continue that tradition in any respect?

A: My father and mother became convinced atheists. They were married in the church and my brother was a confirmed Lutheran, but by the late 1950s, after my father had entered the Party and was rising in the People's Police, he made the switch. My father was married in church, but when he left the Church and entered the Party, his relationship to the Church was completely broken. He used to joke about the nonsense that the minister would say in the pulpit even while he was chauffeuring his mother to her church every week. She was still attending services every Sunday as a loyal believer.

He used to say, "Well, if it provides some people with consolation, it's fine." He came to view religion as a form of superstition, and he said he never needed that. Occasionally, he would attend the Protestant and Catholic services in the jail, for whatever reason. It could have been that he did so to have a better relationship with the clergy who worked with the prisoners. It was also good to have the visibility and to be perceived as sympathetic to the value of religion for the purpose of reforming criminals.

Q: Did your father defend the Party before 1989?

A: He never really attempted a general defense of the Party, but he would defend particular comrades. He would say "so and so is all right" or "I have no objections to the policies that so and so is advocating," or he would praise the critical stance or sober attitude that a particular Party comrade had shown at a recent Party meeting. But as the 1980s went on, he certainly didn't make any kind of general defense of Honecker or the Party elite.

He was not a defender of the regime in that sense; he simply felt that it was impossible for him to leave the Party, because the consequences would be too devastating for the family. His favorite activity was to tell us the political jokes that were circulating. He would pick a lot of them up at the meetings. At the same time he was well aware that we had to be careful. He would tell them at home, but he certainly wouldn't tell them in the correctional facility. I didn't know anyone who was openly defiant toward the system. My friends, like me, had just learned to live with the system and accepted it for what it was. Some of them thought that it could be improved a bit, some others said it was getting worse or that it was beyond redemption, but nobody was willing to stand up or sacrifice a great deal to change it or to expose its weaknesses.

One of the turning points in our family was in 1984, when one of my older brother's best friends applied for an exit visa to emigrate. That was also a decisive turning point for me, because I got to know him better and we became good friends. That opened my eyes.

For the first time, I began to see what kind of petty injustices were routine in the DDR. They were being imposed on this young man as a result of his wanting to leave the country. At about this time, there was a rise in the number of applications for emigration. This was also about the time that the economy was slowing down. The economic prosperity, which had been with us for many years and had allowed us to forget about a third world war waiting to happen on our turf, disappeared. The great successes that we had been having in the 1970s were not continuing into the 1980s. Instead there was anxiety about rearmament. Opposition against entering into the peace process with West Germany was a growing theme.

Q: By this point your father had climbed quite high up on the Party ladder.

A: Yes. My father was, especially by the 1980s, a highly trusted Party figure. He entered negotiations with other wardens in West Germany to exchange some prisoners, especially East German hardened criminals who had committed crimes in West Germany or the East. Again, these were not political prisoners, so these were not political exchanges that West Germans were paying for. The fact that he was in contact with West Germans was a sign of Party trust. This activity brought him into frequent contact with the DDR foreign ministry—with people at the second- and third-tier levels. Of course, that meant that he had important connections in the Party. He was also well-regarded in Party circles as a district official.

Q: Did he ever work for the Stasi?

A: My father was never a Stasi agent, but he is in the Stasi files as an IM [*inoffizieler Mitarbeiter,* unofficial employee or Stasi informant]. He regularly submitted reports to the Stasi about the criminals in the prison and about his conversations with West German wardens. So he had a lot of contact with the Stasi, which he called *Gummiohr* [plastic ear]. Once in a while he would say, "The Stasi is the worst." He didn't attempt to rationalize Stasi spying or justify it as some necessary evil.

But he wasn't without sympathy for some of the Stasi careerists or for the Stasi agents and individuals. He knew many Stasi people and would often say, "Well, so and so is with the Stasi and joined during his time in the army so he could have a few hundred extra marks per month, and I'm sure his family appreciates it," or "He's getting quite a few perks from the Stasi for his conscientious reports and he just wants a better life." In other words, he saw some Stasi people as motivated by the same concerns for economic security that he had. Of course, that was also the attitude that brought Hitler to power in the 1930s—people just thought that they would benefit more if the Nazis were in control.

Q: What did your father do for the Stasi?

A: I should emphasize that my dad was a Party man, not a Stasi man. He had contact with the Stasi, but he wasn't doing any spying and he was not profiteering from the Stasi. He was just making his and our lives easier by cooperating with the Stasi when he was asked to. His activity as a Party district leader never extended to filing reports on neighbors; rather, it was limited to his activity as a warden. He always wondered who it was in our neighborhood that was the head spy that fingered people as being disloyal or critical of the state. These people played a major role in improving or hurting the lives of other people. Whenever you applied to visit a sick relative in the West, or to attend the eightieth birthday party of an uncle who was in the West, or to attend the wedding of a child who had gone to the West, Stasi documents were consulted. If there was something negative there on you, you were simply refused without explanation. You needed to have a clean record so you wouldn't ruin your chances in case some opportunity arose to travel that was justifiable within the state law. The Stasi agents could ruin your chances with a lie—and without your ever even clearly knowing it.

The Stasi would, however, occasionally approach my father and ask him about a certain individual. For instance, they would ask him about a person who was applying for a ten-day visa to go to West Germany. "Is he merely going to visit a relative?" they would ask. My father would typically say, "Well, yes, I know him well and he's a good neighbor. There won't be any trouble with him. He'll be back."

He didn't write formal Stasi reports. He gave information to their agents in interviews. And, of course, our family was spied upon intensely. I'm still waiting for our family's complete file of Stasi documents. My father occupied an important position and he was regularly screened at a distance by the Stasi. People were spying on him to make sure that he was trustworthy, because he was interacting with high-level officials in the West. He was called a *Geheimnisträger* [carrier of state secrets]. So he had to be closely screened for a clean record, which was referred to as a "white vest"—which we jokingly considered a clean bib. My father knew this, of course, and occasionally told us that he was often spied upon.

Q: Has your father read his Stasi files?

A: My father doesn't want to see his Stasi files. He says, "I know my old friends were probably reporting on me regularly. But I don't have a lot of friends from those days anymore." He doesn't want to ruin his remaining friendships or rake up the past. He's annoyed by the *Wendehälse* [turncoats], who have suddenly decided that they've been capitalists all along. "Those hypocrites upset me!" he says.

Interview #2: Grit

Q: You came from a Red family?

A: Yes. My parents were members of the SED since its founding in 1946. My father was born in 1925 and my mother in 1928. They came from working-class families that were left-wing during the Weimar Republic.

My father supervised the business end of a large agriculture cooperative, a VEB [People's Own Enterprise]. He was the *Betriebsleiter* [manager] who was responsible for keeping the books, helping organize personnel. My mother was a child care worker in the *Hort* [after-school child care center] for the POS in our town. She really specialized in the kindergarten-age children.

Q: Where did your parents come from?

A: Both of my parents come from an iron ore mining region, the Erzgebirge in Saxony, located near what had been called Karl Marx City during the DDR and has reverted since the *Wende* to its original name, Chemnitz.

I'm from a small town called Meller. My father was born in the same small town. My grandparents on both sides of the family also came from this small town. So we had deep roots there. I didn't know my grandparents very well on my mother's side. They died when I was child. The only thing I know today about them was that my grandfather was severely wounded in World War II.

My grandparents were oriented toward the left but were not persecuted during the Third Reich; they remained very quiet and just went along. Both of my grandfathers were soldiers in the war. So they did cooperate to that extent with the Third Reich even though they disagreed with its policies. They didn't try to flee the country, nor did they refuse to be drafted, which would have certainly meant persecution and jail, maybe execution.

Q: So both of your parents were raised in leftist families.

A: Yes. Both grandfathers were members of the KPD in the 1930s—quite a statement to be making at that time. One of them was even in a KPD functionary position in our small town.

I don't think there was a great deal of difference in the early post-war years between my grandparents and parents. Such great optimism about a new beginning after the war prevailed among most KPD members that their attitude was similar to the idealism of youth. The idealistic attitudes of my grandparents about socialism resembled the youthful idealism about building a good socialist Germany that my parents felt as teenagers after the war. The differences between the two generations developed much later. As prospects for a better socialist Germany dimmed, a cynicism developed in the younger generation. Skeptical thinkers proclaimed that all politics was a scam, and that socialism was just another "ism" no better than capitalism.

Q: When did that "great optimism" of the post-war era end for your father?

A: Probably the decisive event that occurred during the early life of our family—well before I was born—was the Workers' Uprising in June 1953. My father was one of the members of a battle unit [*Kampfgruppe*] that was sent out to quell the rebellion and stand up to these counter-revolutionary workers, as they were officially condemned. In later years, my brother—who was in the POS at that time—would often talk about June 1953 as the betrayal of the workers. He would either implicitly or explicitly indict my father for having betrayed the workers. Of course, my father's view was that he was simply carrying out orders and that the uprising was really western-inspired.

My father was always very defensive about being part of this battle unit sent out to put down the rebellion in Chemnitz. His position as a member of the battle unit owed to his management position in the industrial VEB. Already by his late 20's, he was entering lower- or middle-level management, which meant that he had to organize the VEB workers who would support the regime's policies. In the case of the June 1953 uprising, that meant organizing units in the firm to serve as army reserve units. At this time, the NVA [People's National Army] had not yet been founded. That occurred in 1956. [The NVA had not yet come into being partly in order to discourage the talk about DDR militarism and discourage any additional reason young men would have to emigrate to West Germany—since they still could flee easily, because the Wall had not yet arisen.]

So these battle units, located in every VEB, were the only military force that the DDR had except for the *Vopos* [*Volkspolizei*, People's Police]. These factory battle units were treated as army reserve soldiers—and actually wore soldiers' uniforms. They were quite official—they were DDR defense units that were designed to supplement the Russian army of occupation and the People's Police.

Despite his rationalizations, my father was very ambivalent about quelling the worker's rebellion. He thought of himself as a worker and, as the son of a KPD member, came out of the worker's revolutionary tradition. In later years, his embarrassment about his participation in the 1953 rebellion only increased. It was a real sore point between my brother and my father. I think my father was ashamed that he had participated. That accounted for his sometimes aggressive defense of the action, when he voiced accusations of "counter-revolutionary workers" leading the uprising and spoke about the legitimacy of the DDR government's response.

Q: Did this disillusionment tear your family apart?

A: Despite the fact that my brother and I never joined the Party—unlike our parents and even more so unlike our grandparents, who were if anything more fervently left-wing than our parents—there never arose any great debate in our family. Nor did these differences in opinion cause a split in the family. Instead, there were simply large taboo areas in our family, topics that were off-limits for discussion. That's how we arrived at a *modus vivendi* for getting along.

Q: What were your father's duties in the Party?

A: My father never talked much about his Party activities. He was a faithful participant at the regional and district Party meetings, but he didn't talk a lot about them at home. I know just from his regular attendance and general attitude that he strongly supported the Party until the mid-1980s. He was a loyal Party supporter, not just a member. He began to question the Party more critically by the late 1980s, but he was one of the conservatives in the district and advocated taking harsh measures against protestors. He deplored the Monday night *Demos* in Leipzig and felt that the protest leaders were being dealt with much too leniently. He argued that the problem was in the top Party echelon, that the Party leaders were out of touch with the attitudes of the rank and file. They were too old in the case of Honecker, and they were too comfortable in the case of most Politburo members. Some of them had been in their positions for decades and were insulated from the daily life of the rank-and-file Party members.

Q: What sort of "harsh measures" against the protestors did your father advocate?

A: My father never perceived the protestors in 1989 as counter-revolutionaries or enemies of the state, nor in any of these official terms of condemnation that the government was constantly blaring in the media. He simply saw them as DDR citizens who were in disagreement with the state. He shared some of this discontent, but he felt that this was not a proper way to work through things. The proper way was to work through the Party, to voice disagreement in Party meetings, and to work within the Party structure, which included taking on some positions whereby you could influence events or have the ear of more powerful Party members who could make important changes.

So his loyalty to the state and to the Party still extended to believing it was the sole legitimate vehicle for running the country and achieving reform. The Party would have to reform itself from within; pressure from without would only weaken the DDR. Certainly he never anticipated that the *Demos* would bring down the regime or that these marches would eventually topple not only Party leaders, but destroy the Party itself and lead to the collapse of DDR. Well, almost no one foresaw that, but least of all my dad.

Q: Did you or your brother join the Party?

A: No. My brother studied music and was a bit of an alternative thinker. That's probably the reason he never joined the Party. He simply couldn't or didn't want to participate in something so organized. He wasn't so much left-wing as he was simply independent. I probably didn't become a member of the Party because of the critical attitude that my brother expressed, which imprinted itself deeply on my consciousness as a young girl. My brother is forty-two, so he's quite a lot older than me. I am twenty-six. My siblings, my parents, and I really belonged to three different DDR generations. Whereas my parents were convinced socialists, my brother was completely unpolitical and indeed skeptical of all ideology, whether capitalist or communist.

My brother was involved in the *Demos* fairly early on. Already in early 1989 he belonged to a circle of artists who, though basically unpolitical, became more politicized and outspoken against the regime as it dragged its feet on *perestroika* and *glasnost*. I think their opposition to the DDR arose because the regime was being perceived as increasingly behind the times, untrendy. My brother was a big fan of Gorbachev, who was seen among some artists and intellectuals as leading a "revolution from above" in the Soviet Union. But that was impossible in the DDR—our Party hierarchy was backward, decrepit, and arch-conservative.

Q: How did your brother's participation in the protests affect your family?

A: It seldom came to open argument between my brother and father. Again, it was rather that numerous topics were simply avoided. On Monday nights, my brother would visit home, even though my father knew where he had been. After awhile, the protest marches were never even mentioned. My father and brother had simply and tacitly agreed to disagree. This opposition by silence was a common pattern in the DDR. A great deal was left unsaid. A great deal wouldn't and couldn't be said—because who knows where it might lead and who might be listening?

Such an attitude about public talk filtered very easily into private homes. After the *Wende* in November 1989, tensions in the family dissipated. There was so much upheaval that my brother and father just buried the hatchet. Whatever they disagreed about in the DDR days just didn't seem relevant any more. "It is a new world, so let's begin anew," they thought. It's also the case that they shared sharp criticism of the changes in new federal states after the *Wende*. My father did, because he believed a lot of aspects of the DDR were better; my brother did, because he reacted against the naive hope of the typical DDR citizen that we would be soon ushered into some paradise.

Q: What was your father's view of the West?

A: My father definitely had a *Feindbild*. There was a class enemy, there was KA, which meant to him West Germany, capitalism—these were real threats to socialism, he said, and it's important to know who your enemy is. He felt for a long time that you had to do everything possible to fight this class enemy and these capitalist exploiters. I think he really saw the West as a substitute for the Nazis. Living in the closed cage of the DDR, coming from an old KPD family, working in a VEB, and carrying responsibility as a Party member, it was understandable that he would transfer his enemy image from Nazi Germany to West Germany. Of course, the DDR media constantly blared that the Nazi war criminals had taken up residence in West Germany and were living a good life there. The propaganda was that West Germany was continuous with Nazi Germany. My father believed that to some extent. We had no relatives in West Germany. We had no contact with West Germany after the Wall went up.

Q: Your father represented the Party line toward the major post-war political events—essentially the Cold War positions that the schoolbooks reflect.

A: Yes. What came first was the textbook *Feindbild*, and then everything else was fit into that. It wasn't as if all kinds of substantive facts and data from current events added up and formed the enemy image. Rather, it simply existed and little bits of information were used to reinforce it. It had come out of our [KPD] family background and out of the Nazi past. It was easy for the government to keep reinforcing it because there were enough incidents and images in the West to support some version of such an image even if it was a gross caricature.

Q: How could your father continue to be a true believer in the face of socialism's economic failure?

A: My father really believed that it was better to live in an inefficient socialism than a sleek, exploitative western capitalism that creates such extreme inequalities. But his fragile faith to the end had also to do with his desperate defense of his ideals and his personal past. You see, my father had also served with a battle unit that supervised the construction of the Berlin Wall, which was an even more embarrassing assignment than that which occurred with the suppression of the Workers' Uprising in 1953. He talked very seldom about the Berlin Wall, and even my brother rarely brought it up—because they both knew it was an atom bomb ready to explode between them if they did. But it was obvious to me that my father believed it was a necessary evil in order to stave off a bleeding to economic death of the DDR via mass emigration.

Q: Did your father have any connection to the Stasi?

A: My father was no fan of the Stasi, but he had the attitude of a man who wielded some power in a responsible position. "You Americans have your CIA and FBI. So we need the MFS [*Ministerium für Staatssicherheit*, Ministry of State Security] and Stasi," he would have said to you. "These are just political realities, given that we have two opposing systems."

Of course, he did occasionally in his position have to talk to the Stasi about employees in the VEB, other VEB directors, or figures in the government. So he came to rationalize the Stasi as an unfortunate but necessary presence in order to maintain law and order. While he deplored its excesses and thought much of its activities were needless, he fully cooperated. This was the pragmatist in him.

But he spoke very guardedly about anything having to do with the Stasi, even after the *Wende* in 1989. I've never had an open conversation with him about his activities with it. Again, I think there was an element of shame, at least after the *Wende*, when all of the scandals related to the Stasi and its horrible excesses were exposed. Anyone who had any connection with the Stasi seemed to be tainted by mere association.

Q: How has your father come to terms with his role in the old regime?

A: In hindsight, his whole adult life sometimes seems to me to have been a struggle with self-justification and rationalization: first with my brother for almost three decades, and since then with himself after 1989. He's still working through his personal history. How and why did he dedicate himself to this ideal—which proved in many ways to be an apple rotten at the core? I think he ruminates about that. It pains him to admit the truth: for a long time he only saw its shiny exterior.

EIGHT

EDUCATION FOR TOLERANCE
Of Ideology, Identity, and Intolerance

Among (German and Jewish) Schoolchildren

A prominent theme of this study has been how DDR education shaped young eastern Germans' minds—and the conversations in Part 2 thus far have sought to explore whether and how that "textbook mentality" lives on today among easterners. In this chapter, we will examine a post-reunification pedagogical initiative—which is active and ongoing in western as well as eastern Germany—to foster a different, more nuanced, and more flexible outlook toward otherness: "Education for Tolerance." As we shall see, that phrase covers a wide range of programs and efforts, all of them designed to cope with eastern problems arising in the wake of the DDR's collapse and nationwide problems exacerbated by German reunification and the dramatic rise in the non-German population since 1989. Our focus will continue to be on eastern German educators and youths, but in the special context of German-Jewish relations.

Before examining that specific theme, however, let us re-emphasize that much of DDR schooling was directed toward promoting Marxist-Leninist ideology and legitimating the DDR as a socialist state. The vacuum left by the DDR's collapse was partly filled during the 1990s by xenophobia and youth violence. And so, the most pressing question for German educational policymakers since reunification has necessarily concerned the theme of "education for tolerance." In the twenty-first century, Germany is still asking: To what extent should German education be directed toward a greater tolerance of non-Germans, especially given their significantly increased numbers since reunification?[1]

And that remains a compelling issue for German policymakers today, particularly for eastern German educators, because a frightening post-reunification development has indeed been the increase in *Ausländerfeindlichkeit* [xenophobia].[2]

The right-wing message—keep the New Germany "clean" of foreigners (*ausländerfrei*), prevent racial mixing, intimidate "un-German" elements—has had particular appeal for all German youth.[3] In the east, what the communist regime once proudly referred to as anti-capitalist, anti-bourgeois "Education for Hate" ("Comrade, carry hatred in your heart!") gave way in the 1990s to an anti-foreigner hate speech and hate crimes that many observers regard as the legacy of the DDR "hate" programs.[4] "DDR Education Causes Hostility Toward Foreigners" run the newspaper headlines.[5]

The challenge of the twenty-first century, many German educators agree, is to reverse trends that have turned the nation's schools into breeding grounds of intolerance and violence. To stem the youth violence and tendencies toward nationalism and racism, educators have developed diverse programs, such as promoting contacts between schools and refugee hostels, arranging for German students to tutor immigrants in German, coordinating student volunteer activities with immigrant welfare agencies, sponsoring friendly sport competitions with immigrant teams, and financing multi-racial student performances and art exhibits.[6] Germany has also strongly supported the Education for Tolerance initiative administered by UNESCO (United Nations Educational, Scientific, and Cultural Organization) and endorsed by most EU nations.[7] This initiative approaches intolerance as a worldwide problem and defines tolerance not as mere toleration, but rather as acceptance, affirmation, and charity.

Education for Tolerance is, in effect, peace education for the new millennium. A hard-headed European version of the "politics of meaning" once promoted by the Clinton administration in Washington, it manifests a post–Cold War educational sensibility focused not upon the old politics of international nuclear disarmament but rather on the cultural issues of interracial respect, interpersonal harmony, and inner peace.[8] Since the early 1990s, some German *Länder* have developed special "intercultural courses" in schools, courses that range from exercises to promote reflection on acts of (verbal and physical) violence in daily life (e.g., hypothetical letter-writing to victims) to week-long, school-sponsored study of and participation in cultural celebrations of other nationalities and races.[9]

And so, both eastern and western German educators have united in their determination to fight intolerance. Many of them believe that whatever legislation may be passed to forbid violence and racism, only a revolution in German pedagogy—toward character education rather than the traditional German concentration on knowledge acquisition and skills training—will eliminate racial stereotypes, dissolve centuries of bigotry, and instill intercultural understanding. The old DDR appeals to Education for Socialist Patriotism ("love of the socialist Fatherland") have evolved into programs that promote a non-socialist form of internationalism. In a sense, the nationwide Education for Tolerance initiative does indeed bear resemblance to DDR campaigns such as Education for Socialist Internationalism, which had been the positive counterpart to Education for Hate. Certainly one concern of Education for Tolerance has been to promote a form of cross-cultural understanding, even if that understanding has not been limited to, or explicitly framed within, a fraternity of working-class or socialist countries.

One of the deepest forms of racism in Germany, involving indeed both racial stereotypes and long-standing bigotry, is anti-Semitism. Polls in the twenty-first century continue to show that anti-Semitism is prevalent in Germany.[10] Thus, perhaps those most concerned with fostering Education for Tolerance are the Jewish residents in Germany. Likewise, a site where the fate of such initiatives will undergo a critical test is the handful of Jewish schools throughout Germany. For these reasons, our closing chapter examines Jewish issues and the struggle to revive Jewish education in post-reunification Germany.

Renewed consideration of such efforts is timely, given the new agreement negotiated in June 2003 between the German government and the Central Council of Jews in Germany, which tripled official support for Jewish congregations (to 3 million euros per year) and which German politicians have hailed as "opening a new chapter in the cooperation" between the government and Germany's eighty-three Jewish congregations (with a total of 100,000 members). Various government spokespersons have noted that more Jews today emigrate to Germany than to Israel and that the new treaty constituted "an impressive sign of trust" from Jewish citizens in Germany.[11]

Our emphasis in this chapter on German-Jewish relations as the context for understanding Education for Tolerance also has another purpose. It explores an eastern German educational setting in which a radically new consciousness is in process, showing the gradual, painful evolution away from the DDR's Education for Hate. Instead, in all Jewish and some eastern German schools, Education for Tolerance has been explicitly embraced. In this chapter, we encounter it in all the richness of its challenges, tensions, successes, and shortcomings. Given the twin burden of both the

Nazi and communist pasts in eastern Germany, such experiments in cross-cultural understanding are regarded by some observers as involving not simply education for tolerance but indeed *re*-education for tolerance. The reason is that fully inculcating an ethics of tolerance in eastern Germany means overcoming a legacy burdened by totalitarian ideologies of both the Right and the Left. In a sense, DDR citizens were re-educated for *in*tolerance after World War II. Nazi ideology was replaced by the Soviet-ordained *Antifa* (anti-fascist) programs, which, as we saw in the introduction, supplanted fascism with Stalinist ideology.

Thus, as we shall see in the following vignettes and interviews with both Jews and Germans, the re-education that has been occurring since 1990 must work through a doubly onerous past: both the original intolerance of the Right and the newer intolerance of the Left thereby to cultivate a genuine tolerance of all points of view without simply devolving into postmodernist permissiveness or indifference. For the latter would probably fester into a seedbed facilitating a dangerous new authoritarianism to arise, precisely because of the lack of any political backbone to oppose it.

1. Border-Crossing After Checkpoint Charlie

8:05. A typical school morning on a beautiful October day in 1994 at the Jewish Oberschule of Berlin. Commotion in the hallways as the school bell rings. Students dash to their seats; shouts and cries die to whispers.

Yes, for a moment, it seems as if life here is the same as in any other German school.

But the sights, if not the sounds, immediately belie this impression. A glance out the window shows that what's abnormal elsewhere is typical here: Police wagons sit in the courtyard; armed police officers check visitors at every school entrance.

Herr Bruno Landthaler, thirty-seven, greets me as I explain that I'm here to observe his religion class. We reflect that the majority of the students are not German Jews; a quarter are Russian Jews and another 30 to 40 percent are Germans, most of them from eastern German families that were agnostic or atheist before 1989. He notes that most students in eastern German schools choose to take ethics, not religion classes—whether in the Lutheran or Catholic faith.

"Of course, German state schools have no religion classes in Judaism," he remarks off-handedly. "Most young Germans have never even met a Jew until they enter this school."

Herr Landthaler brings his seventh-grade religion class to order. Today's topic: God's eternal covenant with the Jewish people.

"What does it mean to say . . . ?"

Herr Landthaler stops in mid-question, his voice trailing off. His eyes scan the rows of students, thirteen girls and eight boys. Given my research interests, what is immediately noticeable to me is that nobody has a textbook—or a book of any kind. They simply take notes from Herr Landthaler, who teaches via a lecture-discussion format.

What is also noticeable—as it was to me on my earlier visit to the school—is the yarmulke atop each male head, which is part of the school dress code required of all boys, Jewish or Gentile. The teacher raises his own head, which also bears a black skullcap.

"What does it mean to say . . ."—Herr Landthaler enunciates each word carefully in his acrid Berliner accent:

"*Ich bin Jude* [I am a Jew]"?

A simple question? Outside its context, perhaps. But any considered response to it here is endlessly ramified, for history casts a dark and lengthy shadow in the Great Hamburg Street in eastern Berlin, site of what was until 1995 (when it relocated to Charlottenburg in western Berlin) the nation's first and only Jewish high school in five decades.

Herr Landthaler's question about what it means to say one is a Jew, in light of my research for this book, is both compelling and jarring. For I have been pondering a very difficult question related to his in complicated ways: What does it mean to be "a German"? The issue of the German identity and the DDR's attempts at national self-legitimation have been a leitmotif of this study, as the DDR's textbook material in Part 1 and the interviewees in Chapters 6 and 7 have made clear. Yet a glance around the room reminds me that class is under way, and it's Herr Landthaler's question about Jewish identity that is the immediate topic for consideration. But it is not a simple question at all. For the past lives on in the present: Yes, like it or not, this school is different indeed from other German schools.

And how could it be otherwise? For on this very spot there once existed a thriving school for Jewish boys, in what had been the heart of Berlin's Jewish quarter in the center of Berlin, a few minutes from the Alexanderplatz. Established as a state-supported Jewish boys' school in 1826, in a building that had previously housed the first private Jewish school in Germany—co-founded in 1778 by the Jewish philosopher and community leader Moses Mendelssohn—the school swelled to more than a thousand students during the early years of the war, since the Nazis forbade most Jews to attend state schools. The school survived until May 1942, when the National Socialists closed down all Jewish-run educational facilities in Berlin; it was the last Jewish educational institution to resist Nazi pressure to shut its doors. Most of its students were rounded up and deported to concentration camps. Shortly thereafter, the SS commandeered the building and turned it into an assembly point for Jews destined for Auschwitz and Theresienstadt. (The German communists transformed the school after the war into a non-Jewish vocational training center.)

The past lives on in the present: Before World War II, 530,000 Jews resided in Germany. (That figure does, however, somewhat underestimate the total, since it included only those who were registered as religiously Jewish.) In 1994 the number of registered Jews in Germany was 60,000. In 1933, Berlin's Jewish population totaled 171,000; in 1994, it was only 9,200—nonetheless the largest of any German city. (By 2005, this figure had almost doubled.)

These numbers are relatively small. But these figures, small as they are, represent a huge increase in Berlin's Jewish population since reunification. Indeed, the Jewish influx since the Berlin Wall fell in 1989 and the Soviet Union collapsed in 1991 has been dramatic: in 1989, 5,000 Jews resided in West Berlin and exactly 208 in East Berlin, most of them aged. (The Jewish population in all of East Germany totaled a mere 400—in a population of 17 million.) The number of Soviet Jews in Berlin now constitutes about one-fifth of the German total; roughly 40,000 Soviet Jews, most of them from Russia and the Ukraine, entered Germany between 1989 and 1994; despite sharp general curbs on immigration imposed by Bonn in 1993, the German government has issued residence permits of unlimited duration to all immigrant Jews.

Equally dramatic is the change in the Jewish school population. Whereas more than 30,000 Jewish students attended community-run schools in the 1920s, approximately 700 Jewish children did so in the late 1990s (up from 200 in 1989). The first Jewish elementary school opened in Frankfurt in the late 1960s. Not until German reunification and the immigration flow from the former USSR, however, did enough Jews reside in Berlin for the community to open a high school.

Mendelssohn (1729–86), who urged that education promote tolerance and understanding among peoples, founded the famed Jewish Freyschule [free school], a mixed school for Jews and Gentiles. That integrative concept has been revived in the new Jewish Oberschule—if only out of necessity, given the small size of the Jewish community in Berlin. The

Oberschule, which reopened in August 1993, numbers only ninety-five pupils, grouped into two sets of seventh- and eighth-grade classes, an academically oriented, college preparatory *Gymnasium* and a technical training *Realschule*. The elementary school, which consists of kindergarten through sixth grade, is housed in the same building and has almost two hundred students; roughly 60 percent of the total student body is Jewish. Both the Oberschule and the elementary school have grown considerably since their relocation to the Charlottenburg school, each of them almost doubling in size by 2005.

The Oberschule is supported by funds from the German government, from the Berlin Jewish community, and from the families of students. Tuition is scaled according to parental income; those who cannot afford to pay have their tuition waived. The Oberschule curriculum is identical to that of other German high schools, except for the addition of three subjects: Bible history, Judaism (religion class), and Hebrew. German schools do not offer classes in Jewish history and religion; Jews who attend non-Jewish schools in Germany must take courses in the Catholic or Lutheran religion, or a non-sectarian course in ethics.

At the center of the city's rich yet tragic Jewish history, the school lies in the *Scheunenviertel* [barn quarter] of eastern Berlin. Traditionally a working class area, indeed almost a Jewish ghetto by the 1930s, the neighborhood was once a center of devout religious activity by day and a racy red-light district by night—and word has it that the latter reputation is also on the upswing.

Yes, the contradictions are dizzying. Next door to the school is what had been a home for the elderly, until the Gestapo turned it into a depot from which Jews were shipped to the death camps. A small statue informs passersby that 55,000 Berlin Jews were sent to camps from this site. It exhorts the reader: *"Nie vergessen."* "Never forget."

Indeed, a journey to Berlin's sole Jewish Oberschule is a passage through a graveyard of memorials next to streets of sacrileges. Take just a few steps in any direction from the Oberschule and you find yourself treading and retreading more historic paths, confronting more exhortations, and struggling lamely to connect the frayed thread between past and present. A short stroll to the end of the Great Hamburg Street and you enter an austere park, which had been Berlin's oldest Jewish cemetery before it was defiled and obliterated during the war years. Only a single gravestone has been restored: Moses Mendelssohn. His tombstone is covered with small stones, the traditional remembrance of a nomadic people who lived in deserts bereft of flowers. In the Auguststrasse, less than five minutes away, lies a building that was once a Jewish hospital, then in the 1930s a home for poor children, and finally a concentration camp for old Jews. Its name is AHAWAH, which in Hebrew means "love."

"What does it mean to say, *"Ich bin Jude"*?

The mere question itself—voiced in this street and in German—sends a slight *frisson* through my body.

Herr Landthaler, a thin man with ravenblack hair, black-rimmed glasses, and much nervous energy, pauses for a response.

Benjamin raises his hand. "It means you are bound by the Law."

"And what does that mean?"

Immediately Holger (who like the other Christian boys in class also wears a yarmulke) answers: "You are born a Jew, and you must observe God's commandments."

"Yes, a Christian must profess Christianity, but a Jew is born into Judaism," says Herr Landthaler. "This is the essential difference between Judaism and all other religions: A Jew does not have the choice of whether or not to be a Jew, only whether he will observe the commandments or not. God has a special covenant with Israel, and his People are bound by the commandments of this covenant. You do not 'profess' Judaism; it is not a personal decision. You choose only to obey or disobey."

Herr Landthaler removes his glasses, twirls them a couple of times. Then he writes on the blackboard:

Judentum—Erziehung—Bund. [Judaism—Education—Covenant.]

He turns again to face the class.

"Judaism is a culture and a religion," says Herr Landthaler, laying his glasses on his desk. "As a Jew, you either embody Judaism or you reject it. Your parents give you the tradition and you can choose to continue it or not. It is our task—my task and your parents'—to pass on to you the content of the eternal Covenant with God that the Sinai generation received."

Jakob objects: "But doesn't every religion believe that it's the Chosen People? Christianity too?"

"Yes, in a way; but each individual *professes* his membership in those religions. The single individual decides. As a Christian, you decide whether Christ is to be your savior or not; you are baptized a Christian. But you are a Jew from the beginning: You are born a Jew, and you only decide whether you will remain 'chosen' by honoring the commandments and the tradition or not. A Christian joins an association; a Jew belongs to a family."

"Which is better?" Rachel asks. It is a question that seems to be on everyone's lips.

"Neither! It isn't a matter of 'better' or 'worse,'" says Herr Landthaler quickly. "The issue is to understand what Judaism and Jewishness mean. The 'Chosen People' are not better, but they have a different calling—and they are 'special' by virtue of this distinctive calling. The calling is to maintain the eternal Covenant. Why don't we eat pork?"

Rafael answers: "Because it would violate the Law."

"And why do we observe the Law?"

Rafael: "Because it is the Law."

"Yes," says Herr Landthaler. "We observe the Law because God commands it. We respect the Covenant; the Covenant exists between God and each one of us. At what age are you obliged to observe the commandments?"

Several students call out, "Girls, beginning at twelve; boys, beginning at thirteen!" Other students add that, now that they are seventh-graders, the obligation starts this very year.

"Right," says Herr Landthaler. "But Christians can always think it over. But you don't think over the fact of your birth into a family: You are simply born into it."

Benjamin waves his hand impatiently. "But devout Moslems aren't allowed to eat various meats either! And other religions have commandments too! And it's hard for their members to uphold them!"

"Yes, but we renounce pork and observe our commandments for different reasons than the other religions. For us, the only ground is obedience. To have all kinds of proscriptions about food is not rational. There is no rational ground for it. We observe Shabbat in order to show respect and obedience."

Other hands go flying; it is obvious that many students find it difficult to understand such religious practices as Shabbat within a secular society whose individualistic, even hedonistic values are so much at odds with Jewish tradition—not to mention the difficulty of conveying Jewish beliefs against the immediate backdrop of the Holocaust. Even the Jewish students have trouble with what seems to be the rules-observing emphasis governing their teacher's presentation of (Orthodox) Judaism—Herr Landthaler does not distinguish among Orthodox, liberal, and conservative viewpoints—for the students profoundly believe in liberal values and freedom of choice. The school's self-inquiring education for tolerance seems already to be exemplified in the outlooks of these pupils. Has education for tolerance already worked in this school? Or has it been largely unnecessary, given the school's history and the composition of its student body? Perhaps it is the case that the schools that take a pedagogy based in tolerance most seriously are those that need it least.

But Herr Landthaler seems unimpressed by the pupils' attitudes: they exemplify an ethic of tolerance that he regards as permissiveness.

Benjamin above all remains unsatisfied.

"So: let me pose a thought experiment," he says. "I found a new religion. I make new laws, and I call them the truth. And I seek to keep my followers apart from others, so as to prevent their leaving my religion. Who is to say that isn't the way Judaism started? Shouldn't a religion have to justify itself rationally? Isn't Judaism too possessive of its People if it claims their allegiance from birth and expects them to obey without rational grounds for obedience?"

I am struck by Benjamin's audacity—and maturity. Herr Landthaler smiles. He welcomes the challenge.

"Tradition is crucially important to Judaism: Yes, you must be acculturated to the Jewish faith. And when we talk of the Jewish faith, we are talking about the Jewish community as a family. Such membership goes deeper than human reason can justify. You don't 'select' membership in Judaism and you can't determine the Covenant; the Covenant simply applies—to the whole People, including you. Not just to the Sinai generation, but to all descendants; the Covenant applies to all Jews everywhere. A Christian can change religions; if a Jew subsequently professes another religion, he remains a Jew."

Herr Landthaler addresses the relation between culture and religion, noting that Germany and Israel have different cultures, just as the DDR and West Germany also had different cultures and correspondingly different allegiances.

The students' questions turn toward practical matters.

"Why aren't there Jewish holidays on the calendar, and not just Christian ones?" asks Rafael.

"In Israel there are," answers Herr Landthaler.

"But we're in Germany."

"Yes, Germany is chiefly a Christian country."

"We celebrate both Jewish *and* Christian holidays in the school," says Rachel. "Both Passover and Christmas."

Herr Landthaler nods.

"Different countries have different cultures and religions and traditions," Herr Landthaler says. He pauses, then asks: "Would it be better if there were only one religion and one tradition?"

"The DDR opposed religion and advocated Marxism," Dietmar says.

The observation surprises; it takes the discussion in a new direction—and shows how many barriers and boundary lines exist in this eastern Berlin school.

"Yes, the DDR was different from West Germany," says Herr Landthaler, nodding again. "Very different."

Benjamin's hand is up, swaying in the stillness. He seems poised to force the issue: "But was it *better?*"

Instead the class bell slices the air.

"Next time," Herr Landthaler shouts above the rustling of books, "we'll discuss the differences between Judaism in the east and west!"

"A daring attempt to revive Judaism," Herr Landthaler sums up his class and the mission of the Jewish Oberschule to me later that morning after my tour of the school.

"How do we convey the history, the tradition, the culture to these young people?" he asks. He addresses me, but he is really putting the question to himself. He glances out the window as police officers check the identification of two visitors. He shakes his head.

No, we seem to silently agree, this variety of sights, if not sounds, are not to be seen in other high schools in Germany: neither the police with their pistols and bullet-proof vests, nor the yarmulkes, nor the stars of David, nor the Hebrew lettering gracing clothing and blackboards, nor the Hebrew conversation among several teachers and staff members.

Herr Landthaler relates two anecdotes about the challenges that he must overcome. On seeing him wearing a yarmulke on the first day of school, a new Christian girl entering the school asked him, "Do you have a bald spot?" During the first week, when Herr Landthaler assigned the class to write papers on an exemplary Jew in the history of Germany or Israel, a boy—a half-Jew—submitted an essay on Jesus.

Only a few Jewish children in the school—no more than a dozen—are religious believers, Herr Landthaler explains. The German Jews, who have no religious practice at home, find Bible class and Judaism class—and most especially Hebrew lessons—difficult and abstract. The Russian Jews, cut off from their religious traditions by seventy years of Soviet communist persecution, know little about Judaism; they find it overwhelming just to cope with Germany. Because their parents can't speak German, these children become the de facto heads of the household—they fill out applications, answer the telephone, even do much of the shopping in German stores. Christian believers possess at least an atmosphere that provides them with an orientation toward a Judeo-Christian tradition; but it is near impossible for them to understand Jewish life from the inside. It is perhaps most difficult of all for those students from agnostic or atheistic families from the former DDR, where religious belief was treated as superstitious or politically reactionary.

"They are *gewaltig. Gewaltig,*" repeats Herr Landthaler, when I ask him about the specific challenges that he and his colleagues face. "Formidable."

"Our main goal with the Jewish students," he explains, "is to teach them enough about Judaism so that they can later observe the commandments—if they choose to do so. Not to pressure them into it—you saw this morning their independence of mind—even a hint of coercion would backfire, anyway. I want to present Judaism to them so that they might, if they choose to do so, begin to live as Jews consciously and intelligently—or, if they deviate, they will do so in an aware, informed way, and not because of ignorance. I want them to be able to engage in a searching discussion about Judaism with others and with themselves.

"And I also keep fully in mind the Christians and the non-believers in the class," Herr Landthaler continues. "Even though we require non-Jews to take the Jewish subjects—and even require the non-Jewish boys to wear the yarmulke, at least during their Jewish lessons—none of that means that we seek to convert non-Jews to Judaism."

Not even the Jewish students—not even he himself—wears the yarmulke on the street, Herr Landthaler adds. "That might be taken by rightwing Germans as a provocation."

"But we want the students to experience a specifically Jewish atmosphere here; we stress that this is a Jewish school," he continues, explaining why the yarmulke is required of Gentile boys too. All teachers, Jewish and Gentile alike, attend synagogue every Friday; even parents must attend synagogue once per year. "For the non-Jews, we strive to foster mutual understanding. This is not *Erziehung zum Glauben* [education toward belief], but *Erziehung zur Toleranz*. That was also a major goal of Mendelssohn's Freyschule, and it is one reason why we are a mixed school. Perhaps we have learned some valuable lessons from German history, so that we can succeed where past attempts have failed."

Signs of progress are visible. Several German cities are in the process of integrating Jewish subjects into their schools' curricula, so that they can be taught to those Jews who attend Berlin public schools. Moreover, in 1996 the first interdisciplinary program in Jewish studies began at Potsdam University, near Berlin, and plans are underway to introduce similar programs in Halle, Leipzig, Oldenburg, and Duisburg. Formerly, Germans could only study Jewish theology; their exposure to "Jewish studies" was restricted to courses in theology departments that included offerings in Judaism.

Herr Landthaler mentions another, more practical challenge for the Oberschule: to "integrate the Russian families" more fully into Berliner life. Given German history, Herr Landthaler worries about Jews—Orthodox or not—who want to keep to themselves.

"Many of the Russian parents and grandparents do not mix with Germans—not out of any antagonism, but because the language and culture are so alien to them," Herr Landthaler says. "And then, of course, they do have fears about anti-Semitism. We teachers here worry that it may be too late to integrate the older adults; we aim to make sure that we integrate"—he is careful not so say "assimilate"—"the children."

Because more than a quarter of the students are Christian, Herr Landthaler teaches his Judaism class as a comparative religion course.

"I know Christianity and have taken seminars in it," he says. "I can thematize both sides, the Jewish and the Christian." Herr Landthaler is from East Berlin and pursued his Jewish university studies in Berlin, Munich, and, eventually, Jerusalem; he specialized in medieval theology, especially the work of such major figures as the twelfth-century scholastic philosopher Moses Maimonides. He is the only native-born German in all of Germany who is teaching Jewish subjects in a Jewish school, which are otherwise taught by certified teachers from Israel.

I ask about the personal challenge—as a German Jew—that his teaching poses.

"As teacher here, you are a role model," Herr Landthaler says. "It's probably easier for me because I'm a believer. Most of the religion teachers are liberal; I'm Orthodox and I observe Shabbat. Because I'm observant, I think I'm more credible to the Jewish students; when they imply that it's impossible in this secular society to observe the commandments, I say, 'That's an excuse. *My family is doing it. It's difficult, yes, but it's possible.*' But with Germans, it's harder to be an Orthodox Jew—the differences between us are more conspicuous: meals can't be shared so easily, greater distance is maintained, our religious *Weltanschauung* is alien."

"Do you have many German friends?" I ask Herr Landthaler.

"Yes," he says. "Several." He mentions again that he is German and has lived in Berlin most of his life. He pauses. He starts to speak, then hesitates.

"Yes," he goes on, "because of my family, I have several old German friends—and I understand the tensions of German-Jewish friendships from the inside." He pauses again. My eyes are fixed on him; I wait for his words to come.

"I am a convert," he says quietly.

The statement takes me slightly aback; Herr Landthaler says the students and most parents don't know that he is a former Catholic theology student who converted to Judaism two years ago.

"And it's not important that they know," Herr Landthaler quickly adds. "In Judaism, what matters is that I *am* a Jew, not how I became one. Also, if they knew there might be some confusion. Something along the lines: 'He isn't a proper Jew. How can he teach these subjects?'"

I mention his emphasis in class this morning that Jews are "born into" rather than "join" the Jewish community.

"Yes, that's certainly the norm," says Herr Landthaler. He says he doesn't want to confuse the students with his exceptional case: you can count on one hand the number of Germans in the entire country who have converted to Orthodox Judaism. Twenty or so Germans convert to liberal or reformed Judaism each year; but conversion to Orthodox Judaism is rare, perhaps two or three times in a decade.

Yes, his case is exceptional. And yet, it strikes me that he is somehow representative by virtue of his distinctiveness. For his example—as a German and a Jew, as a *Wossi* in eastern Berlin—elucidates the unique identity issues faced by the school and by Jewish education in Germany generally.

Why did you convert?

Herr Landthaler says there were a number of reasons, both theological and personal. "I wanted a different relationship to God: I find the supposedly 'rigid' quality of Orthodox Judaism invaluable for giving structure and meaning to my life. It creates order and discipline. I wanted to be permeated and pervaded by my faith; only priests have that possibility in Catholicism, and I didn't want to be a priest. And I sought to be immersed in history, integrated within a salvation history that constitutes a powerful tradition of belief. History—and I don't primarily mean twentieth-century history—plays a much greater role for the consciousness of Jews than it does for Christians. I don't understand why people convert to liberal Judaism. In German, maybe it is to make a gesture, and even to relieve guilt by being—at last!—on the 'other side' or the 'better side.' Or strictly for practical and family reasons. It's so much easier. To me, however, conversion makes sense only if you convert to Orthodox Judaism."

We talk about Herr Landthaler's own rationale for conversion and his new identity. How do you cope, I ask him, with the paradox that we witnessed in class this morning—you teach that a Jew is "born"—and yet you yourself made a profession of faith to become a Jew? How do you explain this irony to the students?

"I don't. You're right: I had to make a decision to become a Jew. But I'm the great exception and therefore in class I stress the norm. I must live as a Jew, not just believe."

I ask how his German acquaintances and Jewish colleagues have responded to his decision to convert.

"Most Germans have taken it well, even if they wonder about my motives," Herr Landthaler replies. "Some older Germans have reacted uneasily, partly because simple routines get upset. Because I don't eat what they do anymore, my decision can seem like a provocation. Others—including some of my family members—don't understand at all. They don't want to understand. And the Israelis? Often they say: 'You're crazy!'—since I'm Orthodox and most of them are liberal. But they say it with fondness and respect.

"The biggest challenge emerges in small moments, such as the exchanges in class this morning," Herr Landthaler continues. He pauses and quotes a line that echoes Albert Schweitzer: "My argument—my pedagogy—is my life."

"I embody the tensions and challenges that I spoke of in class in my own life. Every time I teach, I confront the grounds for my own conversion. I understand Christianity from the inside and from the outside. I can *live* a mutual understanding of the two religions. I can help foster Christian-Jewish dialogue, not only by word but also by example. Not only in the scholarly or pedagogical sense, but directly in my daily life. I feel as if I'm part of a process of understanding the Judeo-Christian tradition better. The Old Testament is the foundation of Christianity: both Judaism and Christianity have the same roots. By converting, I am not rejecting but rather extending Christianity, helping it to reach back and reconnect to a tradition from which it departed."

He stops short. And it occurs to me that I too am now part of the ongoing argument within himself, a second self—another Christian (indeed Catholic) self, and another teacher, too—voicing the questions that endlessly traverse his professional and personal life. And I realize further that, though he seems excessively rules-oriented to some of the students, his genuine openness to freewheeling debate—in the classroom and with himself—marks the governing principle of his being. His trust in searching self-inquiry—his own internal theological dialectic—derives from his dialectical duels with Marxism, Christianity, and Judaism together.

Yes, Herr Landthaler takes his responsibility as a role model in this school seriously—just as Mendelssohn did in his Freyschule. And I see now, despite his Orthodox strictness, that Herr Landthaler is, in his own distinctive way, broadly in the spirit of the *Haskalah* [Enlightenment], Mendelssohn's movement that urged Jews to open themselves to Europe and yet remain Jews. No, Herr Landthaler is certainly not a Reform Jew, as the main line of Mendelssohn's spiritual descendents became, but his intellectual cosmopolitanism carries on Mendelssohn's tradition nonetheless. For Mendelssohn was, above all, devoted to exploring and reconciling opposites. He was both a German Enlightenment philosopher (and close friend of Lessing) and an adherent to traditional Jewish law. He translated the Torah into literary German and urged Jews to expose themselves to German culture and Enlightenment ideas. He was the first notable European thinker to confront the issue of how to reconcile the Age of Reason with Jewish religious tradition. And his followers, the *Maskilim* [enlightened ones], honored his legacy by erecting and teaching in schools that offered both secular and Jewish subjects.

Herr Landthaler sits pensively. He takes off his glasses and looks at me squarely. He smiles.

"I suppose I'm a *Grenzgänger* in Berlin," he chuckles.

A "border-crosser." We both nod our heads. He is a religious and cultural *Grenzgänger*.

The usage is fitting. For the word is overdetermined, possessing a wealth of associations, particularly for Berliners and eastern Germans. It is a political concept that describes those Berliners who, before the Berlin Wall went up in August 1961, traveled back and forth frequently between the DDR and West Germany. Because the *Grenzgänger* lived and worked in the east and the west, they understood both sides better—and usually supported cordial relations between (and even reunification of) the two Germanies. But the *Grenzgänger* were often suspected of national "disloyalty" by fellow Germans, especially by DDR officialdom, who made life difficult for East Berliners who worked in the West, fearing that they might emigrate, or at least become "infected" with western ideology.

In the years immediately before the erection of the Wall, *Grenzgänger* became a special term of abuse by the East German government to describe workers whose home was in East Berlin (where housing was cheaper) and whose employment was in West Berlin (where wages were higher), the implication being that they were exploiting the Cold War for personal gain.

Border-crossing is especially difficult when the terrain is unfamiliar,

Herr Landthaler concedes. It is hard to be an Orthodox Jew, particularly in Germany, when one lacks the personal history.

"Or I should say: It's another challenge. I don't possess the history of the Jews, but of a German. And I can't change my history. I haven't lived through their family history, and history is very important in Judaism. So I must work harder. I don't put it under the table. I work to understand it better. Now that I'm a member of this family, it's my task to recover the history as best I can."

Herr Landthaler says that his wife, a German Orthodox Jew, has helped him enormously to understand Jewish history from the inside. At the age of thirty, he began to consider conversion seriously. At thirty-five, he completed the process. He started teaching school; his wife commenced her dissertation in Jewish theology. Indeed, Herr and Frau Landthaler share similar intellectual interests: Her dissertation will be an edition and commentary on a Hebrew manuscript by the medieval pietist Eleazer ben Judah of Wurms, a contemporary of Moses Maimonides.

"But she isn't the reason I converted," Herr Landthaler repeats. "It wasn't an expedient or socially convenient decision at all. It was a religious and theological matter."

The class bell rings for lunch. The children skip toward the cafeteria, where two Russian Jewish cooks serve kosher meals.

"My wife and I think about emigrating to Israel," Herr Landthaler concludes. "But for now we're staying.

He looks out the window. Then he turns and grins.

"After all, we're both *Grenzgänger* in Germany."

Stepping outside into the sunshine, I speak briefly to the grandfather of one of the students, who has come early to pick her up from school. I tell him about my conversations with the school's staff, especially my classroom visit this morning. He tells me that he had emigrated as a boy to England, in the late 1930s, and spent the war years there, returning in the late 1940s to Berlin, where he has spent most of his life.

Together we muse on the plaque near the entrance to the school that honors Mendelssohn. "The third Moses," says the old grandfather with admiration. "From Moses to Moses to Moses," he says, as if quoting a Talmudic commentary. He sighs. "The history of our people lives on." The sweep of ancient, medieval, and modern Jewish history evoked by this single name—from the Old Testament prophet to Maimonides to Mendelssohn—a name borne by leaders and lawgivers braving challenges in the wilderness. Yes, the journey goes on.

As the students stream by us, to play outside in the autumn warmth during their lunch break, the old man points to the plaque bearing Mendelssohn's words, which ring with the Enlightenment hope that young Germans and Jews, young Jews and Gentiles, learn to live together in peace, that they not re-enact the tragic history of preceding generations:

> Seek truth, love beauty, wish good,
> and do your best.

2. Forward and Never Forget—Tolerance?
A Berlin Teacher's Post-Communist "Class" Struggles

I'm visiting after school with Frau Ulla Berhau, thirty-three, a colleague of Herr Landthaler. She too was just hired [1994]; she teaches German and history in the recently opened Jewish Oberschule in eastern Berlin. We have met twice before to discuss her family past; she doesn't want to address it further. This time, she says, she'd like to talk with me about her past as a DDR citizen—and how it shaped her teaching and exerts ongoing influence on her classroom pedagogy and overall thinking as a teacher in this school.

A slight woman with short black hair cut in a close crop, Frau Berhau speaks in even tones and in a sharp Saxon accent about her past. Like many eastern German women, she wears no makeup, but her face lights up with animated expression as she tells her story, whose newest chapter has much to do with the historical challenges facing the Jewish Oberschule at Great Hamburg Street 27 in eastern Berlin.

Frau Berhau taught history and Russian in an elite Berlin EOS during the DDR days. But I am not here to ask about her experience in Germany's sole Jewish high school, but rather about how her classroom teaching methods have changed since 1989–90.

To my surprise, she says she never wanted to become a teacher.

"I'm a teacher because the Party wouldn't let me become what I wanted to be," Frau Berhau says. She pauses and looks out the window.

What was that?

"A minister!" She laughs, as I acknowledge once again my surprise. She says her special interest in Judaism is also connected with a personal struggle for religious freedom and represents another dimension of the ambiguous legacy of the SED and DDR.

"I really wanted to be a [Lutheran] minister," she says. "Our local minister encouraged me. I announced in eleventh grade that I was going to be a minister and my teachers were at the end of their ropes! But we had to list two choices, and for my second choice I put down 'teacher.' So they pushed that on me. But at first, even that didn't fly with them. They said, 'You could be, at best, a butcher or a baker, but not a teacher!' Eventually they relented.

"I'm interested in the relation between Judaism and Christianity: how they mutually relate and how they cope. I'm still a Christian, even though I attend church only every month or two."

I ask about her relation to the Party, since history and Russian teachers were often regarded as the "cultural cadre."

Frau Berhau says she never joined the Party. Most of her friends did, but her Christian background gave her a reasonable excuse.

"And the Party didn't pressure me," she says. "Because the Party didn't want idealists. They were just problems, because they *believed* in communism. As soon as they saw what was happening from the inside, they knew full well that the DDR wasn't on track toward 'really existing socialism.' Idealists were far more dangerous than apathetic Party or even hostile non-Party members. Because the idealists believed in communism, but they didn't believe that it was being executed right in the DDR. And because they really wanted to transform the Party."

Young Ulla was too idealistic for the Party, and her chief allegiance was to the Church, anyway. But she had belonged to the JP and the FDJ and all their ancillary youth organizations. And her participation had influenced her against the West.

"Yes, I did possess a certain *Feindbild* of the West, especially West Germany and the United States. And so did my classmates. But by the mid-1980s, it simply wasn't credible to vilify the West in such terms any more: We all watched western TV programs and bought western products; we knew too much to be deceived by the blatant old propaganda."

The last time she gave full credence to the DDR version of events was in 1977, in her penultimate high school year at the Brecht EOS located near the Czech border in Schwarzenberg, when the school lavishly celebrated its twentieth anniversary.

"Given the school's name, we had a relationship with the Berlin Ensemble, Brecht's acting company," Frau Berhau recalls. "And on May 1, the leading actors came to visit and we all honored Brecht. We sang the *Solidaritätslied* [hymn of solidarity, composed by Brecht]. 'Forward and never forget—SOLIDARITY!' We spoke of how the world was divided into 'oppressor' and 'oppressed' states. We praised DDR agitation for the liberation of oppressed Third World states such as Ethiopia and Cuba, all under the guidance of the 'glorious' USSR. You see, there was no '1968' in East Germany. Only a decade later did any kind of freethinking begin in the east."

No breezes of radical protest, no counterculture, no student movement blew over the Wall into the DDR until the end of the 1970s and the beginning of the 1980s, Frau Berhau says.

And so, Ulla's intellectual awakening began in college, during her studies at the Pedagogical College in Magdeburg from 1983 to 1988.

"Since I couldn't travel, I learned about the world outside the Wall from the foreign students," Frau Berhau says. "Many foreigners explained their lives in their native countries to me. They were the only contact we had with the outside world, and they were the living—even 'state-approved'—truth that our media were lying to us."

Eventually Frau Berhau secured a job in an East Berlin polytechnical *Oberschule*. She taught Russian and German to seventh- and eighth-graders. Many Stasi agents had children who attended the school.

"I didn't have too much room to maneuver. The best way to express disapproval of the standard line was simply to skip the author or work altogether. You could always say that you hadn't had enough time to get to the work. Better not to do anything than to deviate from the directive on how the work should be taught. Just not handle the work: That was the easiest and most convenient method of dissent."

But it wasn't always possible to operate this way, Frau Berhau admits. For instance, her teacher certification examiner was very strict: The examiner insisted that her student teachers adhere strictly to the directives of the Ministry of Education on content and approach.

"She was a true believer in the system," says Frau Berhau. She shakes her head in disbelief. "Right up to November 1989!"

In terms of her current teaching at the Jewish Oberschule, Frau Berhau sees the differences between East and West in the presence of the Russian and Ukrainian pupils: Most German students take the *Gymnasium* track; almost all of the foreign students take the *Realschule* track. But even among the Germans, differences are evident: the eastern German students are much more traditional and respectful of authority than are those from the west. Geography also deepens differences. One-third of the students are from eastern Berlin and know the neighborhood; two-thirds are from western Berlin, where most Berlin Jews live—and hang around after school.

"Everything for me in the BRD schooling system is so different," says Frau Berhau. "Literature, history, all methods of pedagogy—I'm still adjusting." For instance, she says, when she taught Brecht's *Solidaritätslied* in DDR days, she treated it as a clarion call to DDR socialism; now she sees it simply as anti-fascist—rather than explicitly pro-communist.

"When I teach history, all the concepts are different. We talked in the DDR about the 'original classless society' and the 'slave societies' that followed; the West talks about the Stone Age and classical Greece and Rome.

"You need to understand the personal histories of people who grew up in the DDR educational system," Frau Berhau continues. "Everything was controlled in school through the group, the 'collective.' Old DDR colleagues say that the West is cold and individualistic. But that's not quite right. The fact is that you must be better organized here and more self-reliant. Because the *Zusammengehörigkeitsgefühl* [feeling of belonging, community togetherness] that we had in the DDR isn't here.

"It's hard for me to appreciate a variety of opinions. We had only one opinion—which was handed down to us, not thought through by us ourselves—and it was invariably right. So I'm not used to accepting lots of opinions.

"My pedagogical method was oriented toward a single question: How can I teach them so that they will be useful to society? As soon as any teaching called into question social norms or hurt society, I stopped it. *Erziehung zur Gemeinschaft.* Education toward community-thinking. If you wanted to help the individual, you really couldn't. You had to suppress the uniqueness of the individual for the presumed good of society. I was concerned with the *class*'s best development.

"Today I see the individual student better. My teaching is much more varied and student-centered. I'm concerned with the personal development of each child. Now I try to give each child something he or she can take home. My new pedagogy promotes the free exchange of opinions in class. I think that different opinions aren't threatening; they enrich the class.

"Still it's hard for me—it's hard for me to accept when the students disagree with what I've presented and believe is a sound, cogent view point."

We joke for a moment about Frau Berhau's "class struggles." "Yes, that's it!" Frau Berhau laughs. "My style used to be: X is right, Y is false. I had a *Feindbild* always available and operating, even if only subconsciously. The authoritarian mind-set is still strong in me. Many of us former DDR teachers are walking contradictions in the classroom. We say that the DDR was an oppressive, regimented nightmare, but we ourselves are still authoritarian and tied to the old ideology."

She pauses, then she adds abruptly:

"But still I want to know: how does one *care*—and still *tolerate* so much—?"

She stops in mid-sentence. Again the difficulty of distinguishing permissiveness and tolerance that I observed in Herr Lanthaler's firm convictions about Judaism and religious practice, though Frau Berhau's orthodoxies were Marxist-oriented. Still, this similarity between the two teachers is noticeable. What seems to be slack and permissive to Frau Berhau is tolerant and flexible to her western colleagues.

"—so much—well, all right, I'll say it—*deviation!* It seems often to me in this country [reunited Germany] that so-called tolerance derives from a lack of caring—of genuine, deep concern. If you really care, you want to influence and even prevail. Nobody in the west seems to care about anything very much, nobody is passionate about anything—except their own small selves.

"It's a question of feeling adrift, without allegiances. It's difficult to support this state, the BRD. On the other hand, you don't have to support it. In the DDR, you did. The teacher was a political propagandist. You had to support it, conform, or make some compromising arrangement.

"But it's getting easier for me. I used to try to persuade the students to think in a socialist direction. Not any more."

Her college experience had given her a keen interest in life outside the DDR and she had mixed frequently with foreigners. So frequently that she eventually married one: an Ethiopian student engineer. As a result of his experience as a black man, she became more sensitive to the problems faced by members of other minorities—including Jews. She also found herself reacting to what she sees as the hypersensitivity of minorities to being slighted, and their often exaggerated perceptions of discrimination. She says that many members of minority groups imagine that the majority group discriminates against them—including her own husband sometimes.

"But it's not discrimination—it's just his subjective view, with no ill intent. So don't read into it!" Ulla says.

She admits that her husband's sensitivities are not baseless. But most of the threatening words and gestures perceived by foreigners dwelling in the east, she says, arise from eastern Germans' ignorance and smugness, rather than outright antipathy. Her own mother, Frau Berhau says, is a case in point. "My mother had problems with my choice of an Ethiopian husband. Not only because of her Nazi-influenced racial thinking. Most DDR citizens would also have had reservations, if only due to ignorance, because one seldom met foreigners in the DDR. There simply were very few, no more than two hundred thousand, and they didn't interact with most citizens.

"All that is true. But on that score, my mother was the exception: she had plenty of contact with foreigners. We had three [North] Vietnamese tenants living with us for several years. My mother was very friendly to them; she even treated them like her boys. But sons don't marry daughters: it was all fine, just as long as they had nothing whatsoever to do with her girls—or any German girls, for that matter.

"Fortunately, I was already pregnant before I told my mother about my Ethiopian boyfriend. It was too late to abort. So now she had a socially difficult choice: Accept an unwed mother or accept a daughter married to a colored man. I knew that, for her, it was just a question of which was worse, which was more embarrassing socially. To be the parent of a single mother? Or the mother-in-law of a black foreigner? What a dilemma for her!" Frau Berhau's laugh is heavy with sarcasm. "Fortunately, she came to support what I had planned to do anyway—get married."

"But it's not entirely a happy ending," she adds quickly. Her husband is scared to go out in Berlin during the evening hours.

"Before the Wall fell, he had no fear at all," Frau Berhau explains. "He feels that people are prejudiced against him [as a black man]. He never felt this way before."

As another class bell chimes, Frau Berhau rises to leave for her noon class. She points out the window at the police guards.

"And he associates it all with the New Germany: the Wall is down, the 'anti-fascist state' has given way to right-wing terror in the streets. And he sees all this as a specifically eastern problem. He thinks western Berliners are much more tolerant, and he wants us to move there. Perhaps we will. But I've always lived in the east; I feel myself an easterner. I don't want to live in western Germany or western Berlin."

3. Return of the Pink Rabbit?

Bleibtreustrasse 43. "Keep Faithful Street." Or "Remain True Street."

The address itself expresses the challenge. "School spirit" has an entirely different meaning here than in American schools—or, for that matter, in other German schools.

Keep the faith. Remain true to the heritage. History lends those exhortations special force in a Jewish school in Germany.

It is September 1995, and I am visiting the elementary school in the Bleibtreustrasse, located in the Charlottenburg district of western Berlin. The school is one of only four such schools in all of Germany. Founded in 1986, it was the first post-war Jewish school set up in Berlin—and the lone Jewish school to exist before the Wall came down in November 1989. (Two other Jewish elementary schools and one high school were established in Berlin after German reunification in October 1990. We have just visited one of those schools—the Jewish Oberschule in Great Hamburg Street in eastern Berlin. Both the Oberschule and the Jewish elementary school at that location were closed in 1995.)

A glance out the window suggests the dimensions of the challenge. The substantial police presence has been fortified since April, when skinheads defaced Jewish graves throughout Berlin. For months now, the Berlin Jewish community has been shaken by German neo-Nazis chanting *"Deutschland den Deutschen"* ("Germany for the Germans") in the streets, and by Palestinian radicals plotting to disrupt the peace process in Israel by attacking Jews in Germany and thereby undermining Arab-Israeli relations. The Berlin police also announced that they had uncovered and foiled a shocking plan by the Palestinian terrorist Abu Nidal ("Father of the Struggle") to blow up Berlin's main synagogue and to assassinate Ignatz Bubis, president of the Central Council of Jews in Germany.

Inside the school, I am again struck immediately, as I was in the Jewish Oberschule, by the visual contrast between these pupils and those in most German schools I've visited. Indeed, even a casual look shows in a different way how the Bleibtreustrasse school differs from most German schools. As elsewhere, boys race through the corridors to their next class. But these boys have yarmulkes atop their heads. Some wear stars of David; several have books and schoolbags covered with Hebrew letters in Cyrillic script. The reason, of course, owes to an ethnic factor that also distinguished the previous two portraits of this chapter: Approximately 80 percent of the student body is Jewish.

8:30 am. Room 211. Teachers are chatting in the staff conference room about next month's preparations for Chanukah, the Feast of Lights, an eight-day Jewish commemoration of the rededication of the Jerusalem Temple dating to the second century. One teacher notes that the Bleibtreustrasse school observes both Jewish and German holidays. Another teacher remarks that the inclusive stance extends to the composition of the school administration: an Israeli principal and a German assistant principal.

Hebrew conversation peppers the conference room before the class bell for the second period; one Hebrew teacher prepares a crossword puzzle for his Hebrew language class. It's a challenging one: even the hints are in Hebrew. I remark on the absence of a textbook; the teachers reply that they do consult a Hebrew textbook, but that teachers are encouraged to craft their own classroom materials, and to adapt all Israeli-design textual materials to the special needs of a German school. The school requires all of its three hundred students in grades one through six—Gentiles as well as Jews—to take Hebrew, Judaism, and bible history; all eight teachers for these subjects are Israelis. (Germans teach the secular subjects.) Judaism class deals with the feast days, holy days, dietary laws, prayer rituals, holy symbols, and other aspects of religious observance. Bible history class addresses the salvation story of the Jewish people. The Israeli teachers possess the same qualifications as any religion instruction teacher in Israel.

A fourth-grade reading teacher mentions that some of the students in her class will soon begin Judith Kerr's children's novel, *When Hitler Stole Pink Rabbit* (1971), based on the author's experience of her family's flight from Nazi Germany. Here again, I notice that the class is not using a *Lehrbuch* or *Fibel*; unlike during the DDR days, when reading class in early grades consisted of selections from an anthology, these children are reading from a serious novel—an opportunity not permitted DDR pupils until the upper grades.

When Hitler Stole Pink Rabbit has received many prizes and is recognized as a children's classic. Anna, a nine-year-old Jewish girl in Berlin, must suddenly leave Germany with her family on Hitler's accession to power in 1933. Shortly thereafter, her parents receive word from acquaintances that the Nazis have expropriated all their property. Her older brother explains that all her toys are now gone. Anna is distraught, above all because she has lost her favorite friend: her stuffed pink rabbit with its familiar soft fur, large black eyes, and endearing way of rolling on its paws. "Hitler is probably snuggling my pink rabbit!" wails Anna inconsolably. By the end of the novel, however, she has learned to adapt to her refugee status in Switzerland and then France, and is about to emigrate to London. The reading teacher notes that a public school in Berlin was recently named after Judith Kerr, who—like most German Jewish exiles of her generation—did not resettle in Germany after the war. Kerr (1922–) has spent her entire adulthood in London.

Room 211 also witnesses several "caretakers" pass in and out to speak with classroom teachers. Most are German; three are Russian, since 60 percent of the student body consists of Russian and Ukrainian Jews who have fled from the former Soviet Union since its collapse in 1991. One German caretaker, Frau Maya Kupfenberg, a young woman in her late twenties, informs me proudly that the caretakers handle all after-school supervision of the students, sponsoring and helping to organize extracurricular activities. Most students belong to several activity groups, choosing among chess, soccer, knitting, carving, basket-weaving, dancing, ceramics, music, drawing, and painting. Caretakers work closely with teachers and parents; some caretakers even sit in on classes and help with homework. Frau Kupferberg, who has worked in the school since 1988, points out that, though there are Jewish schools in Munich, Frankfurt, and Düsseldorf, the Bleibtreustrasse school is the only one with caretakers, the only *Ganztagsschule* [all-day school].

"If the parents must work during the school holidays," says Frau Kupferberg, "we also take care of the children. That's another advantage of our school."

We talk about why Gentile parents choose to send their children to a Jewish school. The reasons are varied, she says. Some parents want to promote tolerance. Others with religious interests want their children to understand the roots of Christianity in Judaism. Many simply acknowledge the excellence of the classes and extracurricular offerings.

"And the after-class services in the school are unique," repeats Frau Kupferberg. "It's a wonderful school."

I ask her about the police presence.

"I don't think that the students notice it overmuch," she says. "But the parents are very concerned."

And with good reason. As I have repeatedly noticed, history casts a lengthy shadow across the Jewish life in Berlin. Frau Kupferberg and two other teachers mention the decline of the Jewish community since the Nazi era. She repeats statistics that I have already heard the Oberschule teachers cite. In January 1933, when Hitler rose to power, Berlin's Jewish community totaled 171,000—the largest in Europe, the fifth biggest in the world. Today [1995], it numbers 9,200—double the figure of 1989—with almost half that population consisting of Russian and Ukrainian émigré Jews. Much ferment has occurred in Berlin's Jewish community, and the existence of the Bleibtreustrasse schools, and other Jewish schools in Germany, are indeed hopeful signs, everyone agrees.

But the pink rabbit has not yet been returned to Germany's Jews.

Frau Kupferberg takes her leave as the class bell to announce the second period rings, and I chat in the hallway with a trio of third-graders as we wait together for their bible history teacher to arrive. They show me their work from yesterday's after-school art group: A colorful drawing of Moses' flight from Egypt and escape across the Red Sea. They agree with Frau Kupferberg that the school has special advantages.

The excellence of the school is cogently argued by David, eight, who elucidates concisely its main advantage:

"We get more holidays."

Not exactly what the Jewish elders may have had in mind, but nonetheless a wholly positive response.

9:20. Bible class is about to commence. Herr Eliahu Avital is writing on the blackboard in Hebrew. The class of eight boys and eight girls copy the names: Jacob, Rachel, Leah. As in the Oberschule, all boys—Gentile as well as Jew—wear yarmulkes. In a locked cabinet window stand two wine goblets and a slice of unleavened bread; a large star of David, awkwardly crayoned on colored construction paper, forms the background. An anonymous quotation in the corner of the room reads: "All human beings, animals, and plants have names."

Two German girls admit that they have trouble writing in Hebrew. They lament that Hebrew is "not their *Muttersprache*"—and that "the Hebrew alphabet is hard." Andreas, a caretaker—one of two male caretakers in the school—watches closely, then helps them form the letters. Although this is not Hebrew class—the discussions are conducted in German—the teachers of Bible literature endeavor, when relevant, to introduce Hebrew words. In Bible history class, there is also no conventional textbook—rather, a German-language children's Bible serves as the textbook.

Today's topic: The Genesis story of Jacob and his wives Leah and Rachel.

We turn to Genesis 25 and read about Jacob, the second son of Isaac, the twin brother of Esau, and father of the twelve patriarchs of Israel. And Rachel, his favorite wife, mother of Joseph and Benjamin.

"How long did Jacob labor to win the hand of Rachel?" asks Herr Avital.

"Seven years!" several students answer.

"That's a long time! Imagine! You'd all be in the tenth grade by then. Another three years and you'd be old enough to graduate!"

The students nod. Seven years is a long time.

Herr Avital smiles broadly, his white teeth sharply contrasting with his jet-black hair and shoes. A young man of about thirty, he dresses in blue jeans and a purple sweatshirt, and sports a gold ring in his left ear. I admire how artfully Herr Avital manages the difficulty, which I well remember from my own days as a schoolteacher, of establishing a relaxed yet authoritative presence in the classroom. He knows how to make history come alive for his students; he wittily relates the three-thousand-year-old story of Jacob as if it were happening today.

Leah, Jacob's first wife, feels bad about Jacob's love for Rachel, says Herr Avital. She feels sad and abandoned. She speaks to God about her feelings. She asks God to help her. So what does she say to Him?

"Jacob doesn't love me anymore, he has a different woman now and loves Rachel instead of me," explains Judith.

"And what do you think she asks from God?"

"A man of her own."

"Well, no, not that." Herr Avital lets out a slight chuckle, directed at Andreas and myself. Judith's answer is a bit *too* contemporary. She wants Jacob back, he says. So what else might she ask for?

"A baby," says Ute.

"Right, that's what she asks God for. You see, back then, if a woman brought babies into the world, the community showered honors upon her. In fact, women were valued according to the number of children, especially sons, that they bore.

"So: What does she say to God?" Herr Avital reads from Genesis 29: "I will be blessed and happy. The daughters of Israel will praise me, because I'll have more sons."

Herr Avital explicates the passage, omitting mention of its sexual politics. Evidently that theme is also a bit too contemporary.

"The people will take her as a praiseworthy example of a fruitful woman," he says. "Isn't that just like our society—how we praise people and they get known for their achievements?" asks Herr Avital. "We praise someone for his strength: You're strong like Arnold Schwarzenegger! Well, Leah is the Arnold Schwarzenegger of mothers! The bible even has a special word with which to praise her. She is praised for her *Leibesfrucht* [fruit of the womb or body]. Isn't that a beautiful word? They didn't call infants 'babies'; they called them *Leibesfrucht*."

Herr Avital summarizes: All right, Leah already has four sons. But she wants another baby, because that will bring her more honor—and maybe win back Jacob too. So how does she go about it?

"She gets Zilpah to bear it and give it to her," says Heike.

"Right," says Herr Avital. "Leah says to herself: 'Zilpah can bear the baby, and it will go into my account. Then I'll have five sons.' But why does Zilpah give Leah her baby?"

"Because Zilpah was Leah's slave," says Heike.

Uwe asks: "So people owned other people in the Bible?"

"Yes. That's the way it was in that society," replies Herr Avital.

"The awful way Leah treats Zilpah—I think it's vulgar," says Heike. "She just expected her to give up her baby. As if Zilpah were a dog or a horse."

"But it was an acceptable practice in that society," repeats Herr Avital.

I am reminded that it was the acceptance of precisely such practices by religious communities that led DDR educators to condemn them as "priest-ridden slave societies."

Heike remains dissatisfied, protesting: "But a human being shouldn't be treated like a dog or a horse!"

"And who said it should be 'acceptable'?" objects Uwe. "Did good people accept it?"

"Take the observance of the Sabbath," says Herr Avital. Shabbat is a day of rest, a holy day in Judaism. "The day of rest applies to every head of household, every family member, all slaves, and all animals. The head of household isn't permitted to work on the Sabbath. But the slave can't work for the head of the household on the Sabbath either. What do you think that means?"

The students sit quietly, uncertain how to respond. Herr Avital glances at his watch.

"Maybe it means that we're all equal in God's sight. Maybe only humans make such distinctions—like 'owner' and 'slave.' Maybe it means that God honors the dignity of every person—even every creature."

"Yes, let us remember: the dignity of all persons is all-important. And respect for their independence is all-important. Thankfully, we human beings have become better in more recent centuries."

The class bell rings.

The Fall into the twentieth century—the nightmare of the Jews that transpired in these very streets—goes unmentioned.

I wonder: A lost opportunity?

10:15. Herr Avital and I chat after class.

I mention the problem of cultural relativism, and specifically the twentieth-century feminist and Jewish issues lurking in the subtext of today's lesson.

Herr Avital acknowledges that it's a dilemma—even (or sometimes especially) with the younger students: to reconstruct history "as it was" (insofar as we can aspire to that) or to render it accessible in present-day terms. When do you simply attempt to comprehend the past? When can you "judge" earlier generations?

As fellow teachers, we mull the difficulties together, fully aware that, in the Bleibtreustrasse, those questions are not merely academic. If you try to walk the fine, unmarked line between contextualizing to understand the past, do you wind up historicizing and thereby whitewashing it?

Herr Avital acknowledges that there are contemporary Jewish, and also feminist, issues in the Bible story of Jacob and Leah and Rachel, but says it's more appropriate to address such stories later, in junior high school.

"I don't want to confuse the students too much by introducing contemporary issues," he says. "We want to show in bible class the changing values and customs of the people of Israel. Of course, you're right: there have been many backward steps in the last several decades—so much so that the Jewish people were almost wiped out altogether. If a young student seems bothered or raises a question about slavery in the Bible, I do discuss the idea of *Untermenschen* [subhumans] and the Holocaust. The older students immediately connect the concept of *Untermenschen* to the history of slavery. And then we discuss the struggle to attain and maintain human dignity by peoples of all kinds. But with the younger ones I don't—unless they initiate it, or unless it seems necessary to explain how one could conceive of human beings as property."

Again the class bell rings. Herr Avital heads off for his fourth-grade Judaism class. This month he is teaching the ten commandments. Today the students will be learning about the third commandment: Honor your father and your mother.

"And teachers too," Herr Avital jokes.

11:45. Some students head for the lunchroom—the school serves kosher meals. Others head for the playground in the schoolyard.

Frau Kupferberg is outside, watching the children play. They do not go outside the school gates. We watch as police officers check the identification cards of would-be school visitors.

"The school is like a ghetto, and that's a danger," says Frau Kupferberg. "Many students have contact only with other Jews." In some cases, she acknowledges, the primary problem is linguistic: the new arrivals from the former USSR don't speak German yet. But there is also fear. Like Frau Berhau at the Jewish Oberschule, she believes that the fear is both understandable and overblown.

"I'm a German, and it's nonsense to say that all Germans are Nazis," Frau Kupferberg says. "And it makes our work harder if we believe things like, 'All German grandparents are Nazis.' That's a dangerous overgeneralization—just as dangerous as 'all Jews are. . . .'" Her voice trails off. "And what does that mean, anyway, '*All* Germans are X, or *all* Jews are Y? You should never generalize like that."

I mention Herr Avital's emphasis on human dignity in his bible history class.

Frau Kupferberg is pleased.

"This school's main goal is to combat and dissolve prejudice," she says. "We can and must reach out to Jews and non-Jews: *Erziehung zur Toleranz*. We must show how Judaism, Christianity, and Islam all have common historical roots. To truly see those shared legacies will mean seeing the dignity of each person."

Another bell. I look toward the Bleibtreustrasse as Frau Kupferberg turns to face toward the school.

"But the special task for the Jewish students here remains," Frau Kupferberg continues. "*Erziehung zum Glauben* [education toward faith] is our main task with the Jewish students. Education toward an open stance within the Jewish heritage, toward a willingness to think about their history and its legacy. It begins with education."

Tolerance toward differences with others, faith in one's own heritage. It's a unique dual mission for a school—and also a daunting responsibility, I think, as I reflect on my own life as a teacher. Yes, the task of rebuilding a tradition is indeed quite a responsibility to invest in a school and its teachers.

Bleib treu. Keep the faith. It begins with education.

4. Breaching Walls, Breaching Faith

Back in the Bleibtreustrasse, in October 1995, for a look at how east meets west. Herr Miron Schumälder, thirty-one, a first-grade teacher, has a free period and stays in the teacher's room to chat. He says that he has come to the Bleibtreustrasse school by an unusual route. Whereas most teachers in the school are Israelis or western Germans, he is one of two eastern German teachers.

Beneath the obvious tensions between Germans and Jews, he says, is the more subtle conflict between western and eastern Germans.

"Walls within walls," he says. At times Herr Schumälder feels as if the *Ossis* are treated as second-class citizens by the *Wessis;* one colleague, also an experienced high school teacher in the east German communist system, had to undergo a special "competence" examination by the administration of the Bleibtreustrasse school, an ordeal to which no western teacher was subjected. At least he was spared that humiliation, he says.

Born in Erfurt in the eastern province of Saxony, Herr Schumälder lived his whole life in eastern Germany. He says he never got to know a single Jew in the DDR: only four hundred Jews lived in post-war East Germany, i.e., Jews who were officially registered with a Jewish synagogue. As a teacher at the Friedrich Liszt Oberschule in Pankow, an elite high school in East Berlin where the children of the communist regime's politicians and diplomats attended school, Herr Schumälder taught Russian, history, and sports before the Wall fell. One month before the protests began against the DDR government, he was fired: August 31, 1989. He had made a few critical remarks of the school administration's opposition to Mikhail Gorbachev's *perestroika* program. He was deemed "not sufficiently committed politically."

Herr Schumälder was later "rehabilitated." He got a letter apologizing for his dismissal. But he never received his old job back, nor were any of the orthodox Party teachers fired, or even those who informed to the secret police. "That's all I got—a letter," he says.

"The *Seilschaft* [old comrades' network] still functions," Herr Schumälder continues. The expression refers to the SED network of "old comrades" who pull each other through tight places in the new system. Nobody campaigned for the ouster of the Party teachers, Herr Schumälder says. That angers him. Despite his qualifications, he couldn't get a teaching job anywhere in Germany after the Wall collapsed.

"I worked a whole year in a restaurant after I was fired," he says with an edge of bitterness.

Finally, primarily because of his fluency in Russian, he was hired to teach in the Bleibtreustrasse; he teaches Russian immigrant children in their native language in all subjects, until their German skills are adequate. He also serves as a liaison with Russian parents. Fifty percent of the school's students are Russian immigrants. Herr Schumälder is grateful to be teaching in the school, but points out testily that he is overqualified to be teaching primary school. As much as the political anxieties facing the Jewish school concern him, he is preoccupied by the uncertainties of his own future. Above all, he wants to teach his special subjects in a German public high school.

Herr Schumälder explains that teaching in a Jewish school—or in any private school in Germany—is a comedown for him because it means "No money, no security, and no status." Public school teachers in Germany are civil servants who are well paid, are guaranteed lifetime appointments, and have traditionally received high social status.

But what frustrates him most is that he's not challenged intellectually—he's not teaching the subjects that he is highly trained to teach. And it galls him that teachers with credentials far inferior to his are allowed to do so.

If Herr Schumälder harbors a feeling of bitterness, it is understandable. Indeed, his qualifications are impressive. His Russian is fluent: he spent one-and-a-half years [1983–84] at the prestigious Kluga Institute for Languages and Literature in Moscow, where top foreign language teachers from the East bloc countries received their training. Herr Schumälder traveled widely in the USSR and spoke with a wide range of Soviet citizens. He visited during the presidency of Yuri Andropov, who had headed the Soviet Communist Party since 1980 and who died in February 1984; it was a relatively progressive period in the USSR.

Another unusual accomplishment—and quite a qualification for a sports teacher, one would think—is that Herr Schumälder was a near-Olympic-level swimmer in the 100- and 200-meter butterfly. In 1973, he placed in the finals in the European Youth Championships. In 1976, he qualified for the DDR National Championships and placed fourth, narrowly missing a berth on a DDR Olympic squad that won an astounding 70 percent of the swimming medals that year in Montreal. If he had been from any other country, including the United States, he would have easily qualified to compete. Later, he graduated from the special Brandenburg School for Sports Teachers.

As if all that weren't enough, Herr Schumälder never joined the Communist Party, the normal pathway to such opportunities and achievements. It was almost unheard of for a Russian and history teacher at an elite East Berlin high school—given that he taught the two most ideologically sensitive subjects—to remain outside the Party. Or for a DDR athlete to travel abroad to Western swimming meets.

"Everyone would say to me: 'What?! You're a Russian and history teacher, and you're not in the Party?! What gives?! And you've spent one-and-a-half years in the USSR?! And gained permission to travel abroad as part of the international swimming squad?! I don't believe it.' Some of them probably thought that I was lying about the Party membership; others may have thought I worked secretly for the Stasi. But you could refuse Party membership and gain such privileges if you fulfilled two conditions:

First, you were top-notch. Merit did count in the DDR. Second, if you kept your mouth shut. Nobody ever doubted my abilities, and I proved them over and over again. But I finally slipped up on the second criterion."

Herr Schumälder anticipates my own reply to him—I assumed that he could only have traveled so widely if he had some relationship to the DDR state authorities. (Indeed, I later asked a fellow DDR history teacher about Schumälder's story—and was told: "He's lying—certainly he was a Stasi informant—and he won't admit it.")

Whatever the truth, in February 1989, according to Herr Schumälder, he curtly told the school principal that she was stifling the exchange of opinions in the school by her strong support of the DDR opposition to Gorbachev's reforms.

"From then on, I was observed daily. Outside examiners from the Party would drop in on my class regularly. Finally, they caught me on some minor error and told me that I could be either demoted to a provincial elementary school or fired. I chose to be fired."

Sometimes he regrets the choice. Although he never joined the Party and thus could be assumed to be untainted, "that doesn't help me get a teaching job," he laments. Precisely because his subjects were ruled "ideologically tainted" by the western German school examining commission after reunification, he lacks the necessary qualifications to teach in western Germany. "And all the jobs in eastern Germany are filled, since so few Party *Bonzen* [bigwigs] were fired. I can't even coach or teach sports, because—despite my swimming record—the academic part of my qualification is judged to be ideologically suspect.

"August 31, 1989: I was fired just ten weeks before the Wall fell! If only I'd lasted another two months, I'd still be teaching in that school today.

"It's six years—SIX YEARS!—since the Berlin Wall fell! Why can't eastern teachers get jobs in western Germany? We're united, aren't we?" He pauses. He waits for me to respond. Herr Schumälder answers his own question.

"No. In name only: even here in eastern Berlin, public school teachers get only 80 percent of the salaries of the *Wessis*. This isn't what I expected in a reunited Germany."

He glances out the window. "The physical Wall may have fallen." He gestures toward the street; Checkpoint Charlie is just a few blocks east.

"But the bigger wall—the wall in our heads—remains."

5. The Strains of Silence II: Hospitality or Hitlerism in Weimar?

A return visit in October 1994 to Frau Ehspanner, formerly a music teacher in the DDR and currently the principal of the Goethe Gymnasium for the Humanities in Weimar, whom we met in Chapter 6, Section 5. The Goethe Gymnasium was hosting an official delegation of pupils and teachers from Tel Aviv during the month of this second interview. Our exchange about that difficult visit discloses another way in which eastern German life has utterly changed from the DDR years. Such a visit was never conducted during the DDR years—nor were there public controversies about anti-Semitism or widespread concerns about violence in the schools. All this is part of the transformation of life in post-reunification eastern Germany. Even a courageous and independent thinker such as Frau Ehspanner found it quite a strain to cope with the upheaval in eastern life.

Q: What have been the negative consequences of reunification?

A: Above all, violence in the schools. It's an indirect outcome of reunification that it has increased dramatically. The media, especially with respect to Germany in this region, also plays it up since Buchenwald is around the corner from Weimar. But it's also true because extracurricular institutions and non-school activities have disappeared. All of the organizations that used to be there for the youth are no longer available and churches can't fill the void. As a working mother in the DDR, you could have a child cared for until six PM every day free of charge. Some members of the child care staff were not good, that's true, but many or most were. The children were in good hands. It was an ideal arrangement. Admittedly, some child care workers were true believers in socialism, and would ram their socialist ideas into kids' heads. Fortunately, this wasn't so common. Most of the women who worked with kids loved kids. They played with them and taught them about music, ceramics, and sports.

The state did exploit sports that showcased performance before spectators. *Leistungssport* [competitive athletics] was a vanity of the state and it was used in order to boost its international profile. That was deplorable. There were doping scandals and everything else, but a lot of the responsibility lay with the parents too. I never permitted that to happen to my kids. I didn't want my kids pushed into that kind of suffocating environment, wherein their bodies and spirits would be strained. The question is, "How ambitious are you and how much of a risk are you going to take at the expense of your children's welfare?"

But the point is that children in the DDR were supervised, and cared for, and not left to themselves to form gangs and hang out on streets. The so-called freedom that exists now is partly a freedom to abuse freedom. Too much freedom at a young age can be reckless. Child care doesn't exist and teachers don't stay after school like they used to. This system functions on a pay-as-you-go basis and teachers are not going to stay after school for three or four hours with the children unless they are paid for it.

Q: Could this surge of violence in the east have been avoided? Or at least minimized?

A: That is one area in which the western Germans could have learned something from us. They could have learned how to tend to children in such a way that you tap into their natural abilities and help them grow while turning them away from violence. But that possibility was never realized because of the working assumption that everything over here [in the east] was bad. Everything we had that was outstanding in the artistic realm, such as our orchestras and our symphonies, was made *kaputt* [destroyed]. The naive assumption that everything in the west was naturally better wasn't true. There was a lot of good talent over here—especially in the cultural area. Many choirs have died. In theater, of course, we are now in a position where we need to discover new plays and dramas, but what was produced was already at a high level. What pupils and we teachers cooperatively accomplished in choirs, recitals, and band performances in school were astounding. These teachers never left for home at 2 in the afternoon; rather, they'd stay until 5 or 6 in the evening! The result was performances that were nearly professional.

Before a choir recital, practice was held from 7 to 9 every night. The level of chamber music was excellent and was also a product of the same type of diligent preparation. Of course, DDR excellence in athletics was internationally known. There were lots of DDR extracurricular activities whereby children thought, "I can cultivate a talent that I possess."

The worst problem with violence is in the *Realschule,* not in the *Gymnasium.* I think the *Realschule* has been nothing better than a version of *Hauptschule.* In both cases, the problem is traceable to the violent neighborhoods and households that these children come from. Schools can't rear children starting from infancy, and they can't reverse the effects of poor parenting. Schools take over what they receive. They must have the cooperation of parents; otherwise, we can't do it alone. The result is violence and aggression.

Here again, however, problems have been played up too much in comparison with western Germany. Most eastern German areas are not bad at all. We always had tight discipline in the DDR, whereas in West Germany there was a complete lack of it.

Q: The problem is really the sudden explosion of violence—it was unknown in the DDR days.

A: Right. The problem of youth violence is not worse today in the east than in the west. It's new here. It didn't exist under communism. It is much worse today than it was in the DDR days, but it's still no worse than in West Germany. It's safer to go through Weimar, Berlin, and Dresden than it is to go through Frankfurt or Hamburg.

Q: You currently have a group of teachers and students from Israel visiting your school. I've heard that the visit has gone poorly.

A: I feel awful about this—angry, distraught, exhausted. One of the Israeli teachers wants to believe that Jews are still being persecuted in Germany and he overreacts and imagines that he is being slighted. He imagines a neutral look from a German to be something other than it is, when usually it's simply a different culture's way of interacting with people. It isn't an insult toward a foreigner, let alone anything particular toward a Jew. Certainly he is right that there are right-wing activists in Germany and there are kids who hang out on the corner in Weimar. They may have a Nazi salute or loud joke about Hitler. But there's nothing anti-Semitic here in this school.

Q: So, what is this visitor claiming?

A: This Israeli would like to believe that our school is a microcosm of the Third Reich. He claims two men in school have been constantly threatening him and his group, but he's dreaming, because it is untrue. "Show me who the men are. I want to confront them," I've said to him. I meet with the entire group of guests at my school every day. He can easily say, "Come with me today and I'll show you who they are." He won't do that. He's refused me the opportunity because he can't come up with them. He claims this every day, but it's his imagination. He simply wants to go back home and claim that there is prejudice in Germany, that he was badly treated, and that nothing has changed since 1945. Worst of all for many of us here, his attitude reinforces a perception that exists elsewhere in Europe and in western Germany that eastern Germany equals neo-fascism. It's untrue. I tell you it's untrue.

Q: Some teachers in your school have told me that the Israeli visit has been a "disaster."

A: It's been a horrible disappointment to me. We had spent months preparing ourselves to host these Israeli guests and were looking forward to it immensely. The whole school was prepared for this. We worked endless hours with parents in various neighborhoods to make this visit a success. Really, only one man is ruining it and I find it awful that this should happen—that he should be saying, "I'm calling the police because Israelis are being trailed and persecuted by Nazis everywhere." He calls and informs the police about this and doesn't even tell me. It's a humiliation for me too. He does this despite my asking for information on these alleged persecutors, so that it could be stopped immediately.

These reports have gone all the way up to the foreign ministry in Berlin. The embassy is expressing its displeasure with my school. It's even gone to the German embassy in Tel Aviv and also to the Israeli embassy in Bonn. Headlines are already coming out: "Israeli guests at Goethe Gymnasium in Weimar Are Badly Treated."

I won't permit that to be said. I won't remain publicly silent about such distortions any longer. I'll defend our school against that kind of rumor. It is being caused by a single man and no one else. He is now influencing other people. Every time he enters the school, he begins to announce that his pupils aren't getting enough to eat. That's absurd. They're getting the best and plenty to eat. "We are being poorly housed," he said to me. "We should be in a Hilton hotel." But I can't afford that. My budget won't allow me to put twenty Israelis in the Hilton for two weeks. We're putting them with lovely German families. I don't believe it's a requirement of good hosting that he should be put in a Hilton.

This is a tragic backward step. It destroys so much that has been worked on and so much that has been done to improve relations between the eastern states and Israel since 1990. The children [visiting Israeli pupils and German pupils] actually understand one another very well and are getting along.

It is extremely frustrating. It's really an outrage.

Q: But the surge in youth violence does have a right-wing, and even neo-Nazi, dimension to it.

A: Yes, of course. No one can dispute that. Ironically and tragically, it's the case that a few of our region's youth have turned toward this awful movement. There are only a few hundred of them [skinheads] in the east—and they have been schooled into it by long-time Nazis from the west. The Nazis have come east in an effort to exploit the difficulties associated with the transition: the unemployment and the uncertainty about our future as well as the inexperience that our people have with foreigners. These professional neo-Nazis in the west are experts at heating things up and exploiting the freedoms of democracy to promote their movement. People who have had the floor fall out from under them are especially vulnerable to such appeals.

6. "Re-Education for Tolerance": A Civic Leader Speaks Out

Interview with the late Ignatz Bubis (1927–99), the former political leader of Germany's Jewish community, which consists of seventy-one congregations totaling more than 50,000 registered members.

Elected chair of the Central Council of Jews in Germany in September 1992, Bubis did not have long to wait before he was plunged into the political turmoil that has plagued Germany since reunification. Bubis was in office less than two weeks before young skinheads set fire to the area surrounding the former Jewish barracks in the Sachsenhausen concentration camp outside Berlin. He became a familiar figure on the German political scene, addressing issues sometimes ranging far beyond the immediate topic of the condition of Jews in Germany, such as the responsibilities of European education, the task of integrating eastern and western Europe, the proper qualifications for a German president—not to mention subjects that are his direct concerns, such as immigration policy and anti-foreigner violence. (Bubis delivered a widely quoted memorial address at the May 1994 service for five Turkish victims of a neo-Nazi arson attack at Solingen, in western Germany.)

Despite his political battles against reactionary elements in Germany, Bubis was a moderate and a strong admirer of post-war Germany's political system. He repeatedly emphasized that he was a German citizen—not an easy step for German Jews and one that remains unusual among his generation. Unlike his predecessor, Heinz Galinksi—another survivor of Nazi camps—Bubis did not adopt a combative or confrontational style with politicians in Bonn and Berlin; instead he preferred to work behind the scenes and to cooperate with Germany's leaders whenever possible.

This new, politic approach exhibited by the leader of Germany's Jews won

Bubis praise and gratitude from both Social Democrats and Conservatives; in 1993, several Bundestag members, along with prominent editorialists, even proposed that Bubis succeed President Richard von Weizsäcker, who was not eligible for re-election. "A Jew as president of united Germany?" asked Hans-Ulrich Joerges in Die Woche, *endorsing the suggestion in February 1993. "Yes, and not just for the sake of the outside world but for our own sake. What could be more fruitful, more healing, more purifying?" (Bubis immediately disavowed any interest in the German presidency.)*[12]

A strong believer that education can promote tolerance and world peace, Bubis was also an active educator himself, both in Israel and Germany. In Jerusalem, a school for disabled children was named after him during the early 1990s; he was part owner of the Tel Aviv Sheraton, which was the major donor to the school. In Germany, he spearheaded the "Schools without Racism" initiative. When I interviewed him, he was in the middle of promoting this nationwide, voluntary, anti-racism and anti-Semitism program, which was just being introduced to schools in the fall of 1995; more than five hundred German schools had signed up immediately. His main theme was "education for tolerance." Bubis spoke to more than 500,000 schoolchildren in Germany on that theme during his tenure as the head of Germany's Jewish community.

Short and rotund, Bubis was an avuncular, friendly man, but one who was also capable of going on the offensive and responding sharply to his critics. Witty and jocular, he nevertheless did not brook intimidation— whether by anti-Semites on the Right or by feminists on the Left critical of the "patriarchal" aspects of Orthodox Judaism.

The following interview was conducted in two parts, on October 5 and 6, 1995, first in Bubis's office in the Schumannstrasse, where he pursued his real estate business in Frankfurt's West End, and later in the lobby of the Steinberger Hotel in eastern Berlin.

Q: What do you say to a young Jew who asks, "Why should I stay in Germany and live in the shadow of the past?"

A: First of all, I don't simply say: "You should stay." Each person must inquire and decide for himself on that issue.

I tell nobody that he should stay. I don't have the right to tell young people to stay here. I don't even cite reasons why a person should stay here. I do, however, point out one fact to young people: If you can't cope with the past that your parents or grandparents suffered, then you won't be able to thrive here, because the burden will overwhelm you.

Each person must decide for himself whether the current Germany is really a "new" Germany—and not merely some form of continuation of Nazi Germany. If you can accept that a new start has been made—and that a different country has developed over the last half-century—then it's possible to live a good life here.

People have a wide range of different reasons for staying and leaving. For instance, my daughter decided to stay because her parents are here and she wants to remain close to us.

Q: Why have you yourself decided to remain in Germany?

A: That's not a simple question. I'm not even sure *when* I decided to resettle permanently in Germany. I was in Poland—in Breslau—when the war ended and didn't want to stay there.[13] In November 1945, I returned to Germany with the intention to emigrate. And I toyed with this idea for a long time. Over the years, the idea became weaker. But I was still considering it in the 1950s, and that is the reason why I was constantly on the move for a decade: I lived in West Berlin, Stuttgart, Pfortsheim, Dresden, and finally came to Frankfurt in 1956. I kept looking for a place in Germany that I could call home.

It was probably around 1956 that I reached the decision to stay in Germany.[14] By that time I had also been abroad, and I had considered and rejected places outside Germany. In 1951, I visited Israel for the first time. It was a difficult time. I visited the United States and Canada. I thought about emigrating to North America. But the pace felt too hectic. Canada is a bit more European than the U.S., but it still didn't feel right. I had also married by that time, and my wife didn't want to go that far away from Europe. She was born in Poland and grew up in Paris. She wanted to settle in Paris. I told her that, given its proximity, we could pick up and go to Paris at any time—we didn't need to make elaborate plans for a decision to move there.

So, by 1956, I'd decided that I was living in a different Germany than existed in the previous two decades, and I decided to remain. But, as you can see, no single reason accounts for that decision.

Q: You grew up in an Orthodox home.

A: Yes, my parents' home was very Orthodox, and Jewish traditions mean a great deal to me. And even though I don't follow Orthodox observance now, the tradition remains very important to me.

Q: When did you stop living as an Orthodox Jew?

A: My first step away was in 1945, right after the end of the war. I wasn't near my parents' home anymore. That's when the backsliding began.

Q: Have you found it at all difficult to reconcile the Orthodox tradition with a worldly life? Did your business career ultimately contribute to the "backsliding"?

A: No. I don't think that the one conflicts with the other. You can settle your worldly matters from Sunday to Friday—and even eat kosher throughout the week, if you choose. My Orthodox education and rearing expresses itself by my occasional attendance at synagogue and my active participation in the life of the Jewish community in Germany. Everyone knows that I'm the chair of the Central Council of Jews in Germany, and that I take pains to assure that the interests of the Orthodox Jews in Germany are also given proper attention.

I take the position that a Liberal/Reformed Jew can also feel at home in some observances of Orthodox Judaism, insofar as no "sin" is involved for him in accommodating some Orthodox views and practices. But only with great difficulty can an Orthodox Jew participate in the Liberal/Reformed tradition. So I think it's always crucial to attend especially to the needs of the Orthodox members in the community, since they have fewer options.

Q: To return to the tasks facing younger Jews in the "new" Germany of the mid-1990s: Since German reunification in 1990, several Jewish schools have been opened in Germany. What are the special challenges and burdens of the Jewish school in Germany?

A: The Jewish school does indeed have a special task in Germany: In full awareness of German history in this century, we aim to pass on Jewish traditions. Children are our hope for the future, and we want to make certain that young Jews understand what Judaism is: whatever they do with that knowledge and however they later decide to shape their lives is their own decision. Because of the small number of Jews in Germany, we know that young Jews won't learn much about Jewish life in the public schools or in the wider culture: we must give them as much education about Jewish life as possible.

Q: You've often spoken about the goal of *Erziehung zur Toleranz*. Do you see it as part of the special educational task of the Jewish school in Germany?

A: Yes, but we must understand that term in the richest sense: not mere toleration, but rather acceptance and responsibility. "Tolerance" could mean simply "putting up with" others. It doesn't necessarily mean that I accept that the Other is different from me and that he lives according to his own vision. This struggle for tolerance is a long-standing problem in Germany—we should properly speak of "re-education for tolerance."

All this applies to Jews, too. A Jew should respect and accept that there are other religions. And others should respect and accept that there is a Jewish religion. And this acceptance—in one's deepest being—of the whole culture of the Other, and of the right of the Other to live exactly as he chooses, goes beyond mere toleration. It is a kind of affirmation of the Other.

Q: Apart from living in the shadow of the past, what are the greatest difficulties facing Jews living in Germany?

A: The biggest difficulty has relatively little to do with the Nazi era, because most Jews living in Germany today are not German Jews. Our biggest challenge involves integrating the tens of thousands of immigrants from the former USSR who have come to Germany since 1989. They are in tough economic straits and know little, if anything, about Judaism. Only a handful practice the faith. We must make certain that, when these people settle in Germany, they don't live as outsiders, but rather that they are welcomed and integrated into the Jewish community. This means helping them find work and living arrangements, as well as informing them about Judaism and giving them the means to become full members of the Jewish community.

Q: What specific steps are you taking to bridge the division between German Jews and Russian or Ukrainian Jews?

A: I wouldn't call it a "division." It's just a certain incomprehension, mostly on the side of Jews from the former USSR, who don't understand the history and conditions of the German Jews.

Q: You note that the integration of immigrants from the former USSR is the chief task of the Jewish community. What are some other major tasks?

A: To reach out to other groups, to establish that we care not just about fellow Jews or about members in our own community. At the moment, I'm trying—just trying, mind you—to help improve the mood in the country toward foreigners. That's not really an official responsibility of mine or of the Central Council of Jews in Germany. But whenever I see the opportunity to speak out about it, I do so.

Because if we're just concerned about injustices toward Jews and don't express concern about others, then we really shouldn't be surprised when others in Germany don't care about us when *we* get threatened.

Q: Let me turn to political issues in Germany's past that still shape Jewish life in Germany today. Recently, Federal President [Roman] Herzog called upon citizens and residents of Germany to develop a "relaxed relationship to the past." His remark was condemned in some quarters as "irresponsible" and provoked widespread controversy among those who fear that it paves the way for Germans to forget about or jettison the Nazi past and the Holocaust. But you defended Herzog's statement as constructive. Could you elaborate on your reasoning?

A: First, let's remember that Herzog never used the word "Jew." Secondly, while some media did at first criticize the remark as "irresponsible," most commentators later reconsidered and praised it as courageous and timely. It took the media awhile to understand what Herzog meant by it.

I said from the start that the federal president is right and that he meant the following: How else is the younger generation to come to terms with itself here if it has an awkward relationship to the past? And how can those born before or during the war live here if they can only have a tense relationship to the past?

You must know history, understand it, and learn from it—but you don't need to feel awkward about it or ambivalent toward it. Because when your stance remains cramped or tense over many years, it eventually will lead to an explosive release via acts of aggression. When someone who is twenty-five or thirty or forty feels awkward speaking to me, when he feels tense just to be in my presence, then he begins to hate me—because I seem to be the one who is *making* him feel so uncomfortable. And he then shifts his guilt—which is the cause of his anxiety and tenseness—onto me. And thereupon I become the object of his anger and rage.

And the fact is that he doesn't have any personal reason to feel so awkward about the past. Yes, he should inform himself about what happened and know that it did indeed happen. But he doesn't need to remain in a state of anxiety or tension about it.

Q: To return to questions of identity that specifically confront a Jew living in Germany: Do you feel that you are a "German"? Or a "Jew of German heritage"? Or something else? How important is the issue of self-designation to your identity and to the identity of Jews living in Germany?

A: I consider myself a German citizen of the Jewish faith. In that sense, I'm not a "German"—though I'm still a German citizen—because the Germans themselves make a distinction between Jewish and non-Jewish Germans.

I am a citizen of Germany, and as a German citizen, I have the rights and duties of other Germans. And I have my Jewish faith, which is just as important to me as my German citizenship.

Q: There are many Jews in Germany who describe themselves differently.

A: Yes. Many of them describe themselves as Jews, and they say that they are just living in Germany—because they don't want to identify with Germany. And there are some Jews who consider themselves Germans first and Jews second. [Michael] Wolfsohn [professor of history at the National College of the Armed Forces in Munich], for instance, is a German nationalist first. And somewhere down the line he also regards himself as a Jew. But for me, Judaism plays a more important role than for him.

Q: You yourself were proposed as a candidate for Federal President of Germany in 1993, and the suggestion was widely discussed in the German media. Did you consider the possibility seriously?

A: No, not for a second. First I laughed. I considered it a joke. I thought it might be a bad prank. The suggestion came from a Bundestag representative who was also a former secretary in the Ministry of Defense. The media took it up then, but the proposal never came to an official meeting between [Chancellor] Kohl, or his representatives, and me. And I would have turned down even a meeting to discuss the proposal. I said on every occasion when I was asked about it: "I don't know of anyone more unsuitable than me!" (Laughter)

Q: Do you think Germans could accept a Jew in the office of Federal President?

A: No, I don't—just as I don't think that most Americans could accept a Jew as their president.

Q: Does the development of that form of acceptance also belong to your call to foster "education for tolerance"?

A: No. The resistance to a Jewish head of state in a non-Jewish nation indicates only that the relations between Jews and non-Jews remain problematic. And these relations will remain problematic for a long time to come—not only in Germany but also in the rest of the world. But you are right that the *recognition* of that problem does belong to the task of education for tolerance.

To some extent, the resistance [to a Jewish head of state] involves symbolic issues: the top man is invariably a symbol of his nation. There's no problem being a Jewish parliamentary representative, a cabinet minister, or a state president in most Western countries, even in Germany. Right now, there is a Jew heading the Ministry of the Interior in Nordrhein-Westphalen, the biggest state in Germany. He emigrated to Palestine before the war and came back to Germany after it.

But a minister is one thing, and a federal president is another. To a degree, the whole problem of resistance to Jewish visibility or prominence in a nation's political life is less an issue in Germany than elsewhere—and precisely because of the history of the Jews in modern Germany: since there are so few of us here now, nobody—ourselves included—really has much of an expectation that we'll play a big role in Germany's political life.

EPILOGUE
Curriculum Without a Core

> Things fall apart;
> the center cannot hold
> —William Butler Yeats, "The Second Coming"

Perhaps no other regime in history has expended so much energy in educational reform with such miserable results than did the DDR. As we have seen, the DDR schoolbook was a strategic weapon in that educational campaign, with immense resources of time, talent, and teacher training invested in its production.

Indeed, the herculean efforts of SED leaders to capture "the citadel of learning" could be summed up in the popular Party slogan of the 1960s and 1970s: "*Wo ein Parteimitglied ist, da ist die Partei!*" [Wherever one member of the Party is, there too is the Party!] The Scriptural echoes are unmistakable: the Party-inspired and -written textbook was, as it were, an omnipresent, omniscient Party member. Through its approved textbooks, the Party was always in attendance in DDR schools. The textbooks did not aim to describe, or even interpret, the world as it was, but to change it. The textbooks did not represent reality; they served as SED educators' key pedagogical instrument for the revolutionary transformation of reality via the transformation of public consciousness.

And yet, despite (or rather because of) the SED's relentless educational battle—featuring a core curriculum aimed at winning nothing less than the hearts and minds of East German youth—"really existing socialism" never came into existence, except in fanciful M-L theory. Likewise, the Party drive to "storm the citadel of learning": the SED captured the commanding heights governing the citadel, but never the hearts and minds of the majority of the rank-and-file.

Not that SED educators ever stopped trying. "*Die Partei hat immer recht!*" [The Party is always right!] went the refrain of the venerable SED hymn composed by Louis Fürnberg, which had echoed through the halls of Party meetings in the 1940s and 1950s. True believers such as Erich and Margot Honecker voiced its hard-line sentiments through their last days in office in mid-October 1989. Theirs was a textbook campaign that made ideology the core curriculum and targeted the planned human being (*Planmensch*) as the production norm.

But by the fall of 1989, the core could not hold DDR pupils; the *Planmensch* norm was going grossly under-fulfilled. Indeed, the overwhelming majority of DDR youth were refusing to turn into model "socialist personalities." They were not becoming "textbook Reds."

"Who has the youth, has the future," ran another old Party slogan, which was derived from a speech by the nineteenth-century Social Democratic leader, Wilhelm Liebknecht. The SED adopted the slogan as its call to arms—but the DDR's youth ultimately refused to heed it. Instead they came, in effect, to believe:

"The Party, the Party / It's *never* right!"

By October 1989, the DDR no longer had the youth. By early 1990, it no longer had a future.

And thereupon eastern Germans lurched into a new round of *Umerziehung* and western re-education. As the two dozen portraits and interviews in Part 2 evinced, they have entered a brave new world in which the old communist values and verities no longer apply. Yes, they have entered a new territory, an unmapped *Neuland* marked both by complex continuities and by discontinuities with their immediate past, a post-communist wilderness both exciting and threatening in which, as they cope with the traumatic aftereffects of national reunification that persist into the twenty-first century, many of them wander still.

Notes

Although each entry in the primary bibliography contains the full listing for all sources, the East German textbooks cited below include, where relevant to the immediate argument, the date of publication. *Lehrbuch* is the general name for "textbook"; *Unterrichtshilfen* is common usage for "teacher's guide."

As in the main text, I have translated all titles of and quotations from DDR textbook selections (short stories, memoirs, poems, songs, and so forth) into English for the convenience of the non-German reader. All German book titles are, however, cited in the original. Unless otherwise noted, all translations from the German are my own.

PROLOGUE: CREATING YOUNG COMRADES

1. See Alberta Phillips, "Cutting Corners on Texas' Textbooks Is A Lot of Bull," *Austin American-Statesman*, 20 April 2003, H3. Among the thirty-six works of fiction currently banned in some Texas public school districts are Orwell's *1984* (for its sex scene) and the Harry Potter series by J. K. Rowling (for its "mystical content"). Until recently, the American Heritage Dictionary was also banned because some parents objected that certain listed words were obscene. See Molly Wardlaw, "Texas School Libraries Keep 36 Books Off Shelves," *Daily Texan*, 23 September 2003.

2. Volk und Wissen is still publishing textbooks today in reunified Germany—though, of course, the DDR's system of socialist editorial collectives has been replaced by a conventional Western model of editorial staffing.

3. Helmut Roske, "The Textbook Factory," *Atlantic Monthly*, December 1963, 91–92. Roske committed *Republikflucht* in 1961.

4. Quoted in Hans Mieskes, *Die Pädagogik der DDR in Theorie, Forschung, und Praxis* (Oberursel: Taunus Finken-Verlag, 1971), 2:267.

5. For two West German studies of DDR textbooks, see Gerhard Möbus, *Unterwerfung durch Erziehung: Zur politischen Pädagogik im sowjetisch besetzten Deutschland* (Mainz: Verlag Hase und Koehler, 1965) and Horst Siebert, *"Bildung"spraxis in Deutschland: BRD und DDR im Vergleich* (Düsseldorf: Bertelsmann Universitätsverlag, 1970), respectively.

6. I use the term "eastern Germany identity" in the book's subtitle—rather than "character" or "soul"—quite deliberately. The latter terms are quite compromised, especially in the context of fascist or Nazi history. The [eastern] "German soul" actually doesn't exist and is a mere construction (just as is the alleged "Jewish character"). It would be misguided to propound such an entity in the pages of this book, as if there were no discontinuities within East German society, as if the whole DDR populace had been so overwhelmingly dominated by M-L ideology dictated by the Party that there were only two ways of reacting: full submission or *Republikflucht*. Such a picture is too simplistic. Historians need to study the numerous and complex ways in which people negotiated and adapted to the ideology, the diverse means whereby they aimed to integrate or exclude Party ideology from their private lives.

The artifact that I have selected to examine the intersections of East German life and ideology—the school textbook—is a source seldom chosen by historians, despite the opportunities that this source has to offer: DDR school textbooks provide direct insight into Party political and educational ideology. Why have historians been reluctant to use textbooks as a source for assessing the impact of DDR official Party ideology on its citizens' lives? The reason is simply this: A textbook can show—literally—only what is written in it. It does not answer any questions as to how much of its contents were taught, whether teachers wholeheartedly agreed with its data and claims, or whether schoolchildren laughed at its ideological assertions about "dialectical processes" in atoms and molecules. It is quite impossible to extrapolate from the textbook contents to the attitudes of students and teachers. Let me emphasize again the limits of my material: Textbooks can tell us what DDR citizens were *supposed* to think. So my occasional forays into the question of the influence of textbooks on East German pupils and teachers must remain highly speculative. Current research (especially historical research in communication studies, propaganda, advertising, etc.) stresses the ways in which participants in all communication networks construct meanings and selectively acknowledge parts of the communication exchange while overlooking those parts that do not fit into their own mental frameworks. One has to avoid the trap of saying: "Because it is *there*—in the textbooks—it *must* have been in the heads of the people."

For the DDR citizenry was not one block of people, but rather a society defined by internal ruptures and strong generational tensions. Reputable historiography of the DDR has long dropped the Cold War view of the DDR as a homogeneous society and now stresses its growing diversity since the 1960s as the most important reason for the collapse of the DDR in 1989.

7. See Peter Grothe, *To Win the Minds of Men: The Story of the Communist Propaganda War in East Germany* (Palo Alto: Pacific Books, 1958).

8. Let me also note here that most of the textbooks analyzed in this study were donated to me by families and schoolteachers whom I interviewed.

INTRODUCTION: IDEOLOGY AS CORE CURRICULUM

1. Gottfried Uhlig, *Monumenta Paedagogica. Band 2. Der Beginn der antifaschistisch-demokratischen Schulreform, 1945–1946* (Berlin [East]: Akademie-Verlag, 1965), 281, 283. The word "re-education" originated in American psychiatry in the 1930s and described the effort to convert, or rather "re-convert," people from one belief system to another: it was a technique of "brainwashing" people back to their original ideology (e.g., from fanatical religious fundamentalism back to respectable middle-class thinking, or from a newfound capitalistic or fascistic outlook back to a communist Weltanschauung.)

Some critical German historians have referred to the Allied occupation, both in the east and west, as the *Charakterwäsche* [character-washing] of the Germans, but the German language has no word precisely corresponding to re-education. The usual translation is *Umerziehung*, a word that traditionally refers explicitly to schooling or rearing. For linguistic reasons and because the Soviet Military Administration (the occupation government, known as SMAD) mandated sweeping educational reforms, the familiar German word *Umerziehung* was more commonly used in the SBZ (Soviet Occupation Zone). Both words were used in the western zones. Our English word became colloquial for referring to the western Allies' wide-ranging psychological approach to German political re-orientation (e.g., via international student exchanges, western-oriented magazines, and American films and cartoons).

2. Grothe, *To Win the Minds of Men*, 164.

3. Already in February 1945, German communists in Moscow had determined that the Weimar schoolbooks would be unsuitable in the SBZ. As one DDR historian later wrote: "They glorified wars, war experiences, and war heroes of the Prussian-German military, and included the biographies of such figures as Frederick the Great, Queen Luise, Bismarck, and others, thereby distorting German history and promoting nationalism. Many books of the 1920s must be seen as

predecessors to the fascist books. Some schoolbooks of the Weimar Republic were relatively progressive. But even they, in many cases, were not free from reactionary influences."

Education officials objected to such poems in the Weimar books as "The Farewell of the Army Reserve Soldier," as well as the "Austrian Cavalry Song," a dying soldier's rhapsody about the conquest of Yugoslavia, an adversary of Germany and Austria in World War I. Given that post-war Yugoslavia was, under Soviet occupation, about to become a "socialist brotherland" of the SBZ, this poem was obviously objectionable:

> Over there in the setting sun / two vultures are hovering
> When does the Grim Reaper / arrive to take us?
> But it is a consolation / if only to see our flag
> swaying in the wind / toward Belgrade.

Uhlig, *Monumenta Paedagogica*, 2:281–83.

4. Quoted in Grothe, *To Win the Minds of Men*, 164.
5. Uhlig, *Monumenta Paedagogica*, 2:281–83.
6. David Childs, *Germany in the Twentieth Century*. London, 1991, 169.
7. Childs notes that when the DDR was founded in 1949, there were 65,207 teachers, 45,244—or almost 70 percent—of whom were new teachers.
8. Quoted in Uhlig, *Monumenta Paedagogica*, 2:281.
9. Quoted in Uhlig, *Monumenta Paedagogica*, 2:283.
10. Of course, when Volk und Wissen itself could not keep pace with sudden Party line changes—as both occurred in 1956, when DDR children went on learning from textbooks proclaiming the "Great Stalin" long after Khrushchev's Secret Speech that February, and in the 1980s, when Soviet *perestroika* was in full swing—the inflexibility of DDR schooling proved quite embarrassing. In each case, as history seemed to change overnight, thousands of teachers—and students—simply ceased believing the textbooks, which now contained material that the regime was publicly denying every day. As we shall see, however, after these and other crises of faith, the official charade of Party "truth" continued, as if nothing were amiss.
11. But what about *unofficially*? Yes, indeed, the teachers were *told* to "teach the textbook to the letter"—but *did* they?

Not always. As we shall see in the portraits in Chapters 6 and 7, DDR teachers could—and did—treat the Party's pedagogical directives in the teaching guides rather with laxity. Nor did their pupils swallow whole their textbooks' lessons. And that is another compelling reason why any investigation into the "influence" of DDR textbooks or discussions of an abstraction such as the "DDR mind" should remain, at most, highly speculative.

12. To achieve similar ends, some stories even demonized grandparents, featuring young heroes defiant toward their "Nazi" elders. One such work was Erwin Strittmatter's *Tinko*, a novel frequently excerpted in DDR readers of the 1950s.
13. Quoted in Möbus, *Unterwerfung durch Erziehung*, 199. One gets a sense of the scope of the "unlearning" at work here if one recalls the Nazi schoolbooks. Is "When Stalin Came" much different from "The *Führer* Comes"?

> Today Klaus's mother does not need to wake him. He springs from bed on his own. Today is an important holiday. . . .
> From the windows, the swastika flags wave. . . . In the shop windows stand pictures of the *Führer*. . . . The boys climb up trees. . . . When a flag-bearer passes, Klaus raises his right arm in salute. All at once, Klaus hears *Heil!* salutes from afar. The shouts resound, [growing] ever nearer.
> And then Klaus sees the *Führer*. He stands in the car and waves in a friendly manner. *Heil! Heil!* calls Klaus, as loud as he can.
> What a pity, the *Führer* is already past! But Klaus continues to call: *Heil Hitler! Heil Hitler!*

Quoted in Gilmer W. Blackburn, *Education in the Third Reich: Race and History in Nazi Textbooks* (Albany: SUNY Press, 1985), 32.

14. *Geschichte 5* (1968 [1965]), 5.

15. "Textbook Writers," *Soviet Education,* April 1960. See also Mieskes, *Pädagogik der DDR,* 2:25–71.

16. I elaborate on this theme in an interview devoted to the "lessons" of DDR education for concerned Americans. See Megan Gilles, "Illiberal Education: An Interview with John Rodden," *The Texas Observer,* 7 January 2005, 30–31.

CHAPTER 1. GERMAN FOR THE EAST GERMANS: LANGUAGE AND LITERATURE

1. Val Rust and Diane Rust, *The Unification of German Education* (New York: Garland, 1995), 74–75.

2. Among other researchers, scholars affiliated with the Georg Eckert Institute of Textbook Research in Braunschweig (western Germany) have conducted studies since the 1960s regarding German textbooks. (See the institute's website at http://www.gei.de/.) For a sample of their scholarly studies that differ from my own, see Georg Stober, ed., *Der Transformationsprozess in Ostdeutschland und in Polen,* Georg-Eckert-Institut (Braunschweig: Georg-Eckert-Institut, 2003); and Verena Radkau Garcia and Heike Chr. Matzing, eds., *Zehn Jahre nach der Wiedervereinigung—die DDR im Geschichtsbewusstsein der Deutschen,* vol. 22 (2000). See also "Deutschlandbild und Deutsche Frage," in *Studien zur internationalen Schulbuchforschung,* ed. Wolfgang Jacobmeyer, vol. 43 (1986), which specifically addresses DDR textbooks.

3. *Literaturunterricht 5* (1979 [1966]), 23–24.

4. *Lesebuch 3* (1980 [1970]), 171; *Lesebuch 4* (1978 [1977]), 169.

5. *Unterrichtshilfen Deutsch 1* (1977, 1973 [1970], 122.

6. *Unterrichtshilfen Deutsch. Klasse 2* (1977, 1973 [1970]), 123.

7. *Lesebuch 3,* 3.

8. Here again, while American elementary textbooks from an earlier era have had the same kind of simple-minded ideological stories about the founders of the nation, DDR textbooks differed: unlike George Washington, Ulbricht was a brutal and unjust dictator. Moreover, DDR textbooks mythologize numerous living Party leaders, such as Ulbricht, whereas no living American presidents or statesmen have been similarly enshrined in our textbooks since the nineteenth century.

9. A change first appears in the fifth-grade readers. For instance, *Unser Lehrbuch. 5. Schuljahr* (1965 [1959]) features sections on various genres, including sagas and fairy tales. The selections include writings by Erich Weinert, Erwin Strittmatter, Hoffmann von Fallersleben, Mark Twain (an excerpt from *The Adventures of Tom Sawyer*), Goethe (two lyric poems), Johann Peter Hebel, Brecht, Heine, and fairy tales from the Brothers Grimm, Hans Christian Andersen, and Martin Luther ("The Raven and the Fox").

10. *Lesebuch 3,* 4; *Lesebuch 4,* 19; *Lesebuch 4,* 20; *Heimatkunde 4* (1979 [1978]), 61.

11. *Unterrichtshilfen Deutsch 1,* 122.

12. *Lesebuch 3,* 41. Or see the "Song of Friendship" in *Lesebuch 3,* 26, which presents Soviet cosmonauts as personal friends of DDR schoolchildren:

> Let's greet the bold pilots of the cosmos
> All children love them.
> Juri and Valia, victors over the heavens
> Nobody will ever forget your feat.
> Children in the Soviet Union
> We extend the hand of friendship
> Drushba, Drushba! On the wind
> Our greeting flies quickly to you.

13. *Lesebuch 2* (1978 [1977]), 65. See also the poem "Transformation," in *Lesebuch 5* (1978 [1977]), 167, on the metamorphosis of Pjotr from an "enemy" during the Nazi era to a "friend" during the DDR era.

14. *Lesebuch 3*, 30–31, 46.

15. *Literaturunterricht 5*, 23.

16. Ibid., 24.

17. Honecker's words are from his greeting to the Seventh Writers' Congress (1977). This quotation and the following ones appear in *Literaturunterricht 5*, 7–9, 33.

18. Exceptions include excerpts from children's books such as Max Zimmering's *Buttje Pieter and His Hero*.

19. See the table of contents in *Unser Lesebuch. Klasse 7* (1977 [1968]), 6–7, includes anti-American agitprop stories about Hiroshima and poetry about the Vietnam War. But *Lesebuch 7* does also leave some room for fantasy and the more childlike concerns of the textbooks in earlier grades: two short sections are still devoted to fables and anecdotes.

20. Like the selection of Dickens, those from Keller and Hugo were well-suited to the DDR's progressive purposes. Keller's story—a masterpiece of realistic fiction—appealed to SED educators because it could be turned into a critique of class pride and bourgeois conventions: a tailor's apprentice dresses in the clothes of the gentry and is ultimately unmasked as an imposter—but not before being mistakenly feted by the town's pompous gullible dignitaries as a visiting aristocrat. Keller was also an approved author because he had been the subject of an admiring 1947 study by the renowned Hungarian Marxist scholar-critic, Georg Lukács.

Throughout the post-war era, *Gavroche* was a school requirement in the communist world, and the DDR in particular treated Hugo as a nineteenth-century Mayakovsky: a poet of the Revolution. The eight-year-old Gavroche is the prototype of the "little person" who revolts. Derived from Hugo's *Les Miserables* (1862), the novella features a plucky street urchin who dies a heroic death as he aids the populist students at the barricades during France's nineteenth-century post-revolutionary uprisings.

21. *Unser Lesebuch. Klasse 7* (1964 [1962]); *Literatur. Klasse 7. Unterrichtshilfen* (1978), 100, 111–12; *Unser Lesebuch 7*, 208. On Becher's poem, which was written in 1949 to celebrate the founding of what the new government called the First German Workers' and Peasants' State, the teaching guide advises: "[Pupils] should adopt the conviction of the poet that 'such a state'—their Fatherland—must receive the comprehensive approval of all classes and groups of the People. And they feel pride as citizens of such a state—and a sense of obligation to represent this state via actions and with a perception of their rights and duties."

One imagines that "The Great October" would rather have been forgotten by such a hardened cynic as Brecht. Written in 1937, on the twentieth anniversary of the October Revolution ("O great October of the working class!"), the poem is not just embarrassing but corrupt: a hymn to Soviet Russia ("Moscow, the famous capital of all workers") at the very height of the purges and show trials.

> Since then the world has Hope.
> The comrade in Wales and the Manchurian coolie
> and the Pennsylvania worker, who lives worse than a dog
> and the German worker, my brother, whom everyone still envies
> They all know, there is
> an October.

22. *Literaturunterricht 5* (1979), 27–29.

23. Ibid., 29.

24. *Unsere Muttersprache 7* (1979), 15–16; *Unsere Muttersprache. Klasse 8*, 36, 42.

25. *Unsere Muttersprache 7* (1979), 15–16, 30–31; *Unsere Muttersprache 8* (1979 [1969]), 36, 42.

26. *Unsere Muttersprache 7* (1977 [1968]), 30–31.

27. Ibid., 39.

28. Ibid., 135.

29. *Muttersprache 5* (1968), 121.
30. *Unsere Muttersprache 2* (1979), 13, 24.
31. *Unsere Muttersprache 9 und 10* (1979 [1970]), 10, 98.
32. *Unsere Muttersprache 9 und 10*, 28, 46.
33. *Arbeit am Ausdruck Klasse 9/10* (1977 [1975]), 164, 171.
34. *Unterrichtshilfen Deutsch 4* [1977], 183–86, 196.
35. *Unterrichtshilfen Deutsch 2* [1977], 130.
36. *Unterrichtshilfen Deutsch 2* [1977], 136.
37. *Unterrichtshilfen Deutsch 2* [1977], 15. For a more extensive discussion of the DDR's "hate pedagogy," see "Education for Hatred" in Chapter Three.
38. *Deutsch Muttersprache Klasse 6. Unterrichtshilfen*, 146.
39. *Deutsch. Muttersprache. Klasse 5. Unterrichtshilfen* [1971], 72–73.
40. *Arbeit am Ausdruck 9/10* [1975], 124.
41. *Arbeit am Ausdruck 9/10* [1975], 151.
42. *Unsere Muttersprache 8* [1979], 5.
43. *Heimatkunde 3* [1979], 3–6; *Heimatkunde 4* [1979], 188–90.
44. *Unterrichtshilfen Deutsch 4*, 145.
45. Quoted in *Bildungspolitik in der DDR, 1963–76*, ed. Siegfried Baske (Wiesbaden: Harrassowitz, 1979), 253.
46. Dr. Werner Lindner, 5 October 1961. Quoted in Baske, *Bildungspolitik in der DDR, 1963–76*, 287.
47. For instance, "Somebody Has To Risk It," the story of Hennecke's exploits in October 1948 and how he became a "Hero of Labor." *Heimatkunde 3*, 84–86.
48. The phrase is from Lionel Trilling, "Reality in America," in *The Liberal Imagination: Essays on Literature and Society* (New York: Viking Press, 1950), 11.
49. *Unser Lesebuch. Klasse 5* (1979 [1966]), 166.
50. *Unterrichtshilfen Deutsch 2* (1977) advises the teacher: "The students should take up such persons as models" (11). When *Heimatkunde* teachers addressed the topic of the Wall and its erection, their goal was to make even more explicit the message that the stories of military heroism in the primers delivered: "We boys will replace the soldiers." *Unterrichtshilfen Deutsch 4* explicitly instructed teachers:

> Goal: Pupils can prove why it is especially necessary to protect the Berlin state border. They recognize that on August 13, 1961, the National People's Army blocked the route of the enemy to our Republic and protected us from invasion. An emotionally effective class presentation will develop feelings of security and trust toward our border soldiers. Our border soldiers are proud to protect our Republic. . . .
> The teachers should inspire the pupil to activities (diligent study and socially useful work, visits to the border soldiers, letters to a unit, etc). He should lead the pupil to the insight: We boys will replace the soldiers. It is an honor to serve as a soldier on the border! (182–83)

51. *Lesebuch 4* (1978 [1977]), 63.
52. *Lesebuch 4* (1978 [1977]), 52–53.
53. *Lesebuch 4* (1978 [1977]), 51.
54. See, for instance, the poem "Socialist Competition," by Ho Chi Minh, in *Lesebuch 4*, 14.
55. The SPD heroes featured in the primers include Karl Liebknecht, Rosa Luxemburg, and August Bebel. The poem "Worth the Effort" in *Lesebuch 4* refers affectionately to the first pair as "Karl and Rosa" (53). See also the Liebknecht story in *Heimatkunde 4*, "Karl Liebknecht Fights Against the War," 100–102; and the Bebel story in *Lesebuch 4* (1978), "A Suitcase Full of Dynamite," 48–50.
56. *Lesebuch 4* (1977), 56–58.
57. For instance, "How Friedrich Engels Got to Know the Life of the English Worker,"

which portrays Engels's life in Manchester, and two Marx stories, "How Karl Marx Lived and Worked in London" and "A Diligent Reader," *Heimatkunde 4,* 82–86.

58. Occasionally a story or poem featuring President Otto Grotewohl, Rosa Luxemburg, or a minor figure in DDR or German socialist history also appears.

59. *Lesebuch 2* (1978 [1977]), 34.

60. *Lesebuch 3,* 64–66.

61. Krupskaya herself disputed the "many stories about [Lenin's] playful relations with children as sentimental twaddle." In truth, Lenin had little or no love even for Krupskaya—she begged him several times for a divorce, but he refused—let alone children or anyone else. "Sentimentality" was a favorite term of abuse for him.

Lenin was a pure, indeed obsessional, revolutionary. Other people were useful as comrades or dangerous as enemies. In fact, he avoided close attachments precisely because they might "inhibit ruthless actions." "Practically all the 'friends' who helped him were eventually discarded, often in a humiliating manner." Lenin had no time for friendship, intimacy, and even sexuality; probably the only person whom he ever treated with a modicum of gentleness was Inessa Armand, his sometime mistress.

Historians estimate that Lenin's rule cost at least 10 million people their lives: 200,000 to 1,500,000 people were killed through terror, 5 million perished from famine, and at least 4 million more died in the civil war.

The quotations and statistics are from Stefan Possony, *Lenin: The Compulsive Revolutionary* (Chicago: Regnery, 1964), 147, 360–61, 383–84, 387. New scholarship based on recently opened Soviet archives confirms these conclusions. Stalin's views on dictatorship, terror, the one-party state, the banning of elections, a secret police, and slave labor camps all originated with Lenin. See, for example, Hélène Carrere d'Encausse, *Lenin* (New York: Holmes and Meier, 2001) and Robert Service, *Lenin: A Biography* (Cambridge, Mass.: Harvard University Press, 2001).

62. *Lesebuch 4,* 148–49.

63. For example, the following stories: "The Visitor," "Lenin in Siberian Exile," and "The Overthrow of the Capitalists and Landowners in Russia," *Heimatkunde 4,* 92–100. Such stories are, generally, pure fantasy: Lenin never lived in a working-class urban district or even befriended workers, but rather lived his entire life among bourgeois intellectuals.

64. Mieskes, *Pädagogik der DDR,* 2: 381.

65. Ibid.

66. *Lesebuch 2,* 78.

67. *Lesebuch 4,* 72.

68. *Unser Lesebuch. 5. Schuljahr* (1965 [1959]), 5–6, 88–90.

69. Ziegelhaus is still today a pilgrimage site for elder PDS members and former SED officials.

70. *Leben, Singen, Kämpfen. Liederbuch der deutschen Jugend* (Berlin [East], 1954), 260.

71. Irma Thälmann's fortitude, grit, and endurance marked her as her father's daughter. She spent twenty-eight years in an ultimately futile effort to identify and punish her father's murderers. In 1986, Wolfgang Otto, a former Nazi SS sergeant suspected of the 1944 death camp execution of Thälmann, was found guilty of complicity in the murder. He was sentenced to four years, but the case was later overturned and he never served time. Otto, then seventy-eight, was a retired DDR schoolteacher who had been in charge of the Buchenwald camp office. (He was forced by DDR authorities to resign his teaching position in 1962, after Irma Thälmann's lawyers brought charges against him in connection with her father's murder.)

For her part, Irma also suffered during the war—and thereafter became a DDR celebrity. She herself was imprisoned in the Ravensbrück concentration camp. After the war ended, she was brought to Moscow for several months to recover her health. When she returned, she was immediately taken up by the SED as a symbolic figure. In 1990 she campaigned for the Bundestag in Friedrichshain on the ticket of the newly founded PDS.

See also the 8th-grade stories "Ernst Thälmann Shows a Peasant the Way" and "Encounter with Ernst Thälmann," *Unser Lesebuch. Klasse 8* (1964; 1959), 113–17, 121–23.

72. See *Ernst Thälmann. An Stalin. Briefe aus dem Zuchthaus 1939 bis 1941*, ed. Wolfram Adolphi and Jörn Schütrumf (Berlin: Dietz Verlag, 1996).

73. See "Wie ein Fest war es, wenn Thälmann im Beiwagen kam," *Frankfurter Allgemeine Zeitung*, 29 August 2000, 3. New details of the so-called Wittorf Affair are available in a recent second volume of Thälmann's correspondence with Stalin that covers the period mid-1927 to March 1929. See Hermann Weber and Bernhard H. Bayerlein, *Der Thälmann-Skandal. Geheime Korrespondenzen mit Stalin* (Berlin: Aufbau Verlag, 2003).

74. *Lesebuch 3*, 61–64; see also *Wilhelm Pieck: Unser Präsident* (Berlin: Kinderbuchverlag, 1954). In *Unser Lesebuch. 5. Schuljahr*,"Wilhelm Pieck's Apprenticeship" (another excerpt from Bartel's hagiography of Pieck) tells the story of Pieck's journeyman years at greater length (86–88). Young Wilhelm gains a worker's class consciousness through the apprenticeship, which opens his eyes to the exploitative practices of capitalism. The excerpt's title alludes to Goethe's "Wilhelm Meister's Apprenticeship" and contributes to the SED's aim of turning Pieck into a mythic character worthy of a *Bildungsroman*.

75. "Wilhelm Pieck is Back in the *Heimat*," *Heimatkunde 3*, 62–65.

76. *Heimatkunde 3*, 72–73, 74–75. A first-grade story from the 1950s, "Our President, Wilhelm Pieck," contained all the foregoing themes:

> Our president Wilhelm Pieck is a friend of children. He wants all children to be happy and healthy and smart. That's why they should learn in their beautiful schools and enjoy playing in their playgrounds.
>
> He wants children to get to know our beautiful Germany. That's why they should travel during holidays to the sea and the mountains and live in the camps of the Young Pioneers.
>
> He also visits schools. Children look forward to his visit and give him flowers. He says to boys and girls, "Study diligently! Become good workers! Then we can build up our Fatherland to be more and more beautiful."
>
> Our president is a friend of the workers. He himself was once a cabinet maker. Frequently he visits the People's Own Firms [state-run industries] and says to the workers:
>
> "These factories belong to all of us. When we work better, we'll live better. Think how you can work better! We need more machines, more clothes, more food, if everyone is to feel good."
>
> And the workers think it over together. They make a plan, and they reach [the norm] they have intended.
>
> Many persons, men and women from the city and country, visit our president in Berlin. They express their wishes to him. He listens to everyone, he speaks with everyone. He helps those whom he can help. That's why our people love our president Wilhelm Pieck.

77. Baske, *Bildungspolitik in der DDR, 1963–76*, 245.

78. Mieskes, *Pädagogik der DDR*, 2:244–46.

79. *Unser Lesebuch 5*, 54–56.

80. *Unser Lesebuch. 5. Schuljahr*, 97–98. Some stories also sought to burnish Ulbricht's antifascist record. For a story of Ulbricht's courageous outspokenness at a local Nazi Party meeting in 1931, see "How the Communists Fought Against the Fascists," *Heimatkunde 4*, 103–104.

81. *Neue Erziehung im Kindergarten*, July 1962, cited in Carola Stern, *Ulbricht: A Political Biography* (New York: Praeger, 1965), 193–94.

82. Quoted in *Literaturunterricht 9 und 10. Klasse* (1979), 8.

83. Ibid., 12–13.

84. Ibid., 13.

85. This change occurred after passage of the 1965 Education Act. For example, earlier editions of *Unser Lesebuch. 8. Schuljahr* (Berlin, 1964 [1959]), like the readers in lower grades, are

organized according to topics such as "From the Life of Boys and Girls in Our Republic" and "From the Struggle of the German Working Class."

86. *Unser Lesebuch. Klasse 8*, 122.
87. *Literatur. Klasse 8. Unterrichtshilfen* (1979), 66, 68
88. Ibid., 99, 103.
89. Ibid., 137.
90. *Lehrbuch für den Literaturunterricht in den Klassen 8–10. Zur Entwicklung der Literatur und bedeutenden Dichterpersönlichkeiten* (1979 [1974]), 181.
91. Ibid., 9.
92. Ibid., 16–17.
93. Ibid., 198–200.
94. *Literaturunterricht 9 und 10. Klasse* (1979), 65.
95. Ibid., 64–65.
96. Ibid., 69. See also *Lehrbuch für den Literaturunterricht 8–10*, 193–97.
97. *Literaturunterricht 9 und 10. Klasse*, 22–23.
98. *Lehrbuch für den Literaturunterricht 8–10*, 126–34.
99. Freely adapted from Gorky's novel *The Mother*, Brecht's play was, according to the teaching guide, "the first work in which the principles of socialist realism are fully worked out." A portrayal of the early years of the Russian revolutionary underground, the play also marks Brecht's "transition from an anti-bourgeois position to the *Weltanschauung* of the revolutionary worker class." It depicts an illiterate working-class woman who is converted to the revolutionary cause, opens her heart to all Humanity, and seeks to educate the People by distributing propaganda literature: the mother is a metaphor for the Party, through which the masses will be reborn. The teaching guide stresses the importance of the play's production history: it opened in Berlin on the thirteenth anniversary of Rosa Luxemburg's death, and more than 150,000 German working-class women saw it during its Berlin run. *Lehrbuch für den Literaturunterricht 8–10*, 180–81.

Gorky's *The Mother* was also frequently an upper-grade POS assignment. For insight into the recommended pedagogical approach, see "Love of Man and Hatred Toward His Enemies," *Lehrbuch für den Literaturunterricht 8–10*, 162–64.

100. Noll's novel was widely read in the DDR. It deals with the fate of a young German who tries to build a new life for himself after service in the *Wehrmacht*. For the approved pedagogical approach to Noll, see *Lehrbuch für den Literaturunterricht 8–10*, 211–12.
101. Ibid., 114.
102. *Lehrbuch für den Literaturunterricht 8–10*, 193.
103. *Literaturunterricht 9 und 10. Klasse*, 128–33.
104. Ibid., 133.
105. Ibid., 120–21, 127, 193.
106. It is worth mentioning the difference between the textbook "collectives" of the Soviet era and how this process is undergoing change in post-Soviet Russia. For example, the 1996 *Russkaia literatura* for tenth graders indicates that the publishing house Prosveshchenie contracted Yuri Lebedev, an individual author, to produce the textbook. The one-author system reflects a shift to a more Western model of textbook production. However, both volumes of the 1996 *Russkaia literatura* for eleventh graders list more than twenty authors as contributors. Such diversity indicates that textbook production in Russia is a hybrid of Soviet and Western practices, a mix of communism and capitalism that reflects the competing ideologies and methodologies also prevailing in other Russian institutions of the post-Soviet era.
107. N. N. Shneidman, *Literature and Ideology in Soviet Education* (Toronto: Lexington Books), 333.
108. N. N. Shneidman, "Soviet Approaches to the Teaching of Literature," *Canadian Slavonic Papers* 15.3 (1973): 332.
109. Yuri Lebedev, *Russkaia literatura, desiatyi klass* [Russian literature textbook for the tenth grade] (Moscow: Prosveshchenie, 1996), 296.
110. Shneidman, *Literature and Ideology in Soviet Education*, 47.

111. Ibid., 48.
112. R. F. Christian, *Tolstoy: A Critical Introduction* (Cambridge: Cambridge University Press, 1969), 145–46.
113. G. Struve, "Tolstoy in Soviet Criticism," *Russian Review* 19.2 (1960): 181.
114. Shneidman, *Literature and Ideology in Soviet Education*, 52.
115. Ibid., 337.
116. Shneidman asks: "What about the university student who studies the foundations of Marxism-Leninism and is being trained to approach a work of literature from a class point of view, and realizes that, in spite of the fact that *War and Peace* conceptualizes the common people and the problem of the masses, the main characters in the plot are not people belonging to the camp of the oppressed and those deprived of civil rights?" "Soviet Approaches to the Teaching of Literature," 338.
117. The textbook states: "The fundamental contradiction in Tolstoy's world view—the contradiction between his spiritual aspiration to unite with the *narod*, i.e., to live with their interests while denying the revolutionary path of the liberation of the people—intensifies in the years of the new revolutionary situation (1879–1881)." B. I. Bursov, *Russkaia literatura, deviatyi klass* . . . [Russian literature textbook for the ninth grade] (Moscow: Prosveshchenie, 1973), 273.
118. When justifying the salvaging and use of many nineteenth-century authors who were in fact aristocrats, one Soviet scholar explains:

> In reality classes are not isolated from one another, but find themselves in a complex interaction. Owing to this, the ideologies of writers belonging to different classes often have, along with marked differences, similar, common traits. These similar, sometimes common, traits are the reason for the fact that a writer, while being a representative of a certain class, also expresses to a degree the feelings, moods, strivings, and interests of persons belonging to other classes. (Shneidman, *Literature and Ideology in Soviet Education*, 36

119. Bursov, *Russkaia Literatura, deviatyi klass*, 274.
120. Consider also the introductory statement in the 1991 Syllabus for General Institutions of Learning: "The goal of literature education is to shape the spiritual world of a person, the creation of the conditions for the formation of the inner needs of the personality for continuous improvement, to realize each person's creative potential." *Programmy dlia srednikh obshcheobrazovatel'nykh uchebnykh zavedenii—literatura* [Syllabus for secondary school general institutions of learning—literature] (Moscow: Prosveshchenie, n.d.), 41. Compare the above statement to the first sentence a student encounters in the 1973 ninth-grade literature textbook: "The history of progressive Russian literature cannot be separated from the history of the liberation movement in Russia" (Bursov, *Russkaia Literatura, deviatyi klass*, 5).
121. Lebedev, *Russkaia Literatura, desiatyi klass*, 296.
122. Ibid.
123. See the table of contents to *Literatur. Klassen 11 und 12* (Berlin, 1980), 3–14.
124. Freya Klier, *Lüg Vaterland: Erziehung in der DDR* (Berlin: Kindler, 1990).
125. I am grateful to Frau Bärbel Hintze of the Friedrich Schiller Gymnasium in Weimar for sharing these examination materials with me.

CHAPTER 2. TERRA VERDE, TERRA RUSSO: GEOGRAPHY

1. Early editions of the fifth-grade geography text, *Lehrbuch der Erdkunde für die 5. Klasse* (1968 [1966]), were subtitled "The German Democratic Republic, Our Socialist Fatherland." Here and elsewhere, M-L educators, following Stalin, conveniently forgot Marx and Engels's ringing words in the *Communist Manifesto* that a communist "has no fatherland."
2. See *Atlas der Erdkunde: Für die allgemeinbildenden polytechnischen Oberschulen* (1968 [1962]). A related "march" is depicted later in the atlas via four historical maps (1914, 1922, 1949,

1961). They highlight "socialist countries" in bright red and "young nations" (newly independent states) in pink. The map is titled: "The Collapse of the Imperialist Colonial System in Africa and Asia."

3. *Geographie 5* (1980 [1977]), 6.
4. *Unterrichtshilfen für den Geographieunterricht in der 5. Klasse*, 10–11, 19.
5. *Geographie 5*, 51.
6. *Unterrichtshilfen für den Geographieunterricht in der 5. Klasse* (1967), 161.

7. The SED abolished the old *Land* system of German states and principalities in 1952. It was formally reintroduced to eastern Germany after German reunification in October 1990.

8. In the first edition of 1960, however—before de-Stalinization swept the DDR—the city is still referred to as "Stalinstadt." The strong ideological flavor of the 1960 text reflects the historical crisis of the moment. Whereas the 1980 edition stresses the close working relationship between Eisenhüttenstadt and iron ore locales in the Soviet Union, the 1960 edition treats Stalinstadt as a showcase city of socialism:

> A new and beautiful city, Stalinstadt, has been built in the vicinity of the iron ore factory in a former forest area.
>
> In Stalinstadt there are only HO- and consumer stores. They are, like all buildings of the city, socialist property. All skilled workers—tailors, carpenters, painters, etc—are also members of comrade associations. That is why Stalinstadt is a socialist city, the first of our Republic. It is a model for our socialist cities. (*Lehrbuch der Erdkunde für die 5. Klasse*, 1960, 1966)

9. *Geographie 5* (1980), 11.

10. Chapters on other cities are similar. For instance, the chapter on Dresden opens: "Dresden was cruelly destroyed on February 13, 1945, by American and English bombers. In a single night, the city was transformed into a river of flames. Tens of thousands of people were killed, irreplaceable cultural objects were destroyed." *Geographie 5* (1967 [1966]), 167.

The 1960 edition goes even further in its denunciation of the bombings, and it concludes by thanking "our Soviet friends" for refurbishing the "art treasures" of the Dresden Art Museum: "Every visitor, when viewing the paintings, should be reminded of the magnanimous deed of our friends, the Soviets" (33). The text makes no mention of how Dresden's art treasures wound up in the USSR in the first place (the Soviet occupation army seized hundreds of paintings), or that the USSR refused to return many paintings and charged the DDR exorbitant prices for those they did return.

11. *Geographie für die 5. Klasse. Unsere Deutsche Demokratische Republik* (1967 [1966]), 52–53. The language was even stronger in the 1960 edition: "Through the fault of the imperialists, Berlin is divided into two parts" (70).

The units on Berlin and other cities, in all editions of fifth-grade geography textbooks, offer sketches of urban history in order to show the revolutionary progress of socialism. DDR cities went from rubble in 1945 to "modern socialist cities" by the 1960s. The fifth-grade teaching guide also stresses that pupils should "understand that Berlin was largely destroyed in the Second World War and that our capital, through systematic work, has been wonderfully rebuilt" (68). Similarly, the "formerly backward area of Mecklenburg has developed into a modern rural and industrial *Bezirk*" (50).

12. *Geographie für die 5. Klasse*, 53.
13. Ibid., 52.
14. Ibid., 161.
15. *Geographie 6* (1979 [1975]), 8.

16. I am reminded of a casual remark to me by a Humboldt university student in 1990, as we rode the subway in East Berlin and discussed his schooldays: "Every time I looked at the Tower of Nations clock"—which features a map of the world's time zones—"I was reminded that I couldn't travel."

During my school visits to the POS and EOS that fall, teachers and pupils told me much the same about geography class: for many of them, it had been a constant reminder, particularly when it covered the topic of KA, of what they *couldn't* do. It reminded them that they might never be able to visit their *republikflüchtig* brother in West Germany or their relatives in America. It reminded them of the wonders of the world that they might never glimpse, except on their television sets. And thus, like the East Berlin clock, it was cause for anger.

17. *Geographie 6* (1960), 9–10. As elsewhere, the 1960 edition makes a similar point in stronger language via a story of a delegation of DDR coal miners who visit the BRD:

"The people speak German like us at home. Here too there are signs and billboards. But they say: 'Drink Coca-Cola! Tank up with Shell!' No flags on the houses, no word about peace and reunification. We realize: Yes, we've crossed the border all right!" (5).

18. *Geographie 6,* 10. *Arbeitsmaterialien 6,* a seatwork handbook that featured questions based on maps, has several exercises of the same sort. This handbook series was in use in all grades of POS geography.

19. *Geographie 6,* 55.
20. Ibid., 91–92.
21. Ibid., 98–99.
22. Ibid., 166.
23. *Geographie. Lehrbuch für Klasse 7* (Berlin (1980 [1968]), 10–11.
24. *Geographie. Klasse 7. Unterrichtshilfen* (1978 [1968]), 12, 29. Teachers are advised to show a film about the Russian Revolution, *The Russian Miracle.* Here and elsewhere, teachers should stress the "legacy" that young socialists have inherited from the revolutionaries of 1917 and "the overwhelming successes in all areas of life" that the USSR has achieved. The teaching guide makes clear that geography teachers belong to the cultural cadre:

> A strong accent on the emotional moment [1917] should flow from the teacher with an exemplary partisan demeanor. The teacher can fulfill the assignment of the syllabus, which should build [these] convictions [in youth]: Strengthen feelings of friendship toward the Soviet Union, heighten pupils' respect for the achievements of the Soviet working people, educate technicians and scientists and produce certainty in them of the firm alliance between our *Volk* and the peoples of the Soviet Union. (35)

25. *Geographie. Klasse 7. Unterrichtshilfen* (1st ed., 1968), 133.
26. *Geographie. Lehrbuch für Klasse 7,* 130.
27. *Geographie. Lehrbuch für Klasse 7* (1st ed., 1968), 155.
28. *Geographie. Klasse 7. Unterrichtshilfen* (5th ed., 1978), 13.
29. *Geographie. Lehrbuch für Klasse 7* (1st ed., 1968), 155, 159
30. *Geographie 8* (1979 [1969]). See also the detailed unit on Cuba, titled "The First Socialist State of the Americas," 166–73. Among the "educational emphases" of the Cuba unit, notes the eighth-grade teaching guide, should be:

—Education toward Hatred against aggressive U.S. imperialism and strengthened conviction of the unstoppable march of socialism.
—Deepening of the perception that oppressed and exploited peoples will win their political and economic independence through the revolutionary transformation of productive relations.
—Strengthening of the recognition that, under socialist relations, the consequences of imperialistic exploitation and oppression can be quickly overcome. (115)

31. *Geographie 8* (1979), 9–10.
32. But this explanation is cited as just a single instance in the chapter's list of the eleven "neocolonial methods of the imperialistic countries." The 1978 teaching guide, *Geographie. Klasse 8 Unterrichtshilfen* (1978), conveniently summarizes them:

1. Export of capital (foreign or "developmental" aid) with political and economic stipulations.
2. Export of capital or investments of monopolies in order to take control of the economy.

3. Exploitation of dependence on exports and imports for economic and political blackmail.
4. Support of reactionary forces (including the preparation of putsches against progressive governments).
5. Dispatch of advisors and educators to expand political and economic influence.
6. Military aid (arms and advisors) to influence the military apparatus.
7. Ideological poisoning through the distribution of anti-communist and pro-capitalist ideas.
8. Support of right-wing political parties and labor unions as opposing forces to progressive movements.
9. Exploitation of cultural, religious, and economic institutions of the imperialistic states for ideological, political, and economic influence.
10. Joint measures of the imperialistic states through the use of collective institutions (e.g., the World Bank) and alliances (e.g., the Common Market).
11. Classical methods of colonialism also applied (e.g., aggression). (64)

33. *Geographie. Klasse 8 Unterrichtshilfen*, 63.
34. *Geographie 8*, 72–75, 78.
35. *Geographie. Klasse 8. Unterrichtshilfen*, 15.
36. *Geographie 8*, 111.
37. *Geographie. Klasse 8. Unterrichtshilfen*, 73, 85.
38. *Geographie 8*, 86–88.
39. Ibid., 109, 111.
40. Ibid., 110–11, 126. Exercises in the 1968 edition also alert pupils to "important concepts" such as "conglomerate," "slum quarter," "seasonal worker," "exhaustion of the soil," "soil erosion," "petrochemical," "plantation," "slave system," "racial discrimination," "land reform," "indentured servitude," and "great estates"(105–40).
41. Ibid., 135–36, 145.
42. *Geographie. Klasse 8. Unterrichtshilfen*, 69, 73.
43. Letter to the author from Stefan Schwarzkopf, 6 May 2004.
44. *Geographie. Unterrichtshilfen. 9. Klasse* (1978), 113. An earlier edition of the ninth-grade geography textbook, *Lehrbuch der Erdkunde für die 9. Klasse. Grundzüge der allgemeinen physischen Erdkunde* (1961), was more concrete and went further:

> The Soviet Union and China show us most clearly how Nature can be changed for the welfare of all people and, through the careful respect for natural laws, the geographical milieu can be constantly improved. In our DDR too, the first socialist state on German soil, we can almost daily gather examples of this. That gives us the certainty that a restructuring of nature, through a thorough knowledge of all her appearances and contexts, is only possible in socialism. (132)

45. *Geographie. Klasse 9. Unterrichtshilfen* (1978), 6.
46. See *Lehrbuch der Erdkunde für die 9. Klasse. Ökonomische Geographie sozialistischer Länder* (4th ed., 1967).
47. See *Geographie 10. Ökonomische Geographie der sozialistischen Staatengemeinschaft und der DDR* (2nd ed., 1979); and *Ökonomische Geographie der beiden deutschen Staaten. 9. Klasse* (6th ed., 1967).
48. *Ökonomische Geographie der beiden deutschen Staaten 9. Klasse* (1967), 107–17.
49. *Geographie 10. Ökonomische Geographie der sozialistischen Staatengemeinschaft und der DDR*, 5–6.
50. *Geographie 10. Ökonomische Geographie der sozialistischen Staatengemeinschaft und der DDR*, 9.
51. *Geographie. Klasse 10. Unterrichtshilfen* (1979 [1978]), 37, 47, 97.
52. See *Lehrbuch der ökonomischen Geographie. Klasse 10a, 10c, 11b* (4th ed., 1967).
53. See "Cuba's National Democratic Road of Development from a Half-Colony to the

Building of Socialism," *Lehrbuch der ökonomischen Geographie. Klasse 11a, 11c, 12b,* 5th ed. (1967), 121–32.

54. *Lehrheft der Erdkunde für die 11. Klasse der erweiterten Oberschule, Teil II* (1961), quoted in Peter R. Lucke, *Lehrbuch der Erdkunde in der Sowjetzone* (Berlin, 1964), 45.

CHAPTER 3. MY COUNTRY, LEFT OR WRONG? CIVICS

1. *Staatsbürgerkunde. 7. Klasse. Unterrichtshilfen* (1976 [1974]), 10.
2. See Gerhard Moldenhauer, "2 x Deutschland, 2 x politische Bildung," *Schulpraxis* 6 (1989).
3. On the early history of *Staatsbürgerkunde* as a school subject, see Siebert, *"Bildung"spraxis in Deutschland.*
4. Until the mid-1970s, *Staatsbürgerkunde* began in the eighth grade, where it was chiefly devoted to an intensive history of Marxism and SED policies. Pupils learned that "the names of the great Germans MARX and ENGELS are eternalized in human history." The text briefly discusses utopian socialists such as Fourier and (purported) forefathers of Marxism such as Thomas More and Tomasso Campanella. Several units are given over to the work of Marx and Engels after the revolutions of 1848–49, to Lenin's "world-historical achievement," and even to the "democratic school reform" in the SBZ. *Staatsbürgerkunde 1: Weg und Ziel des Sozialismus in der DDR* (1968).
5. Historical events were, however, addressed in order to inflame socialist patriotism. As the teaching guide specified: "The teacher reactivates pupils' knowledge about the danger of BRD imperialism, which tried in 1953 and 1961, with the help of world imperialism to destroy our Workers' and Peasants' State and to devour the DDR. It is well established that leading BRD politicians do indeed constantly speak of their love of peace, but their plans for armaments speak another language." *Unterrichtshilfen. 8. Klasse. Staatsbürgerkunde* (1975).
6. *Staatsbürgerkunde* (2nd ed., 1978), 26, 56, 62. The *Staatsbürgerkunde* texts contain very few examples of wisdom from "real existing workers." A lone example from *Staatsbürgerkunde 8* (1978 [1977]) is from Comrade Friedrich Lehmann, a skilled worker in the printing factory "Victory" in Heidenau: "Through good work, we earn time and money, more joy in daily life, and an ever higher reputation with our partners abroad" (12).
7. *Unterrichtshilfen. 8. Klasse. Staatsbürgerkunde,* 22, 26, 27, 72, 136.
8. Ibid., 26.
9. In a supplementary text, pupils were also introduced to many primary sources in their entirety. For instance, *Staatsbürgerkunde 9 und 10. Dokumente und Materialien* (1976) includes Engels's eulogy of Marx, seven different prefaces to various language editions (including Polish and Italian) of the *Communist Manifesto,* lengthy selections from Lenin, and Honecker's 1976 report to the SED Ninth Party Congress.
10. See *Staatsbürgerkunde. Klasse 9. Unterrichtschilfen* (1979 [1975]), 20–21.
11. See Kurt Schneider, *Staatsbürgerkunde* (1968 [1966]), 7.
12. *Staatsbürgerkunde 9* (1979 [1977]), 14. But the quotations from Ulbricht about Marx, which appeared in chapter one in earlier editions, are gone—as are all quotations and references to Ulbricht (and also Pieck) in the 1979 edition.

For comparison, see *Staatsbürgerkunde 9* (1st ed., 1970), in which Ulbricht is quoted dozens of times (more often than even Lenin) and pictured holding a tapestry of Thälmann. Pieck is depicted tutoring a girl on the cover of this edition.

13. *Staatsbürgerkunde. Klasse 9. Unterrichtschilfen,* 26, 27, 34, 70, 72.
14. In editions of ninth-grade *Staatsbürgerkunde* from the 1960s, "socialist morality" is also briefly covered. See *Staatsbürgerkunde 2. Der umfassende Aufbau des Sozialismus* (1968), 115–25.
15. *Staatsbürgerkunde 10* (1971), 6–7, 9, 137–38.
16. *Staatsbürgerkunde 3: Die sozialistische Weltanschauung* (1983), 200.
17. Ibid., 204–5.
18. *Staatsbürgerkunde 10* (1971), 241, 243, 245, 248.

19. *Staatsbürgerkunde 10* (2nd ed., 1983), 163.
20. *Staatsbürgerkunde. Klasse 10.Unterrichtshilfen* (1979), 90, 91, 99, 140, 141, 143, 176, 180–81, 183, 185, 198, 200, 223–24, 226, 230/
21. *Staatsbürgerkunde. 7. Klasse. Unterrichtshilfen* (1976 [1974]), 10.
22. *Staatsbürgerkunde 2. Der umfassende Aufbau des Sozialismus* (1968), 144, 200.
23. See Mieskes, *Pädagogik der DDR*, 2:308. On socialist patriotism, see *Zwei Jahrzehnte Bildungspolitik in der Sowjetzone Deutschlands*, ed. Siegfried Baske and Martha Engelbert (Berlin: Freie Universität, 1966), 238–41. On the pedagogy of love and hate, see Möbus, *Unterwerfung durch Erziehung*, 132–40, 173–82.
24. The portrayal of heroic workers, which formed a significant part of *Heimatkunde*, continues in the historically oriented units of seventh-grade *Staatsbürgerkunde*. For instance, chapter two relates the story of early post-war eastern Germany. "Sunrise in the East" is the theme. The exploits of Adolf Hennecke, the "coal-pit comrade," are discussed in detail, accompanied by a large photo of Hennecke, "a model for the new attitude toward work" distinguished with the title "Hero of Labor." Hennecke's "example," we are told, "led to a quick increase in production results." The text also dwells on a female "Hennecke," the weaver Frida Hockauf, who in September 1953 produced forty-five meters more fabric than her previous best. She is credited having said, "How we work today will be how we live tomorrow!" which became an SED slogan during the first Five-Year Plan (1951–55). Even three young "Henneckes"—two male lathe operators and one female lamp maker—are exalted as *"Aktivisten." Staatsbürgerkunde 7* (1979 [1978]).
25. Ibid., 10–12.
26. Ibid., 89.
27. Ibid., 94–95.
28. Ibid., 96.
29. Ibid., 99, 103.
30. On the contribution expected of the music curriculum to *weltanschauliche Erziehung*, see, for example *Unterrichtshilfen Musik. 5 und 6. Klasse* (1st ed., 1973). The chapter titles of this text indicate its ideological emphasis: "The Pioneer Song in the Life of the Pupils' Collective"; "Workers' Songs and Marches in their Social Significance"; "Pioneer Songs for Holidays and Friendship Rallies." For further discussion of ideological uses to which music education was put in DDR schools, see the interview with Frau Christine Ehspanner, a former POS music teacher, in Chapter 6.
31. Louis Fürnberg, "Unser Lied," in *Leben, Singen, Kämpfen. Liederbuch der FDJ*. 12th ed. (Leipzig: F. Hofmeister, 1973), 28.
32. *Staatsbürgerkunde 7*, 158. The *Staatsbürgerkunde* textbooks also contain lists and summaries of similar "recommended books," many of which focus on the duty to put state above personal loyalty. Among the works were the following:

1. Peter Jacobs, *Weil ich Jane Fonda bin: Absage an eine Traumfabrik* (Berlin, 1976). Based on interviews with Jane Fonda by an East German journalist, this book spotlights Fonda's anti-war activism and criticism of American values during the Vietnam War, both of which make her, as the jacket cover puts it, "an ally in the worldwide anti-imperialist battle" and "an example of healthy-minded youth in capitalist countries."
2. *No Turning Back for Elke* (Berlin, 1974). In this book, a POS pupil discovers her brother is making espionage drops for a West German agent. She is uncertain about whether to tell the Stasi or wait until he turns himself in—or gets caught. "Her indecisiveness almost costs her boyfriend, who works as a border soldier, his life."
3. *Out of the Clouds* (Berlin, 1970). Here, a lieutenant is worried about his new bride. He travels to see her, forgetting that he is on military alert. This leads to "conflicts between him and the collective in his bomber fighter unit."

33. *Staatsbürgerkunde 9* (1970), 64–65. Brecht's song and a lithograph specially made to illustrate it by DDR sculptor Fritz Cremer are also included in this textbook (22).
34. Ibid., 246.

35. Ibid., 106.
36. Ibid., 165.
37. *Staatsbürgerkunde. Klasse 9.Unterrichtshilfen* (1979 [1975]), 229.
38. Or consider the poem "Learn from Lenin," in which a child declares that the greatest dead saint of communism preached not only a gospel of love but also hate:

> I've looked it up
> in books about him—
> and I'd like to tell you:
> Learn from Lenin!
> He could hate—
> he defended against betrayal
> and taught the masses to battle boldly.
> His hatred was his sharpest sword.
>
> I've looked it up in books about him—
> and I'd like to tell you
> Learn from Lenin!
> He could love—
> He had the brightest sunshine
> radiating into the heart of the People.
> His was a life like bread and wine.

Both the poem and the Thälmann song are quoted in Möbus, *Unterwerfung durch Erziehung*, 135–36.

39. *Leben, Singen, Kämpfen*, 30.
40. Quoted in Baske and Englebert, *Zwei Jahrzehnte Bildungspolitik in der Sowjetzone Deutschlands*, 245.
41. See Siebert, *"Bildung"spraxis in Deutschland*, 23.
42. Baske, *Bildungspolitik in der DDR, 1963–76*, 262, 350, 359.
43. Ibid., 301.
44. Among the most popular NVA documentaries designed for use in DDR schools were *Trained to Triumph* (about a group of artillerymen), *I'm Going to Be an Officer* (about an NVA company commander), *Nobody Is a Born Hero* (about how dedicated Pioneers become heroic soldiers), *Tomorrow's Soldiers* (about how GST training prepares for good soldiering), and *A Dialogue with Friedrich Engels* (about "the first military theoretician of the working class"). See *Wehrkunde in der DDR: Die neue Regelung ab 1. September 1978* (East Berlin: Hohwecht, 1978), 134–36.
45. Quoted in *Wehrkunde in der DDR*, 90.
46. Quoted in Thomas Beck, *Liebe zum Sozialismus, Hass auf den Klassenfeind: Sozialistisches Wehrmotiv und Wehrerziehung in der DDR* (Berlin: Ost-Akademie, 1983), 58–59. On the revival of the *Erziehung zum Hass* programs in the 1970s and 1980s, see Ulrike Enders, "Erziehung zum Hass," *Kirche im Sozialismus* 2 (1987).

CHAPTER 4. PROGRESSIVE LESSONS OF THE PAST: HISTORY

1. Mieskes, *Pädagogik der DDR*, 2:233.
2. *Geschichte 5* (10th ed., 1980), 5, 6.
3. Ibid.
4. Ibid., 48–49. DDR historians did not use reckonings such as BC or AD, but rather the secular *v.u.Z.* (*vor unserer Zeitrechnung*, before our chronology).
5. Ibid., 32.
6. Ibid., 50.
7. Ibid., 76–77.

8. Ibid., 112.
9. Ibid.
10. Ibid., 59, 71, 123, 126.
11. Ibid., 129.
12. *Geschichte: Lehrbuch für die Abiturstufe.* (1989), part 1, 72.
13. *Geschichte 6* (1968), 9–10.
14. *Geschichte 6* (1980), 28, 159.
15. *Geschichte 6* (1966), 131, 193. The 1954 edition of *Lehrbuch für den Geschichtsunterricht. 6. Schuljahr* is much tougher on Luther, even titling one subsection "Luther's Betrayal of the Peasants" (153).
16. *Geschichte 7* (1980 [1968]), 124.
17. Ibid., 226.
18. Indeed, whole units of sixth- and seventh-grade history are devoted to analyzing Engels's remark (from *The German Peasants' War*) that Luther was "a lightning bolt that struck" European history, or to passages from his impressionistic book, written when he was twenty-three and a newly arrived immigrant in Britain, *The Condition of the English Working Classes in 1844*.
19. *Geschichte 7* (1980 [1968]), 72, 73, 88.
20. I should note, however, that by the 1970s, West German textbooks also focused on the twentieth century—even if not so heavily as did DDR history books and with a lighter version of the Whiggish interpretation of history.

Nonetheless, the similar emphasis on modern history does have a historical explanation. The traumatic experiences of emerging from two world wars and living under a murderous regime between 1933 and 1945 ultimately led both the West and the East German societies to adopt the same heavy focus on teaching twentieth-century history. As if to follow an extreme variant of the *Sonderwegsthese,* the historiographical thesis postulating modern Germany's "special path" of development, West German history textbooks since the 1970s concentrated on contemporary history and culminated in the foundation of the West Germans state as the true and only heir of the full breadth of German history. The rupture of German civilization between 1933 and 1945 resulted in a near-obsessive focus on the present in both German societies.

21. Even for fifth graders studying prehistoric and ancient civilizations, the priority of contemporary socialist history was made explicit. *Geschichte 5* closes with the observation:

> There are many important events in history, and we must know when—on what date—they occurred.
> Every student knows:
> 1949 was the founding of the German Democratic Republic.
> 1945 was the end of the Second World War and liberation of the German *Volk* from fascism.
> 1917 was the Great Socialist October Revolution. (120)

Moreover, to elucidate the reckoning of historical chronology and concepts such as *v.u.Z.* and "century," the editors of *Geschichte 5* repeatedly ask questions such as: "In which century did the revolt of Spartacus take place?" "How many years ago did the revolt of Spartacus begin?" "How many years before the revolt of Spartacus did Hammurabi reign?"

22. *Geschichte 8* (1979 [1969]), 5.
23. Ibid., 46, 111.
24. *Geschichte 8. Klasse 8. Unterrichtshilfen* (1979 [1969]), 131, 135.
25. *Geschichte 8* (1970), 139.
26. Ibid., 77. The text makes it clear that a successful class struggle can only be waged by a Leninist "party of the new type," i.e., a workers' party allied with the peasants and all other working people. (Significantly, however, despite extensive attention devoted to German socialists such as Rosa Luxemburg, the text omits mention of her numerous strategic and philosophical disagreements with Lenin.)

27. Ibid., 88.

28. *Lesebuch 4*, 42–44.

29. Of special interest is the repeated effort by the textbook writers to depict Marx the scholar as a "brain worker." Here and elsewhere, the textbooks stress that Marx plowed through more than 1,500 books to write *Das Kapital;* when asked about Marx, a librarian of the British Museum tells a patron in "A Diligent Reader": "For many years Dr. Marx has worked day after day here, at least ten hours. He is the most diligent and most punctual worker that I have ever seen in this library. And I've been here twenty years, sir, so I know my patrons!" (85)

30. Frank Manuel, *A Requiem for Karl Marx* (Cambridge, Mass: Harvard University Press, 1995).

31. *Geschichte 8* (1979), 23–24. See H. F. Peters, *Red Jenny: A Life with Karl Marx* (London: Allen & Unwin, 1986), 101–66; Yvonne Kapp, "Karl Marx's Children: Family Life 1844–55," in *Karl Marx: 100 Years* (London, 1983), 273–85; and Yvonne Kapp, *Eleanor Marx* (London: Pantheon, 1972).

32. For the foregoing examples, see *Geschichte 11* (1968).

33. Meanwhile, the ninth-grade teaching guide suggests discussions such as the following: "Explain the statement of Lenin: 'The Soviet Union is a million times more democratic than any democratic bourgeois republic!'" *Unterrichtshilfen. Geschichte. 9. Klasse.* Berlin, 1976 [1970], 27.

34. *Geschichte 9* (1970), 217, 224. These pictures do not appear in subsequent editions, nor is Ulbricht's name even mentioned.

35. Ibid., 5, 7.

36. *Unterrichtshilfen. Geschichte. 9. Klasse* (1976 [1970]), 78.

37. *Geschichte 8. Klasse 8. Unterrichtshilfen* (1979), 197, 271; *Unterrichtshilfen. Geschichte. 9. Klasse* (1976 [1970]), 74.

38. Although our focus here is upon the history texts used in the ten-year general POS—only 10 to 12 percent of DDR students advanced to the EOS, and even fewer students attended university—discussion of ideologically sensitive events in DDR history in EOS and university texts also warrants mention. In general, the advanced history texts phrase the SED line in harsher, more aggressively anti-Western language. While this was not always true of other school subjects, such as German literature, history was an even more politicized subject than German literature. Other ideologically oriented subjects, such as *Staatsbürgerkunde,* made much use of literary agitprop. Moreover, the majority of university history students came from families loyal to the SED.

In the eleventh-grade history of the Party, *Geschichte der SED,* events are consistently portrayed according to a strict ideological orthodoxy. The importance attached to *Geschichte der SED* is indicated by the fact that the volume was issued not by the Ministry of Education but directly by the Institute of Marxism-Leninism under the supervision of a commission (whose members included Erich Honecker) that reported to the SED Central Committee.

39. On the shortcomings of the secondary school history texts of the early post-war *Bundesrepublik,* see John Dornberg, *Schizophrenic Germany* (New York: Macmillan, 1961). In his trips throughout the BRD schools in the 1950s, Dornberg noted that students in history classes were rarely taken beyond World War I. Although this is certainly no longer the case today, it apparently continued—in at least a few select instances—until the mid-1980s in CDU *Länder,* as my classroom visits to schools in Rhineland-Palinate in 1987 confirmed.

40. *Geschichte 9* (3rd ed., 1986), 170, 172. The text is virtually unchanged from its first edition (1970); in contrast to DDR history schoolbooks of the 1950s and 1960s, which sometimes altered considerably as SED historians adjusted to changing Party lines, history textbooks of later decades underwent little or no revision. This is generally the case with DDR textbooks of the 1970s and 1980s.

41. The ninth-grade teaching guide notes the "pedagogical emphasis" to apply to Dimitroff's story: "The courageous fight of Dimitroff against Nazi executioners is a radiant example of an unbowed fighter of the Party and a yardstick for [pupils'] personal action." *Unterrichtshilfen. Geschichte. 9. Klasse* (1976 [1970]), 159.

A further sign of the importance that DDR textbook writers attached to Dimitroff's version of the Reichstag fire is that his speech was among a handful of works—by Marx, Engels, Lenin, and Honecker—excerpted for study in the eleventh-grade course of the 1980s in Party history. *Dokumente und Materialien: Geschichte 11* (Berlin: Dietz Verlag, 1986), 66–70.

42. *Geschichte 9*, 162.

43. The eleventh-grade text in Party history, *Geschichte der SED. Abriss* (Berlin [East]: Dietz Verlag, 1978), discussed the Nazi-Soviet pact at greater length:

> Until late August 1939, the Soviet Union had sought to organize a common defense against fascist aggression with Great Britain and France. After its efforts failed due to the anti-Soviet stance of the ruling circles in London and Paris, however, the Soviet Union saw itself compelled to sign a non-aggression pact with Germany. The USSR thereby escaped the danger of confronting in isolation a unified bloc of imperialistic powers. The pact helped gain the USSR time for the further development of the construction of socialism and, above all, for the strengthening of its defense capabilities. The KPD greeted the Non-Aggression Pact and called upon the German *Volk* to struggle in support of its observance. The KPD thus consistently pursued the interests of peace and socialism.
>
> With its murderous, traitorous attack on the Soviet Union in June 1941, the fascist aggression reached its peak. . . . (65)

44. Indeed, Stalin's name appears only three times in all of *Geschichte 9*.

45. The ninth-grade teaching guide is especially passionate about the Nazi invasion of the USSR. Teachers are to "establish the connection between the heroic battle of the peoples of the USSR and the related superiority of the socialist social order. . . . *Pedagogical emphases:* Honoring of the heroic defensive war of the Soviet people. Solidarity with them. Condemnation of the criminal attack on the Soviet Union" (201).

46. *Geschichte 9*, 169.

47. Ibid., 176.

48. Commenting on these parallels after a 1954 visit to East German schools, one British observer wrote: "Again the allusions to machinations by World War II enemies sustain the older German grievances against [Britain and the U.S.], while ingeniously linking the latter with Nazism, so that the old animosity will be carried over." He noted that East German history classes "show up imperialist Britain as the father of slavery and the master exploiter of the coloured races. It needs no great effort to follow that line back to Nazi agitation over colonies." "Lessons of Their Neighbors: Nazi Themes Reversed in East Germany," *Times Educational Supplement*, 18 June 1954.

Indeed, the worst excesses of SED historiography bring to mind a line of Hitler from *Mein Kampf:* "Especially in history an abridgment of the materials is necessary."

49. *Geschichte 10* (4th ed., 1986), 42.

50. Ibid., 46.

51. Ibid., 44.

52. Ibid., 43.

53. Ibid., 44. The eleventh-grade *Geschichte der SED* is even more blunt: The Marshall Plan was extended "under the cover of so-called economic aid," but actually "served the expansion of U.S. imperialism." The text continues:

> The U.S. sought to exploit the weakened West European capitalist countries; the Marshall Plan furthered its goal of building American economic, political, and military dominance over Europe; intensifying the "Cold War"; and creating the preconditions for a military bloc against the Soviet Union and the People's Democracies. . . .
>
> American aid [for the SBZ] was designed to wipe out anti-fascist-democratic rela-

tions in the Soviet occupation zone, incorporate eastern Germany into the power sphere of imperialism, and gain a carefully premeditated strategic position in the heart of Europe. From this base, the People's Democracies in Poland, Czechoslovakia, Hungary, and other countries in Middle and Southern Europe were supposed to be undermined and wiped out. In league with the other Western powers, imperialistic circles of the U.S. forced the restoration of the West German monopoly bourgeoisie and their political representatives in the bourgeois parties, along with right-wing SPD leaders. They all prepared systematically the division of Germany and Berlin. A step here was that both the Western zones of Germany and West Berlin were included in the Marshall Plan. (156)

54. *Geschichte der SED* also throws a veil over these events. The 667-page EOS text does not mention Khrushchev's speech, though it acknowledges "the overemphasis of the role and the achievements of J. V. Stalin," which "led to the violation of the Leninist norms of Party life and the laws of the Soviet state." Then comes a note of self-congratulation: "It is testimony to the power of the revolutionary spirit of the CPSU that, once having uncovered this kind of development, it undertook to act decisively against the cult of personality, which is fundamentally foreign to Marxism-Leninism and socialism. It sought to expel its consequences in all areas of Party work, and in state and ideological activities" (343). The EOS text *does* discuss the Berlin Blockade—albeit in just three sentences:

To defend against currency speculation and economic sabotage conducted from the Western zones and western sectors of Berlin, the SMAD temporarily interrupted traffic between the Western zones and Berlin. At the same time, the Soviet government suggested that it would provide the residents of West Berlin with foodstuffs and other necessities. But the imperialistic occupying powers and the [West Berlin] Senate refused and began to transform West Berlin into a beachhead for the Cold War. (174)

Geschichte der SED makes no mention of the Berlin Airlift, nor indeed how—or even of the fact that—the temporary "interruption" of traffic was resumed eleven months later.

55. *Geschichte 10* (1986), 130.
56. Ibid., 155. To make these conclusions plausible, the unit in the tenth-grade teaching guide told teachers to underline four "background" points: "1. Hungary had been a satellite of fascist German imperialism. 2. Catholicism had a great influence on all classes. 3. Weak workers' movement. 4. Part of the bourgeoisie was against Hitler, but for western imperialism" (139).
57. Ibid., 130–31. Both *der 17. Juni* and the Hungarian revolt are dealt with at greater length and in more ideologically tinged language in *Geschichte der SED*, 294–95 and 356–57.
58. Ibid., 160–63, 176.
59. Ibid., 161.
60. Ibid., 162.
61. Ibid., 163.
62. Ibid., 190.
63. Ibid., 191. Once again, the erection of the Berlin Wall and the suppression of the Prague Spring are presented much more strongly to EOS students. *Geschichte der SED* speaks proudly of the "excellently planned and outstandingly organized operation." It claims that the Wall "foiled" the plan of "fascist German imperialism" to "annex" the DDR. Likewise, *Geschichte der SED* does not hesitate to note that NVA troops marched "alongside their brothers-in-arms of the other socialistic states" to "defend socialism against the counter-revolutionary assaults of its enemies." Their action rendered the "plans of imperialism to liquidate" Czech socialism "a fiasco" (417, 517–18).
64. It was testimony to the importance of history to the Party—and to how the march of events directly affected the history curriculum above all—that history was the only school subject in which a strong eleventh-hour effort was launched in mid-1989 to update DDR textbooks in light of *glasnost* and *perestroika*.

65. *Geschichte: Lehrbuch für die Abiturstufe,* part 1, 5. Meanwhile, in the USSR, nationwide examinations in history had simply been cancelled in 1988. Gorbachev had made the famous pronouncements in 1987 that "history must be seen as it is" and "blank spaces" must be removed from the historical record, leading within two years to the rehabilitation of numerous Old Bolsheviks (ultimately including Trotsky) and a revolution in Soviet historiography.

The DDR Ministry of Education did not administer nationwide examinations in history, and given the speed with which the DDR fell apart, a level of confusion comparable to that in the USSR never took place. As we have seen—and as the DDR's banning of *Sputnik* in 1988, after it compared Stalin with Hitler, suggests—*glasnost* did not arrive in the DDR until after the breaching of the Wall.

66. A few pages later, the forced collectivization of the kulaks in 1933–34 is acknowledged to have caused the starvation of "more than 4 million people." (According to Western estimates, the figure is three to four times more.) Stalin is also charged with having "incarcerated" "more than" 10 million people in the 1930s—a gross underestimate, by at least half—and silence prevails on the number of deaths during the decade. *Geschichte: Lehrbuch für die Abiturstufe,* part 1, 46–47.

67. Ibid., 42, 51.

68. Ibid., 26–27. All this was a major advance on the CPSU history course traditionally taught in the twelfth grade. In *Geschichte der Kommunistischen Partei der Sowjetunion* (1971)—which was little more than a German translation, with minor editing, of the standard advanced high school Soviet text—Stalin's murder of Trotsky is omitted, as is any mention of the scale of Stalin's crimes. Turning adversity to opportunity, Stalin is merely faulted for "serious mistakes," above all for having violated Lenin's sacred principle of collective leadership; the Party is, here again, congratulated for its act of "bold self-criticism": "This decisive self-criticism is visible proof of the strength and soundness of the Communist Party and the socialist Soviet order" (869).

69. *Geschichte: Lehrbuch für die Abiturstufe,* part 2, 26, 24, 32.

70. Ibid., 92, 93, 107. The upgrading of Stauffenberg and the July 20 conspirators had already begun in the 1987 edition of *Geschichte 9,* where they are praised as "anti-imperialists and democratic reformers" worthy of becoming part of the DDR's *Erbe* [inheritance] (170).

71. One of Germany's leading scholars of contemporary history, Heinrich August Winkler, predicted the *Black Book*'s influence in the near future on German textbooks as follows: "The central feature of the *Black Book* is a highly productive contribution to the [long-standing Holocaust] discussion. The *Black Book* refutes the notion that the Left can focus its attention exclusively on the Holocaust and need not occupy itself with the crimes of Stalin, Mao, or Pol Pot." Quoted in Michael Berger and Hans-Ulrich Joerges, "Eine Aufgabe für alle Zeit," *Die Woche,* 3 July 1998, 32.

72. Textbooks are typically revised every five to seven years, so it usually takes at least that long for a new scholarly consensus to be reflected in schoolbooks.

A recent collection of scholarly essays suggests the range of strategies and methods of comparative history—including cross-national approaches—designed to overcome collective "amnesia" about the Holocaust and/or Gulag. See Norbert Frei, Dirk van Laak, and Michael Stolleis, *"Geschichte vor Gericht." Historiker, Richter und die Suche nach Gerechtigkeit* (Munich, 2000). For a discussion of resistance toward the *Vergangenheitsbewältigung* (coping with the past) of French Communism, see Thankmar von Münchhausen, "Jospins Stolz auf seine kommunistischen Partner," *FAZ,* 14 November 1997, 16.

In Italy, the *Black Book* has intensified recurrent conservative demands for a more severe treatment of communism and Stalinism. The book was widely distributed at the national conference of Forza Italia, Italy's ruling political party. The Alleanza Nationale, the nation's leading party on the far Right, has organized a commission to review textbooks of twentieth-century history. This commission aims to stymie what it terms "vulgar Marxism," excessively anti-fascist "gas-oven romanticism," and the decades-long "communist cultural dictatorship" of Italy. Italian leftists warn in reply about a "fascist coup in the schools." Several reactionary organizations have erected websites that denounce leftist history teachers. Various Italian publications have published lists of alleged "historical falsifications" in current Italian schoolbooks.

Partly because of tighter laws restricting both neo-Nazi activity and public expression of fascist sentiments, such developments have not yet occurred in Germany. See F. Haas, "Zeitzeichen: Vulgärmarxismus contra Faschismusrevision," *Neue Zürcher Zeitung*, 30 December 2000, 57.

73. *The God that Failed*, ed. Richard Crossman (London, 1950).

74. On the story of the unsuccessful prosecution against these Berlin protesters, see Dirk Hempel, "Dunkle Erinnerung im Zeugenstand," *Die Tageszeitung*, 15 February 2000. For an 816-page left-wing reply to Courtois that indicts capitalism's crimes, see Robert Kurz, *Das Schwarzbuch des Kapitalismus* (Frankfurt: Ullstein, 1999).

75. Stéphane Courtois et. al., *The Black Book of Communism: Crimes, Terror, Repression* (Cambridge, Mass: Harvard University Press, 1999), 30. References hereafter are cited parenthetically in the main text. Unless otherwise noted, I am quoting from the English edition.

76. In *Das Schwarzbuch des Kommunismus:* Ehrhart Neubert, "Politische Verbrechen in der DDR," 829–84; and Joachim Gauck, "Vom schwierigen Umgang mit der Wahrnehmung," 885–94.

77. Quoted in Hempel, "Dunkle Erinnerung im Zeugenstand," *Die Tageszeitung*, 15 February 2000.

78. Courtois and his French contributors have remained, however, men of the Left. Some conservative and centrist German critics of the *Black Book* deplored that, by indicting Lenin yet exempting Marx and Engels, the *Black Book* authors did not go far enough in their critique. Courtois maintained during his German book tour that Lenin and Stalin had radicalized and brutalized Marx's theory of revolution. This line of argumentation led a few conservative German critics to brand him an apologist for Karl Marx.

So, just as Courtois was castigated in Paris from the Left for having argued that violence was integral to Lenin's (not just Stalin's) USSR, he was attacked in Germany from the Center-Right for "exculpating" Marx and Engels. See, for instance, the full-length reply to the *Black Book* by Konrad Loew, *Das Rotbuch der kommunistischen Ideologie: Marx & Engels—Die Väter des Terrors* (Munich, 1999). Loew insists that Lenin and Stalin "rightly understood themselves as Marxists."

79. Courtois, *Black Book*, 17.

80. Quoted in Reinhard Mohr, "Die Wirklichkeit ausgepfiffen," *Der Spiegel*, 30 June 1998, 172.

81. Courtois, *Black Book*, 23.

82. See Robert von Rimscha, *"Politische Korrektheit" in Deutschland* (Bonn: Bouvier, 1995).

83. Quoted in Michael Berger and Hans-Ulrich Joerges, "Eine Aufgabe für alle Zeit," *Die Woche*, 3 July 1998, 32.

84. Not only because the *Black Book* addressed issues central to German identity does it bid likely to contribute to the comparative historiography of totalitarianism. It also arrived in the aftermath of shattering events that "set the stage" on the German scene: Newly reunified Germany had just witnessed in the mid-1990s three major historical controversies that had dominated German news headlines for months. These discussions—the Botho Strauss dispute, the Holocaust Memorial controversy, and the debate occasioned by the German publication of Daniel Goldhagen's *Hitler's Willing Executioners*—had already directed Germans' attention not merely to the Nazi atrocities but also to communist crimes. And they in turn evince further why the *Black Book*, which concentrates almost exclusively on the history of communist crimes, also had the inevitable effect of triggering discussion about the Nazi evils: in German public life, like Siamese twins, they cannot be separated from each other.

But it must be emphasized: the focus of all of these post-reunification debates differed in one crucial respect from that of the *Black Book*. Whereas these debates began with the Holocaust and broadened periodically to include comparisons with communism (and with other crimes by other nations), the controversy fueled by the *Black Book* started with the Gulag and widened to include the Holocaust. That different orientation accounts for why I expect the *Black Book* to be the key work of recent scholarship that will influence German pedagogy on communism. See Michael Berger and Hans-Ulrich Joerges, "Eine Aufgabe für alle Zeit," *Die Woche*, 3 July 1998, 32.

85. Courtois's remarks provoked numerous French intellectuals to dismiss his scholarship

as a polemic—and even prompted two of his co-authors to publicly dissociate themselves from his introduction and conclusion to the book.

86. While the overlapping and multilayered context of this triad of reunification-era debates formed the historical-political scene that the *Black Book* entered on its 1998 German publication, another event also exerted a shaping influence. It bears noting that, perhaps as much or more than these debates of the 1990s, an earlier debate—which had shaped these debates, too—explicitly and directly conditioned the reception of the *Black Book:* the so-called *Historikerstreit* ("historians' debate") of 1986-87. In turn, it had followed upon the controversy aroused by Ronald Reagan's decision to visit the Bitburg cemetery in June 1985. Amid much controversy, Reagan accepted Chancellor Kohl's invitation to visit the Bitburg gravesite, which included not just Wehrmacht soldiers but also twenty-eight Waffen SS soldiers as part of a fiftieth anniversary memorial.

The *Black Book* does not specifically mention the *Historikerstreit*. Between the lines, however, it acknowledges its relevance. The *Historikerstreit* had spotlighted precisely the same issue as does the *Black Book:* the comparative evils of communism and Nazism. It was set off by the historian Ernst Nolte's argument in a 1986 essay that a "causal nexus" existed between Bolshevism and Nazism, with Lenin's "class genocide" having exerted exemplary influence on the Nazi "race genocide." Nolte's thesis was soon branded as right-wing revisionism and disputed by Jürgen Habermas; numerous other liberal-Left intellectuals and historians labeled Nolte's argument "proto-fascist." *Die Zeit,* 18 September 1986.

87. On Germany's need to grieve, see E. Gujer, "Kein Schlussstrich unter Deutschlands Geschichte," *Neue Zürcher Zeitung,* 5 December 1998, 3. See also the classic work of Alexander Mitscherlich, *Die Unfähigkeit zu Trauern. Grundlagen des kollektiven Verhaltens* (Munich: Piper, 1967).

88. Courtois, *Black Book,* 27.

89. Jürgen Habermas "Die Leere der Geschichte," *Süddeutsche Zeitung,* 12 March 1997.

CHAPTER 5. SOCIALIST SCIENCE: BIOLOGY, CHEMISTRY, MATHEMATICS

1. *Biologie: Ein Lehrbuch für die EOS 11. Klasse* (1967), 5.
2. *Biologie. Klasse 5. Unterrichtshilfen* (1978), 14–15.
3. Trofim D. Lysenko (1890–1976) was the Soviet Union's leading authority on evolution and heredity. Lysenko, a Soviet agronomist, came to prominence as the proponent of a theory that fit nicely with Soviet ideology. His opinions were declared to be dogma by the Kremlin, and those who disagreed were systematically purged from the Soviet system. Lysenkoism was a return to the evolutionary theories of Jean Lamarck, who was the first to put forward the idea that biological characteristics could be passed on from generation to generation. Lamarck believed that traits acquired by organisms in response to their surroundings were passed on to future generations: for example, if we cut the tails off of rats, they will breed rats with no tails, since it is the "will" of an organism that passes on traits to offspring. Lysenkoism was thus adopted by the Soviets because it introduced the will into evolution—supporting the implied M-L claim that a backward people could transform itself into "new Soviet man" in a few generations, if only they had the will to do it.

The rise of this doctrine in the Soviet Union in the late 1940s is one of the most tragic pages in the history of science. Many scientists who refused to submit to this silliness were executed, sent to the Gulag, or discredited, leaving only a cadre of Stalinist sycophants who parroted the Party line.

4. *Biologie: Ein Lehrbuch für die EOS 11. Klasse,* 5.
5. *Biologie. Klasse 5. Unterrichtshilfen* (1978) 16.
6. Here again, it bears repeating that biology teachers were *supposed* to link the "science of M-L" with their biology lessons. As the interviews in Part 2 make clear, some teachers did nothing of the kind. (My impression, based on dozens of interviews that I conducted in the east in the course of a decade of research, is that science teachers were most likely to treat such Party directives blithely. I estimate that by the 1980s the vast majority of science teachers—except if

they were being officially monitored or evaluated by Party representatives—largely ignored such official pronouncements.

7. In *On the Aesthetic Education of Man* (1795), Schiller gives the philosophical basis for his doctrine of art and indicates his view of the place of beauty in human life. Although Marx's fantasy about "unalienated labor" owes a great deal to Schiller's warning about man becoming "merely the imprint of his occupation," Schiller's insistence on the irreducible nature of aesthetic experience, his linking of aesthetic with moral freedom, and his celebration of ornament and the free play of imagination were decidedly contrary to Marx—or at least M-L doctrine.

8. *Biologie. Klasse 5. Unterrichtshilfen* (1978), 17.
9. Ibid.
10. *Biologie 8* (1968), 119.
11. Ibid., 120.
12. *Biologie. 9. Klasse* (1967), 111–13.
13. *Der Mensch: Ein Lehrbuch für den Biologieunterricht. Klasse 9* (1967), 106–7.
14. *Frauenruheräume* were designated rest areas for women in companies with a sizable female workforce. They were the DDR's attempt to make life for working women a little easier. If a female employee needed rest or felt sick (due to pregnancy or for other reasons), this was her designated area—complete with beds where women could nap until they felt ready to return to work.

Progressives and women's activists in the 1890s campaigned for such special relaxation areas for women, which became widespread throughout Europe in large factories and offices. Because 95 percent of DDR women worked, *Frauenruheräume* were quite common there. Today, although the term is no longer in use, the rooms themselves still exist, even if on a more sophisticated basis: paragraph 31 of Germany's employment conditions code states that employers must provide a private space where pregnant women can lie down to rest.

15. *Biologie. 9. Klasse* (1967), 118.
16. Ibid., 108, 109.
17. Ibid., 121.
18. See, for instance, *Biologie 4: Ein Lehrbuch für die erweiterte Oberschule. 12 Klasse* (1967).
19. *Biologie 4: Ein Lehrbuch für die erweiterte Oberschule. 12 Klasse*, 252–58.
20. *Biologie: Ein Lehrbuch für die EOS 11. Klasse* (1967), 252–53, 257–58.
21. See, for instance, *Physik. Klasse 8. Unterrichtshilfen* (1978), 17, 85–86.
22. *Chemie 9* (1979 [1970]), 162.
23. *Unterrichtshilfen. Chemie. Klasse 9.* (1979 [1970]), 10–11.
24. Ibid., 192.
25. Ibid., 76–77.
26. *Anorganische Chemie. Ein Lehrbuch für die 8. Klasse* (1967), 137–38.
27. *Anorganische Chemie. Ein Lehrbuch für die 9. Klasse* (1967), 73–75.
28. Ibid., 23–24.
29. *Chemie. Ein Lehrbuch für die EOS 12. Klasse* (1967–68).
30. *Organische Chemie. Lehrbuch für die Oberschule. 9. und 10. Klasse* (1967), 63–65, 224–26.
31. Ibid., 79.
32. *Unterrichtshilfen. Chemie. Klasse 9* (1979 [1970]), 169.
33. *Organische Chemie. Lehrbuch für die Oberschule. 9. und 10. Klasse* (1967), 292–94.
34. *Mathematik 2* (1968), 117.
35. *Mathematik 4* (1968), 109.
36. *Mathematik. Klasse 4. Unterrichtshilfen* (1978), 12.
37. *Mathematik 4* (1980), 65–67.
38. *Mathematik 4* (1968), 109.
39. *Mathematik 5* (1968), 108.
40. *Mathematik 7* (1967), 176.
41. *Mathematik 4* (1980), 55.
42. *Mathematik. Klasse 4. Unterrichtshilfen,* 127.
43. Many such exercises contain "agitprop bites" inserted in the middle. For instance:

Because of the rapid development of the DDR People's Economy, the demand for electrical energy rose from year to year. Our Republic is today one of the leading countries in the world in the per capita production of electrical energy.

In 1960, the production of electrical energy was roughly W = 40 × 10 kWh. With an average annual growth rate of 5 percent, the development of electrical energy production from 1960 to 1980 can be described as

Wn = Wo × 1.05 n (n e V; O = n = 20).

That means that the production of electrical energy—in order to keep pace with the level of 1960—must rise by more than 2 1/2 times above its present level. (*Mathematik 9* [1979], 146)

44. Ibid., 158.
45. Ibid., 126. See also the 1967 edition (93).
46. *Mathematik 9* (1979), 100.
47. Ibid., 128, 189.

CHAPTER 6. ARTS AND HUMANITIES
"History Lessons" for Would-Be Revolutionaries

1. On the face of it, this lesson may be a foolish and unnecessary distortion of history. One is tempted to suggest a different ideological tack to the DDR historians: Why didn't Soviet (and other Communist educators) simply turn the USSR's unpreparedness to wage war in 1941 into an advantage? They could more easily (and consistently, given other agitprop claims) have argued that their relative lack of preparation testified to the peaceful nature of international communism and the noble, trusting ideals of the model worker state—and also to the obsessive warmongering of the fascist powers and the "fascistic" social democracies. This argument also would have made the USSR's initial defeat quite forgivable, and rendered their ultimate victory over the Nazis seem even more heroic.

2. The colloquial term *astrein* derives from woodworking and carpentry. Timbers without dark spots or knobs, which make sawing and processing difficult, are *astrein*.

CHAPTER 8. EDUCATION FOR TOLERANCE:
OF IDEOLOGY, IDENTITY, AND INTOLERANCE
Among (German and Jewish) Schoolchildren

1. One cannot forget the terrifying events of the early 1990s, which witnessed an explosion of neo-Nazi activity partly triggered by an influx of foreigners into Germany in greater numbers than the immigrant flow into the rest of the European Union combined.

2. Although the entire nation of Germany harbors no more than fifty thousand active neo-Nazis, right-wing political parties have exploited the continuing high unemployment rates and perceptions of "second-class" status among easterners. Polls show that only one-third of eastern Germans consider Germany's western-style democracy "defensible"; right-wing parties have attracted up to 13 percent of the vote and up to a third of all voters under thirty—in various eastern state elections since 1990.

3. The youth violence reflects Germany's national anxiety over the upheavals that have come in the wake of unification, as well as popular resistance to top-down, government-sponsored initiatives in "re-education." Indeed, although the German government carefully avoids mentioning that particular "unword"—*Umerziehung* (re-education)—because of its negative associations acquired during the Allied occupation, German educators have in fact launched a wide range of re-education activities in the schools.

In a nationwide study in 1998, the Munich Institute for Youth Research reported that 67 percent of German students (ages six to nineteen) have witnessed "violent acts," with an astounding one-third claiming to have been victims themselves. These figures constitute "a significantly higher percentage of violent acts than in American schools," the Munich Institute noted. The Institute's report concluded that German youth violence was equally worrisome in both west and east: "Brutal violence has become an everyday occurrence in almost every German school." "Faustrecht macht Schule," *Focus Magazin*, 21 March 1998, 72–84.

4. A 1998 report noted that 10 percent of the able-bodied DDR population—at least 750,000 people—were "employed in varying degrees in the DDR's military or paramilitary security forces." "When one adds that to the 643,000 members of the paramilitary GST, the 490,000 members of the civil defense program, and the 2.6 million members of the NVA reserves," concludes the report, "the dimensions stretch into the sheer unbelievable." Günter Holzweissig, "Ungezügelte Erziehung zum Hass," *Frankfurter Allgemeine Zeitung*, 15 May 1998. See also *Im Dienste der Partei* (Berlin, 1998), from which these figures were taken.

Other reports note that former DDR teachers still harbor vestiges of their "friend-enemy mentality" and their training in "unconditional obedience" and the glorification of military heroism that the Education for Hate programs fostered. *Frankfurter Allgemeine Zeitung*, 25 September 2000 and 13 July 2001.

5. See, for instance, "Wenn anerzogener Hass übertragen wird," *Frankfurter Allgemeine Zeitung*, 10 March 1999, a letter to the editor written by a professor from the eastern town of Geschwend. The subhead reads: "DDR Education Causes Hostility Toward Foreigners." Indeed, a prominent western German criminologist, Christian Pfeiffer, has outspokenly promoted the controversial thesis that the collectivist pedagogy of the DDR has directly facilitated neo-Nazi battle units and other ideological cells of the New Right that have mushroomed in the east since 1990. Pfeiffer notes that the risk of assault on a foreigner in the east is twenty-five times higher than in the West—and that a woman (German or foreigner) is 500 percent more likely to be raped in the east. Moreover, the incidences of eastern youth violence exceed the western figures by 500 to 600 percent. He also argues that, because the violence emerges from group settings twice as often in the east as in the west, the group mentality inculcated by DDR pedagogy is obviously a chief contributing factor. Pfeiffer lays stress on the fact that, in the DDR, "the nursery and kindergarden were very strongly group-oriented." Edith Kresta, "Familienkultur der Intoleranz und des Hasses," *Die Tageszeitung*, 22 March 1999.

6. Since the early 1990s, social workers have organized weekend seminars that bring together neo-Nazi and Turkish youths, aiming to foster mutual perspective-taking, "foreigner identification," and good will between Germans and foreigners "through music, dance, graffiti—whatever works," as one organizer stated. *Times Educational Supplement*, 11 September 1992. See also Toby Axelrod, "Lessing's Tale of Tolerance Unites," *Jerusalem Post*, 18 January 2002, which reports on the competition "Remembering for the Past and Future: In Dialogue for Tolerance." Sponsored by film director Steven Spielberg's Shoah Visual History Foundation, the winning submission was a production of *Nathan der Weise* by Jewish, Arab, and German students, who rehearsed and performed together in all three languages. For tolerance initiatives linked to *Kristallnacht* (Night of the Broken Glass), the pogrom inflicted upon the German Jews on November 9, 1938, see Philipp Gessler, "Ein Datum wie ein Geschichtsbuch," *Die Tageszeitung*, 8 November 2001. See also Belinda Cooper, "Berlin's Jewish High School Teaches Tolerance to All," *Christian Science Monitor*, 14 June 1995.

7. "UNESCO-Seminar zu Menschenrechten in Nürnberg eröffnet," *AP Worldstream*, 20 August 1998.

8. See Barbara Hasler, "Erziehung zur Toleranz," *Tages-Anzeiger*, 27 May 1998.

9. *Süddeutsche Zeitung*, 28 June 1993. See also *AP Worldstream*, 20 August 1999; and *Neue Zürcher Zeitung*, 1 July 1999. The European Union's version of the Education for Tolerance initiative includes recommendations for increases in international teacher- and student-exchange programs, closer contacts with schools in eastern Europe, professional development courses in "diversity appreciation" for teachers, and intercultural projects sponsored by companies active in work-study apprentice programs of German schools.

Steven Spielberg has applauded German initiatives in education for tolerance, commenting in 2003 to Germany's Education Minister: "I'd like to clone you, so that you could perform your outstanding work in the U.S., where education for tolerance is not in the curriculum." "Vermischtes," *Deutsche Presse-Agentur*, 26 January 2003.

10. A survey by EMNID, the opinion research institute based in Bielefeld, in 2000 showed that 75 percent of Germans are convinced that "prejudices exist toward citizens of the Jewish faith." But only 43 percent of easterners (vs. 57 percent of westerners) regard it as a citizen's responsibility to take a firm stand against right-wing violence. "So denken die Deutschen," *News Aktuell,* 13 October 2000.

Another EMNID poll disclosed that almost two-thirds of Germans support the contention of Norman Finkelstein, in his recent book *The Holocaust Industry,* that Jewish institutions are enriching themselves through Holocaust-related indemnities from German (and Swiss) government and industry. "Umfrage: Zwei Drittel aller Deutschen teilen Finkelsteins Thesen," *Agence France Presse,* 10 February 2001.

An Allensbach survey of western Germans estimated that up to 15 percent of FDP voters are "secret anti-Semites." The poll was conducted in the 1990s and re-checked a decade later, in light of FDP attempts to cultivate votes by appealing to latent anti-Semitism. The most blatant appeals came from the FDP Vice Chair, Jürgen Mölleman, who died in 2003. "Inszenierter Tabubruch," *Der Spiegel,* 3 June 2002. The poll data are from Marcus Krämer, *Süddeutsche Zeitung,* 25 May 2002. See also *Süddeutsche Zeitung,* 12 December 1992; 26 June 1993; 11 November 1993.

11. "Einstimmiges Ja zum Staatsvertrag mit Zentralrat der Juden," *Associated Press Worldstream,* 6 June 2003. The first quote is from the subheadline; the second quote is from CDU vice chair Wolfgang Bosbach.

"Re-Education for Tolerance": A Civic Leader Speaks Out

12. It was a shock, both to Germans and Jews, when Bubis's last will and testament stipulated his desire to be buried in Israel. Many observers took that decision as a direct slap at the BRD and as an expression of Bubis's disgust with half-hearted official attempts to combat neo-Nazism and anti-foreigner violence.

13. Bubis was no stranger to controversy—or to adversity borne of German politics and history. Indeed, his life had hardly begun before he and his family found themselves on the run from the Nazis. Born in January 1927 in Breslau in German Silesia (now Wroclaw, Poland), Bubis fled with his family to Poland in 1935, settling in the town of Deblin. When the war ended, he turned out to be the only member of his family to have survived the Nazi terror. His mother had died of cancer in 1940, just a few months after the outset of World War II; his father had been sent in 1942 to Treblinka and perished in the concentration camp; his sister and brother had escaped eastward into Soviet-occupied Poland—and had disappeared without a trace. Young Bubis himself worked in two Polish labor camps during the war, in Deblin and Czestochowa.

14. When Czestochowa labor camps were liberated by the Red Army in the winter of 1945, Bubis was an emaciated slave laborer in a Nazi munitions factory. Even his name had changed: Shortly before entering the camps, he had acquired, at the age of sixteen, the Christian name "Ignatz" (derived from Ignatius) from members of the Polish resistance. Polish partisans employed him to smuggle goods into the Warsaw ghetto during a time when the Nazis made him a mail carrier in the ghetto. Bubis kept the name; his childhood name is Yisrael. (When he was summoned to the Torah, he was still called Yisrael ben Yehoshua.)

When eighteen-year-old Ignatz returned to Germany after a decade's absence, he felt like an alien in a hostile land. He took up residence briefly in Dresden, then soon moved to West Berlin. Bubis dreamed of becoming a lawyer, but instead entered business. After several more moves, he arrived in Stuttgart in 1949, where he opened an office dealing in jewelry and precious metals. Finally, in 1956, he put down roots in Frankfurt; by the mid-1960s, he had established himself as a developer and real estate broker, occupations that were soon to make him a wealthy man.

Bibliography

A. PRIMARY

Listed below are textbooks, teachers' handbooks, songbooks, and youth organization manuals pertaining to education in the DDR. All items were issued by the central publishing house, Volk und Wissen Volkseigener Verlag of East Berlin, except where otherwise noted.

Anorganische Chemie. Ein Lehrbuch für die 8. Klasse. Ed. Werner Renneberg et al. Berlin, 1967 [1960].
Anorganische Chemie. Ein Lehrbuch für die 9. Klasse. Ed. Werner Renneberg et al. Berlin, 1967 [1960].
Arbeit am Ausdruck. 9/10. Klasse. Berlin, 1977 [1975].
Atlas der Erdkunde: Für die allgemeinbildenden polytechnischen Oberschulen. Berlin, 1968 [1962].
Biologie. Ed. Johannes Müller et al. Berlin, 1979.
Biologie 4: Ein Lehrbuch für die erweiterte Oberschule. 12. Klasse. Berlin, 1967.
Biologie. Klasse 5. Unterrichtshilfen. Berlin, 1978 [1966].
Biologie 8. Klasse. Berlin, 1968.
Biologie. 9. Klasse. Berlin, 1967.
Biologie. Ein Lehrbuch für die EOS 11. Klasse. Berlin, 1967.
Chemie. Ed. Jochen Teichmann, Heinz Obst, and Barbara Arndt. Berlin, 1979.
Chemie 9. Berlin, 1979 [1970].
Chemie. Ein Lehrbuch für die EOS 12. Klasse. Berlin, 1967–68.
Chemie in Übersichten: Kompendium für die Oberschule. Bearbeitet von Wolfgang Eisenhuth. Berlin, 1967.
Der Mensch: ein Lehrbuch für den Biologieunterricht. Klasse 9. Berlin, 1967 [1959].
Deutsch. Ed. Gerhard Dathe et al. Berlin, 1977.
Deutsche Rechtschreibung. Ed. Otto Bauerfeind et al. Berlin, 1979.
Deutsch 2. Unterrichtshilfen. Berlin, 1974.
Deutsch. Klasse 4. Unterrichtshilfen. Berlin, 1978.
Dokumente und Materialien: Geschichte 11. Berlin: Dietz Verlag, 1986.
Entwicklung der Organismen: Lehrbuch der Biologie. Berlin, 1968.
Ergänzungslesestoffe für den Literaturunterricht. Ed. Alfred Antkowiak et al. Berlin, 1978.
Geographie. Ed. Hella Kinzel et al. Berlin, 1968.
Geographie 5. Berlin, 1980 [1977].
Geographie für die 5. Klasse. Unsere Deutsche Demokratische Republik. Berlin, 1960.
Geographie für die 5. Klasse. Unsere Deutsche Demokratische Republik. Berlin, 1967 [1966].
Geographie 6. Berlin, 1960.
Geographie 6. Berlin, 1971.
Geographie 6. Berlin, 1979 [1975].

Geographie. Klasse 7. Unterrichtshilfen. Berlin, 1978 [1968].
Geographie. Lehrbuch für die Klasse 7. Berlin, 1980 [1968].
Geographie. Unterrichtshilfen. Klasse 7. Berlin, 1968.
Geographie 8. Berlin, 1979 [1969].
Geographie. Klasse 8. Unterrichtshilfen. Berlin, 1978 [1969].
Geographie 9. Zur allgemeinen physischen Geographie. Berlin, 1979 [1970].
Geographie. Unterrichtshilfen. 9. Klasse. Berlin, 1978 [1970].
Geographie 10. Ökonomische Geographie der sozialistischen Staatengemeinschaft und der DDR. Berlin, 1979 [1978].
Geographie. Klasse 10. Unterrichtshilfen. 1979 [1978].
Geographie 11. Berlin, 1983 [1981].
Geschichte. Dieter Behrendt et al. Berlin, 1967–68.
Geschichte der Kommunistischen Partei der Sowjetunion. Berlin: Dietz Verlag, 1971.
Geschichte der SED. Abriss. Gerhard Rossmann et al. Berlin (East): Dietz Verlag, 1978.
Geschichte 5. Berlin, 1968 [1965].
Geschichte 5. Berlin, 1980 [1971].
Geschichte 6. Berlin, 1968 [1967].
Geschichte 6. Berlin, 1980 [1978].
Geschichte 6. Lehrbuch für die Abiturstufe. Berlin, 1964.
Geschichte 7. Berlin, 1980 [1968].
Geschichte 8. Berlin, 1970.
Geschichte 8. Berlin, 1979 [1969].
Geschichte Klasse 8. Unterrichtshilfen. Berlin, 1979 [1969].
Geschichte 9. Berlin, 1968 [1965].
Geschichte 9. Berlin, 1970.
Geschichte 9. Berlin, 1986 [1980, 1970].
Geschichte 9. Berlin, 1987.
Geschichte 10. Berlin, 1986 [1980, 1977, 1970]
Geschichte 11. Berlin, 1968 [1967].
Geschichte: Lehrbuch für die Abiturstufe. Berlin, 1989.
Grammatik und Orthographieunterricht: Arbeit am Ausdruck: fachwissenschaftliche und methodische Anleitung. 8. Klasse. Ed. Anneliese Claus-Schulze et al. Berlin, 1978 [1969].
Heimatkunde 3. Berlin, 1979 [1978].
Heimatkunde 3. Ed. Brigitta Drefenstedt et al. Berlin, 1980 [1978].
Heimatkunde 4. Berlin, 1979 [1978].
Leben, Singen, Kämpfen. Liederbuch der deutschen Jugend. Berlin (East), 1954.
Lehrbuch der Erdkunde für die 8. Klasse. Berlin, 1968 [1966].
Lehrbuch der Erdkunde für die 9. Klasse. Grundzüge der allgemeinen physischen Erdkunde. Berlin, 1961.
Lehrbuch der Erdkunde für die 9. Klasse. Ökonomische Geographie sozialistischer Länder. Berlin, 1967.
Lehrbuch der Erdkunde in der Sowjetzone. Ed. Peter R. Lücke. Berlin, 1964.
Lehrbuch der ökonomischen Geographie. Klasse 10a, 10c, 11b. Berlin, 1967 [1964].
Lehrbuch der ökonomischen Geographie. Klasse 11a, 11c, 12b. Berlin, 1967 [1963].
Lehrbuch für den Geschichtsunterricht. 5. Schuljahr. Berlin, 1951.
Lehrbuch für den Geschichtsunterricht. 6. Schuljahr. Berlin, 1954.
Lehrbuch für den Geschichtsunterricht. 8. Jahr. Berlin, 1953.
Lehrbuch für den Geschichtsunterricht. 10. Schuljahr. Berlin, 1956 [1953].

Lehrbuch für den Literaturunterricht in den Klassen 8–10: Zur Entwicklung der Literatur und bedeutender Dichterpersönlichkeiten. Ed. Ernst-Ludwig Zacharias et al. Berlin, 1979 [1974].
Lesebuch 2. Berlin, 1978 [1977].
Lesebuch 3. Ed. Anneliese Lücke-Gruse et al. Berlin, 1980 [1970].
Lesebuch 4. Berlin, 1978 [1977].
Lesebuch 4. Berlin, 1980 [1971].
Lesebuch 5. Berlin, 1978 [1977].
Literatur. Klasse 7. Unterrichtshilfen. Berlin, 1978.
Literatur. Klasse 8. Unterrichtshilfen. Berlin, 1979.
Literatur. Klassen 11 und 12. Berlin, 1980.
Literaturunterricht. 5. Klasse. Berlin, 1979 [1966].
Literaturunterricht. 6. Klasse. Berlin, 1978 [1967].
Literaturunterricht. 9 und 10. Klasse. Berlin, 1979.
Literaturunterricht. Fachwissenschaftliche und methodische Anleitung. Ed. Hans Marnette et al. Berlin, 1978–79.
Marxistische-leninistische Philosophie: Geschrieben für die Jugend. Ed. Erich Hahn and Alfred Kosing. Berlin: Dietz Verlag, 1979 [1978].
Mathematik. Ed. Artur Wolf et al. Berlin, 1976.
Mathematik 2. Berlin, 1968.
Mathematik 4. Berlin, 1968.
Mathematik 4. Berlin, 1980 [1978].
Mathematik. Klasse 4. Unterrichtshilfen. Berlin, 1978 [1971].
Mathematik 5. Berlin, 1968.
Mathematik 7. Berlin, 1967.
Mathematik 9. Berlin, 1967.
Mathematik 9. Berlin, 1979.
Muttersprache 4. Berlin, 1968.
Muttersprache 5. Berlin, 1968.
Muttersprache. Klasse 5. Unterrichtshilfen. Berlin, 1979 [1977].
Muttersprache. Klasse 6. Unterrichtshilfen. Berlin, 1978.
Muttersprache. Klasse 7. Unterrichtshilfen. Berlin, 1979.
Ökonomische Geographie der beiden deutschen Staaten. 9. Klasse. Berlin, 1967 [1962].
Ökonomische Geographie sozialistischer Länder. 10. Klasse. Berlin, 1967 [1964].
Organische Chemie. Lehrbuch für die Oberschule. 9. und 10. Klasse. Berlin, 1967 [1964].
Physik. Ed. Rolf Grabow et al. Berlin, 1967–68.
Physik in Übersichten. Ed. Werner Golm et al. Berlin, 1966.
Physik. Klasse 8. Unterrichtshilfen. Berlin, 1978 [1969].
Physik 9. Berlin, 1968 [1965].
Physik 10. Berlin, 1968 [1965].
Physik 11. Berlin, 1968 [1964].
Politische Ökonomie. Geschrieben für die Jugend. Ed. Otto Reinhold and Karl-Heinz Stiemerling. Berlin: Dietz Verlag, 1982.
Staatsbürgerkunde. Ed. Rudolf Hellborn et al. Berlin, 1968.
Staatsbürgerkunde. Ed. Kurt Schneider. Berlin, 1968 [1966].
Staatsbürgerkunde 1: Weg und Ziel des Sozialismus in der DDR. Berlin, 1968.
Staatsbürgerkunde 2: Der umfassende Aufbau des Sozialismus. Berlin, 1968.
Staatsbürgerkunde 3: Die sozialistische Weltanschauung. Berlin, 1968.
Staatsbürgerkunde 7. Berlin, 1979 [1978].

Staatsbürgerkunde. 7. Klasse. Unterrichtshilfen. Berlin, 1976 [1974].
Staatsbürgerkunde 8. Berlin, 1978 [1977].
Staatsbürgerkunde 9. Berlin, 1970.
Staatsbürgerkunde 9. Berlin, 1979 [1977].
Staatsbürgerkunde. Klasse 9. Unterrichtshilfen. Berlin, 1979 [1975].
Staatsbürgerkunde 9. und 10. Dokumente und Materialien. Berlin: Dietz Verlag, 1976.
Staatsbürgerkunde 10. Berlin, 1971.
Staatsbürgerkunde 10. Berlin, 1971 [1968].
Staatsbürgerkunde 10. Berlin, 1983 [1982].
Staatsbürgerkunde. Klasse 10. Unterrichtshilfen. Berlin, 1979.
Tafelwerk. Mathematik, Physik, Chemie. Zahlentafeln, Wertetabellen und Formeln für die Klassen 7 bis 12. Berlin, 1967.
Unser Lesebuch. Klasse 5. Berlin, 1979 [1966].
Unser Lesebuch. 5. Schuljahr. Berlin, 1965 [1959].
Unser Lesebuch. Klasse 7. Berlin, 1964 [1962].
Unser Lesebuch. Klasse 7. Berlin, 1977.
Unser Lesebuch. Klasse 8. Berlin, 1979.
Unser Lesebuch. Klasse 8. Berlin, 1979 [1969].
Unser Lesebuch. 8. Schuljahr. Berlin, 1964 [1959].
Unsere Muttersprache. Ed. Gerhard Dathe et al. Berlin, 1978–80.
Unsere Muttersprache 2. Berlin, 1979 [1969].
Unsere Muttersprache 3. Berlin, 1979 [1970].
Unsere Muttersprache 4. Berlin, 1980 [1978].
Unsere Muttersprache 7. Berlin, 1977 [1968].
Unsere Muttersprache. Klasse 7. Berlin, 1977 [1968].
Unsere Muttersprache 8. Berlin, 1979 [1969].
Unsere Muttersprache 9 und 10. Berlin, 1979 [1970].
Unterrichtshilfen. Chemie. Klasse 9. Berlin, 1979 [1970].
Unterrichtshilfen Deutsch 1. Berlin, 1977, 1973 [1970].
Unterrichtshilfen Deutsch. Klasse 2. Berlin, 1977, 1973 [1970].
Unterrichtshilfen Deutsch 4. Berlin, 1978, 1977, 1973 [1970].
Unterrichtshilfen für den Geographieunterricht in der 5. Klasse. Berlin, 1967.
Unterrichtshilfen. Geschichte. Klasse 5. Berlin, 1977 [1971].
Unterrichtshilfen. Geschichte. Klasse 6. Berlin, 1979 [1978].
Unterrichtshilfen. Geschichte. Klasse 7. Berlin, 1977 [1968].
Unterrichtshilfen. Geschichte. 9. Klasse. Berlin, 1976 [1970].
Unterrichtshilfen. Geschichte. 9. Klasse. Berlin, 1977 [1970].
Unterrichtshilfen. Geschichte. Klasse 10. Berlin, 1977.
Unterrichtshilfen. Musik. 5. und 6. Klasse. Berlin, 1973.
Unterrichtshilfen. 8. Klasse. Staatsbürgerkunde. Berlin, 1975.
Wissenschaftlicher Kommunismus. Lehrbuch für das marxistisch-leninistische Grundlagenstudium. Berlin: VEB Deutscher Verlag der Wissenschaften, 1985 [1974].
Zeittafel für den Geschichtsunterricht. Ed. Jander Eckhard. Berlin, 1967.
Zirkel junger Sozialisten zum Studium der Biographien von Karl Marx und Friedrich Engels. Berlin: Verlag Junge Welt, 1980.

B. SECONDARY

The following bibliography covers all books, memoirs, monographs, and scholarly articles that are cited in the text and notes, along with the most significant reviews and periodical articles. It also includes numerous other items that have exerted an influence on my thinking.

Adamovitch, G. "Tolstoy as an Artist." *Russian Review* 19.2 (1960): 141–49.
Adolphi, Wolfram, and Jörn Schütrumf, eds. *Ernst Thälmann. An Stalin. Briefe aus dem Zuchthaus 1939 bis 1941.* Berlin: Dietz Verlag, 1996.
Allan, Sean, and John Sanford. *DEFA: East German Cinema 1946–1992.* New York: Berghahn Books, 1999.
Anweiler, Oskar, and Siegfried Baske, eds. *Die sowjetische Bildungspolitik, 1917–60.* Wiesbaden: Harrassowitz, 1979.
Arnold, Heinz Ludwig, and Frauke Meyer Gosau, eds. *Die Abwicklung der DDR.* Göttingen: Wallstein, 1992.
Autorenkollektiv. *Dialektischer und historischer Materialismus. Lehrbuch für das marxistisch-leninistische Grundlagenstudium.* Berlin (East): Dietz Verlag, 1987.
Babakian, Genine. "Textbook Shortages at the Start of School." *Moscow Times*, August 28, 1996, sec. 1034.
Badstubner, Evemarie. *Befremdlich anders: Leben in der DDR.* Berlin: Dietz, 2000.
Bartley, D. E. "The Foreign Language Curriculum at the Level of the General Secondary Polytechnical Special School in Foreign Languages in the R.S.F.S.R." Ph.D. diss., Stanford University, 1970.
Balluseck, Lothar von. *Die guten und die bösen Deutschen: das Freund-Feind-Bild im Schrifttum der DDR.* Bonn: Hohwacht Verlag, 1972.
Bambach, Jürgen. "The Transformation of East German Education: A Comparison between the Federal States of Berlin and Brandenburg," *European Education* 25.2 (Summer 1993): 58–65.
Bartel, Walter. *Unser Präsident Wilhelm Pieck-Erzählungen aus seinem Leben.* Berlin (East): Kinderbuchverlag, 1954.
Baske, Siegfried, ed. *Bildungspolitik in der DDR, 1963–76.* Wiesbaden: Harrassowitz, 1979.
Baske, Siegfried, and Martha Engelbert, ed. *Zwei Jahrzehnte Bildungspolitik in der Sowjetzone Deutschlands.* Berlin: Freie Universität, 1966.
Bauerkämper, Arnd, Martin Sabrow, and Bernd Stover. *Doppelte Zeitgeschichte: deutsch-deutsche Beziehungen 1945–1990.* Bonn: J. H. W. Dietz, 1998.
Baumann, Edith. *Geschichte der deutschen Jugendbewegung.* Berlin (East), 1947.
Beck, Thomas. *Liebe zum Sozialismus, Hass auf den Klassenfeind. Sozialistisches Wehrmotiv und Wehrerziehung in der DDR.* Berlin: Ost-Akademie, 1983.
Behrends, Jan C., Thomas Lindenberger, and Patrice G. Poutrus. *Fremde und Fremdsein in der DDR: zu historischen Ursachen der Fremdenfeindlichkeit in Ostdeutschland.* Berlin: Metropol, 2003.
Belen'kii, G. I. "The Program of the Communist Party of the Soviet Union and Some Problems in the Teaching of Literature." *Literatura v shkole* 5 (1962): 21–30.
Bennett, Vanora. "No More Lessons from the Revolution: Post-Soviet Schools in Russia Have Dropped the Heavy-Handed Ideology and Teaching Methods. But With New Freedom Comes New Ignorance As Pupils Ask, 'Lenin Who?'" *Los Angeles Times,* October 21, 1996, A1.
Bertram, Hans, and Raj Kollmorgen. *Die Transformation Ostdeutschlands: Berichte zum sozialen und politischen Wandel in den neuen Bundesländern.* Opladen: Leske & Budrich, 2001.

Billerbeck, Liane. *Generation Ost: aumfmüpfig, angepasst, ehrgeizig? Jugendliche nach der Wende; zwölf Selbstaussagen*. Berlin: Christoph Links, 1999.
Blackburn, Gilmer W. *Education in the Third Reich: Race and History in Nazi Textbooks*. Albany: SUNY Press, 1985.
Bode, Dirk. *Polytechnischer Unterricht in der DDR*. Frankfurt: Campus Verlag, 1978.
Bredel, Willi. *Ernst Thälmann*. Berlin (East): Dietz, 1961.
Brenner, Michael, and Derek J. Penslar. *In Search of Jewish Community: Jewish Identities in Germany and Austria, 1918–1933*. Bloomington: Indiana University Press, 1998.
Brinks, Jan Herman. *Children of a New Fatherland: Germany's Post-War Right-Wing Politics*. London: I. B. Taruis, 2000.
Bungenstab, Karl-Ernst. *Umerziehung zur Demokratie? Re-education Politik im Bildungswesen der US-Zone, 1945–49*. Düsseldorf: Bertelsmann Universitätsverlag, 1970.
Bursov, B. I. *Russkaia Literatura, deviatyi klass*. Moscow: Prosveshchenie, 1973.
Carrere d'Encausse, Hélène. *Lenin*. New York: Holmes and Meier, 2001.
Childs, David. *Germany in the Twentieth Century*. London, 1991.
Christian, R. F. *Tolstoy: A Critical Introduction*. Cambridge: Cambridge University Press, 1969.
Clark, K. *The Soviet Novel: History as Ritual*. Chicago: University of Chicago Press, 1981.
Crossman, Richard, ed. *The God that Failed*. New York: Harper, 1950.
Connelly, John. *Captive University: The Sovietization of East German, Czech, and Polish Higher Education, 1945–1956*. Chapel Hill: University of North Carolina Press, 2000.
Courtois, Stéphane, et al. *The Black Book of Communism: Crimes, Terror, Repression*. Cambridge, Mass.: Harvard University Press, 1999.
Detjen, Claus. *Die anderen Deutschen: wie der Osten die Republik verändert*. Bonn: Bouvier, 1999.
Dialektischer und historischer Materialismus. Lehrbuch für das marxistisch-leninistische Grundlagenstudium. Berlin (East): Dietz Verlag, 1974.
Diefendorf, Jeffry M. "Teaching History in the Polytechnical Schools of the German Democratic Republic." *History Teacher* 15.3 (1982): 347–62.
Doppelte Last–doppelte Herausforderung: Gedenkstättenarbeit und Diktaturenvergleich an Orten mit doppelter Vergangenheit. Frankfurt: Peter Lang, 1998.
Dornberg, John. *The New Germans: Thirty Years After*. New York: Macmillan, 1976.
———. *The Other Germany*. New York: Doubleday, 1968.
———. *Schizophrenic Germany*. New York: Macmillan, 1961.
Enders, Ulrike. "Erziehung zum Hass." *Kirche im Sozialismus* 2 (1987): 52–55.
Erbe, Günter. *Die verfemte Moderne: die Auseinandersetzung mit dem "Modernismus" in Kulturpolitik, Literaturwissenschaft und Literatur der DDR*. Opladen: Westdeutscher Verlag, 1993.
Ernst Thälmann. Vorbild der Jugend als wahrer Patriot und Kämpfer für den Frieden. Berlin (East): Plambeck & Co., 1952.
Bernd Faulenbach and Rainer Eckert. *Auf dem Weg zur Zivilgesellschaft? Mythos und Realität der 60er und 70er Jahre in Ost und West*. Essen: Klartext, 2003.
Fishman, Sterling. *Estranged Twins: Education and Society in the Two Germanies*. New York: Praeger, 1987.
Flockton, Christopher. *The New Germany in the East: Policy Agendas and Social Developments since Unification*. London: Portland, 2000.

Foitzik, Jan. *Sowjetische Militäradministration in Deutschland (SMAD) 1945–1949: Struktur und Funktion*. Berlin: Akademie Verlag, 1999.
Frank, Mario. *Walter Ulbricht: eine deutsche Biografie*. Berlin: Seidler, 2001.
Frei, Norbert, Dirk van Laak, and Michael Stolleis, *"Geschichte vor Gericht." Historiker, Richter und die Suche nach Gerechtigkeit*. Munich, 2000.
Fuhr, Christoph. *Deutsches Bildungswesen seit 1945*. Bonn: Inter Nationes, 1996.
Fulbrook, Mary. *Anatomy of a Dictatorship: Inside the GDR, 1945–1949*. Oxford: Oxford University Press, 1995.
———. *Interpretations of the Two Germanies*. New York: St. Martin's Press, 2000.
Furet, François. *The Passing of an Illusion*. Chicago: University of Chicago Press, 1999.
Fürnberg, Louis. "Die Partei hat immer recht." In *Auferstanden*, ed. Michael Gläser. Deutsche Schallplatten, 1990.
Geissler, Gert. *Geschichte des Schulwesens*. Frankfurt: Peter Lang, 2000.
Geschichtsbilder, Weichenstellungen deutscher Geschichte nach 1945, Originalauzug. Freiburg: Herder, 2003.
Gibas, Monika. *Propaganda in der DDR (1945–1989)*. Erfurt: Leipziger Universitätsverlag, 2000.
Glaessner, Gert-Joachim, ed. *Der lange Weg zur Einheit: Studien zum Transformationsprozess in Ostdeutschland*. Berlin: Dietz, 1993.
Glaessner, Gert-Joachim, and Irmhild Rudolph. *Macht durch Wissen: zum Zusammenhang von Bildungspolitik, Bildungssystem und Kaderqualifizierung in der DDR*. Opladen: Westdeutscher Verlag, 1978.
Gottschlich, Helga. *Aber nicht im Gleichschritt. Zur Enstehung der FDJ*. Berlin: Metropol, 1997.
Griese, Christiane. *"Bin ich ein guter Staatsbürger, wenn ich mein Kind nicht zur Jugendweihe schicke": die Deutung von Phänomenen der Erziehungsrealität*. Baltmannsweiler: Schneider Verlag Hohengehren, 2001.
Grix, Jonathan, and Paul Cooke. *East German Distinctiveness in a Unified Germany*. Birmingham: University of Birmingham Press, 2002.
Grossbölting, Thomas. *Die Errichtung der Diktatur: Transformationsprozesse in der Sowjetischen Besatzungzone und in der frühen DDR*. Münster: Aschendorff, 2003.
Grothe, Peter. *To Win the Minds of Men: The Story of the Communist Propaganda War in East Germany*. Palo Alto: Pacific Books, 1958.
Gurevich, I. A. *Russkaia klassika xix v. kak literaturnoe iavlenie: uchebnoe posobie* [The Russian 19th century classic as a literary phenomenon: Teaching aid]. Moscow: Rossiiskii otkrytyi universitet, 1991.
Hahn, Hans J. *Education and Society in Germany*. Oxford: Berg, 1998.
Hannig, Waltraud. "The GDR—A Country of Books and Readers." *Contemporary Review* 244 (1984): 43–44.
Haveman, Katja. *Robert Havemann, oder, Wie die DDR sich erledigte*. Berlin: Ullstein, 2003.
Hensel, Jana. *Zonenkinder*. Reinbeck: Rowohlt, 2002.
Hoffman, Dierk. *Die DDR unter Ulbricht: gewaltsame Neuordnung und gescheiterte Modernisierung*. Zurich: Pendo Verlag, 2003.
Honecker, Lorenzen. *Erich Honecker: eine Biographie*. Reinbeck: Rowohlt, 2001.
Iggers, George. *Marxist Historiography in Transformation: New Orientations in Recent East German History*. New York: St. Martin's Press, 1991.
Jahnke, Karl Heinze. "Aus einm Brief Ernst Thälmanns an seine Tochter Irma." In *Ernst Thälmann—Freund und Vorbild*. Berlin (East): 1974.

Joachim, Scholtyseck. *Die Aussenpolitik der DDR*. Munich: R. Oldenbourg, 2003.
Kapp, Yvonne. *Eleanor Marx*. London: Pantheon, 1972.
———. *Karl Marx: 100 Years*. London, 1983.
Kersten, Heinze. *Das Filmwesen in der sowjetischen Besatzungszone*. Bonn and Berlin: Bundesministerium für Gesamtdeutsche Fragen, 1963.
Khrapchenko, M. B. *Lev Tolstoi kak khudozhnik* [Leo Tolstoy as Artist], 654–59. Moscow: Sov. Pisatel', 1963.
Klier, Freya. *Lüg Vaterland: Erziehung in der DDR*. Berlin: Kindler, 1990.
Kravchenko, Viktor. *I Chose Freedom: The Personal and Political Life of a Soviet Official*. Garden City, NY: Garden City Publishing, 1947.
Kudriashev, N. 1. 1965. "The Literature Course in the Secondary School." *Soviet Education* 7.7 (1965): 3544.
Kuhrt, Eberhard, and Henning von Lowis. *Griff nach der deutschen Geschichte: Erbeaneignung und Traditionspflege in der DDR*. Paderborn: F. Schöningh, 1988.
Kunze, Reiner. *The Wonderful Years*. Trans. Joachim Neugroschel. New York: G. Braziller, 1977.
Kurz, Robert. *Das Schwarzbuch des Kapitalismus*. Frankfurt: Ullstein, 1999.
Lebedev, Yuri. *Russkaia literatura, desiatyi klass* [Russian Literature Textbook for the Tenth Grade]. Moscow: Prosveshchenie, 1996.
Leben-Singen-Kämpfen. Liederbuch der FDJ. 12th ed. Leipzig: F. Hofmeister, 1973.
Lemke, Michael. *Sowjetisierung und Eigenständigkeit in der SBZ/DDR (1945–1953)*. Köln: Böhlau, 1999.
Lokatis, Siegfried. *Der rote Faden: Kommunistische Parteigeschichte und Zensur unter Walter Ulbricht*. Köln: Böhlau, 2003.
Loth, Wilfried. *Stalins ungeliebtes Kind*. Berlin: Rowholt, 1994.
Maaz, Hans-Joachim. *Der Gefühlsstau: Ein Psychogramm der DDR*. Berlin: Argon, 1990.
———. *Das gestürzte Volk: die unglückliche Einheit*. Berlin: Argon, 1991.
———. *Die Entrüstung: Deutschland, Deutschland, Stasi, Schuld und Sündenbock*. Berlin: Argon, 1992.
Maier, Helmut, and Walter Schmidt, eds. *Erbe und Tradition in der DDR: Die Diskussion der Historiker*. Köln: Pahl-Rugenstein, 1989.
Makarenko, A. S. *Das deutschsprachige Schrifttum bis 1962*. Berlin (West): Akademie Verlag, 1963.
Markovits, Andrei, and Simon Reich. *From Bundesrepublik to Deutschland: German Politics after Unification*. Ann Arbor: University of Michigan Press, 1993.
Marx, Karl, and Friedrich Engels. *The German Ideology*. New York: International Publishers, 1939.
Maus, Andreas. *Drüben: Alltagsgeschichten aus Ost und West*. Munich: DTV, 1999.
McAdams, A. James. *East Germany and Detente: Building Authority After the Wall*. New York: Cambridge University Press, 1985.
———. *Germany Divided: From the Wall to Unification*. Princeton: Princeton University Press, 1993.
McFalls, Laurence H. *Communism's Collapse, Democracy's Demise: The Cultural Context and Consequence of the East German Revolution*. New York: New York University Press, 1995.
Meier, Andres. *Jugendweihe—JugendFEIER: ein deutsches nostalgisches Fest vor und nach 1990*. Munich: Deutscher Taschenbuch Verlag, 1998.
Mertens, Lothar. *Rote Denkfabrik? die Akademie für Gesellschaftswissenschaften*. Munster: Lit, 2004.

———. *Unter dem Deckel der Diktatur: Soziale und kulturelle Aspekte des DDR-Alltags.* Berlin: Duncker & Humblot, 2003.
Meuschel, Sigrid. *Legitimation und Parteiherrschaft: zum Paradox von Stabilität und Revolution in der DDR, 1945–1989.* Frankfurt: Suhrkamp, 1992.
Mieskes, Hans. *Die Pädagogik der DDR in Theorie, Forschung, und Praxis.* 2 vols. Oberursel: Taunus Finken-Verlag, 1971.
Mitscherlich, Alexander. *Die Unfähigkeit zu Trauern. Grundlagen des kollektiven Verhaltens.* Munich: Piper, 1967.
Mittenzwei, Werner. *Die Intellektuellen: Literatur und Politik in Ostdeutschland von 1945 bis 2000.* Leipzig: Faber & Faber, 2001.
Möbus, Gerhard. *Unterwerfung durch Erziehung: Zur politischen Pädagogik im sowjetisch besetzten Deutschland.* Mainz: Verlag Hase und Koehler, 1965.
Moldenhauer, Gerhard. "2 x Deutschland, 2 x politische Bildung." *Schulpraxis* 6 (1989): 35–37.
Mueller, Marianne. *Stürmt die Festung Wissenschaft.* Berlin: Colloquium-Verlag, 1953.
Muller, Jerry. *The Other God that Failed: Hans Freyer and the Deradicalization of German Conservatism.* Princeton: Princeton University Press, 1987.
Manuel, Frank. *A Requiem for Karl Marx.* Cambridge, Mass: Harvard University Press, 1995.
Naimark, Norman. *The Russians in Germany: A History of the Soviet Zone of Occupation, 1945–49.* Cambridge, Mass.: Harvard University Press, 1995.
Niemann, Heinz. *Meinungsforschung in der DDR. Die geheimen Berichte des Instituts für Meinungsforschung an das Politbüro der SED.* Cologne: Bund-Verlag, 1993.
Niermann, Johannes. *Sozialistische Pädagogik in der DDR: Eine wissenschaftstheoretische Untersuchung.* Heidelberg: Quelle und Meyer, 1972.
Niethammer, Lutz. *Der "gesäuberte" Antifaschismus: die SED und die roten Kapos von Buchenwald: Dokumente.* Berlin: Akademie Verlag, 1994.
Niethammer, Lutz, et al. *Die volkseigene Erfahrung. Eine Archäologie des Lebens in der Industrieprovinz der DDR.* Berlin: Rowohlt, 1991.
Nothnagle, Alan L. *Building the East German Myth: Historical Mythology and Youth Propaganda in the German Democratic Republic, 1945–89.* Ann Arbor: University of Michigan Press, 1999.
Peters. H. F. *Red Jenny: A Life with Karl Marx.* London: Allen & Unwin, 1986.
Pike, David. *The Politics of Culture in Soviet-Occupied Germany, 1945–1949.* Stanford: Stanford University Press, 1992.
Pritchard, Rosalind. *Reconstructing Education: East German Schools and Universities after Unification.* New York: Berghahn Books, 1999.
Programmy dlia srednikh obshcheobrazovatel'nykh uchebnykh zavedenii—literatura [Syllabus for secondary school general institutions of learning—literature]. Moscow: Prosveshchenie, n.d.
Possony, Stefan. *Lenin: The Compulsive Revolutionary.* Chicago: Regnery, 1964.
Reuter, Frank. *Geschichtsbewusstein in der DDR. Programm und Aktion.* Cologne: Verlag Wissenschaft und Politik, 1973.
Riesnberger, Dieter. *Geschichte und Geschichtswissenschaft in der DDR.* Göttingen, 1973.
Rimscha, Robert von. *"Politische Korrektheit" in Deutschland: Eine Gefahr für die Demokratie.* Bonn: Bouvier, 1995.
Roske, Helmut. "The Textbook Factory." *Atlantic Monthly,* December 1963, 91–92.
Ross, Corey. *The East German Dictatorship: Problems and Perspectives in the Interpretation of the GDR.* London: Oxford University Press, 2002.

Rust, Val, and Diane Rust. *The Unification of German Education*. New York: Garland, 1995.
Sabrow, Martin. *Geschichte als Herrschaftsdiskurs: der Umgang mit der Vergangenheit in der DDR*. Köln: Böhlau, 2000.
———. *Das Diktat des Konsenses: Geschichtswissenschaft in der DDR 1949–1969*. Munich: Oldenbourg, 2001.
Schmidt, Hans-Dieter. *Geschichtsunterricht in der DDR. Eine Einführung*. Stuttgart, 1979.
Schmitt, Karl. *Politische Erziehung in der DDR*. Paderborn: Schöningh, 1980.
Schneider, Peter. *The German Comedy*. New York: Garland, 1991.
Schneider, Rolf. *Frühling im Herbst: Notizen vom Untergang der DDR*. Göttingen: Steidl, 1991.
Schnoor, Rainer. *Amerikanistik in der DDR: Geschichte-Analysen-Zeitzeugenberichte*. Berlin: Trafo Verlag, 1999.
Service, Robert. *Lenin: A Biography*. Cambridge, Mass.: Harvard University Press, 2001.
Shneidman, N. N. *Literature and Ideology in Soviet Education*. Toronto: Lexington Books, 1973.
———. "Soviet Approaches to the Teaching of Literature." *Canadian Slavonic Papers* 15.3 (1973): 324–49.
Sidenko, N. V. *Sochinenie po literature: metodicheskoe posobie dlia uchashchikhsia 9–11 klassov, no. 2* [The literature essay: study guide for students in grades 9–11, no. 2]. Volgograd: Brat'ia Grininy, 1996.
Siebert, Horst. *"Bildung"spraxis in Deutschland: BRD und DDR im Vergleich*. Düsseldorf: Bertelsmann Universitätsverlag, 1970.
Sievert, Christel, and Herbert Mühlstädt, eds. *Zu Fragen der Erziehung im Geschichtsunterricht*. Berlin (East): Volk und Wissen, 1955.
Skyba, Peter. *Vom Hoffnungsträger zum Sicherheitsrisiko: Jugend in der DDR und Jugendpolitik der SED 1949–1961*. Köln: Böhlau, 2000.
Solov'eva, I. N. *101 luchshee sochinenie vypusknykh i vstupitel'nykh ekzamenov za 1995 god* [101 Best Essays of Final and Entrance Exams for 1995]. Saint Petersburg: Khardford, 1996.
Solzhenitsyn, Alexander. *Gulag Archipelago*. New York: Harper and Row, 1974.
Spittmann, Ilse, and Gisela Helwig. *DDR Lesebuch: Stalinisierung, 1949–1955*. Köln: Volk und Wissen, 1991.
"Stalin Still a Hero to German Pupils." *New York Times*, 15 July 1956, p. 8.
Steele, Jonathan. *Inside East Germany: The State That Came In from the Cold*. New York: Urizen Books, 1977.
Steiner, Andre. *Von Plan zu Plan: Eine Wirtschaftsgeschichte der DDR*. Munich: Deutsche Verlags-Anstalt, 2004.
Stern, Carola. *Ulbricht: A Political Biography*. New York: Praeger, 1965.
Struve, G. "Tolstoy in Soviet Criticism." *Russian Review* 19.2 (1960): 1180–86.
Thälmanns Namen tragen wir. Berlin (East), 1968.
Timmerman, Heiner. *Die DDR in Deutschland: Ein Rückblick auf 50 Jahre*. Berlin: Duncker & Humblot, 2001.
———. *Die DDR zwischen Mauerbau und Mauerfall*. Münster: Lit, 2003.
Traxler, Arthur E. "The Re-education of German Youth—What Kind of a Job Are We Doing?" *Yale Review* 69 (June 1949): 393–97.
Treichel, Hans. "Probleme bei der Behandlung hervorragender Persönlichkeiten der Geschichte." *Geschichtsunterricht und Staatsbürgerkunde* 7 (1963): 600–617.

Trilling, Lionel. *The Liberal Imagination: Essays on Literature and Society.* New York: Viking Press, 1950.
Uhlig, Gottfried. *Monumenta Paedagogica. Band 2. Der Beginn der antifaschistisch-demokratischen Schulreform, 1945–1946.* Berlin (East): Akademie-Verlag, 1965.
———. *Monumenta Paedagogica. Band 14. Zur Entwicklung des Volksbildungswesens in der Deutschen Demokratischen Republik in den Jahren 1949–1956.* Berlin (East): Akademie-Verlag, 1974.
Ulbricht, Walter. "10 Gebote der sozialistischen Moral, 10. Juli 1958. In *DDR. Dokumente zur Geschichte der Deutschen Demokratischen Republik 1945–1985*, ed. Hermann Weber. Munich, 1987.
Voelmy, Willi. *Polytechnischer Unterricht in der zehnklassigen allgemeinbildenden Oberschule der DDR seit 1964.* Frankfurt: Diesterweg, 1968.
Vogt, Hartmut. *DDR: Theorie und Praxis der Lehrplanrevision in der Deutschen Demokratischen Republik.* München: Ehrenwirth, 1972.
Vogt, Hartmut, et al. *Schule und Betrieb in der DDR.* Köln: Verlag Wissenschaft und Politik, 1970.
Volken, Ulrich. *Honecker: eine Biographie.* Berlin: Aufbau Taschenbuch, 2003.
von Borries, Bodo. *Kindlich-jugendliche Geschichtsverarbeitung in West- und Ostdeutschland 1990: ein empirischer Vergleich.* Pfaffenweiler: Centaurus-Verlagsgesellschaft, 1992.
Vorsteher, Dieter. *Parteiauftrag: Ein neues Deutschland. Bilder, Rituale und Symbole der frühen DDR.* Munich: Koehler & Amelang, 1997.
Vorwärts und nichts vergessen: Sprache in der DDR: was war, was ist, was bleibt. Berlin: Aufbau Taschenbuch, 2004.
Weber, Hermann. *DDR: Grundriss der Geschichte 1945–1990.* Revised and expanded Hannover: Fackelträger, 1991.
———. *Die DDR 1945–1990.* München, 1993.
Weber, Hermann, and Bernhard H. Bayerlein. *Der Thälmann-Skandal. Geheime Korrespondenen mit Stalin.* Berlin: Aufbau Verlag, 2003.
Wegner, Gregory P. "The Legacy of Nazism and the History Curriculum in the Secondary Schools." *History Teacher* 25.4 (August 1992): 471–87.
———. "Ideological Change and Curriculum Transition: Teaching About the Legacy of the Third Reich in East German Secondary Schools." *Education Today* 44 (1994): 14–21.
Wehrkunde in der DDR: Die neue Regelung ab 1. September 1978. Berlin (East): Hohwecht, 1978.
Weissenthal, Helmut. *Die Transformation der DDR: Verfahren und Resultate.* Gütersloh: Bertelsmann Stiftung, 1999.
Wilhelm, Jutta. *Jugend in der DDR: Der Weg zur "sozialistischen Persönlichkeit."* Berlin (West): Holzapfel, 1983.
Winkler, Karl. *Made in the GDR: Jugendszenen aus Ost Berlin.* Berlin (West): Oberbaumverlag, 1983.
Wolf, Hans-Georg. *Zur Entwicklung des Geschichtsunterrichts in der DDR.* Paderborn: Schöningh, 1978.
Zharavina, L. V. *Sochinenie po literature: metodicheskoe posobie dlia uchashchikhsia 9–11 klassov, no. 1 Idassov, no.* [The Literature Essay: Methodological Aids for Students in Grades 9–11, n. 1]. Volgograd: Brat'ia Grininy, 1996.
Zimmermann, Hans Dieter. *Literaturbetrieb Ost/West: die Spaltung der deutschen Literatur von 1948 bis 1998.* Stuttgart: Kohlhammer, 2000.

Index

ABF. See GDR ideology, and Marxist-Leninist ideological apparatus
Abgrenzung. See GDR-BRD relations
Abitur. See GDR education, primary and secondary education; Weimar Germany, education
Abwicklung. See reunified Germany, "annexation" of eastern states
Africa, 74, 76, 80–81, 83, 130, 313, 403 n. 2
American education. See USA
American zone. See occupation-era Germany, Western occupation zones
Andropov, Yuri, 377
antifaschistischer Schutzwall. See Berlin Wall
anti-fascism, 5, 142–43, 205, 208
anti-Semitism, 4, 347, 357, 379, 384, 419 n. 10
Apitz, Bruno: *Naked Among the Wolves*, 54–56
APW (*Akademie der Pädagogischen Wissenschaften*), xv, 136
astrein (politically untainted), 255–56, 417 n. 2
Auschwitz
  and German guilt, 144, 291, 294
  relativizing of, 140
  and *The Black Book of Communism*, 140, 143
Ausländerfeindlichkeit, Ausländerhass. See reunified Germany, social problems
ausländerfrei (free of foreigners), 346
Avital, Eliahu, 371–75

Bachmann, Ingeborg, 66
Barbusse, Henri, 66
Bartel, Kurt, 20
BDM. See Nazi Germany, Nazi youth organizations
Bebel, August, 123, 398 n. 55
Becher, Johannes, 19, 20, 48, 104, 204
  as leading GDR writer, 17, 101
  works: "Great October," 100, 397 n. 21; "We are Soldiers of the People," 104
Becker, Artur, 29
Beethoven, Ludwig von, 233–36, 244
Berlin airlift, 2, 132, 412 n. 54
Berlin Blockade, 132, 412 n. 54
Berlin Wall, 75, 90, 99. See also Honecker; Ulbricht
  as *antifaschistischer Schutzwall* (anti-fascist wall of protection), xix, 134, 322
  building of, 18, 134, 204, 329, 342, 360, 412 n. 63
  Checkpoint Charlie, 378
  as *die Schandmauer* (wall of outrage), 323
  fall of, xxxi, 10, 199, 279, 321, 350, 378
  post-Wall era. See reunification; reunified Germany
Berhau, Ulla, 362–67, 374
Bernstein, Eduard, 123
Biermann, Wolf, 123
Bildung. See German educational tradition
Bismarck, Otto von, 121, 292, 394 n. 3
Bolshevik Revolution, 196
Brant, Sebastian, 48
BRD (*Bundesrepublik Deutschland*, Federal Republic of Germany, a.k.a. West Germany, 1949–90), xv, 81, 98–107 passim, 322, 410 n. 35, 419 n. 12. See also reunified Germany
BRD education, 85, 269: as compared with GDR education, 129, 320, 364, 366; universities/higher education. See names of individual institutions
BRD political parties. See CDU; DKP; FDP; SPD
  as capitalist state, 24, 76, 313
  and imperialism, 99–100, 103, 107, 133–35, 406 n. 5
  relations with GDR. See GDR-BRD relations
  transition to reunification, 200, 220, 328
Brecht, Bertolt, 19, 48, 56, 200, 202, 205–15, 396 n. 9, 407 n. 33
  quoted, 15, 69, 89, 199, 208, 211
  status in GDR, 17, 20, 212
  works: "Five Difficulties with Writing the Truth," 203; *Life of Galileo, The*, 199, 206, 212–13; *Mother, The*, 54, 401 n. 99; "Senora Carrar's Rifles," 50, 205; "Solidaritätslied" ("Solidarity Song"), 69–70, 87, 205, 363, 365; "Song of the Class Enemy," 101; "To Posterity," 207, 210, 213
Brezhnev, Leonid, 58

Bruderländer, xix
Bubis, Ignatz, 368, 383–90, 419 nn. 12–14
Buchenwald, 34, 39, 55–56, 129, 209, 213, 379, 399 n. 71
Büchner, Georg, 48
Bukharin, Nicolai, 148
Bulgaria, 23, 77, 85, 246
Bundesrepublik Deutschland. See BRD; reunified Germany
Bursov, Boris, 57, 61, 402 n. 117
Busch, W., 25

"Carry Hatred in Your Heart," 99, 105, 346
Carter, James, 303
Catholic Church. See GDR, churches in
CDU (*Christlich-Demokratische Union*, Christian Democratic Union), xvi, 198, 288, 410 n. 39, 419 n. 11
Central Council of Jews in Germany, 368, 383, 386, 388
Checkpoint Charlie. See Berlin Wall
Chekhov, Anton, 49
Chernyshevsky, Nikolai, 62
China, 79, 405 n. 44, 411 n. 48
Chotzejitz, Peter O., 142
Christian Democratic Union. See CDU
Christianity, 104, 115, 119, 319, 352, 357, 359, 363, 370, 375
churches. See GDR, churches in; German Jews
Clinton, Bill, 346
Cold War, 14, 129, 144–45, 202, 360, 394 n. 6, 411 n. 53, 412 n. 54
  and GDR education, 131, 133–35, 198, 265, 342, 346
COMECON (Council for Mutual Economic Assistance), xvi, xix, 245, 273
Commission on Post-War Political Monuments in the Former East Berlin, 40
communism, ix, xxxii, 3–9 passim, 15, 70, 235, 299, 319–33 passim, 363, 381, 408 n. 38, 413 n. 72
  and Brecht, 214
  and "convinced Communists," xxix, 222, 276
  crimes of, 138–45, 316, 413 n. 72, 414 n. 84, 415 n. 86
  and Eastern Europe, 133
  and GDR leadership, 52
  and Marxism-Leninism, 9, 93
  and *Staatsbürgerkunde* (civics), 106, 113
  and USSR, 122, 126, 401 n. 106
communist political parties. See DKP; KPD; USSR, CPSU

concentration camps, 54, 209, 289, 399 n. 71, 419 n. 13
  Auschwitz. See Auschwitz
  Buchenwald. See Buchenwald
  GDR use of for propaganda purposes, 36, 52, 130
  imprisonment of Jews, 350, 352, 383
  Nazi, 296
Courtois, Stéphane: *The Black Book of Communism*, 140–45, 414 n. 78, n. 85,
CPSU. See USSR
Czechoslovakia, x, 77, 85, 96, 134–36, 200, 261, 412 n. 53
Czesko, Bogdan, 49

Daniel, Yuli, 52
Darwin, Charles, 98, 143, 317
das bessere Deutschland, xix
Daudet, Alphonse, 49
Davis, Angela, 66
D-Day, 130
Deicke, Günther, 48
DEFA (GDR state film company), xv, 38, 101
Demuth, Frederick, 124
denazification. See occupation-era Germany, aims of Allied occupation
Derrida, Jacques, 292
Deutsche Demokratische Republik. See GDR
"*Deutschland einig Vaterland*" (GDR national anthem), 37, 95, 117, 160, 346, 358
Deutschlandlied (German and West German national anthem), 68, 186
Deutschlandpolitik. See GDR-BRD relations
Deutschtum (Germanness), 7–8
DIAMAT (dialectical materialism). See GDR ideology, and Marxism-Leninism; GDR education, primary and secondary education, curriculum; GDR education, universities/higher education, curriculum
Dickens, Charles: *Oliver Twist*, 20, 66
die neue schule (the new school), xx, 5
Dimitroff, Georgi, 129, 410 n. 41
DKP (*Deutsche Kommunistische Partei*, Communist Party of [West] Germany), xv, 76
"D-mark nationalism," 297
Dorfschule. See GDR education, primary and secondary education

Eastern Europe, xxi, 14, 71, 74–75, 77, 85, 136, 195, 287, 325–26, 418 n. 9
East Germany. See GDR
eastern German education (since 1990)
  and Humanities, 13–87, 111–46, 195–298
  in reunified Germany, 39, 63–65, 83–84,

136–44, 226, 246, 300, 314, 345–50 passim, 368, 386, 392
  in Saxony, 6, 265–68, 337, 376
  and Social Sciences, 89–109
  and tolerance initiatives, xxxiii, 345–390, 418 n. 914
economic initiatives. *See* GDR ideology, and state policy
education. *See also* BRD education; GDR education; eastern German education; German educational tradition; reunified Germany, education; and education entries for German Jews; Nazi Germany; occupation-era Germany; USA; USSR; Weimar Germany; Wilhelmine Germany
  as "citadel of learning," 3, 391
  Education for Hatred, xx, 79, 97–109, 228, 262
  as political re-education, xxi, 1–10, 63, 348, 383, 387, 392, 394 n. 1, 417 n. 3
  as unlearning, 2, 7, 136–38, 200, 395 n. 13
Ehspanner, Christine, 232–33, 243, 272, 379, 407 n. 30
Eisler, Hanns, "The Secret of Youth," 53
EMNID, 419 n. 10
Endlösung. *See* German Jews, history of, in Nazi Germany
Engels, Friedrich, 7–8, 29–40 passim, 50, 93–97 passim, 111, 399 n. 57, 402 n. 1, 406 n. 4, 410 n. 29, 414 n. 78
  in GDR iconography, 31–32, 34, 40, 93, 120–27 passim, 159, 406 n. 4
  works: *Communist Manifesto, The*, 402 n. 1; *Dialectics of Nature, The*, 91, 126; *German Ideology, The*, 7; *German Peasants' War, The*, 409 n. 18; *History of the Ur-Germans*, 126; *Origin of Family, Private Property, and the State, The*, 95, 126
Entnazifizierung. *See* occupation-era Germany, aims of Allied occupation, denazification
EOS. *See* GDR education, primary and secondary education
Erweiterte Oberschule. *See* GDR education, primary and secondary education, EOS
Erziehung zum Hass. *See* GDR ideology, and state policy, educational initiatives and youth laws
European identity, 296–97

Fachhochschule. *See* reunified Germany, education, universities/higher education
Fachschule. *See* GDR education, universities/higher education
von Fallersleben, Hoffmann, 48, 396 n. 9

FDJ. *See* GDR youth organizations
FDP (Free Democratic Party), 419 n. 10
Feindbild (enemy image), xx, 202, 262, 342, 363, 365
Fichte, Johann Gottlieb, 121
Finkelstein, Norman: *The Holocaust Industry*, 419 n. 10
First German Workers' and Peasants' State, 7, 9, 114, 397 n. 21
Fleming, Paul, 48
Fontane, Theodor, 19–20
Frankewicz, Heinz, xxiv–xv
Free German Youth. *See* GDR youth organizations, FDJ
Freiligrath, Ferdinand, 48
Freiraum, xx, 67, 150, 202, 233
Freischule. *See* German Jews, education
Friedrich Wilhelm University (Berlin), *See also* Humboldt University; University of Berlin
Frisch, Max, 66
Fuchs, Jürgen, 151
Fühmann, Franz, 48
Furet, François: *The Passing of an Illusion*, 140
Fürnberg, Louis, 20, 48, 204
  Die Partei hat immer recht (The Party Is Always Right), 99, 392
  "Our Song," 100

Gadamer, Hans Georg, 307
Galileo, 199, 206. *See also* Brecht, works, *Life of Galileo*
Gauck, Joachim, 141
GDR (*Deutsche Demokratische Republik*, German Democratic Republic, a.k.a. East Germany, 1949–90)
  as compared with Nazi Germany, 160, 342, 385
  as compared with SBZ, 5, 42, 129–30
  as *das bessere Deutschland*, xix, 236, 314. *See also* utopianism
  as *der erste Deutsche Arbeiter-und-Bauernstaat* (First German Workers' and Peasants' State), 7, 9, 114, 397 n. 21
  and Ministry of Education, ix, xxiv, xxv, xxvii, 3–5, 9, 44, 58, 68, 101, 112, 137, 207, 213, 245, 410 n. 38, 413 n. 65
  Orwellian dimensions of, 21, 94, 109, 141
  and relation to COMECON members, 73, 85, 157, 160 245
  and relation to Warsaw Pact members, 135–36, 274
  relations with West Germany. *See* GDR-BRD relations

GDR (*continued*)
  and "textbook mentality," x, xxvi, xxiv, 168, 195, 214, 220, 274, 279, 288, 322, 345
  and USSR, 2–8 passim, 17–18, 32, 74–98 passim, 126, 130–38, 145, 149, 160, 197–98, 201, 203, 210, 244, 413 n. 65, 414 n. 78
GDR, churches in. *See also* German Jews
  Catholic Church, 231, 242, 270, 348, 412 n. 56
  Lutheran (German Evangelical) Church, 242, 270
  state promotion of atheism, 14, 115, 155, 271
GDR culture
  artists and intellectuals, 31, 41, 121, 127, 144, 341
  worker's uprisings 133–34, 326–27
  youth protest,
GDR education. *See also* GDR ideology; eastern German education; German educational tradition; primary and secondary education
  Abitur (high school diploma), xix, 67–68, 167, 240–41, 249, 272–74, 280–82, 308
  curriculum: biology, 148–55, 158, 161, 216, 415n6; chemistry, 25, 3, 148, 155–65, 246, 270; civics, ix, xxi, xvi, 70, 89–109, 128, 195, 240–45 passim, 267, 272, 276, 313; *Gegenwartskunde* (Marxist-Leninist current events), 90; geography, ix, xix, 27, 69–87, 150–52, 224, 245, 267, 270, 276, 364, 402 n. 1, 403 n. 11, 404 nn. 16, 24, 405 n. 44; grammar, 21–25, 161, 164; history, ix–xiii, xxv–xxxii, 3–5, 9, 15, 18, 27, 29, 34, 36, 41, 48, 54, 111–47, 150, 159, 195–98, 201–3, 214, 221, 224–25, 246, 264–70, 286–88; language and literature, ix, xxvii, 13–68; Marxism-Leninism, ix, xvi, xxvii, 2–26 passim, 40, 60–65, 71–72, 84–94 passim, 120–21, 126, 136–37, 145–49, 154–67 passim, 200, 213–14, 221–24, 244, 246, 266, 275–76, 331, 391, 402 n. 116, 410 n. 38, 412 n. 54; mathematics, ix, xxvii, 3, 161–68, 270; penmanship, 3, 21, 25, 42; physics, 155, 299, 308, 312–13; reading comprehension, 15, 369; rhetoric and composition, 25–27; spelling, 3, 21, 25–27, 161; *Staatsbürgerkunde*, xxi, xxvii, 69, 87–113 passim, 150–53, 243, 245–46, 406 n. 4, 407 n. 24, 410 n. 38; *Wehrerziehung*, xxi, 107–8, 165–66
  EOS (*Erweiterte Oberschule*, advanced high school), xvi, xxvii–xxvii, 47, 51, 53–54, 65–71 passim, 86, 119–22, 127, 136–38, 148–65 passim, 201, 215–18, 233, 240, 249, 269, 272–73, 362–63, 403 n. 16, 410 n. 38, 412 nn. 54, 63

  POS (*Polytechnische Oberschule*, 10-year uniform school), xvi, xxvii, 13, 15, 27, 47, 53–54, 65–71 passim, 84–89 passim, 98, 100, 119, 121, 131, 136, 151, 155, 160–65 passim, 195, 234, 239, 266, 273, 337–38, 401 n. 99, 403 n. 16, 404 n. 18, 407 n. 2, 410 n. 38
  post-Wall *Abwicklung* of the schools, xix, 227, 240
  schools: Friedrich Schiller EOS (Weimar), 199–201; universities/higher education, xi, xii, xiv, xix, 6–7, 54, 67, 89, 105–6, 112, 127, 201, 215, 218, 225, 226, 241, 255, 266–69, 279–87 passim, 300–312, 321–27 passim, 410 n. 38
GDR emigration, 232, 252, 335, 343
  Grenzgänger (border-crossers), xx, 360–61
  as *Republikflucht* (flight from the Republic), xxi, 90, 247, 253, 258, 323, 332, 393 n. 6
GDR identity, 1–10, 112–14, 232–47, 299–312, 321–29, 345–48
GDR ideology, 7–10, 14, 27–46, 72–74, 95–108, 104
  Erziehung zum Hass (Education for Hatred), xx, 79, 97–109, 128, 262, 408 n. 46
  and Marxism-Leninism, ix, xvi, xxvii, 2–26 passim, 40, 60–65, 71–72, 84–94 passim, 120–21, 126, 136–37, 145–49, 154–67 passim, 200, 213–14, 221–24, 244, 246, 266, 275–76, 331, 391, 402 n. 116, 410 n. 38, 412 n. 54
  polytechnical education, 7, 70, 84, 156, 364
GDR military and police
  Grenzpolizei (Grepos, border police), xx, 29, 134–35
  NVA (*Nationale Volksarmee*, National People's Army), xvi, 25, 29, 99, 108, 136, 165–66, 256, 339, 408 n. 44, 418 n. 4; role in Prague Spring, 18, 106, 136, 412 n. 63
  Stasi (*Staatssicherheitsdienst*, State Security Service, i.e., Secret Police), xvi, xxi, 196, 206, 237, 253, 261, 314, 326; cooperation of educators with, 240–41, 267; and family life, 250, 329, 335–57, 343, 364; fate in reunified Germany, 141; use of informants, 335, 378
GDR political parties. *See* CDU; FDP; KPD; LDPD; PDS; SED; SPD
GDR sports, xvi, 45, 248, 270, 274, 312, 337, 378–79
GDR universities. *See* GDR education, universities/higher education; and names of individual institutions
GDR youth organizations, 207, 217, 259, 363
  FDJ (Freie Deutsche Jugend, Free German

Youth, a.k.a. Blueshirts), xvi, 23, 33, 70, 104–5, 164, 218, 255, 278, 323, 326, 363; and GDR leadership, 29, 36, 41, 46, 216
JP (*Junge Pioniere*, Young Pioneers), xvi, 23, 30, 36, 216, 363; commandments of, 16–17; slogans and songs, 17, 43
TP (*Thälmann Pioniere*, Thälmann Pioneers), xvii, 33–38, 43, 104, 108
Gegenwartskunde, 90
Georg Eckert Institute of Textbook Research, 396 n. 2
Gerlach, Jens, 49
German education. *See* BRD education; GDR education; eastern German education; German educational tradition; reunified Germany, education; and education entries for German Jews; Nazi Germany; occupation-era Germany; USA; Weimar Germany; Wilhelmine Germany
German educational tradition, 1–10, 220–32
Bildung (education, culture, self-development), 230, 300, 307
as compared with American, 300–12
German Evangelical Church. *See* GDR, churches in, Lutheran Church
German identity, 7–10, 14, 27–46, 72–74, 95–108, 104
and "the German question," 98
and Germany's Sonderweg (special path), 409 n. 20
and *Vergangenheitsbewältigung* (overcoming the past), xxi, 198–211 232–43, 413 n. 72
German Jews
education, 348–90
Freischule (Berlin Jewish Free School), 350
history of: education, 348–52, 361; Holocaust, the, xx, xxi, xxxiii, 142–44, 203, 287, 294, 296, 322, 353, 274, 388, 413 n. 71, 414 n. 84, 419 n. 10; *Kristallnacht* (Night of the Broken Glass), 418 n. 6; in Nazi Germany, 55, 104, 130, 350; neo-Nazis, 144, 288, 291, 368, 383, 414 n. 72, 417 n. 1, 418 nn. 5, 6
Jewish Oberschule (high school), 348–55 passim, 362–74 passim
Scheunenviertel (barn quarter), 351
German political parties. *See* CDU; DKP; FDP; KPD; LDPD; PDS; SED; SPD
German reunification. *See* reunification; reunified Germany
Germany. *See* BRD; GDR; Nazi Germany; occupation-era Germany; reunified Germany; Weimar Germany; Wilhelmine Germany

glasnost (openness), 6, 137, 201, 218, 221, 341, 412 n. 64, 413 n. 65
Glassbrenner, Adolf, 48
God That Failed, The (ed. Richard Crossman), 139, 141
Goering, Hermann, 129
Goethe, Johann Wolfgang von, 19–20, 48–49, 245, 400 n. 74
works: *Faust*, 57; "Prometheus," 51
Goethe Gymnasium for the Humanities (Weimar), 207, 232, 244, 246, 313, 317, 379, 382
Goethe-Schiller Archive (Weimar), 303, 357
Gorbachev, Mikhail
ascent to power, 137, 221
and glasnost and perestroika, 6, 201, 218, 221, 341, 376
and Honecker, 40, 201
as inspirational figure, 123, 341
popularity with GDR youth, 218, 221, 341
support for GDR dissent, 123, 218, 221, 341, 376
as threat to GDR leadership, 123, 201, 341, 376, 378
Gorky, Max, 19, 49, 66, 401 n. 99
Grass, Günter, 212
Green Party, 288
Grenzpolizei. *See* GDR military and police
Grepos. *See* GDR military and police, *Grenzpolizei*
Grotewohl, Otto, 13, 34, 68, 399 n. 58
quoted, 13, 68
GST. *See* GDR sports
Gulag, 32, 143, 210, 294, 413 n. 72, 414 n. 84, 415 n. 3
Gulf War, 291
Gymnasium. *See* German educational tradition, three-track secondary education; reunified Germany, education, schools
Gypsies, 104, 231

Habermas, Jürgen, 145, 297, 415 n. 86
Hajek, Jaroslav, 49
Hamburg schools, 13
Harich, Wolfgang, 123, 127
Hauptmann, Gerhart: "The Weavers," 48
Hauptschule. *See* German educational tradition, three-track secondary education
Havemann, Robert, 123, 127, 206
Hebel, Johann Peter, 20, 396 n. 9
Hegel, G. W. F., 7, 122, 318
Heidegger, Martin, 307
Heimat (homeland), xx, 25, 32, 72, 98, 105–6, 159

INDEX

Heimatkunde (local and regional studies), 27–47 passim, 69–70, 73, 89–90, 98, 101, 151, 157
  and cult of personality, 30, 47
  and GDR heroes, 28, 30–32, 34–35, 39, 42, 47, 407 n. 24
  and Lenin, 30–32
  and Marx, 28, 30–31, 124
Hein, Christoph, 204
Hennecke, Adolf, 29, 407 n. 24
Herder, Johann Gottfried von, 66
Hermlin, Stephan, 19
Herwegh, Georg, 48
Herzog, Roman, 388
Heym, Stefan, 204
Hindenburg, Paul von, 41
Hintze, Bärbel, 199–206, 402 n. 125
Historikerstreit (historians' conflict), xx, 415 n. 86
Hitler Jugend. *See* Nazi Germany, Nazi youth organizations, HJ
Hitler, Adolf
  and education, 6, 8, 131, 137, 198, 276, 369, 395 n. 13, 412 n. 56, 413 n. 65
  and German heritage, 6, 143, 208–9, 287, 291–93, 332
  and German Jews, 104, 369–70, 381
HJ. *See* Nazi Germany, Nazi youth organizations
Hobsbawm, Eric, 117
Ho Chi Minh, 30
Hofmannsthal, Hugo von, 66
Holocaust, the. *See* German Jews, history of, in Nazi Germany
Honecker, Erich, 22, 42, 67, 406 n. 9, 410 n. 38, 411 n. 41
  and Berlin Wall, 134
  career, 46
  and cult of personality, 46–47
  and GDR education, ix, 119
  quoted, 20, 40, 67, 90, 397 n. 17
  regime, 104, 334, 340
Honecker, Margot, 201, 392
  as Minister of Education, 42, 106–7
  quoted, 147
Huch, Ricarda, 48
Hugo, Victor: *Gavroche*, 20, 397 n. 20
Humboldt University (Berlin), 99. *See also* Friedrich Wilhelm University
  faculty and students, 220–26, 247, 257, 403 n. 16
Hungary, 77, 86, 96, 107, 132–35, 203, 253, 261–62, 412 n. 53, 56
Husserl, Edmund, 307

IM (*inoffizieller Mitarbeiter*, unofficial employee), 335. *See also* GDR military and police, Stasi, use of informants
international proletarianism, ix, xxvii
Israel, 80, 291, 293, 347, 352–85 passim, 419 nn. 12, 14
Italian occupation, 1

Jammerossi, xx, 220, 230–32
Jefferson, Thomas, 125
Jewish Oberschule of Berlin, 348
Jews. *See* German Jews
JP. *See* GDR youth organizations
Judaism, 348–89 passim
Jugendweihe (youth consecration ceremony), xx, 56, 104, 115, 213
July 20 Movement, 129, 131, 138
June 17 uprising. *See* GDR dissent, *Arbeiteraufstand*
Junge Pioniere. *See* GDR youth organizations, JP

Kahlau, Heinz, 48
Kafka, Franz, 66, 204
Kant, Hermann: *Auditorium, The*, 49, 66
Kapelle, Heinz, 129
kapitalistisches Ausland (KA), xvi, 71, 74, 76, 98, 111, 114, 136, 255, 322, 342, 404 n. 16
Keller, Gottfried: *Clothes Make the Man*, 20–21, 397 n. 20
Kerr, Judith: *When Hitler Stole Pink Rabbit*, 369
KJVD (*Kommunistischer Jugendverband Deutschlands*), xvi, 29, 129
Krupskaya, Nadezhda, 32, 399 n. 61
Khrushchev, Nikita: "Secret Speech," 132, 203, 395 n. 10, 412 n. 54
Klier, Freya, 66
Koestler, Arthur, 141
Kohl, Helmut, 210, 290, 389, 415 n. 86
Komsomol, xx, 52
Korea, 79
KPD (*Kommunistische Partei Deutschlands*, Communist Party of Germany), xvi, 16, 33, 66, 123, 338–42 passim, 411 n. 43
  and leadership, 33–34, 39–40, 42–45, 129–30
  in Nazi Germany, 33–34, 129, 342
  and SPD, 1
Kravchenko, Victor: *I Chose Freedom*, 139
Kristallnacht. *See* German Jews, history of, in Nazi Germany
Krupskaya, Nadesha, 32, 399 n. 61
Kuczynski, Jürgen, 126
Kunze, Reiner, 206

Labs, Helga, 108
Landthaler, Bruno, 348–62
Lassalle, Ferdinand, 123–24
Lavoisier, Antoine 159
LDPD (*Liberaldemokratische Partei Deutschlands*, Liberal Democratic Party), xvi
Lebedev, Yuri, 57–58, 64, 401 n. 106
Lehrbuch, 19, 20, 51, 137, 369, 393
Leipzig University, 204, 321, 326
Lenin Pioneers. *See* USSR, youth organizations
Lenin, Vladimir Ilych, 24–49 passim, 81, 103–4, 112–13, 399 n. 61, 409 n. 26, 411 n. 41, 414 n. 78, 415 n. 86
 and cult of personality, 30
 and Fürnberg's SED hymn, 100
 and heroic image in GDR textbooks, 25, 31–33, 35, 37, 45, 138, 145, 408 n. 38
 place in GDR education, 8–9, 91, 96, 103, 122–23, 127, 159, 166–67, 406 n. 4
 principle of collective leadership, 47, 413 n. 68
 slogans and quotations, 65, 95, 109, 126, 166, 211, 215, 220, 410 n. 33
 and Tolstoy, 58–63
Liberal Democratic Party. *See* LDPD
Lichtenberg, Georg Christoph, 66, 157
Liebknecht, Karl, 28, 42, 123, 128, 398 n. 5
Liebknecht, Wilhelm, 70, 123, 392
Luechow, Johann Christian, 48
Lunacharsky, Anatoly, 58
Luther, Martin, 242, 252, 270, 292, 334, 348, 351, 362
 and education, 120, 396 n. 9, 409 nn. 15, 18
 and German heritage, 265, 304
Lutheran Church. *See* GDR, churches in
Luxemburg, Rosa, 42, 123
 as inspirational figure, 28, 128, 398 n. 55, 399 n. 58, 401 n. 99
 vs. Lenin, 409 n. 26
Lysenkoism, 149, 415 n. 3
Lysenko, T. D., 415 n. 3

Maimonides, Moses, 357, 361
Makarenko, Anton, 21
Mann, Heinrich: *The Vassal*, 53
Mann, Thomas: "Mario and the Magician," 53
Manuel, Frank, 125
Mao Zedong, 30, 141–42, 413 n. 71
Marshall Plan. *See* occupation-era Germany, Western occupation zones
Marx, Jenny, 95, 124, 126
Marx, Karl, 45, 111, 113, 156, 213, 220, 313–18 passim, 337, 414 n. 78, 416 n. 7
 and burnishing of his image, 124–26
 and communist ideology, 7–9
 and family life, 95, 124
 in GDR textbooks, 28–37 passim, 50, 66, 93, 120, 122, 127, 149, 215, 399 n. 57, 406 nn. 4, 9, 410 n. 29, 411 n. 41
 works: *Communist Manifesto, The*, 106, 139, 402 n. 1, 406 n. 9; *Das Kapital*, 121, 314, 410 n. 29
Marxism-Leninism. *See* GDR ideology, and Marxism-Leninism; GDR education, primary and secondary education, curriculum; GDR education, universities/higher education, curriculum
de Maupassant, Guy, 49
Mayakovsky, Vladimir, 52, 100, 204, 397 n. 20
 "Good and Beautiful," 100
Mehring, Franz, 42, 66, 123, 126
Mendeleev, Dmitri, 159
Mendelssohn, Moses, 349–51, 356, 360–62
Meyer, Laurenz, 288
MfS. *See* GDR military and police, Stasi
Ministry of Education, ix, xxv, xxvii, 3–5, 9, 44, 58, 68, 101, 112, 137, 207, 213, 232, 245, 364, 410 n. 38, 413 n. 65
M-L. *See* GDR ideology, and Marxism-Leninism; GDR education, primary and secondary education, curriculum; GDR education, universities/higher education, curriculum
Mohr, Reinhard, 124, 142
Molotov, Vyacheslav Mikhailovich, 45
Mommsen, Hans, 141
More, Thomas: *Utopia*, 120–21, 406 n. 4
Möerike, Eduard, 20
Morrison, Toni, 309
Munich Institute for Youth, 417 n. 3
Munich University, 129
Mussolini, Benito, 53
MVD. *See* USSR, NKVD

National Socialists, 7, 350
NATO, 83, 99, 134
Nazi Germany (1933–45), 138, 160, 342, 369, 385. *See also* German Jews, history of, in Nazi Germany
KJVD (*Kommunistischer Jugendverband Deutschlands*, Communist Youth League of Germany, a.k.a. Young Spartacists), xvi, 29, 129
National Socialism, 121
NSDAP (*Nationalsozialistische Deutsche Arbeiterpartei*, National Socialist German Workers' Party, i.e., Nazi Party), 5, 45, 290, 400 n. 80

neo-Nazis, 288, 268, 383
Neubert, Erhard, 141
Neues Deutschland (New Germany), xx, xxv, 47, 277
Neulehrer (new teacher), xx, 5, 7
Newspeak ("Ostspeak"), 21
Nexø, Martin Andersen, 90
Nidal, Abu, 368
Niebelungenlied, 20
Niethammer, Lutz, iv
Nietzsche, Friedrich Wilhelm, 111
  Gay Science, The, 128
NKVD. *See* USSR
Noll, Dieter: *The Adventures of Werner Holt*, 54, 404 n. 100
Nolte, Ernst, 415 n. 86
NSDAP. *See* Nazi Germany
NVA. *See* GDR military and police

Oberschule. *See* GDR education, primary and secondary education, EOS and POS; German educational tradition; German Jews, education
occupation-era Germany (1945–49)
  SBZ (Sowjetische Besatzungszone, Soviet Occupation Zone), 5, 7, 42, 129–37 passim, 394 nn. 1, 3, 406 n. 4, 411 n. 53
  Soviet Military Administration in Germany. *See* SMAD
  Western occupation zones, 1–2
October Revolution, 17, 51, 78, 80, 90, 107, 127, 159, 196, 397 n. 21
Odyssey, The, 20
Orthodox Judaism, 353, 358, 384, 386
Orwell, George
  Nineteen Eighty-Four, xxiii, 109, 393 n. 1
  Orwellian dimensions of life in GDR, 21, 94, 141
Ossis (eastern Germans), xx, 222–23, 227, 260
  and effects of reunification, 325, 375
"*Ostalgie*" (easterners' nostalgia for GDR era), xxx, 231
Ostpolitik. See GDR-BRD relations
Ostrowski, Nikolai: *How Steel is Made Hard*, 50
Otto, Wolfgang, 399 n. 71

Panitz, Eberhard, 48
Paris Commune, 122, 124
Party of Democratic Socialism. *See* PDS
Pasternak, Boris, 204
Patton, General George S., 56
Paustowski, Konstantin, 49
PDS (*Partei des demokratischen Sozialismus*, Party of Democratic Socialism), xvi, 41, 139, 313–323 passim, 399 n. 69,
  1990 (March) GDR election, 399 n. 71
  as "the party of youth," 316, 321
perestroika (restructuring), 136, 201, 218, 221, 341, 376, 395 n. 10, 412 n. 64
Pieck, Wilhelm, 26, 45, 56, 216, 400 n. 74, 406 n. 12
  death, 34
  as "Father of the Nation," 30, 41–43
  and KPD, 66, 130
Planmenschen. *See* GDR ideology, and Marxist-Leninist pedagogy
Plekhanov, Georgi, 58
Poland, 10, 22, 77, 85, 138, 203, 274, 303, 332, 385, 412 n. 53, 419 n. 13
Polytechnische Oberschule. See GDR education, primary and secondary education, POS
Pope Innocent III, 51
POS. *See* GDR education, primary and secondary education
Prague, 44, 200
Prague Spring, 18, 106
  as presented in GDR textbooks, 135–36, 412 n. 63
Preissler, Helmut, 48
"proud to be German," 287–97
Pushkin, G. M., 49

Quayle, Dan, 303

Raebiger, Fritz, 48
Reagan, Ronald, 317, 415 n. 86
Realschule. *See* German educational tradition, three-track secondary education
Red Army. *See* USSR
Reformpädagogik. See GDR ideology, and Marxist-Leninist pedagogy; German educational tradition
religion. *See* GDR, churches in; German Jews
Republikflucht (Flight from the Republic), xxi, 90, 247, 253, 258, 323, 332
reunification, xxix–xxx, xxxiii, 144, 220–246 passim, 266, 278, 379–83, 403 n. 7, 404 n. 17, 414 n. 84, 415 n. 86. *See also* German identity
  problems with, 144, 200, 231, 238–41, 314, 379, 383, 392
reunified Germany (BRD, Bundesrepublik Deutschland, Federal Republic of Germany, 1990–) and GDR history, 142, 393 n. 2, 414 n. 84
  anti-semitism, 4, 291, 347, 357, 379, 389, 419 n. 10

INDEX

Ausländerfeindlichkeit, Ausländerhass (hostility, fear toward foreigners), 294, 346, 366, 418 n. 5
and German identity, xxx, 288, 296, 322, 349, 414 n. 84
neo-Nazi youth culture, 418 n. 6
political parties. *See* CDU; DKP; FDP; PDS; SPD
tensions between Ossis and Wessis, 222, 227, 230, 260, 325, 375
violence, 345, 346, 379, 380, 381, 382, 383, 414 n. 78, 417 n. 3, 418 n. 5, 419 nn. 10, 12
reunified Germany, education, 393 n. 2
"Education for Tolerance," xx, xxxiii, 345–48, 353, 383–90, 418 n. 9
schools, xxxiii, 353, 418n9; Friedrich Schiller Gymnasium (Weimar), 199, 402 n. 195; Goethe Gymnasium (Weimar), 207, 244, 246, 317, 379, 382; universities/higher education. *See* names of individual institutions
Rilke, 66
Rimbaud, 66
RGW. *See* international organizations and accords (Communist), COMECON
RIAS (Radio in the American Sector), 202
Rodden, John: *Repainting the Little Red Schoolhouse: A History of Eastern German Education, 1945–1995*, xi, xxvii
Romania, 23, 77
Roeske, Helmut, xxiv–xxv
Russia, 45, 57–62 passim, 122, 126, 131, 143, 221, 243, 274, 350, 397 n. 21, 401 n. 106
Russian Jews, 348, 355
Russian Olympics, 271–78
Russian Revolution, 52, 59, 62, 100, 122, 123, 401 n. 99, 404 n. 24
Russian teachers, 89, 242, 243, 269, 271, 363
Russian zone. *See* occupation-era Germany, SBZ

SBZ. *See* occupation-era Germany
Scheindemokratie. See SMAD
Schiller, Friedrich von, 49, 53, 150, 199, 201–6 passim, 402 n. 125, 416 n. 7
and Bildung, 230, 300, 307, 393 n. 5, 406 n. 2, 406 n. 3, 408 n. 41
works: *Cranes of Ibykus, The* 48
Schnitzler, Karl-Eduard von: *The Black Channel*, 108, 202, 327
Scholl, Hans, 129
Scholl, Sophie, 129
Schultz, Egon, 29, 30
Schumälder, Miron, 375

Schwarzenegger, Arnold, 372
SED (*Sozialistische Einheitspartei Deutschlands*, Socialist Unity Party), xvi, xvii, xx, xxi, xxvi, 9, 14–21 passim, 26–36 passim, 42–54 passim, 67, 87, 98–99, 104–8, 112–56 passim, 215–18, 221, 226–27, 232–34, 251, 277, 313, 337, 362, 376, 399 n. 71, 403 n. 7, 407 n. 24, 411 n. 48. *See also* GDR ideology
Party leadership, 16, 20, 30, 42–45, 148, 201, 257, 391, 400 n. 74, 406 n. 9, 410 n. 38
and PDS, xvi, 315, 318, 321, 399 n. 69
Politburo, 46, 332, 340
and polytechnical education. *See* GDR ideology.
and SED educators, xxiv, 6, 10, 14–15, 28, 33, 47–48, 52, 69, 75–76, 89, 95, 109, 122, 124, 146, 151, 154–56, 161, 166–67, 288, 365, 391–92, 397 n. 20
and textbook collectives, 59, 60, 65, 198
Seghers, Anna, 20, 48, 201
Duel, The, 54
Seventh Cross, The, 204
Senkbeil, Heinz, 48
Shakespeare, William
Hamlet, 309
Macbeth, 51
Sholokhov, Michail Aleksandrovich
"Fate of a Man," 52, 204
New Country Under Way, 204
Silone, Ignazio, 141
Sinyavsky, Andrei, 52
Sluckis, Mykolas, 49
SMAD (Soviet Military Administration in Germany), xvii, 2–6, 394 n. 1, 412 n. 54
Social Democratic Party of Germany/Social Democrats. *See* SPD
socialism, xii, 36, 67, 70, 121, 137, 139, 234, 250, 262, 276–77, 338, 265, 379, 403 n. 8, 412 n. 54
and capitalism, xxx, 2, 14, 75, 78, 87, 90, 93, 99–100, 122, 135, 259, 315–16, 321, 342
and Lenin, 32, 127, 138
and Marx, 81, 121, 125–26, 318
and model "socialist personality," 14, 54, 103, 205, 259
and morality, ix, xxvii, 16, 94, 95, 96, 140, 148, 150, 151, 157, 406 n. 14
and patriotism, ix, xxvii, 5, 14, 28, 59, 90, 92, 95, 98, 100, 112, 136, 151, 167, 262, 347, 406 n. 5, 407 n. 23
and "real existing," 9, 57, 273, 333, 363, 391, 406 n. 6
"scientific socialism," 72, 93, 95, 147–49, 154, 159

socialism (*continued*)
  in textbooks, 15, 22, 26, 28, 34, 83, 92, 96, 103, 105–8, 112–113, 119, 130–34, 156, 162, 198, 213–15, 404 n. 30, 405 n. 44, 411 n. 43, 412 n. 54
Socialist Unity Party. *See* SED
Solzhenitsyn, Aleksandr, 52, 139, 203–4
  Gulag Archipelago, 139
  One Day in the Life of Ivan Denisovich, 204
Soviet Military Administration in Germany. *See* SMAD
Spartacus, 117–22 passim, 196–98, 409 n. 21
SPD (Sozialdemokratische Partei Deutschlands, Social Democratic Party of Germany), xvii, 1, 33, 41–42, 70, 123, 128, 287, 398 n. 55, 412 n. 53
  and KPD, 33
Spender, Stephen, 141
Spielberg, Steven, 418 nn. 6, 9
SSD. *See* GDR military and police, Stasi
Staatsbürgerkunde, xxi, xxvii, 69, 406 nn. 1, 6, 407 nn. 24, 32
  and capitalism, 93
  and duties of citizenship, 95–97
  and Education for Hatred, 97–109
  and ideology, 89–90, 150–51, 243, 245–46, 410 n. 38
  and Lenin, 95–97
  and Marxism-Leninism, 91–93
  and socialist morality, 92–95
Stacheldrahtsonntag. *See* Berlin Wall, building of
Stalin, Josef Vissarionovich, ix, x, 7–9, 105–06, 111, 199–211 passim, 218, 399 n. 61, 400 n. 73, 415 n. 3
  compared to Hitler, 395 n. 13, 413 n. 65
  cult of personality, 9, 30–53
  in GDR textbooks, 8, 126–44, 395 n. 10, 402 n. 1, 403 n. 8, 411 n. 44, 412 n. 54, 413 nn. 66, 68
  German re-education, 1, 348
  slogans and quotations of, 98
  "Stürmt die Festung Wissenschaft!" ("Storm the citadel of learning!"), 3, 391
  and *The Black Book of Communism*, 413 nn. 71, 72, 414 n. 78
Stasi. *See* GDR military and police
Stauffenberg, Count Klaus von, 129, 138, 413 n. 70
Stern, Fritz, 7
Storm, Theodor, 19
Strauss, Botho, 414 n. 84
Strittmatter, Erwin, 19–20, 48, 204, 395 n. 12, 396 n. 9

Süddeutsche Zeitung, 415 n. 89, 418 n. 9, 419 n. 10

Teachers
  unemployed, 270
  unemployment, 86, 270
  retirement, 75, 285, 327, 364
  salary, 227, 257, 267
Teachers College (Columbia University), 1
Technical University (Berlin), 364
Ten Commandments of Socialist Morality, 16
Texas, xxiii, 81, 279, 289, 300–301, 311, 393 n. 1
Thälmann Brigade, 29, 34
Thälmann, Ernst, 13, 26, 28, 30–45, 104, 108, 129, 213, 217, 399 n. 71
  as communist hero, 30, 33, 129
  and cult of personality, 30, 41, 45, 104
  in DEFA film 39
  execution in Buchenwald, 34, 399 n. 71
  fate after reunification, 40, 41
  in GDR textbooks, 35
  as KPD chief, 33, 40
  life and career, 33
Thompson, E.P., 117
Tito, Josip Broz, 30
Tolstoy, Lev Nikolayevich (Leo), 57–65, 402 n. 117
  War and Peace, 57–62, 65
Trakl, Georg, 66
Treuhand Agency, 220, 226–29 passim
Trittin, Jürgen, 288
Trotsky, Leon, 33, 137, 316, 413 nn. 65, 68
Tucholsky, Kurt, 48, 53–54
Twain, Mark: *The Adventures of Tom Sawyer*, 19, 396 n. 9

Uhlig, Gottfried: *Monumenta Paedagogica*, 394 n. 1
Ulbricht, Walter, xxv, 74, 214, 400 n. 80, 406 n. 12
  background, 44–46
  and Berlin Wall, 94
  and cult of personality, 30, 43, 46
  and GDR education, 43–46, 105
  in GDR iconography, 156, 158
  in GDR textbooks, 17, 31, 127, 130, 396 n. 8
  and Honecker, 47, 104
  quoted, 160
  and Stalin, 30, 33
  "Ten Commandments of Socialist Morality," 16
Umerziehung (re-education), xxi, 392, 394 n. 1, 417 n. 3
University of Jena, xii, 278

University of Texas at Austin, 279, 299
University of Würzburg 299, 301, 307
USA, 43, 256, 284, 295, 343, 394 n. 1, 411 n. 53
  American education, xxiii, xxviii, 10, 125, 259, 279–85, 299–312, 367, 393 n. 1, 396 n. 8, 417 n. 2
  as depicted in GDR textbooks, 18–26 passim, 81–86, 130–32, 135, 161, 397 n. 19, 403 n. 10, 407 n. 32
USSR, 2, 30, 149, 201, 203–10, 244, 364, 377, 414 n. 78, 417 n. 1
  and CPSU (Communist Party of the Soviet Union), 52, 91, 122, 130, 137–38, 145, 412 n. 54, 413 n. 68
  as depicted in GDR texbooks, 17–18, 32, 52, 74–79 passim, 85–86, 96–98, 126, 130, 135–38, 160, 197–98, 403 n. 10, 404 n. 24, 411 nn. 43, 45
  and education, 6–7, 374, 413 n. 65
  immigration from, 350, 374, 387–88
  and Prague Spring, 136
utopianism, 52, 125, 318, 406 n. 4

VEB (*Volkseigener Betrieb*, People's Own Enterprise), xvii, 99, 157, 337, 339, 342–43
Vergangenheitsbewältigung (coping with the past), 21, 206, 413 n. 72
Verlaine, 66
Vietnam, 18, 20–21, 26, 32, 79, 82–83, 120, 162, 164, 197, 295, 367, 397 n. 19, 407 n. 32
Vogelweide, Walter von der, 48
Volkskammer. *See* GDR government
Volkspolizei. *See* GDR military and police
Volk und Wissen Volkseigner Verlag (GDR state publishing house for educational and pedagogical materials), xxi, xxiv, 2, 9, 266, 393 n. 2, 395 n. 10
Vopos. *See* GDR military and police, Volkspolizei

Walden, Matthias, 202
Walker, Alice: *The Color Purple*, 309
Walser, Martin, 66
Walter, Bernd: "October Ballad," 107
Wandervögel. *See* Wilhemine Germany, youth organizations
Warsaw Pact, 135–36, 273–74
Webb, Beatrice and Sidney: *Industrial Democracy*, 123

Weber, Franz, 265
Weerth, Georg: "Hunger Song," 48
Wehrerziehung. *See* GDR education, primary and secondary education, curriculum
Wehrmacht, 293, 401 n. 100, 415 n. 86
Weimar Germany (1918–33), 40, 53, 337
  and education, 2, 394 n. 3
Weinert, Erich, 48, 215, 396 n. 9
Weizsäcker, Richard von, 384
weltanschauliche Erziehung (education for a world outlook), xxi, 3, 14, 21, 66, 74, 111, 149, 407 n. 30
Wende (turn). *See also* reunification; reunified Germany, xxi, 127, 200, 205, 222, 232, 239, 249, 251, 260, 306, 337, 341, 343
Wessis (western Germans), xxi, 195, 222, 375, 378
  as *Besserwessis* (West German know-it-alls), xxxi, 230, 232
  as *Wossis* (westerners going east), xi, 195, 222, 230
West Germany. *See* BRD
Wilhelm I, 215
Wipperman, Wolfgang, 141–42
Wittenberg, 265, 268, 270
Wolf, Christa, 201, 204
Wolf, Friedrich, 48, 53, 68
  Cyankali, 68
  Professor Mamlock, 48
women
  children, 372
  image in textbooks, 29, 201, 401 n. 99
  in labor force, 152, 154, 231, 234, 271, 328, 379, 416 n. 14
  students, 270
Wright, Richard, 141

xenophobia, xix, 117, 145–46

Yeltsin, Boris, 40
Young Pioneers. *See* GDR youth organizations, JP
Young Spartacists. *See* Nazi Germany, anti-Nazi youth organizations, KJVD

Zetkin, Clara, 42, 123, 156
Ziegelhaus, 38, 399 n. 69

Post-Communist Cultural Studies Series
Thomas Cushman, General Editor

The Culture of Lies
Antipolitical Essays
Dubravka Ugresic

Burden of Dreams
History and Identity in Post-Soviet Ukraine
Catherine Wanner

Gender Politics in the Western Balkans
Women, Society, and Politics in Yugoslavia and
the Yugoslav Successor States
Sabrina P. Ramet, ed.

The Radical Right in Central and Eastern Europe Since 1989
Sabrina P. Ramet, ed.

The Culture of Power in Serbia
Nationalism and the Destruction of Alternatives
Eric D. Gordy

Russia's Liberal Project
State-Society Relations in the Transition from Communism
Marcia A. Weigle

Revolt of the Filmmakers
The Struggle for Artistic Autonomy and
the Fall of the Soviet Film Industry
George Faraday

The Denial of Bosnia
Rusmir Mahmutcehajic

Tundra Passages
Gender and History in the Russian Far East
Petra Rethmann

Up from the Underground
The Culture of Rock Music in Postsocialist Hungary
Anna Szemere

Looking West?
Cultural Globalization and Russian Youth Cultures
Hilary Pilkington, Elena Omel'chenko, Moya Flynn,
Ul'iana Bliudina, and Elena Starkova

Imagining the Nation
History, Modernity, and Revolution in Latvia
Daina Stukuls Eglitis

www.ingramcontent.com/pod-product-compliance
Lightning Source LLC
Chambersburg PA
CBHW021926290426
44108CB00012B/739